Head-Driven Phrase Structure Grammar

Studies in Contemporary Linguistics

A series edited by
John Goldsmith, James D. McCawley, and Jerrold M. Sadock

Previously published by the University of Chicago Press:
Autolexical Syntax: A Theory of
Parallel Grammatical Representations
Jerrold M. Sadock

Syntax and Human Experience
Nicolas Ruwet
Edited and translated by John Goldsmith

The Last Phonological Rule: Reflections on
Constraints and Derivations
Edited by John Goldsmith

HEAD-DRIVEN PHRASE STRUCTURE GRAMMAR

Carl Pollard and Ivan A. Sag

Center for the Study of Language and Information
Stanford

The University of Chicago Press
Chicago & London

Carl Pollard is associate professor of linguistics at Ohio State University. Ivan A. Sag is professor of linguistics and symbolic systems at Stanford University.

The University of Chicago Press, Chicago 60637
The University of Chicago Press, Ltd., London
© 1994 by The University of Chicago
All rights reserved. Published 1994
Printed in the United States of America

03 02 01 00 99 98 97 96 95 94   1 2 3 4 5

ISBN: 0-226-67446-0 (cloth)
        0-226-67447-9 (paper)

Library of Congress Cataloging-in-Publication Data

Pollard, Carl Jesse.
    Head-driven phrase structure grammar / by Carl Pollard and Ivan A. Sag.
        p.   cm. — (Studies in contemporary linguistics)
    Includes bibliographical references and index.
    1. Head-driven phrase structure grammar.   I. Sag, Ivan A., 1949–   .
II. Title.   III. Series.
P158.4.P65   1994
415—dc20   93-17533
                                                                    CIP

⊗ The paper used in this publication meets the minimum requirements of the American National Standard for Information Sciences—Permanence of Paper for Printed Library Materials, ANSI Z39.48-1984.

To Lucie and Penny

Contents

Preface

When we began the present volume, we fully intended it to be the successor to our *Information-Based Syntax and Semantics, Volume 1* (1987). As was duly noted by various reviewers, that volume issued numerous promissory notes regarding precise grammatical analyses that were to be honored by the successor volume. But in the years that have elapsed since 1987, we have revised a number of the technical assumptions made in that work. These revisions in fact play such a critical role in the analyses we present here that it would be misleading at best to call the present work *Information-Based Syntax and Semantics, Volume 2*. For this reason, the present volume is intended to be logically self-contained; it does not presuppose a familiarity with Pollard and Sag 1987. On the other hand, since we have every intention of honoring the many promissory notes issued in our earlier work, we have endeavored to explicate as clearly as possible the nature of the revisions we have made, usually in footnotes.[1]

We owe our deepest debt of gratitude to Georgia Green of the University of Illinois. From the earliest partial drafts through the final cycle of revisions, the shape of this work has been influenced, indeed inspired by her commentary, critique, and colleagueship. Had we taken more of her advice, doubtless a better book would have been the result.

There are a number of other colleagues who gave us detailed comments on earlier drafts, in addition to providing valuable sustained interaction. To them we are especially indebted: Sergio Balari (Universitat Autònoma de Barcelona), J. Mark Gawron (SRI International), Tilman Höhle (University of Tübingen), Polly Jacobson (Brown University), Andreas Kathol (Ohio State University), John Nerbonne (University of Groningen), and Peter Sells (Stanford University). Special thanks are also due to Bob Borsley (University of Wales), whose theoretical and analytic innovations form the basis of our ninth chapter.

It would be difficult indeed for us to thank everyone who had an influence

1. We are pleased to note that there have been numerous attempts by others to build on or improve the general approach to grammatical analysis we sketched in 1987. No doubt we have failed to do justice here to that body of research, and must be content to refer the reader to the bibliography in Calcagno et al. 1993.

on the ideas presented here. Although some attributions appear in footnotes in various chapters, there is no doubt that these are inadequate. In the last five years, we have learned a great deal, more than we can acknowledge here, from the various students and colleagues who were present when we lectured at Stanford University, Ohio State University, the 1991 European Summer School on Language, Logic, and Information, and the 1991 Linguistic Institute at the University of California, Santa Cruz. The same is true of those occasions when we have had the opportunity to present our research at institutions in England, Germany, Hungary, Japan, Korea, the Netherlands, Scotland, Spain, Switzerland, and Taiwan, as well as various places in the United States. We are in the debt of many, but we would particularly like to acknowledge the contributions, suggestions, and corrections of our writing made by the following individuals: David Adger (University of Edinburgh), Sondra Ahlen (Carnegie Mellon University), Kathy Baker (Carnegie Mellon University), Michael Barlow (San Diego State University), Guy Barry (Cambridge University), Tom Bever (University of Rochester), Liz Bratt (Stanford University), Joan Bresnan (Stanford University), Claudia Brugman (University of California, San Diego), Stephan Busemann (DFKI/University of the Saarland), Mike Calcagno (Ohio State University), Jo Calder (University of Arizona), Bob Carpenter (Carnegie Mellon University), Suk-Jin Chang (Seoul National University), Cleo Condoravdi (Stanford University and Yale University), Chris Culy (University of Iowa), Mary Dalrymple (Xerox PARC), Tony Davis (Stanford University), Elisabet Engdahl (University of Edinburgh), Donka Farkas (University of California, Santa Cruz), Dan Flickinger (Hewlett Packard Laboratories), Janet Fodor (City University of New York Graduate Center), Dean Forbes (Hewlett Packard Laboratories), Alex Franz (Carnegie Mellon University), Jonathan Ginzburg (University of Edinburgh), Jeffrey Goldberg (Stanford University), John Goldsmith (University of Chicago), Takao Gunji (Osaka University), Aaron Halpern (Ohio State University), Eunjoo Han (Stanford University), Yasunari Harada (Waseda University), Kathryn Henniss (Stanford University), Mark Hepple (Cambridge University), Arild Hestvik (University of Stuttgart), Erhard Hinrichs (University of Tübingen), Molly Homer (University of Illinois), Larry Horn (Yale University), Masayo Iida (Stanford University), Khalil Iskarous (University of Illinois), Eric Jackson (Stanford University), David Johnson (IBM Watson Research Center), Michael Johnston (University of California, Santa Cruz), Ron Kaplan (Xerox PARC and Stanford University), Bob Kasper (Ohio State University), Graham Katz (University of Rochester), Martin Kay (Stanford University and Xerox PARC), Jongbok Kim (Stanford University), Paul King (University of Tübingen), Tibor Kiss (IBM Germany), Tony Kroch (University of Pennsylvania), Bill Ladusaw (University of California, Santa Cruz), Mike Lake (University of Illinois), Charles Lee (Stanford University), Bob Levine (Ohio State University), Chris Manning (Stanford University), Mayumi Masuko (Cambridge University), Dan Maxwell (BSO/

Language Technology), Jim McCawley (University of Chicago), K. P. Mohanan (Singapore National University), Lynn Murphy (University of Illinois), Tsuneko Nakazawa (NTT), Klaus Netter (DFKI/University of the Saarland), Dick Oehrle (University of Arizona), Karel Oliva (DFKI/University of the Saarland), Maike Paritong (DFKI/University of the Saarland), Byung-Soo Park (Kyung-Hee University), Barbara Partee (University of Massachusetts at Amherst), Gerald Penn (Carnegie Mellon University), David M. Perlmutter (University of California, San Diego), Stanley Peters (Stanford University), Paul M. Postal (IBM Watson Research Center), Geoffrey K. Pullum (University of California, Santa Cruz), Alan Ramaley (Stanford University), Nalini Rau (University of Illinois), John Richardson (University of Chicago), Susanne Riehemann (Stanford University), Dale Russell (University of Illinois), Jerrold Sadock (University of Chicago), Hinrich Schütze (Stanford University), Stuart Shieber (Harvard University), Jeff Smith (San Jose State University), Peter Svenonius (University of California, Santa Cruz), Whitney Tabor (Stanford University), Mike Tanenhaus (University of Rochester), Hans Uszkoreit (DFKI/University of the Saarland), Tom Wasow (Stanford University), Steve Wechsler (University of Texas), Mary Wu (University of Illinois), Dieter Wunderlich (Heinrich Heine–Universität), and Annie Zaenen (Xerox PARC and Stanford University).

We also gratefully acknowledge various kinds of assistance with matters related to the production of this book from Tom Burke, Emma Pease, Gabriel Amores, Beth Bryson, Tilman Höhle, Jongbok Kim, Susanne Riehemann, Karen Peterson, Dikran Karagueuzian, Tony Davis, and Geoffrey Huck. Finally, we want to thank our respective families—Lucie, Becca, and Claire Pollard and Penny Eckert—who are doubtless more relieved than anyone that this volume is seeing the light of day.

Chapter 6, "Binding Theory," is a version of Carl Pollard and Ivan Sag, "A Nonconfigurational Binding Theory," in J. Wedekind and C. Rohrer, eds., *Unification in Grammar* (Cambridge, MA: MIT Press, 1993). Chapter 7, "Complement Control," is reprinted with revisions from *Language* 67: 63–113 by permission of the Linguistic Society of America.

Head-Driven Phrase Structure Grammar

Introduction

In *Information-Based Syntax and Semantics, Volume 1* (Pollard and Sag 1987; henceforth P&S-87), we sketched the fundamentals of head-driven phrase structure grammar (HPSG), an integrated theory of natural language syntax and semantics. There our focus was on foundational issues, such as the nature of features, categories, lexical entries, rules, and principles; the relationship between syntax and semantics; and technical aspects of formalization. We were at pains to emphasize the extent to which HPSG was intellectually indebted to a wide range of recent research traditions in syntax (principally nonderivational approaches such as categorial grammar (CG), generalized phrase structure grammar (GPSG), arc pair grammar (APG), and lexical-functional grammar (LFG)), semantics (especially situation semantics), and computer science (data type theory, knowledge representation, unification-based formalisms).

But the range of linguistic facts that we considered was quite narrow, being limited for the most part to matters such as subcategorization, the distinction between complements and adjuncts, constituent ordering, and inflection. In this volume, our goal is to demonstrate the applicability of a theory like the one described in P&S-87 to a wide range of empirical problems. The phenomena with which we will be concerned are among those that have occupied center stage within syntactic theory for well over thirty years: the control of 'understood' subjects, long-distance dependencies conventionally treated in terms of *wh*-movement, and syntactic constraints on the relationship between various kinds of pronouns and their antecedents.

Within that time period, detailed accounts of these phenomena—and of the relationships among them—have been developed within the research framework established by Noam Chomsky and known in its successive stages as the 'standard' theory, the 'extended standard' theory, the 'revised extended standard' theory, and 'government-binding' theory (GB, or the 'principles-and-parameters' approach). But given the widespread acceptance of that framework as a standard in recent years, especially among an extensive community of syntacticians in the United States and much of continental western Europe, it is incumbent on the proponents of a competing framework to explicate the sense in and extent to which the proposed alternative addresses the concerns of that community. For that reason, we will be relatively less concerned in this volume with paying our intellectual debts and correspondingly more concerned with making our proposals intelligible to workers within Chomsky's paradigm. More than that, we will try to make clear in what respects our accounts resemble those provided within GB theory and—more importantly—in what respects they differ.

A number of similarities between GB theory and the theory advocated here will be apparent. For example, in both theories, structure is determined chiefly by the interaction between highly articulated lexical entries and parametrized universal principles of grammatical well-formedness, with rules reduced to a handful of highly general and universally available phrase structure (or immediate dominance) schemata. In both theories, phonetically empty constituents (GB's variables, HPSG's traces) are central to the account of unbounded dependency (*wh*-movement) phenomena. A number of key GB principles (such as Principles A, B, and C of the binding theory, subjacency, and the empty category principle) have more or less direct analogs in HPSG; and two other HPSG principles (the head feature principle and the subcategorization principle) play a role in the theory roughly comparable to that of the projection principle in GB. Moreover, in both GB and HPSG, there are assumed to be several distinct 'levels' (or, as we will call them, *attributes* or *features*) of linguistic structure.

At the same time, however, there are a great many differences between the two theories, with respect to both global theory architecture and matters of technical detail. One key architectural difference is the absence from HPSG of any notion of transformation. Unlike GB levels (at least as they are most commonly explicated[1]), the attributes of linguistic structure in HPSG are related not by movement but rather by *structure sharing*, that is, token identity between substructures of a given structure in accordance with lexical specifications or grammatical principles (or complex interactions between the two).[2] In common, then, with a number of linguistic theories (including those commonly referred to as 'unification-based'), HPSG is *nonderivational*, in contradistinction to nearly all variants of GB and its forebears, wherein distinct levels of syntactic structure are sequentially derived by means of transformational op-

---

1. See, e.g., Chomsky 1986b, 1991, 1992; Chomsky and Lasnik, to appear; and Haegeman 1991.

2. The notion of structure sharing has a somewhat obscure origin in modern linguistics. As noted by Johnson and Postal (1980: 479–483), it has played a central role (under various names, e.g., 'loops,' 'vines,' 'multiattachment,' and 'overlapping arcs') in various theoretical frameworks and a body of research in relational grammar and arc pair grammar (see especially the formulation in Johnson and Postal (1980) and the references cited therein).

erations (e.g. move-α).[3] We will argue that, far from being a matter of indifference or mere notational variance, the derivational/nonderivational distinction has important empirical consequences.

A second essential difference between GB and HPSG has to do with the number and nature of structural levels posited. Although both theories posit multiple levels of structure, the inventory is somewhat different. A *sign* (i.e. a word or phrase, the HPSG analog of an expression in GB) is assumed to have (at least) the attributes PHONOLOGY (PHON), SYNTAX-SEMANTICS (SYNSEM), and (in the case of phrases) DAUGHTERS (DTRS).[4] Here PHON and DTRS can be regarded as rough analogs of the GB levels PF (phonetic form) and S-structure. But the SYNSEM attribute does not correspond directly to any one level of GB syntactic structure. Rather, it in turn has (at least) three attributes of its own called CATEGORY (CAT), CONTENT (CONT), and CONTEXT (CONX).[5] Here CAT plays a role roughly analogous to that of D-structure in GB; CONTENT, on the other hand, is concerned principally with linguistic information that bears directly on semantic interpretation (and is therefore most closely analogous to GB's level of LF (logical form)).[6] It should also be emphasized here that, unlike the situation in GB theory, where only sentences are assumed to have the levels of representation PF, LF, S-structure, and D-structure, in HPSG it is assumed that all signs, be they sentences, subsentential phrases, or words (i.e. lexical signs), have the attributes PHON and SYNSEM and that all phrasal signs have the attribute DTRS as well.

Technical detail, of course, is mostly what this book will consist of. Just a few salient respects in which HPSG differs from GB will be mentioned here, to give something of the flavor of the theory; all will be discussed in full in the chapters to come. Perhaps most characteristically, in HPSG, tree-configurational notions such as government and c-command are not regarded as linguistically significant; instead, their role is taken over by the relation of *relative obliqueness* that obtains between syntactic dependents of the same head (P&S-87, secs. 3.2 and 5.2). For example, in HPSG, the subject is defined not in terms of a D-structure configurational position, but rather as the

3. Exceptional in this respect is the nonderivational GB model developed by Koster (1987).

4. This inventory of attributes differs from the one assumed in the version of HPSG presented in P&S-87. This and other differences between the two versions will be discussed in full in Chapter 1.

5. For expository simplicity, we are ignoring the distinction within SYNSEM values between LOCAL (LOC) and NONLOCAL (NONLOC) features, which will be discussed in Chapter 1.

6. The CONTEXT attribute contains linguistic information that bears on certain context-dependent aspects of semantic interpretation. As we will explain below, the CONTEXT attribute supersedes the INDICES attribute of P&S-87.

least oblique complement of the relevant head, where relative obliqueness is modelled by position on the list that forms the SUBCATEGORIZATION (SUB-CAT) value of that head. To give another example, in HPSG, Principle A (which constrains the possible antecedents of anaphors) makes no reference to c-command or government, merely requiring that an anaphor be coindexed with some less oblique argument (provided such exists). We will try to show that such nonconfigurational formulations are not only conceivable alterna-tives, perhaps to be preferred on grounds of simplicity and conceptual clarity, but are also superior with respect to conformity with the facts.

As mentioned above, although HPSG does not employ movement, the ac-count that we propose for phenomena traditionally treated under the rubric of *wh*-movement does resemble the GB account inasmuch as phonetically null constituents—traces—are assumed to occupy the 'gap' position;[7] however, we will argue that the relationship between the gap and its 'filler' is more clearly understood as a matter of structure sharing than as one of movement.[8]

To put it another way, we deny that transformations themselves model any-thing in the empirical domain (and therefore HPSG shares the property of 'non-derivationality' with CG, GPSG, APG, and LFG, in contradistinction to GB and its derivational kin).[9] Similarly, raising will be treated in terms of structure sharing between a matrix argument and the complement's SUBCAT specifica-tion corresponding to the complement subject. In this case, however, there is no need to posit an actual constituent (e.g. NP-trace) corresponding to that specification, and hence the complement will simply be a VP, not an S.[10] Thus HPSG has no analog of GB's 'extended' projection principle, which appears to us to have been introduced by Chomsky (1982) essentially without argument: lexical requirements (as expressed in SUBCAT lists) do *not* always have to be satisfied on the surface (i.e. in the DAUGHTERS attribute).

Another GB assumption explicitly denied in HPSG is the principle, pro-

---

7. But we will propose an alternative, traceless analysis in Chapter 9.

8. The proposal to treat extraction phenomena in terms of structure sharing (or 'over-lapping arcs,' in their terms) was first made, we believe, by Johnson and Postal (1980). Our proposals for the analysis of extraction, coreference, and a variety of other linguis-tic phenomena, though differing in many points of detail from those of Johnson and Postal, nonetheless share the important feature of being based on structure sharing rather than derivational processes.

9. If one adopts the distinction between *level* and *stratum* proposed by Ladusaw (1988), then HPSG would be said to be a *multilevel* theory, in that it posits more than one kind of representation, but *monostratal* (like GPSG and CG), in that there is only one representation of each such kind.

10. Moreover, since passive is handled by lexical rule rather than within the syntax, the necessity for an analog of NP-trace is obviated altogether. See P&S-87, Chapter 8.

posed by Chomsky (1981), that every (nonsubject) subcategorized element must be assigned a semantic role.[11] Thus there is no obstacle to a 'raising-to-object' analysis of sentences like *Kim believes Sandy to be happy*. In HPSG, this amounts to structure sharing between the matrix object and the subject specification on the complement's SUBCAT list. Thus raising to subject and raising to object are handled in entirely parallel fashion: by sharing of structure between the complement subject and the matrix controller at the 'level' of subcategorization.

As we have seen, the closest HPSG analog of movement is structure sharing either with a phonetically null constituent (unbounded dependencies) or with a SUBCAT element that is not realized as a constituent at all (raising). But not all instances of movement in GB correspond to structure sharing in HPSG; passive, for example, as mentioned above, is not treated in the syntax at all but rather by lexical rule. Another case in which movement in GB has a 'non-movement' (i.e. non-structure-sharing) account in HPSG is that of 'head movement,' as manifested, for example, in VSO word order or in English 'subject-auxiliary inversion.' On our account, such structures simply arise from the existence of a phrase-structure schema, utilized (like all schemata) to different extents by different languages, that permits the realization of all complements (including the subject) as sisters of the lexical head (P&S-87, sec. 6.2); the orderings are the consequence of independently motivated language-specific constituent ordering principles (P&S-87, scc. 7.2). But in Chapter 9, we will consider the possibility that inverted structures are licensed by the same schema as typical head-complement structures (i.e. that inverted 'subjects' are actually nonsubject complements).

The other core case of head movement in GB, namely, movement of the head of VP into INFL, does not require any treatment at all in HPSG, for HPSG does not posit an independent category INFL to serve as a repository of tense and subject agreement features. Instead, subject agreement features (like object agreement features, in languages that have object agreement) occur within the corresponding SUBCAT element of the verb; and the role of the tense element of INFL is taken over by the head feature VERB-INFLECTIONAL-FORM (VFORM). Thus whether the verb is tensed is simply a question of whether the VFORM value is *finite* (*fin*) or some other (nonfinite) value; and the independent question of whether the verb is an auxiliary (and therefore can license VP deletion, contracted negation, etc.) is treated in terms of another (binary) head feature AUXILIARY (AUX).

---

11. Postal and Pullum (1988) argue persuasively that this assumption, though conventional, is justified by neither empirical nor GB-internal theoretical considerations. We return to these issues in Chapter 3.

Indeed, from the point of view of HPSG, Chomsky's rule move-α must be seen as a kind of procrustean bed. On our account, the phenomena that have been relegated to it are a heterogeneous assemblage, each of which deserves a more comfortable resting place of its own, be it in the lexicon (passive and verb inflection), in the phrase structure schemata (verb-object nonadjacency), or in structure sharings that accord with different kinds of interactions between lexical specifications and universal principles (raising and unbounded dependencies).[12]

The Nature of Linguistic Theory

Let us begin by making explicit some methodological assumptions. In any mathematical theory about an empirical domain, the phenomena of interest are *modelled* by mathematical structures, certain aspects of which are conventionally understood as corresponding to observables of the domain. The theory itself does not talk directly about the empirical phenomena; instead, it talks about, or is *interpreted by*, the modelling structures. Thus the predictive power of the theory arises from the conventional correspondence between the model and the empirical domain.

An informal theory is one that talks about the model in natural language, say a technical dialect of English, German, or Japanese. But as theories become more complicated and their empirical consequences less straightforwardly apparent, the need for formalization arises. In cases of extreme formalization, of course, the empirical hypotheses are cast as a set of axioms in a logical language, where the modelling structures serve as the intended interpretations of expressions in the logic.

For example, in one kind of standard model of celestial mechanics, the positions and velocities of bodies subject to mutual gravitation are represented by vectors in a higher-dimensional Euclidean space ('phase space'), the masses of the bodies by positive real numbers, and their motions by paths along certain smooth vector fields ('flows') on the space. Of course such a model is not the same thing as what it models (e.g. the solar system), but certain formal properties of such a model may represent aspects of the solar system of interest to a physicist. In a formal theory based on such a model, the underlying logic is just a standard first-order language (e.g. the language of Zermelo-Fraenkel set theory), and the axioms are certain systems of differential equations (e.g. Hamiltonian systems) that the flows are required to satisfy. An observed motion of

12. For an analogous critique of the notion of *metarule* employed in GPSG, see Pollard 1985.

the solar system is then predicted by the theory insofar as it agrees—under the conventional correspondence—with an admissible flow (i.e. one that satisfies the equations). This state of affairs is summarized in (1):

(1)

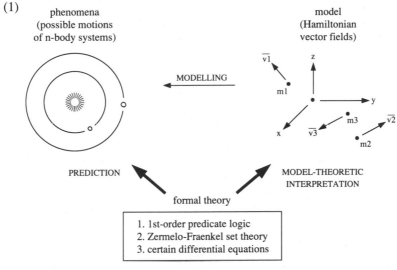

phenomena
(possible motions
of n-body systems)

model
(Hamiltonian
vector fields)

MODELLING

PREDICTION

MODEL-THEORETIC
INTERPRETATION

formal theory

1. 1st-order predicate logic
2. Zermelo-Fraenkel set theory
3. certain differential equations

In our view, a linguistic theory should bear exactly the same relation to the empirical domain of natural language, namely, the universe of possible linguistic objects, as a mathematical theory of celestial mechanics bears to the possible motions of n-body systems. Thus we insist on being explicit as to what sorts of constructs are assumed (i.e. what ontological categories of linguistic objects we suppose to populate the empirical domain) and on being mathematically rigorous as to what structures are used to model them. Moreover, we require that the theory itself actually count as a theory in the technical sense of precisely characterizing those modelling structures that are regarded as admissible or well-formed (i.e. corresponding to those imaginable linguistic objects that are actually predicted to be possible ones). This does not mean that the empirical hypotheses must be rendered in a formal logic as long as their content can be made clear and unambiguous in natural language (the same holds true in mathematical physics), but in principle they must be capable of being so rendered. Unless these criteria are satisfied, an enterprise purporting to be a theory cannot have any determinate empirical consequences. Thus we emphatically reject the currently widespread view which holds that linguistic theory need not be formalized. Rather, our position is the same as the one advocated by Chomsky (1957: 5):

> Precisely constructed models for linguistic structure can play an important
> role, both negative and positive, in the process of discovery itself. By pushing

a precise but inadequate formulation to an unacceptable conclusion, we can often expose the exact source of this inadequacy and, consequently, gain a deeper understanding of the linguistic data. More positively, a formalized theory may automatically provide solutions for many problems other than those for which it was explicitly designed. Obscure and intuition-bound notions can neither lead to absurd conclusions nor provide new and correct ones, and hence they fail to be useful in two important respects. I think that some of those linguists who have questioned the value of precise and technical development of linguistic theory have failed to recognize the productive potential in the method of rigorously stating a proposed theory and applying it strictly to linguistic material with no attempt to avoid unacceptable conclusions by *ad hoc* adjustments or loose formulation.

In HPSG, the modelling domain—the analog of the physicist's flows—is a system of *sorted feature structures* (Moshier 1988; Pollard and Moshier 1990), that are intended to stand in a one-to-one relation with types of natural language expressions and their subparts. The role of the linguistic theory is to give a precise specification of which feature structures are to be considered admissible; the types of linguistic entities that correspond to the admissible feature structures constitute the predictions of the theory.

Just as in other empirical domains, linguistic theory has become sufficiently modular, complex, and deductive that a need for formalization has become apparent, especially to researchers concerned with the computational implementation of current theories. Thus in the past few years, a number of specialized 'feature logics' have been proposed (Kasper and Rounds 1986; Johnson 1988, 1991; Gazdar et al. 1988) for specifying constraints on the feature structures used in linguistic analysis. At the same time, theoretical computer scientists have proposed various constraint languages for programming language description (e.g. Moshier 1988) and knowledge representation (e.g. Höhfeld and Smolka 1988; Ait-Kaci and Nasr 1986) that are easily adapted to this end. A very recent integration of these lines of work is the development of feature logics appropriate for the formalization of linguistic theories, languages whose formulas serve as the linguist's analog of the space physicist's differential equations (see Carpenter 1990; Carpenter et al. 1991; Carpenter and Pollard 1991; King 1989; Pollard, n.d.; Pollard and Carpenter 1990; and Carpenter 1992). The last-mentioned work in particular sets forth a logic very close to the one that we assume will underlie a fully formalized version of our theory. In very general terms, this can be characterized as a sorted variant of Kasper and Rounds's (1986) logic augmented with path inequalities, definite relations, and set values.

Our research program thus assumes the following three-way relation connecting theory, model, and the empirical domain of language:

(2)

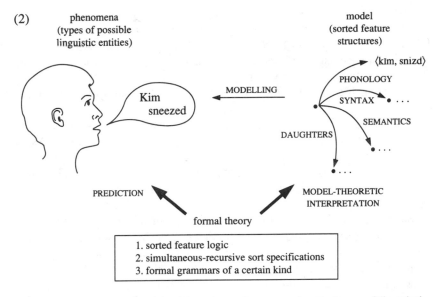

1. sorted feature logic	
2. simultaneous-recursive sort specifications	
3. formal grammars of a certain kind	

Since our principal goal in this volume is to propose analyses of linguistic phenomena and make them intelligible to the linguistic community, we eschew extreme formalization here and thereby avoid the many technical design decisions associated with the problem of choosing a feature logic; our rules and principles, in the form of feature structure constraints, will be expressed— clearly and unambiguously, we hope—variously in English or in a quasi-formal description language that we turn to directly. We doubt that the relative informality of analyses such as those presented here is likely to impede understanding; if anything, probably the reverse is true. Nevertheless we consider formalization of the theory an important goal, indeed a necessary one for the proof of computational properties (see below).

A further methodological principle, shared by the scientific community at large, is that of ontological parsimony: insofar as it is possible without doing violence to the simplicity and elegance of the theory, we do not posit constructs that do not correspond to observables of the empirical domain. Of course, all scientific theories contain such constructs. An obsolete example is the phlogiston that used to form the basis for the theory of combustion; a contemporary one is the quarks that are posited to account for the observed variety of sub-atomic particles. But with respect to nonobservable constructs the parsimony principle dictates: use only as needed. Perhaps phrase structure itself (variously manifested as, e.g, GB's S-structure, LFG's c-structure, and HPSG's DAUGH-TERS attribute) is the nonobservable linguistic construct that enjoys the widest acceptance in current theoretical work. Surely the evidence for it is far less direct, robust, and compelling than that for phonological structure (e.g. GB's

PF, HPSG's PHONOLOGY), logical predicate-argument structure (GB's LF, HPSG's CONTENT), or underlying grammatical relations (GB's D-structure, HPSG's SUBCATEGORIZATION attribute, LFG's f-structure). But for all that a theory that successfully dispenses with a notion of surface constituent structure is to be preferred (other things being equal, of course), the explanatory power of such a notion is too great for many syntacticians to be willing to relinquish it.[13]

But if phrase structures are current syntactic theory's quarks, move-α—as Koster (1987) has remarked—might well be regarded as its phlogiston. As we hope to have made clear by now, we regard transformational operations between levels as constructs that are not motivated by empirical considerations. What we observe, albeit indirectly, is sharing of certain subparts (e.g. between a filler and a gap, between an anaphor and a binder, between an 'understood' subject and a controller). But such sharing is straightforwardly and neutrally accounted for as simple identity; attributing it to derivational processes at best contributes nothing to the theory and at worst introduces complications and confusions (e.g. ordering paradoxes) of a completely artifactual nature.[14]

There is a further condition of *decidability* that we impose on a linguistic theory, a condition that has no real analog in (say) celestial mechanics.[15] That is, we require that for a substantial fragment of candidate expressions (i.e. expressions and nonexpressions) for a given language under study, it must be determinable by algorithm whether each candidate expression is assigned a well-formed structure by the theory and, if so, what that structure is. Inasmuch as an algorithm can operate only over a set of precisely specified syntactic objects, of course a rigorous demonstration of decidability in this sense depends on the selection of a formal language in which to express the content of the theory (see above). The condition of decidability is the theory's reflection of two fundamental facts about language use: first, that the structures of linguistic expressions are capable in principle of being computed by the resource-

13. Notable exceptions in this respect are Hudson's (1984, 1990) word grammar and certain varieties of categorial grammar wherein the particular order in which lexical items are assembled into larger units is viewed as an epiphenomenon lacking in linguistic significance.

14. For further arguments in support of the view that grammars should be formulated as declarative systems of constraints rather than derivational processes, see Johnson and Postal 1980 and Langendoen and Postal 1984.

15. The reason the decidability condition lacks an analog in celestial mechanics is that the system of differential equations does not describe a system of knowledge embodied by some information-processing organism (at least, not by a resource-bounded one): there is no requirement that there be an algorithm for determining whether a candidate solution (say, given as a Fourier series) satisfies the equations, nor in general are we guaranteed a method of solution (say, relative to a specification of initial positions and velocities).

bounded information-processing organisms that successfully employ them in a communicative function; second, that language users are able to render judgments as to the well-formedness of candidate expressions (generally taken as the primary data to be accounted for by the theory). On the other hand, in order to circumscribe our task, we do not charge our theory with providing a specific algorithm, though we would expect an adequate theory of language use to provide one.

Of course, decidability of this sort, in and of itself, is a modest criterion to impose on a linguistic theory. If the grammars offered by a linguistic theory are to be embedded into a theory of human language processing, then there is a variety of properties of language processing that might be expected to inform the design of grammar. For example, even the most superficial observation of actual language use makes plain the fact that language processing is typically highly incremental: speakers are able to assign partial interpretations to partial utterances (and quite rapidly, in fact). Thus, other things being equal, a theory of grammar that provides linguistic descriptions that can be shown to be incrementally processable should be regarded as superior to one that does not.

Similarly, we know that language processing is highly integrative—information about the world, the context, and the topic at hand is skillfully woven together with linguistic information whenever utterances are successfully decoded. For example, it is the encyclopedic fact that books don't fit on atoms—integrated mid-sentence—that allows the correct attachment of the prepositional phrase *on the atom* to be determined well before word-by-word processing of a sentence like (3) is complete:[16]

(3)   After finding the book on the atom, Kim decided that the library really wasn't as bad as people had been claiming.

Without such nonlinguistic sources of constraint, the interpretation of even the most mundane of utterances can become highly indeterminate. So profound, in fact, is this indeterminacy (and the concomitant reliance of language on situational information) that the very fact that communication is possible using natural language acquires an air of considerable mystery. Although we lack at present any well-developed scientific theory of how linguistic and nonlinguistic information are brought together to resolve such indeterminacy, it is nonetheless clear that we must prefer a linguistic theory whose grammars provide partial linguistic descriptions of a sort that can be flexibly integrated with nonlinguistic information in a model of language processing.

In addition to the incremental and integrative nature of human language processing, we may also observe that there is no one order in which information is consulted that can be fixed for all language use situations. In fact, an even stronger claim can be justified. In examples like (4), early accessing of mor-

16. Example (6) is an adaptation of an example of Graeme Hirst's (see Hirst 1987).

phological information allows the cardinality of the set of sheep under discussion to be determined incrementally, and well before the world knowledge necessary to select the 'fenced enclosure' sense of *pen* rather than its 'writing implement' sense: [17]

(4)   The sheep that was sleeping in the pen stood up.

In (5), on the other hand, the relevant information about the world (the information, however represented, that allows a hearer to determine that sheep might fit inside a fenced enclosure but not inside a writing implement) seems to be accessed well before the relevant morphological information constraining the cardinality of the set of sheep:

(5)   The sheep in the pen had been sleeping and were about to wake up.

What contrasts like these suggest is that the order in which information is accessed in language understanding, linguistic or otherwise, is tied fairly directly to the order of the words being processed. Assuming then that it is the particular language process that will in general dictate the order in which linguistic (and other) information is consulted, a grammar—if it is to play the role, as we assume, of information that fits directly into a model of processing—should be unbiased as to order. Grammars that are to fit into realistic models of processing should be completely order-independent.

Finally, we know that linguistic information, in the main, functions with like effect in many diverse kinds of processing activity, including comprehension, production, translation, playing language games, and the like. By 'like effect,' we mean, for example, that the set of sentences potentially produceable by a given speaker-hearer is quite similar to, in fact bears a natural relation (presumably proper inclusion) to, the set of sentences that that speaker-hearer can comprehend. This might well have been otherwise. The fact that there is so close and predictable a relation between the production activity and the comprehension activity of any given speaker of a natural language argues strongly against any theory where production grammars are independent from comprehension grammars, for instance. Rather, this simple observation suggests that the differences between, say, comprehension and production should be explained by a theory that posits different kinds of processing regimes based on a single linguistic description—a process-neutral grammar of the language that is consulted by the various processors that function in linguistic activity. The fact that production is more restricted than comprehension can then be explained within a theory of comprehension that allows certain kinds of linguistic constraints to be relaxed, or even word-by-word processing to be suspended, when situational information is sufficient to signal partial communicative intent. Suspension of word-by-word processing clearly cannot enter into production in the

17. We owe this sort of example to Martin Kay.

same way (though incomplete sentences sometimes achieve communicative success). Hence, if we appeal to differences of process—not differences of grammar—there is at least the beginning of a natural account for why production should lag behind comprehension. Speakers who stray very far from the grammar of their language run a serious risk of not being understood; yet hearers who allow grammatical principles to relax when necessary may understand more than those who do not. There is thus a deep functional motivation for why the two kinds of processing might differ as they appear to.

Observations of this sort about real language use and language processing are quite robust. Yet, given our current understanding, it is not completely clear how to convert such intuitive observations into criteria for evaluating linguistic theories. The problem is in essence that our understanding of language processing lags well behind our understanding of linguistic structure. Whereas it is reasonable to expect that further research into human language processing will produce specific results that inform the minute details of future linguistic theories, we do not yet know how to bring these considerations to bear.

Despite this uncertainty, the foregoing observations about human language processing suggest certain conclusions about the design of grammar. Grammars whose constructs are truly process-neutral, for example, hold the best hope for the development of processing models. And the best known way to ensure process-neutrality is to formulate a grammar as a declarative system of constraints.[18] Such systems of constraints fit well into models of processing precisely because all the information they provide is on an equal footing. To see this, consider a theory of grammar that does not meet this criterion. A grammar of the sort proposed by Chomsky (1965), for example, embodies transformational rules whose application is order-dependent. The fixed order imposed on such rules is one that is more compatible with models of production than models of comprehension. This is so because production models may plausibly be closely associated with the *application* of transformations, and the information that must be accessible to determine transformational applicability is localized within a single structural description (a phrase marker) at some level in the transformational derivation. Comprehension models based on transformational grammar, by contrast, seem ineluctably saddled with the problem of systematically *applying transformations in reverse*, and this is a problem that no one, to our knowledge, has ever solved.

Declaratively formulated grammars like those we develop in this book exhibit no biases toward one mode of processing rather than another. Because each partial linguistic description is to be viewed denotatively, that is, as being satisfied by a certain set of linguistic structures (see above), the constructs of such grammars (e.g. words, rules, or principles) can be consulted in whatever

18. A similar point is made by Bresnan and Kaplan (1982). See also Halvorsen 1983; Sag et al. 1985; and Fenstad et al. 1987.

order a process may dictate—the constructs are all constraints that, by their very nature, are order-independent and that allow themselves to be processed in a monotonic fashion. Given the current state of our knowledge of language use, a constraint-based architecture of this sort would seem to be the most plausible choice for the design of the theory of language, at least if the goal of embedding that theory within a model of language processing is ever to be realized.

In our concern for processing issues like those we have touched on briefly here, we have accepted the conventional wisdom that linguistic theory must account for linguistic knowledge (a recursively definable system of linguistic types) but not necessarily for processes by which that knowledge is brought to bear in the case of individual linguistic tokens. Indeed, we take it to be the central goal of linguistic theory to characterize what it is that every linguistically mature human being knows by virtue of being a linguistic creature, namely, universal grammar. And a theory of a particular language—a grammar—characterizes what linguistic knowledge (beyond universal grammar) is shared by the community of speakers of that language. Indeed, from the linguist's point of view, that is what the language is.

But what does language consist of? One thing that it certainly does not consist of is individual linguistic events or utterance tokens, for knowledge of these is not what is shared among the members of a linguistic community. Instead, what is known in common, that makes communication possible, is the system of linguistic types. For example, the type of the sentence *I'm sleepy* is part of that system, but no individual token of it is.

Just what sorts of things these linguistic types are is another question. Indeed, the precise ontological status of linguistic types is the subject of a very long-standing debate among various schools of conceptualists (e.g. Ferdinand de Saussure, Noam Chomsky), who take them to be mental objects, and realists (e.g. Leonard Bloomfield, Jerrold Katz, Paul Postal, Jon Barwise), who consider them to belong to extramental reality.[19] Thus we might identify linguistic types with such psychological entities as Saussure's signs or with certain presumably nonmental objects of situation theory (situation types or perhaps infons).[20] For our part, we doubt that the question of whether objects of knowledge are mental or extramental is an empirical one. Fortunately, as Rich Thomason has pointed out, a successful science does not have to have solved its foundational problems: the interminable philosophical debate over the meaning of quantum mechanics has failed to diminish its predictive power. Our concern in this book will be with the internal architecture of the system that the linguistic types form, not with that system's ultimate ontological status.

19. For a recent, slightly different assessment of the possible stances on the foundations of linguistics, see Katz and Postal 1991.

20. For further discussion of this point, see P&S-87, secs. 1.1–2.

1

HPSG: A System of Signs

1.1 The Structure of the Sign

In the early days of generative grammar (e.g. Chomsky 1957), the linguistic types singled out for attention were the sentences, considered as strings of phonetic shapes. Correspondingly, a grammar was just a computational device, for example, a context-free grammar or a transformational grammar, that enumerated a set of strings. Most current linguistic theories, of course, are much more demanding: the linguistic types par excellence, the expressions—or signs (in roughly the Saussurean sense)—include not only sentences, but also the words and subsentential phrases, even multisentence discourses. And a sign is taken to consist not only of a phonetic form, but of other attributes or features as well. That is, we conceive of signs as structured complexes of phonological, syntactic, semantic, discourse, and phrase-structural information.

As we noted in the introduction, most current syntactic theories posit two or more levels of representation. In the present formulation of HPSG theory, we assume that all signs at minimum possess the two attributes PHON and SYN-SEM.[1] Here the value of the PHON attribute is assumed to be some kind of feature representation of the sign's sound content that serves as the basis for phonological and phonetic interpretation. We will have nothing to say about the nature of PHON in this book, and will content ourselves with glossing PHON values as lists of phoneme strings, or often, to enhance readability, lists of English orthographies. The SYNSEM attribute includes a complex of linguistic information that was distributed among the two attributes SYNTAX and SE-MANTICS employed in P&S-87.[2] As we will see, this complex of information is more or less analogous to the information that is distributed between the levels of D-structure and LF in current transformational models. Thus the top-

---

1. A third attribute of signs, called the QUANTIFIER-STORE (QSTORE), will be discussed below.

2. However, certain information about 'unscoped' quantifiers contained within the SEMANTICS attribute in P&S-87 will now be treated in terms of the QSTORE attribute. For further discussion, see Chapter 8.

level structure of a sign posited in the present theory is as shown in (1):[3]

(1)

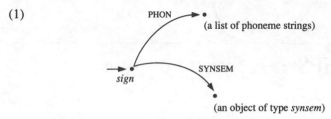

The information brought together within the SYNSEM attribute forms a natural class in the sense that it is precisely this information that has the potential of being subcategorized for by other signs; in addition it is SYNSEM information that is shared by the complement subject and the controller in raising (Chapter 3). It is these facts that justify the localization of this particular complex of information into a single structure.

Thus the value of the SYNSEM attribute is another structured object, of a type that we will call a *synsem* object, with attributes of its own called LOCAL (LOC) and NONLOCAL (NONLOC). NONLOC information figures centrally in the analysis of unbounded dependency phenomena (Chapter 4). LOC information in turn is divided into CATEGORY, CONTENT, and CONTEXT attributes. What these three pieces of information have in common, which justifies their being viewed as attributes of a single structure, is that they and they alone are shared between a trace and its filler in an unbounded dependency; we return to this topic in Chapter 4.

Before explicating these notions, we digress briefly to explain a few technical points about feature structures as employed in our theory. Some readers, particularly those steeped in the tradition of generative grammar, may prefer to proceed directly to section 1.4, where we sketch the nature of phrase structure schemata, referring back to sections 1.2 and 1.3 as needed. A summary of sorts

---

3. This should be compared with the following structure, which was assumed in P&S-87:

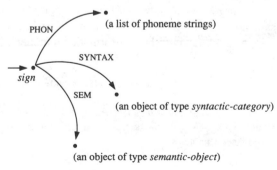

of objects, appropriate attributes, rule schemata, and universal principles can also be found in the appendix.

1.2 Some Formal Properties of HPSG Feature Structures

The structure for the English pronoun *she* is shown in (2):[4]

(2)

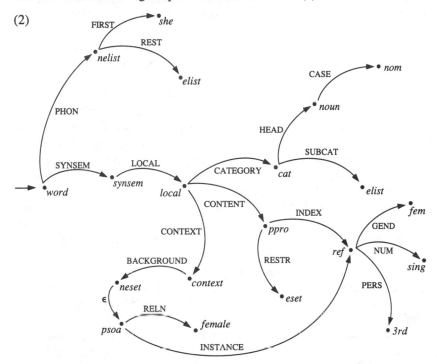

A few purely formal properties of feature structures such as the one depicted in (2) should be noted; the linguistic significance of this structure will be explained in the next section. We presuppose some familiarity with the use of feature structures in linguistics; for introductory accounts, see Shieber 1986 or Pereira and Shieber 1987; for a full formal account of feature structures and feature logic as employed here, see Carpenter 1992.

The first formal point to note is that the feature structures employed in HPSG are *sorted*. This means simply that each node is labelled with a *sort symbol* that tells what type of object the structure is modelling; that is, there is one sort symbol for each basic type (ontological category) of construct. It is the labels on the nodes in (2) that specify such sort assignments (for notational ease, the sort symbol labelling a node in a feature structure will often be deleted when it can be recovered from the context). The (finite) set of all sort symbols is as-

4. For simplicity, QSTORE and SYNSEM | NONLOCAL values are omitted here.

sumed to be partially ordered, with sort symbols corresponding to more inclusive types lower in the ordering.[5] For example, the sort *sign* is ordered below the sort *phrase* or *word* because signs include both phrases and words; we say, for example, that *word* is a *subsort* of *sign* and *accusative* is a subsort of *case*.

Second, we require feature structures to be *well-typed* (Carpenter 1992). This means that what attribute (or, equivalently, feature) labels can appear in a feature structure are determined by its sort; this fact is the reflection within the model of the fact that what attributes (or, equivalently, features or components of structure) an empirical object has depends on its ontological category. Thus a feature structure of sort *word* can have the attribute labels PHON and SYN-SEM; a feature structure of sort *synsem* can have the attribute labels LOC and NONLOC; and a feature structure of sort *local* (*loc*) can have the attribute labels CATEGORY, CONTENT, and CONTEXT. In addition, given a sort of feature structure and an attribute label appropriate for that sort, the value of that attribute must also be of a sort appropriate for the given sort and attribute label. For example, the value of the CATEGORY attribute in a feature structure of sort *loc* must be of sort *category* (*cat*), and the value of the CASE attribute in a feature structure of sort *noun* must be one of the most specific subsorts of the sort *case* (for English, assumed to be *nominative* (*nom*) or *accusative* (*acc*)). In a completely formalized HPSG grammar, it must be stated explicitly what the sort symbols are, how the sort symbols are ordered, and what the appropriate attribute labels and value sorts are for each sort.

Third, feature structures that serve as models of linguistic entities are required to satisfy further criteria of completeness. Roughly what this means is that they are total (not merely partial) models of the objects that they represent. More precisely, they are required to be both *totally well-typed* (Carpenter 1992) and *sort-resolved*. A feature structure is *totally* well-typed in case it is well-typed, and, moreover, for each node, every feature that is appropriate for the sort assigned to that node is actually present. Thus for any node labelled *local*, there must actually be an outgoing edge from that node for each of the three appropriate feature labels CATEGORY, CONTENT, and CONTEXT. A feature structure is *sort-resolved* provided every node is assigned a sort label that is maximal (i.e. most specific) in the sort ordering. For example, the CASE value of a node labelled *noun* must be labelled either *nom* or *acc*; it cannot be labelled *case* (which subsumes both *nom* and *acc* in the sort ordering).[6]

It should be observed that a linguistic entity, or some subpart of one, can be

5. This reverses the ordering convention employed in P&S-87, which was regarded as confusing by many readers. The mnemonic in force here is that 'bigger' corresponds to 'more informative.'

6. Of course, precisely which features and feature values a given language avails itself of must be permitted to vary from language to language. We will not take a position as to whether each feature (e.g. CASE) selects its values from among some fixed set of universally available values.

a list or a set of linguistic entities of a certain kind. For example, the value of the SUBCAT feature of a sign is always a list each of whose members is an entity of sort *synsem*. And the value of the BACKGROUND feature is a set of *parametrized states of affairs* (psoas). For the sake of specificity and familiarity, we have chosen to model nonempty lists as a sort of feature structure—*nelist*—specified for the two attributes FIRST and REST; the empty list is modelled by another sort—*elist*—for which no attribute labels are appropriate. Set values are modelled by nodes with arcs labelled 'ϵ' leading to the nodes of the graph that model the members of the set. For notational convenience, such nodes bear the label *neset* (if there are outgoing ϵ arcs) or *eset* (otherwise), but technically speaking *neset* and *eset* are not sort symbols.

It is crucially important that two distinct paths in a feature structure can lead to one and the same node: for example, the paths SYNSEM | LOC | CONTENT | INDEX and SYNSEM | LOC | CONTEXT | BACKGROUND | ϵ | INSTANCE in (2). In such cases, we speak of *structure sharing*: two paths share the same structure as their common value. Informally (but not quite correctly), the values of the two paths are often said to be *unified*. It is important to be clear that structure sharing involves token identity of values, not just values that are structurally identical feature structures; identity of the latter kind is referred to as *type identity* or *structural identity*. It is unification in this sense of structure sharing that gives its name to the family of 'unification-based' linguistic frameworks, of which HPSG is an exemplar. It is not going too far to say that in HPSG structure sharing is the central explanatory mechanism, much as move-α is the central explanatory mechanism in GB theory; indeed, the relationships between fillers and traces, between 'understood' subjects and their controllers, between pronouns and their antecedents, between 'agreement sources' and 'agreement targets,' and between the category of a word and the category of its phrasal projections will all be analyzed as instances of structure sharing.

A final formal point to note is that for some sorts, no attribute labels are appropriate. Such sorts are called *atoms*. Examples are *case* and its subsorts *nom* and *acc*; *number* (*num*) and its subsorts *singular* (*sing*) and *plural* (*plu*); and *elist*. A feature structure consisting of a single node labelled by an atom will sometimes be called an atom itself, though 'atomic feature structure' is more technically correct.

As noted above, we often formulate constraints on modelling structures like (2) in terms of an appropriately designed description language. In one easily imagined such language, essentially a quantifier-free predicate calculus with sorts and features represented as unary and binary predicates, respectively, a reasonably complete description of a word like (2) might be given as (3):

(3)   rooted-at(X1) & *word*(X1) & PHON(X1,X2) & *nelist* (X2) &
        FIRST(X2,X3) & *she*(X3) & REST(X2,X4) & *elist*(X4) &

SYNSEM(X1,X5) & *synsem*(X5) & LOCAL(X5,X6) & *local*(X6) &
CAT(X6,X7) & *cat*(X7) & HEAD(X7,X8) & *noun*(X8) & CASE(X8,X9) &
nom(X9) & SUBCAT(X7,X10) & *elist*(X10) & CONTENT(X6,X11) &
ppro(X11) & INDEX(X11,X12) & *ref*(X12) & PERSON(X12,X14) &
3rd(X14) & NUMBER(X12,X15) & *sing*(X15) & GENDER(X12,X16) &
fem(X16) & RESTRICTION(X11,X17) & *eset*(X17) & CONTEXT(X6,X18)
& *context*(X18) & BACKGROUND(X18,X19) & SINGLETON-
OF(X19,X20) & *psoa*(X20) & INSTANCE(X20,X12) &
RELATION(X20,X21) & *female*(X21)

We say that (3) *describes* (2), or that (2) *satisfies* (3) relative to some assignment of the variables in (3) to nodes of (2). Note that the conjuncts IN-
DEX(X11,X12) and INSTANCE(X20,X12) clearly express the structure sharing
appropriate to (2).

In a proper formalization of linguistic theory, grammars, universal and language-particular principles, and lexical entries will all be given as logical formulas that are interpreted as denoting the set of feature structures that satisfy
those formulas. Throughout this volume, however, we will describe feature
structures using *attribute-value matrix* (AVM) diagrams. The perspicuity
gained by this choice of description language can readily be appreciated by
comparing (3) with the AVM description of (2) shown in (4):

(4)

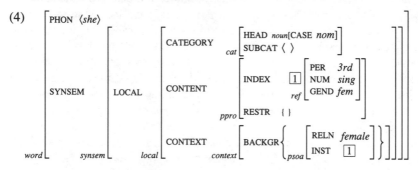

Note that descriptions of (or, equivalently, constraints on) feature structures, be
they first-order formulas like (3) or AVM diagrams like (4), need not be
complete. For example, although satisfied by the feature structure (2), the
AVM diagram

$$(4') \quad \text{sign} \left[\text{SYNSEM} \ \text{synsem} \left[\text{LOCAL} \ \text{local} \left[\text{CATEGORY} \ \text{cat} \left[\begin{array}{l} \text{HEAD} \ \textit{noun} \\ \text{SUBCAT} \ \langle \ \rangle \end{array} \right] \right] \right] \right]$$

provides only a partial description of (2). For instance, the sort is given not as
word, but as the less specific supersort *sign*; the value of the path SYNSEM |
LOC | CAT | HEAD is specified only as *noun*, with no indication of the CASE
value; and only the CATEGORY value is described for the path SYNSEM | LOC,

not the CONTENT or CONTEXT value. Of course the description (4′) is also satisfied by many feature structures in addition to the one in (2); in general, the more specific (or explicit, or informative) a description, the fewer feature structures satisfy it.

A common source of confusion is that feature structures themselves can be used as descriptions of other feature structures. Since feature structures that are not totally well-typed and sort-resolved can be arranged into a partial ordering relation (called the *subsumption* relation; see Shieber 1986 or P&S-87, Chapter 2), any feature structure can be thought of as partially describing any of the feature structures that it subsumes. Similarly, a feature structure can be taken as a partial description of any of the well-typed (or totally well-typed, or totally well-typed and sort-resolved) feature structures that it subsumes.[7] We choose to eliminate this possible source of confusion by using only totally well-typed, sort-resolved feature structures as (total) models of linguistic entities and AVM diagrams (not feature structures) as descriptions.

The following matters of notation should be observed with respect to AVM descriptions like (4). First, sort assignments are indicated by left subscripts (e.g. *word*) if the object in question has one or more of its attributes specified, and by an atomic symbol (e.g. *feminine (fem)*) otherwise. Second, structure sharing is indicated by multiple occurrences of boxed numerals called *tags*, for example, '$\boxed{1}$.' Third, descriptions of sets are given within curly braces, with '{ }' describing the empty set. And fourth, descriptions of lists are usually abbreviated by the use of angle-bracket notation (instead of the attribute labels FIRST and REST), with '⟨ ⟩' describing the empty list. These notations are modelled after those of Shieber 1986 and those of P&S-87. AVM descriptions will also employ functional or relational symbols such as append, union (∪), and ≠, all of which we consider to be necessary in a linguistically adequate description language; the use and interpretation of such symbols will be explained as they are introduced.

1.3 The Linguistic Application of Feature Structure Descriptions

We turn now to the linguistic significance of the various substructures contained within the feature structure (2) described in (4). First, note that the indicated sort of the whole structure is *word*. Now let us consider the structure of sort *loc* that lies at the end of the path SYNSEM | LOC. As noted above, this structure has the three attributes CATEGORY (CAT), CONTENT (CONT), and CONTEXT (CONX). Here the CATEGORY value includes not only what would be regarded by most syntacticians as the syntactic category of the word in question, but also the grammatical arguments it requires. The CONTENT value

---

7. More precisely, feature structures can be viewed as representing logical equivalence classes of nondisjunctive formulas in certain feature logics.

constitutes the word's contribution to (context-independent) aspects of the semantic interpretation of any phrase that contains it. And the CONTEXT value contains certain context-dependent linguistic information usually discussed under such rubrics as indexicality, presupposition, and/or conventional implicature. Let us examine these three structures more closely.

The CATEGORY value is an object of sort *category* (*cat*), and it contains the two attributes HEAD and SUBCAT.[8] Roughly speaking, the HEAD value of a sign is its part of speech, analogous to the information contained in an X̄-theory category stripped of bar level information. As we will discuss in the following section, a principle of universal grammar (the Head Feature Principle) requires that the HEAD value of any sign is always structure-shared with that of its phrasal projections. The appropriate values for HEAD are divided into the two sorts *substantive* (*subst*) and *functional* (*funct*). Subsorts of the sort *substantive* are *noun, verb, adjective* (*adj*), and *preposition* (*prep*), whereas *determiner* (*det*) and *marker* (*mark*) (e.g. complementizers) are the two subsorts of the sort *functional* that we will deal with here. For the sake of familiarity, we will refer to all these sorts as *parts of speech*.[9] This list is not intended to be exhaustive; we leave open the question of the precise inventory of the parts of speech. Some parts of speech have attributes of their own.[10] For example, *noun* has the

---

8. In P&S-87, a sort *syntactic-category* was employed for values of the SYNTAX attribute. This sort had the two attributes BINDING (similar to the NONLOCAL attribute of SYNSEM values in the present arrangement) and LOCAL (essentially the same as the present attribute CAT). The revision of the top-level structure of signs can be summarized as in P&S-87 (i) and this volume (ii), respectively:

(i)
$$
\begin{bmatrix}
\text{SYN} \begin{bmatrix} \text{LOC} \begin{bmatrix} \text{HEAD} \dots \\ \text{LEX} \\ \text{SUBCAT} \dots \end{bmatrix} \\ \text{BINDING} \dots \end{bmatrix} \\
\text{SEM} \begin{bmatrix} \text{CONTENT} \dots \\ \text{INDICES} \dots \end{bmatrix}
\end{bmatrix}
$$

(ii)
$$
\begin{bmatrix}
\text{SYNSEM} \begin{bmatrix} \text{LOC} \begin{bmatrix} \text{CAT} \begin{bmatrix} \text{HEAD} \dots \\ \text{SUBCAT} \dots \end{bmatrix} \\ \text{CONTENT} \dots \\ \text{CONTEXT} \dots \end{bmatrix} \\ \text{NONLOC} \dots \end{bmatrix}
\end{bmatrix}
$$

A third LOCAL attribute, LEXICAL (LEX), was employed in Chapter 7 of P&S-87, in the account of English constituent ordering principles. In order to carry that account over into the present system, LEX should be added to the inventory of CAT attributes; but since we will not touch on questions of constituent ordering in this volume, the LEX feature will not be employed in this volume.

9. The part of speech *marker* is introduced for the analysis of complementizers and certain other 'minor' words, discussed below.

10. Such attributes correspond for the most part to the HEAD features of P&S-87. But note that the HEAD feature MAJOR (MAJ) of P&S-87 is superseded here by the sort of the HEAD value; also, as explained below, the function of the old HEAD feature NOUN-FORM (NFORM) for nouns is taken over by the sort of the INDEX value.

feature CASE, prepositions have the attribute PREPOSITION-FORM (PFORM), and verbs have the attribute VFORM as well as the boolean features AUX and INVERTED (INV). In addition, the boolean feature PREDICATIVE (PRD) is appropriate for the sort *subst* (i.e. for all the parts of speech *noun, adj, verb,* and *prep*),[11] and the feature SPECIFIED (SPEC) is appropriate only for the sort *funct.*[12] In the present case, the HEAD value is specified as *noun*[CASE *nom*].

The SUBCAT value of a sign is in essence the sign's valence, that is, a specification of what other signs the sign in question must combine with in order to become *saturated*. More precisely, the SUBCAT value is a list of *synsem* objects, corresponding to the SYNSEM values of the other signs selected as complements by the sign in question. Here the notion *complement* is broadly construed to include not only sisters of lexical heads but also certain dependent elements classified as specifiers in GB theory (i.e. subjects, including determiner subjects of NPs). The condition that the SYNSEM value of a complement is structure-shared with the corresponding specification within the SUBCAT value of the sign that selects the complement is required by another universal principle to be discussed in the following section (the Subcategorization Principle). In the present case the SUBCAT value is ⟨ ⟩ because pronouns do not require any complements in order to become saturated; more complex cases will be considered below. It is noteworthy that only the SYNSEM values of complements are selected, not any of their other attributes (e.g. PHON and DTRS).[13] We thus eliminate a defect of the account of subcategorization given in P&S-87, wherein the SUBCAT value was assumed to be a list of *signs*. Because that account did not constrain what attributes of complements can be subcategorized for, a *Locality Principle* had to be introduced in order to disallow the possibility of heads imposing conditions on the internal constituent structure of their complements (P&S-87, pp. 143–144). In the current theory, the essential content of the Locality Principle follows immediately from the internal structure of signs. That is, because of the particular information that is included in objects of the sort *synsem* (e.g. information about part of speech, agreement features, case and referential index), we derive the effect that category selection, head-dependent agreement, case assignment, and semantic role assignment are all strictly local. Looking at this from a somewhat different perspective, precisely because such information about subconstituents of a

---

11. The motivation for these features and inventories of their possible values are given in P&S-87, sec. 3.1.

12. The feature SPEC will play a crucial role in our analysis (section 1.6) of complementizers as markers that select the kind of phrase they 'mark' and our treatment of noun phrases (sections 1.7 and 1.8), wherein determiners select the kind of nominal they combine with.

13. The DAUGHTERS attribute, which is defined for phrases but not for words, will be introduced in the following section.

complement is *absent* from *synsem* objects, it follows that no head can select for, agree with, or assign a role to such a subconstituent.

As justified at length in P&S-87, we assume that the ordering of elements on the SUBCAT list corresponds not to surface order, but rather to a version of the traditional obliqueness hierarchy. Thus subjects appear first (leftmost), followed by other complements (if any) in the order primary object, secondary object, then oblique PP and verbal and/or predicative complements.[14] As explained in P&S-87 (see also Sag and Pollard 1989), this ordering is broadly similar to other proposed hierarchies of grammatical relations such as the Keenan-Comrie accessibility hierarchy, the 1-2-3-oblique ordering of relational grammar, and the SUBJ-OBJ-OBJ2 hierarchy employed in the LFG Lexical Rule of Functional Control. Our obliqueness order also corresponds closely to the semantic order of arguments assumed in categorial grammar accounts such as that of Dowty 1982a, 1982b. However, under the set of semantic assumptions that we adopt here, where the contents of grammatical arguments are structure-shared with substructures of the head's content (rather than being taken as arguments), the categorial notion of semantic argument order does not have any analog.

We now turn to the CONTENT value, which (together with CONTEXT) specifies the sign's contribution to semantic interpretation, especially with respect to matters of reference.[15]

For the CONTENT value of nominals (i.e. lexical nouns and their phrasal projections), we will employ a feature structure sort called *nominal-object* (*nom-obj*), which in turn bears an attribute called INDEX (IND). The INDEX value, a structure of sort *index*, should be thought of as the HPSG analog of a reference marker in discourse representation theory (DRT: Kamp 1981) or of a parameter introduced by an NP use in situation semantics. As we will soon see, it is to indices that semantic (or thematic) roles are assigned.[16] Indices themselves are classified into subsorts, according to what might be called their 'mode of referring.' Thus *index* has the three subsorts *referential* (*ref*), *there*, and *it*. Indices of the latter two sorts are used only for the expletive (dummy or pleonastic) pronouns *there* and *it*, respectively. Referential indices are used for semantically contentful nouns as well as for nonpredicative PPs (i.e. PPs in

14. Unlike P&S-87, however, left-to-right order on the SUBCAT list corresponds to increasing, rather than decreasing, obliqueness. This is more mnemonic, since it corresponds roughly to English surface order (rather than its reverse).

15. The way that the CONTENT-related notions presented here figure in a situation-based account of semantic interpretation will be discussed at length in Chapter 8. For background on relevant situation-semantic notions, see Gawron and Peters 1990, Devlin 1991, Cooper 1990, and Ginzburg 1992.

16. Our approach thus differs in detail from most work in situation semantics, where the objects to which roles are assigned are restricted parameters, which are roughly analogous to our nominal-objects.

which the head preposition functions analogously to a case marking, so that the whole PP gets its content from the prepositional object NP).

Nominal-objects are further divided into the two subsorts *nonpronoun* (*npro*) and *pronoun* (*pron*), with the latter sort itself subdivided into the subsorts *personal-pronoun* (*ppro*) and *anaphor* (*ana*). Finally, *anaphor* has the two (maximal) subsorts *reflexive* (*refl*) and *reciprocal* (*recp*). The three subsorts *ppro, ana,* and *npro* correspond roughly to the classification within GB theory of NPs as pure pronominals (+p, −a), pure anaphors (−p, +a), or R-expressions (−p, −a). In the present example, the CONTENT value is of sort *ppro*, which entails that *she* will be subject to a certain principle of the HPSG binding theory (Chapter 6) analogous to GB's Principle B.

Indices in turn have the three agreement features PERSON (PER), NUMBER (NUM), and GENDER (GEND). Indices play a role in our theory analogous to that of NP indices in GB theory: two nominals are said to be *coindexed* if their indices are token-identical (structure-shared). For example, in the sentence *he shaved himself* the indices of *he* and *himself* will be structure-shared. Their CONTENT values, however, will not be; indeed, the CONTENT value of *he* is of sort *ppro*, while that of *himself* is of sort *refl*. Since agreement features are internal to indices, it follows that coindexed elements always agree.[17] This in turn has important consequences for the HPSG theory of agreement, presented in Chapter 2.

We also allow for the possibility that the content of a (nonexpletive) nominal introduces a semantic restriction on its index, which, when present, will be the value of the RESTRICTION attribute of the nominal-object. The value of the RESTRICTION attribute is a set of parametrized states-of-affairs (psoas).[18] Expletive pronouns, which are always nonreferential, are specified as [RESTRICTION { }].

Within a psoa, the values of the attributes other than the RELATION attribute (i.e. the arguments of the psoa) can be either referential indices or psoas (which may in turn contain further indices of their own). In general the referential index arguments will originate in the contents of NPs or nonpredicative PPs, while the psoa arguments will arise from predicative phrases (such as sentential

17. At present, we have no account of such colloquialisms as *everyone has behaved themselves* (pointed out to us by Tom Wasow), which are counterexamples to all theories of agreement that we are familiar with.

18. States-of-affairs (soas) were called 'circumstances' in P&S-87. In recent situation semantics literature, the term 'infon' is also frequently employed in this connection (see Devlin 1991). A (p)soa is represented by a feature structure that specifies a relation (for us, the value of the RELATION (RELN) attribute) together with values for the (argument) roles of that relation (for us, represented by the other attributes). In situation theory, a soa also specifies a polarity (either *1* or *0*), but since we will not be concerned with the analysis of negation, we suppress the POLARITY attribute, which can always be assumed to have the value *1*.

and VP complements, or predicative APs and PPs). Each psoa in the RESTRIC-
TION value is interpreted as placing semantic conditions on the entities that the
indices appearing in them can be anchored to in a given context (or range over,
in case an index is quantified over). In the present example, the set of restrictions is empty; but nonempty restrictions are introduced in the case of common
nouns. For example, the CONTENT value of the common noun *book* would be
as in (5):

(5)

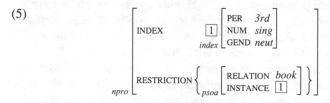

The significance of the RESTRICTION value is that when the word *book*
is used referentially (e.g. in a referential use of the phrase *a book*), the index
1 introduced by that use must be anchored to an entity that renders each psoa
in the set (in this case, a single psoa) factual; that is, the index must be anchored
to a book.[19] And when the index is bound by quantification (e.g. in a use of the
expression *every book*), the quantification is constrained to range over a set of
entities that render the psoa factual; that is, it will range over some contextually
salient set of books.[20]

19. When an NP is used referentially, its referent is just the object that its index is
anchored to. If two NPs are coindexed (i.e. they share a common index) and one of the
NPs refers to some entity X (which is then the anchor of that NP's index), then the other
NP necessarily also refers to X. Similarly, if some index is bound by a quantifier, then
any other occurrence of the same index must also be bound by the same quantifier. For
further discussion of these and related issues, see Chapter 8.

20. The present terminology and structuring of information within CONTENT values
differ in numerous respects from those employed in P&S-87. The differences can
be summarized by comparing the CONTENT value for *book* in (5) with the diagram
in (i), which shows how (roughly) the same information would have been structured
in P&S-87:

(i)

Restructuring along these lines leads to numerous simplifications in the theory with
respect to expletive pronouns (Chapter 3), binding (Chapter 6), control (Chapters 3 and
7), and quantification (Chapter 8).

Finally, we consider the CONTEXT value, which is a structure of sort *context*. For the moment we consider a single *context* attribute called BACKGROUND (BACKGR), whose value is a set of psoas.[21] Like the psoas in RESTRICTION values, each of these background psoas restricts the possible anchors of indices. Unlike RESTRICTION psoas, however, BACKGROUND psoas are not part of the CONTENT value but should rather be considered as felicity conditions on the utterance context. To put it another way, CONTENT values represent contributions to literal (truth-conditional) meaning, while BACKGROUND values represent conditions on anchors that correspond to presuppositions or conventional implicatures. For example, in the present case the single background psoa corresponds to the presupposition that the referent of the English feminine pronoun *she* must be female. This is how we capture the fact that English is a 'natural gender' language (as opposed to, say, French, which is a standard example of a 'grammatical gender' language). By contrast, the French feminine pronoun *elle* does not introduce this BACKGROUND psoa: the referent of *elle* need not be a female. (For further discussion of these and related issues, see Chapter 2).

To take another example, the BACKGROUND value of the proper NP *John* would contain the psoa shown in (6):

(6)
$$\begin{bmatrix} \text{RELATION} & naming \\ \text{BEARER} & \boxed{1} \\ \text{NAME} & John \end{bmatrix}$$

Here the atomic value *John* refers to the name *John*, not to an individual named John. The psoa (6) corresponds to the presupposition that the referent of a use of the name *John* be named John, or, to be somewhat more precise, that the referent be identifiable in the utterance context by means of the name *John*. A somewhat different kind of example will be provided in Chapter 2, where we analyze Korean honorific verbs as introducing a background psoa corresponding to the condition that the speaker be honoring the referent of the verb's subject. Such conditions have often been regarded as a kind of conventional implicature.

Let us now examine lexical entries for some verbs. To ease the notation, we introduce in (7) some abbreviations for certain AVM diagrams of sort *synsem* that will be employed repeatedly; as always, sort symbols will be omitted when recoverable from context:

---

21. The BACKGROUND attribute fulfills much the same function as the INDICES attribute in P&S-87. Later, we will add a second *context* attribute called CONTEXTUAL-INDICES (C-INDS), which represents information about various indexical coordinates such as SPEAKER, ADDRESSEE, indices of spatiotemporal location, etc.

(7)   Abbreviation: Abbreviated AVM Diagram:

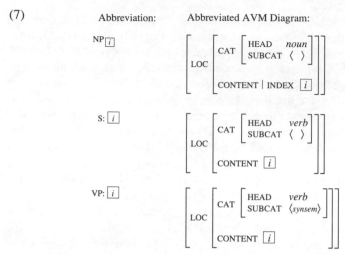

Thus the meaning of NP is the SYNSEM value of a saturated ([SUBCAT ⟨ ⟩]) nominal ([HEAD *noun*]) sign; the index, if mentioned, is written as a right subscript. S denotes the SYNSEM value of a saturated verbal sign, while VP denotes the SYNSEM value of a verbal sign that is saturated except for a single element (as always, of sort *synsem*) that corresponds to the subject. The CONTENT value may also be mentioned in the abbreviation, in which case it is notated after a colon. Abbreviatory symbols such as those in (7) may also be augmented with feature specifications in square brackets. In such cases the feature value appears without the feature or path label when no confusion can result, for example, VP[*fin*] or NP[*acc*]. In the case of a boolean feature, the feature label conventionally appears *preceded* by the value, for example S[+INV] or VP[−PRD]. Information internal to indices can also be abbreviated. NP$_{\boxed{1}[3rd,sing,fem]}$ abbreviates an NP whose index is $\boxed{1}$, where $\boxed{1}$ is specified as [PER *3rd*], [NUM *sing*], and [GEND *fem*]; NP:*ppro* abbreviates an NP whose content is of sort *ppro*. We will employ other such abbreviations, explaining them when necessary.

With these notational conventions out of the way, we can now present some lexical entries for verbs. Only the LOC values are shown.[22] The lexical entry for the verb *walks* is shown in (8):

(8)   *walks*
$$\begin{bmatrix} \text{CAT} & \begin{bmatrix} \text{HEAD} & \textit{verb} \, [\textit{fin}] \\ \text{SUBCAT} & \langle \text{NP}[\textit{nom}]_{\boxed{1}[3rd,\,sing]} \rangle \end{bmatrix} \\ \text{CONTENT} & \begin{bmatrix} \text{RELN} & \textit{walk} \\ \text{WALKER} & \boxed{1} \end{bmatrix} \end{bmatrix}$$

22. The discussion of NONLOC features is postponed until Chapter 4. Unless otherwise specified, lexical entries can be assumed to bear the value { } for all NONLOC features. This is only a matter of expository convenience; the theory itself does not employ any notion of defaults.

Like all tensed verbs in English, this bears the VFORM value *finite* (*fin*) and subcategorizes for a nominative subject.[23] And like all third-singular verbs, it requires that the index on the subject be [PER *3rd*, NUM *sing*]; in other words, for a verb, being third-singular is simply a matter of selecting a third-singular subject. Finally, the CONTENT value expresses the fact that the verb *walks* makes reference to the walk relation, and that the WALKER role of the walk relation is filled by the referential index of the subject.

The lexical entry for *sees*—(9)—is similar, but now in addition to a third-singular nominative subject (whose index fills the SEER role), an accusative primary object is also selected whose index is assigned to the SEEN role. And *gives* (in one of its valence alternants) further selects an accusative secondary object, with the assignment to semantic roles as shown in (10). Note that the order of the SUBCAT elements in (10), in virtue of English-specific principles of linear precedence, will correspond to the (focus-neutral) order in which the corresponding complements are realized (see P&S-87, Chapter 7):

(9)   *sees*
$$\begin{bmatrix} \text{CAT} & \begin{bmatrix} \text{HEAD} & verb[fin] \\ \text{SUBCAT} & \langle \text{NP}[nom]_{\boxed{1}\,[3rd,\,sing]},\ \text{NP}[acc]_{\boxed{2}} \rangle \end{bmatrix} \\ \text{CONTENT} & \begin{bmatrix} \text{RELN} & see \\ \text{SEER} & \boxed{1} \\ \text{SEEN} & \boxed{2} \end{bmatrix} \end{bmatrix}$$

(10)   *gives*
$$\begin{bmatrix} \text{CAT} & \begin{bmatrix} \text{HEAD} & verb[fin] \\ \text{SUBCAT} & \langle \text{NP}[nom]_{\boxed{1}\,[3rd,\,sing]},\ \text{NP}[acc]_{\boxed{2}},\ \text{NP}[acc]_{\boxed{3}} \rangle \end{bmatrix} \\ \text{CONTENT} & \begin{bmatrix} \text{RELN} & give \\ \text{GIVER} & \boxed{1} \\ \text{GIVEN} & \boxed{2} \\ \text{GIFT} & \boxed{3} \end{bmatrix} \end{bmatrix}$$

There are a number of general points to be noted with respect to lexical entries like those in (8)-(10). First, unlike most work in GB and GPSG (but

---

23. We disregard tense in this volume. But we assume that the proper way to handle it is in terms of an additional LOCATION role in the CONTENT value together with certain *context* attributes concerning temporal location, corresponding (say) to Reichenbach's utterance time, reference time, and event time. For example, present tense might be treated by structure sharing the EVENT-TIME value in the CONTEXT with the index of the LOCATION value in the CONTENT, and adding a BACKGROUND psoa restricting the EVENT-TIME value to temporally overlap the UTTERANCE-TIME value. For some discussion of these and related topics, see Fenstad et al. 1987, Crow 1990, and Cooper 1990.

like LFG), we assume that subjects are selected by verbs just as nonsubject complements are. (For a defense of this position, see P&S-87, sec. 5.4.)[24]

Second, assignment of case to complements, including nominative case assignment to the subject of finite verbs, is simply treated as part of subcategorization, no different in principle from selection of a VP complement bearing a particular VFORM value or of a PP complement bearing a particular PFORM value. There is no separate theory of case (or of Case). Nominative case assignment takes place directly within the lexical entry of the finite verb, without the intercession of an abstract INFL element. Loosely speaking, though, we might say that nominative case in English is assigned by the VFORM value *finite*, which is HPSG's closest analog to GB theory's AGR-bearing INFL. As in GB, we assume that the subject SUBCAT element of a nonfinite verb (as well as a predicative PP, AP, or NP) does not have a CASE value specified.[25]

Third, the assignment of semantic roles is uniform, with all roles, including that of the subject, being assigned directly within the verb's lexical entry; in particular, there is no notion of the subject's role being assigned 'externally' or by the intercession of the verb's phrasal projection.[26] In all cases the role assignment comes about by structure sharing of a SUBCAT element's index with the value of some attribute (i.e. semantic role) of the verb's CONTENT value; thus it is not the complements themselves (subject, object, etc.) that are assigned roles, but rather their indices.[27] Thus the CONTENT value of a verb directly embodies the verb's underlying predicate-argument structure; however, unlike the GB account of θ-role assignment under subcategorization, roles are explicitly modelled as attributes of the verb's CONTENT.[28] To summarize, in HPSG the selection of complements (including subjects), as well as the assignment of their cases and semantic roles, all takes place within the lexicon.

24. This assumption bears comparison to certain proposals within GB (e.g. Kitagawa 1986) to the effect that subjects originate under the maximal projection of V. In Chapter 9, we will consider an alternative position, wherein subjects and (nonsubject) complements are selected by distinct SUBJ and COMPS features.

25. We do acknowledge, however, that for languages with more complex case systems, some sort of distinction analogous to the one characterized in GB work as 'inherent' vs. 'structural' is required. For example, the analysis of Icelandic case assignment proposed in Sag et al. 1992 also distinguishes between structural (default) case and lexically assigned case specifications. For some discussion in the context of German, see Pollard, to appear.

26. This feature is shared with GB proposals wherein subjects originate under VP. See n. 24 above.

27. A similar intuition seems to underlie the suggestion by Williams (1989) that the binding theory applies to θ-roles.

28. As mentioned above, another difference is that we do not assume that every nonsubject complement is assigned a role. We return to this question in our account of 'subject-to-object raising' (Chapter 3).

1.4 Phrasal Signs and Principles of Universal Grammar

The principal type of object with which our theory is concerned, of course, is the sign (corresponding to the feature structure sort *sign*); and we assume that signs fall into two disjoint subtypes, *phrasal* signs (sort *phrase*) and *lexical* signs (sort *word*).[29] We have seen in the previous section some representative words, though these need not be given simply as a list; considerable redundancy can be eliminated by organizing the lexicon as a multiple-inheritance hierarchy along the lines proposed in Chapter 8 of P&S-87 (see below).

But how do we specify the well-formed phrases of a given language? The answer we give is similar to the one given in GB theory: a candidate phrase will be well-formed provided it satisfies all the principles of grammar, including both universal principles and language-specific principles. We do not rule out as a possible long-term goal the elimination of language-specific principles (e.g. principles of constituent ordering) in favor of 'parametrized' universal principles; and we will from time to time propose certain variants of universal principles in response to the empirical demands of some language or other, which might be regarded as parametrized forms of some more general principle. But in our opinion the notion of a parameter as it is currently employed in much syntactic research is not sufficiently constrained and well-defined to bear much real empirical weight. In the absence of a list, however tentative, of posited parameters and their range of settings, together with a substantial, worked-out fragment for at least one language, a specification of the settings for that language, and a reasonably detailed account of how those settings account for the array of facts covered in the fragment, we are inclined to view parameter-based accounts of cross-linguistic variation as highly speculative.

In this section, we consider the structure of some simple phrases and explicate two of the universal principles proposed in HPSG, the *Head Feature Principle* (HFP) and the *Subcategorization Principle*, which function as rough analogs of GB's Projection Principle.

Unlike words, phrases have the attribute DAUGHTERS (DTRS) (in addition to PHON and SYNSEM), whose value is a feature structure of sort *constituent-structure* (*con-struc*) representing the immediate constituent structure of the phrase. The sort *con-struc* has various subsorts characterized by the kinds of daughters that appear in them.[30] For the most part we will be concerned in this book with the constituent structure subsort *headed-structure* (*head-struc*),

---

29. Formally, this assumption is expressed by statements to the effect that, in the partial ordering of the sorts, *sign* is the meet or greatest lower bound of *word* and *phrase*, but *word* and *phrase* have no join or least upper bound (i.e. they are mutually inconsistent).

30. For further discussion, see P&S-87, pp. 55–59. Our view of hierarchically classified sorts of structures, or constructions, bears a striking resemblance to independent work on 'construction grammar.' See, e.g., Fillmore and Kay to appear.

which is employed in all headed constructions. Appropriate attributes for the sort *head-struc* include HEAD-DAUGHTER (HEAD-DTR) and COMPLEMENT-DAUGHTERS (COMP-DTRS); other attributes such as ADJUNCT-DAUGHTER (ADJ-DTR), FILLER-DAUGHTER (FILLER-DTR), and MARKER-DAUGHTER (MARKER-DTR) appear on more specific subsorts of *head-struc* to be discussed later. Thus we assume the minimal overall structure of a headed structure to be as shown in (11):

(11)
$$\begin{bmatrix} \text{HEAD-DTR} \quad \text{(a sign)} \\ \text{COMP-DTRS} \quad \text{(a list of signs)} \end{bmatrix}_{head\text{-}struc}$$

Note that every headed structure has a unique head daughter, but there may be many (or no) complement daughters; as with SUBCAT lists, order on the COMP-DTRS list is by increasing obliqueness.[31]

We now consider certain subsorts of *head-struc*, beginning with the sort *head-complement-structure* (*head-comp-struc*). In this sort, the only daughters are the head daughter and complement daughters (if any).[32] The structure of a very simple phrase whose DTRS value is a head-complement structure is sketched in (12); numerous inessential details are omitted:

(12)

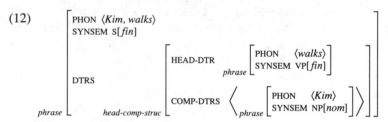

For the sake of familiarity—and typographical convenience—we adopt certain abbreviatory conventions for displaying phrasal structures as illustrated in (13):

(13)

```
                    S[fin]
              C  /‾‾‾‾‾‾\  H
          NP[nom]      VP[fin]
             |           /\
             |          /‾‾\
            Kim        walks
```

---

31. Again, this reverses the convention of P&S-87.

32. We make the standard assumption that there are head-complement structures where the list of complement daughters is empty. Such structures are employed to form phrases whose only daughter is a noun or verb lexical head, so that there is a distinction, say, between the word *walk* and the VP *walk* with the word *walk* as its head (and only) daughter.

In such abbreviated diagrams, a phrasal sign is represented by a node labelled with (an abbreviation of) the SYNSEM value of the sign in question, while the various daughters of that sign appear at the ends of labelled arcs originating from that node; such arcs are labelled H (HEAD-DTR), C (COMP-DTRS), A (ADJUNCT-DTR), F (FILLER-DTR), or M (MARKER-DTR); in the case of multiple complement daughters, the arcs are labelled C_1, C_2, . . . in order of increasing obliqueness. Finally, PHON values for lexical signs are written below the corresponding nodes (usually abbreviated by English orthography). Thus the specification of the DTRS value for a phrase can be seen to carry much the same information as a traditional phrase structure tree diagram, but additionally each daughter is characterized as to its 'grammatical role' (head, complement, adjunct, etc.).

In order to explicate the HFP and the Subcategorization Principle, we now consider another example in somewhat more detail. This is shown in (14):

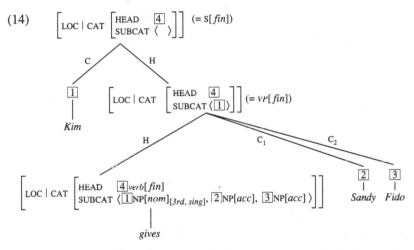

Let us consider (14) in bottom-up fashion, beginning with the lexical head *gives*. Note that this is the same as the lexical entry (10).[33] The next node up, representing the VP *gives Sandy Fido*, has three daughters: the lexical head already considered (H), the primary object *Sandy* (C_1), and the secondary object *Fido* (C_2). There are two important points to note here. First, each of the complement daughters of the VP has its SYNSEM value (indicated by the tags '②' and '③') token-identical to one of the elements on the SUBCAT list of the head daughter, while the SUBCAT value of the VP itself consists of the head daughter's SUBCAT list minus those requirements that were satisfied by one of the complement daughters. This state of affairs exemplifies the *Subcategorization Principle*, which is stated in (15):

33. Note that here the numerical tags within the SUBCAT value refer to the *synsem* objects on the SUBCAT list, not to their indices as in (10).

(15)   SUBCATEGORIZATION PRINCIPLE:

In a headed phrase (i.e. a phrasal sign whose DTRS value is of sort *head-struc*), the SUBCAT value of the head daughter is the concatenation of the phrase's SUBCAT list with the list (in order of increasing obliqueness) of SYNSEM values of the complement daughters.

The effect of this principle is to 'check off' the subcategorization requirements of the lexical head as they become satisfied by the complement daughters of its phrasal projections; at the same time, the SUBCAT elements themselves are token-identical to the SYNSEM values of the corresponding complements. Thus the Subcategorization Principle works much the same way as cancellation in categorial grammar.

The second point to note with respect to the VP node is that its HEAD value (indicated by the tag '$\boxed{4}$') is token-identical to that of *gives*. This state of affairs exemplifies the *Head Feature Principle*, which is stated in (16):

(16)   HEAD FEATURE PRINCIPLE (HFP):

The HEAD value of any headed phrase is structure-shared with the HEAD value of the head daughter.

The effect of the HFP is to guarantee that headed phrases really are 'projections' of their head daughters. Notice that when the token identities in (14)— indicated by '$\boxed{1}$' and '$\boxed{4}$'—are taken into consideration, the CAT value of the VP node is as shown in (17), namely, the category of VP[*fin*]:

(17)
$$\begin{bmatrix} \text{HEAD} & verb[\mathit{fin}] \\ \text{SUBCAT} & \langle NP[\mathit{nom}]_{[3rd,\ sing]} \rangle \end{bmatrix}$$

Finally, we consider the top node, representing the whole sentence, which has two daughters. One, the head daughter (H), is the VP just considered, while the complement daughter (C) is the subject *Kim*. In accordance with the Subcategorization Principle, the SYNSEM value of the subject is token-identical to the remaining element (indicated by '$\boxed{1}$' on the SUBCAT list of the VP); and in accordance with the HFP, the HEAD value is token-identical to that of the VP (and therefore to that of the head verb). Taking into consideration the token identity indicated by '$\boxed{4}$,' the CAT value of the S node is as shown in (18), namely, the category of S[*fin*]:

(18)
$$\begin{bmatrix} \text{HEAD} & verb[\mathit{fin}] \\ \text{SUBCAT} & \langle\ \rangle \end{bmatrix}$$

It should be clear from the consideration of this example that in any saturated ([SUBCAT $\langle\ \rangle$]) phrase where every phrasal constituent is headed, it will always be the case that (1) every SUBCAT requirement of the lexical head is satisfied by (i.e. token-identical to the SYNSEM value of) precisely one complement daughter of one of the lexical head's phrasal projections; and (2) the HEAD value of the entire phrase will be token-identical to that of the lexical head. Thus the combined effect of the Subcategorization Principle and the HFP is somewhat analogous to that of GB's Projection Principle, inasmuch as it guarantees that the information in the CAT of the lexical head (which should be seen as analogous to the D-structure of the whole sentence) is in some sense respected in the sentence itself. However, unlike GB, HPSG does not adopt the hypothesis that every lexical sign have a saturated projection;[34] we will see some examples of lexical signs that do not in the following section.

It should be noted in passing that the example in (14) also illustrates the handling of subject-verb agreement in HPSG: it arises from the token identity of the subject's SYNSEM value (and therefore the INDEX value) with that of the least oblique SUBCAT element of the lexical head. This should be compared with the GB analysis sketched in (19):

(19)

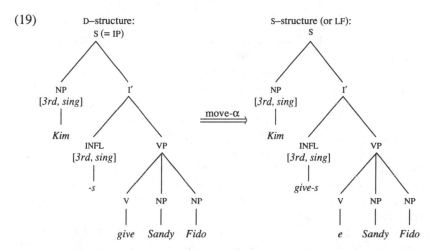

Unlike the GB account (Chomsky 1986b, 4–6, 68–69; Chomsky and Lasnik, to appear), there is no movement from V to INFL (or from INFL to V— see, e.g., Chomsky and Lasnik, to appear). Indeed, verb inflection, which we view as a lexical matter, is not accounted for within the syntax at all. There is no INFL node, which we consider an unmotivated conflation of two pieces of information (tense and agreement) that are best kept apart.[35] Neither is there any need to explain how INFL becomes coindexed with the subject NP, or how it is that coindexing causes the agreement features to be copied (if indeed they

34. But we will posit a weakened form of this hypothesis in Chapter 9.

35. Proposals by Pollock (1989) and others to eliminate the INFL node in favor of distinct nodes for tense, agreement, and modality are perhaps motivated by analogous considerations. Our analysis differs in the respect that we do not propose distinct phrase-structural nodes for these different features.

are copied). Instead, our account has the general form shown in (20) (which abbreviates the relevant aspects of (14)): subject-verb agreement arises directly from the lexical specifications of the finite verb in conjunction with the structure sharing imposed by the Subcategorization Principle.

(20)

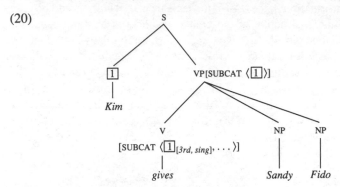

As is evident from this discussion, the theory of grammar presented here relies crucially on complex lexical information, which determines, in accordance with general principles such as the HFP and the Subcategorization Principle, the essential grammatical properties of phrasal expressions. This does not mean, however, that HPSG relies on complex lexical stipulations, or that the presence of distinct lexical entries with shared properties leads to massive redundancy within the lexicon. As described in P&S-87 and Flickinger 1987 (see also Flickinger et al. 1985; Flickinger and Nerbonne 1992; and Fraser and Hudson 1992), properties of lexical entries and relationships among them are expressed in a concise and principled fashion in terms of classification by a multiple inheritance hierarchy (P&S-87, sec. 8.1) and lexical (redundancy) rules (P&S-87, sec. 8.2), respectively.

The multiple-inheritance architecture for the lexicon employs standard knowledge-representation techniques to cross-classify words according to properties shared across word-classes (which are represented by 'generic' lexical entries, similar to defined types in knowledge representation systems). Thus, each generic lexical entry specifies certain constraints (i.e. values of certain features or relationships among values of different features) that must hold of all actual lexical entries that instantiate the generic entry. The hierarchical organization of lexical entries (both generic and actual) has the effect of amalgamating the information associated with any one actual entry with the information associated with all of the generic entries that it instantiates, thus requiring that a word inherit the properties of all word classes to which it (directly or indirectly) belongs. For example, one lexical entry for the word *gives*

---

36. For an initial attempt at formulating a 'linking theory' for HPSG, i.e. a theory of the relation between semantic roles and grammatical relations, see Wechsler 1991.

might specify that it inherits all constraints imposed by the two generic entries *ditransitive* and *third-singular-finite* (each of which in turn will inherit other properties from more general generic entries higher in the hierarchy); the only specific information about *gives* that has to be stipulated is the phonology of the base form, the semantic relation of its CONTENT value, and the assignment of semantic roles to grammatical relations.[36] In consequence of this architecture, the lexical entry in question acquires its seemingly complex syntactic information in a maximally general and highly deductive fashion.

Lexical rules, similar to those employed in early lexical-functional grammar (Bresnan ed. 1982), may be interpreted as rules of inference that derive lexical entries of inflected, derived, or compound words from those of simpler words. Passive (see Chapter 3) is one such lexical rule in our treatment of English; others include rules to produce inflected verb forms, valence alternants of 'the same verb' (e.g. the inchoative/causative alternation), nominalizations, etc. Thus lexical rules too have a highly deductive character.

For detailed discussion of both lexical hierarchy and lexical rules, the reader is referred to the relevant sections of P&S-87 cited above. Although numerous technical aspects of the syntactic theory have been revised since that account was presented, we do not anticipate any particular difficulties in adapting this overall lexical architecture to the current theory.

1.5 Immediate Dominance Schemata

Among the principles of universal grammar, there is a set of principles that have occupied a distinguished status within syntactic theory. These are the principles, variously known as 'grammar rules,' 'immediate dominance (ID) rules,' 'phrase structure rules,' or 'X-schemata,' that in effect serve as templates for permissible local phrase structure trees or configurations of immediate constituency. In the past decade, there has been a continuation of the general trend in syntactic theory toward the 'lexicalization of grammar,' and concomitantly a tendency to collapse or eliminate construction-specific rules in favor of highly schematic immediate dominance templates. For example, most GB work assumes the existence of schematic $\bar{X}$-rules such as those shown in (21):[37]

(21)   *a.* $X'' \rightarrow$ Y'' X'
                  (specifier)

         b. $X' \rightarrow$ X Y''
                                    (complement)

37. It is frequently assumed that such X-schemata should be derivable from deeper principles. We are sympathetic with such a view, but are not aware of any proposal in this regard that is worked out with sufficient precision to qualify as a genuine theory of possible ID configurations.

The set of such schemata should be regarded as a disjunctively specified principle of universal grammar. That is, one of the universal well-formedness conditions on a phrase is that its set of immediate constituents satisfy one of the schemata.[38]

Immediate dominance (ID) schemata in HPSG occupy a position in the theory analogous to that of X̄-schemata in GB theory: they are a small, universally available set of disjunctive constraints on the immediate constituency of phrases, from among which each language makes a selection. Thus the disjunction of the ID schemata itself constitutes a universal principle, which we call the *Immediate Dominance Principle* (IDP). A preliminary version, containing only two disjuncts (schemata), is stated informally in (22); successive versions will include more—but not many more—schemata:[39]

(22)   IMMEDIATE DOMINANCE PRINCIPLE (IDP, preliminary version):

The universally available options for a well-formed phrase are:

(SCHEMA 1) a saturated ([SUBCAT ⟨ ⟩]) phrase with DTRS value of sort *head-comp-struc* in which the HEAD-DTR value is a phrasal sign and the COMP-DTRS value is a list of length one; or

(SCHEMA 2) an almost-saturated (SUBCAT list of length one) phrase with DTRS value of sort *head-comp-struc* in which the HEAD-DTR value is a lexical sign; or

. . .

Let us consider these schemata one by one. Schema 1 (called 'Rule 1' in P&S-87, p. 149) is analogous to the X̄-schema (21a): it licenses saturated phrases with a phrasal head daughter and one other daughter that is a complement. It is an immediate consequence of the Subcategorization Principle that this complement daughter must have its SYNSEM value token-identical to the single element on the SUBCAT list of the head daughter, and that moreover that element must be the subject (least oblique SUBCAT element) of the lexical head. Thus any phrase licensed by Schema 1 will have the general form shown in (23) (disregarding the surface order of the daughters); note the structure sharings indicated by the tags '⒈' and '⒉,' which arise from the HFP and the Subcategorization Principle, respectively:[40]

---

38. Thus X̄-theory has the same status as any other disjunctively specified principle of UG, e.g. versions of the ECP (Empty Category Principle) that require that any non-pronominal empty category be either lexically governed or antecedent governed.

39. As with all disjunctive principles, it is a goal of the theory to have the precise inventory of posited disjuncts follow from deeper principles.

40. To enhance readability, nodes in constituent structure tree diagrams will often be labelled with only the LOC | CAT value at each node, rather than the entire SYNSEM value.

(23)

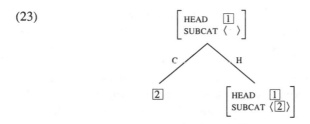

'Such phrases include sentences (S → NP VP), including 'small clauses' (i.e. saturated phrases headed by nonfinite verbs or nonverbal predicative phrases), as well as noun phrases consisting of a determiner and a nominal head (NP → Det N').[41] For example, the S[*fin*] node in (14) is licensed by this schema.

Schema 2 (called 'Rule 2' in P&S-87, p. 151) is analogous to the X̄-schema (21b); it licenses phrases that have a lexical head daughter and zero or more complement daughters, and that have satisfied all their subcategorization requirements except the least oblique one (the subject). By the HFP and the Subcategorization Principle, any phrase licensed by Schema 2 will have the general form shown in (24) (again disregarding the surface order of the daughters):

(24)

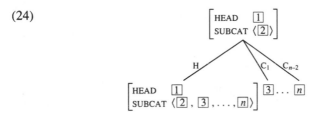

Thus Schema 2 subsumes all conventional phrase structure rules that expand a phrase as a lexical head together with its (nonsubject) complements; an example is the VP[*fin*] node in (14).

For all that the schemata in (22) are analogous to X̄-schemata, two important differences should be noted.[42] First, the notion of 'bar level' plays no role, being superseded in part by the lexical/phrasal distinction and in part by the relative degree of saturation. Second and more important is a difference in the relationship between the schemata and notions of grammatical function such as subject/specifier and object/(nonsubject) complement. In X̄-theory, such no-

41. Thus, if the least oblique position in the SUBCAT list is taken as the HPSG analog of the GB notion 'specifier,' we treat determiners, including possessive phrases, as the specifiers of their NPs. However, for reasons to be discussed below, we do not adopt here the *Barriers*-style analysis of complementized sentences as projections of the complementizer and 'topic' position as their specifiers.

42. But see Chapter 9, where we posit a lexically based reformulation of X̄-theory.

tions are *defined* by the schemata; for example, the subject/specifier in a phrase is the subject/specifier by virtue of occupying a particular position in (some instantiation of) a particular schema, namely, the *Y″* position in (21a). Thus in GB grammatical functions are wholly configurational notions, where 'configurational' in turn is understood in terms of immediate dominance trees. In HPSG, though, such notions as subject and (nonsubject) complement are *lexically* defined in terms of position on the SUBCAT list of lexical heads. ID schemata, then, do not *define* grammatical functions, but only constrain how they can be *realized* configurationally.

This last point can be made clearer by introducing our third ID schema, given in (25):

(25)   (SCHEMA 3) a saturated ([SUBCAT ⟨ ⟩]) phrase with DTRS value of
         sort *head-comp-struc* in which the HEAD-DTR value is a lexical sign.

By the HFP and the Subcategorization Principle, any phrase licensed by Schema 3 will have the general form shown in (26), that is, a phrase in which all complements (including the subject) are realized as sisters of the lexical head:

(26)

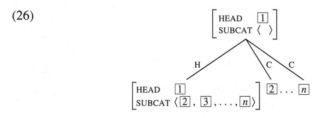

It is this schema, we assume, that licenses clausal structures, standardly analyzed by GB in terms of 'scrambling,' in free constituent order languages such as Warlpiri; languages like Japanese and German where the complements (including the subject) can be more or less freely ordered are analyzed in a similar fashion, except that parochial conditions require the verb to be clause-final in Japanese and either clause-initial or clause-final in German according as the clause is root or subordinate.[43] We also consider VSO structures such as Welsh finite clauses or English 'subject-auxiliary inversion' clauses, sometimes analyzed by GB in terms of head movement of the auxiliary from INFL into complementizer position (Sproat 1985), to be instances of Schema 3.[44]

---

43. We follow much recent work in analyzing V2 word order in German root clauses in terms of fronting of a constituent from a verb-initial finite clause.

44. Thus 'Rule 3' of P&S-87 (p. 156) should be regarded as a special case of Schema 3. In Chapter 9, we will consider an alternative view of this matter.

By way of illustration, we consider briefly an example of subject-auxiliary inversion. The heart of the analysis lies in the lexical entry of the auxiliary verb, exemplified by (27):

(27)   CAT value of the auxiliary verb *can*:

$$\begin{bmatrix} \text{HEAD} & verb[fin, +\text{AUX}] \\ \text{SUBCAT} & \langle \boxed{1}\text{NP}[nom], \text{VP}[bse] \rangle \end{bmatrix}$$

Note that auxiliaries are simply treated as verbs bearing the specification [+AUX]; there is another head feature INV (INVERTED) appropriate for verbs, for which most finite auxiliaries are unspecified.[45] Like all finite verbs, *can* subcategorizes for a nominative subject; and in common with other modals, it subcategorizes for a base-form VP complement.[46] Now in languages like English, where only auxiliaries can invert, we assume that Schemata 1 and 2 are employed in uninverted structures, while Schema 3 is employed in inverted structures. Technically, this means that, in availing itself of Schemata 1 and 2, English imposes on them the further parochial condition that the HEAD value must bear the specification [−INV], while in availing itself of Schema 3, English imposes on it the parochial condition that the HEAD value must bear the specification [+INV], which arises only in case the lexical head is a finite auxiliary.[47]

Thus an uninverted sentence like *Kim can go* is analyzed as in (28):

45. But auxiliaries like first-singular *aren't* that must invert are lexically specified as [+INV], while those like *better* that must not, as well as all verbs that are nonfinite or nonauxiliary, are [−INV]. It is these subtle distributional facts, to the best of our knowledge not treated in other accounts, that motivate the INV feature. For further discussion, see P&S-87, pp. 63–64.

46. In fact the VP complement will be further specified as [SUBCAT $\langle \boxed{1} \rangle$], i.e. the subject of the auxiliary is structure-shared with the complement subject. This kind of sharing is characteristic of raising-to-subject verbs (discussed in Chapter 3), of which we consider auxiliaries to be a subspecies.

47. Such parochial conditions on ID schemata can be regarded as candidates for parameters of cross-linguistic variation; but as a point of methodology, we are cautious about proposing parameters in the absence of a precise specification of the range of possible values for the parameter. The important point is that the same schemata might well be employed in other languages, with gross typological differences corresponding to different parochial conditions on the structures that realize those schemata. For example, in languages such as Welsh, where finite clauses are VSO but nonfinite VPs and clauses (S)VO, we might propose that Schema 3 carry the further condition (roughly) that the HEAD value be specified as *fin* while Schemata 1 and 2 are *nonfinite*.

(28)

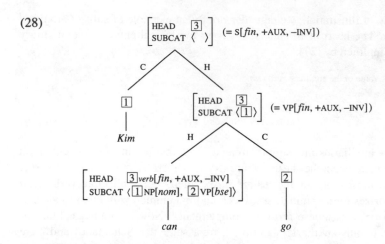

Here the S and VP nodes are licensed by Schema 1 and Schema 2, respectively. Except for the fact that the auxiliary is taken to be a verb rather than INFL, this is grossly similar to the standard GB analysis shown in (29):

(29)

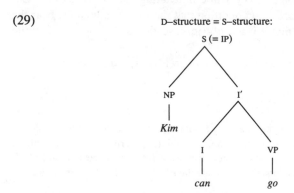

In the case of an inverted sentence like *can Kim go*, however, the situation is quite different. On the HPSG analysis, the structure is licensed by Schema 3, as in (30):

(30)

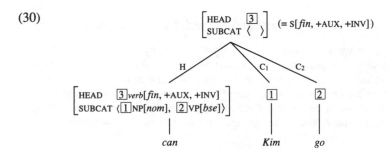

Suppressing the internal category structure of the lexical head, this is just the flat structure shown in (31):

(31)

There is no sense in which *can go* figures as a constituent in this structure at any level of analysis. By contrast, the standard GB analysis of such an example is in terms of head movement from INFL to COMP as shown in (32):

(32)

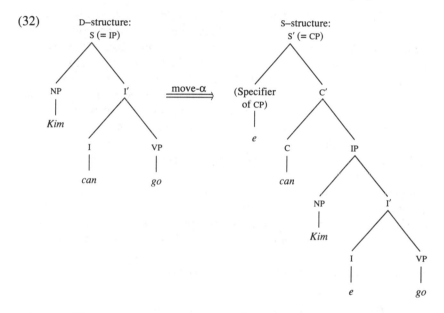

Presumably, in most general terms, the point of such an analysis is to capture the relationship between the two sentences. But on our view, the relationship between *Kim can go* and *can Kim go* is captured perfectly in the lexical heads of (30) and (28), which are identical except that the values of the INV feature are instantiated as − and +, respectively. In both cases the NP[*nom*] *Kim* is the subject and the VP[*bse*] *go* the oblique complement (whose own subject is controlled by *Kim*). But these facts arise out of the subcategorization of the lexical head, not from the way that the different grammatical functions are variously realized configurationally in (29) and (32). (For a more complete HPSG analysis of the English auxiliary system, see Warner (1992, to appear).)

1.6 Complementizers

In Chomsky 1986b and much subsequent GB work it is assumed that complementizers are heads. Thus, for example, the gross structure of the complementized clause *that John left* is taken to be that shown in (33):

(33)

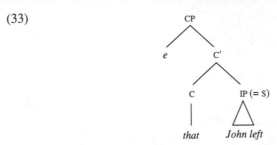

Among the arguments adduced for this structure are the following: (1) it extends the $\overline{\text{X}}$ system to complementizers, thereby contributing to greater uniformity of the overall grammar; (2) if we assume, as much current GB research does, that many instances of VSO word order (including subject-auxiliary inversion) arise from movement of the finite verb from INFL to COMP (see (32)), then we predict that inverted sentences do not occur with complementizers; and (3) if we further adopt the standard GB assumption that unbounded dependency constructions (such as *wh*-questions and relativization) arise from movement of a constituent into the specifier of CP position, then we also predict that 'dislocated' constituents appear to the left of the complementizer (e.g. in Scandinavian languages).

Suggestive though they may be, we do not consider such arguments persuasive, inasmuch as all three arguments depend on GB-internal assumptions that we have not adopted here (e.g. $\overline{\text{X}}$-theory, the analysis of inversion as movement to COMP, and the analysis of unbounded dependencies as movement to specifier of CP). In addition, as is well known, some verbs select a complementized sentential complement headed by a base-form (rather than finite) verb, as in (34):

(34)   I demand that he leave/*leaves immediately.

If the complementizer heads the complementized clause, then it seems difficult to explain how *demand* selects the complement's head verb inflection. On the other hand, if S is the head of *that*-S, then we need only assume that *demand* subcategorizes for S[*bse*] rather than S[*fin*].

We are not claiming that the analysis of complementizers as heads is untenable, only that the fundamental intuition underlying such proposals raises as many questions as it answers; enough questions, in fact, to lead one to consider alternative approaches. But if complementizers are not heads, then what are they? We will take the position that they are a subspecies of *marker*. On our account, a marker is a word that is 'functional' or 'grammatical' as opposed to substantive, in the sense that its semantic content is purely logical in nature (perhaps even vacuous). A marker, so-called because it formally *marks* the constituent in which it occurs, combines with another element that heads that constituent. In addition to the complementizers *that* and *for*,[48] other examples of markers include the comparative words *than* and *as*, the case-marking post-clitics of Japanese and Korean,[49] and perhaps nonpredicative adpositions in (the vast majority of) languages where adposition stranding does not occur.

Technically, as noted above, we posit a new part of speech *marker* (*mark*). Markers are distinguished from each other, and from nonmarkers, by a new attribute of categories (in addition to HEAD and SUBCAT) called MARKING, with values of sort *marking*. The sort *marking* in turn has the subsorts *marked* and *unmarked*. Here *unmarked* is the default value, in the sense that it is the value borne by words other than markers. As we will see presently, constituents with a marker daughter inherit the MARKING value from that daughter. Different classes of markers are distinguished by different subsorts of *marked*. For present purposes, we need consider only the subsort *complementizer* (*comp*), with subsorts of its own *that* and *for*.

Although markers are not heads, we assume that they resemble heads inasmuch as they select the phrases that they mark; for example, *that* selects S[*fin* ∨ *base*] while *for* selects S[*inf*].[50] To this end, we propose that markers bear the head feature SPECIFIED (SPEC) whose value is of sort *synsem*. This value will be structure-shared with the SYNSEM value of the (head) sign that the marker combines with to form a phrase. And such combinations are effected by the new ID schema given in (35):[51]

48. It is unclear whether interrogative *whether* is best treated as a marker or as an adjunct.

49. For arguments that Japanese case clitics are markers rather than heads ('postpositions'), see Tomabechi 1989.

50. In fact, finite and 'subjunctive' forms of English verbs are probably best analyzed in terms of two subsorts of a *tensed* sort (rather than the two unrelated sorts *finite* and *base* that we assume here, borrowing from work in GPSG). Under this alternative, the disjunction S[*fin* ∨ *bse*] is replaced by the supersort *tensed* in the description of the type of phrase that *that* selects.

51. We must also ensure that phrases without marker daughters are specified [MARKING *unmarked*]. One way to do this is to assume that each ID schema except the head-marker schema introduces this specification on the mother. Alternatively, we could let MARKING values be determined by a principle along the lines of (i):

(i)   MARKING PRINCIPLE:
        In a headed structure, the MARKING value coincides with that of the marker daughter if there is one, and with that of the head daughter otherwise.

We do not know of any empirical basis for choosing between these alternatives.

(35)   (SCHEMA 4) a phrase with DTRS value of sort *head-marker-structure*
          whose marker daughter is a marker whose SPEC value is structure-
          shared with the SYNSEM value of the head daughter, and whose
          MARKING value is structure-shared with that of the mother.

Here the sort *head-marker-structure* (*head-mark-struc*) is a subsort of
headed-structure that has no complement daughters (i.e. it is specified as
[COMP-DTRS ⟨ ⟩]) and that bears an additional attribute MARKER-DTR. Thus
Schema 4 licenses phrases of the form shown in (36):

(36)

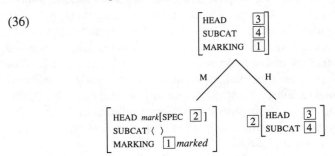

Given complementizer lexical entries like the one in (37), the analysis of
that John left will be as in (38):[52]

(37) CAT value of complementizer *that*:

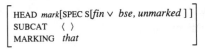

(38)

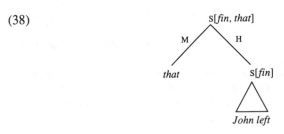

---

52. The SPEC value of *that* is specified as *unmarked*, thus blocking **that that John*
left.

1.7 Determiners, Quantifiers, and Quantifier Storage

In this and the following section we present a new analysis of determiners, which we will assume to include both quantificational determiners like *every* and possessive phrases such as *her* and *Mary's*.[53] We consider quantificational determiners first.

We begin by asking, what should the CONTENT value of a quantificational NP like *every book* be? In P&S-87 we assumed that it would be a structure of sort *quantifier* (*quant*), which, given the structuring of NP content information presented above, would have the form shown in (39), where the index $\boxed{1}$ has the internal structure given in (40):[54]

(39)

$$
quant \begin{bmatrix} \text{DET } forall \\ \text{RESTIND} \begin{bmatrix} \text{INDEX} & \boxed{1}ref \\ \text{RESTR} & \left\{ \begin{bmatrix} \text{RELN} & book \\ \text{INST} & \boxed{1} \end{bmatrix} \right\} \end{bmatrix} \end{bmatrix}
$$

(40)

$$
ref \begin{bmatrix} \text{PER} & 3rd \\ \text{NUM} & sing \\ \text{GEND} & neut \end{bmatrix}
$$

However, in making this assumption we were working within a simplified set of assumptions about the nature of natural language quantification, one that ignored the well-known scopal ambiguities exhibited by such sentences as (41):[55]

(41)   Every man loves some woman.

We now abandon that analysis. In Chapter 8 we will present an alternative account of quantification that uses a version of Cooper's (1975, 1983) storage technique to account for scope ambiguity. A key element of that account will

---

53. Since the principal concerns of these sections are semantic, some readers may prefer to omit them initially (except for the last three paragraphs of this section), or to read them later in conjunction with Chapter 8.

54. Here the RESTRICTED-INDEX (RESTIND) attribute takes as its value a kind of nominal-object (an object of sort *npro*, in fact) that specifies both an index and a non-empty restriction on that index.

55. The main ingredients in that analysis were a certain recursive function called *successively-combine-semantics* (P&S-87, p. 111) and a grammatical principle (the Semantics Principle, P&S-87, p. 110) that employed that function to define 'default' readings (contents) for sentences containing quantifiers; here the default reading is the one in which each quantifier receives the narrowest scope possible while still binding every instance of the appropriate index.

be the assumption that *all* quantifiers 'start out in storage'; the final scope that a quantifier receives will depend on which node it is retrieved at and on the order of its retrieval relative to other quantifiers retrieved at the same node. Roughly speaking, stored quantifiers can be thought of as being passed from constituents to their mothers according to the principle stated in (42):[56]

(42)   QUANTIFIER INHERITANCE PRINCIPLE (QIP, informal version):

The QUANTIFIER-STORE (QSTORE) value of a phrasal node is the union of the QSTORE values of the daughters less those quantifiers that are retrieved at that node.

The retrieved quantifiers themselves will then appear, with their scopes determined, in the CONTENT value of that node.

In anticipation of this analysis, we now revise the treatment of quantificational NPs like *every book* as follows. Instead of appearing as the CONTENT value, the quantifier (39) will appear in the QSTORE value. Only the nominal-object (an object of sort *npro*) of that quantifier will be 'left behind' as the CONTENT value. Thus the phrase *every book* will have QSTORE and CONTENT as shown in (43):

(43)
$$\begin{bmatrix} \text{SYNSEM | LOCAL | CONTENT} & \boxed{2} \\ \text{QSTORE} & \left\{ \begin{bmatrix} \text{DET } forall \\ \text{RESTIND} & \boxed{2} \begin{bmatrix} \text{INDEX} & \boxed{1}ref \\ \text{RESTR} & \left\{ \begin{bmatrix} \text{RELN} & book \\ \text{INST} & \boxed{1} \end{bmatrix} \right\} \end{bmatrix} \end{bmatrix} \right\} \end{bmatrix}$$

Notice that on this analysis a quantificational NP's CONTENT value is of the same sort as that of a nonquantificational NP (e.g. *she* in (5)), namely *nominal-object* (i.e. an index together with a restriction on that index). In fact, the CONTENT value of *every book* will be precisely the same as that of the head N′ *book*. This is an instance of a general constraint that we state provisionally as (44):[57]

(44)   SEMANTICS PRINCIPLE (preliminary version):

The CONTENT value of a phrase is token-identical to that of the head daughter.

56. In spite of the procedural ring of this informal description, in Chapter 8 quantifier retrieval will actually be formulated declaratively as a relation among the CONTENT and QSTORE values of a sign and those of the sign's daughters.

57. A careful formulation of the Semantics Principle will be given in Chapter 8. Two important cases not covered by the version given here are (1) the case where a quantifier is retrieved, and (2) the case where there is an adjunct daughter. In the former case, any retrieved quantifiers will have to be scoped (in some order) over the head daughter's content. In the latter case, as we will see in the next section, the mother's content must come not from the head daughter, but rather from the adjunct daughter.

Now according to the Quantifier Inheritance Principle, the stored quantifier in (43) must have been present on either the head noun or the determiner. There is good reason to assume that the quantifier does not originate from the head noun. For one thing, we would like to leave open the possibility that a non-quantificational analysis is available for indefinite NPs like *a book* (perhaps along the lines suggested by Kamp (1981)); moreover, some uses of common nouns (e.g. as prenominal modifiers) never become quantified. For these reasons, we assume that the stored quantifier in (43) arises from the determiner.

Let us now consider the phrase structure (i.e. the DTRS value) of *every book*. We assume that common nouns subcategorize for their determiners (perhaps optionally in the case of plural common nouns).[58] Thus the lexical sign for *book* is as shown in (45):

(45)

$$
\begin{bmatrix}
\text{PHON } \langle book \rangle \\[2pt]
\text{SYNSEM | LOC}
\begin{bmatrix}
\text{CAT}
\begin{bmatrix}
\text{HEAD} & noun \\
\text{SUBCAT } \langle \text{DetP} \rangle
\end{bmatrix} \\[6pt]
\text{CONT}
\begin{bmatrix}
\text{INDEX} & \boxed{1} \\
\text{RESTR } \left\{ \begin{bmatrix} \text{RELN} & book \\ \text{INST} & \boxed{1} \end{bmatrix} \right\}
\end{bmatrix}
\end{bmatrix}
\end{bmatrix}
$$

Here the symbol 'DetP' abbreviates the *synsem* structure given in (46):

(46)

$$
\begin{bmatrix}
\text{LOC | CAT}
\begin{bmatrix}
\text{HEAD} & det \\
\text{SUBCAT } \langle \ \rangle
\end{bmatrix}
\end{bmatrix}
$$

Schema 1 will now license the phrase *every book* with complement daughter *every* and head daughter *book* as shown in (47):

(47)

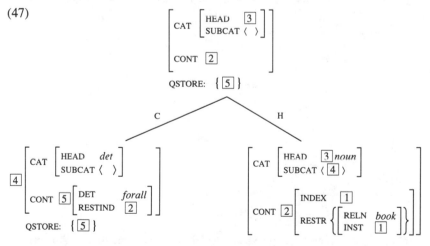

58. We leave open here the question of whether bare plural NPs should be analyzed as having phonetically null determiners.

Note that (47) incorporates a specific hypothesis about the CONTENT value of quantificational determiners (that it is token-identical to the stored quantifier). This analysis satisfies all four of the universal principles posited thus far: the HFP, the Subcategorization Principle, the QIP, and the Semantics Principle.

However, one important question about the analysis remains. How does it come about that the *npro* element (the RESTIND value) within the content of the determiner is token-identical to the content of the noun? At first blush it might be thought that this identity could be lexically specified within the SUB-CAT value of the noun. This will not work, however, since if the head noun were modified (say, by relative clauses or attributive adjectives), the semantic contribution of the modifiers would not be taken into consideration in the content of the determiner (or in the RESTIND value of the stored quantifier). Under present assumptions, it is clear that the determiner must in some sense be able to select its N′ sister, in order to 'have its hands on' the N′ sister's content. This situation bears comparison with the widely adopted hypothesis that determiners head NPs and therefore select their N′s, rather than the other way around.[59]

We will make a more conservative move, however. While continuing to assume that N′s are the heads of NPs and subcategorize for their determiners, we will also assume that determiners reciprocally select their N′ sisters. We effect this selection by means of a mechanism introduced in the preceding section, namely, the SPEC feature. Recall that this is a head feature, appropriate for markers, by which the marker selects (the SYNSEM value of) the phrase that it marks. We now assume that determiners also bear the SPEC feature. That is, both kinds of functional categories, markers and determiners, will be assumed to share the property that they select their head sisters. Thus far, our only argument that determiners select their N′ sisters is a semantic one. In Chapter 9, we will present evidence from German that this selection is (at least sometimes) syntactic as well. Under this assumption, the lexical sign for *every* is as in (48):

(48)

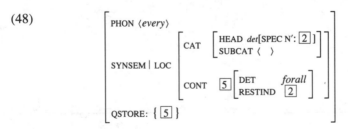

Here 'N′:☐2' abbreviates the *synsem* structure in (49):

59. See, e.g., Brame 1982, Hoeksema 1984, Hellan 1986, and Abney 1987. We will discuss this hypothesis in more detail in Chapter 9.

(49)

$$\left[\text{LOC} \begin{bmatrix} \text{CAT} \begin{bmatrix} \text{HEAD} & noun \\ \text{SUBCAT} & \langle \text{DetP} \rangle \end{bmatrix} \\ \text{CONT} \boxed{2} \end{bmatrix} \right]$$

Finally, we adopt the following general principle to ensure that SPEC values of nonheads get the right values:

(50)   SPEC PRINCIPLE:

If a nonhead daughter in a headed structure bears a SPEC value, it is token-identical to the SYNSEM value of the head daughter.

This concludes our analysis of quantificational determiners. Incidentally, (50) applies to markers as well as to determiners. As a consequence, Schema 4 in (35) can now be simplified to the form (51):

(51)   (SCHEMA 4) a phrase with DTRS value of sort *head-marker-structure* whose marker daughter is a marker with MARKING value token-identical to that of the mother.

1.8 Possessives

We turn next to possessives, such as *my* and *Mary's*.[60] The analysis of these items might be thought to pose something of a challenge, inasmuch as they behave like determiners in some respects but like pronouns in others. More specifically, on the one hand forms like *my* form NPs in combination with Ns and introduce a stored quantifier; on the other hand they pattern like personal pronoun subjects with respect to the binding theory (Chapter 6). In HPSG, however, the coexistence of these properties in a single expression does not pose an insurmountable problem. To see why, consider the lexical entry for *my* in (52):

---

60. In P&S-87 we assumed that such signs had a part of speech distinct from *det*, provisionally called *pos*. This assumption entailed that all lexical common nouns have two lexical entries, one subcategorizing for a determiner and the other for a possessive phrase. With possessives assimilated to determiners, this is no longer necessary, although this may still be the analysis of choice for languages like Hungarian where nouns exhibit different forms according as they appear with nonpossessive or possessive determiners. See also Chapter 9.

(52)

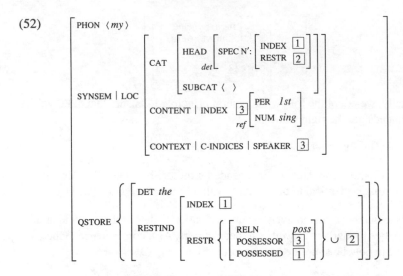

There are a number of points to note here. First, observe that the CAT value is exactly as for the determiner *every*, except that we have identified the index and restriction of the selected N′ head with tags ('[1]' and '[2],' respectively) so that they can be referred to elsewhere in the structure. The reason for this will be explained presently. Second, the CONTENT is exactly as for the first singular personal pronoun *I*: the agreement features of the referential index (labelled '[3]') identify it as first-singular. Together, the CAT and CONTENT values explain how it is that *my* behaves like a determiner in some respects, and like a personal pronoun in others. The CONTEXT value, which shows that the index introduced by *my* is structure-shared with the SPEAKER value, provides a typical example of how indexicality is handled in HPSG. Finally, we consider the stored quantifier, with which the NP mother of *my* will eventually make its contribution to semantic interpretation. Of course the index bound by this quantifier is [1], the index introduced by the determiner's N′ sister. Particular attention should be paid to the restriction on this index (the set value of the RESTR feature within the stored quantifier): it is the union of the restrictions contributed by the N′ itself ([2]) with the singleton set containing the psoa (53):

(53)

$$\begin{bmatrix} \text{RELN} & poss \\ \text{POSSESSOR} & 3 \\ \text{POSSESSED} & 1 \end{bmatrix}$$

The RELATION value *poss* should be understood here as a 'wild card' that will be instantiated, in a given context, as some contextually salient binary relation R (see Downing 1977); likewise, POSSESSOR and POSSESSED will be instantiated as the roles of R. And $\boxed{3}$ indicates the index introduced by *my*, which as we noted is coindexed with the speaker. If *my* combines with (say) *book* (see (45)) to form the NP *my book*, the stored quantifier (which will be passed up to the NP by the QIP) will be as in (54):[61]

(54)
$$
\begin{bmatrix}
\text{DET } the \\
\text{RESTIND}
\begin{bmatrix}
\text{INDEX } \boxed{1} \\
\text{RESTR}
\left\{
\begin{bmatrix} \text{RELN } book \\ \text{INST } \boxed{1} \end{bmatrix},
\begin{bmatrix} \text{RELN} & poss \\ \text{POSSESSOR} & \boxed{3} \\ \text{POSSESSED} & \boxed{1} \end{bmatrix}
\right\}
\end{bmatrix}
\end{bmatrix}
$$

We conclude this section with an analysis of possessive *'s*. The basic idea is that *'s* combines with an NP sister to form a sign that is essentially like a possessive determiner, except that (CONTENT or CONTEXT) restrictions on the possessor will now come from the NP sister. More precisely, we analyze *'s* as an unsaturated determiner that subcategorizes for a nonpronominal NP sister, as shown in (55):

(55)
$$
\begin{bmatrix}
\text{PHON } \langle 's \rangle \\
\text{SYNSEM | LOC}
\begin{bmatrix}
\text{CAT}
\begin{bmatrix}
\text{HEAD} \begin{bmatrix} \text{SPEC N'}: \begin{bmatrix} \text{INDEX } \boxed{1} \\ \text{RESTR } \boxed{2} \end{bmatrix} \end{bmatrix} \\
det \\
\text{SUBCAT } \langle \text{NP}: \boxed{5}npro[\text{INDEX } \boxed{3}]\rangle
\end{bmatrix} \\
\text{CONTENT } \boxed{5}
\end{bmatrix} \\
\text{QSTORE}
\left\{
\begin{bmatrix}
\text{DET } the \\
\text{RESTIND}
\begin{bmatrix}
\text{INDEX } \boxed{1} \\
\text{RESTR}
\left\{
\begin{bmatrix} \text{RELN} & poss \\ \text{POSSESSOR} & \boxed{3} \\ \text{POSSESSED} & \boxed{1} \end{bmatrix}
\right\}
\end{bmatrix}
\end{bmatrix}
\cup \boxed{2}
\right\}
\end{bmatrix}
$$

Now suppose *'s* takes as complement the NP *Mary*, whose SYNSEM|LOC value is shown in (56):

61. By the way, (52) provides a good illustration of the fact that lexical entries, like ID schemata ((22), (25)) and principles of UG ((15), (16)), must be represented theoretically as *constraints* on (i.e. descriptions of) feature structures, not simply as feature structures. That is, (52) constitutes a constraint that (the feature structure models of) any token of *my* must satisfy; but there is no one feature structure that satisfies (52), since for different tokens of *my*, the set value indicated by $\boxed{2}$ will be instantiated by different sets of psoas. By the same token, it is the description (4), not the feature structure (2), that should be thought of as the lexical entry for *she*; the difference is that in this case, the description is complete, so that (up to structural isomorphism) there is only one (totally well-typed, sort-resolved) feature structure that satisfies it.

(56)

$$
\begin{bmatrix}
\text{CAT} \begin{bmatrix} \text{HEAD} & noun \\ \text{SUBCAT} \ \langle \ \rangle \end{bmatrix} \\[2ex]
\text{CONTENT} \ \boxed{5} \, npro[\text{INDEX} \ \boxed{3}] \\[2ex]
\text{CONTEXT} \mid \text{BACKGR} \left\{ \begin{bmatrix} \text{RELN } naming \\ \text{BEARER } \boxed{3} \\ \text{NAME } Mary \end{bmatrix} \right\}
\end{bmatrix}
$$

Assume also, for the sake of specificity, that the BACKGROUND value of any phrase is the union of its daughters' values.[62] Then the determiner *Mary's* will be as in (57):

(57)

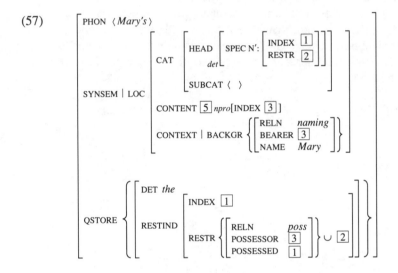

It is of crucial importance here that SPEC is a head feature, and therefore the SPEC value of *'s* is carried up to *Mary's* by the HFP. Notice that, except for the CONTENT and CONTEXT value, (57) has exactly the same structure as (52).[63]

62. We will consider the propagation of CONTEXT information more closely in Chapter 8.

63. There remains the question as to which ID schema licenses signs like (57). The obvious candidate is Schema 1, but it will not apply in its present form because *'s* is not phrasal. Two obvious alternatives are (1) to extend Schema 1 to allow clitic as well as phrasal heads, or (2) to introduce new schemata for clitics (presumably different schemata would be required according as a given clitic is analyzed as a head, a complement, or a marker). We leave this question unresolved here.

1.9 Adjuncts

In P&S-87 we considered the question of whether adjuncts select the heads that they modify or whether heads select their adjuncts. The tentative solution we adopted there assumed the latter, but as it has turned out, that solution has resisted extension to a satisfactory account of how adjuncts contribute their content to the content of the phrases they occur in. In this section we explore an alternative approach, wherein adjuncts select their heads. This approach has much in common with the analysis of adjuncts in categorial grammar, where it is assumed that adjuncts are functions that take heads as arguments. The basic idea of our analysis is that, in a head-adjunct structure, the content of the mother is token-identical to that of the adjunct; the content of the head is incorporated not by functional application but rather by structure sharing with a substructure of the head's content.

In order to explicate this analysis, we take as our point of departure the SYNSEM value of the lexical entry for the attributive adjective *red* given in (58):

(58)
$$
\begin{bmatrix}
\text{CATEGORY} & \begin{bmatrix} \text{HEAD} & adj\begin{bmatrix} \text{MOD N}': \begin{bmatrix} \text{INDEX} & \boxed{1} \\ \text{RESTR} & \boxed{2} \end{bmatrix} \\ \text{PRD} - \end{bmatrix} \\ \text{SUBCAT} \langle\ \rangle \end{bmatrix} \\
\text{CONTENT} & \begin{bmatrix} \text{INDEX} & \boxed{1} \\ \text{RESTR} \left\{ \begin{bmatrix} \text{RELN} & red \\ \text{ARG} & \boxed{1} \end{bmatrix} \right\} \cup \boxed{2} \end{bmatrix}
\end{bmatrix}
$$

To enable an adjunct to select its head, we introduce the head feature MODIFIED (MOD), which is analogous to the SPEC feature employed by markers and determiners for the same purpose. The specification [PRD −] is used to distinguish attributive adjectives from predicative adjectives.[64] For semantically restrictive adjectives like *red*, the content has a particularly simple form: it is just a nominal object whose index ($\boxed{1}$) coincides with that of the head noun, and whose restriction is the set of psoas obtained by adding to the restrictions imposed by the head noun one further restriction imposed by the adjective itself, in this case the psoa in (59):

(59)
$$
\begin{bmatrix} \text{RELN} & red \\ \text{ARG} & \boxed{1} \end{bmatrix}
$$

---

64. For discussion, see P&S-87, pp. 64–67.

An adjunct and a head that it selects can combine via the ID schema in (60):[65]

(60)   (SCHEMA 5) a phrase with DTRS value of sort *head-adjunct-structure* (*head-adj-struc*), such that the MOD value of the adjunct daughter is token-identical to the SYNSEM value of the head daughter.

Here *head-adj-struc* is a subsort of *head-struc* whose COMP-DTRS value is specified as ⟨ ⟩ and that bears an additional attribute ADJ-DTR. For example, Schema 5 will license the N' *red book* with adjunct daughter *red* and head daughter *book*; the SYNSEM phrase will then be as in (61):

(61)
$$
\begin{bmatrix}
\text{CAT} & \begin{bmatrix} \text{HEAD} & noun \\ \text{SUBCAT} & \langle \text{DetP} \rangle \end{bmatrix} \\[4ex]
\text{CONT} & \begin{bmatrix} \text{INDEX} & \boxed{1} \\ \text{RESTR} & \left\{ \begin{bmatrix} \text{RELN } book \\ \text{INST } \boxed{1} \end{bmatrix}, \begin{bmatrix} \text{RELN } red \\ \text{ARG } \boxed{1} \end{bmatrix} \right\} \end{bmatrix}
\end{bmatrix}
$$

One point that remains to be accounted for is the structure sharing of the mother's content with that of the adjunct daughter. This is a consequence of the Semantics Principle, which we now reformulate as in (62):[66]

(62)   SEMANTICS PRINCIPLE (second version):

In a headed phrase, the CONTENT value is token-identical to that of the adjunct daughter if the DTRS value is of sort *head-adj-struc*, and with that of the head daughter otherwise.

Various problems remain in extending this analysis of attributive adjectives to a general theory of adjuncts. One of these is the problem of ensuring that phrasal adjuncts bear the appropriate MOD value. In certain cases this can be handled by introducing the MOD feature on the adjunct's lexical head, letting the HFP carry it to the top of the adjunct. For instance, *with*-predicative adjunct clauses like the one in (63) can be treated this way:

(63)   With Kim gone, the project fell apart.

(64)   *With, the project fell apart.

Roughly, the idea is to treat *with* as the head of the adjunct, letting it select the small clause *Kim gone* via the SUBCAT feature and the finite clause by the MOD

---

65. Our use of MOD to allow adjuncts to select the kind of element they modify is quite like the treatment of modification (in terms of the feature ADJUNCT) proposed for Japanese by Gunji (1987: chap. 2).

66. This reformulation still ignores the effect of quantifier retrieval. We return to this issue in Chapter 8.

feature; we can block the nonsentence (64) by adding to Schema 5 the require-ment that the adjunct daughter be saturated ([SUBCAT ⟨ ⟩]).[67] Further refine-ments are required, however, in light of the fact that some adjuncts are *not* saturated. For example, *with*-less predicative adjuncts can occur either with or without subjects, as illustrated in (65):

(65) *a.* His hands trembling violently, Sandy loomed in the doorway.
      b. Trembling violently, Sandy loomed in the doorway.

Similar problems arise in the grammar of relative clauses, where the value on the whole relative clause for the feature MOD cannot be determined lexi-cally, though languages where the verbal head of a relative clause bears iden-tifying morphology (e.g. Korean) may well be analyzed in terms of lexically specified MOD values. The MOD value of a relative clause in English is inti-mately related to the values of the binding features SLASH and RELATIVE (REL), in ways that are discussed further in Chapters 4 and 5.

Another difficulty is presented by 'polymorphic' adjuncts that can adjoin to different kinds of heads with varying semantic effects. Consider, for example, the uses of the locative PP *in Chicago* in (66):

(66) *a.* A man in Chicago claims that the Axiom of Infinity is
          inconsistent.
      b. Kim slept in Chicago.
      c. In Chicago (at last), Kim slept soundly.
      d. Kim is in Chicago.

In (66a), the adjunct is a postnominal predicative modifer ('reduced relative') that restricts the index introduced by *man*. In (66b), it is a VP adjunct that might be analyzed as restricting an index corresponding to the location of the sleep-ing. In (66c), it is a sentence adjunct that might be analyzed as contributing a background psoa to the effect that Kim is in Chicago. And in (66d), it is not an adjunct at all but a predicative complement to the copula. Such polymorphism might be approached in terms of multiple lexical entries, perhaps related by lexical rules, but we will not speculate further about such matters here.

1.10 Conclusion

In this chapter, we have sketched the outlines of a linguistic theory, one whose descriptive power and empirical adequacy we will examine in detail in the chapters to come. Modelling types of conceivable linguistic entities as rooted labelled graphs of a special kind—totally well-typed, sort-resolved feature

---

67. As discussed in Chapter 9, this can be seen as a special case of the more general principle that nonhead daughters must be saturated with respect to (nonsubject) complements.

structures—we formulate universal grammar and grammars of particular languages as a system of constraints on those feature structures. Only those feature structures that satisfy the constraints are taken to model (types of) grammatically well-formed linguistic entities. The distinction between the system of constraints and the collection of linguistic entities that satisfies it can be viewed as corresponding both to Chomsky's (1986a) distinction between *I-language* and *E-language* and to Saussure's ((1916) 1959) distinction between *langue* and *parole*. Though only the latter is directly observable, only the former can be embodied as a mental computational system shared by members of a linguistic community. The constraints themselves can be classified roughly along the following lines:

(67)   **Universal Grammar:**

Linguistic ontology: the inventory of universally available sorts of linguistic entities, together with a specification of their appropriate attributes and their value sorts.

Schemata: a small, fixed inventory of universally available phrase types (schematic immediate dominance rules), for example, head-complement, head-adjunct, head-marker, etc.

Universal constraints on well-formed phrases: Head Feature Principle, Subcategorization Principle, etc.

Particular Grammar:

Lexicon: a system of lexical entries (possibly interrelated by lexical rules).

Linguistic ontology: selection from and further articulation of the universal linguistic ontology.

Schemata: selection from and further specification (e.g. for the constituent order) of the universally available schemata.

Thus, what expressions (words and phrases) are well-formed in a particular language depends on the interactions among a complex system of universal and parochial constraints, which themselves must ultimately be realized in computable form in the minds of the speakers of that language.

Broadly speaking, this conception of language and of linguistic theory has much in common with the GB approach, for all that HPSG and GB differ with respect to matters of technical detail (e.g. feature structures vs. labelled trees, structure sharing vs. transformation, the formulation of specific constraints). However, the approach we take here is also properly viewed as a further development of the one pioneered in Gazdar et al. 1985, not only because of obvious influences at the technical level (e.g. numerous aspects of the feature system, or constraints like the Head Feature Principle), but more importantly because of methodological commonalities. Principal among these are a concern with analyses of particular phenomena that are worked out in detail; insistence on mathematical precision (at least in principle) with respect to the grammar formalism itself and its intended interpretation; and commitment to the criterion of empirical consequence, that is, the requirement that given a grammar and (a model of) a candidate linguistic expression, it is a determinate matter of fact whether or not the entity satisfies the grammar. This last criterion is fundamental to the scientific method and at the same time provides a point of departure for meeting the more ambitious criterion of decidability (see the introduction). That is, by taking our system of constraints—appropriately formalized—as a hypothesis about the structure of human linguistic knowledge, we hope eventually to exploit formal and computational properties of the theory to develop integrated models of language processing, models that seek to explain how linguistic and nonlinguistic knowledge are effortlessly interleaved in language use, where communication proceeds with remarkable accuracy and efficiency.

2

Agreement

2.1 Two Views of Agreement

Agreement, which we may define quite generally as 'systematic covariation of linguistic forms,' presents an interesting focus of comparison between derivation-based and constraint-based theories of language. The derivational approach to agreement assumes a directional process that either copies or moves bundles of agreement features from a nominal, called the agreement controller, onto something that agrees with it, called the agreement target. On this view, the agreement features of the agreement controller are somehow inherent and logically prior to those of the target; the usual locution is that the verb *agrees with* the subject (or object) and the pronoun with its antecedent (not the other way around).

A constraint-based approach to agreement, by contrast, assumes that two elements that participate in an agreement relation specify partial information about a single linguistic object. Agreement is simply the systematic variation in form that arises from the fact that information coming from two sources about a single object must be compatible. In LFG, for example, the relevant objects are *functional structures*. Thus the initial NP in a canonical English NP-VP sentential structure may provide partial agreement information about the value of the feature SUBJ in the functional structure; and the verb within the VP also provides information about the value of SUBJ. Since verbs vary in shape depending on the agreement information they bear and since that information must be compatible with the agreement information about the SUBJ borne by the initial NP, a systematic variation in form arises. This is illustrated schematically for subject-verb agreement in (1):

(1)
$$\begin{bmatrix} the\ salmon \\ \text{PER } 3rd \end{bmatrix} \quad \begin{bmatrix} swims \\ \text{SUBJ} \begin{bmatrix} \text{PER } 3rd \\ \text{NUM } sing \end{bmatrix} \end{bmatrix} \quad \begin{bmatrix} you \\ \text{PER } 2nd \end{bmatrix}$$

the salmon swims (SUBJ is resolved to third-person singular)
*you swims (information about SUBJ is inconsistent)

But, as we shall argue at length below, the structures that are required to be token-identical in agreement phenomena of this sort are not functional structures, but rather indices. The shape of the verb is constrained when the grammar requires structure sharing between the INDEX value of one expression and an index specified by some other expression. In the present example, *swims* specifies a third-singular index for its subject (as the INDEX of the first member of its SUBCAT list), and token identity of that index with the index of the actual subject of the sentence is required by general principle, namely, the Subcategorization Principle.

From the constraint-based perspective, agreement information might appear to 'flow' in one direction or another not because agreement is inherently directional in nature, but because agreement information is often underspecified in lexical forms. Thus in examples like those in (2), the partial agreement information associated with the noun *salmon* is augmented variously by information contributed by either the main clause verb or the verb within the relative clause:

(2)   *a.* The salmon that had been swimming up the river was returning to
           spawn.
        b. The salmon that was swimming up the river had returned to
           spawn.

In (2a, b), the grammar of relative clauses (Chapter 5) requires that the index of the subject of the relative clause be token-identical to that of the matrix subject, which in turn is required to be token-identical to the index of the word *salmon*. This index is also required, by principles of our theory, to be identical to the index specified for the first SUBCAT member of *was* and the first SUBCAT member of *had*. Since only *was* specifies person and number information about this index, it is only when we encounter that form that the described index is known to be unambiguously singular. Thus, though agreement information may appear to flow sometimes in one direction, sometimes in another, in fact this flow of information is entirely dependent on the happenstance of when the word specifying crucial information is encountered in real time. The grammatical 'process' of, say, a verb agreeing with its subject is thus an illusion. The directional flow of information is essentially a property of language use (or linguistic performance), while the (competence) grammar of agreement is nothing more than a system of constraints requiring certain token identities, and hence inducing compatibility of certain lexically specified information.

A constraint-based analysis of an agreement system must include a theory of what kinds of objects are affected (identified) by agreement processes, an account of partial lexical entries (i.e. an account of their partial specifications), and a general theory of the constraints that establish the token identity of the relevant agreeing structures. In this chapter, we will develop the view that there are at least three kinds of agreement that must be kept analytically distinct: *index agreement* (which arises when indices are required to be token-identical), *syntactic agreement* (which arises when strictly syntactic objects (e.g.

CASE values) are identified), and *pragmatic agreement* (which arises when contextual background assumptions are required to be consistent).

2.2 Problems for Derivation-Based Agreement Theories

The constraint-based view of agreement theory is motivated not only by a certain computational perspective on the facts of language use, but also from a consideration of simple empirical generalizations. The alternative view, accepted by a long tradition of work in transformational grammar, is that agreement information originates on a nominal constituent (the agreement controller) and is transferred, either by movement or copying operations, onto the agreeing element (the agreement target). What has not been properly appreciated is that directional, transformational theories of agreement lead to massive redundancies in linguistic descriptions. We will illustrate this point with respect to the agreement systems of five languages, adapting some arguments due to Mike Barlow, who presents a more fully developed attack on derivation-based theories of agreement (see Barlow 1988).

2.2.1 French

Predicate adjectives in French must agree with their subjects, with respect to number and gender:

(3)   *a.*   Il est heureux. 'He is happy (masc).'
        b.   *Il est heureuse. 'He is happy (fem).'

(4)   *a.*   Ils sont petits. 'They (masc) are small (masc, plur).'
        b.   Elles sont petites. 'They (fem) are small (fem, plur).'
        c.   *Elles sont petits. 'They (fem) are small (masc, plur).'

A derivation-based account of these data would postulate a rule that copies a fully specified bundle of agreement information (presumably a feature structure of some sort) from the subject NP onto the agreement target.

But any such analysis will then have to posit multiple lexical entries for first- and second-person pronouns in order to explain the agreement patterns in (5):

(5)   *a.*   Je suis heureux. 'I am happy (masc).'
        b.   Je suis heureuse. 'I am happy (fem, sing).'
        c.   Tu es heureux. 'You are happy (masc).'
        d.   Tu es heureuse. 'You are happy (fem).'

On a constraint-based account, however, no pronoun proliferation is required. The first- and second-person pronouns are simply unspecified for gender information, and hence are compatible (yielding different results) with either masculine or feminine gender, as specified by the adjective.

2.2.2 Walmanpa

Walmanpa, an Australian aboriginal language studied by Hale (1973), has a first-person pronoun *ŋayu* that co-occurs with the subject clitic typically realized as part of the 'AUX' constituent. However, the clitics of Walmanpa manifest a three-way number distinction and a two-way distinction of exclusivity, as illustrated in (6):

(6)   -ŋa   (1st person, singular)
      -tja   (1st person, dual, exclusive)
      -li   (1st person, dual, inclusive)
      -ŋa-lu   (1st person, plural, exclusive)
      -lpa-lu (1st person, plural, inclusive)

As Hale (1973, p. 321, n. 7) makes clear, there are no distinctively plural pronouns in Walmanpa (and dual marking is optional). The optimal analysis, given derivation-based assumptions, is a transformation of the sort Hale proposes, which copies agreement information from the subject onto the AUX-node. But if such an analysis is adopted, then there must be five pronominal lexemes whose phonology happens to be *ŋayu*—one lexeme corresponding to each of the inflectional categories illustrated in (6).

Such redundancy is avoided in a constraint-based agreement analysis where the pronoun and subject clitic both provide partial information about the subject of the Walmanpa sentence. There need be only one first-person pronoun, whose agreement information is compatible with that associated with any of the clitics in (6).

2.2.3 Onondaga

As pointed out by Chafe (1970), verbs in the Iroquoian language Onondaga are systematically marked for number:

(7)   a. cihá kahnyá-ha?
        dog   barking-singular
        'The dog is barking.'
     b. cihá knihnyá-ha?
        dog   barking-dual
        'The two dogs are barking.'
     c. cihá kọtihnyá-ha?
        dog   barking-plural
        'The dogs are barking.'

Yet, as the data in (7) suggest, nouns in Onondaga are typically unmarked for number (though a plural marker may optionally occur). Thus a feature-copying derivational analysis would in all likelihood require that there be three distinct lexemes for each noun in this language—one singular, one dual, and one plural.

On a constraint-based analysis, there is only one lexeme for each noun—one that is unspecified for number. Information from the verb and information from the subject NP, in virtue of grammatical conditions of identity, both represent information about a single object, and hence must be compatible.

2.2.4 Polish

Polish is one of many languages where 'pro-drop' is the unmarked mode of expression for simple sentences. Yet as the following data show, Polish verbs mark distinctions of person and gender:

(8) a. kochałem   kochałeś   kochał
        'I(masc) loved' 'you(masc) loved' 'he loved'
     b. kochałam   kochałaś   kochała
        'I(fem) loved' 'you(fem) loved' 'she loved'

If the relevant agreement information is copied from phonetically null pronominal subjects onto the verb, as would be the case in standardly accepted derivation-based analyses, then a multiplicity of phonetically null pronominals is required—one for each distinct verbal inflection class.

On a constraint-based analysis of these same data, one may assume that there is one null pronoun, completely unspecified for the relevant agreement information (cf. the analysis of Borer (1986)). All relevant agreement information is supplied by the verbal forms, and the redundancy that accompanies derivation-based analyses is eliminated.

2.2.5 German

German nouns and adjectives typically exhibit far more paradigm slots than distinct lexical forms. The masculine noun *Tisch* 'table,' for instance, has eight paradigm slots, but only four distinct lexical forms:[1]

(9)

	SING	PLUR
NOM	Tisch	Tische
GEN	Tisches	Tische
DAT	Tisch	Tischen
ACC	Tisch	Tische

In a derivation-based account, where fully specified bundles of agreement features are copied onto agreement targets, there must be a distinct lexical entry

1. We are particularly indebted to Klaus Fenchel and Dieter Wunderlich for discussions about German agreement.

corresponding to each paradigm slot. On a constraint-based account, however, which is governed by compatibility of partially specified agreement information, the number of nominal lexemes can be reduced to exactly the number of distinct inflected forms:

(10)   Lexical Forms for the Masculine Noun *Tisch*:

FORM	GEND	NUM	CASE
Tisch	MASC	SING	¬GEN
Tisches	MASC	SING	GEN
Tische	MASC	PLUR	¬DAT
Tischen	MASC	PLUR	DAT

Even more striking is the way a constraint-based approach to agreement can simplify the treatment of German adjectives. An adjective like *klein* 'small' exhibits what is often treated as three distinct inflectional paradigms: weak, strong, and mixed, as illustrated in (11)–(13):

(11)   German Adjectives—Weak Forms:

	SING			PLUR		
	MASC	NEUT	FEM	MASC	NEUT	FEM
NOM	kleine	kleine	kleine	kleinen	kleinen	kleinen
GEN	kleinen	kleinen	kleinen	kleinen	kleinen	kleinen
DAT	kleinen	kleinen	kleinen	kleinen	kleinen	kleinen
ACC	kleinen	kleine	kleine	kleinen	kleinen	kleinen

(12)   German Adjectives—Strong Forms:

	SING			PLUR		
	MASC	NEUT	FEM	MASC	NEUT	FEM
NOM	kleiner	kleines	kleine	kleine	kleine	kleine
GEN	kleinen	kleinen	kleiner	kleiner	kleiner	kleiner
DAT	kleinem	kleinem	kleiner	kleinen	kleinen	kleinen
ACC	kleinen	kleines	kleine	kleine	kleine	kleine

(13)   German Adjectives—Mixed Forms:

	SING			PLUR		
	MASC	NEUT	FEM	MASC	NEUT	FEM
NOM	kleiner	kleines	kleine	kleinen	kleinen	kleinen
GEN	kleinen	kleinen	kleiner	kleinen	kleinen	kleinen
DAT	kleinen	kleinen	kleinen	kleinen	kleinen	kleinen
ACC	kleinen	kleines	kleine	kleinen	kleinen	kleinen

A derivation-based approach that assumes fully-specified lexical forms would have to posit seventy-two distinct adjectival lexemes.

The first step toward eliminating this obvious redundancy is taken by Wunderlich (1988),[2] who treats as strong adjectives those that occur in NPs without determiners, or else combine with weak determiners (e.g. the singular and non-feminine nominative or singular neuter accusative form *ein*), and as weak adjectives those that combine with strong determiners (e.g. all forms of the definite article *der* or all other inflected forms of the determiner *ein*). These combinatoric restrictions constitute an essential part of the lexical entries of these forms. Mixed declension patterns then arise because a determiner like *ein* has a paradigm all of whose singular forms are strong, except for the form *ein* itself.[3]

Once this insight is appreciated, then, using standard techniques for representing partial information, a constraint-based approach can reduce the number of lexical forms for each adjective to fourteen, as shown in (14). Here DTYPE refers to a head feature appropriate only for determiners. More precisely, STRONG means that the adjective indirectly selects a determiner marked [DTYPE *strong*] (see (65) below), while WEAK means that the adjective indirectly selects either a [DTYPE *weak*] determiner or else no determiner at all:

(14)   Adjectival Lexemes:

FORM	DTYPE	NUM	GEND	CASE
kleinen	STRONG	SING	*unspecified*	GEN ∨ DAT
	STRONG	PLUR	*unspecified*	*unspecified*
	unspecified	SING	MASC	ACC
	WEAK	SING	¬FEM	GEN
	WEAK	PLUR	*unspecified*	DAT
kleine	*unspecified*	SING	FEM	NOM ∨ ACC
	STRONG	SING	MASC	NOM
	STRONG	SING	NEUT	NOM ∨ ACC
	WEAK	PLUR	*unspecified*	NOM ∨ ACC
kleines	WEAK	SING	NEUT	NOM ∨ ACC
kleiner	WEAK	SING	FEM	GEN ∨ DAT
	WEAK	PLUR	*unspecified*	GEN
	WEAK	SING	MASC	NOM
kleinem	WEAK	SING	¬FEM	DAT

And the fact that these forms occur only as attributives, never as predicatives, motivates the introduction of one more feature (PRD) for which all the forms in (14) are negatively specified.[4]

2. Wunderlich builds on certain key ideas developed in earlier work by Manfred Bierwisch.

3. We return to this topic in section 2.5, where we formulate a more explicit analysis that incorporates Wunderlich's proposal.

4. The feature PRD, also used to distinguish attributive from predicative adjectives, is independently motivated, as explained in P&S-87, Chapter 3.

The only adjectives that can occur in predicative environments like (15) are those specified as [PRD +], for example, the one illustrated in (16):

(15)   Das Buch ist klein/*kleines.

(16)   FORM DTYPE   NUM   GENDER   CASE   PRD
         klein *inappropriate inappropriate inappropriate inappropriate* +

Thus what is often described as 'lack of agreement' in predicative environments results from the fact that the only adjectives in German that are specified as [+PRD] are those like (16), that is, those that are presumably related to a morphological stem by zero derivation.

We wish to stress that the various observations made in this section do not merely argue that derivation-based approaches to agreement entail minor additions to the lexicons of the languages we have considered here. Rather, we have attempted to show that any theory of agreement that takes fully specified agreement structures as input to a derivational operation will systematically miss generalizations about the lexicon—exactly the generalizations that a constraint-based approach to agreement is able to express.

2.3 How Syntactic Is English Agreement?

2.3.1 The Issue

The conventional wisdom about agreement information in English is that it is syntactic in nature. That is, words are assigned complex syntactic categories that consist of bundles of specifications for such syntactic features as part of speech, case, and verb form; and these features include the agreement features person (PER), number (NUM), and gender (GEND). General constraints, formulated variously as 'feature percolation' or 'feature matching' principles, ensure that phrases inherit agreement information from their lexical heads just as they inherit information about case or verb form.

An alternative view, which we will defend in section 2.4, is that the attributes PER, NUM, and GEND are not specified as part of syntactic categories at all, but rather belong to the internal structure of referential indices.[5] Thus, for example, the index indicated by the subscript '*i*' in *My neighbor$_i$ thinks she$_i$ is a genius* is a third-person singular feminine index. We can think of these indices as abstract objects that function in discourse to keep track of the entities that are being talked about, or (in the case of quantified NPs) the sets of entities that are being quantified over. Thus agreement features serve the practical purpose of helping conversants to keep referential indices distinct from each other by encoding contextually relevant properties of the entities or sets that they are an-

5. The idea that agreement features are not syntactic features but rather are borne by referential indices has been proposed independently in various forms by, inter alia, Lapointe (1980, 1983), Hoeksema (1983), Chierchia (1988), and Wunderlich (1988).

chored to.[6] Just which properties of referents are encoded by agreement features is subject to cross-linguistic variation, but common choices include person (roughly, linguistically encoded distinctions of discourse role relative to the speaker, e.g. self, addressee, or other) and number (linguistically encoded semantic sortal distinctions related to counting, such as cardinality or count vs. mass). Other agreement features are often lumped together as 'gender,' but the collection of distinctions treated under that rubric, as is well known, constitutes a heterogeneous lot. In so-called natural gender languages, gender distinctions correspond to semantic sortal distinctions such as sex (e.g. English third-person singular pronouns), human/nonhuman, animate/inanimate, or shape (e.g. Bantu noun classes). In so-called syntactic gender languages (e.g. French and German), common nouns are more or less arbitrarily (i.e. independently of semantic sortal distinctions) assigned to genders; then a particular referential index will bear a certain value for the gender feature according as the entity to which that index is anchored in the discourse could be appropriately classified by a common noun belonging to the corresponding gender class. (We shall return to this point in section 2.4.1).

We now turn to a number of observations about agreement in English that seem to be problematic for the conventional, purely syntactic view; we will return to the analysis of such facts from our alternative perspective in section 2.4.

2.3.2 Agreement Mismatches

Reference Transfer

The first piece of evidence suggesting that something is wrong with the traditional view of English agreement comes from the phenomenon of reference transfer, as studied by Nunberg (1977) and others. Nunberg argues that metaphorical reference is pervasive in language use. Among the examples he considers are those of the type illustrated in (17):

(17)   *a.* The ham sandwich at table six is getting restless. (said by one
             waitress to another)
         b. Queen-six bets.
         c. The dean's office approved the proposal.

In (17a), the referent of the subject NP is not a ham sandwich, but rather a restaurant customer who ordered one. The referent of the subject of (17b) is not a set of two cards, but rather an individual who holds one. And in (17c), the referent of *the dean's office* is presumably an appropriately authorized in-

---

6. In the tradition of situation semantics, *anchors* play a role analogous to that of variable assignment functions in logic. The referent of a linguistic expression token is the anchor of its index.

dividual who works in the dean's office. In each case, the referent of the relevant phrase is some individual in a contextually appropriate relation to an object of the sort normally picked out by nonmetaphorical utterances of that phrase.

Agreement is in many cases guided by this transferred reference, rather than any inherent agreement properties of the phrase itself. Thus, even though the NP *the hash browns at table nine* is inherently plural, as shown in (18a), when its referent is transferred to a nonaggregate entity, as in (18b), singular subject-verb agreement is observed:

(18)　　*a.* The hash browns at table nine are/*is getting cold.
　　　　b. The hash browns at table nine is/*are getting angry.

Similarly, reference transfers can affect pronoun agreement:

(19)　　*a.* The ham sandwich at table six just made a fool of himself/*itself.
　　　　b. The hash browns at table nine said he/*they can't find the men's room.

Wh-ever Constructions

Wh-ever constructions, illustrated in (20), have usually been taken to be a subtype of the 'free relative' construction (Bresnan and Grimshaw 1978):

(20)　　*a.* Whoever took my teddy bear is in big trouble.
　　　　b. I'll talk to whichever representative comes through the door.

As Richardson (1988) shows, however, *Wh-ever* constructs are both interrogative and quantificational in nature and share numerous properties with 'free choice *any*' phrases.

In a sentence like (20a), it is customary (following Bresnan and Grimshaw 1978) to treat *whoever* as the head of the subject phrase (or else to treat such phrases as headless, as in the 'COMP' analysis (see, e.g., Kuroda 1968; and Chomsky 1973)). By parity of reasoning, it is the plural phrase *whoever's dogs* that is the head of the subject phrase in (21):

(21)　　Whoever's dogs are running around in the garden is in big trouble.

But the matrix verb in this example does not agree with *whoever's dogs*. Instead, perhaps surprisingly, it agrees with the possessor *whoever*, which is singular.

Relative Pronouns

English relative pronouns appear to agree with the head noun with respect to a feature that corresponds closely to the notion of humanness:

(22)   *a.* the man who/*which I saw
        b. the book which/*who I saw

But the feature specification in question cannot simply be a syntactic property of the head noun. As Barlow (1988) points out, the choice of *who* versus *which* is tied to the referent of a given phrase, not its inherent syntactic properties:

(23)   *a.* The volcano which/*who has been dormant for a century erupted.
        b. The volcano who just left the room was Bill's kid.
        c. The soldiers which were made of lead were thrown away.

Singular Plurals

In the examples in (24) and (25), there is an apparent conflict between the agreement features of the subject NP and those that the singular verb normally demands of its subject. As noted by Morgan (1972, 1985), these examples stand as curiosities, at best, for purely syntactic analyses of subject-verb agreement:

(24)   *a.* Eggs is my favorite breakfast.
        b. Eggs bothers me more than okra.

(25)   *a.* Doing phonology problems and drinking vodka makes me sick.
        b. Unleashed dogs on city sidewalks threatens the health and welfare of law-abiding citizens.
        c. Steak and okra appears to bother Kim.

Collectives

It is often assumed that with respect to examples like (26), collective nouns occasion singular agreement in American English and plural agreement in British English:

(26)   The government is/are setting new wage standards.

But it is a fact that many collective nouns in American varieties of English also allow plural agreement:

(27)   *a.* If your family are all going to be here next week, then let's have a party.
        b. The faculty are all agreed on this point.
        c. The faculty have voted themselves a new raise.

Collective nouns appear to allow the objects they denote to be individuated either as a nonaggregate entity or as an aggregate of entities (see Hoeksema 1983 and the references cited there), much in the same way that these nouns admit of multiple interpretations when modified by certain adjectives, as in the ambiguous (28):

(28)   The Chicago Bears are a large football team.

When a nonaggregate entity is referred to, singular agreement arises; when an aggregate is referred to, plural agreement results. The tie between mode of individuation and mode of agreement is essential to understanding this phenomenon, for examples like the following, where an aggregate-entity interpretation is nonsensical, are clearly ungrammatical in all varieties of British and American English:

(29)   *A new committee have been constituted.

Interestingly, in many contexts either the aggregate or the nonaggregate mode of individuation is possible. However, once the choice is made within a particular local context, the mode of individuation is immutable. Thus we find examples like (30a, b), but not (30c) or (30d):

(30)   a.   The faculty is voting itself a raise.
         b.   The faculty are voting themselves a raise.
         c.   *The faculty is voting themselves a raise.
         d.   *The faculty are voting itself a raise.

2.3.3 Is a Purely Semantic Theory of Agreement Possible?

At first blush, facts like those presented in the preceding subsection would appear to argue for a purely semantic agreement theory, perhaps along the lines proposed most recently by Dowty and Jacobson (1989).[7] Indeed, what these agreement mismatch cases all have in common is that the agreement features on some expression seem to be dictated by properties of a certain nominal's referent, rather than by any formal properties of the nominal itself. Thus the verb *is* agrees with the nonaggregate referent of *the hash browns* in (18), and with the nonaggregate referent of the *Wh-ever* phrase (i.e. the owner of the dogs) in (21); in (23) the humanness of the relative pronoun is dictated by the referent of the head noun of the relative; and in (27) the plural number of the verb seems to reflect the fact that the referents of the formally singular subjects are being individuated as aggregate entities.

But however appealing it may seem to conjecture that agreement is determined solely by semantic properties of the relevant nominals' referents, we will argue for a somewhat more complex theory, wherein the connection between agreement and referent is an indirect one, mediated by the referential index that

7. See also Bartsch 1973; Scha 1981; Link 1983; Lapointe 1980, 1983; Hoeksema 1983; Cooper 1975; and Lasersohn 1988.

is anchored to that referent. Noting again the analogy between indices and reference markers in discourse representation theory, it is fair to characterize ours as a pragmatic or discourse-oriented agreement theory, in the sense that formal agreement features (PERSON, NUMBER, and GENDER) are assumed to be linked in various ways (depending on the language in question) to conditions on anchors (expressed as states of affairs in which the corresponding indices appear as arguments) that may be specific to the discourse context of the utterance token. Of course, in some cases, the relevant condition on anchors may turn out to express a property of the referent that is independent of the context (i.e. a purely semantic property), and in such cases, our theory will make much the same predictions as Dowty and Jacobson's.

By way of example, let us return briefly to the facts in (30). A faculty can be individuated either as a nonaggregate entity or as an aggregate entity, and this distinction seems sufficient for a purely semantic theory to explain why either (a) or (b) is possible. What seems harder for a semantic theory to explain is why (c) and (d) are impossible. On our account, though, the faculty is referred to in a given utterance in virtue of being anchored to a particular index, a formal object employed by the language user as a kind of mental tab kept on the things being referred to in the discourse at hand. Indices bear formal agreement features, in much the same way that pushpins employed by military strategists to represent army divisions might come in different colors to represent different countries. Thus a [NUM *sing*] or [NUM *plur*] index is employed according as the anchor is being individuated by the speaker as a nonaggregate or as an aggregate. Now in discourse, there is nothing to stop a speaker from employing a new index for an old referent, in order to signal a change in how that referent is being individuated, as in (31):

(31)   The Senate just voted itself another raise. Most of them were already overpaid to begin with.

Why can't this happen in (30c–d)? On our account, it is because Principle A of the HPSG binding theory (Chapter 6) requires that anaphors (including reflexive pronouns) in certain syntactic environments (including the one exemplified in (30)) be coindexed with their antecedents. Thus the badness of (30c–d) is the result of the incompatibility between [NUM *sing*] and [NUM *plur*], arising from the interaction of a syntactic constraint on indices with pragmatic constraints of English that require that [NUM *sing*] and [NUM *plur*] indices be anchored to referents individuated as nonaggregates and aggregates, respectively.

The same point can be illustrated by examples that have nothing to do with number agreement mismatch. Pragmatic principles of English allow a male dog to be referred to by both masculine ([GEND *masc*]) and neuter ([GEND *neut*]) pronouns, even in the same discourse. Roughly speaking, the masculine pronoun carries some connotation of familiarity or affection that the neuter pronoun lacks. This is illustrated in (32):

(32)   That dog is so stupid, every time I see it I want to kick it. He's a damned good hunter though.

Here the pronoun agreement switch signals a change in the speaker's attitude toward, or mode of individuation of, the dog. But such a switch is impossible if the second pronoun is an anaphor bound to the first, as (33) illustrates:

(33)   *a.*   That dog is so ferocious, it even tried to bite itself.
         b.   That dog is so ferocious, he even tried to bite himself.
         c. * That dog is so ferocious, it even tried to bite himself.
         d. * That dog is so ferocious, he even tried to bite itself.

Our theory of control (Chapters 3 and 7) interacts with our binding theory (Chapter 6) in such a way as to require that the subject pronoun be coindexed with the reflexive. This explains fully the contrasts observed in (33). In addition, since the binding theory requires no structure sharing of indices in examples like (32), the relevant indices in these examples are free to bear discrepant agreement information, modulo the effects of the anchoring conditions of the language (so, e.g., a singular and plural index cannot in general be anchored to the same individual because the former normally requires an aggregate anchor and the latter a nonaggregate).

But the facts in (33) appear to be quite difficult to reconcile with a purely semantic agreement theory. A purely semantic theory, which tries to derive all facts of agreement from denotational compatibilities, must recognize the fact that (male) dogs are among the things in the world that can be referred to by either masculine or neuter pronouns (as demonstrated by the acceptability of (32)). But then nothing in the semantic theory predicts that the subjects and reflexive objects in (33) covary with respect to gender. Surely, no ambiguity could result from a change of pronoun, inasmuch as the antecedent is uniquely determined by purely syntactic conditions. In short, a purely semantic approach to agreement has no obvious way to explain why any of the examples in (33) are ungrammatical.

In the following section, we set forth within the framework of HPSG a theory of agreement that we believe incorporates the insights and advantages of both syntactic and semantic approaches, while avoiding many of their respective pitfalls.

2.4 Agreement in English

In this section, we discuss the three basic types of agreement in English: pronoun-antecedent, subject-verb, and determiner-noun. In presenting our unified treatment of these three types, we will also have occasion to comment on closely related phenomena in other languages, for example, adjective-noun agreement, case concord, and demonstrative pronoun uses.

2.4.1 Pronoun-Antecedent Agreement

In English and a great many other languages, a pronoun agrees in person, number, and gender with its antecedent noun or noun phrase, provided such exists. Agreement of this kind obtains quite generally, whether the pronoun is reflexive, nonreflexive, or relative; whether the antecedent is referential or quantificational; and whether the antecedent is in the same sentence as the pronoun or in an earlier one. We explain the fact that pronouns and antecedents agree by defining the very notion of 'pronoun-antecedent relation' in terms of token-identity of indices, the very objects that specify agreement information. The term 'coindexing' thus has a literal interpretation in our theory and is criterial for the phenomenon of index agreement.[8]

The coindexing relationship is often misleadingly referred to as 'coreference.' Examples where the antecedent is a quantificational NP show clearly that the relationship between the antecedent and the pronoun cannot be generally characterized as a matter of referring to the same thing, for such quantificational NPs do not refer. But even if we limit our attention to cases where the antecedent is a definite description or a proper NP, coreference is not the same thing as coindexing. For example, in (34), the definite description, which is within the scope of a universal quantifier, does not have a referent:

(34)   [The cornerstone]$_i$ of each building bears the initials of the mason
         who laid it$_i$.

And in cases such as (35) and (36), often referred to as 'accidental coreference,' we assume that two NP tokens have distinct indices that are anchored to the same referent (or, equivalently, pick out the same individual):[9]

8. As illustrated in (32) above, a pronoun that refers to an entity already referred to by some earlier expression may have a new index with agreement features different from those of the earlier expression, in order to serve some specific discourse purpose (in the present case, to signal a change of attitude toward the referent). In such cases, according to our definition, the earlier expression does not qualify as an antecedent; to put it another way, instead of being 'referentially dependent' on the earlier expression, such pronoun uses must be regarded as deictic. The same point is illustrated in a somewhat different way by the discourse in (i):

(i)   A: You were mistaken.
         B: Yes, I was.

Here *I* has the same referent as *you* but bears a different PERSON value (and therefore necessarily a different index). The change, of course, serves the crucial discourse function of indicating a switch in conversational turn.

9. The use of bold uppercase in (35) indicates contrastive pitch accent.

(35)   It isn't true that nobody voted for John$_i$. **JOHN**$_j$ voted for him$_i$. (in a context where both uses of *John* refer to the same person)

(36)   He$_i$ [pointing to Richard Nixon] voted for Nixon$_j$.

In short, the identity indicated by coindexing is not at the level of real-world reference. Rather, it is at the level of the indices corresponding to uses of NPs, or, as it is often called, the level of discourse representation. The connection between coindexing and coreference is simply that if two expressions are coindexed *and* one of them refers, then the other expression refers to the same thing.[10]

Let us suppose that the foregoing rough account of the pronoun-antecedent relation is correct. Then the agreement of pronouns with their antecedents follows immediately, provided we assume that the features PER, NUM, and GEND are not attributes of syntactic categories, as generally supposed, but rather are attributes of the indices, as proposed in section 2.3.1 above. Thus variations in the form of pronouns (i.e. the choice of *he* vs. *she, it, we, I, they, you,* etc.) are correlated with differing specifications within the indices.

For example, the nominative third-person singular feminine pronoun *she* is analyzed as shown in (37), while the first-person singular pronoun *I* (which is unspecified for gender) can be partially described as in (38):

(37)
$$
sign\begin{bmatrix} \text{PHONOLOGY } \langle she \rangle \\[1em] \text{SYNSEM} \mid \text{LOCAL } local\begin{bmatrix} \text{CATEGORY } cat\begin{bmatrix} \text{HEAD } noun[\text{CASE } nom] \\ \text{SUBCAT } \langle \ \rangle \end{bmatrix} \\[1em] \text{CONTENT } ppro\begin{bmatrix} \text{INDEX } ref\begin{bmatrix} \text{PER } 3rd \\ \text{NUM } sing \\ \text{GEND } fem \end{bmatrix} \end{bmatrix} \end{bmatrix} \end{bmatrix}
$$

(38)
$$
sign\begin{bmatrix} \text{PHONOLOGY } \langle I \rangle \\[1em] \text{SYNSEM} \mid \text{LOCAL } local\begin{bmatrix} \text{CATEGORY } cat\begin{bmatrix} \text{HEAD } noun[\text{CASE } nom] \\ \text{SUBCAT } \langle \ \rangle \end{bmatrix} \\[1em] \text{CONTENT } ppro\begin{bmatrix} \text{INDEX } ref\begin{bmatrix} \text{PER } 1st \\ \text{NUM } sing \end{bmatrix} \end{bmatrix} \end{bmatrix} \end{bmatrix}
$$

Note that the CONTEXT values are omitted here; we will deal with that detail presently.

10. In some linguistic discussions, the coindexing relation is characterized as 'intended coreference,' in contradistinction to accidental coreference. But this too is misleading; e.g., in an utterance of *He$_i$* [pointing to Richard Nixon] *is Nixon$_j$* it seems clear that the speaker intends to refer to Nixon with both NPs. Yet we would say that the two NPs have distinct indices; the semantic content of the token of *he* does not depend on the semantic content of the token of *Nixon*, but rather gets at the individual Nixon in a different way (namely, by ostension).

Now if we supposed that the proper name *John*, which normally is given only to males, bore a third-singular-masculine index, then it would follow from our assumption that pronouns and their antecedents are coindexed that any pronoun with *John* as its antecedent would also be (i.e. have an index that is) third-singular-masculine. Similarly, if proper nouns such as *Main Street* and NPs headed by singular common nouns like *house* or *theorem*, which normally refer to or quantify over inanimate nonaggregate entities, bore third-singular-neuter indices, then so would any pronouns that had them as antecedents. In fact, however, this account is somewhat simplistic, for (39) is perfectly acceptable in any context where the individual referred to by the use of the name *John* is a woman who, contrary to English naming conventions, is known as 'John':

(39)   John$_i$ thinks she$_i$ is smart.

Perhaps the best approach to this difficulty is to assume not that in 'natural gender' languages (such as English) proper and common nouns lexically specify a gender value on their indices, but rather that there is a pragmatic constraint requiring, roughly, that an index bearing the specification [GEND *fem*] be anchored to a female (or range over a set of females), with analogous constraints linking masculine and neuter gender to male and nonhuman anchors, respectively.[11] The effect of this constraint is that a more complete description of the pronoun *she*, which incorporates the CONTEXT value, will have the form shown in (40):

(40)

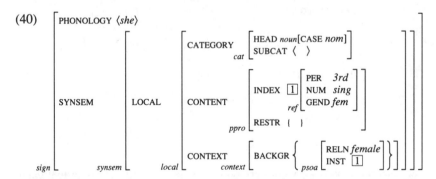

In standard pragmatic terms, this reflects the presupposition introduced by feminine pronouns in natural gender languages that the referent is female. Thus

---

11. We are temporarily disregarding uses of feminine pronouns in reference to ships, and uses of masculine pronouns, sometimes considered sexist uses, whose antecedents are quantificational NPs whose range set is of mixed or unspecified sex.

such constraints explain, for example, why the pronoun choice in (41) is determined by the sex of the referent:

(41)   My neighbor$_i$ thinks he$_i$/she$_i$ is smart.

An additional pleasant consequence is the correct prediction that deictic uses of pronouns such as that in (42) are infelicitous:

(42)   *She is tall. (pointing to a man)

Here, of course, we are making the natural assumption that deictic reference is to be analyzed in terms of an index that is directly anchored to some object salient in the context of utterance.

Similarly, we assume a pragmatic constraint of English (and no doubt a good many other languages) to the effect that, for example, first-singular indices must anchor to the speaker; in accordance with this constraint, the foregoing entry for *I* must be extended to the form (43):

(43)

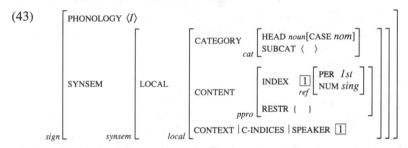

And analogous constraints require that singular (respectively, plural) indices anchor to entities that are individuated in the utterance context as nonaggregates (respectively, aggregates). If we assume that, for example, the RELATION value of the singular noun *book* is *book*, corresponding to the property each of whose instances is a book, these constraints will ensure that token utterances of *book* can introduce only singular indices; similarly, assuming that the plural noun *books* has the RELATION value *books* corresponding to the property each of whose instances is an aggregate of books, then utterances of *books* will introduce only plural indices. However, let us now suppose that the (morphologically) singular word *faculty* introduces the RELATION value *faculty*, corresponding to the property each of whose instances is a faculty. Since a faculty can be individuated as either an aggregate or a nonaggregate, it follows that a use of *faculty* can introduce either a singular or a plural index.

In the case of 'grammatical gender' languages, where the gender of a common noun is in general independent of semantic sortal restrictions on the anchoring (or quantificational domain) of the index of the noun, we assume that common nouns, in addition to pronouns, lexically specify a gender value on the index, but that these gender specifications are not subject to the anchoring constraints mentioned above in connection with natural gender languages. Although it is tempting, as well as traditional, to think that such languages should be subject to a purely syntactic agreement analysis, it is difficult to square such thinking with the well-known fact that such languages also exhibit gender restrictions when pronouns are used deictically. This is illustrated by the following French and German examples, but similar facts hold for gender in many other Romance, Germanic, and Slavic languages as well as for noun class in Bantu languages:

(44)   Elle/*Il est très longue. 'It is very long.' (pointing to a table)

(45)   Ich hoffe, daß er/*es/*sie bald kommt. 'I hope that it soon comes.'
        (said to a stranger while waiting at a bus stop)

Intuitively, the deictic pronoun in (44) must be feminine because the French word for table (*table*) is a feminine noun; likewise in (45) it must be masculine because the German word for bus (*Bus*) is masculine. For such languages, a different pragmatic constraint is evidently at work: roughly, an entity can serve as the anchor of an NP index only if the index's agreement features coincide with those of a common noun (of the language in question) that effectively classifies that entity at a level of granularity appropriate to the context. Much the same point emerges in Johnson's (1984) discussion of these matters:

> In describing a small, somewhat run-down residence, I might use either the term *das Haus* (neuter) 'the house' or *die Hütte* (feminine) 'the hut'. Both refer equally well to the same object, yet the second term conveys the impression to the hearer that I regard the residence as being something less than standard in size or quality. Interestingly, using the deictic pronoun *es* 'it' or *sie* 'she' conveys exactly the same connotation as using the noun it agrees with, *das Haus* or *die Hütte* respectively. A theory in which deictic pronouns refer directly to objects without the mediation of lexical entries would seem to have no way of directly accounting for this fact without marking the connotations of using a deictic pronoun with a particular gender on the object itself.

Thus, we assume natural gender languages and grammatical gender languages to be alike in specifying agreement features on indices, although the pragmatic constraints linking such features to (possibly contextual) properties of referents differ dramatically.[12]

It is perhaps worth reemphasizing at this point that we are not advocating a purely semantic theory of agreement. That is, we are not saying that the world is simply divided into singular, plural, masculine, feminine, and neuter objects,

12. It is in fact a simplification to suppose that in a given language, gender agreement must be uniformly of the 'natural' type or uniformly of the 'grammatical' type. For example, as Johnson (1984) points out, in German natural gender can override grammatical gender in the case of human (but not nonhuman animate) referents:

and that pronouns are restricted as to what sorts of things they may refer to. Indeed, it would appear that such a view is difficult to maintain in light of the existence of grammatical gender languages.[13] But as we saw in connection with examples like (30) and (33) above, there is evidence that it is wrong even for languages like English. Further evidence of a somewhat different kind is provided by the case of boats and ships, which of course exceptionally admit reference by either neuter or feminine pronouns. On a purely semantic view of agreement, this would require us to say that ships belong to two sorts of objects: the sort that can be referred to by neuter pronouns (i.e. inanimates) and the sort that can be referred to by feminine pronouns (e.g. females and boats). In that case nothing would prevent utterances where a given ship was referred to with both a neuter pronoun and a feminine pronoun; but such utterances are often ill-formed or infelicitous:

(46)   *a.* *The ship lurched, and then she righted itself.
        b. *Each yacht that had lost its way found her destination.

On our account, though, English pragmatics constrains [GEND *fem*] indices (such as the indices of feminine pronouns) to have females or boats (inter alia) as anchors. The badness of (46a) then follows (as in (33c–d)) from the demands of binding theory, which requires that the two incompatible indices (those associated with the subject and the object) be the same index. The badness of (46b), on the other hand, follows from the incompatibility of the index corresponding to the quantifier and the index that the quantifier is supposed to bind. More specifically, in order to bind the feminine index of *her*, the quantified NP must bear that same feminine index. But the index of the quantified NP, which originates from the common noun *yacht*, must also be neuter, under the assumption (see Chapter 5) that the head noun *yacht* in (46b) is coindexed with the subject of the relative clause (i.e. the initial SUBCAT element of *lost*, which in turn is the antecedent of the neuter bound pronoun *its*).

(i)   Ich sah das Mädchen,   als   es/sie hereinkam.
        'I   saw the girl (neut) when   it/she came in.'
(ii)   *Ich sah den Hund.   Sie   war   schön.
        'I   saw the dog (masc). She   was   beautiful.'

Here (ii) is infelicitous even in a context where the referent is a female dog. Such considerations indicate that pragmatic constraints between agreement features of indices and their anchors can be quite complex, but this has no bearing on the overall architecture of our analysis.

13. Dowty and Jacobson (1989) point out that it is possible to treat the possibility of being referred to by a word of a certain gender class as a semantic property of a given entity. However, as noted by Chierchia (1988: 150), such approaches seem 'extremely artificial.'

We should point out that our approach does countenance agreement-like effects that are 'purely semantic,' in the sense that they arise solely from anchoring conditions on indices and need not be mediated by agreement features on those indices. For example, following Barlow (1988) (see also Pollard 1989), we treat the distinction between the English relative pronouns *who* and *which* in such terms. Thus our lexical sign for relative *who* is as sketched in (47) (a more detailed rendition is given in Chapter 5):

(47)
$$
\begin{bmatrix}
\text{PHONOLOGY } \langle who \rangle \\[2ex]
\text{SYNSEM} \mid \text{LOCAL}
\begin{bmatrix}
\text{CATEGORY}
\begin{bmatrix}
\text{HEAD } noun \\
\text{SUBCAT } \langle \; \rangle
\end{bmatrix} \\[2ex]
\text{CONTENT} \mid \text{INDEX } \boxed{1} \\[2ex]
\text{CONTEXT} \mid \text{BACKGROUND}
\left\{
\begin{bmatrix}
\text{RELATION } human \\
\text{INSTANCE } \boxed{1}
\end{bmatrix}
\right\}
\end{bmatrix}
\end{bmatrix}
$$

Positing such a sign avoids the use of an otherwise unmotivated agreement feature (HUMAN), and treats the deviance of examples like (48) as arising from the incompatibility of two properties (being human and being a boat) that an entity would have to have in order to serve as an anchor for the NP's index: [14]

(48)   *a.*   #the boat who I like
       b.   the boat which I like

Thus our analysis need not treat all variations in nominal form as index agreement. In consequence of this fact, we have an immediate account for the seemingly puzzling fact that boats can be referred to in English by feminine personal and reflexive pronouns, but not by human relative pronouns. We would expect this fact to pose a serious challenge to any agreement theory that is purely syntactic or purely semantic in nature. At the same time, we account for the fact, noted above in (23), that in a metaphorical use of a common noun, the humanness of the relative pronoun is determined by the referent, not by any inherent property of the noun.

A remaining point to be noted before we turn to nonpronominal agreement phenomena is that CASE is not an attribute of indices; indeed it is not a CONTENT attribute at all. Hence, just as our theory (on the semantically plausible assumption that anaphora involves identity of indices) predicts that anaphoric agreement will affect all features of indices (specifically PER, NUM, and GEND), at the same time, given the stronger and more interesting hypothesis that anaphora involves identity of *nothing other than indices*, it also predicts that there is no agreement between pronouns and their antecedents with respect to

---

14. For a detailed development of the property compatibility approach to agreement, which has influenced numerous aspects of our analysis, see Barlow 1988.

purely syntactic properties like CASE. This is of course the correct prediction, as illustrated in (49):

(49)   We$_i$ can't stand for people to disagree with us$_i$.

Here, we have coindexing between the two plural pronouns, even though they do not agree on values for the syntactic feature CASE. Likewise, other discrepancies of syntactic feature specifications may appear between coindexed expressions, for example the one that distinguishes possessive and nonpossessive pronouns (according to our account in Chapter 1, [HEAD *det*] vs. [HEAD *noun*]):

(50)   She$_i$ claims her$_i$ bike has been stolen.

These predictions are, to the best of our knowledge, cross-linguistically valid.

2.4.2 Verb-Argument Agreement

An important and widespread subspecies of agreement arises when a language has a class of lexical forms (such as verbs, adjectives, prepositions, and determiners) that specify a referential index. In such cases, the possibility exists that members of the inflectional paradigm of that form may contain differing agreement specifications for that index (or may impose differing anchoring conditions). Now it may turn out, in virtue of conditions of identity imposed by principles of grammar, that expressions that combine with the form in question may also specify that same index, and thus be constrained by whatever restrictions were imposed on that index. The most obvious example of this kind in English is subject-verb agreement for person and number. But examples from the languages of the world can be multiplied at will, including: determiner-noun agreement for number in English, and for both number and gender (e.g. in German); agreement for person, number, and gender (or noun class) between verbs and nonsubject complements (primary or secondary objects, e.g. in Bantu); agreement for person, number, and gender between prepositions and pronominal prepositional objects in Celtic languages; agreement for number and gender between attributive adjectives and the nouns they modify; and agreement between predicative adjectives and their controllers.

As argued in P&S-87 (sec. 5.4), there is ample independent evidence that verbs specify information about the indices of their subject NPs. Unless verbs 'had their hands on' (so to speak) their subjects' indices, they would be unable to assign semantic roles to their subjects. It is natural to expect, therefore, that verb forms might vary in accordance with particular feature specifications associated with these indices, or for that matter in accordance with the indices associated with any of the subcategorized-for dependent elements. This observation provides a rationale for the existence of subject-verb agreement in En-

glish, and the agreement of verbs with primary and secondary objects found in
many of the world's languages.

In the framework developed here, a third-person-singular present-tense verb
form in English is characterized as in (51):

(51)

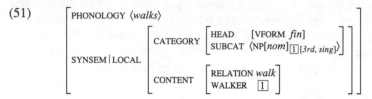

Indeed, *walks* might be said to *assign* third-singular agreement to its subject,
much as it assigns nominative case to its subject; the only difference is that the
agreement specification is located within the CONTENT of the subject subcategorization element, while the case assignment is located within its (syntactic)
head features. To put it another way, on our view, to be a third-singular verb is
nothing more than to assign third-singular agreement to the index associated
with one's subject. That English finite verbs 'inflect for agreement' is just to
say that within the inflectional paradigm we find a correspondence between the
inflectional morphology of the verb and the assignment of agreement features
to the subject. This is just what we mean when we say that the verb agrees with
its subject. Analogous remarks apply, for example, to agreement for noun class
between verbs and direct objects in Bantu languages illustrated in (52),[15] and
to agreement in Celtic languages between prepositions and their objects (when
the latter are pronouns) illustrated by the Welsh examples in (53):

(52)   Njûchi zi-ná-wá-lum-a   alenje.
          bees   SM-PAST-OM-bite-INDIC hunters
          The bees bit the hunters.

(53)   *a.* arnaf   i
              on(1-sing)   I
          b. arnat   ti
              on(2-sing)   you(sing)
          c. arno   ef
              on(3-sing-masc)   he
          d. arni   hi
              on(3-sing-fem)   she

15. The Chicheŵa example in (52) is taken from Bresnan and Mchombo (1987), who
propose an alternative to the familiar verb-object agreement analysis of these data. On
their analysis, the object agreement morpheme in such examples is an incorporated
topic-anaphoric pronoun.

e.	arnom	ni
	on(1-plur)	we
f.	arnoch	chwi
	on(2-plur)	you(plur)
g.	arnynt	hwy
	on(3-plur)	they

A final point to be noted in connection with English subject-verb agreement is that the NUMBER specification on the subject SUBCAT element of a verb will typically, but not always, be reflected by the number morphology of the subject itself. For example, as noted above, the morphologically singular noun *faculty* can bear either a singular or a plural index; as a result, both (30a) and (30b) above are consistent with the assumption that *is* and *are* assign singular and plural number, respectively.

2.4.3 Determiner-Noun Agreement

Our analysis of the syntax and semantics of NPs (Chapter 1, section 7) predicts the possibility of index agreement between nouns and determiners, inasmuch as nouns subcategorize for their determiners (and determiners reciprocally select their nouns via the SPEC feature, as discussed in sections 7–8 of Chapter 1). For example, in the case of quantificational determiners like *every* (Chapter 1, (48)), the CONTENT value of the N′ selected by the determiner is structure-shared with the RESTRICTED-INDEX value in the CONTENT of the determiner itself. Thus we can account for the fact that *every* combines only with singular nouns by further specifying the RESTRICTED-INDEX value of *every* as [INDEX | NUMBER *sing*]. By contrast, the plural determiner *all* will be further specified as [INDEX | NUMBER *plur*]. Given the English constraints between NUMBER specifications on indices and anchors, we thus predict facts such as those in (54):

(54)   *a.*   every man (singular index)
   b.   *every men
   c.   *all man
   d.   all men (plural index)
   e.   every faculty (singular index)
   f.   all faculty (plural index)

In short, *every* is a nonaggregate determiner, while *all* is an aggregate determiner. Given the account of subject-verb agreement in the preceding section, we also predict the following:[16]

16. Other collective nouns that pattern as in (55) include *staff, clergy, laity, peasantry, nobility, aristocracy, lumpenproletariat.* But others, such as *committee, family,* and *government,* disallow aggregate quantification with the singular form (55c).

(55)   *a.* Every faculty is/*are homogeneous.
         b. Every faculty meets/*meet on a monthly basis.
         c. All faculty *is/are required to submit midterm grades by March
              12.
         d. All faculties *meets/meet on a monthly basis.

On the other hand, we assume that determiners such as *the* and *no* do not
specify a NUMBER value, which explains the facts in (56): [17]

(56)   *a.* No/The man sneezes.
         b. No/The men met.

It is worth highlighting here the fact that in English the agreement features
of both VPs and NPs coincide with those of their lexical heads. This fact is no
doubt the reason that agreement has been treated in terms of head features (the
category-valued feature AGR and the atom-valued features PER and PLUR) in
GPSG work (Gazdar et al. 1985). On our account, though, agreement features
are not head features, and therefore the Head Feature Principle cannot play a
role in the explanation.[18] Instead, different principles are at work in the two
cases. NPs share the agreement of their heads because, as noted in Chapter 1,
the Semantics Principle requires them to share their semantic content, to which
the agreement features belong. But (in English at least) the agreement of a verb
or verb phrase is entirely a matter of the index of the SUBCAT element corresponding to the subject, and this element is shared in its entirety by the VP and
its lexical head (by virtue of the Subcategorization Principle).

17. Although English determiners can specify number, in general it is not true that
they *inflect* for number, unless we count the pairs *this/these* and *that/those* as degener-
ate inflectional paradigms. The situation is quite different, e.g., in German, where determiners inflect for both number and gender as well as for case. We return to this subject,
and in particular to the complex relations of agreement, case concord, and determiner
strength among German determiners, adjectives, and nouns, in section 2.5.

18. Our theory thus provides a principled account of a long-standing problem with
GPSG treatments, namely the problem of why agreement features are passed from a
prepositional object to its mother PP when the prepositional head is a case-marking
preposition. In examples like (i), for instance, agreement must be ensured between the
object of *to* and the reflexive pronoun within the VP complement:

(i)   We appealed to them$_i$ to behave themselves$_i$.

The theory of control presented in Chapters 3 and 6 interacts with our agreement theory
to solve this problem.

2.4.4 Agreement Mismatches

Let us return now to the question of agreement mismatches discussed earlier.
Consider first the issue of reference transfer, discussed by Nunberg (1977) (examples repeated here):

(57)   *a*. The ham sandwich at table six is getting restless. (said by one
           waitress to another)
       b. The hash browns at table nine are/*is getting cold.
       c. The hash browns at table nine is/*are getting angry.
       d. The ham sandwich at table six just made a fool of himself/*itself.
       e. The hash browns at table nine said he/*they can't find the men's
           room.

Whatever process governs such transfer of reference from the 'original' or
'natural' referent to a contextually associated entity (we make no attempt here
to characterize the pragmatic constraints that govern such uses),[19] we assume
that it is the *transferred* (or 'final') referent of the NP that is mutually constrained with respect to the NP index by the English anchoring conditions.[20]

For example, if the NP *the hash browns* is used to refer to a male restaurant
customer, then the NP utterance will introduce a third-singular-masculine index. As expected, it is the agreement features induced by the transferred referent that determine the number agreement of the determiner, as (58) and (59)
indicate:[21]

19. But see Nunberg (1977, to appear) for some interesting suggestions.

20. As pointed out to us independently by Andreas Kathol and John Nerbonne, in
analogous German examples the verb shows grammatical number agreement, even with
a transferred referent subject:

(i)   Die Eier wollen/*will   zahlen
         the eggs want(3-plur)/*want(3-sing) pay
         'The eggs wants to pay.'

21. We note that there are many as yet unexplained data regarding the phenomenon
of reference transfer, which apparently must be distinguished from *predicate transfer*
of the sort found in examples like (i):

(i)   I'm parked on 12th Street.

As shown by Nunberg (to appear), if these are analyzed as predicate transfer (roughly,
mapping the property of 'being parked on 12th Street' onto the property of 'having a car
that is parked on 12th Street'), then an explanation is derived for the well-known but
poorly understood fact that only first-person agreement is possible in such examples:

(ii)   *I is parked on 12th Street.

(ii) would be predicted to be grammatical if it, like the examples discussed in the text,
involved transfer of the subject's reference from the speaker to the speaker's car, but it
is correctly predicted to be ungrammatical by a theory that instead transfers the interpretation of the predicate, leaving the subject's reference unaltered. Similarly, distin-

(58)   *a.* Did that hash browns at table nine leave a tip?
        b. * Did those hash browns at table nine leave a tip?

(59)   *a.* Has that hash browns at table nine paid his check?
        b. * Have those hash browns at table nine paid their check?

The same analysis also provides an account of the 'singular plurals' cases (examples repeated):

(60)   *a.* Eggs is my favorite breakfast.
        b. Steak and okra appears to bother Kim.
        c. Doing phonology problems and drinking vodka makes me sick.
        d. Unleashed dogs on city sidewalks threatens the health and welfare of law-abiding citizens.

In each case, there is a nonaggregate entity (a menu item, a complex activity, a social problem) that is referred to, and that object is in some contextually determined relationship to a (generic?) aggregate entity (that could have been referred to by the morphologically plural (or conjunctive) NP without reference transfer). And again, the pragmatic constraints between referent and index induce singular number on the latter.

Our account is borne out by the existence of certain interpretational differences correlating with distinct choices of number for the index in question, as illustrated by the contrasts between the examples in (60) and the corresponding examples in (61):

(61)   *a.* Doing phonology problems and drinking vodka make me sick.
        b. Unleashed dogs on city sidewalks threaten the health and welfare of law-abiding citizens.
        c. Steak and okra appear to bother Kim.

The point to be noted here is that the examples in (61) possess distributive interpretations that are unavailable with the examples in (60). For example, (61a) can be paraphrased as *Doing phonology problems makes me sick, and drinking vodka makes me sick*, while (60c) cannot. Precisely what mechanism is responsible for the existence of such distributive plural readings has been the subject of much semantic research (see, e.g., Link 1983, 1987; Hoeksema

---

guishing between reference and predicate transfer provides an immediate account for such contrasts as the following:

(iii)   The hashbrowns at table nine was smoking a cigar and left without paying.

(iv)   * Dana was parked on 12th Street and wouldn't turn over.

These matters, fascinating though they are, are well beyond the scope of the present inquiry. We believe that a complete account of phenomena studied by Nunberg and others can be provided within the framework presented here.

1983; Dowty and Brodie 1984; Roberts 1987; and Lasersohn 1988). We will not take a position on this complex question here; we simply point out that an account of such contrasts follows from our agreement analysis in conjunction with any semantic theory of plural NPs that allows them to have aggregate referents in distributive contexts and nonaggregate referents in certain nondistributive ('singular plural') contexts.[22]

We should also mention in this connection the well-known phenomenon of morphologically plural nouns that refer to single entities, for example, *scissors*. On our account, these nouns have plural indices, and hence occasion plural agreement in all their occurrences. Given the assumed constraints between indices and anchors, we are driven to the conclusion that scissors and the like are simply individuated as pairs. This view certainly has initial plausibility in consideration of the fact that the referents of all the words in this class are artifacts with a certain bipartite structure, for example, *pliers, tongs, tweezers, shears, glasses, goggles, shades, pants, trousers, pantaloons, shorts*, etc. Independent linguistic confirmation is provided by the striking fact that deictic reference to such objects is effected by using a plural pronoun: *Give me those!* These observations would appear to make little or no sense on the standard view of number as a syntactic distinction.

To conclude this section, we return briefly to the matter of collective nouns. As noted above, there is good reason to believe that the referents of such nouns as *faculty, staff*, etc. can be individuated as either nonaggregate or aggregate entities, thus giving rise to the patterning of data in (30) and (55). This word class can be roughly characterized as referring to social/professional castes or classes. However, there is another class of collective nouns roughly characterizable as denoting social organizations, including (with a certain amount of dialect variation) such words as *committee, family*, and *government*, that systematically depart from this patterning, as seen in (62) and (63):

(62)　　*a.*　　John's family is destroying itself.
　　　　b.　　John's family are destroying themselves.
　　　　c.　　*John's family is destroying themselves.
　　　　d.　　*John's family are destroying itself.

(63)　　*a.*　　Every family has problems.
　　　　b.　　Every family gets together for the holidays.
　　　　c.　　All family *is/*are asked to bring a dessert or a salad.
　　　　d.　　All families are asked to bring a dessert or a salad.

The difference between the two semantic classes of collectives is signalled by the contrast between (55c) and (63c), which seems to suggest that, unlike class/

---

22. Remaining puzzles in this domain of facts include the unacceptability of such examples as *Raccoons is getting to be a big problem in this neighborhood* and *Kim and Sandy is carrying the piano upstairs (together)* (cf. (60c)).

caste collective nouns, the social-organization collectives denote entities that are individuated as nonaggregate. This hypothesis seems at first to be inconsistent with the datum (62b); but this too might be accounted for as reference transfer from John's family (individuated as a nonaggregate) to the aggregate entity made up of the *members* of John's family. We leave as an unresolved mystery why castes and social organizations should differ with respect to mode of individuation in this particular fashion.

2.5 Further Issues

2.5.1 Agreement and Case Concord within German NPs

The noun inflection paradigms in languages like German exemplify another phenomenon, *case concord*, which is a kind of syntactic agreement that must be sharply distinguished from index agreement. Case concord arises from language-specific constraints requiring structure sharing between a noun's CASE value and that of another sign (e.g. a determiner or adjective) that is dependent on the noun, in the sense that its projection selects a projection of the noun (via MOD or SPEC). Index agreement and case concord must be distinguished, for, as we have seen, we can have agreement between elements with differing case specifications in situations, such as antecedent-pronoun relationships, that involve coindexing but not the selection of one sign by another. On our account, case concord and index agreement within NPs are both consequences of lexically specified identities.

To see this, consider the following description of the nongenitive singular form of the German noun *Mädchen*:

(64)

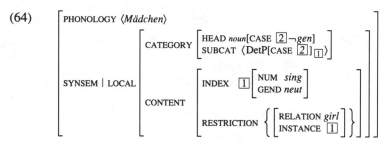

Note that the structure sharing of case value between this noun and the determiner it selects is independent of the structure sharing of indices, as INDEX is an attribute of CONTENT.[23] Note further that the specification [GEND *neut*] in (64) lacks the anchoring restrictions associated with such a specification in English because German is not a natural gender language.

23. Alternatively, the case concord and number-gender agreement can be imposed by the determiner on its N′ sister via the SPEC feature. We consider this alternative in detail in Chapter 9, section 4.4.

Attributive adjectives in German also have indices specified for number and gender, and these are structure-shared with the index of the nominal that the adjective modifies. This is illustrated in (65), which partially exhibits the SYN-SEM | LOCAL | CAT value for one of the four lexical forms (see section 2.2) of the attributive adjective *kluge*. (The reader may find it useful to compare this with the corresponding, somewhat simpler, value for an English attributive adjective where considerations of gender and case do not arise (Chapter 1, (58)).)

$$(65) \quad \begin{bmatrix} \text{HEAD} \begin{bmatrix} \text{MOD} \begin{bmatrix} \text{LOC} \begin{bmatrix} \text{CATEGORY} \begin{bmatrix} \text{HEAD } noun[\text{CASE } nom \lor acc] \\ \text{SUBCAT } \langle \text{DetP}[strong] \rangle \end{bmatrix} \\ \text{CONTENT} \mid \text{INDEX} \begin{bmatrix} \text{GEND } neut \\ \text{NUM } sing \end{bmatrix} \end{bmatrix} \\ synsem \\ \text{PRD} - \end{bmatrix} \\ adjective \\ \text{SUBCAT } \langle \; \rangle \end{bmatrix}$$

Note that this is traditionally regarded as a *weak* adjectival form. On our analysis, weak adjectival forms are those that impose the restriction that the NP's determiner must be strong.

As explained in Chapter 1, section 9, adjuncts bear a head feature MOD whose value is a *synsem* object; moreover, Schema 5 ensures that in a head-adjunct structure the adjunct daughter's MOD value is structure-shared with the head daughter's SYNSEM value. These assumptions, together with the lexical entries sketched in (64) and (65), yield (66) as the category of the head-adjunct structure *kluge Mädchen*:

$$(66) \quad \begin{bmatrix} \text{HEAD } noun[\text{CASE } \boxed{2} \, nom \lor acc] \\ \text{SUBCAT } \langle \text{DetP}[strong, \text{CASE } \boxed{2}]_{[sing, neut]} \rangle \end{bmatrix}$$

Here, combination of the noun with the adjectival form has three effects: (1) the determiner that the nominal phrase subcategorizes for is required to be strong; (2) the case of the nominal phrase is now further restricted to be either nominative or accusative; and (3) the index of the noun and that of the adjective are identical (hence ensuring index agreement between the adjective and the noun).[24] Thus *kluge Mädchen* can combine only with a neuter nominative or accusative form of a strong determiner (e.g. *das* or *dieses*) to form an NP like *das kluge Mädchen* or *dieses kluge Mädchen* (but not **kluge Mädchen* or **ein kluge Mädchen*).

By contrast, a strong adjective like the neuter nominative or accusative form *kluges* imposes the requirement (through its MOD value) that the NP's deter-

---

24. In addition, the set of restrictions on the nominal's index now contains two states-of-affairs, one originating from the adjective and one from the lexical noun (cf. Chapter 1, section 9).

miner be absent or else weak (e.g. *ein*).[25] This guarantees that NPs like *ein kluges Mädchen* are well formed, but those like **das kluges Mädchen* are not.

Note that this analysis, which is based entirely on the notion of simultaneous constraint satisfaction, makes a subtly different prediction from a generalization that is traditionally taught about so-called mixed declension patterns in German.[26] That generalization runs something like this: *A strong inflection must be realized exactly once within the NP—if the determiner is weak, then the adjective must be strong; if the determiner is strong, then the adjective must be weak.* This traditional generalization seems to make predictions identical to those of the analysis just sketched; however, there is a crucial difference. If a weak determiner is followed by two or more adjectives, the traditional generalization would lead one to expect that only the first adjective exhibits strong inflection, the others presumably being realized as weak. On our analysis, however, the MOD value of adjacent adjectives must be consistent, as the SYNSEM values of each N′ in a nested modifier structure are structure-shared. Hence the contrasts in (67) follow to the letter under our proposal, but not under the traditional analysis:

(67)   *a.*   ein kleines kluges Mädchen
         b.   *ein kleines kluge Mädchen
         c.   *ein kleine kluges Mädchen

The traditional analysis could of course be supplemented by additional rules or principles to render it consistent with facts such as these (case spreading principles or case copying transformations), but no such complications are required under our proposal.

Predicative adjectives in German, as noted in section 2.2, are unspecified for agreement (and concord) features. Hence the index of the [+PRD] adjectival form *klug* is compatible with that of any subject NP in such sentences as (68):

(68)   *a.* Der Junge(masc sing) ist klug.
         b. Die Frau(fem sing) ist klug.
         c. Das Mädchen(neut sing) ist klug.
         d. Die Frauen(fem plur) sind klug.
         e. Die Mädchen(neut plur) sind klug.

25. A question remains as to how an adjective can be permitted to combine with a noun that does not seek a determiner, while ruling out the possibility of combining with a noun that does not seek a determiner merely because it has already combined with one. That is, we must somehow block **kluges ein Mädchen*. One solution to this problem (which arises in English as well) is to employ phonetically empty determiners in 'bare plural' and mass NPs. The lexical entries for attributive adjectives can thus remain as formulated in the text, i.e. as modifying only nominal phrases that subcategorize for a determiner phrase.

26. Here we are indebted to conversations with Thomas G. Bever.

Thus by distinguishing between predicative and attributive forms of adjectives in German, we provide an account of what is standardly described as 'lack of agreement' in predicative constructions. From our perspective, this description is grossly inaccurate. There *is* index agreement (structure-sharing of indices) in predicative constructions; predicative adjectival forms happen to exhibit no inflectional morphology, bear less information than their attributive counterparts, and hence are compatible with a wider, perhaps even completely unrestricted, class of nominals.

2.5.2 Polite Plurals

Polite plural pronouns of the sort found in German and many other languages are problematic for many approaches to agreement.[27] These are readily treated in terms of conditions on anchors, a technique we have already seen to be useful for the analysis of English relative pronouns. Thus to express paradigmatic regularities in German, we would want to posit a single lexeme for such plural finite verb forms as *essen* 'eat,' *gehen* 'go,' and *sind* 'are.' And these uniformly select for subjects whose indices are specified as [NUM *plur*]. Now [NUM *plur*] indices in German (as in English) are in general anchored to aggregates, but the polite pronoun *Sie*, whose SYNSEM | LOCAL value is given in (69), is an exception:

(69)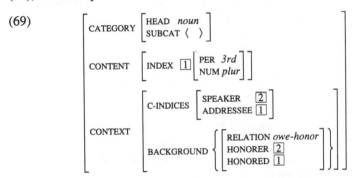

Polite *Sie* thus has a third-person plural index, but is exceptionally specified as allowing either an aggregate or a nonaggregate as an anchor. That is to say, it lacks the contextual restriction (present in the lexical signs of other plural nominals) that requires an aggregate as anchor. Hence *Sie*, despite its potential for singular reference, combines only with third-person-plural verb forms. In (69), we have employed both the CONTEXTUAL-INDICES and the BACKGROUND values of the CONTEXT attribute to build into the lexical entry the pragmatic ap-

27. For further discussion of this problem, see Barlow 1988, whose analysis in terms of compatibility of properties has had considerable influence on the treatment presented here.

propriateness condition that, in the context of utterance, the addressee—who is also the referent of *Sie*—is being honored by the speaker. It appears to us that a purely semantic theory such as that of Dowty and Jacobson (1989) would find the phenomenon of polite plurals something of a challenge. Evidently the move made in that theory in order to deal with syntactic gender (i.e. treating the potential for reference by nouns of certain gender classes as a semantic property of the referent) is not available here. It seems to make little sense to say that *Sie* can be used only to refer to things that have the property of being referable to by the word *Sie*. Rather, it is a pragmatic fact about *Sie* that it can be used only when it is appropriate that the speaker show honor to the addressee.

2.5.3 Honorific Agreement

The CONTEXT attribute also plays a crucial role in the analysis of various kinds of pragmatic agreement, for example, the honorific agreement found in languages such as Japanese and Korean, inter alia. In Korean, for example, the nominal honorific marker -*nim* is used to mark an NP whose referent is owed honor. Also the suffix -*si*- is present on the matrix verb or adjective if and only if honor is owed to the subject's referent. That is, the absence of -*si*- constitutes a positive indication that honor is not owed to the subject's referent (as opposed to merely failing to indicate that honor *is* owed). These facts are illustrated in (70):[28]

(70)   *a.*   Kim   sacang-i   o-ass-ta.
              Kim   President-NOM   come-PAST-DECL
              'President Kim has come.'
      b.   Kim   sacang-nim-i   o-si-ess-ta.
              Kim   President-HON-NOM   come-HON-PAST-DECL
      c. #Kim   sacang-i   o-si-ess-ta.
              Kim   President-NOM   come-HON-PAST-DECL
      d. #Kim   sacang-nim-i   o-ass-ta.
              Kim   President-HON-NOM   come-PAST-DECL

Most typically, honorific verbal morphology and honorific subject marking are both present or else both absent, as in (70a, b). However, (70c) and (70d) are in general infelicitous, inasmuch as the honorific marking of the subject (sig-

---

28. The analysis sketched here draws freely from the work of Han (1990), Kang (1991), and Park (1992); we are especially grateful to Hyeonseok Kang, Byung-Soo Park, Suk-Jin Chang, and Jongbok Kim for valuable discussions. None of these authors necessarily accepts the conclusions we have drawn here. See also Paolillo 1992.

nalled by presence or absence of *-nim*) and that of the verb (presence or absence of the affix *-si-*) make conflicting indications about the facts of the social context.[29]

In order to account for such facts as (70), we must first recognize certain nonlinguistic facts about Korean society. In certain social contexts, a relation of owing honor may obtain between two individuals, for example, between superordinate and subordinate in a work situation, between teacher and student (or between members of a relatively senior cohort and a relatively junior one) in a school-related situation, or between a member of an older generation and a member of a younger one in a family situation. We do not attempt here to state the precise social conditions under which this relation obtains. As a first approximation, the linguistic relevance of such social facts is this: in an utterance context where the speaker owes honor to the referent of the subject, the speaker is required to employ the *-si-* form of the matrix predicate, and may mark the subject with *-nim* as well; if the speaker does not owe honor to the subject's referent, then the uses of *-nim* and *-si-* are both disallowed.

However, the facts are somewhat more complex: in certain contexts, the usage of *-nim* and *-si-* is dictated not by the social relation of the speaker to the subject referent, but rather by the social relation of the addressee to the subject referent. We are not in a position to exhaustively catalog the kinds of contexts in which the social relations of the addressee enter into determination of who the speaker may owe honor to. Two such examples are (1) contexts in which the speaker also owes honor to the addressee, where the latter is distinct from the referent of the subject, and (2) certain contexts in which the addressee is a sufficiently junior relative of the speaker (including, e.g., cases where the former is a young child whom the latter intends to instruct in politeness).

For present purposes, we will abstract away from the fine details of the (nonlinguistic) social rules that underlie such uses and will treat honorification via constraints on when the speaker owes honor to the referent of the subject. With such nonlinguistic assumptions in place, we can now account for the linguistic honorification facts as follows.

First, we assume that *-nim* introduces into the BACKGROUND the psoa that the speaker owes honor to the referent of the NP that *-nim* attaches to. Ignoring technical details (e.g. whether *-nim* is to be treated as an inflectional suffix or a clitic), the result will be that the LOCAL value for an honorific NP such as *Kim sacang-nim* will be as shown in (71):

---

29. However, Park (1992) suggests that usages such as (70c) and (70d) are appropriate in certain contexts. (70d), for example, may be appropriate for registering the fact that the social relations of speaker and addressee are different with respect to the subject's referent.

(71)

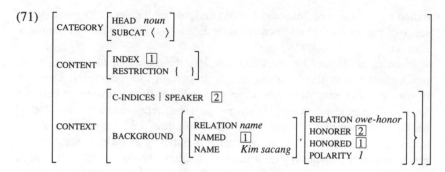

Note that for explicitness we have indicated the positive polarity (*1*) in the psoa of owing honor. This background psoa constitutes what might be regarded by a pragmatist as a conventional implicature. As we shall see in Chapter 8, we assume that all such psoas are inherited by phrasal signs from their constituents.[30] In the honorifically neutral NP *Kim sacang*, this psoa would simply be absent.

Next, we assume that the *-si-* form of the verb likewise imposes the same contextual requirement (that the speaker owes honor to the subject referent), as shown in the LOCAL value for *o-si-ess-ta* in (72):

(72)

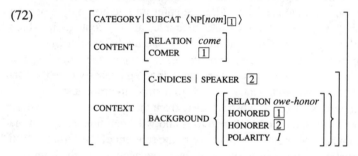

Because the background condition specified by this verb is identical to that of the NP in (71), a sentence like (70b), whose subject is (71) and whose VP is (72), involves no inconsistency and is therefore felicitous (in appropriate contexts); (70c) likewise involves no inconsistency, though in this case it is because the subject specifies nothing at all about owing honor.

Finally, we assume that the nonhonorific (*-si*-less) verb forms contribute a *negative* ([POLARITY *0*]) condition to the pool of BACKGROUND information. Thus the LOCAL value for the verb *o-ass-ta* is as shown in (73):

30. Unfortunately, this simple assumption cannot be maintained for all types of BACKGROUND information. (Otherwise the projection problem for presupposition would be trivial!)

(73)

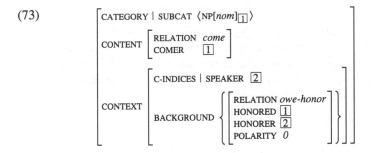

Since this verb form specifies background information that is inconsistent with that of an honorifically marked NP, we predict that, while violating no grammatical constraints, sentence (70d) necessarily involves contradictory background assumptions and is therefore infelicitous.

Pragmatic agreement, such as that examined here, thus differs from both index agreement and syntactic agreement in a fundamental way. In the case of the latter two types, lack of agreement leads to linguistic descriptions that are inconsistent in the strong sense that no linguistic entity can satisfy them. Thus, for example, speakers of (standard varieties of) English, French, and German all agree that examples like those in (74) are ungrammatical:

(74) *a.* *We is . . . , He are . . . , You am . . . (English)
  b. *Nous est . . . , Il sont . . . , Vous suis . . . (French)
  c. *Wir ist . . . , Er sind . . . , Sie bin . . . (German)

However, an example like (70d) leads to inconsistency in a different and arguably weaker sense: any context in which it could be uttered would have to be one that involved mutually inconsistent background assumptions.[31] Various accounts might then be developed (e.g. that offered by Park (1992)) for the special communicative effect that is derived from utterances that give rise to such background inconsistencies but that are nevertheless part of the language in question.

Here we have presented just the rudiments of the analysis of Korean honorification as pragmatic agreement. Both Han 1990 and Park 1992 contain a more detailed discussion of 'optional' honorific agreement and in addition provide analyses of cases where more than one honorific marker must appear. The basic technique of both proposals, however—compatibility of conditions on anchors (background conditions)—is suitable for providing a natural account of all phenomena discussed under the general rubric of 'honorification' in particular, and pragmatic agreement in general.

31. Our treatment of German examples like *Sie bist . . .* actually involves assigning both kinds of deviance, i.e. impossible structure sharing and inconsistent background assumptions.

2.6 Hybrid Agreement

For any given language, then, the question arises for each observed agreement phenomenon as to whether it is an instance of index agreement, syntactic agreement, pragmatic agreement, or some combination of these. The answer to this question in particular cases may not always be obvious. In French, for example, the following data pose an interesting problem: [32]

(75)   *a.* Vous êtes   belle.
            you are-2nd-plur beautiful-fem-sing
       b. Vous êtes   belles.
            you are-2nd-plur beautiful-fem-plur

Although the verb form is second-person-plural in both cases, the predicate adjective is singular in (75a) and plural in (75b). And the difference in adjectival form corresponds to a difference in interpretation: (75a) can be said only to an individual (and female) addressee with whom the speaker is 'on *vous* terms,' while (75b) can be said only to an aggregate of female individuals (with no restriction on the social relationship of the speaker to the addressees).

If we adopt a treatment of the polite second-person *vous* in French analogous to the one proposed earlier for the polite pronoun *Sie* in German, then we will posit a lexical sign whose SYNSEM | LOCAL value is as shown in (76): [33]

(76)

$$
\begin{bmatrix}
\text{CATEGORY} & \begin{bmatrix} \text{HEAD} & \textit{noun} \\ \text{SUBCAT} \langle \ \rangle \end{bmatrix} \\[2ex]
\text{CONTENT} & \begin{bmatrix} \text{INDEX} & \boxed{1} \begin{bmatrix} \text{PER } \textit{2nd} \\ \text{NUM } \textit{plur} \end{bmatrix} \end{bmatrix} \\[3ex]
\text{CONTEXT} & \begin{bmatrix} \text{C-INDICES} & \begin{bmatrix} \text{SPEAKER} & \boxed{2} \\ \text{ADDRESSEE} & \boxed{1} \end{bmatrix} \\[3ex] \text{BACKGROUND} & \left\{ \begin{bmatrix} \text{RELATION } \textit{honor} \\ \text{HONORER } \boxed{2} \\ \text{HONORED } \boxed{1} \end{bmatrix} \right\} \end{bmatrix}
\end{bmatrix}
$$

This sign, like its German counterpart, is exceptional in not requiring that its [NUM *plur*] index be anchored to an aggregate. The second-person-plural verb form *êtes* requires a subject whose index is specified as [PER *2nd*] and [NUM *plur*], which is compatible with the index of polite *vous*, thus accounting for the subject-verb agreement in (75a). But then how can the index of *belle*, presumably specified as [NUM *sing*], be identified with that of the subject? And

---

32. This problem and its solution were pointed out to us by Dieter Wunderlich.

33. We leave open the precise relation between the notion of honor relevant for the analysis of polite forms in Western languages and the notion that is relevant for honorific forms in Korean, Japanese, etc.

how does the feminine plural form *belles* force an aggregate interpretation on the subject?

The suggested answer to these questions is that in French, predicative adjectives have gender specifications on indices (as discussed earlier) but introduce no specifications for the feature NUM. Rather, morphologically singular or plural predicative adjectives impose the condition that the index be anchored to a nonaggregate or an aggregate, respectively. In this way, the index of the predicate adjective *belle* can be token-identical with the second-person-plural index of the subject pronoun in (75a) (rendering it also [GEND *fem*]). In this case, the adjective introduces a constraint that the anchor of that index be a nonaggregate. Similarly, the index of the plural form *belles*, unspecified for NUM, can be structure-shared with the subject's index, and bears the restriction that the anchor of the index be an aggregate (of females). The French agreement system thus employs a combination of index features and anchoring conditions. It is our expectation that a conventional, purely syntactic analysis of agreement, or a purely semantic Dowty-Jacobson-style one, will be hard put to account for these facts.

Finally, we note that in some languages certain forms seem to be in flux between specifying features of indices and conditions on anchors. For example, Corbett (1988: 35) (see also Barlow 1988: 121ff.) notes interesting variation in Serbo-Croat. Some nouns in Serbo-Croat (e.g. *gazda* 'master') have a 'feminine form' but typically denote a male. In this case, a possessive pronoun may show feminine agreement, as in (77):

(77) naše   gazde
      our-fem-plur masters-fem-plur

However, natural agreement is also possible, as in (78):

(78) naši   gazde
      our-masc-plur masters-fem-plur

Such variation, on our view, is indicative of a competition between two different analyses of gender agreement in Serbo-Croat. The agreement pattern of (77) requires an analysis of possessive pronouns stated in terms of features of indices; the pattern in (78) implies that varying possessive forms are correlated with differences in anchoring conditions. We speculate that such a competition is unstable and will be resolved as the language evolves.

2.7 Conclusion

We began this chapter by considering two views of agreement—the widely held derivation-based approach and the constraint-based alternative. Our comparison led to the conclusion that the principles of agreement theory should not be cast in directional terms, as they are in most transformational analyses, but rather should be formulated as a static set of identity conditions. The appearance of directionality in agreement processes, we argued, is the result of lexical underspecification, that is, forms whose underspecified lexical entry allows them to be identified (with respect to the relevant properties) with a larger class of forms, and has no status in the formulation of universal or language-particular agreement rules. Standard directional accounts, as we showed, lead to massive redundancy in the grammars of languages where agreement targets specify more information than the agreement source.

We then considered the role of semantics in agreement, arguing that standard theories of agreement, where person, number, and gender information are treated as purely syntactic in nature, fail to express the fact that agreement for such features is tied to reference in fundamental ways. These theories fail, for example, to explain the systematic cross-linguistic fact that, under appropriate syntactic conditions, coreferential nominals agree for these features (and not, say, for case). In addition they fail to provide an account of a wide range of facts we have examined suggesting that there is a fundamentally semantic nature to agreement.

At the other extreme is the purely semantic theory of agreement advanced by Dowty and Jacobson (1989). On their view, which we examined in detail, all patterns of agreement result from compatibility of conditions on denotation. In the course of this chapter, we isolated a number of problems for a purely semantic theory of agreement whose solution is not apparent. These problems are summarized in (79):

(79)   Problems facing a purely semantic theory of agreement (e.g. that of Dowty and Jacobson 1989):

1. The existence of 'grammatical gender' languages defies a purely semantic analysis (potential solutions seem artificial).
2. Number variation (*family is/are*) must remain fixed within grammatically specified domains (**My family are destroying itself*).
3. Gender variation (*ship$_i$ ... it$_i$/she$_i$*) must remain fixed within grammatically specified domains (**The ship lurched, and then she righted itself*).
4. Polite plurals may involve plural agreement properties, but singular (i.e. nonaggregate) reference (German polite *Sie*).
5. Polite plurals may involve plural agreement distinct from the truly denotative plurality of predicative adjectives (French *Vous êtes belle* (sing)/*belles* (plur)).

For this reason, our analysis of person, number, and gender agreement phenomena (in a wide range of languages) encodes this agreement information in terms of features of indices, which function as the vehicle of reference and coreference in our theory. This sort of agreement is thus conventional (linguistic systems vary with respect to features of indices) and at the same time crucially tied to matters of reference.

Finally, we have distinguished this index-based agreement from two other kinds: (1) syntactic agreement (e.g. case concord), which occurs when two elements are in construction with one another, never across discourse, and (2) pragmatic agreement (e.g. Korean honorific agreement), which involves compatibility of contextual information requirements contributed by co-occurring expressions.

3

Complement Structures

3.1 Introduction

This chapter presents an overview of a lexically-based analysis of complementation in English and a comparison with competing analyses commonly accepted within GB.[1] Among the topics treated here are 'equi' constructions, 'raising' constructions, and the analysis of the expletive pronouns *it* and *there*. In Chapter 7, we will present a modification that will allow many aspects of the analysis presented here to be derived from the interaction of more general principles.

3.2 Category Selection and Small Clauses

In much current work in syntactic theory, specifically within the framework of GB, it is assumed that all the verbs in (1) subcategorize for a single complement, as indicated:

(1)   *a.* Kim said [that Sandy left].
       b. Dana preferred [for Pat to get the job].
       c. Kim said [Sandy left].
       d. Leslie wanted [Chris to go].
       e. Lee believed [Dominique to have made a mistake].
       f. René tried [PRO to win].
       g. Terry preferred [PRO to go to Florida].
       h. Tracy proved [the theorem false].
       i. Bo considered [Lou a friend].
       j. Gerry expects [those children off the ship].

1. We would particularly like to thank Peter Sells for his help to us in revising this chapter.

The syntactic analysis of these and other complements as single constituents is in fact necessitated in GB by the Projection Principle, which requires that all mappings between levels of linguistic representation be homomorphic with respect to argument structure. That is, since the verb *believe* is assumed to be logically dyadic (designating, say, a relation between individuals and propositions), all of the syntactic representations (specifically D-structure and S-structure) where the verb *believe* occurs must also have exactly two syntactic dependents—one an NP (the subject), the other a clause.[2]

But, assuming the constituency indicated in (1), an issue arises as to the categorial status of the complements in (1h–j). As noted by Stowell (1983: 301), if these complements are treated as 'small clauses,' then:

> [a]t Logical Form, the verb assigns a theta-role to the clause as a whole, so it should be unable to specify the categorial features of anything other than the entire clause, given the restricted theory of subcategorization [that Stowell advocates]. In particular, the verb should be indifferent to the categorial status of the [small clause] predicate. But this is not the case:

(32)   a. *I consider [John *off my ship*].
        b. *I proved [the weapon *in his possession*].
        c. *I expect [that man *stupid*].
        d. *We all feared [John *unfriendly*].

> This kind of selection for the category of the predicate is never permitted with infinitival complements. (Note that insertion of *to be* before the [italicized] predicates in (32) renders the sentences grammatical.)

Stowell's observation then is that a standardly accepted constraint on subcategorization (namely the *locality of subcategorization*) is inconsistent with clausal analyses of the complements of verbs like *prove, expect*, and *consider*, for these verbs must select for the category of the phrase that follows. This criticism remains valid, not only against the S̄ analysis of NP-AP and NP-PP sequences that Stowell attacks, but also against any version of the CP/IP analysis (Chomsky 1986b) of small clauses. Stowell's observations thus lead to the conclusion that both of the following analyses of *expect* and *consider* must be rejected:

2. For a critical discussion of these and related issues, see Postal and Pullum 1988.

(2)

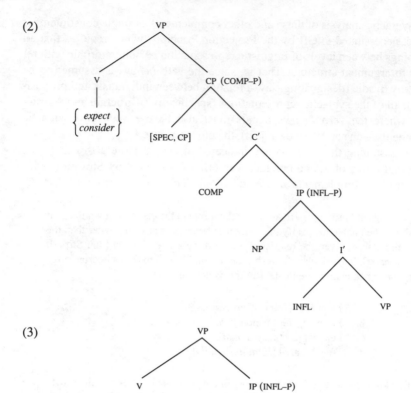

(3)

Kitagawa (1985) seeks to defend the small clause analysis of the complements in question by arguing that they involve a purely semantic selection, rather than selection for category, as Stowell assumes. Kitagawa discusses examples like the following:

(4)   *a.* *The doctor considers that patient *dead* tomorrow.
        b. Unfortunately, our pilot considers that island *off* the route.

(5)   *a.* *I expect that island *off* the route.
        b. I expect that man *dead* by tomorrow.

From these examples, Kitagawa (1985: 3) concludes that '*consider* selects a complement expressing [a] 'state of affairs', but not a complement expressing

[a] 'change of state'. The selectional property of *expect*, on the other hand, is exactly the opposite.' Kitagawa's conclusion then is that no category selection is involved with respect to the complements of *consider* and *expect*, a conclusion that renders the locality of subcategorization consistent with any small clause analysis of the complements in question, including the widely accepted CP/IP analysis.[3]

But the analysis of the complements of verbs of this sort must involve more than just semantic selection. If *off the route* fails to denote a 'change of state' and thus is incompatible with the semantics of *expect*, then why are examples with *to be* well-formed (as Stowell notes)?

(6)   I expect that island to be off the route.

And if *expect* has no access via subcategorization to the categorial properties of its complements, then why is there a contrast between (7a) and (7b)?

(7)   *a.*   I expect that island to be a good vacation spot.
         b.   *I expect that island a good vacation spot.

Note that all of these complement types are possible with *consider*:

(8)   *a.* I consider that island to be off the route.
         b. I consider that island to be a good vacation spot.
         c. I consider that island a good vacation spot.

What these facts demonstrate is that (1) *expect* and *consider* both allow AP, PP, and infinitival complements; (2) when *expect* and *consider* subcategorize for AP or PP complements (but not when they combine with infinitival complements), semantic properties of the verbs in question interact with the semantic

---

3. There is reason to question Kitagawa's assumption that the complements in question inherently express different kinds of properties. The semantics of *expect*, when it takes an AP or PP complement, involves a state of affairs that is expected to be different from some previously existing state of affairs. Hence all such complements express states of affairs. Acceptability is reduced when the complement of *expect* expresses a state of affairs that is difficult to construe as a change from some other state of affairs. The proof of this is that the examples presumed to be ungrammatical by Kitagawa can in fact be contextualized. Suppose, for instance, that the manager of a cruise ship company suddenly discovers that a coup d'état is about to take place on an island that is currently on the route of the company's premier cruiseship. She might then with complete felicity say to her assistant: *I expect that island off the route by tomorrow*. Similarly, the semantics of *consider* involves a judgment that a certain state of affairs holds at the moment of considering. *That patient dead tomorrow* is not such a state of affairs, as the adverb introduces conflicting temporal information.

nature of the complements to make certain examples uninterpretable or hard to contextualize (see n. 3); and (3) *consider*, but not *expect*, also allows NP complements of the sort illustrated in (8c) (cf. *(7b)). These conclusions constitute an argument that the subcategorization properties of *expect* are inconsistent with the clausal analysis of its complements, given the familiar principle that subcategorization is local.

Of course the issue of semantic selection versus selection by syntactic subcategorization is notoriously vexed, plagued as it is by the difficulty of knowing whether our inability to explain a particular selection in semantic terms is due to the inadequacy of currently available semantic tools or else to the nonsemantic nature of the selection in question. For example, perhaps the unacceptability of *I expect Kim a success* is due to the same kind of semantic factors that affect *I expect that island off the route*. To make good on this explanation, one would need to develop a precise account of how the denotations of predicative NPs are systematically different from those of other predicative expressions, and how this semantic difference renders predicative NPs inconsistent with the semantics of *expect*. This seems to us to be unlikely, as it is quite impossible to contextualize any examples like those in (9):

(9)   *a.* *We expect Kim a doctor (by the end of the year).
        b. *We expect that island a safe place (after the revolution).
        c. *We expect him a dead man (by tomorrow).

These remarks should not be interpreted as implying skepticism on our part about the possibility of adjudicating particular cases, or as indicating a bias toward syntactic explanations. Consider the following contrast, standardly taken to demonstrate that the verb *seem* must subcategorize for an AP (rather than a PP) complement:

(10)   *a.* *Sandy seems out of town.
        b. Sandy seems clever.

As argued by Maling (1983: 256), the selection in question must be semantic in nature, as *seem* allows a class of PPs that she terms 'metaphorical' PPs:

(11)   *a.* Lee sure seems out of it.
        b. Lee sure seems out of his mind.
        c. Lee sure seems under the weather.

Citing further contrasts like (12), Maling concludes that *seem* allows PP, AP, and NP complements, as long as they involve 'gradable predicates':

(12)   *a.* Robin seems a fool.
        b. *Robin seems prime-minister.

This conclusion seems reasonable enough,[4] though one might quibble with Maling's characterization of the semantic difference in question.

On the basis of similar contrasts, Maling (1983, p. 282, n. 9) also offers a semantic account of the complement selection exhibited by the verb *become*:

(13)   *a.*   Lee became mad.
        b. *Lee became out of his mind.
        c. *Lee became lunatic.
        d. Robin became more and more like her brother.
        e. Robin became more and more unlike his former self.
        f. *Robin has become near the edge of bankruptcy.

Her analysis is that *become* selects 'gradable, non-locative' complements 'of any category.' The conclusion that semantic selection is at work here also seems plausible, though certain problems remain.[5]

Thus there are clear cases where it can be demonstrated that an apparently syntactic selection is really semantic in nature. But this is not to say that all selections can or should be explained in semantic terms. Our own view of these matters is essentially that of Grimshaw (1979), namely that semantic selection must work hand in hand with syntactic subcategorization, in particular category selection, to explain the complex dependencies that particular lexical items exhibit.

This having been said, let us again turn to the small clause type of analysis. Problems of the sort Stowell raises for clausal analyses are pervasive. In P&S-87 (see also Sag and Pollard 1989), we pointed out the contrasts illustrated in (14)–(18), which involve a semantically-related class of verbs that we may refer to as 'verbs of becoming':

(14)   *a.*   Kim grew political.
        b. *Kim grew a success.
        c. *Kim grew sent more and more leaflets.
        d. *Kim grew doing all the work.
        e. Kim grew to like anchovies.

(15)   *a.*   Kim got political.
        b. *Kim got a success.

4. Jackendoff (1985: 280) reasons similarly (citing observations of Jane Grimshaw's) to the conclusion that verbs like *last* and *take* select for complements of any syntactic category, as long as they 'denote a period of time.' The relevant examples are *The meeting lasted/took two hours/much too long/until midnight.*

5. For example, if the nongradability of *prime-minister* is supposed to be responsible for the deviance of **Robin seems prime-minister*, then why is *Kim became prime-minister* well-formed?

    c.   Kim got sent more and more leaflets.
    d.   *Kim got doing all the work.
    e.   Kim got to like anchovies.

(16)   *a.*   Kim turned out political.
        b.   Kim turned out a success.
        c.   *Kim turned out sent more and more leaflets.
        d.   *Kim turned out doing all the work.
        e.   Kim turned out to like anchovies.

(17)   *a.*   Kim ended up political.
        b.   Kim ended up a success.
        c.   *Kim ended up sent more and more leaflets.
        d.   Kim ended up doing all the work.
        e.   *Kim ended up to like anchovies.

(18)   *a.*   Kim waxed political.
        b.   *Kim waxed a success.
        c.   *Kim waxed sent more and more leaflets.
        d.   *Kim waxed doing all the work.
        e.   *Kim waxed to like anchovies.

Let us add to the discussion the verb *become*, as well as further data about the PPs discussed by Maling:

(19)   *a.*   Kim became political.
        b.   Kim became a success.
        c.   *Kim became sent more and more leaflets.
        d.   *Kim became doing all the work.
        e.   *Kim became to like anchovies.

(20)   *a.*   Kim became more and more like her brother.
        b.   Kim grew more and more like her brother.
        c.   Kim got more and more like her brother.
        d.   Kim turned out more and more like her brother.
        e.   Kim ended up more and more like her brother.
        f.   *Kim waxed more and more like her brother.

Are these contrasts reducible to semantic selection? We think not. These verbs of becoming are all closely related semantically, and whatever differences in meaning may exist among them seem insufficient to explain the full range of their subcategorizational differences. Whereas all verbs of becoming except *wax* allow PP complements (of the appropriate semantic type), only *turn out, end up*, and *become* allow predicative NP complements. What possible semantic difference between *get* and *grow* on the one hand and *become* on the other could explain this difference in complement selection? Similarly, what difference in meaning between *end up* and *turn out* could explain why only the former allows a present participial complement? Why does *get*, but not *grow*, allow a passive complement? Why does *wax*[6] allow only AP complements? And so forth. In the absence of any semantic explanation for the contrasts in (14)–(20), we cannot avoid the conclusion that purely syntactic subcategorization plays a significant role in explaining these data.

This conclusion is crucial, for it leads directly to the rejection of the CP/IP analysis of these complements. It is possible to imagine reconciling the CP/IP analysis with selections for infinitivals, *that*-clauses, or even gerund complements, but if NP, PP, AP, passive, and participial complements may be subcategorized for, then, in virtue of the uncontroversial locality of subcategorization, these phrases must be locally accessible to (i.e. presumably, sisters of) the verbs that select them, and this is simply not the case in the CP/IP analysis. Nor would matters be helped by allowing some of these verbs to take IP complements directly, for such a proposal would still not render IP-internal NPs, APs, PPs, and VPs local to the verbs that must subcategorize for them.

Much the same conclusion follows from an examination of examples like (21)–(24), involving 'verbs of considering':[7]

(21) *a.* We consider Kim to be an acceptable candidate.
      b. We consider Kim an acceptable candidate.
      c. We consider Kim quite acceptable.
      d. We consider Kim among the most acceptable candidates.
      e. *We consider Kim as an acceptable candidate.
      f. *We consider Kim as quite acceptable.
      g. *We consider Kim as among the most acceptable candidates.
      h. ?*We consider Kim as being among the most acceptable candidates.

(22) *a.* *We regard Kim to be an acceptable candidate.
      b. *We regard Kim an acceptable candidate.
      c. *We regard Kim quite acceptable.

6. Historically, *wax* (cognate with German *wachsen*, 'to grow') occurred with a wider range of complements than at present. In present-day American usage, *wax* occurs most frequently with a handful of adjectives (e.g. *poetical, lyrical*), but is not restricted to that class.

7. We are grateful to the late Dwight Bolinger for helpful discussion of these contrasts. For attempts to explain in purely semantic terms contrasts of the sort discussed here, see Wierzbicka 1988 and Peeters 1989 (n.v.).

   d. ?*We regard Kim among the most acceptable candidates.
   e. We regard Kim as an acceptable candidate.
   f. We regard Kim as quite acceptable.
   g. We regard Kim as among the most acceptable candidates.
   h. We regard Kim as being among the most acceptable
     candidates.

(23) *a.* We rate Kim to be an acceptable candidate.
   b. We rate Kim an acceptable candidate.
   c. We rate Kim quite acceptable.
   d. We rate Kim among the most acceptable candidates.
   e. We rate Kim as an acceptable candidate.
   f. We rate Kim as quite acceptable.
   g. We rate Kim as among the most acceptable candidates.
   h. We rate Kim as being among the most acceptable
     candidates.

(24) *a.* *We count Kim to be an acceptable candidate.
   b. *We count Kim an acceptable candidate.
   c. *We count Kim quite acceptable.
   d. We count Kim among the most acceptable candidates.
   e. We count Kim as an acceptable candidate.
   f. We count Kim as quite acceptable.
   g. We count Kim as among the most acceptable candidates.
   h. We count Kim as being among the most acceptable
     candidates.

Here too, we find a class of verbs that are very closely related semantically, but whose complement selection properties vary considerably. Although future research could, of course, prove us wrong, we find it unlikely that there is a purely semantic account of the contrasts in (21)–(24). Our conclusion is that verbs must be able to select for the syntactic category of their complements. *Consider*, for example, allows infinitival, NP, AP, or PP complements, but not *as*-phrases, whereas *regard* allows only *as*-phrases. *Rate* allows any of the complements illustrated here, while *count* appears to allow only PPs or *as*-phrases. If the NP-XP sequences in these examples form small clauses (whether CPs S̄s, Ss, or IPs), then the required subcategorization violates locality.

Note that even under the assumption that the immediately postverbal NPs in these examples are primary objects, assigned semantic roles by the matrix verb (an assumption that is difficult to reconcile with the grammaticality of such examples as *We regard there as being no solution to this problem* or *We con-*

sider it likely to rain), the small clause analysis must countenance nonlocal subcategorization restrictions, as illustrated in (25):

(25)

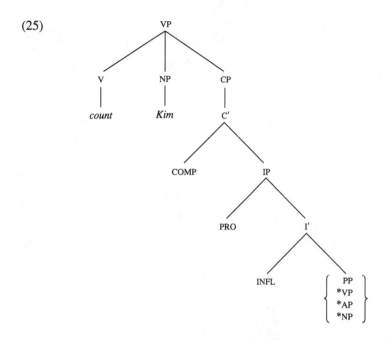

In short, we see no way of reconciling the data considered here with a CP or an IP analysis unless (1) a semantic account of all the dependencies illustrated in (21)–(24) can be motivated or (2) the well-established principle of the locality of subcategorization is abandoned.[8]

3.3 Stowell Structures

An alternative (and considerably more satisfactory) GB analysis of the phenomena at hand is developed by Stowell (1981, 1983). Stowell treats many of the complements discussed above as projections of the major categories N, V, A, and P, crucially modifying the X-theory he assumes in order to allow NPs, VPs, APs, and PPs to take subjects. His analysis is illustrated in (26):

8. For further discussion of problems associated with small clause analyses, see Williams 1983 and Lasnik and Saito 1991.

(26)

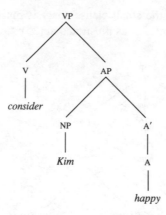

Stowell's approach solves a number of the problems discussed above, for the categorial information that we have argued must be subcategorized for is indeed locally accessible to the matrix verb. It is unclear, however, how Stowell's analysis would deal with *as*-phrase selection. If *as* is treated as a preposition, then we should expect all verbs that select PPs to also allow *as*-phrases, and vice versa. But, as we have seen, this is not the case (e.g. *consider* vs. *regard* vs. *count*). Perhaps this problem could be solved by introducing a syntactic feature (let us call it [+/− AS]) that is projected onto the AP from its lexical head (in accordance with general principles analogous to the Head Feature Principle of GPSG and HPSG). In this way, the relevant information about the nature of the preposition selected for would be locally available to the matrix verb.

These 'Stowell structures' (henceforth SSs) seem plausible for a number of syntactic constructions. In P&S-87, for example, we analyzed certain absolutive constructions, for example, *With Noriega in power (, we'll have to cancel our vacation)*, in terms of SSs, as illustrated in (27):

(27)

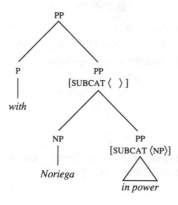

And SSs appear in other contexts as well, for example, in examples like (28): [9]

(28)   a. We feared [Noriega in power].
        b. We didn't like [the party on a Tuesday].
        c. They wanted [the party on a Tuesday].
        d. What, [me worry]?

However, there are compelling, independent reasons for rejecting the treatment of verbs of considering in terms of SSs.[10] First, there is the matter of constituency. If the NP-XP sequences occurring after *consider* and the like were SS constituents, then we should expect to find corresponding pseudocleft and *it*-cleft sentences like (29):

(29)   a. *What we considered was [Leslie in complete control of the situation].
        b. *It was [Leslie in complete control of the situation] that we considered.

However, these are systematically ill-formed.

Note that there is nothing otherwise preventing SSs of this form from appearing as a focussed constituent in either kind of cleft-sentence, as the examples in (30) are perfectly grammatical:

(30)   a. What we feared most was [Leslie in complete control of the situation].
        b. It was [Leslie in complete control of the situation] that we feared most.

Note that (29a)/(30a) and (29b)/(30b) are minimal pairs. The NP-PP sequences occur in identical matrix environments, yet only *fear* allows a missing small clause or SS complement. Hence one cannot explain the deviance of (29a, b) by appeal to such GB principles as the *Case Filter*,[11] which fails to distinguish between (29) and (30), or to any constraint barring clauses without complementizers from appearing in positions not adjacent to a governing verb.[12]

The most straightforward explanation of these contrasts is that the verbs of considering take two complements (in addition to the subject): a primary object NP and a predicative complement. In this way, the deviance of the examples in (29) follows from the fact that the cleft clauses (i.e. *what we considered* __ __ in (29a) and *that we considered* __ __ in (29b)) would have to contain

9. For some discussion of examples like (28d), see Akmajian 1984 and Zhang 1990, 1992.

10. Here, and throughout, we are indebted to Joan Bresnan for valuable discussion.

11. Such an appeal would involve the claim that the NP *Leslie* in (29) cannot be assigned case. See below (section 3.4).

12. See the discussion in Postal (1974: 128ff.), in response to a suggestion made by Howard Lasnik.

two gaps, a highly restricted circumstance in English (see Chapter 4)—and certainly a circumstance inconsistent with the presence of a single focussed constituent, as in these examples. These data thus provide significant evidence against the Stowell-type analysis of these structures (as well as evidence against any small clause analysis), which treats the complements of *consider* and the like as a single constituent.

Clearly relevant to the matter of the constituency of the complements under discussion here is the debate about the status of the transformation of 'Subject-to-Object Raising' (SOR), which began in the early 1970s (see, inter alia, Chomsky 1973; Postal 1974, 1977; Bresnan 1976; Bach 1977; and Postal and Pullum 1988). At stake in this controversy has been the status of not just verbs of considering, but rather the full range of examples where a given verb occurs followed by an NP and an infinitive VP or other predicative complement, that is, all the examples in (31):

(31)   *a.* Pat believes Chris (to be) a spy.
        b. Kim expects Sandy (to be) on time.
        c. Terry proved Dana (to be) wrong about the regulations.
        d. Lee prevented Dominique from being a scapegoat.

The structure proposed for such examples by Chomsky (1973), not different in essential respects from the small clause structures currently assumed within GB, is illustrated in (32):

(32)

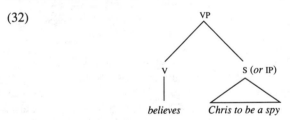

In this structure, the NP *Chris* remains the subject of the embedded clause throughout the transformational derivation.

On the analysis advocated by Postal (1974), the same example is assigned the structure in (33) through the application of the SOR transformation:

(33)

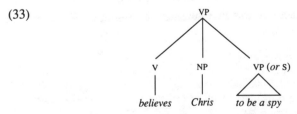

Postal offers numerous arguments for the SOR structure, many of which are disputed by Bresnan (1976), and two of which are of immediate relevance here.

Postal's first argument concerns the 'complex NP shift' phenomenon exemplified in (34)–(35):

(34)　　*a.* Kim bought a book from René.
　　　　b. Kim bought from René—a book which taught him organic knitting.

(35)　　*a.* I showed the cookies to Dana.
　　　　b. I showed to Dana—all of the cookies that could be made from betel nuts and molasses.

On the basis of such examples as those in (36), Postal (1974: 83) offers the generalization in (37):

(36)　　*a.* *Are happy—all of the men who recovered from mononucleosis?
　　　　b. *I regret the fact that were destroyed—so many of our priceless relics.

(37)　　Complex NP shift does *not* operate on NPs that are subjects at the point of application.

This generalization supports the SOR analysis in virtue of the fact that the NPs whose object status is in question clearly do undergo complex NP shift: [13]

(38)　　*a.* Pat believes to be a spy—everyone who was working for the Warren Commission.
　　　　b. ?Kim expects to be on time—every employee who was hired for the Christmas rush.
　　　　c. Terry proved to be wrong—virtually everyone who challenged her.
　　　　d. Lee prevented from being a scapegoat—that nice old professor who introduced the modification without prior approval.

This conclusion also bears directly on the analysis of verbs of considering discussed above, as the immediately postverbal NPs in these examples freely undergo complex NP shift:

(39)　　*a.* We would consider acceptable—any candidate who supports the proposed amendment.
　　　　b. We would regard as acceptable—any candidate who supports the proposed amendment.

13. Bresnan (1976: 486) disputes the correctness of Postal's generalization on the basis of 'locative inversion' examples like *Near that town was situated for many years after the war an old ruin that the Germans had bombed*, where the subject phrase (on her analysis) *an old ruin that the Germans had bombed* has been shifted. Her objections are countered by Postal (1977), and are in any case obviated by the analysis of locative inversion developed in Bresnan (n.d.). Hence, we will not review the details of this controversy here.

    c. We would rate among the acceptable candidates—any one of
    them who supports the proposed amendment.
    d. We would count among the acceptable candidates—any one of
    them who supports the proposed amendment.

Since the NPs that immediately follow verbs of considering freely undergo
complex NP shift, they cannot be subjects. Hence we have another piece of
evidence that the correct structure for these examples is the SOR structure illustrated in (40), rather than the small clause analysis or the alternative suggested by Stowell:

(40)

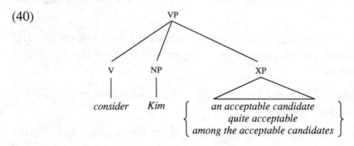

    But this argument rests on the correctness of Postal's generalization that
subjects cannot be shifted, a generalization that one might challenge. In particular, one might propose to replace Postal's condition with the one in (41):

(41)   Complex NP shift leaves a trace, which must be properly governed.

The ungrammatical shifts in (36a, b) would involve traces that were subjects of
finite verbs, and hence not properly governed. On an analysis in terms of SSs
(or small clauses), on the other hand, the traces in (38) and (39) are all properly
governed under the standard assumption that the matrix verbs occasion exceptional case marking (possibly accompanied by CP erasure).

    To see that this alternative proposal fails to explain the data in question, we
must compare the behavior of these complements with that of gerund phrases,
illustrated in (42):

(42)

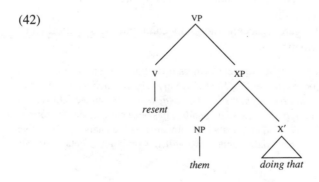

The constituency indicated here is motivated by such facts as the possibility of clefting and pseudoclefting gerund phrases (these examples should be compared with *(29) and (30)):

(43)   *a.* It was [him doing that] that I resented ___.
         b. What I resented ___ was [him doing that].

We assume, following Postal (1974, 1977), that the subjects of gerunds never undergo raising. And, in keeping with Postal's generalization, gerunds may not undergo complex NP shift (as noted by Postal (1977: 152, n. 15); see also Kayne (1984a, chap. 2)):

(44)   *I resented doing that—the doctor that treated your pig.

Rizzi (1990: 35) seeks to explain the ungrammaticality of (44) as a violation of the condition (41) (slightly revised to require trace to be properly *head*-governed by its inflection). However, his approach fails to explain the fact that the accusative subject of a gerund phrase may be a trace in unbounded leftward extraction constructions:

(45)   *a.* The man that I resented ___ stepping in front of me in line.
         b. Which man did you resent ___ stepping in front of you in line?
         c. It was Sandy that I resented ___ stepping in front of me in line.

Under standard GB assumptions, these traces must be properly governed (or properly head-governed). But this in turn undermines the alternative account of the condition on complex NP shift. That account fails to distinguish subjects of small clauses (which are properly governed and may be shifted) from gerund subjects (which are properly governed yet may not be shifted).[14] On our view, complex NP shift involves linear ordering principles that sanction alternative 'shifted' orders of sister constituents.[15] This analysis involves no traces at all. Leftward extractions like those illustrated in (45) are possible because of the existence of the Subject Extraction Lexical Rule presented in section 4 of Chapter 4.

14. One might attempt to salvage the proposed alternative generalization by imposing a further condition that traces left by rightward movement must be properly governed by a verb (presuming, following Reuland (1983), that the subjects of gerunds are governed by the inflection of the gerund). Such a proposal, though observationally adequate, lacks independent motivation.

15. This in turn requires that we regard examples like (i) as being free of parasitic gaps, which we take to occur only in unbounded dependency constructions analyzed in terms of the feature SLASH (see Chapter 4):

(i)   The twins insulted, by not recognizing immediately, their favorite uncle from Cleveland.

Such examples may be a kind of Right Node Raising. We lack any precise analysis as yet.

A second of Postal's arguments for the SOR structure, based on the positioning and interpretation of certain adverbs, is also worth reexamining in the present context. Postal (1974: 147) argues that the adverb in (46a) can only modify the verb of the embedded clause (*outweigh*), whereas the adverb in (46b) may modify the matrix verb *prove*:

(46)   *a.* I can prove that Bob easily outweighed Martha's goat.
        b. I can prove Bob easily to have outweighed Martha's goat.

He offers an account of this in terms of the following principle:

(47)   A 'sentential' adverb cannot be inserted in a complement clause.

This principle, together with the SOR analysis of [*prove* NP VP[*inf*]] constructions, would explain the contrast in (46).

Bresnan (1976: 496) challenges this claim, arguing that the SOR analysis, taken together with Postal's generalization, fails to explain such contrasts as (48) (due to Huddleston):

(48)   *a.* *I expected John quite confidently to give the lecture.
        b. I persuaded John quite easily to give the lecture.

Postal (1974: 153–154) accepts the data in (48), but claims that the contrasts necessary to motivate the SOR analysis can be reconstructed on the basis of different adverbials, such as *quite without reason, in spite of protests, with my usual false optimism*, etc.

However, as Bresnan (1976: 496) points out, these *parenthetical* adverbs, typically set off as an intonational phrase, have quite generally a wider distribution. In particular, they can appear within embedded clauses with matrix-modifying interpretation:

(49)   *a.* I arranged [for my relatives, in spite of protests, to have jobs in our department].
        b. I had hoped [for the deanship, with my usual false optimism, to be given to Uncle Buddy].

While we accept Bresnan's observations about the data in (49), it is nonetheless true that Postal's argument for the SOR structure can be resurrected if even one class of adverbials can be found that obeys the generalization in (47), yet occurs (with matrix interpretation) between the postverbal NP and the infinitival VP. Moreover, it appears that there is such a class of adverbs, one that includes *in spite of myself* and *to this very day*. These adverbials, unlike those considered by Postal, Huddleston, and Bresnan, cannot receive matrix interpretation when they appear within an embedded clause. Thus (50b) and (51b), constructed so as to make sense only if the adverbial has the matrix interpretation of the corresponding examples in (50a) and (51a), lack any sensible interpretation:

(50)   *a.*   To this very day, I have been hoping for Kim to be proven
               innocent.
         b.   #I have been hoping for Kim to this very day to be proven
               innocent.

(51)   *a.*   In spite of myself, I have been hoping for Kim to get the job.
         b.   #I have been hoping for Kim in spite of myself to get the job.

Yet the adverbs illustrated here seem perfectly acceptable with matrix interpretation in examples like the following:

(52)   *a.*   I believe George Washington to this very day to have been a great
               statesman.
         b.   I believed Kim in spite of myself to be the most qualified
               candidate.

And, predictably, such adverbs (with matrix modification) are also to be found
after the primary objects of verbs of considering:

(53)   *a.*   I consider George Washington to this very day to have been a
               great statesman.
         b.   I regard Kim in spite of myself as the most qualified candidate.
         c.   I count George Washington to this very day as one of the nation's
               greatest statesmen.

Thus, on the basis of these adverbials one can in fact resurrect Postal's second
argument for the SOR structures,[16] structures that have been consistently rejected by Chomsky, Stowell, and most researchers working within the tradition
of GB.[17]

    The reason that such structures have been rejected, of course, is that they are
inconsistent with the part of GB's Projection Principle stated in (54):

(54)   If α subcategorizes the position β, then α θ-marks β.

That is, (54) would be contradicted by the assumption of the SOR structures
for examples like (55), where the expletive pronouns are presumably assigned
no θ-role:

(55)   *a.*   We believe *it* to be obvious that Sandy will win.
         b.   We believed *there* to be no alternative.

    However, as Postal and Pullum (1988) show in detail, the part of the Projec-
tion Principle stated in (54) must be abandoned. In particular, the clausal treatment of phrases like *it to be obvious that Sandy will win* and *there to be no*

---

16. For an analogous argument, based on adverbials, for SOR structures in Icelandic,
see Andrews 1982.
   17. Williams (1983) is a notable exception.

alternative that is required in order to reconcile the examples in (55) with the Projection Principle is unavailable in a large class of well-known cases where expletives may appear. Among the examples they cite in drawing this conclusion are those in (56):

(56)   *a.* We can prevent *there* from being a riot on Sunday.
         b. We take *it* as obvious that Sandy is qualified for the job.
         c. You owe *it* to yourself, in my opinion, to get an annual checkup.
         d. He never gave *it* a thought that Bolshies are human beings.
         e. I regret *it* very much that we could not hire Mosconi.
         f. We're going to have to wing *it*.

Given Postal and Pullum's conclusion, which we accept, that the part of the Projection Principle stated in (54) must be abandoned, it is plain that there is no theoretical obstacle to positing the SOR structures for all the verbs discussed above (i.e. *believe, expect*, and the verbs of considering). This conclusion, as we have seen, is motivated by other empirical considerations as well.[18]

These differing hypotheses about the nature of infinitival complements lead in turn to differing hypotheses about the nature of passivization. Under the standard GB assumption that the NP immediately following *believe* and the like is part of a small clause or a Stowell structure, it follows that passive must involve a movement transformation in order to allow for examples like those in (57):

18. Note that contrasts like (i)–(ii), due originally to Mark Baltin, have sometimes been taken as evidence against assigning object raising sentences the same structures as object equi sentences:

(i)   *John believes me himself to be aggressive.

(ii)   John persuaded me himself to be aggressive.

But, in fact, such contrasts involving the positioning of emphatic reflexives seem to provide no evidence for the constituency of *me to be aggressive* because of contrasts like (iii)–(iv):

(iii)   John prevented me himself from causing a riot.

(iv)   *John prevented there himself from being a riot.

(iii) and (iv), as Postal and Pullum argue, cannot be treated in terms of a small clause structure, yet only (iii) allows the emphatic reflexive after the object NP. The conclusion we draw from these data (though we present no precise analysis here) is that emphatic reflexives may appear after an object NP only if the latter is assigned a semantic role. Assuming that the object of *prevent* is optionally assigned such a role (an assumption that is motivated on purely semantic grounds), this generalization extends to all of (i)–(iv) under the assumption that none of these examples involves a small clause structure.

(57) *a.* Sandy was believed to be a spy (by almost everyone).
      b. Terry was expected to win the prize (by almost everyone).
      c. Bo was considered a great athlete (by all her coaches).
      d. Dana was regarded as among the leading candidates (by everyone).
      e. Gerry was counted among the leading contenders (by the entire committee).

These should be contrasted with the following examples, where the immediately postverbal NP cannot passivize (contrasts due to Postal (1974; 1977: 152, n. 15)):

(58) *a.* *The doctor was resented examining Kim (by our whole family).
      b. *Dana was resented having been chosen (by almost everyone).

What is the explanation for such contrasts in passivizability? In GB, the answer is that passivization (an instance of NP-movement) affects only those NPs that cannot be assigned case. The passive verbal forms in (57) have 'absorbed case,' and hence cannot assign case to the following NP. Movement is thus obligatory, because every NP must be assigned case in accordance with the case filter. But in (58), the postverbal NP is assigned case by the inflection of the gerund, and hence cannot be fronted by passivization, because case must be assigned uniquely. We will return to the matter of the case filter, on which this entire analysis hinges, in the next section.

By contrast, the HPSG account of these contrasts turns on the assumption that an immediately postverbal NP may passivize only if it is a primary object of the verb. Passive is an operation on grammatical relations, one that 'demotes' subject arguments (universally, including impersonal passivization in many languages) and, in many instances, additionally 'promotes' more oblique syntactic dependents (e.g. primary objects in English, or perhaps primary and secondary objects in other languages) to subject status. This *relational* characterization of passivization represents a significant point of agreement among researchers working in diverse theoretical frameworks.[19] The relational character of passive also explains the contrasts just noted: only in (57) is there a primary object to be passivized.

We note in passing that the arguments denying the relational nature of passive offered by Chomsky (1981) have no force in the present context. In discussing the examples in (59), for example, Chomsky (1981: 123) asserts that 'there is no independent sense of 'object' in which such examples . . . are instances of change of grammatical relation from object to subject':

19. For example, relational grammar (Perlmutter and Postal 1977, 1983), arc pair grammar (Johnson and Postal 1980; Postal 1986), lexical functional grammar (Bresnan ed. 1982; Bresnan 1982), generalized phrase structure grammar (Gazdar 1982; Gazdar et al. 1985), and categorial grammar (Dowty 1982a, 1982b), to name but a few.

(59)   *a.* The Cadillac was driven away in.
       b. John was spoken to.
       c. The bed was slept in.
       d. John was believed to be stupid.
       e. He was pronounced dead on arrival.

We have already reviewed some of the evidence for the primary object status of the active counterparts of (59d) and (59e). As for (59a–c), Chomsky accepts the conclusion that the relevant prepositional objects are reanalyzed as primary objects (in his terms, assigned the GF [NP,VP]), objecting only that 'such derivative GF's, assigned through reanalysis, do not seem to affect θ-role assignment.' With this we agree, but once the Projection Principle is modified in the manner summarized above, there is nothing of consequence that follows from this observation.

Chomsky (1981: 124) concludes that '[the] traditional characterization of passive as involving a change of object to subject . . . is otherwise unacceptable on grounds of factual inaccuracy, . . . incompleteness, . . . circularity, . . . and redundancy.' His charge of 'inaccuracy' is based on the existence of passivized expletives (e.g. *it was believed that the conclusion was false*), which he assumes correspond to active small clause structures lacking direct objects, an assumption we have already seen to be problematic. The 'incompleteness' he refers to is the possibility of passive nominalizations, e.g. *Rome's destruction.* But in any lexical theory of grammar, nominal argument structures are determined at least in part by verbal argument structures. Hence once passive is cast as a lexical rule (see below), the syntactic argument structures it assigns to verbs give rise to corresponding nominal argument structures. Chomsky has not shown that the lexical theory of passive is in any way incomplete.

Chomsky's charge of 'circularity' is rather curious. It is based on examples like those in (59a–c), where, as noted above, Chomsky finds no appropriate independent sense of 'object' that can be applied. But on Chomsky's (1981: 124ff.) own account of prepositional passives, where 'passive morphology . . . in effect 'absorbs' case,' no account is given of why certain intransitive verbs may absorb the case of the object of an adjacent (or, in cases like (59a), a nonadjacent) preposition. The lexical, semantic, and pragmatic idiosyncrasies surrounding the entire issue of prepositional passives, discussed originally by Chomsky (1955) and subsequently in great detail by numerous researchers,[20] pose at least as many problems for Chomsky's case absorption, structure-blind theory of passives as they do for analyses based on lexical rules that affect grammatical relations.

20. See, e.g., Lakoff (1965), Johnson (1974), Bolinger (1975), Riddle and Sheintuch (1983), Couper-Kuhlen (1979), Bresnan (1982), Davison (1980), Ziv and Sheintuch (1981), and Postal (1986).

Finally, Chomsky's charge of 'redundancy' is based on his claim that 'independent principles of much broader scope determine both when movement is necessary and that the new grammatical function assigned is that of subject.' This claim, however, appeals to various principles that we regard as untenable, for example, the Projection Principle (see above) and the Case Filter (see section 3.4). In addition, some of the other 'principles' Chomsky is referring to are quite arcane in nature, for example, principles governing 'function chains'; others, for example, the stipulation that passive morphology is 'case-absorbing,' have no independent motivation outside of the technical apparatus of GB theory.

In sum, the arguments against the relational formulation of passive are tied to a number of assumptions that are internal to GB and the utilization of movement rules rather than lexical rules. In the theory we develop here, these arguments have little, if any, force. In light of the successful analyses of passivization in numerous languages attained by researchers working within such frameworks as relational grammar, arc-pair grammar, (early) lexical-functional grammar, and categorial grammar, we would prefer to regard the relational analysis of passive as one of the established results of modern syntactic theory—a result that is inconsistent with assumptions standard in transformational syntax from Chomsky 1973 to the present day.

Our own account of passive, sketched in P&S-87,[21] is stated in terms of a lexical rule that permutes the SUBCAT list of active transitive verb forms. Thus the SUBCAT lists for active forms of verbs of considering and other verbs that occur in the SOR structures, sketched in (60), are mapped into the corresponding SUBCAT lists in (61):

(60)   *a.* SUBCAT $\langle$NP, NP, XP[+PRD]$\rangle$ (*consider, rate*)

   b. SUBCAT $\langle$NP, NP, PP[*as*]$\rangle$ (*regard, rate, count*)

   c. SUBCAT $\langle$NP, NP, PP[+PRD]$\rangle$ (*count*)

   d. SUBCAT $\langle$NP, NP, VP[*inf*]$\rangle$ (*believe, expect*)

(61)   *a.* SUBCAT $\langle$NP, XP[+PRD], PP[*by*]$\rangle$ (*considered, rated*)

   b. SUBCAT $\langle$NP, PP[*as*], PP[*by*]$\rangle$ (*regarded, rated, counted*)

   c. SUBCAT $\langle$NP, PP[+PRD], PP[*by*]$\rangle$ (*counted*)

   d. SUBCAT $\langle$NP, VP[*inf*], PP[*by*]$\rangle$ (*believed, expected*)

And in virtue of Rule Schema 2, discussed in Chapter 1, these lexical entries give rise to passive phrases like (62):

21. It should be noted that this analysis of passive bears a strong family resemblance to those developed in the various frameworks mentioned in n. 19. Moreover, the lexical analysis we propose can be modified in various minor ways to provide successful HPSG reanalyses of various RG, LFG, and CG accounts.

(62)

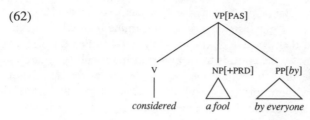

It should be noted that, although we explicitly abandon, for the reasons summarized above, GB's Projection Principle, HPSG theory nonetheless embodies a strong theory of the nature of syntactic and semantic structures and the relation between the two. As explained in Chapter 1, the CONTENT values employed in HPSG are *parametrized states of affairs* (psoas), which are constellations of relations, roles, and polarities. Relations differ as to which roles they permit, and roles differ as to what type of objects they take as value. The nature of these objects is motivated on purely semantic grounds.

Our syntactic structures are the restricted subset of constituent structures given by the various universal schemata sketched in Chapter 1. These are subject to a certain degree of language-particular parametric variation. In contrast to the relatively 'flat' architecture of psoas (modulo embedding of psoas), these constituent structures may exhibit a certain hierarchical nature, for example, in the combination of subject and VP in English permitted as an instance of Schema 1. The arguments for such structures, at odds with aspects of semantic structures that can be *semantically* motivated, are too familiar to warrant repeating here, but are one of the important ways in which semantic and syntactic structures diverge.

The relation between syntactic and semantic structures is constrained in two fundamental ways: by the nature and structure of lexical signs and by universal and language-particular constraints. Thus in HPSG, as in virtually all approaches to syntax that are equally concerned with semantic analysis, the question of the relation between form and content is not a matter to be legislated in advance of empirical investigation (as is done, in essence, by simply asserting (Chomsky 1981: 29) that the Projection Principle will be taken 'as a guiding principle for the theory to be developed'). The precise nature of the syntax-semantics interface is an important empirical issue, one that is the topic of intense ongoing inquiry.

Lexical items have various kinds of semantic objects as their content, often critically linked to aspects of the context of utterance. For example, a verb has a psoa as its content and specifies the relation of that psoa as well as certain roles that are to be specified. The various dependents that a lexical item subcategorizes for may be semantically associated with other aspects of that lexical item's content. One important instance of such an association is role assignment, which is simply a lexically specified identification of all or part of the content of a syntactic dependent with the value of some role in the head's content. Not all dependents are assigned a role, however, and not all roles are linked to a dependent. Our theory thus countenances both unassigned syntactic arguments and 'implicit' arguments, hence explicitly denying in its totality Chomsky's θ-Criterion.[22]

The various principles of universal grammar that we have put forth, for example, the Subcategorization Principle, the Head Feature Principle, and the Semantics Principle, interact with the token-identities specified within lexical signs to 'project' many of the syntactic and semantic properties of a phrase from those of the phrase's lexical head. Form and content are thus mutually constraining in HPSG, rather than isomorphic, as entailed by the Projection Principle.

The specific nature of the relation between form and content that emerges from HPSG theory will become apparent as we consider in more detail the analysis of various complement constructions.

3.4 Unsaturated Complements

In the previous section, we presented evidence for rejecting the CP and IP analyses (and the alternative proposed by Stowell) of infinitival and other predicative complements. This evidence, as noted, leads to the conclusion that many verbs and adjectives in English subcategorize for a complement that is itself *unsaturated*, that is, a complement that is specified as [SUBCAT⟨NP⟩], rather than [SUBCAT ⟨ ⟩]. Following the treatment sketched in P&S-87, we analyze not only VP complements as unsaturated, but also [+PRD] complements, such as *among the acceptable candidates* (PP[+PRD]), *quite acceptable* (AP[+PRD]), and *an acceptable candidate* (NP[+PRD]). We posit no phonetically unrealized PRO as a constituent in syntactic representations, though, as will become apparent, the NP within the SUBCAT value of unsaturated complements performs many similar functions.

---

22. There are of course canonical relations between syntactic and semantic argument structure. Oblique prepositional phrases that are syntactically selected are associated with a restricted set of semantic roles, as are primary and secondary objects in most, if not all, languages. Such canonical associations, which doubtless play a key role in the language acquisition process, may be cast as general principles constraining the nature of a particular language's lexicon, or of lexicons quite generally. Thus abandoning the Projection Principle as formulated in GB in no way entails abandoning the search for strong constraints on the relation between form and content. It simply moves the search into the lexicon, where generalizations about the relation between syntactic and semantic argument structure can be expressed. For some specific proposals concerning the structure of the lexicon, see P&S-87, Chapter 8.

Before proceeding, it is perhaps worthwhile to consider various possible objections to the VP complement analysis that we adopt (following, inter alia, Brame (1976) and Bresnan (1978)). Such objections have been raised by Koster and May and by Chomsky. Koster and May (1982) argue on the basis of examples like those in (63) that a grammar for English that allowed VP complements, as well as S complements, would need to posit redundant phrase structure rules:

(63)   Sandy preferred [(for Lee) to leave].
         We have plans [(for Dana) to leave].
         It is possible [(for Leslie) to leave].
         [(For him) to prove the continuum hypothesis] would have been Gödel's greatest achievement.

The rules they consider as necessary under the VP complement analysis are those sketched in (64):

(64)   VP → V {S, VP}
         NP → N {S, VP}
         AP → A {S, VP}
         NP → NP {S, VP}

The redundancy that they allege to be unavoidable clearly turns on the assumption that the class {S,VP} is not a natural class, and hence must be specified disjunctively, as in (64).

Chomsky (1981: 25ff.) reasons similarly, rejecting the 'considerably clumsier system of rules' in (65), and with it any analysis of English that fails to acknowledge the clausal character of superficially subjectless infinitival phrases, that is, any analysis that fails to recognize PRO subjects, as assumed within GB:

(65)   *i.* $\overline{\text{VP}}$ → COMP VP_1
         ii. $\overline{\text{S}}$ → COMP S
         iii. S → NP VP_1 when COMP = *for*;
                S → NP VP_2 otherwise
         iv. VP_1 is *to*-VP and VP_2 is Tense-VP

These arguments, however, fall short of invalidating the VP complement analysis of subjectless infinitivals: from the fact that some PRO-less phrase structure analyses fail to express certain generalizations, it does not follow that all PRO-less phrase structure analyses fail to express those generalizations. The theory of complementation we develop here suffers from none of the inadequacies alleged by Chomsky and by Koster and May.

Our universal theory of immediate dominance schemata, summarized in Chapter 1, makes available head-marker structures like the following:

(66)

MARKER–DTR   HEAD–DTR

The mother and the MARKER-DTR in such structures, licensed by Schema 4, share a specification for the attribute MARKING, while the HEAD-DTR is specified as [MARKING *unmarked*].[23] The MARKING values *that* and *for* are two subsorts of the sort *comp*; hence we will use the abbreviations S[*comp*] and S[*unmarked*] to distinguish clauses with [MARKING *marked*] from those specified as [MARKING *unmarked*]. The MARKER-DTR, it will be recalled, also specifies a SPEC value that must be token-identical with the SYNSEM value of the HEAD-DTR. The complementizer *for*, for example, is a marker specified as [HEAD | SPEC S[*inf*]], and the complementizer *that* as [HEAD | SPEC S[*fin*∨ *base*]].

If, as in P&S-87, we follow Pullum (1982) and Gazdar et al. (1985) in treating the infinitive marker *to* as a defective auxiliary verb whose head features include the specification [VFORM *inf*], then there are three kinds of infinitival ([VFORM *inf*]) phrases in English, as shown in (67):

(67)   *a.* for Kim to resign (S[*inf,comp*])
       b. Kim to resign (S[*inf,unmarked*])
       c. to resign (VP[*inf*])

The question then is: Why are (67a, c), but not (67b), possible in the contexts Koster and May discuss? Are (67a, c) a syntactic natural class?

The answer to this question is to be found by considering a broader range of data. It is commonly observed that in numerous syntactic environments a clause must appear with a complementizer. This set of environments includes at least sentence fragments, subject position, and the focus position in various copular constructions:

(68)   What did they prefer?
       – For Kim to be reassigned
       –*Kim to be reassigned
       – That Kim be reassigned
       –*Kim be reassigned

(69)   What did they believe?
       – That they will be reassigned
       –*They will be reassigned

23. This is due to the SPEC value of English complementizers (see Chapter 1, (37)). In other languages, a marker daughter may select for a specific MARKING value on the HEAD-DTR.

(70)   *a.* [That Dana was unhappy] was obvious.
         b. *[Dana was unhappy] was obvious.
         c. [For Pat to resign] would be unfortunate.
         d. *[Pat to resign] would be unfortunate.

(71)   What did they prefer?
         – It was [for Kim to be reassigned]
         –*It was [Kim to be reassigned]
         – It was [that Kim be reassigned]
         –*It was [Kim be reassigned]

(72)   What did they believe?
         – It was [that they will be reassigned]
         –*It was [they will be reassigned]

(73)   *a.* What they promised was [that Kim would be reassigned].
         b. *What they promised was [Kim will be reassigned].
         c. What they preferred was [for Kim to be reassigned].
         d. *What they preferred was [Kim to be reassigned].

These environments—let us call them *free* environments—are all to be analyzed in terms of S[*comp*].

Crucially, subjectless infinitival VPs like *to be reassigned* also occur in all
the free environments:

(74)   What did they promise you?
         –To attend the ceremony on Sunday
         –It was to attend the ceremony on Sunday

(75)   What they preferred was [to be reassigned at the end of the year].

A natural conclusion to draw from this observation is that infinitival VPs also
lead a life as [*comp*] expressions, and that the specification relevant for the
analysis of free environments should not be S[*comp*], but rather just [*comp*]
(with SUBCAT value unspecified, hence allowing the description to be satisfied
by either S or VP).

One might imagine that this result should be achieved by treating *to* as a
marker specified as [HEAD | SPEC VP[*base*]], but in light of the numerous argu-
ments cited by Pullum to the effect that *to* is a defective auxiliary, not a complementizer, this analysis would appear to be unavailable.[24] A preferable alternative is simply to posit a phonetically null complementizer in English that is
specified as [HEAD | SPEC VP[*inf*]].[25] This analysis requires no new grammar

---

24. For detailed justification of the claim that auxiliaries, including modals, are
verbs, see Gazdar, Pullum, and Sag 1982.

25. In older forms of English, and in certain varieties of modern English (e.g. Ozark
dialects), this null complementizer is realized as *for*.

rules or otherwise unmotivated complications of existing devices. In virtue of the independently motivated, universal schema for head-marker constructions, this complementizer will occur in structures like (76):

(76)

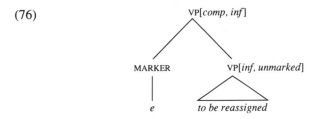

The analysis just sketched effectively answers the objections raised by Koster and May and by Chomsky. The disjunctive category specifications in the rules Koster and May propose are replaced by the specification [*inf, comp*], a partial category specification that can be realized in exactly two ways: as a *for-to* clause or as an infinitival VP.

In addition, it is plain that the 'considerably clumsier' system of rules Chomsky considers (see (65)) has been replaced by an elegant and streamlined system under our proposal. His rules (i) and (ii) are two instances of the head-marker schema, corresponding to two different lexical SUBCAT specifications. The two rules he gives in (65iii) are both instances of Schema 1, which allows a single complement as sister to a phrasal head. Chomsky's stipulations (*when COMP = for* and *otherwise* in (65)) are eliminated entirely. Finite verb forms never co-occur with the complementizer *for* because finiteness (encoded as the head feature specification [VFORM *fin*]) is projected onto the clause from the finite verb, in accordance with the Head Feature Principle, and the complementizer *for* selects clauses specified as [VFORM *inf*], as illustrated in (77):

(77)

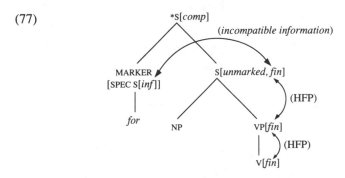

Hence the constraints that Chomsky assumes must be stipulated are actually derived through the interaction of lexical selection, universal rule schemata, and principles of the HPSG theory of universal grammar (e.g. the Head Feature Principle).

Compare this with the GB account of these same facts. In GB, it is assumed that PRO may never be governed[26] and that all overt NPs must be assigned case, or else violations of the Case Filter are occasioned. Such case assignment is assumed, following Stowell (1981), to be subject to an adjacency condition. That is, it is assumed that every overt NP in a well-formed syntactic structure is adjacent to some lexical item that both governs and assigns case to that NP.[27]

The Case Filter (Chomsky 1981; Stowell 1983) is often assumed to be responsible for the deviance of many of the complementizerless examples considered above, for example, those in (78):

(78)   a. *It was [*Kim* to be reassigned].
        b. *What they preferred was [*Kim* to be reassigned].
        c. *What they considered was [*Sandy* a fool].

In these examples, the italicized NP, properly contained within the clefted clause (or Stowell structure), is not governed by the copula. Hence the examples are ill-formed because these NPs must be assigned case, yet there is no governing case-assigner available. The analogs of (78a, b) where the small clause is replaced by a *for-to* clause are grammatical, on this account, because the complementizer *for* assigns case to the relevant NP.

Exceptional case assignment may take place in structurally similar examples involving verbs like *believe* and *expect* in examples like (79), because it is stipulated either that these verbs trigger '$\bar{S}$-deletion' or else that their complements are disjunctively specified as either CP or IP. Under either analysis, it becomes possible for the verb to govern, and hence assign case to, the adjacent NP, even though it is properly contained within the clause that these verbs subcategorize:[28]

(79)   a. Sandy believes [*Kim* to be unpopular].
        b. We expect [*Dana* to leave].

The same is assumed to be true under the small clause analysis of verbs of considering:[29]

(80)   a. Sandy considers [*Kim* unpopularⱼ.
        b. Sandy regards [*Kim* as unpopular].

26. For a critical assessment of this assumption, see Chapter 6.

27. There are various modifications and complications of this basic characterization of the Case Filter that have been proposed in the GB literature. For example, Chomsky (1986a: chap. 3) seeks to derive the relevant aspects of the Case Filter from his 'visibility condition.' However, the various alternative formulations that have been proposed do not, as far as we are aware, avoid the criticisms we make below.

28. As Postal and Pullum (1988) point out, interclausal case marking of this sort has in all likelihood never been attested in languages with nondegenerate case systems.

29. See Stowell 1983 for an alternative account of why case assignment is possible into a Stowell structure complement.

Note that this GB account fails to relate the impossibility of clefted and pseudoclefted small clauses (e.g. (78a–c)) to the impossibility of clefted and pseudoclefted *that*-less finite clauses like the ones in (81):

(81) *a.* *It was [Kim was reassigned].
      b. *What they preferred was [Kim is reassigned].
      c. *What they considered was [Kim was a fool].

This is because tense is assumed to be a governor that assigns case to the subject of finite clauses (with or without the complementizer *that*).

However, quite apart from this *argumentum ad generalisationem omissam*, there are serious problems facing this appeal to the Case Filter. First, it is well-known that in many languages case assignment obeys no adjacency condition whatsoever. Relatively well-known facts of Icelandic, for example, demonstrate that verbs may assign marked case values to their subjects. In each of the following examples (from Andrews 1982; see also Thráinsson 1979) the indicated case of the subject is the only possible choice:

(82) Mig   langar að fara til   Íslands.
      me.ACC longs to to go to(LOC) Iceland
      'I long to go to Iceland.'

(83) Honum mæltist vel í kirkjunni.
      He.DAT spoke   well in the church
      'He spoke well in church.'

(84) Verkjanna   gætir   ekki.
      the-pains.GEN is noticeable not
      'The pains are not noticeable'

These contrast with the default subject case, namely, nominative, that must appear in examples like (85):

(85) Drengurinn   kyssti stúlkuna   í bílnum
      the-boy.NOM kissed the-girl.ACC in the-car.DAT
      'The boy kissed the girl in the car.'

Icelandic word order exhibits more flexibility than English, however. Subjects are always case-marked in the way illustrated in (85), but they may sometimes be separated from their assigning verb by adverbs or other types of phrases, as in the following example from Maling 1980:

(86) Thegar mer   allt i einu datt i hug að ...
      when   me.DAT all at once fell in mind that ...
      'when it suddenly occurred to me that . . .'

Facts such as these call into question the idea that case assignment is based on the notion of adjacency. At the very least, these data require appeal to otherwise unmotivated representations where the relevant notion of adjacency is assumed to hold prior to scrambling operations that are classified as part of the mapping from S-structure to phonetic forms.[30]

A second argument of this same form can be based on languages where verbs assign case to more than one nonsubject dependent. We mention only in passing double object constructions in English, which are potentially counterexamples of this type (as recognized by Chomsky (1981: 94)). Such examples abound, however, in other Indo-European languages. In Sanskrit, for example, there is a class of verbs that allow accusative-marked objects and ablative-marked dependents as well as a subject. But among this class of verbs, there are some that also allow two accusative-marked objects (with the same interpretation). Examples of this kind must surely be treated in terms of case assignment, yet only one of the two accusative-marked objects can reasonably be analyzed as adjacent to the verb, even granting the questionable assumption of fixed-order S-structures for Sanskrit. Such widely known and well-documented examples from diverse languages can be multiplied at will.

A third objection to analyses that appeal to the Case Filter and case marking under adjacency is raised by the fact that there are numerous environments where NPs occur without any adjacent lexical item to function as their case assigner. Without appeal to ancillary principles, the Case Filter predicts that all of the following well-formed NPs should be ungrammatical:

(87)   *a.* NP fragments:
         Who left?—*Pat.*
         Ouch. *My leg*!
         Ms. Gilbert! *Your briefcase.*
      b. Vocatives:
         Professor Harris!
         Dana!
      c. Nonfinite main clause constructions:
         Me worry?
         George Bush in the White House?
      d. Imperatives:
         You get yourself a new whipping boy!
         Nobody move!
      e. Absolutives:
         His army in retreat, the general had no choice but to surrender.
         Her castle a ruin, she was forced to take refuge at the Hilton.

30. Note in addition that the very existence of quirky case subjects in Icelandic causes otherwise unmotivated complications in the formulation of GB's case theory, which includes the claim that nominative case in finite clauses is assigned by INFL, rather than by the verb.

  f. Possessors in NPs:
  Kim's books
  Sandy's resignation
  g. ACC-ing nominals:
  I resent [*Pat* getting the job].
  [*Pat* getting the job] was outrageous.
  h. Coordinate nominals:
  [*Sandy*, *Kim*, and *Dana*] get along with each other just fine.
  We compared [*Bo*, *Terry*, and *Gerry*] with each other.

In none of these environments is there a tense element or an adjacent lexical governor to assign case.

Chomsky (1981) recognizes one of these problems ((87f)) and suggests that genitive case is assigned by a special rule that is not contingent on government by a lexical head (see Stowell (1983: 293) for a more precise formulation). And, as noted earlier, a similar assumption must be made for the *accusative* case assignment in (87g). But following this approach, six further ad hoc case assignment rules will be necessary to account for the data in (87), which most certainly do not exhaust the domain of counterexamples to the Case Filter.[31] In our view, facts such as these suggest that the generalization embodied in the Case Filter is incorrect. There is no requirement that NPs be assigned case by an adjacent, governing lexical head.

Note finally that even if various devices were introduced to assign case in (87a–h), it is still left unexplained why clefts and pseudoclefts do not also allow this device to assign case in the examples in (78). The potential for explanation in terms of case theory seems very low indeed. In fact, the potential for explanation seems nonexistent, for true Stowell structures, for example, those that occur as the complement of verbs like *fear*, can appear in focus position of both pseudoclefts and *it*-clefts, as noted earlier ((89) = (30) above):

(88)   *a.* We feared [Noriega in power].
       b. What we feared most was [Noriega in power].
       c. [Noriega in power] was what we feared most.
       d. It was [Noriega in power] that we feared most.

(89)   *a.* What we feared most was [Leslie in complete control of the situation].
       b. It was [Leslie in complete control of the situation] that we feared most.

---

31. Further arguments against the view that case must be assigned under adjacency are provided by Postal and Pullum (1988: 644). For additional critical discussion of GB's case theory, see Hudson (1992).

And the examples in (89) provide crucial minimal contrasts with those in (90) (= (29) above), which are systematically ill-formed:

(90)   *a.* * What we considered was [Leslie in complete control of the situation].

         b. * It was [Leslie in complete control of the situation] that we considered.

Thus it cannot even be stipulated that cleft constructions fail to assign case, for examples like (89a, b), which involve true Stowell structures (PPs with subject, let us assume), are completely well-formed. Under standard GB assumptions, there is nothing in the syntactic context of (89) and (90) that can be appealed to in order to explain why case assignment is possible in the former case, but not in the latter.

In our view, the best explanation for the contrast between these clefts and the impossibility of similar examples involving verbs of considering has nothing to do with case assignment. The contrasts follow directly from the hypothesis, motivated in the previous section, that verbs of considering take SOR (NP+XP) complement sequences, rather than small clauses or Stowell structures. This proposal has the further pleasant consequences that (1) the constraints on complementizerless clauses (both finite and infinitival) are given a unified account (as they are not, under the Case Filter analysis) in terms of the specification [MARKING *comp*]; (2) no appeal whatsoever is made to the Case Filter, which, as we have seen, makes numerous incorrect predictions (or else, if arbitrary case assignment rules are permitted, makes no empirical predictions whatsoever); and (3), in virtue of (2), the Case Filter can be eliminated entirely from the theory of grammar, allowing the theory of case to be formulated in terms of lexically specified syntactic argument structure (SUBCAT lists). This in turn has the consequence that subjects may be assigned case lexically (which, as we have seen, is the simplest analysis available for Icelandic (and many other languages)) and that interclausal case assignment is ruled out in principle—a highly desirable strengthening of the theory of grammar.

3.5 Equi and Raising

We now turn to the lexical treatment of controlled complements. As we have seen, unsaturated complements are of diverse syntactic types. However, verbs must be classified not only with respect to the syntactic category of the unsaturated complement they take, but also with respect to the standard distinction between *equi* and *raising* verbs, as illustrated in (91):[32]

32. The terms 'equi' and 'raising' derive from the names of the rules posited for the analysis of the two constructions within one highly influential version of transformational grammar (see, e.g., Soames and Perlmutter 1979). The transformation of 'Sub-

(91)   Equi verbs and adjectives:

VP[*inf*] complements	try, hope, eager, persuade, promise [try *to leave*, persuade Sandy *to leave*]
VP[*ger*] complements	consider, try [considered *dropping the course*]
AP[+PRD] complements	feel, look [felt *sick*]
NP[+PRD] complements	make [made the boys *good little housekeepers*]
PP[+PRD] complements	got, count [got *under the table*, count Kim *among our friends*]

(92)   Raising verbs and adjectives:

VP[*inf*] complements	appear, seem, likely, believe, expect [seem *to be happy*, expect Sandy *to leave*]
VP[*prp*] complements	begin, keep, be [kept *sleeping late*]
AP[+PRD] complements	become, seem, be [became *sick*]
NP[+PRD] complements	become, be [were *good little housekeepers*]
PP[+PRD] complements marked by *as*	regard, strike [strikes them *as a disaster*]
PP[+PRD] complements	be, seem [be *in trouble*]

The reasons for drawing a careful distinction between these two classes of complement-taking expressions are well-established in the literature. First, equi verbs (and adjectives) systematically assign one more semantic role than their raising counterparts. This is illustrated by the difference in CONTENT for the superficially similar examples in (93) and (94):[33]

---

ject-to-Subject Raising' mapped deep structures like *[[for Kim to be happy] seems]* onto structures like *[Kim [seems to be happy]]* by 'raising' the embedded subject into subject position of the embedding clause. Similarly, the transformation of 'equi NP deletion' created structures like *[Sandy wants [to go]]* from deep structures like *[Sandy wants [Sandy to go]]* by deleting the subject of the embedded clause. Variants of these analyses have been proposed under a variety of names, but the terminology adopted here has become a kind of lingua franca for discussions of these and related phenomena.

33. Here and throughout, we assume that the semantic content of a VP complement, like that of an S, is a psoa; we defend this assumption in section 1 of Chapter 7. We also make various simplifying assumptions here about the nature of the roles that are appropriate for the semantic analysis of control verbs. A more precise proposal, which countenances generalized semantic roles that are appropriate for larger classes of relations, is presented in Chapter 7.

(93)   a. They try to run.

b.

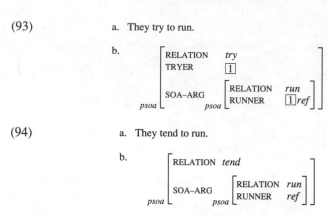

(94)   a. They tend to run.

b.

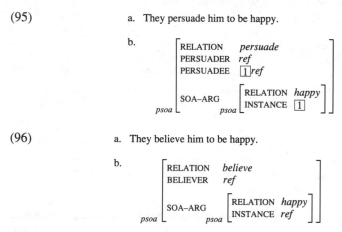

In short, the referential index associated with the subject of an equi verb (like *try*) is assigned a role in the psoa that is the verb's content, but in addition that index is structure-shared with that of the unexpressed subject of the VP complement inside the embedded psoa argument (in this case the psoa corresponding to the circumstance that the tryer is trying to bring about). The subjects of superficially similar subject raising verbs (like *tend*) are assigned no role in the matrix psoa.

Exactly the same contrast obtains between the objects of object equi verbs like *persuade* and those of object raising verbs like *believe*:

(95)   a. They persuade him to be happy.

b.

(96)   a. They believe him to be happy.

b.

This is in fact the essence of the equi/raising distinction: all subcategorized dependents of equi verbs are assigned a semantic role; raising verbs always fail to assign a semantic role to one of the dependents that they subcategorize for.[34]

34. Correlated with this difference in semantic argument structure is a second difference between equi and raising expressions. Role assignment in the 'upstairs' psoa gives

The lexical signs for the subject equi verb *try* and the subject raising verb *tend* thus differ in the way illustrated in (97) and (98) (here and throughout we illustrate LOCAL values only):[35]

(97)

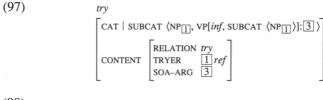

$$try$$

$$\left[\begin{array}{l} \text{CAT} \mid \text{SUBCAT } \langle \text{NP}_{\boxed{1}}, \text{VP}[inf, \text{SUBCAT } \langle \text{NP}_{\boxed{1}}\rangle]:\boxed{3} \rangle \\[1em] \text{CONTENT} \begin{bmatrix} \text{RELATION } try \\ \text{TRYER} \quad \boxed{1}\,ref \\ \text{SOA–ARG} \quad \boxed{3} \end{bmatrix} \end{array}\right]$$

(98)

$$tend$$

$$\left[\begin{array}{l} \text{CAT} \mid \text{SUBCAT } \langle \boxed{2}, \text{VP}[inf, \text{SUBCAT } \langle\boxed{2}\rangle]:\boxed{1} \rangle \\[1em] \text{CONTENT} \begin{bmatrix} \text{RELATION } tend \\ \text{SOA–ARG} \quad \boxed{1} \end{bmatrix} \end{array}\right]$$

And the differences between the object equi verb *persuade* and the object raising verb *believe* are illustrated in (99)–(100):

(99)

$$persuade$$

$$\left[\begin{array}{l} \text{CAT} \mid \text{SUBCAT } \langle \text{NP}_{\boxed{1}}, \text{NP}_{\boxed{2}}, \text{VP}[inf, \text{SUBCAT } \langle \text{NP}_{\boxed{2}}\rangle]:\boxed{4} \rangle \\[1em] \text{CONTENT} \begin{bmatrix} \text{RELATION} \quad persuade \\ \text{PERSUADER} \quad \boxed{1}\,ref \\ \text{PERSUADEE} \quad \boxed{2}\,ref \\ \text{SOA–ARG} \quad \boxed{4} \end{bmatrix} \end{array}\right]$$

---

rise to existential entailments in equi sentences. Thus (ii) is entailed by (i) (an equi sentence), but (iv) is not entailed by the raising sentence (iii):

(i)   Kim persuaded a unicorn to approach.

(ii)   There was a unicorn.

(iii)   Kim believed a unicorn to be approaching.

(iv)   There was a unicorn.

Although this difference in entailment possibilities is often regarded as critical for the semantic analysis of these verbs, it is difficult to know how much significance to attach to the difference in light of the fact that role assignment does not always give rise to existential entailments, as in the well-known examples in (v) and (vi):

(v)   They are looking for a unicorn.

(vi)   A page is missing from this book.

35. Recall from Chapter 1 that we use NP$_{\boxed{1}}$ to abbreviate an NP whose index is $\boxed{1}$.

(100)

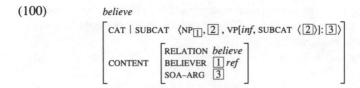

Apart from differing role assignments, there are two other important differences between the equi verbs in (97) and (99) on the one hand, and the raising verbs in (98) and (100) on the other. First, in the signs for equi verbs, the VP complement's unexpressed subject (its SUBCAT member) is coindexed with one of the other syntactic dependents (the subject in (97), the object in (99)). But in the case of raising verbs, the entire SYNSEM value of the subject of the VP complement is structure-shared with (that of) another subcategorized for dependent (the subject in (98), the object in (100)). It follows from this that the SYNSEM value of the raising controller, i.e. the NP standardly considered to have been raised, need not be specified, since that information will be provided by the unexpressed subject of the complement.[36] In addition, the index of the role-assigned subject in (97) is of sort *ref* (i.e. it is not a dummy), whereas no such restriction appears on the subject of *tend* in the lexical sign (98). We will discuss each of these differences in turn.

Note first that from the fact that equi controllers are assigned semantic roles, it follows that examples like (101a, b) and (102a, b) will be associated with distinct CONTENT values:

(101)   *a.* The doctor tried to examine Sandy.
         b. Sandy tried to be examined by the doctor.

(102)   *a.* Kim persuaded the doctor to examine Sandy.
         b. Kim persuaded Sandy to be examined by the doctor.

In (101a), the doctor is assigned the role of TRYER; in (101b), this role is assigned to Sandy. And in (102a), the doctor functions as PERSUADEE, while in (102b), it is Sandy who is assigned to this role. Analogous examples with raising verbs, however, are assigned the same CONTENT:

(103)   *a.* Kim believed the doctor to have examined Sandy.
         b. Kim believed Sandy to have been examined by the doctor.

This is so because the index of the raising controller in both (103a) and (103b) is assigned no semantic role in the belief situation. Hence, under the assumption that passivization affects CONTENT only insofar as it realigns sub-

---

36. We follow standard usage in referring to the elements so linked to the unexpressed subjects of unsaturated complements as *controllers*.

categorized dependents with semantic roles,[37] (103a, b) have the same CON-
TENT value—a psoa whose RELATION is *believe* and whose SOA-ARG
argument has the doctor associated with the EXAMINER role and Sandy associated with the EXAMINEE role. Thus the differing role assignments posited in
our account of the equi/raising distinction immediately predict key differences
in paraphrase relations between the two classes of verbs.

Another important difference between equi and raising expressions is that
only the latter allow expletive *there* as a complement—as a subject in the case
of subject raising verbs, as an object in the case of object raising verbs. This is
illustrated in (104) and (105):

(104) *a.* There tends to be disorder after a revolution.
       b. There seems to be some misunderstanding about these issues.
       c. There kept being problems with the analysis.
       d. Kim believed there to be some misunderstanding about these
             issues.

(105) *a.* *There tries to be disorder after a revolution.
       b. *There hopes to be some misunderstanding about these issues.
       c. *There resented being problems with the analysis.
       d. *Kim persuaded there to be some misunderstanding about these
             issues.

And the expletive pronoun *it* exhibits virtually identical behavior:

(106) *a.* It tends to be warm in September.
       b. It seems to bother Kim that they resigned.
       c. It kept bothering Kim that they resigned.
       d. Lee believes it to bother Kim that Sandy snores.

(107) *a.* *It tries to be warm in September.
       b. *It hopes to bother Kim that they resigned.
       c. *It resented bothering Kim that they resigned.
       d. *Lee persuaded it to bother Kim that Sandy snores.

These familiar yet theoretically critical contrasts follow directly from our
theory of indices and role arguments, as sketched in Chapter 1. Indices, it will
be recalled, are classified into sorts as shown in (108):

---

37. Since lexical rules define relations among lexical signs, and since both CONTENT
and CONTEXT are part of all lexical signs, it would be a simple matter to formulate the
passive lexical rule in such a way that it manipulated semantic or discourse information.
In the absence of a clear understanding of the difference in meaning between active
and passive forms, however, we make the simplifying assumption here that, modulo
quantifier scope preferences, active sentences and their corresponding passives are
synonymous.

(108)

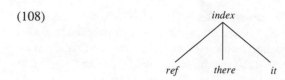

ref   there   it

And, as also explained in Chapter 1, the only indices that may bear semantic roles are those of the *ref* sort. Hence, from the fact that equi controllers are assigned semantic roles, it follows immediately, on essentially semantic grounds, that the indices of equi controllers are referential (i.e. belong to the sort *ref*), and hence can never be realized as expletives, the only nominals whose indices are not of this sort. Since the referentiality of equi controllers is completely predictable in this way, the *ref* specifications in the lexical entries given above need not be lexically stipulated.

Raising controllers, on the other hand, are not constrained in this way, as they are assigned no semantic role in the CONTENT of the raising verb. As we will see, it is a consequence of our analysis that raising controllers are expletives just in case the unsaturated complement of the raising verb subcategorizes for an expletive subject and that they will have referential indices (i.e. will be realized as nonexpletives) just in case they are assigned a semantic role within the unsaturated complement.[38]

There remains one final difference between the lexical signs of raising and equi verbs. As noted above (see (98) and (100)), the SUBCAT list of a raising verb identifies the SYNSEM value of the raising controller with that of the unexpressed subject of the unsaturated complement. In the case of equi verbs, however (see (97) and (99)), only the equi controller's index is identified with that of the unexpressed subject. The analysis of equi in terms of coindexing is well-established, but the issue of how much information is shared between the raising controller and the unsaturated complement's unexpressed subject is more subtle.

In Icelandic, the effects of shared syntactic information in raising constructions are quite robust, as the verbs that assign 'quirky' case to their subject cause these nondefault case values to be inherited by raising controllers, as in examples like the following:

(109)   Hana   virðist vanta   peninga.
         her.ACC   seems to lack   money
         'She seems to lack money.'

---

38. It is generally assumed within GB that semantic incompatibility guarantees that expletives do not occur in θ-positions, but no explicit account of this incompatibility, to our knowledge, has ever been given.

(110)   Barninu   virðist hafa   batnað   veikin.
         the-child.DAT seems   to have recovered from the disease
         'The child seems to have recovered from the disease.'

(111)   Verkjanna   virðist ekki gæta.
         the-pains.GEN seem   not to be noticeable
         'The pains don't seem to be noticeable.'

(112)   Hann   telur   mig   vanta   peninga.
         he.NOM believes me.ACC to lack money
         'He believes that I lack money.'

(113)   Hann telur   barninu   hafa   batnað   vcikin.
         he   believes the-child.DAT to have recovered from the disease
         'He believes the child to have recovered from the disease.'

(114)   Hann telur   verkjanna   ekki gæta.
         he   believes the-pains.GEN not to be noticeable
         'He believes the pains to be not noticeable.'

There is ample evidence that the relevant quirky-case NPs in these examples
are subjects in (109) – (111) and primary objects in (112) – (114), as discussed
at length by Andrews (1982), *Thráinsson* (1979), and Zaenen et al. (1985).
These examples thus show, minimally, that raising controllers in Icelandic
share CASE values with the unexpressed subjects of unsaturated complements.[39]

In English, there is somewhat sparser evidence for the sharing of syntactic
information in raising constructions. One suggestive piece of evidence, however, is the well-known fact that in English PP objects may be equi controllers,
but not raising controllers. That is, there are object equi verbs like *appeal*,
whose infinitive complement's subject is interpreted on the basis of the object
of the prepositional phrase, as in (115):

(115)   Kim appealed to Sandy to cooperate.

But there are no analogous object raising verbs, that is, no verbs whose PP
complement is not assigned a semantic role. We find no verbs otherwise like
the raising verb *believe* that take PP complements whose prepositional object
is a raising controller. Thus there are no verbs in English like the hypothetical
kekieve in the following examples:

(116)   *a.* Kim kekieved to there to be some misunderstanding about these
             issues.
         b. Lee kekieved from it to bother Kim that they resigned.

---

39. For a more complete analysis along these lines of quirky-case propagation in
Icelandic raising constructions, see Sag et al. 1992.

Under our assumption that raising controllers share SYNSEM values with the unexpressed subjects of unsaturated complements, these facts follow immediately, for verbs in general require nominal, not prepositional, subjects.[40]

The structure sharing illustrated above for raising verbs need not be stipulated for individual lexical items—a single generalization may be observed, namely, that unassigned arguments must be raising controllers. This generalization is expressed more precisely as the principle in (117):[41]

(117)   RAISING PRINCIPLE:

Let E be a lexical entry whose SUBCAT list L contains an element X not specified as expletive.

Then X is lexically assigned no semantic role in the content of E if and only if L also contains a (nonsubject) Y[SUBCAT $\langle X \rangle$].

The Raising Principle, which should be interpreted as a constraint on lexical entries, ensures that the relevant *synsem* objects in the lexical entries for *tend* and *believe* (as opposed to *try* and *persuade*) are exactly as illustrated earlier. It also predicts that unassigned arguments (other than lexically selected expletives) can appear on SUBCAT lists only when an unsaturated phrase is also present.

This last property of the Raising Principle is of particular importance, for it provides an immediate account of a number of observations that Jacobson (1990) uses to motivate a categorial grammar analysis of raising in terms of function composition. In particular, Jacobson (1990: 438ff.) observes that the complement omission phenomenon known as null complement anaphora (Hankamer and Sag 1976; Grimshaw 1977, 1979) applies to the complements of many equi expressions, but never applies to raising complements:[42]

40. Of course such facts might also follow under the assumption that the information shared in raising constructions is some subset of the SYNSEM information. That is, we have not fully motivated the particular choice of SYNSEM objects cross-linguistically in our analysis (though see the discussion of the Subject Condition in section 5 of Chapter 4). Note further that our theory does not prevent the possibility of SYNSEM sharing in equi constructions. Thus it is not surprising to learn, as Andrews (1982) reports, that some Icelandic speakers allow (optionally) case agreement in equi constructions.

41. If the Raising Principle is taken as universal, then it rules out analyses like those of Joseph (1979) and McCloskey (1984), where rules of raising to prepositional object are posited for Greek and Irish, respectively. Within the framework of the revised theory in Chapter 9, it is possible to reformulate this principle to eliminate the 'nonsubject' stipulation present in (117).

42. Possible counterexamples to this generalization, e.g. (i)—acceptable to a certain number of speakers—are discussed by Jacobson (1990: 444):

(i)   Sandy is likely to succeed, but I don't think Pat is particularly likely.

(118)   *a.* Pat took out the garbage yesterday and Dana tried/forgot/remem-
        bered/refused.
        b. Sandy is eager/willing to go to the movies and I think Chris is
        also eager/willing.

(119)

They $\left\{\begin{array}{c} \text{persuaded} \\ \text{convinced} \\ \text{asked} \\ \text{told} \\ \text{ordered} \end{array}\right\}$ Jan to leave,

but I don't think they've $\left\{\begin{array}{c} \text{persuaded} \\ \text{convinced} \\ \text{asked} \\ \text{told} \\ \text{ordered} \end{array}\right\}$ Gerry yet.

(120)

*Bo $\left\{\begin{array}{c} \text{seems} \\ \text{happens} \\ \text{turns out} \\ \text{appears} \\ \text{tends} \end{array}\right\}$ to be obnoxious,

but I don't think that Gerry $\left\{\begin{array}{c} \text{seems} \\ \text{happens} \\ \text{turns out} \\ \text{appears} \\ \text{tends} \end{array}\right\}$.

(121)

*They $\left\{\begin{array}{c} \text{expected} \\ \text{believed} \\ \text{imagined} \\ \text{reported} \\ \text{considered} \end{array}\right\}$ Taylor to be obnoxious,

but I don't think they $\left\{\begin{array}{c} \text{expected} \\ \text{believed} \\ \text{imagined} \\ \text{reported} \\ \text{considered} \end{array}\right\}$ Jean.

Under the assumption that null complement anaphora is a lexical process that removes an infinitival complement (inter alia) from the SUBCAT list of verbs or adjectives, the systematic inability of raising complements to undergo that process is an immediate consequence of the Raising Principle: removing the unsaturated complement from a raising verb's SUBCAT list would leave a semantically unassigned SUBCAT element that was not raised.

Jacobson also observes that, whereas equi verbs often allow NPs (or PPs) instead of their VP complements, this is never true for raising verbs:

(122)

Leslie $\left\{\begin{array}{c} \text{tried} \\ \text{attempted} \\ \text{wants} \end{array}\right\}$ $\left\{\begin{array}{c} \text{to win} \\ \text{something} \\ \text{it} \end{array}\right\}$.

(123)

$$\text{*Whitney} \left\{ \begin{array}{l} \text{seems} \\ \text{appears} \\ \text{turns out} \\ \text{happens} \\ \text{tends} \end{array} \right\} \left\{ \begin{array}{c} \text{something} \\ \text{it} \end{array} \right\}.$$

These contrasts too follow directly from the Raising Principle. Since the raising verbs in (123) assign no semantic role to their subject argument, there must be an unsaturated complement on the same SUBCAT list. But NPs like *something* or *it* are saturated, and hence the SUBCAT list required for examples like those in (123) is systematically excluded.[43]

In sum, the Raising Principle is the closest analog to function composition within our framework, and it is capable of explaining the data adduced by Jacobson in favor of the function composition analysis of raising.[44] In fact, the claims made by our analysis are somewhat stronger than Jacobson's. Her analysis treats raising in terms of lexically specified function composition with an S argument, rather than the familiar analysis involving combination with a VP (S/NP) complement via function application. But her system also recognizes 'lexical inheritors,' for example, expressions of category $(S/\alpha)/(A/\alpha)$, that assign no role to their subject, but that combine via function application, rather than function composition. Hence nothing in Jacobson's analysis excludes a verb of this latter kind from undergoing null complement anaphora. Similarly, nothing in her analysis excludes a verb like the raising verbs in (123), that is, a verb that assigns no role to its subject and that combines with an NP or a PP complement via function application, rather than function composition.[45] Our own analysis, by contrast, excludes such lexical items on principled grounds.

To complete the picture of the system of infinitival complements in English,

---

43. Note that verb phrase ellipsis does affect raising verbs, as shown in (i), and hence cannot be collapsed with, or treated in the same lexical fashion as, null complement anaphora:

(i)   Sandy will/couldn't ___.

Independent arguments for distinguishing these two phenomena are given by Hankamer and Sag (1976).

44. Jacobson gives a third kind of argument in favor of the function composition analysis. This has to do with the impossibility of extraction of infinitival complements of raising verbs. Although the data here are quite uncertain (as Jacobson notes), it is possible that the contrasts she notes may reduce to the very matter just discussed, i.e. the fact that raising verbs never allow NP complements. To make this point clear, however, would require developing an analysis of topicalized sentences that abandons strong connectivity (i.e. allows an NP gap to be bound by a non-NP filler), an analysis that we suspect may be called for in any case. See Chapter 4, n. 6.

45. Jacobson (1990: 429, n. 10) does note the correlation of feature inheritance and lack of role assignment.

we need only add the lexical sign for the auxiliary element *to*, which is given in (124):

(124)   *to*

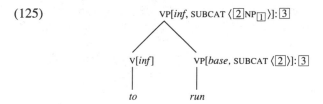

$$\left[\begin{array}{l} \text{CAT} \left[\begin{array}{l} \text{HEAD} \left[\begin{array}{ll} \text{VFORM} & \textit{inf} \\ \text{AUX} & + \end{array}\right] \\ \text{SUBCAT} \ \langle \boxed{2}, \text{VP}[\textit{base}, \text{SUBCAT} \ \langle \boxed{2}\rangle]{:}\boxed{1}\rangle \end{array}\right] \\ \text{CONTENT} \ \boxed{1} \end{array}\right]$$

Note that *to*, like other auxiliaries in English, is in fact a raising verb; that is, it obeys the Raising Principle in (117).

An infinitival phrase like *to run* is assigned the structure shown in (125):

(125)   VP[*inf*, SUBCAT ⟨$\boxed{2}$NP$_{\boxed{1}}$⟩]: $\boxed{3}$

                  V[*inf*]   VP[*base*, SUBCAT ⟨$\boxed{2}$⟩]: $\boxed{3}$

                    | |
                   to   *run*

And the CONTENT of this phrase, tagged as $\boxed{3}$ in (125), is the psoa shown in (126):

(126) $psoa\left[\begin{array}{ll} \text{RELATION} & \textit{run} \\ \text{RUNNER} & \boxed{1} \end{array}\right]$

This phrase may appear as the complement of a raising verb, such as *tend*, in which case the structure in (127) will have the content shown in (128):

(127)   VP[*fin*, SUBCAT ⟨$\boxed{2}$NP$_{\boxed{1}}$⟩]: $\boxed{4}$

                   V[*fin*]   VP[*inf*, SUBCAT ⟨$\boxed{2}$⟩]

                     | △
                   tends   *to run*

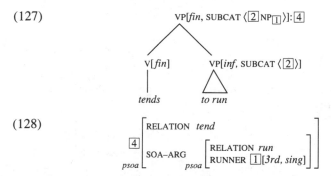

(128) $\boxed{4}\ psoa\left[\begin{array}{l} \text{RELATION} \ \ \textit{tend} \\ \text{SOA–ARG} \ \ psoa\left[\begin{array}{ll} \text{RELATION} & \textit{run} \\ \text{RUNNER} & \boxed{1}[\textit{3rd, sing}] \end{array}\right] \end{array}\right]$

Alternatively, if the infinitival phrase appears as the complement of an equi verb like *try*, the structure will be as in (129), with the CONTENT value as shown in (130):

(129)

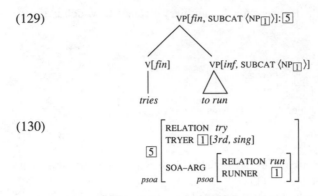

(130)

$$\boxed{5}\begin{bmatrix} \text{RELATION } \textit{try} \\ \text{TRYER } \boxed{1}[\textit{3rd, sing}] \\ \text{SOA–ARG } \begin{bmatrix} \text{RELATION } \textit{run} \\ \text{RUNNER } \boxed{1} \end{bmatrix}_{psoa} \end{bmatrix}_{psoa}$$

The analysis of *believe* versus *persuade* is parallel in all relevant respects.

Note that in the analyses just illustrated the VP complements of both equi and raising verbs are *not* treated as VP[*comp*]. The reason for this in the case of raising verbs is quite clear. In the free environments discussed above, the unexpressed subject of the infinitival VP is always referential. That is, all of the following examples, where the italicized VPs require expletive subjects, are clearly ungrammatical:

(131) *a.* *To rain would be ridiculous.
       b. *To be obvious that Sandy was a spy would be unfortunate.
       c. *To be nothing they could do about it would be unfortunate.

(132) *a.* *What they preferred was *to rain.*
       b. *What they preferred was *to be obvious that Sandy was a spy.*
       c. *What they were afraid of was *to be nothing they could do about it.*

(133) *a.* *It was *to rain* that they were afraid of.
       b. *It was *to be no easy solution to the problem* that they were afraid of.

The grammar of free environments then must minimally guarantee that the index of the unexpressed subject of VP[*comp*] is of the sort *ref.* This is easily accomplished by formulating the lexical entry of the phonetically null complementizer in the following way:

(134)

$$\begin{bmatrix} \text{PHONOLOGY } \langle \quad \rangle \\ \text{SYNSEM|LOCAL|CAT} \begin{bmatrix} \text{HEAD } \quad \textit{marker}[\text{SPEC } [\textit{inf}, \text{SUBCAT } \langle \text{NP}_{ref} \rangle]] \\ \text{MARKING } \textit{for} \end{bmatrix} \end{bmatrix}$$

But since a raising controller will be structure-shared with the unexpressed subject of the unsaturated complement, and since raising controllers, as we have seen, may sometimes be expletives, it follows that the unsaturated complements of raising verbs cannot be VP[*comp*].

The matter is less clear in the case of equi verbs, however, since the equi controller's index and that of the unexpressed subject are always of the *ref* sort, as we have seen. Many equi expressions allow both *for-to* clauses and infinitival VP complements (as noted by Koster and May). Hence it may be preferable to formulate their lexical entries in terms of the natural class [*inf, comp*]. On the other hand, the number of equi verbs that allow only VP complements is quite large, and for these there would be no motivation for positing VP[*comp*] complements. We will not resolve these issues here, turning instead to a more detailed examination of how the analysis of raising and equi constructions just sketched interacts with other aspects of the grammar of the expletive pronouns *it* and *there*.

3.6 Expletive Pronoun Constructions

The expletive pronouns *it* and *there* have an extremely restricted distribution, which follows on semantic grounds. Thus whenever a semantic role is assigned to the index of an NP dependent, that index must be of the *ref* sort. Role-assigned dependents can thus never be expletives:[46]

(135)   *a.* *There died.
        b. *We like there very much.
        c. *You sent a book to there.

(136)   *a.* *It died.
        b. *We talked to it.

The expletive pronoun *there* typically occurs as the subject of the copula,[47] when an additional postcopular indefinite NP also occurs, as illustrated in (137):

(137)   *a.* There were five students protesting the decision.
        b. There is a Santa Claus.

And expletive *it* occurs in a number of environments, especially as the subject of 'weather' verbs, temporal expressions, or verbs and adjectives that also combine with 'extraposed' clauses:

46. Of course the homophonous *locative* pronoun *there* may occur in numerous syntactic environments where its spatial interpretation is semantically compatible. And the referential pronoun *it*, homophonous with the other expletive pronoun, may also occur in many syntactic environments such as these.

47. However, see Aissen 1975 and McCawley n.d. for a more thorough investigation of the verbs that admit *there* subjects.

(138)   *a.* It rained last night.
           b. It is five o'clock.
           c. It bothers me that Sandy snores.

However, as shown by Postal and Pullum (1988), there exists a large class of expressions where expletive *it* occurs in primary object and even prepositional object position, as illustrated in (139):

(139)   *a.* I'm going to wing it tonight.
           b. Make it snappy!
           c. You should take it easy.
           d. They were really going at it.
           e. The president seems completely out of it.

And, following a tradition dating back at least to Jespersen (1937: 63), we take it as established (again, see Postal and Pullum 1988) that expletive *it* may also occur as an object in construction with an extraposed clause:

(140)   *a.* I take it that you will pay.
           b. He never gave it a thought that Bolshies are human beings.
           c. I regret it very much that we could not hire Mosconi.
           d. Don't spread it around that I'm giving you this assignment.
           e. You may depend upon it that their paper will expose crooked politicians. (Emonds 1976: 76)

Examples like these constitute part of the evidence presented by Postal and Pullum against the Projection Principle, and hence part of the motivation for allowing verbs to subcategorize for elements that are assigned no semantic role, as noted above.[48]
Our analysis of expletives makes use of the following two lexical signs:[49]

48. Readers who are in doubt about the expletive status of *it* in any of the examples cited here should consult Postal and Pullum 1988, which presents a variety of arguments to this effect, based in part on a set of descriptive diagnostics for expletivehood, namely:

1.   Expletive NPs do not support emphatic reflexives:
     *It is itself illegal for him to smoke.
2.   Expletive NPs do not coordinate:
     *It and there were/was respectively proved to be raining and claimed to be floods in the valley.
3.   Expletive NPs do not appear in nominalization *of*-phrases:
     * my observation/description of it falling/*raining.
4.   Expletive NPs do not appear as *tough* movement subjects:
     *It was tough to prevent from becoming obvious that things were out of control.

49. The analysis sketched here has an obvious intellectual debt to pay to earlier work by Klein and Sag (see Sag and Klein 1982; and Klein and Sag 1985) and to Bresnan (1982).

(141)
$$\begin{bmatrix} \text{PHONOLOGY} & \langle there \rangle \\ \\ \text{SYNSEM} \mid \text{LOCAL} & \begin{bmatrix} \text{CAT} & \begin{bmatrix} \text{HEAD} & noun \\ \text{SUBCAT} & \langle \ \rangle \end{bmatrix} \\ \\ \text{CONTENT} \mid \text{INDEX} & there[3rd] \end{bmatrix} \end{bmatrix}$$

(142)
$$\begin{bmatrix} \text{PHONOLOGY} & \langle it \rangle \\ \\ \text{SYNSEM} \mid \text{LOCAL} & \begin{bmatrix} \text{CAT} & \begin{bmatrix} \text{HEAD} & noun \\ \text{SUBCAT} & \langle \ \rangle \end{bmatrix} \\ \\ \text{CONTENT} \mid \text{INDEX} & it[3rd, sing] \end{bmatrix} \end{bmatrix}$$

Foremost among the expressions that select for *there*-subjects is the copula *be*, which in our analysis is associated with a small set of lexical entries with different SUBCAT lists corresponding to its different privileges of occurrence. One of these, possibly derived by lexical rule, is illustrated in (143):

(143) *be*
$$\begin{bmatrix} \text{CAT} & \begin{bmatrix} \text{HEAD} & verb[+\text{AUX}] \\ \text{SUBCAT} & \langle \text{NP}_{there[\text{NUM} \boxed{4}]}, \boxed{2}\,\text{NP}_{[\text{NUM} \boxed{4}]}, \text{XP}[+\text{PRD, SUBCAT} \langle \boxed{2} \rangle]{:}\boxed{1} \rangle \end{bmatrix} \\ \text{CONTENT} & \boxed{1} \end{bmatrix}$$

Note that this lexical entry takes as its CONTENT the CONTENT of its [+PRD] complement, whose unexpressed subject's SYNSEM value is token-identical with that of the 'object' NP complement of *be* (as guaranteed without stipulation by the Raising Principle). The CONTENT of a *there*-sentence will thus be determined by these two elements, with the subject *there* making no substantive contribution.

The lexical entry in (143) undergoes the lexical rules creating finite verb forms (P&S-87, Chapter 8) in an unremarkable fashion. The third-singular-present form derived from (143), which, like all forms of this class, specifies that its subject's index must be [*3rd, sing*], combines with the last two of its subcategorized complements in accordance with Schema 2. Thus, once lexical operations derive the appropriate lexical entries, no new rules are needed to characterize verb phrases like the one shown in (144):

(144)
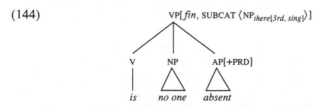

VP[*fin*, SUBCAT ⟨NP*there*[3rd, sing]⟩]

And this VP, whose CONTENT is already 'complete' (roughly corresponding to the state of affairs of 'no one being absent'),[50] can combine with nothing other than an expletive *there* subject, to give the sentence:

(145)   There is no one absent.

The lexical treatment of expletive *there* constructions just sketched posits no ad hoc devices or principles (other than number agreement in *there* construction, which must be treated in a parochial fashion in all accounts we are aware of), but leaves certain matters unresolved, for example, the optionality of the XP[+PRD] complement, which entails only a minor modification of the lexical sign we have given.

We take it as established, however, that no modification should be introduced to take into account the so-called definiteness restriction on the object of *be*, illustrated in (146):

(146)   *a.* *There was every man in the park.
         b. *There is Sandy absent.

Following Milsark (1977), Barwise and Cooper (1981), and Keenan (1987), we assume that some semantic constraint is responsible for whatever deviance inheres in examples such as these, many of which are contextualizable in simple cases:

(147)   *a.* There was every reason to believe him.
         b. There's Sandy. (in response to: *Who is available for this job?*)

Our analysis provides a treatment of the basic facts of agreement in the *there* construction, that is, of the contrasts in (148):

(148)   *a.* There is/*are no one absent.
         b. There are/*is no students absent.

These agreements are predicted because of the lexically specified structure sharing of the NUM value of the *there* subject and that of the postcopular NP (as shown in (143)). It is a general property of all *is*-forms in English that they take subjects whose indices are specified as [PER *3rd*] and [NUM *sing*], and analogously for other finite forms of the copula. Since the value of the *there* subject's NUM is structure-shared with that of the postcopular NP complement, the observed agreement follows. Note that only agreement of number (not of person) is involved here—the index of the *there* subject in (149a) must always

---

50. As in the case of the active-passive relation, the decision to render *there* sentences (e.g. (145)) equivalent to corresponding sentences lacking *there* (e.g. *No one is absent*) is in no way forced by the theory we propose. Should it become possible to characterize precisely whatever subtle interpretational differences distinguish such pairs, the lexical signs we have introduced can be readily modified in an appropriate fashion.

be third-person, whatever the person of the postcopular NP, as the deviance of (149b, c) shows: [51]

(149) *a.* I never heard them at all till there was you $_{sing}$.
       b. *I never heard them at all till there were you $_{sing}$.
       c. *Everyone else has left and now there am only I/me.

The analysis of expletive *it* constructions is quite like the treatment of *there* constructions just sketched. Certain lexical items subcategorize for a subject whose index is of the *it* sort and hence may never combine with referential subjects or expletive *there*. Meteorological expressions, for example *rain* and *snow*, fall in this category, as do temporal expressions like *late* or *five o' clock*. In the latter case, the selection for an expletive subject is transmitted through the copula, which, in its basic lexical entry, is a special class of subject raising verb. Thus once the predicative adjective *late* is lexically specified as allowing an expletive *it* subject, this will be inherited by VPs headed by forms of *be*, hence allowing for sentences like

(150) It is late.

Of particular interest are the verbs and adjectives that combine with an extraposed clause and an expletive *it* subject, as illustrated in (151):

(151) *a.* It bothers Kim that Sandy snores.
       b. It is obvious that Sandy snores.
       c. It seems (to me) that Sandy snores.

The relevant lexical entries for such verbs are as illustrated in (152):

(152)   *bother*

$$
\left[
\begin{array}{l}
\text{CAT} \mid \text{SUBCAT} \quad \langle \text{NP}_{it}, \text{NP}_{\boxed{2}}, \text{S}[comp]{:}\boxed{3} \rangle \\[2ex]
\text{CONTENT} \quad
\left[
\begin{array}{ll}
\text{RELATION} & \textit{bother} \\
\text{BOTHERED} & \boxed{2} \\
\text{SOA–ARG} & \boxed{3}
\end{array}
\right]
\end{array}
\right]
$$

51. This contrast was first pointed out to us by Tom Wasow. As Georgia Green and Dale Russell (personal communications, 1992) point out, examples like (i) should be grammatical according to our analysis:

(i)   . . . until there were you $_{plur}$ (y'all)

Considerations of definiteness aside, we believe this is a correct prediction. We do not explore here the modifications of our analysis necessary to analyze those varieties of English where (ii) or (iii) are acceptable:

(ii)   There's flies in my soup.

(iii)   There is flies in my soup.

Lexical entries like this give rise to finite and other inflected forms in virtue of lexical rules. The third-singular finite form of (152) allows for VPs like (153), again in virtue of Schema 2:

(153)

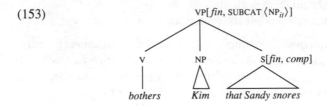

And VPs like these can combine only with an expletive *it* subject, as required. As in the case of *there*-taking VPs, the CONTENT of the S is determined entirely by elements of the VP, the subject expletive being required only by the nature of lexical specifications and general principles of grammatical theory.

Lexical entries like the one just illustrated are related by lexical rule to 'basic' lexical entries like (154):

(154) *bother*

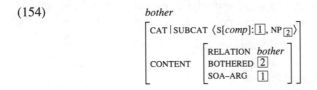

But there are a number of verbs whose basic *it*-taking form must simply be listed, as they have no corresponding entry permitting a sentential subject:

(155) *a.* It seems/appears that Sandy is snoring.
       b. *That Sandy is snoring seems/appears.

Our analysis thus correctly treats a regularity with lexical exceptions as a lexical matter.

The Extraposition Lexical Rule removes an S[*comp*] from a SUBCAT list, replacing it by NP$_{it}$, and appends the S[*comp*] to the end of the SUBCAT list, preserving role assignment. If no further constraints are imposed, a single lexical rule will suffice to account for both subject and object extraposition. That is, in addition to relating lexical entries of the sort just illustrated, extraposition will relate lexical entries with SUBCAT lists like (156a, b) to entries with the corresponding SUBCAT lists (157a, b):

(156) *a.* SUBCAT ⟨NP, S[*comp*], PP[*to*]⟩ (*explain, mention, . . .*)
       b. SUBCAT ⟨NP, S[*comp*]⟩ (*resent, regret, . . .*)

(157)   *a.* SUBCAT $\langle$NP, NP$_{it}$, PP[*to*], S[*comp*]$\rangle$
        b. SUBCAT $\langle$NP, NP$_{it}$, S[*comp*]$\rangle$

Entries like (157b) will, again without positing new rules, give us VP structures like (158), where the expletive object is a syntactic placeholder, and the extraposed clause is assigned a semantic role:

(158)

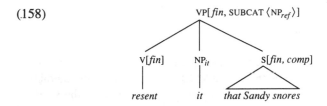

As many have noted, there is a certain variability in judgment about some (but not all) examples of object extraposition, again supporting our decision to treat it lexically.[52]

3.7 Raised Expletives

We are now in a position to illustrate more complex structures involving raised expletives. The examples considered in the previous section all involved finite verbal forms. Nonfinite forms of expletive-subject verbs, however, may appear in embedded structures of various kinds. Base forms of the expletive-subject verbs *be* and *bother*, for example, may head the complement of the infinitive marker *to*:

(159)

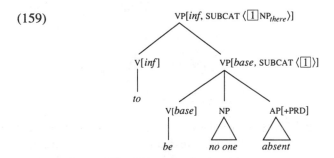

52. Certain seemingly exceptional properties of extraposition, e.g. the impossibility of double extraposition (**It proved [that the earth was flat] [that Columbus was never heard from again]*), are perhaps best treated in terms of general constraints on SUBCAT lists.

(160)

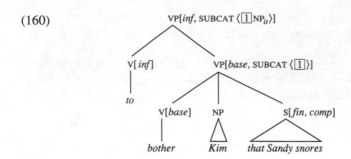

Note that in each of these structures, the expletive-subject requirement of the lower VP has been inherited by the higher VP. This is a result of the interaction of the lexical entry for *to* and the Subcategorization Principle. In the SUBCAT list of *to* (as in the case of all subject raising expressions) the subject SYNSEM value is token-identical to the SYNSEM value of the unexpressed subject of the unsaturated complement. This guarantees that the subject of *to* is *there* in (159) and *it* in (160). The Subcategorization Principle guarantees that the expletive subject of *to* is also the subject of the VP it heads.

The structures in (159) – (160) may appear as complements of raising verbs, as illustrated in (161) – (162):

(161)

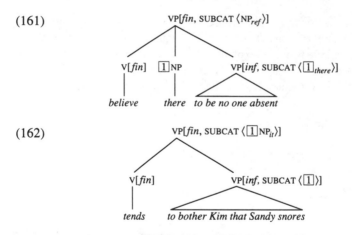

(162)

In each case, because the raising controller on the SUBCAT list of the raising verb shares its SYNSEM value with the unexpressed subject of the unsaturated complement, it is constrained to have an index of the appropriate sort. This has the consequence that the primary object of the object raising verb in (161) must be the expletive *there* and the subject of the subject raising verb in (162) must be the expletive *it*. In the latter case, again in virtue of the Subcategorization Principle, the entire VP inherits the requirement for the appropriate expletive subject. Note that this account, which projects grammatical phrases from lexi-

cal structures using in essence only two universally available schemata and two
principles of grammar, immediately accounts for all of the following examples:

(163) *a.* There [is [likely [to [be a riot in the park]]]].
       b. There [tended [not [to [appear [to [be any solutions to that
            problem]]]]]].
       c. We believe there [to [have [been many solutions to that
            problem]]].

(164) *a.* It [continues [to [appear [to [bother Kim that Sandy snores]]]]].
       b. We believe it [not [to [have [been [obvious that Kim was
            upset]]]]].
       c. Pat believes it [to [have [appeared [to [bother Kim that Sandy
            snores]]]]].

Consider again the lexical entry for an object raising verb like *believe*:

(165)   *believe*

$$\begin{bmatrix} \text{CAT} \mid \text{SUBCAT} \ \langle \text{NP}_{\boxed{1}}, \boxed{2}, \text{VP}[\textit{inf}, \text{SUBCAT} \ \langle \boxed{2} \rangle] : \boxed{3} \rangle \\ \text{CONTENT} \begin{bmatrix} \text{RELATION } \textit{believe} \\ \text{BELIEVER} \quad \boxed{1} \\ \text{SOA–ARG} \quad \boxed{3} \end{bmatrix} \end{bmatrix}$$

Following Pollard 1984 and P&S-87, we treat passivization in terms of a lexical rule that cyclically permutes SUBCAT lists, as illustrated in (166):

(166) *read, devour, . . . :*
       SUBCAT $\langle \text{NP}_1, \text{NP}_2 \rangle \mapsto$ SUBCAT $\langle \text{NP}_2, \text{PP}[by]_1 \rangle$

       give, donate, . . . :
       SUBCAT $\langle \text{NP}_1, \text{NP}_2, \text{PP}[to]_3 \rangle \mapsto$ SUBCAT $\langle \text{NP}_2, \text{PP}[to]_3, \text{PP}[by]_1 \rangle$

       give, hand, . . . :
       SUBCAT $\langle \text{NP}_1, \text{NP}_2, \text{NP}_3 \rangle \mapsto$ SUBCAT $\langle \text{NP}_2, \text{NP}_3, \text{PP}[by]_1, \rangle$

       promise, persuade, . . . :
       SUBCAT $\langle \text{NP}_1, \text{NP}_2, \text{VP}[inf] \rangle \mapsto$ SUBCAT $\langle \text{NP}_2, \text{VP}[inf], \text{PP}[by]_1 \rangle$

The lexical entry in (165) may thus undergo the Passive Lexical Rule, which
will then give rise to the entry in (167):

(167)   *believed*

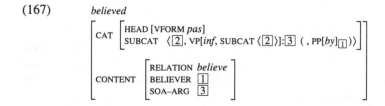

Passives of SOR verbs are in essence subject raising verbs: the SYNSEM value of the subject is token-identical to the SYNSEM value of the unexpressed subject of the unsaturated complement (as guaranteed by the Raising Principle). Hence, our analysis of passive and the treatment of raising interact, and through this interaction, again without introducing any new rules, principles, or constraints, we have an account of structures like (168):

(168)

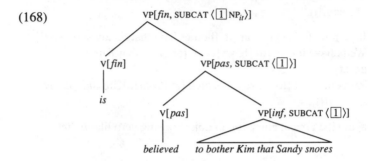

And this account immediately extends to the full range of examples illustrated in (169):

(169) *a.* It [was [believed [to [be [bothering Kim that Sandy snores]]]]].
  b. We expected it [to [have [been [believed [to [be [bothering Kim that Sandy snores]]]]]]].
  c. There [was [believed [to [be [likely [to [be no one absent]]]]]]].
  d. We believed there [to [have [been [believed [to [be a riot in the park]]]]]].

It should be observed that the account of raised expletives we have presented also accounts for 'long-distance' number agreement in *there* constructions. To see this, reconsider the lexical entry for a *there*-subject verb like *be* (repeated here as (170)):

(170) *be*

$$\begin{bmatrix} \text{CAT} & \begin{bmatrix} \text{HEAD } \textit{verb}[\text{+AUX}] \\ \text{SUBCAT } \langle \text{NP}_{\textit{there}[\text{NUM }\boxed{4}]}, \boxed{2}\text{NP}_{[\text{NUM }\boxed{4}]}, \text{XP}[\text{+PRD, SUBCAT }\langle\boxed{2}\rangle]:\boxed{1}\rangle \end{bmatrix} \\ \text{CONTENT } \boxed{1} \end{bmatrix}$$

The NUM value of this verb's subject is token-identical to the NUM value of the second member of its SUBCAT list (corresponding to the postcopular NP). Since raising, on our analysis, involves structure sharing of the entire SYNSEM value of the complement's subject with that of the raising controller, it follows that number agreement with the postcopular NP is propagated over potentially unbounded distances, as illustrated in (171):

(171)

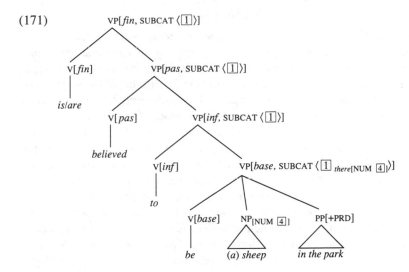

Hence, in complex examples involving subject raising predicates (including passives of SOR verbs), our analysis predicts there will be agreement with the postcopular NP in the most embedded VP, as in (172):[53]

(172)   a. There is/*are believed to be a sheep in the park.
        b. There *is/are believed to be sheep in the park.
        c. There seems/*seem to be no student absent.
        d. There is/*are likely to be no student absent.

Finally, our analysis of raising and equi also correctly guarantees that expletive subject VPs never occur as complements of equi verbs, as the following ungrammatical examples illustrate:

(173)   a. *Sandy tried to be no sheep in the park.
        b. *Pat tried to rain.
        c. *They wanted to bother Kim that Sandy was a spy.

This follows directly from the general principle that all role-assigned indices are referential (of sort *ref*).[54]

---

53. Again, we do not explore the modifications required to analyze those varieties of English where agreement with plurals is optional.

54. We make no attempt here to provide a syntactic treatment of the syntactic flexibility of idiomatic expressions. For some justification of a fundamentally semantic approach to idioms, see Gazdar et al. (1985:236ff.) and Nunberg et al. in preparation.

3.8 Conclusion

In this chapter, we have considered a number of widely held assumptions about the nature of complementation in English, arguing in particular that small clause analyses fail to explain a variety of important facts. We have also presented an analysis of infinitival complements in English based on the premise, which we have justified at length, that such complements are not clausal as standardly assumed. In the analysis we have sketched, the interpretation of the unexpressed subjects of these complements is determined by lexical properties of the verbs and adjectives that co-occur with them. We have summarized the familiar distinction between raising and equi expressions and provided an account of their differing properties. Equi dependencies are treated in terms of coindexing, and nothing more. The dependency in raising constructions, on the other hand, is both syntactic and semantic in nature. This dependency is correctly treated by our Raising Principle, which, as we have shown, also predicts key properties of raising constructions discussed by Jacobson (1990). We have also sketched our treatment of expletive pronoun constructions, presenting a detailed treatment of their behavior in raising constructions.

In Chapter 7, we return to the analysis of unsaturated complements, showing that the dependencies isolated here need not be lexically stipulated, but rather follow from the interaction of principles of syntactic argument structure and semantically based principles of controller assignment whose application is more general than the complements of verbal expressions.

4

Unbounded Dependency Constructions

4.1 Introduction

In this chapter, we discuss in some detail how the theory of HPSG can be brought to bear on the analysis of *unbounded dependency constructions* (UDCs).[1] This term was introduced by Gazdar (1981) to refer to a class of constructions standardly analyzed by transformational grammarians in terms of *wh-movement*, or—to use more recent transformational terminology—movement to the nonargument position SPECIFIER of CP (Chomsky 1986b). For English, the class of unbounded dependency constructions includes such phenomena as *topicalization, wh-questions, relative clauses, it-clefts, pseudoclefts, purpose infinitives*, and *tough 'movement'*, which are illustrated in (1) and (2):

(1)   *a.* Kim$_1$, Sandy loves ___$_1$.   (topicalization)
         b. I wonder [who$_1$ Sandy loves ___$_1$].   (*wh*-question)
         c. This is the politician [who$_1$ Sandy loves ___$_1$]. (*wh*-relative clause)
         d. It's Kim [who$_1$ Sandy loves ___$_1$].   (*it*-cleft)
         e. [What$_1$ Kim loves ___$_1$] is Sandy.   (pseudocleft)

(2)   *a.* I bought it$_1$ for Sandy to eat ___$_1$.   (purpose infinitive)
         b. Sandy$_1$ is hard to love ___$_1$.   (*tough* 'movement')
         c. This is the politician$_1$ [Sandy loves ___$_1$].   (relative clause)
         d. It's Kim$_1$ [Sandy loves ___$_1$].   (*it*-cleft)

Such constructions fall naturally into two classes. In those in (1), there is an overt constituent in a nonargument position—either a topic or an expression containing a *wh*-phrase—that can be thought of as strongly associated with (or *filling*) the gap or trace, indicated by ___. We will refer to the constructions in this class as *filler-gap* constructions, or *strong* UDCs.

In the second class of unbounded dependency constructions, such as those in (2), there is no overt filler in a nonargument position; instead there is a con-

1. We thank Georgia Green and Elisabet Engdahl for detailed comments on earlier drafts of this chapter and for numerous improvements.

stituent in an argument position that is—loosely speaking—interpreted as co-referential with the trace. Constructions of this subclass are the ones that are analyzed by current transformational grammar in terms of an empty operator. The analysis we will propose, however, involves no such empty operators. Rather, it will treat the relation between the argument and the trace as one of coindexing. We will refer to these constructions as *weak* UDCs.

Initially, we will be concerned with topicalization and *tough* movement as representative of the two main subtypes of unbounded dependency, but the analyses we will propose can be extended or adapted in natural ways to deal with UDCs in general. Before turning to specifics of the analyses, however, we must mention two basic points about unbounded dependencies that should be borne in mind. One is that they are indeed *unbounded*, which means that the dependency in question may extend across arbitrarily many clause boundaries; and the other is that, at least in the case of strong UDCs, there is a syntactic-category *matching condition* between the filler and the gap. Both of these points are illustrated by the examples in (3)–(5):

(3)   *a.*   Kim$_1$, Sandy trusts ___$_1$.
        b.   [On Kim]$_1$, Sandy depends ___$_1$.
        c.   *[On Kim]$_1$, Sandy trusts ___$_1$.
        d.   *Kim$_1$, Sandy depends ___$_1$.

(4)   *a.*   Kim$_1$, Chris knows Sandy trusts ___$_1$.
        b.   [On Kim]$_1$, Chris knows Sandy depends ___$_1$.
        c.   *[On Kim]$_1$, Chris knows Sandy trusts ___$_1$.
        d.   *Kim$_1$, Chris knows Sandy depends ___$_1$.

(5)   *a.*   Kim$_1$, Dana believes Chris knows Sandy trusts ___$_1$.
        b.   [On Kim]$_1$, Dana believes Chris knows Sandy depends ___$_1$.
        c.   *[On Kim]$_1$, Dana believes Chris knows Sandy trusts ___$_1$.
        d.   *Kim$_1$, Dana believes Chris knows Sandy depends ___$_1$.

In (3) the trace is an argument of the main clause, in (4) it is an argument of an embedded complement clause, and in (5) it is an argument of a doubly embedded complement clause *within* a complement clause; in principle there is no bound on the depth of embedding.

The other point is illustrated by the contrast between the (a) examples, where the trace is in the object position of *trust*, which requires a noun phrase, and the (b) examples, where the trace is in the object position of *depend*, which requires a prepositional phrase headed by the preposition *on*. In either case, the filler must respect the syntactic category requirements imposed by the local environment of the trace; thus the (c) and (d) examples where it does not are ungrammatical. The point here is simply that in filler-gap constructions (strong UDCs) there is a genuine *syntactic* dependency between the filler and the gap.

4.2 Filler-Gap Constructions

As mentioned in Chapter 1, the NONLOCAL features are analogous to GPSG's foot features. However, there are two important differences that we want to mention here. First, the inventory of features is different. Both GPSG and HPSG employ a SLASH feature for dealing with traces, but unlike GPSG, HPSG does not use a REFL feature for analyzing reflexive pronouns. In fact, in HPSG reflexives are not treated as unbounded dependencies at all, but instead are handled by the binding theory developed in Chapter 6. In addition, instead of a single *wh*-feature, HPSG employs distinct features QUE and REL for interrogatives[2] and relatives. This distinction is motivated, among other things, by familiar distributional differences between interrogative and relative pronouns, for example, with respect to 'pied piping,' as shown in (6):

(6)   *a.*   This is the farmer pictures of whom appeared in *Newsweek*.

        b.   *Pictures of whom appeared in *Newsweek*?

The second difference between HPSG nonlocal features and GPSG foot features is that the data types are different. In GPSG all foot features take the same kind of value, namely a syntactic category. But in HPSG (following a suggestion made originally by Maling and Zaenen (1982)), nonlocal features take *sets* as values. This will allow for the treatment of *multiple* unbounded dependencies, such as those illustrated in (7):[3]

(7)   *a.*   [A violin this well crafted]$_1$, even [the most difficult sonata]$_2$ will
                be easy to play ___$_2$ on ___$_1$.

        b.   This is a problem which$_1$ John$_2$ is difficult to talk to ___$_2$ about
                ___$_1$.

What kind of members those set values have depends on the feature, as shown in (8). This is because in an interrogative dependency, the only information that has to be kept track of is the nominal-object corresponding to the *wh*-phrase,[4] and in a relative dependency, all that is needed is the referential index associated with the relative pronoun.

(8)
$$\begin{bmatrix} \text{QUE} & \text{(set of } npros) \\ \text{REL} & \text{(set of } ref \text{ indices)} \\ \text{SLASH} & \text{(set of } local \text{ structures)} \end{bmatrix}$$

2. We provide no HPSG analysis of interrogatives in the present volume. However, this task has been undertaken by Ginzburg (1992).

3. Implicit in our decision to treat the value of nonlocal features as sets, rather than lists, is a decision to treat Fodor's (1978) nested dependency constraint as a matter of processing, rather than grammar. See n. 9 below.

4. See the HPSG analysis of interrogatives of Ginzburg (1992), whose restricted parameters are for present purposes equivalent to our npros. In an alternative approach, alluded to in P&S-87, the value of QUE was assumed to be an interrogative generalized quantifier.

But in a strong UDC, all the local information—including head features, subcategorization, and content, has to be propagated from the trace position up to the filler. To illustrate this, let us first consider a somewhat simplified example of a filler-gap dependency. We will return to the same example below, filling in a number of details. The example in question is the sentence (9a), and the analysis itself is sketched in (9b):

(9) a. Kim$_1$, we know Sandy claims Dana hates ____$_1$.

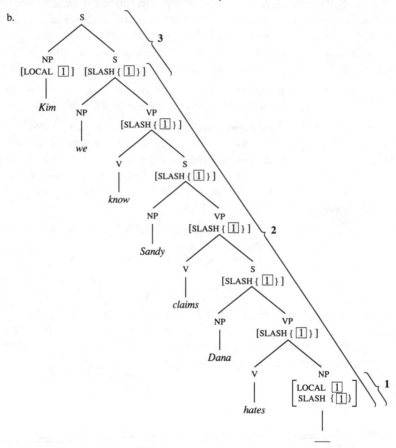

This analysis is similar in spirit to the one proposed by Gazdar (1981), especially as developed by Gazdar et al. (1985), though the technical details are slightly different. The essence of the analysis is that an unbounded dependency has three parts: a bottom, a middle, and a top. These three parts are labelled in (9) as **1, 2,** and **3,** respectively. The bottom of the unbounded dependency construction is where the dependency is introduced; the middle of the dependency is where it is successively passed from daughter to mother up the tree; and the top is where the dependency is discharged or bound off. Let us consider these one by one.

First, the bottom, where the dependency is introduced. We assume that every unbounded dependency is introduced at a terminal node by a special sign that has a nonempty value for the appropriate nonlocal feature. In a relative construction, this sign is a relative word (e.g. *who, which*), containing a nonempty value for the REL feature; and for a *wh*-question, it is an interrogative pronoun with a nonempty value for the QUE feature. In the present case, what we have is a SLASH-type dependency, and the special sign that introduces it is a trace.

But what is a trace? In our theory a trace is just a special lexical item, which is shown in (10a):

(10)   a. Trace as it appears in the lexicon (simplified version):

$$
\begin{bmatrix}
\text{PHONOLOGY } \langle\ \rangle \\
\text{SYNSEM} \begin{bmatrix}
\text{LOCAL } \boxed{1} \\
\text{NONLOCAL} \begin{bmatrix}
\text{SLASH } \{\,\boxed{1}\,\} \\
\text{QUE} \quad \{\ \} \\
\text{REL} \quad \{\ \}
\end{bmatrix}
\end{bmatrix}
\end{bmatrix}
$$

As is clear, a trace is a quite impoverished structure. It has no phonology, of course; it specifies no local features, and as far as nonlocal features go, the only nonempty value is the SLASH value, which is a singleton set. And what is the member of that set? It is just whatever the local features of the trace are. That structure sharing is indicated by the two occurrences of the tag $\boxed{1}$.

Now a trace, as it occurs in the lexicon, appears to be rather useless. But once a trace occurs as a complement of some head, then it will structure-share whatever local features are specified for that complement by the head. And of course whatever those local features are, they will also show up in the SLASH value set of the trace. Thus, the trace in the structure (9b), which is shown in close-up as (10b), has the LOCAL structure imposed by the verb *hates* on its object position, and that same local structure is found in the SLASH value set of the trace:

(10)   b. Trace in (9b) with LOCAL features imposed by *hates*
               on its object position (simplified version):

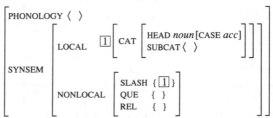

The second part of our unbounded dependency in (9b), labelled **2**, is the middle, where the information that there is an unbound trace is propagated up the tree. The mechanism responsible for this propagation is one of the principles of universal grammar posited in HPSG, called the *Nonlocal Feature Principle*. This is analogous to the *Foot Feature Principle* of GPSG, and a simplified version of it is stated in item (11):

(11)   NONLOCAL FEATURE PRINCIPLE (simplified version):

The value of each nonlocal feature on a phrasal sign is the union of the values on the daughters.

In the case of a structure like (9b), where just one unbounded dependency is introduced, namely the single member of the SLASH value set on the trace, the effect of the Nonlocal Feature Principle is simply that every node in the tree that dominates the trace will also have just that one element in its SLASH value set. Thus the SLASH value is passed from the trace to its mother, then to that node's mother, and so forth up the tree.

Finally, the third part of the unbounded dependency is the top, where the SLASH value introduced by the trace is bound off or discharged, in this case by identification with the local features of the filler, namely the noun phrase *Kim*. Again, as in Gazdar's theory, this is guaranteed by a phrase structure rule, or more properly an *immediate dominance schema*, to the effect that one way to form a phrase is from a finite sentence containing a trace that is unbound within that sentence and a filler whose local features match those of the trace. This rule is expressed informally in rewrite form in (12a), and somewhat more formally as a feature description in (12b). This rule is responsible for licensing the top node in (9b), labelled **3**. All other phrasal nodes in this tree are licensed by the head-complement rules discussed in previous chapters.

(12)   HEAD-FILLER RULE (Schema 6) (preliminary version):

a. X → [LOCAL $\boxed{1}$],   S[*fin*, SLASH { $\boxed{1}$, . . . }]
        FILLER   HEAD

b.
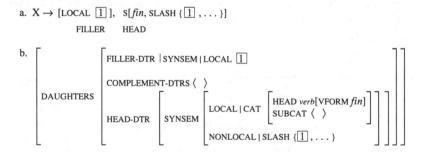

The key point to note about this analysis of strong UDCs is that the local features of the trace position and those of the filler are both identical with the local structure passed up as a SLASH value, and therefore by the transitivity of equality they are identical with each other. In other words, the filler and the trace are the same thing, at least as far as their local structure is concerned. Thus an effect similar to that of *wh*-movement is achieved, without actually moving anything.

This is typical of a more general difference between derivational theories and constraint-based theories. In derivational theories, like GB, the fundamental explanatory mechanisms are transformations, such as move-α, that successively convert one level of structure into another. But, however well the facts may appear to motivate different levels of structure, we are not aware of any evidence that transformations themselves correspond to anything in the empirical domain. In constraint-based theories like HPSG, by contrast, the fundamental explanatory mechanism is conditions of identity or sharing of substructure by different attributes of a common structure.

Before proceeding, we must consider a problem that was glossed over in the simplified analysis of topicalization in (9b). The problem is that in the account we gave of (9), there is nothing in the analysis that prevents the SLASH feature from simply continuing to be passed up the tree, even after it has been identified with the filler, or even from being bound again higher in the tree. Thus, as matters stand, there is nothing in the theory to rule out ungrammatical sentences like the ones in (13):

(13)   *a.* *Bagels$_1$, I know that bagels$_1$, they like ___$_1$.
         b. *Who$_1$ did you wonder who$_1$ Kim saw ___$_1$?
         c. *Kim$_1$ is hard to find the student who$_1$ Sandy met ___$_1$.

What is needed is a mechanism to guarantee that once a trace has been bound, the member of the SLASH value set that corresponds to it will not be passed any further up the tree. What we propose in this connection is to distinguish between unbounded dependencies that are required by the grammar to become bound and those that continue to be inherited upward. More specifically, we replace NONLOCAL structures like that in (8) with structures like the one shown in (14):

(14)   Internal structure of NONLOCAL value:

$$
\begin{bmatrix}
\text{INHERITED} & \begin{bmatrix} \text{QUE} & (\text{set of } npros) \\ \text{REL} & (\text{set of } ref \text{ indices}) \\ \text{SLASH} & (\text{set of } local \text{ structures}) \end{bmatrix} \\
\text{TO-BIND} & \begin{bmatrix} \text{QUE} & (\text{set of } npros) \\ \text{REL} & (\text{set of } ref \text{ indices}) \\ \text{SLASH} & (\text{set of } local \text{ structures}) \end{bmatrix}
\end{bmatrix}
$$

Given this change, the structure of a trace has to be changed correspondingly, from the form given in (10a) to the form shown in (15):

(15)   Trace as it appears in the lexicon (final version):

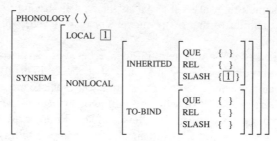

Likewise, the Nonlocal Feature Principle has to be adjusted to guarantee that those nonlocal dependencies that become bound off are subtracted from the set of nonlocal feature values that are passed up to the mother. The way we account for this is by assuming that the binding of a nonlocal dependency is always declared on the head daughter of the structure in question. Thus the Nonlocal Feature Principle has to be changed from the simplified version shown in (11) to the final version given in (16):

(16)   NONLOCAL FEATURE PRINCIPLE (final version):

> For each nonlocal feature, the INHERITED value on the mother is the union of the INHERITED values on the daughters minus the TO-BIND value on the head daughter.

Now one way that a nonlocal dependency can be bound off is for some grammar rule to do it. Our topicalization example (9) is an instance of this. But to make this precise, we must change the rule that licenses head-filler structures from the preliminary version given in (12) to the final version given in (17):[5]

(17)   HEAD-FILLER RULE (Schema 6) (final version):

a. X → [LOCAL $\boxed{1}$], S[*fin*, INHER | SLASH {$\boxed{1}$, . . . }, TO-BIND | SLASH {$\boxed{1}$}]
       FILLER   HEAD

b.

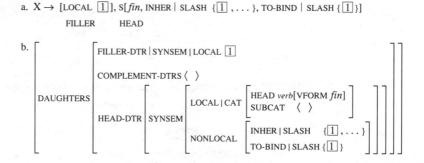

5. In addition, we must modify the other schemata of our theory that introduce phrasal heads so that the specification [TO-BIND|SLASH { }] is added to the head daughter.

With these adjustments in place, the final analysis of our topicalization example is as shown in (18):[6]

(18)   a. Kim$_1$, we know Sandy claims Dana hates ____$_1$.

b.

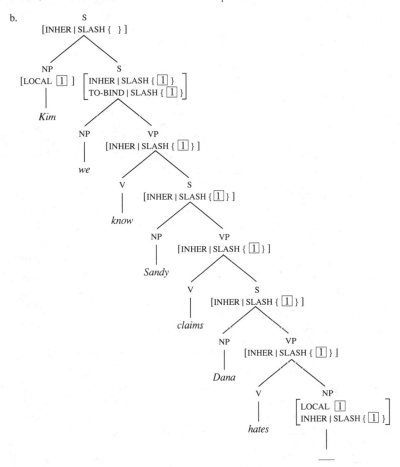

6. In light of the well-known violations of strong connectivity illustrated in (i) and (ii), it may ultimately be necessary to modify the account of topicalized sentences presented in the text:

(i)   * You can rely on that Kim will help you.
(ii)   That Kim will help you, you can rely on.

Such a modification might involve classifying head-filler structures into a variety of subsorts, one of which involves a filler that is merely coindexed with the INHER|SLASH value of the sentential head. In this way, a kind of topicalization would be recognized (e.g. (ii)) that involved only a weak UDC, i.e. where no identity is required between the category of the filler and that of the gap. This analysis would of course have to be

4.3 *Tough* Constructions

Let us now turn to the phenomenon known as *tough* movement. This term refers to examples like the ones in (19), but the analysis we will provide can also be adapted to deal with examples involving verbs like *cost* and *take*, as shown in (20) and (21):

(19)   *a.* Kim₁ would be easy to bribe ___₁.
       b. Kim₁ would be easy to prove Sandy bribed ___₁.

(20)   *a.* [This theorem]₁ will take only five minutes to prove ___₁.
       b. [This theorem]₁ will take only five minutes to establish that Gödel proved ___ᵢ in 1930.

(21)   *a.* [This widget]₁ will cost Kim $500 to fix ___₁.
       b. [This $500 bribe]₁ will cost the government $500,000 to prove that Senator Jones accepted ___₁.

Examples like these all belong to the subclass of unbounded dependency constructions that we referred to as weak UDCs, and they differ from strong UDCs in the key respect that there is no filler corresponding to the trace. Instead there is a constituent in an argument position that is coindexed with—that is, has the same referential index as—the trace. In all the examples in (19)–(21), this constituent is the subject. The fact that this is not a filler-gap dependency is underscored by the fact, illustrated in all of (19)–(21), that the trace and the coindexed subject need not have the same case:[7]

(22)   I₁(*nom*) am easy to please ___₁ (*acc*).

Such constructions have been problematic for transformational grammar because they do not fit comfortably with any of the usual subvarieties of move-α. On the one hand they cannot be *wh*-movement, since the constituent coindexed with the trace is in an argument position; but on the other hand they cannot be NP-movement either, since the trace is in a case-assigned position.

---

executed in such a way that topicalized PPs could not be associated with NP gaps. Alternatively, it may be that the deviance of (i) should be explained simply in terms of a morphophonological constraint that rules out preposition-marker sequences. Such an account is supported by the contrast between (iii) and (iv):

(iii)   You can count on Kim's support and that he will be at the meeting.
(iv)   *You can count on that Kim will be at the meeting and his support.

7. For some discussion of the motivation for distinguishing between strong and weak UDCs (with particular reference to *tough* constructions), see Jacobson (1984, 1987, 1992) and Hukari and Levine (1987b, 1991).

GB theory's solution to this problem (Chomsky 1977) is to propose an empty operator, a phonetically null constituent in a nonargument topic position that binds the trace and is coindexed with the subject, as shown in (23):

(23)   Empty operator analysis:

I$_1$ am easy [$_{\overline{S}}$ O$_1$ [$_S$ PRO to please ___$_1$]]

On our analysis, by contrast, it is just a lexical fact about predicates like *easy*, *take*, and *cost* that they subcategorize for infinitive complements containing an accusative NP gap coindexed with the subject. Thus the heart of our analysis is captured in item (24), which is a partial representation of the SYNSEM value of the lexical entry for the *tough*-class adjective *easy*:[8]

(24)   Partial representation of SYNSEM value for *easy*:

$$
\left[
\begin{array}{l}
\text{LOCAL | CAT}
\left[
\begin{array}{ll}
\text{HEAD} & \textit{adjective} \\
\text{SUBCAT} & \langle \text{NP}_{\boxed{1}}, (\text{PP}[\textit{for}],) \\
 & \text{VP}[\textit{inf}, \text{INHER | SLASH}\, \{\,\boxed{2}\,\text{NP}[\textit{acc}]:ppro\,_{\boxed{1}}, \dots\,\}]\rangle
\end{array}
\right] \\[1.5em]
\text{NONLOCAL | TO-BIND | SLASH}\, \{\,\boxed{2}\,\}
\end{array}
\right]
$$

8. Here NP[*acc*]:*ppro*$_{\boxed{1}}$ abbreviates an accusative NP whose content is of sort *ppro* and whose index is tagged as $\boxed{1}$. We are assuming here that the subject of *easy*-class adjectives is assigned a semantic role and hence that lexical forms like (24) do not constitute a violation of the Raising Principle. To see the potential problem here, consider the fact that identifying the unexpressed subject of the VP complement with the subject of *easy* would produce the wrong interpretation (the unexpressed subject must be associated with the *for* phrase, if the latter is expressed). Yet the Raising Principle requires that any SUBCAT member not assigned a role (other than a lexically specified expletive) be a raising controller.

There is considerable evidence in favor of our claim that the subject of *easy* is role-assigned. First, this immediately explains why examples like (i) are ill-formed, since the expletive *there* bears an index that is nonreferential:

(i)   *There is easy to believe to be a unicorn in the garden.

Second, we also obtain an explanation for the fact that *easy* and the like may undergo null complement anaphora (see section 5 of Chapter 3), as illustrated in (ii):

(ii)   Kim is hard to talk to but Sandy is easy.

Finally, assigning the subject of *easy* a role allows an account of the well-known fact that examples like (iii) and (iv) differ in interpretation:

(iii)   This sonata is easy to play on that violin.
(iv)   That violin is easy to play this sonata on.

Thus sentence (22) is assigned the structure sketched in (25):

(25)

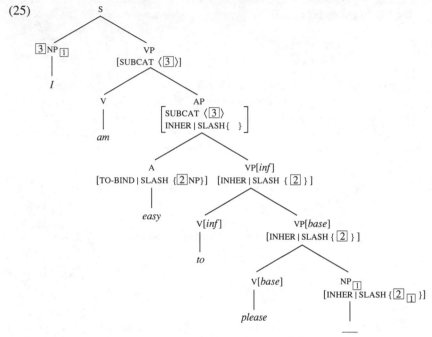

Note that this structure is generated by the usual head-complement rules. The coindexing of the trace with the subject obtains because it is directly specified in the lexical entry for *easy*. And the SLASH value corresponding to the trace is not inherited beyond the infinitive VP because the head daughter of the dominating AP, namely the adjective *easy*, specifies that the inherited SLASH value in the infinitive complement is to be bound.

We should point out here that the idea of having *tough*-class adjectives subcategorize for a complement containing an accusative gap is borrowed from the GPSG analysis of *tough*-movement presented in Gazdar, Klein, Pullum, and Sag 1985 (hereafter, GKPS). And, like that analysis, our account predicts facts like those shown in (26):

(26) *a.* John is easy to please ___.
      b. John is easy to persuade ___ to be reasonable.
      c. John is easy to believe ___ capable of doing something that stupid.
      d. John is easy to persuade Mary to kiss ___.
      e. John is easy to believe Mary would kiss ___.
      f. *John is easy to persuade Mary ___ is capable of doing something that stupid.

g. *John is easy to believe ___ is capable of doing something that stupid.

Here the (f) and (g) examples are ungrammatical because the infinitive complements would have to contain *nominative* gaps.

There are a couple of significant differences between our analysis of weak UDCs and the GKPS analysis, however. First, the GKPS account runs into difficulties explaining why a case conflict does not arise between the subject and the gap in examples like (26) (see Hukari and Levine 1991 for some discussion). Our account avoids this problem because it requires identity only of the referential index, not of any syntactic features.

Second, on our analysis the trace is assumed to be pronominal, in the sense to be explicitly defined in Chapter 6; as explained there, our theory differs from GB in not requiring that a trace be nonpronominal. If the trace were an anaphor, Principle A of our binding theory (also set forth in Chapter 6) would wrongly require it to be coindexed with the subject of *please* in (26)a; and if it were a nonpronoun, coindexation with *John* in (26)a would constitute a violation of our Principle C.

And third, since the GKPS account does not permit set values for foot features, it disallows the possibility of a constituent containing more than one unbound trace. Thus it is unable to account for well-known 'multiple extraction' examples like those in (7), repeated here as (27):[9]

(27)   *a.* [A violin this well crafted]$_1$, even [the most difficult sonata]$_2$ will be easy to play ___$_2$ on ___$_1$.
         b. This is a problem which$_1$ John$_2$ is difficult to talk to ___$_2$ about ___$_1$.

But in HPSG, since nonlocal features have set values, this problem does not arise. For example, the relative clause in (27b) will be assigned a structure like the one sketched in (28):

9. We do not attempt here to deal with nested dependency constraint effects such as the contrast between (27a) and (i):

(i)   *A sonata this simple, even the most crudely crafted violin would be easy to play on.

It is likely that a plausible solution is available in terms of a modification to the theory wherein the value of SLASH is treated as a list rather than a set, and TO-BIND values always coincide with the FIRST of the SLASH list (when this is an NP, at least). In order to develop this analysis, however, a number of technical issues involving parasitic gaps remain to be worked out.

(28)

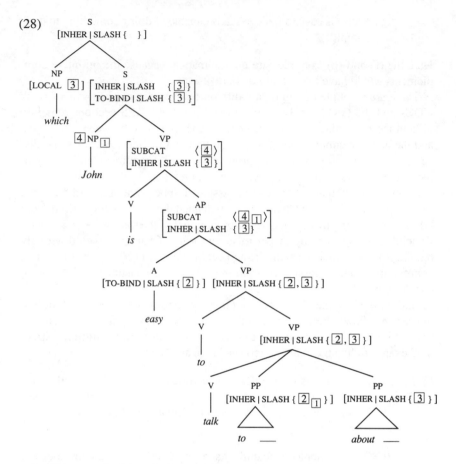

In this example the verb phrase *talk to __ about __* has two unbound traces. One, the object of the preposition *to*, gives rise to the INHER | SLASH element labelled ②; the other, the object of *about*, gives rise to the INHER | SLASH value element ③. The first of these becomes bound as specified on the adjective *easy*, and at the same time is coindexed with the subject of *easy*. Notice that this element is not inherited onto the AP node. The remaining SLASH element, the one labelled ③, is bound at the top of the tree, where it is identified with the local features of the relative pronoun, in accordance with the filler-gap rule that licenses the top node. At the top of the relative clause, the INHER | SLASH value is empty.

As noted by Maling and Zaenen (1982), there are severe constraints on where doubleton INHER | SLASH values can occur in English. On the basis of the ungrammaticality of examples like (29), Maling and Zaenen assume that English obeys a constraint preventing finite clauses from being doubly 'slashed':

(29) *a.* * Violins this well crafted, even the most difficult sonata will be easy to guarantee that Winnie can play ___ on ___.

  b. * Violins made this badly, even the easiest sonata would be hard to make it possible for Winnie to play ___ on ___.

Although some such constraint is doubtless at work, the acceptability for many speakers of examples like (30) suggests that Maling and Zaenen's formulation may not be correct:

(30) Someone that stupid, how much time [$_S$ do we really want to waste ___ arguing with ___]?

Finally, we should point out that the lexically based analysis of the *easy*-class of expressions we have presented is consistent with the observation made by Elisabet Engdahl (personal communication, 1992) that languages vary considerably with respect to which predicates allow gap-containing complements. For a more complete discussion of how HPSG lexicons express the relevant generalizations about these and related expressions, see Flickinger and Nerbonne 1992.

4.4 The Trace Principle

One of the most important issues in modern syntactic theory has been the question of where traces can occur. This question has a long history, dating back to Ross's dissertation (Ross 1967), and since that time a great many so-called *island constraints* have been proposed in the literature. But in recent years, many have attempted to deduce extraction islands from a very small number of universal principles, perhaps involving certain parameters of cross-linguistic variation. For example, in GB theory, the distribution of *wh*-traces is constrained by two principles, the *Empty Category Principle* (or ECP) and *Subjacency* (Chomsky 1981). It would be too much of a digression to discuss these two principles in detail here, but in essence the ECP says that a *wh*-trace has to occur in the right kind of local environment, while Subjacency says that the movement from trace position to the final landing site has to proceed step-by-step, with each step being permissibly small in some appropriate sense. Note that the effect of Subjacency is closely paralleled by that of the Nonlocal Feature Principle, which enforces a particular step-by-step constraint on the inheritance of all NONLOCAL information, including SLASH. In the next section, we will consider an additional principle that places further constraints on the local inheritance of SLASH, and hence functions as an even closer HPSG analog of Subjacency, but here we will direct our attention to a constraint on traces whose role in the theory is largely analogous to that of the ECP in GB.

The Trace Principle is stated as in (31): [10]

(31)   TRACE PRINCIPLE:

Every trace must be subcategorized by a substantive head.

For all the analogies between GB and HPSG, however, we believe that once one unravels the chains of definitions that the GB trace theory depends on, the HPSG theory of traces can be seen to be much clearer and simpler.[11] There are also some important differences of a more specific nature. For example, unlike the GB account, there is nothing in our theory of universal grammar that rules out so-called *that*-trace sentences like the one in (32a). Given the fact that similar sentences in certain Scandinavian languages are grammatical, we think our approach is preferable. Relevant examples are the Icelandic sentence (32b) cited by Maling and Zaenen (1982), and the Norwegian sentence (32c) cited by Engdahl (1983):

(32)   *a.* *Who$_1$ did Kim claim that ___$_1$ left?
         b. Hver   sagðir þu að   væri kominn til Rekyavíkur.
               who(NOM) said   you that was come   to Reykjavik
               'Who did you say came to Reykjavik?'
         c. Desse konstruksjonar trur eg at   er   meir
               these constructions think I   that are more

               naturlege uttrykksmåtar.
               natural   expressions
               'These constructions, I think (*that) are more natural expressions.'

To account for the badness of (32a), we simply propose a further English-

---

10. The locution 'subcategorized by' is here to be understood as 'having its SYNSEM value on the SUBCAT list of.'

11. Our formulation of trace theory carries with it an implicit denial of the central claim embodied in analyses that appeal to the ECP as a constraint on logical forms— namely the claim that quantifier scope, trace binding, and negative particles in various Romance languages all exhibit certain 'subject-object asymmetries' that must be given a unified account in terms of a prohibition (the ECP) against binding from 'too far away.' Indeed, Ladusaw (n.d.) casts doubt on the semantic predictions made by the widely accepted analyses of Romance negative particles put forth by, e.g., Kayne (1984b) and Rizzi (1982). Ladusaw also presents a plausible alternative account of these data that makes different semantic predictions and that, as we have assumed here, separates the account of negative particles from considerations of extraction phenomena. Similarly, as May's (1984) discussion makes clear, the ECP can provide a treatment of quantifier scope asymmetries in English only at the cost of abandoning the idea that logical forms (for us, CONTENT values) represent relative scope information, a consequence that we regard as both unwarranted and unnecessary. For these reasons, we have formulated our Trace Principle as a constraint on the distribution of traces that is unrelated to constraints on the scoping of quantifiers or the interpretation of negative particles.

specific constraint on the distribution of traces, a constraint we will formulate as an English-particular parametrization of the Trace Principle:

(33)   TRACE PRINCIPLE (parametrized for English):

         Every trace must be *strictly* subcategorized by a substantive head.

This modification adds the condition that traces not only be subcategorized, but also be *strictly* subcategorized, in the sense that its SYNSEM value must be a noninitial member of a substantive head's SUBCAT list.[12] We assume that languages simply differ with respect to whether or not this further constraint exists. The revised Trace Principle predicts the ungrammaticality of (32a), as that example contains a subject trace.

There is still more to be said about subjects, of course, since nothing we have said so far accounts for the grammaticality of apparent subject extractions like the one in (34a):

(34)   *a.* Who₁ did Kim claim ___₁ left?

The solution we suggest here, adapting an idea originally proposed by Gazdar (1981), is that such sentences do not actually contain finite sentential complements at all. Instead, we analyze such examples as having a structure like the one in (34b):

(34) b.

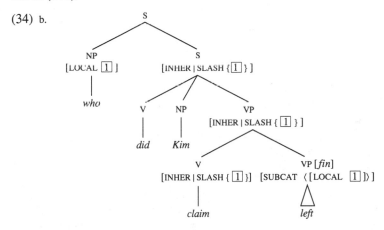

12. Note that we have said nothing thus far that would differentiate objects of case-marking prepositions like *of* from subjects, since both involve initial members of SUBCAT lists. Hence we have not yet provided an account of why traces are permitted in examples like (i):

(i)   What were you thinking of ___?

This deficiency will be remedied in the analysis of Chapter 9, where subject and nonsubject complements are selected by different features.

In order to license such structures, we posit the lexical rule sketched informally in (35):

(35)   SUBJECT EXTRACTION LEXICAL RULE (SELR):

$$
\begin{array}{c}
\text{X} \\
[\text{SUBCAT } \langle \text{Y}, \ldots, \text{S}[\textit{unmarked}], \ldots \rangle]
\end{array}
$$

$$\Downarrow$$

$$
\begin{bmatrix}
& \text{X} & \\
\text{INHER | SLASH } \{\,\boxed{1}\,\} & & \\
& & \text{VP} \\
\text{SUBCAT}\left\langle \text{Y}, \ldots, \begin{bmatrix} \text{SUBCAT } \langle [\text{LOC}\,\boxed{1}\,] \rangle \\ \text{INHER | SLASH } \{\ \} \end{bmatrix}, \ldots \right\rangle
\end{bmatrix}
$$

The idea here is that any English verb that subcategorizes for a nonsubject[13] S complement gives rise to a new lexical entry that subcategorizes for an (unslashed) VP complement. Readers familiar with GPSG will recognize the similarity between this lexical rule and GKPS's SLASH Termination Metarule 2 (sometimes referred to as the Finite VP Metarule). Note in particular that SELR, like the GKPS metarule, applies only if the sentential complement in the input is compatible with the specification [MARKING *unmarked*], and hence produces no violations of Bresnan's (1972) 'Fixed Subject Condition.' Unlike the GKPS account, however, the outputs of this lexical rule will interact with the binding theory presented in Chapter 6 to provide an account of the strong crossover examples in (36):

(36)   *a.*   *Who$_i$ did he$_i$ say Mary likes ___$_i$?
         b.   *Who$_i$ did he$_i$ say ___$_i$ likes Mary?

Under the assumption that gerund phrases are projections of V[*ger*] (i.e. that a gerund phrase like *him stepping in front of me* is also an instance of S[*unmarked*]), SELR will also provide an account of the fact (mentioned in section 3 of Chapter 3) that subjects of gerunds may also be extracted, as in (37):

(37)   *a.* The man that I resented ___ stepping in front of me in line.
         b. Which man did you resent ___ stepping in front of you in line?
         c. It was Sandy that I resented ___ stepping in front of me in line.

In these examples, the SELR output is a slashed form of *resent* that subcategorizes for a subject and an unsaturated gerund complement.

---

13. Y is a variable ranging over *synsem* objects. Hence the presence of Y in (35) guarantees that the S[*unmarked*] is not a subject. This apparently ad hoc restriction will be eliminated in Chapter 9.

The formulation of the Trace Principle in (33) might be strengthened in a number of ways, with varying effects. For example, we might also require that traces be assigned a semantic role (cf. the GB notion of θ-*government*), thus ruling out examples like (38):

(38) a. *There, Kris believes ___ to be no solution to our problems.
      b. *It, Mo believes ___ to be obvious that the bill will pass.

This requirement may well be superfluous, however, as the discourse-functional properties of the topicalization construction may be sufficient to guarantee the referentiality of the topicalized NP.[14] We will not explore such refinements here, though they may both ultimately prove to be the preferred way of accounting for the data in question.

The Trace Principle provides an immediate account of a variety of facts that are commonly discussed under the general rubric of 'island constraints.' For example, the contrasts in (39)–(41) have been explained variously in terms of the *Left Branch Condition* (Ross 1967), the *A-over-A Condition* (Chomsky 1973), the *Relativized A-over-A Condition* (Bresnan 1976), the *Generalized Left Branch Condition* (Gazdar 1981), or the ECP (Chomsky 1981, 1986b):

(39) a. How tall do you think the building is ___?
      b. *How do you think the building is ___ tall?

(40) a. That is the building [whose design our architects rejected ___].
      b. *That is the building [whose our architects rejected [___ design]].
      c. *That is thc building [who our architects rejected [___'s design]].

(41) a. The books that I like, Leslie donated ___ to the library.
      b. *The books, Leslie donated [___ that I like] to the library.

All of these contrasts follow directly from the Trace Principle. The traces in (39a), (40a), and (41a) are all strictly subcategorized complements, as required by the Trace Principle, but the same is not true of the traces in (39b), (40b, c), and (41b). In (39b), the trace is a modifier, and hence not subcategorized at all; in (40b), the trace is a possessor phrase subcategorized by the N', but not strictly subcategorized; the trace in (40c) also violates the Trace Principle, as it appears as the complement of the determiner 's, a nonsubstantive category

14. Similarly, one might account for contrasts like those in (i) and (ii) by imposing a further condition that the trace not be subcategorized (or 'governed') by a noun:

(i)   Which movie star did you find a picture of ___?
(ii)   ?Of which movie star did you find a picture ___?

(see Chapter 1, section 8); and in (41b) the trace is the head of its phrase, not a complement at all. The Trace Principle thus provides a unified account of numerous island constraint phenomena.

Two points implicit in these remarks warrant further discussion. First, though prenominal possessor traces are correctly ruled out by the Trace Principle, it is a fact (as noted by Grosu (1974)) that extraction of possessor phrases is quite generally impossible in English. This fact is illustrated by contrasts like the following:

(42)   *a.*   I met a friend of Leslie's.
         b.   *Leslie's, I met a friend of ___.
         c.   *Leslie, I met a friend of ___'s.

The appropriate generalization about possessor extraction is thus expressed by an English-specific constraint that disallows determiners (more precisely local objects whose HEAD value is *determiner*) as members of the values of SLASH. This correctly rules out (42b), where a trace would otherwise be possible as the object of *of*. Example (42c), on the other hand, is excluded on the same grounds as (40c), as it also involves a trace that is the complement of a nonsubstantive category, and hence is a violation of the Trace Principle.

The second further point we wish to raise concerns the treatment of modifiers like those in (43):[15]

(43)   *a.*   When did Pat eat dinner?
         b.   When do you think Pat ate dinner?
         c.   On Saturday, Dana will go to Spain.
         d.   On Saturday, I think Dana will go to Spain.

On the basis of examples like these, it is commonly assumed that the grammar of traces must allow adverbial expressions to participate in unbounded dependency constructions, presumably binding a trace. This conclusion, if accepted, would require us to modify the Trace Principle in some way so as to allow noncomplement traces.

But the view that adverbs participate in unbounded dependency constructions, as noted by Cattell (1978), might be called into question by contrasts like the following:

(44)   *a.*   When do you/they feel (that) Dana should get promoted?
         b.   When do you/they think (that) Pat should get promoted?

---

15. We are particularly indebted to Georgia Green, Larry Horn, Polly Jacobson, and Mark Liberman for helpful discussions about adverbial extraction.

          c. Where do you/they believe (that) she will camp?
          d. On Tuesdays, she thinks (that) Sandy will attend an aerobics
             class.
          e. In this country, I feel (that) Chris will find true happiness.

(45)   *a.* When do you deny (that) Pat should get promoted?
          b. When do they doubt (that) Dana should get promoted?
          c. When did they deny (that) he will resign?

The examples in (44) are all ambiguous—the sentence-initial adverb appears to modify either the matrix clause or the embedded clause. The matrix modification reading requires a slightly unusual contextualization, for example, a sort of psychiatric discussion of someone's thoughts, beliefs, or feelings, but nonetheless is available in principle. This ambiguity would be predicted by a UDC analysis where the adverbial trace can appear in either matrix or embedded clause position.

    However, as noted by Cattell, the examples in (45) appear to be unambiguous, allowing only matrix modification. This apparent lack of ambiguity is quite mysterious from the perspective of any UDC analysis of 'dislocated' adverbials, for, as examples like (46) show, the verbs in (45) cannot be said to disallow extraction in general:

(46)   *a.* Which position do you deny (that) Pat is qualified for ___?
          b. Which problems do they doubt (that) Dana can solve ___?
          c. This class, she doubts (that) Sandy will attend ___.
          d. This country, I deny (that) Chris will find true happiness in ___.

Cattell (1978: 62) also suggests that simply negating a sentence is sufficient to preclude the possibility of embedded modification, as the following contrast illustrates:

(47)   *a.* Why do they think/suppose/say/imagine (that) she killed him?
          b. Why don't they think/suppose/say/imagine (that) she killed him?

He concludes that a syntactic solution to the contrast between (44) and (45) is unlikely.

    Cattell argues further that there is a semantic basis for the contrasts in question here. The matrix verbs in (44) and (47a) differ from those in (45) (and the negated forms in (47b)) in terms of their ability to function as parenthetical tags, as illustrated in (48)–(49):

(48)   *a.*   When should Dana get promoted, do you/they feel?
          b.   When should Pat get promoted, do they think?
          c.   Where will she camp, do you/they believe?

> *d.* On Tuesdays, Sandy will attend an aerobics class, she thinks.
> *e.* In this country, Chris will find true happiness, I feel.

(49) *a.* *When should Pat get promoted, do you deny?
  b. *When should Dana get promoted, do they doubt?
  c. *When should Dana get promoted, don't they think?
  d. *On Tuesdays, Sandy will attend an aerobics class, she denies.
  e. *In this country, Chris will find true happiness, I doubt.
  f. *In this country, Chris will find true happiness, I don't suppose.

It seems that the ability to perform a parenthetical-like function may play an important role in the explanation of the ambiguity differences in (44)–(45).

The problem of providing an exact characterization of the distinction that is relevant to an account of these data is by no means trivial, however. For example, the correlation between parenthetical tags and the possibility of embedded modification may be imperfect. Nonetheless, on the basis of facts such as these, one might attempt to develop a traceless analysis of adverb extraction, one where there is no true modification of the embedded clause.[16] Although Cattell (1978: 66ff.) seeks to explicate the relevant semantic and contextual properties in terms of the notion *volunteered stance*, he offers no mechanism to make sense of his observed correlations and gives no precise formulation of any alternative analysis.

However, the essential ingredients for such an alternative analysis were suggested by Liberman (1973). Building on unpublished work by Bresnan (1968), Liberman offered an analysis of examples like those in (50) and (51):

(50) One more step and I'm afraid I'll have to shoot you.

(51) One more beer and I'm afraid it looks like I'm going to have to drive you home.

The problem noted by Liberman is the following. The semantic analysis of sentences of the form *One more X and Y* is basically that of a conditional 'if P then Q,' with contextual information interacting with the content of *one more X* to determine P, and the content of Y determining Q. But in examples like these, Q is determined not by Y, but rather by the complement of Y, with the highest clause in Y not making a direct contribution to Q, even though it is clearly an essential part of the matrix syntactic environment. Let us refer to such uses as 'annotations,'[17] distinguishing matrix annotations like those considered by Bresnan and Liberman from parenthetical annotations of a familiar sort.

---

16. For additional arguments against treating sentence-initial adverbials in terms of trace binding in GB, see Hegarty 1990.

17. We owe this term to Mark Liberman (personal communication, 1990).

Liberman's solution to the problem of matrix annotations, cast in a generative semantics–like framework, posited a transformational rule that inserts annotative material into the matrix syntactic environment, thus deriving the
second conjunct in (50) (*I'm afraid I'll have to shoot you*) from a semantic
structure like that of *I'll have to shoot you*, with the additional material (*I'm
afraid*) external to the underlying semantic structure of the clause. The semantic structure for the entire sentence (50) then, once contextual material is supplied, is essentially that of 'if you take one more step, then I'll have to shoot
you,' with the 'I'm afraid' annotation being just that—an annotation external
to the semantic content.

Of course the insight of Liberman's analysis could be preserved even if one
discards the transformational assumptions of his presentation. The essential
claim being made, one that could plausibly be expressed equally well via lexical
rules, is that a large class of expressions (e.g. *think, feel,* and *believe*) may receive an annotative interpretation when they occur in syntactic matrix position.
For example, a verb like *think*, even while it occurs in the environment shown
in (52a), may give rise to an interpretation like the one sketched in (52b): [18]

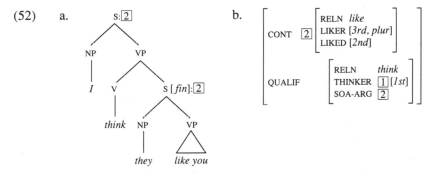

This analysis would thus allow an interpretation of (52a) that can be paraphrased by *They like you, I think* or *They, I think, like you.* The paraphrase is
likely to be only approximate, however, given that there is no reason to believe
that matrix and parenthetical annotations have identical interpretations (or
constraints).

Once structure-interpretation mismatches of this sort are accepted, the Bres-
nan/Liberman-style of analysis allows a biclausal, adverb-initial sentence like
(53) to be assigned two interpretations in simple consequence of the two possible interpretations of the matrix embedding environment (*I feel/think*):

18. We use the attribute QUALIFICATION as an expository convenience, in an attempt
to finesse the host of murky conceptual and representational problems that surround the
construction of a precise theory of annotations, a theory that would presumably include
an account of various prosodic phenomena and discourse particles in addition to matrix
and parenthetical annotations.

(53)

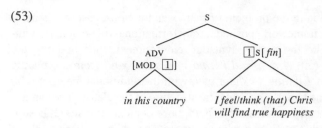

The ambiguity of adverb-initial sentences like (53), which can be analyzed simply in terms of Schema 5 (the head-adjunct schema), is thus explained without any appeal to adverbial traces. If an annotative interpretation is imposed, then the content of S[*fin*] will be the content of the complement, and the modifier in (53) will appear to modify the embedded clause. On the other hand, if the familiar type of interpretation is assigned to (53), then the adverb will modify the psoa whose relation is determined by the matrix verb. In this latter case, the verb's complement will function as an argument of the relation of the matrix verb.

By contrast, the lack of ambiguity in examples like (54) follows directly from the well-known semantic/pragmatic fact that verbs like *deny* and *doubt* cannot function annotatively, as illustrated in (55): [19]

(54)   *a.*   When did they deny (that) Pat should get promoted?
        b.   Where did you deny (that) Chris will find true happiness.

(55)   *a.*   *When should Pat get promoted, do you deny?
        b.   *When should Dana get promoted, do they doubt?

Attractive though the Bresnan/Liberman-style of analysis may seem, we doubt that it can ultimately tell the whole story about adverbial extraction in English. Although it seems clear that there is some relation between parentheticality and the ambiguity differences in (44)–(45), the possibility of adverbial extraction from an embedded clause cannot always be tied to the parentheticality of the matrix environment. Examples like (56) illustrate this point: [20]

(56)   *a.*   When their parents are in town next week, I doubt that the twins will attend any lectures.
        b.   When their parents are in town next week, I don't for a moment think that the twins will attend any lectures.
        c.   When he was president, Reagan denies that he ever received kickbacks from the PLO.

19. The analysis being considered here shares properties with that developed independently by Hegarty (1990), though there are minor differences in assumptions about the relevant data. Hegarty, for example, assumes that the presence of a *that* complementizer prevents the possibility of embedded modification.

20. Here we are indebted to Charles Lee and Chris Manning for persistent construction of counterexamples.

    d. During my term as University President, I deny there were any
       illegitimate appropriations of government money.

Unlike the essentially similar examples in (45), which appear to differ only
inasmuch as they are *wh*-questions rather than topicalizations, the examples in
(56) allow the extracted adverbials to be interpreted as embedded modifiers.
Given the grammaticality of such examples, it would seem to be an unavoidable conclusion that the grammar of English must allow matrix adverbials to
modify semantically embedded complement clauses. There may be complex
semantic and pragmatic factors contributing to the difficulty in assigning a
complement-modifying interpretation to Cattell's examples in (45), but in
the right context even these may prove to be acceptable.[21] The grammar of
English cannot exclude adverbial extractions from the class of unbounded
dependencies.

    In this section we will not revise our analysis of UDCs so as to allow for the
possibility of such embedded modification. Rather, we will take this matter up
again in Chapter 9, once certain modifications of the mechanism for introduc-
ing INHER | SLASH dependencies have been presented.

---

21. As an example of a semantic constraint, we would suggest that only those sentential adjuncts can be extracted that are monotonic in the sense of preserving the entailments of the sentences to which they adjoin. This explains, for example, why
probably cannot be extracted, even across a bridge verb: **Probably, Kim thought that
Sandy stole the books* (on the embedded modification reading).

    Pragmatic constraints that bear on the extraction of (inter alia) adjuncts are exempli-
fied by Kroch's (1989) proposal to block certain 'long' movements (Rizzi 1990; Cinque
1990; Szabolsci and Zwarts 1991) by presupposition failure. On this approach, with
which we are sympathetic, the unacceptability of much-discussed examples like (i),
involving extraction of *wh*-amount phrases out of complement questions, stems from
the difficulty of constructing a context in which the presuppositions of the question are
met:

(i)   #How much did you wonder whether the book cost? [cf. That much, I won-
           der whether any book could cost.]

Thus (i) is acceptable only under the highly improbable presupposition that there exists
a price p (say, $59.95) such that the addressee wonders whether the book in question
costs p. Indeed, we believe this approach can be extended to cover a rather wide range
of other types of extractions, both of adjuncts and of 'nonreferential complements,' as
exemplified in (ii) and (iii):

(ii)   #How did you wonder why Sandy worded the letter? [cf. That rudely, I won-
            der why anyone would ever word a letter.]
(iii)   #How did Kim not know who fixed the disk drive? [cf. With nothing but a
           crowbar and a ballpeen hammer, I don't know who could fix this disk
           drive.]

4.5 Parasitic Gaps

In section 4.3 we considered double gapped examples where the two traces are independent in the sense that they are bound at different places in the structure. However, it can also happen that two or more traces in the same sentence are bound in unison, as shown by the examples in (57):[22]

(57)   *a.* That was the rebel leader who₁ rivals of __₁ shot __₁.
         b. [Those boring old reports]₁, Kim filed __₁ without reading __₁.
         c. Which of our relatives₁ should we send snapshots of __₁ to __₁.
         d. [Someone as vain as Sandy]₁ would be easy to sell pictures of
               __₁ to __₁.

In examples like this, nothing special needs to be said. These are simply cases where two distinct traces happen to structure-share their LOCAL values. For example, the relative clause in (57a) will be assigned the structure sketched in (58):

(58)

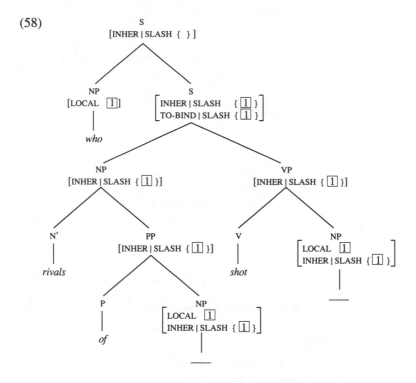

22. We would like to thank Janet Fodor, Polly Jacobson, and Bob Levine for extremely valuable discussions about the analysis of parasitic gaps.

The key point here is that since the two traces have the same LOCAL structure, tagged $\boxed{1}$, the subject NP and the VP have the same INHER | SLASH value, namely the singleton set containing the local structure $\boxed{1}$. It follows from the Nonlocal Feature Principle (stated in (16) above) that the INHER | SLASH value of the lower S must be the same also. When this single SLASH value element is identified with the local structure of the relative pronoun *who*, both traces are bound in unison.

It is well-known that certain traces that are coindexed with another trace can occur in positions where a trace could not otherwise appear, as long as the other trace could have occurred independently. Such traces are known as *parasitic gaps*, and the other, nonparasitic gap is said to *license* the parasitic gap. In cases like this we will refer to the licensing gap as the *host* gap. For example, in (58), the trace within the subject is the parasite, and the object trace is the host. This is because a trace could appear independently as an object but not within the subject, as the facts in (59) show:

(59)   *a.*   *That was the rebel leader who$_1$ rivals of ___$_1$ shot the British consul.
         b.   That was the rebel leader who$_1$ agents of foreign powers shot ___$_1$.

Likewise, it has often been assumed (Huang 1982; Gazdar et al. 1985) that examples like (60a) are ungrammatical and hence that in the case of sentences like (60b), the trace within the adjunct is a parasite and the object trace is its host: [23]

(60)   *a.*   [Those boring old reports]$_1$, Kim went to lunch without reading ___$_1$.
         b.   [Those boring old reports]$_1$, Kim filed ___$_1$ without reading ___$_1$.

GKPS propose a general account of facts such as these: SLASH is both a FOOT feature (one that must be instantiated onto the mother of a local tree if it is instantiated onto a daughter—in accordance with their FOOT Feature Principle) and a HEAD feature (one that must be instantiated onto a head daughter if it is instantiated onto a mother in a local tree—in accordance with their HEAD Feature Convention). The interaction of these two principles of GPSG is sketched in (61):

---

23. In spite of the fact that examples such as (60a) have been treated as ungrammatical in much of the syntactic literature, they are clearly better than ones like (59a). For many speakers, the authors included, examples like (60a) seem completely acceptable.

(61) a. Rule: V[BAR 2] → NP, H[BAR 1]

b.

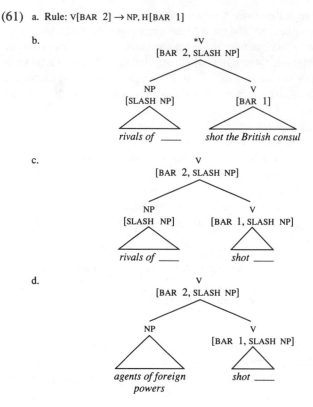

Given the rule in (61a), the structure in (61b) satisfies the FOOT Feature Principle (the precursor of HPSG's Nonlocal Feature Principle), but not the Head Feature Convention (the precursor of HPSG's Head Feature Principle), because the head daughter (the V[BAR 1]) lacks the nonempty specification for the HEAD feature SLASH that is borne by the mother. Hence (59a) and examples like it where only a nonhead daughter contains a gap are predicted to be ungrammatical. The structures in (61c) and (61d), on the other hand, satisfy both relevant grammatical principles. Since SLASH is a HEAD feature, instantiating a nonempty SLASH specification onto the mother necessitates instantiation of the very same specification on the head daughter, and nothing prevents instantiating the very same specification onto the nonhead daughter, as in (61c). In this way, the GKPS treatment of SLASH as both HEAD and FOOT feature renders the presence of [SLASH NP] on the subject NP parasitic on the simultaneous presence of [SLASH NP] on the head V. The GKPS account of contrasts like (60) is similar.

The GKPS analysis of extraction phenomena is perhaps best-known for its explanation of 'across-the-board' exceptions to Ross's (1967) Coordinate Structure Constraint (CSC), a long-standing source of difficulty for transformational analyses of coordination and extraction.[24] Briefly, because each conjunct in a local coordinate structure is treated as a head daughter, it follows from GKPS's Foot Feature Principle that an instantiated nonempty SLASH specification on any daughter will also be present on the mother. And if a nonempty SLASH specification is instantiated on the mother of any structure, then that same specification must be instantiated on the head daughter(s) (in accordance with the Head Feature Convention). Since all conjuncts are taken to be head daughters, it follows that if any conjunct is slashed, then all conjuncts must be slashed. Since being slashed corresponds to containing a gap, this consequence is equivalent to the claim that all conjuncts will contain a gap if any conjunct does, which is precisely Ross's CSC, together with its across-the-board exceptions. The GKPS analysis of filler-gap constructions thus derives the CSC (with its across-the-board exceptions) and the phenomenon of parasitic gaps from a single underlying principle: the principle that SLASH is both a HEAD feature and a FOOT feature.

Elegant though this theory may appear, it suffers from at least one very serious difficulty. As noted by Sells (1984: 307ff.), Swedish differs from English in allowing extractions out of subjects that are not parasitic on the presence of another gap in the sentence. Thus examples like (62), whose structure is identical in all relevant respects to the one in (61b) (which we saw to be ungrammatical in English), are grammatical in Swedish (subject to certain pragmatic conditions):

(62)   den deckare   som de sista sidorna i ___ hade
        that detective novel that the last   pages   in ___ had
        kommit bort
        come   away
        'that detective novel whose last pages had come away . . .'

But Swedish observes the CSC, subject to the very same across-the-board exceptions as English. The GKPS theory, where SLASH is crucially classified as a HEAD feature, apparently predicts that a language like Swedish is impossible. If SLASH is a HEAD feature in Swedish, Sells argues, then examples like (62) should not be grammatical, but they are. And if SLASH is *not* a HEAD feature in Swedish, then Swedish should not obey the CSC, but it does. Either way, the claim that SLASH is doubly classified incorrectly links the phenomenon of parasitic gaps with the CSC and must be abandoned.

We propose, following Sells, to treat the CSC as deriving from a constraint that is particular to coordinate structures, and that in no way involves the assumption that conjuncts are head daughters in those structures. This analysis, which we discuss in section 4.6, leaves the matter of parasitic gaps to an inde-

---

24. For a variety of as yet unanswered arguments demonstrating the superiority of nontransformational analyses of coordination, see Gazdar, Pullum, Sag, and Wasow 1982.

pendent analysis that must deal with cross-linguistic differences such as the one observed by Sells.

But what then is the basis for the analysis of parasitic gaps? One answer to this question might be the introduction of a second universal principle, which we shall refer to as the SLASH Inheritance Principle. This principle, stated in (63), places a further constraint on the inheritance of SLASH value elements:

(63)   SLASH INHERITANCE PRINCIPLE (SIP):

> Every member of the INHER | SLASH set on a headed constituent must be inherited from (i.e. belong to the INHER | SLASH set of) a daughter that is either (a) (strictly) subcategorized by a substantive head, or (b) the head.

SIP would play much the same role in HPSG that is played by Subjacency in GB, in the sense that it places a condition on each step of the unbounded dependency. Readers fam180 with GB will also recognize the close similarity of SIP to Huang's (1982) Condition on Extraction Domains, or to Kayne's (1983) Connectedness Condition (especially as modified by Engdahl (1983)). The main difference is our clause (b) allowing inheritance from the head daughter. This is needed, for example, in order to pass SLASH values up from VP to S. (In then-current GB, of course, this was unnecessary because traces move straight from the topic position of one S to the topic position of the next S up, without having to be passed up one node at a time.)

Let us now return to the question about parasitic gaps that we raised earlier without answering: *Why should traces that would otherwise be impossible become grammatical when licensed by another trace in a normal trace position?* That is, how do we account for the contrast between the grammatical sentence (57a), repeated here as (64a), and the ungrammatical (59a), repeated here as (64b)?

(64)   *a.*   That was the rebel leader who₁ [rivals of ___₁ shot ___₁].
         b.   *That was the rebel leader who₁ [rivals of ___₁ shot the British consul].

The contrast in (64) is predicted by the interaction of the Nonlocal Feature Principle with the Trace Principle and SIP. For reference, this set of principles is recapitulated in (65):

(65)   Summary of HPSG trace theory (preliminary version):

> *a.* Nonlocal Feature Principle: For each nonlocal feature, the INHER-ITED value on the mother is the union of the INHERITED values on the daughters minus the TO-BIND value on the head daughter.
>
> *b.* Trace Principle (English): Every trace must be strictly subcategorized by a substantive head.
>
> *c.* SLASH Inheritance Principle: Every member of the INHERITED |

SLASH set on a headed constituent must be inherited from (i.e. be-
long to the INHERITED | SLASH set of) a daughter that is either (a)
(strictly) subcategorized by a substantive head, or (b) the head.

Now consider the embedded clauses indicated by brackets in (64a) and
(64b). By the Nonlocal Feature Principle, these have the structures sketched
in (66):

(66) a.

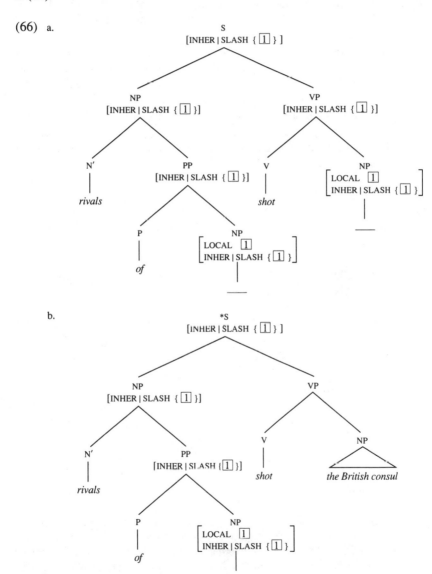

Both of the traces in (66a) are strictly subcategorized, and hence the Trace Principle is satisfied.[25] But what about SIP? The key node to consider is the top node, whose INHER | SLASH set contains exactly one element, labelled $\boxed{1}$. This node satisfies SIP since the element $\boxed{1}$ is also contained in the INHER | SLASH set of the VP head daughter. The fact that this element also appears in the INHER | SLASH set of the subject has no bearing on the grammaticality: all the conditions of the theory are satisfied even though the subject is not strictly subcategorized. Thus (66a) is predicted to be grammatical.

But now consider (66b). The trace is strictly subcategorized, so that the Trace Principle is satisfied. The problem is with SIP. Again, the key node to consider is the top one. As in (66a), the INHER | SLASH set contains one element, labelled $\boxed{1}$. But now SIP is *not* satisfied, for the only daughter that this element is inherited from is the subject. But the subject, of course, is neither strictly subcategorized nor the head. Hence we predict that (66b) is ungrammatical. To put it informally, the gap from the subject in (66a) is parasitic on, or licensed by, the independently permissible object gap, but the one in (66b) is not.

It should also be noted that this analysis of parasitic gaps avoids a further defect of the GKPS analysis pointed out independently by Pollard (1985), Hukari and Levine (1987a), and Jacobson (1987). The GKPS analysis, which relies crucially on the stipulation that SLASH is both a HEAD feature and a FOOT feature, fails to predict the following contrast:

(67)   *a.* *Who did my talking to ___ bother Hilary?
       b. Who did my talking to ___ bother ___?

The problem for the GKPS analysis is that nothing makes a gap within the subject of the S[+INV] dependent on the presence of a gap in the VP, since the latter is not a phrasal head.

On our analysis, illustrated in (68), the relevant structure (i.e. the lower S) is an instance of Schema 3:

25. If nonpredicative prepositions are treated as intransitive (i.e. the prepositional object is the only member of the preposition's SUBCAT list), then we have not yet explained why the trace that follows *of* in (66) is *strictly* subcategorized. In fact, as noted in section 4.4, we have not yet provided a schema for introducing prepositions that take an object but no subject. We return to this problem in Chapter 9.

(68)

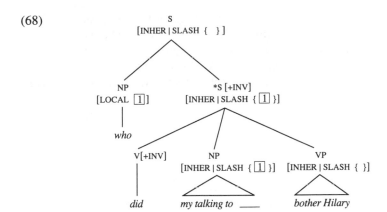

Here, the subject of the inverted auxiliary verb is not strictly subcategorized and hence can contain a gap only if the VP complement (which is strictly subcategorized) also contains a gap, as guaranteed by SIP. Thus the indicated local tree in (68) is ruled out by our theory (but not by the theory of GKPS), and examples like (67a) are correctly deemed ungrammatical.

A number of researchers working within the tradition of phrase structure grammar have pointed out a set of examples that are potentially problematic for the theory of SLASH inheritance we have been considering. For example, contrasts like those in (69) and (70) are discussed by Farkas et al. (1983), by Sells (1984: 309), and by Jacobson (1984: 415):

(69)   a. *Who did you consider friends of ___ angry at Sandy?
        b. Who did you consider friends of Sandy angry at ___?
        c. Who did you consider friends of ___ angry at ___?

(70)   a. *Here's the jerk that I expected my pictures of ___ to bother you.
        b. Here's the jerk that I expected my pictures of you to bother ___.
        c. Here's the jerk that I expected my pictures of ___ to bother ___.

These researchers have argued that examples like (69)–(70) behave like the parasitic gap examples we have been considering; but in (69)–(70) neither the GKPS analysis nor the one based on SIP correctly predicts the observed contrasts. This is illustrated in (71), the structure of the relevant piece of (70a):

(71)

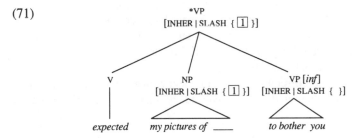

The deviance of (71) follows from nothing in the theory we have been considering; the object NP from which the mother inherits is strictly subcategorized and hence should by itself legitimate SLASH inheritance. And there is nothing about the infinitival VP here (since it is not the head) that would predict that inheriting from it is sufficient to restore acceptability, as in (72), the structure of the relevant piece of (70c):

(72)

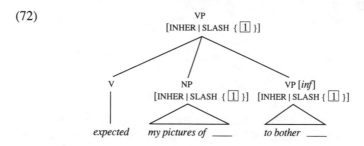

Within the theory of complementation presented in Chapter 3, the problem posed by (69) is the same in all relevant respects.

The solution to this problem that is suggested by Farkas et al. (1983), Jacobson (1983, 1987), and Sells (1984) builds on ideas of Kuno (1973), who argued that English has a constraint legislating that no medial constituent may contain a gap (i.e. no constituent that is nonfinal in its phrase may be 'incomplete'). Kuno's formulation of this constraint did not allow for parasitic gaps (as noted by Jacobson (1987: 415)), but the desired effect—to allow medial phrases containing gaps just in case they are followed by some phrase that also contains a gap—can be obtained by formulating Kuno's (Clause Nonfinal) Incomplete Constituent Constraint as a linear precedence rule like (73). (We have introduced a minor modification of the Farkas et al./Sells/Jacobson proposal to induce compatibility with other aspects of the HPSG analysis of UDCs.)

(73)   INCOMPLETE CONSTITUENT CONSTRAINT:

[INHER | SLASH *empty-set*]   <   [INHER | SLASH *nonempty-set*]

The effect of (73) is to block structures like (71), where a slashed daughter precedes an unslashed daughter, but to allow structures like (72), where a medial slashed daughter precedes another slashed daughter. This formulation of the Incomplete Constituent Constraint is intended to be a complete theory of parasitic gaps, effectively replacing the GKPS theory of SLASH as a head feature or any other alternative such as SIP.

Note that (73) also correctly predicts the behavior of parasitic gaps in sentential structures, whether they are inverted, as in (74a), or uninverted, as in (74b):

(74) a.

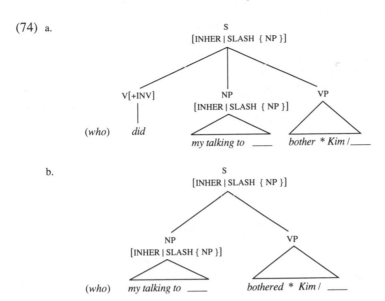

b.

In both these examples, the structures are correctly predicted to be well-formed just in case the VP daughter is slashed.

One important difference should be noted from the outset between the account of parasitic gaps based on the SLASH Inheritance Principle and the one based on the Incomplete Constituent Constraint that we have just sketched. The former account rules out extraction from adverbial modifiers (when not accompanied by extraction from a head daughter), while the latter theory allows these.[26] In light of the grammaticality of a large number of examples of this type, for example, those in (75), the facts would seem to provide strong arguments against most extant analyses of parasitic gaps (including that of GKPS), and strong support for the Farkas et al./Sells/Jacobson reanalysis based on linear precedence (LP) constraints:

(75)   a. That's the symphony that Schubert died [without finishing __].
         b. Which room does Julius teach his class [in __]?
         c. Who did you go to Girona [in order to meet __]? (Hegarty 1990)
         d. What kind of wagon did they use to ride to school [in __]?
         e. How many of the book reports did the teacher smile [after reading __]?
         f. This is the blanket that Rebecca refuses to sleep [without __].

26. See n. 23.

Whatever constraints may affect the possibility of extraction from adverbial modifiers like these, they are considerably more subtle than the absolute constraints on grammatical structures considered thus far.[27]

There are, however, a number of problems facing any attempt to explain English parasitic gaps in terms of the Incomplete Constituent Constraint. First, as noted by Sells (1984: 319–320), there is a potential problem having to do with traces, which, although analyzed as slashed constituents, fail to obey the LP rule in (73):

(76)   Which council members did you [persuade ___ to support the resolution]?

Sells's solution is to stipulate that [+NULL] elements are immune to LP rules; Jacobson's (1987: 416) is to eliminate the analysis of traces as slashed constituents, a proposal we also explore in Chapter 9.

A second problem is that the formulation in (73) disallows structures like the one in (77b), which are required in order to account for the grammaticality of examples like (77a):

(77) a. Those boring old reports, Kim wrote critiques of ____ without falling asleep.

    b.

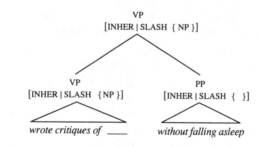

We might seek to remedy this problem by modifying (73) so that slashed daughters are not forbidden to precede *all* nonslashed daughters, but only unslashed *complement* daughters:[28]

---

27. As pointed out to us by Joan Bresnan, similar observations were made in unpublished work by Rothstein (1981). See also Grosu 1972 for some relevant discussion.

28. For a presentation of a linear precedence theory whose rules may make reference to notions such as 'complement,' see Sag 1987 and P&S-87, Chapter 7. For a subtly different reformulation of this constraint with similar consequences, see Sells 1984: 315ff.

(78)   INCOMPLETE CONSTITUENT CONSTRAINT (revised version):

[INHER | SLASH *empty-set*] <
COMPLEMENT[INHER | SLASH *nonempty-set*]

(78) correctly allows for structures like (77).

But even this revised formulation of Kuno's constraint encounters serious difficulties, as pointed out by Hukari and Levine (1991) and Fodor (1992). A few of the various kinds of counterexamples to (78) that can be constructed are given in (79) (from Hukari and Levine 1991 376) and (80) (from Fodor 1992):[29]

(79)   *a.* Who did Kim [argue [with __] about politics]?
        b. What did Kim [argue [about __] with Leslie]?
        c. Who did Kim [have [an argument with __] about politics]?
        d. There are certain heros that Kim [finds [long stories about __]
             very easy to listen to].

(80)   *a.* Which cousin did you [put [a picture of __] in the family
             album]?
        b. Who did you [appeal [to __] to get the requirement waived]?
        c. Which company did you [persuade [the director of __] to make
             an appearance]?

These examples pose a problem for the LP-based theory of parasitic gaps under the assumption that they contain VPs that are instances of Schema 2, that is, that they contain flat VP structures like (81) or (82), which contradict the Incomplete Constituent Constraint:

(81)

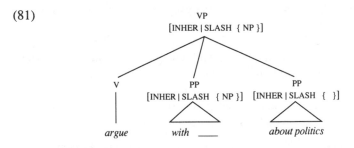

29. Sells and Jacobson both offer examples of equi verbs that they claim obey the same parasitic gap behavior as raising verbs like *consider* and *expect*. However, we do not consider examples like (i) less acceptable than Fodor's example (116c):

(i)   I don't know which children you ordered the parents of __ to stop disturb-
        ing the teachers.

(82)

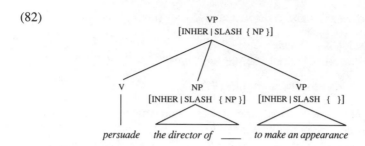

persuade　the director of _____　to make an appearance

For some of these examples, for example, those with the structure of (81), one might attempt to motivate an alternative structure where the first PP forms a constituent with the lexical head, as in (83); that is, the PP[*about*] might be treated as an adjunct:

(83)

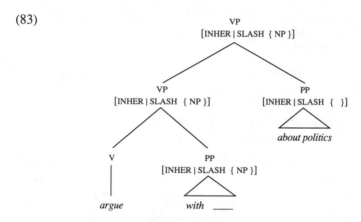

argue　with _____

But even in the unlikely event that this analysis were correct, such a structure is clearly unmotivated for examples like (82).

The conclusion of this discussion, however tentative, is that the attempt to explain parasitic gaps in terms of Kuno's Incomplete Constituent Constraint raises at least as many problems as it might solve.[30] Nonetheless it is perfectly correct, as Farkas et al., Jacobson, and Sells argue, that contrasts like those in (69), (70), and (74) remain unexplained by the GKPS analysis of parasitic gaps. They also remain unexplained by SIP, the HPSG analog of Subjacency.

30. If Fodor (1992) is correct, there is a constraint similar to the Incomplete Constituent Constraint, but that applies only when constituents are not in their unmarked (obliqueness-determined) order. Thus Fodor's theory appeals to a version of Kuno's constraint to explain the deviance of examples like (i) and (ii):

(i)　　　 *Who did you [say [to ___] that you were hungry]?
(ii)　　　 *Who did you [put [on a picture of ___] a hot cup of coffee]?

Assuming that the data are as we have just described them to be, there is a straightforward solution possible within HPSG. The basic intuition is very simple: all the cases of true parasitic gaps are contained within subjects. That is, assuming (1) that extraction from adjuncts is in principle grammatical and (2) that incomplete nonsubject phrases like those discussed by Hukari and Levine and Fodor are grammatical, then the only cases of SLASH inheritance to be blocked are those where a SLASH value has been inherited from a subject (where this notion must include 'raised' subjects like those in (69a) and (70a)) without that SLASH value also being inherited from another daughter. The facts are then predicted by replacing SIP with the following constraint:[31]

(84)   SUBJECT CONDITION:

The initial element of a lexical head's SUBCAT list may be slashed only if that list contains another slashed element.

The Subject Condition predicts the familiar contrast in (85):

(85)   *a.* *That was the rebel leader who rivals of ___ assassinated the British consul.
        b. That was the rebel leader who rivals of ___ assassinated ___.

This is because only in (85b) does the SUBCAT list of the verb *assassinated* satisfy (84). Similarly, the contrast between (86a) and (86b) (discussed above as a problem for the GKPS analysis of parasitic gaps) is accounted for:

(86)   *a.* *Who did my talking to ___ bother Hilary?
        b. Who did my talking to ___ bother ___?

In this case, only in (86b) do the SUBCAT lists of *did* and *bother* satisfy (84). By stating the Subject Condition in terms of SUBCAT lists, the superficial difference between inverted and uninverted clauses is correctly ignored.[32]

The analysis of the Farkas et al./Sells/Jacobson examples in (69) and (70) is

31. It should be noted that our Subject Condition is weaker than the condition of the same name in Chomsky 1973. In Chapter 9, we propose a minor reformulation of (84).

32. We have discovered a number of speakers who accept examples like (85a) and (86a). Such varieties could be described simply by eliminating the Subject Condition. For some of these speakers, however, there appears to be a contrast between (86a, b), both of which are judged to be acceptable, and (i) and (ii), which are judged to be unacceptable:

(i)   Who did rivals of ___ assassinate the British Consul?
(ii)   Who did rivals of ___ assassinate ___?

At present, we have no account of this variety.

more subtle. Here the Subject Condition crucially affects the SUBCAT list of the embedded verb heading the VP complement, rather than that of the matrix verb. Because raising is analyzed as structure sharing between a SUBCAT element and the unexpressed subject of another SUBCAT element (section 3.5), it follows that a raised slashed object will always give rise to an unexpressed slashed subject that must satisfy the Subject Condition, as shown in (87):

(87)

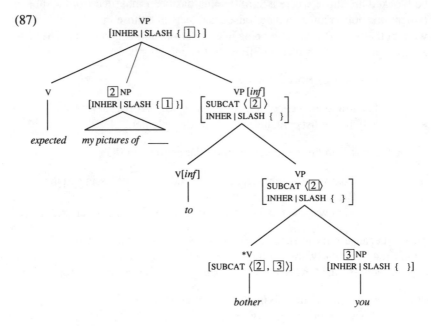

In (87), the subject of *bother*, labelled ②, is a *synsem* object with a nonempty INHER|SLASH value, whereas ③ is a *synsem* object with an empty IN-HER|SLASH value. The SUBCAT list of *bother* in (87) thus violates the Subject Condition.[33] The minimally different structure in (88), on the other hand, produces no such violation:

33. This should be compared with the configurationally similar (82), where the higher VP is headed by an equi verb, rather than a raising verb. As a consequence, the subject SUBCAT element on the head verb (*make*) of the lower VP is merely coindexed with the matrix object and therefore does not share its nonempty SLASH value.

(88)

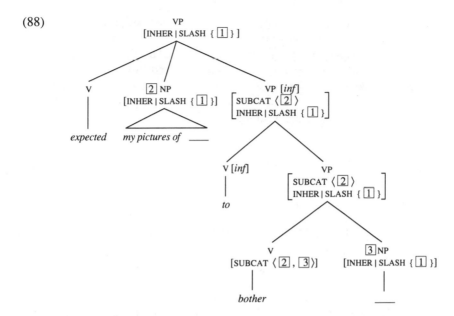

Here, the fact that the object of *bother* is slashed renders that verb's SUBCAT list compatible with (84).[34]

In addition, we now have an account of the differences between English and Swedish noted by Sells (1984: 311ff.): Swedish simply lacks the Subject Condition. In consequence of this fact, not only are examples like (62) above grammatical in Swedish, but so are examples like (89), whose analogs in English violate that constraint:

(89) en symfoni   som många kritiker [anser   [de två sista
      a   symphony that many   critics [consider [the two last
      satserna   i ___] vara oöverträffade]
      movements in ___] to be unsurpassed]

The analysis just sketched, perhaps surprisingly, also provides an account of the behavior of Hukari and Levine's (1991) 'certain heros' examples:

(90) *a.* There are certain heros that Kim finds long stories about ___ very
          easy to listen to ___.
      b. There are certain heros that Kim finds long stories about ___ too
          boring to listen to ___.

34. As pointed out to us by Manfred Sailer and Tilman Höhle (personal communication, 1992), our Subject Condition wrongly rules out the extraction of objects of raising-to-object verbs, e.g. *I wonder who he expected to win.* We provide a solution to this problem in Chapter 9, section 5.1, footnote 38.

Examples like these are argued by Hukari and Levine to be problematic for the Incomplete Constituent Constraint proposed by Jacobson. The problem is that, on virtually any analysis of adjectives like *easy* (see section 4.3), the AP *very easy to listen to* ___ (in spite of containing a slashed VP) is itself unslashed. Hence a VP like (91), which must be part of the structure of the grammatical (90a, b), contains a slashed NP followed by an unslashed phrase, in violation of the Incomplete Constituent Constraint:

(91)

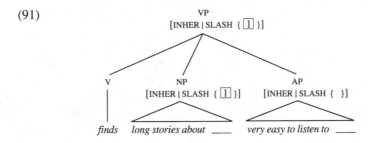

Why are such examples grammatical? The theory we have sketched provides a clear answer to this question: because adjectives like *easy* subcategorize for a slashed complement, a raised, slashed object like the one in (91) will be identified with an unexpressed subject that is less oblique than a slashed element, as shown in (92):

(92)

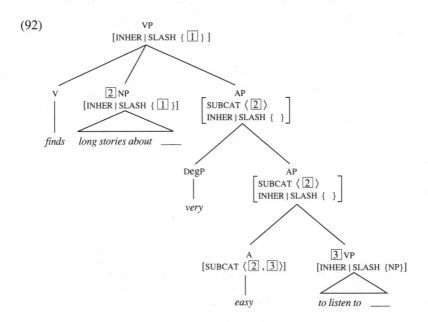

Since the *synsem* objects labelled $\boxed{2}$ and $\boxed{3}$ in (92) are both slashed, it follows that the SUBCAT list of *easy* in (92) satisfies the Subject Condition.[35]

We conclude this discussion of parasitic gaps by considering the facts in (93):

(93)   *a.*   *I never know [which topics]$_j$ jokes about ___$_j$ are likely to offend people.

         b.   I never know [which people]$_j$ jokes about ___$_j$ are likely to offend ___$_j$.

         c.   [People that sensitive]$_i$, I never know [which topics]$_j$ jokes about ___$_j$ are likely to offend ___$_i$.

Like all theories of parasitic gaps with which we are familiar, our account predicts the contrast between (93a) and (93b). In (93a) we have an unlicensed subject-internal gap; but in (93b) the subject-internal gap is licensed by the coindexed object gap. However, nothing in our theory requires that the licensing gap be coindexed with the parasitic gap. Thus our theory also correctly predicts the perhaps surprising grammaticality of (93c).

In sum, a more empirically and theoretically adequate account of parasitic gaps is provided by preserving the essence of the GKPS account (constraints on the inheritance of SLASH specifications in local structures), but abandoning

---

35. A remaining puzzle, pointed out to us by Polly Jacobson, is that phrases containing *easy*-type APs also ameliorate sentences containing subject-internal gaps, as in (i) and (ii):

(i)   There are certain heroes that [[long stories about ___] [are always very easy to listen to ___]].

(ii)   There are certain heroes that [[long stories about ___] [are too boring to listen to ___]].

Examples like these are counterexamples to the GKPS account of parasitic gaps (SLASH is present on the nonhead daughter of S (the subject), but not on the phrasal head (the VP) as well as the account stated in terms of the Incomplete Constituent Constraint. Unfortunately, they are also counterexamples to our theory, inasmuch as they violate the Subject Condition. This is because, even though the SUBCAT lists of the embedded predicates (*easy* and *boring*) in these examples are well-formed, it turns out that in both cases the SUBCAT list of the auxiliary *are* is not. For instance, in (i) this SUBCAT list is of the form (iii):

(iii)   ⟨NP[INHER | SLASH {[1]}], AP[INHER | SLASH { }]⟩

Thus the gap in the AP is already bound, and therefore (on our account) should not be able to license the subject-internal gap. A possible solution to this problem might be to restrict the applicability of the Subject Condition to *role-assigned* subjects. This change has no effect on our analysis of (91), inasmuch as we assume that the subject of *easy* is itself role-assigned (see footnote 8).

the claim that SLASH is a head feature. As we have seen, there are a variety of problems facing the attempt to explain the behavior of parasitic gaps in terms of Kuno's Incomplete Constituent Constraint, and these appear to be adequately accounted for by the Subject Condition.[36] The trace theory we have been led to by these considerations is summarized in (94):

(94)   Summary of HPSG trace theory (final version):

       a. Nonlocal Feature Principle: For each nonlocal feature, the INHER-
          ITED value on the mother is the union of the INHERITED values on
          the daughters minus the TO-BIND value on the head daughter.
       b. Trace Principle (English): Every trace must be strictly subcatego-
          rized by a substantive head.
       c. Subject Condition (English): A lexical head's SUBCAT list may
          contain a slashed subject only if it also contains another slashed
          element.

In Chapter 9, we will return to these matters and consider a revision of this analysis wherein traces, and hence the Trace Principle, are eliminated entirely, their effect being derived from lexical rule application.

4.6 More on Island Constraints

4.6.1 Constraints on Coordinate Structure Extraction

In order to explain the deviance of examples like (95)–(96), Ross proposed that transformations were subject to the Coordinate Structure Constraint (Ross 1967: (4.84)) stated in (97):

(95)   *a.* *Here is the student that [the principal suspended [__ and
          Sandy]].
       b. *Here is the student that [the principal suspended [Sandy and
          —]].

(96)   *a.* *Here is the student that [the principal suspended __ and Sandy
          defended him].
       b. *Here is the student that [the student council passed new rules
          and the principal suspended __].

36. We should note that we have made no attempt here to incorporate the suggestion (Chomsky 1982; Cinque 1990) that all parasitic gaps are pronominal in nature. To do so would require substantial modification of the Nonlocal Feature Principle. A modification along these lines (e.g. replacing the set union condition by a condition allowing daughters to bear distinct but coindexed INHER | SLASH values if one is pronominal), though intriguing, is beyond the scope of the present study. We thank Paul Postal for discussion of this point.

(97)   COORDINATE STRUCTURE CONSTRAINT

In a coordinate structure,

(a) no conjunct may be moved,

(b) nor may any element contained in a conjunct be moved out of that conjunct.

Following Grosu (1973), we may refer to (97a, b) as the *Conjunct Constraint* and the *Element Constraint*, respectively.

Although Ross stipulated (97) as a constraint on variables in transformational rules, subsequent proposals have attempted to derive these generalizations from other principles, as is desirable. The analysis presented above in fact already entails the Conjunct Constraint. Under virtually any assumptions about the nature of coordinate structures, it is the mother of the coordinate structure that is (strictly) subcategorized in examples like (95), not the individual conjuncts.[37] Since a conjunct is never subcategorized for in our theory, it can never be realized as a trace—because of the Trace Principle.

The Element Constraint is another matter altogether. Its factual correctness has been challenged by Goldsmith (1985) and Lakoff (1986), who cite examples like (98) as fully acceptable:

(98)   *a.* How many lakes can we [destroy ___ and not arouse public antipathy]?

      b. How many kinds of tequila has he [snuck off to Mexico, sampled ___, and come back the same day without telling anyone]?

      c. Concerts that short, you can leave work early, hear the entirety of ___, and still be back at the job before anyone notices you are gone.

Goldsmith's discussion of examples like (98a) suggests that these exceptions to the Element Constraint might be explained in terms of a semantically coherent class of subordinate modifiers that have only the appearance of coordinate structures. Lakoff, on the other hand, goes so far as to suggest that Element Constraint effects are to be explained entirely on semantic and pragmatic grounds, rather than in terms of a grammatical constraint. The theory of UDCs we have outlined here is perfectly consistent with such an approach.

But suppose, for the sake of argument, that Lakoff is incorrect in denying the correctness of the Element Constraint. How could the Element Constraint be incorporated into our theory of UDCs?

As we have already seen (section 4.5), our HPSG treatment of coordinate structures differs from the GKPS analysis in at least two fundamental respects: (1) coordinate structures (in English) are *unheaded* (cf. P&S-87, p. 56); (2) SLASH is not treated as a HEAD feature. The identities that must hold among

37. Goodall (1987) attempts to reduce the Conjunct Constraint to Principle C of the binding theory. But this is both too weak and insufficiently general.

conjuncts thus do not follow from the HFP or from any principle of trace theory (summarized in (94) at the end of the previous section), nor do they follow from any other principles external to coordination theory. Aside from the Conjunct Constraint, which, as we have seen, is derived from the Trace Principle, it is left to the theory of coordination to derive whatever further constraints affect coordinate structures.

The consequence of adopting the principle in (99) would be a strong version of coordination theory: [38]

(99)   COORDINATION PRINCIPLE (strong version):

In a coordinate structure, the CATEGORY and NONLOCAL value of each conjunct daughter is identical to that of the mother.

The theory embodied in (99) is strong in that it forces complete categorial identity between the coordinate mother and each conjunct daughter, thereby leaving it to the theory of ellipsis (which might allow *is* or *Kim is* to be omitted from the left periphery of noninitial conjuncts) to provide an account of examples of unlike category coordination like (100):

(100)   Kim is a Republican and proud of it.

The strong version of the Coordination Principle makes a number of correct predictions, including obligatory agreement of CASE in coordinate nominals, but not obligatory agreement of person, number, and gender. These predictions follow because CASE is treated as a HEAD feature (and hence is part of the CATEGORY value that must be shared by all conjuncts), while person, number, and gender are treated as features of indices (Chapter 2), and hence are not constrained by (99).

In addition, (99) derives the Element Constraint, as it entails that the IN-HER | SLASH value of each conjunct is identical to that of the coordinate mother. In fact, (99) also has the effect that the INHER|REL and INHER|QUE values of each conjunct must be identical to those of the mother, thus predicting contrasts like the following:

(101)   *a.*   Here's the student$_i$ [[whose$_i$ mother and whose$_i$ father] both attended the soccer match].

        b.   *Here's the student$_i$ [[Hilary and whose$_i$ father] both attended the soccer match].

(102)   *a.*   I know [[whose mother and whose father] got married in the Poconos].

        b.   *I know [[whose mother and his father] got married in the Poconos].

---

38. The similarity between this principle and the *Conjunct Realization Principle* of Gazdar and Pullum 1982 should be noted.

The theory of coordination just outlined seems too strong, however, inasmuch as it disallows examples like (103):

(103)   *a.* Francis arrived late today but will be on time tomorrow.
         b. Leslie likes that picture and is trying to buy it.

Here the two conjoined VPs have differing values for the feature AUX, and hence are incorrectly predicted to be ungrammatical.

One approach to this problem would be to accept the central claim of the coordination analysis in Sag et al. 1985, namely that coordinate structures may involve 'archicategories,' or partially specified feature structures. If such partial structures are allowed,[39] then we may revise the Coordination Principle as follows:

(104)   COORDINATION PRINCIPLE (weak version):

         In a coordinate structure, the CATEGORY and NONLOCAL value of each conjunct daughter is subsumed by (is an extension of) that of the mother.

This weak version of the Coordination Principle avoids the dilemma of coordinated auxiliary and nonauxiliary VPs by allowing the coordinate mother to be unspecified for AUX in structures like (105):

(105)

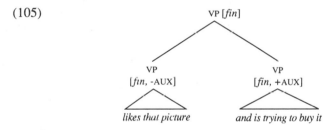

And structures like this are able to appear in any environment where no condition is imposed on the AUX value of the VP. The formulation in (104) also

---

39. The use of partially specified feature structures (or, to put it more technically, feature structures that are merely well-typed, but not necessarily resolved or even totally well-typed) to model linguistic objects raises issues of a foundational nature that we cannot address here. Thus far, we have assumed that all linguistic entities are total objects, in the sense that each feature appropriate for a given entity has a value specified; partial feature structures have arisen only as partial models (or incomplete descriptions) of such entities. The kind of coordination analysis under consideration here requires a fundamental philosophical shift, inasmuch as it becomes necessary to countenance linguistic entities (namely, the mothers in coordinate structures) that are inherently partial; at the same time, presumably, we would want to continue to require that 'normal' linguistic entities be total objects. We do not pretend to have laid the necessary foundations for such an analysis.

allows a straightforward account (without appeal to ellipsis) of examples like *Kim is a Republican and proud of it.*

The principle in (104), though weaker than (99), is stronger than it might appear. It guarantees that whenever a syntactic environment imposes some condition on a phrase in a given position X, that condition is respected by every conjunct of a coordinate structure in position X. For example, as we saw in Chapter 3, the SUBCAT specification of a raising verb like *believe* contains a post-object complement (X in (106)) that is an infinitival VP whose SUBCAT element is required (by the Raising Principle) to be structure-shared with the SYNSEM value of the object NP:

(106)

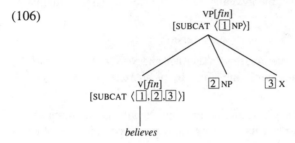

In consequence of (104), if X is realized as a coordinate structure, whatever is required to be true of X (in consequence of the SUBCAT list of *believe* and the Subcategorization Principle) must also be true of each conjunct, as shown in (107):

(107)

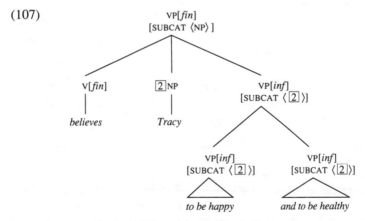

Thus the examples in (108) are correctly ruled out:

(108)   *a.* *Jessie believes Tracy [to be happy and walks].
         b. *Jessie believes Tracy [happy and to be healthy].
         c. *Jessie believes Tracy [am walking to the store and that I left].

In much the same way, this weak version of the Coordination Principle still entails the Element Constraint. The HFP and the information specified in Schema 6 together require that in structures like (109), the head daughter must be a finite S that is further specified as INHER|SLASH {[1]}:

(109)

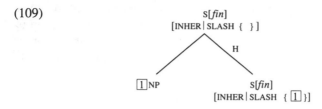

The Coordination Principle in turn guarantees that each conjunct of a coordinate head of (109) also be so specified, as illustrated in (110):

(110)

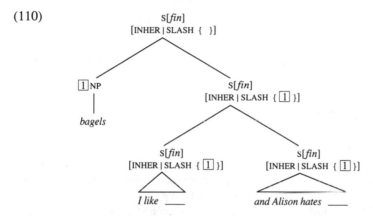

This rules out all Element Constraint violations, as desired, including those involving the features REL and QUE.

In this section, we have explored the consequences of various formulations of coordination theory relevant to the analysis of constraints on coordinate structure extraction. While the exact set of facts to be accounted for remains somewhat unclear (because of the uncertain status of the Element Constraint), we have shown how our analysis can be adapted to derive the Element Constraint or not, all the while deriving the Conjunct Constraint from the Trace Principle, which is independently motivated, as we have seen.

4.6.2 Some Complex Noun Phrases

The fact that filler-gap dependencies cannot penetrate into relative clauses has long been known. To account for this fact, illustrated by the ungrammatical examples in (111), Ross (1967) stipulated that (a certain class of) transformations were subject to his *Complex NP Constraint* (CNPC), which barred movement out of a clause adjoined to a nominal constituent:

(111)   *a.* *Which book do you know [the person [who wrote ___]]?

        b. *Which book do you know [the person [who Allison talked to
             ___ about ___]]?

Ross's theory, like many subsequent theories that attempt to derive the CNPC as a theorem, predicts that factitive (*fact that*) clauses are also extraction islands. However, once one looks past the definiteness factors that are at work in examples like (112), it is not clear that there should be any grammatical constraint barring extraction from a factitive complement:

(112)   *a.* ?*Here is the book that Leslie denied [the claim [that Kris had
             written ___]].

        b. ?*Which book did Dana make [the suggestion [that we should
             read ___]]?

In particular, examples like (113), which are ruled out in some theories of UDCs, including Ross's, seem to be impeccable:[40]

(113)   *a.* Which rebel leader$_i$ would you favor [a proposal [that the CIA
             assassinate ___$_i$]]?

        b. Which Middle East country$_i$ did you hear [rumors [that we had
             infiltrated ___$_i$]]?

If nothing further is said, our analysis of filler-gap dependencies predicts that factitive clauses allow extraction dependencies of this sort. We assume that such clauses are optionally subcategorized for by nouns like *fact, claim,* and *rumor,* with which they form an N' constituent. Assuming this complement analysis is correct, then there is no grammatical principle that prevents the inheritance of nonempty INHER | SLASH values sketched in (114):

(114)

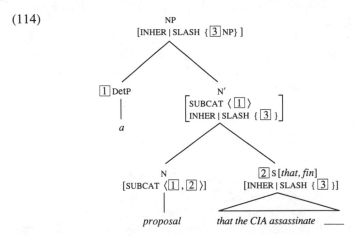

40. This fact is noted by Maling and Zaenen (1982). See also Chung and McCloskey (1983: 706) and Chomsky's (1986b) treatment in terms of L-marking.

As just noted, this appears to be the right prediction, modulo nongrammatical factors such as definiteness.

The remaining data that are usually discussed under the rubric of the Complex NP Constraint concern the impossibility of extracting out of (certain kinds of) relative clauses. We will take up that matter in section 5.2.4, where we present in detail our analysis of relative clauses in a variety of languages.

4.7 Conclusion

In this chapter, we have developed a theory of unbounded dependencies in English that provides the basis for an account of topicalization constructions, extraction in relative and interrogative clauses, and *tough*-constructions. The theory in turn provides an account of constraints on the distribution of traces, so-called *that*-trace facts, and the behavior of parasitic gaps. The essence of our account is the interaction of two principles of universal grammar (the Nonlocal Feature Principle and the Trace Principle) and a language-particular constraint on SUBCAT lists (the Subject Condition).

As we have seen, these principles incorporate important insights from diverse frameworks, including GKPS's Foot Feature Principle and other GPSG proposals due to Jacobson, Farkas et al., Sells, Fodor, and Hukari and Levine, as well as other principles proposed within GB, most notably Chomsky's ECP. Although we have incorporated insights such as these, we have also indicated why we believe our analysis to be both empirically more adequate and conceptually simpler than previous attempts. Yet the integrative approach we have taken in this domain illustrates well the synthetic methodology that we believe is most productive in modern syntactic research.

5

Relative Clauses

5.1 Introduction

Having outlined the basic principles underlying the analysis of unbounded dependency constructions, we are now in a position to consider the grammar of relativization. In this chapter, we consider three types of relative clause that appear in the world's languages: head-modifying relative clauses of the sort found in English, relative-correlative constructions like those in languages of the Indian subcontinent, and internally headed relative clauses found in languages such as Dogon, Quechua, and Navajo.

5.2 English Relative Clauses

5.2.1 Relative Inheritance

Pretheoretically, in English there are two types of relative clauses: *wh*-relatives and non-*wh*-relatives. The former type may be further divided into subject *wh*-relatives and nonsubject *wh*-relatives; the latter type includes *that*-relatives and (finite) *that*-less relatives (as well as infinitival relatives, which we will ignore here). These types are illustrated in (1):

(1)   *a.* the person who I talked to ___.   (nonsubject *wh*-relative)
        b. the person who left.   (subject *wh*-relative)
        c. the person that I talked to ___.   (*that* relative)
        d. the person that left.   (*that* relative)
        e. the person I talked to ___.   (*that*-less relative)

In this section, we will present an analysis of both these relative clause types.

Let us consider *wh*-relatives first. These appear to consist of a *wh*-phrase followed by either an S[INHER|SLASH {NP}] or a finite VP. That is, they appear to be instances of two universal schemata we have already made use of: Schema 6 (the Head-Filler Schema) and Schema 1, as sketched in (2) and (3), respectively:

(2)

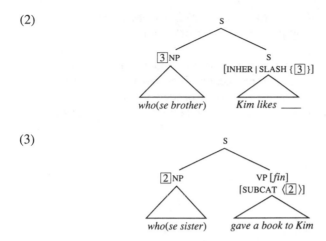

(3)

Indeed, the central tenet of the GPSG analysis of *wh*-relatives developed by Gazdar et al. (1984, 1985) is that such clauses are instances of these basic sentence patterns, rather than otherwise unmotivated structures like (4)–(5), where dislocated phrases occur inside a lexical category (COMP), as was commonly assumed in transformational studies prior to Chomsky 1986b:

(4)

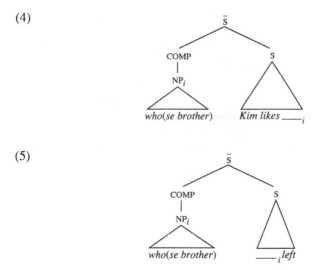

(5)

Let us explore first how the GPSG analysis might be recast within the present framework. The initial constituent in each of the structures in (1)–(3) must be a *wh*-phrase, and it is such in virtue of the fact that it contains a relative *wh*-word. Thus a relative word like *whom* makes a superordinate phrase relative in much the same way that an NP trace makes a phrase [INHER | SLASH {NP}].

This treatment of *wh*-dependencies in relative clauses, as noted in section 4.2, is in fact quite similar to the treatment of filler-gap dependencies outlined in the previous sections: the *wh*-relative dependency consists of a bottom, middle, and top. Relative words serve as the bottom of a *wh*-relative dependency—they introduce a non-null INHER | REL value that will be inherited. The lexical entry of a *wh*-word is illustrated in (6):

(6)   Relative pronoun *whom* as it appears in the lexicon:

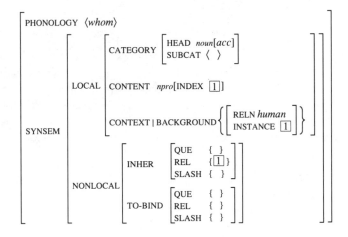

Note that the *wh*-word's index is structure-shared with the INHER | REL value.

Because such lexical entries have nonempty specifications for the path NON-LOCAL | INHER | REL, they give rise to structures like (7)–(the middles of relative dependencies) in virtue of the NONLOCAL Feature Principle (Chapter 4, (16)):

(7)

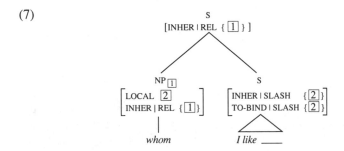

(8)

(9)

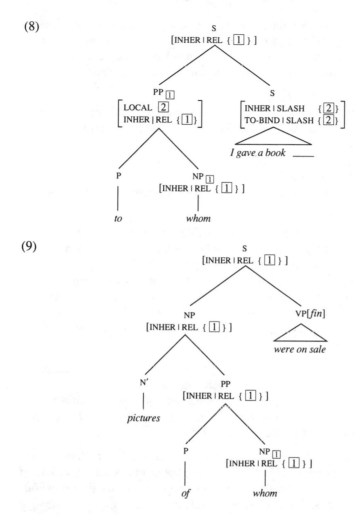

Although the value of REL is a set of indices, we may assume that English obeys the parochial constraint in (10):

(10)   SINGLETON REL CONSTRAINT:

The cardinality of the value of INHER | REL is at most 1.

Thus English differs from languages like Marathi, where adjoined relative clauses may contain multiple relative words (see section 5.3), or from languages like Lakhota, where multiple relative dependencies are manifested in internally headed relative clause structures (see section 5.4).

In relative clauses like (8) and (9) we see that two unbounded dependencies are simultaneously present: the relative dependency (ultimately a dependency between the relative word and the head noun with which it shares an index) encoded by the attribute REL, and the filler-gap dependency encoded by the attribute SLASH. Like the SLASH dependencies discussed earlier, REL dependencies are unbounded:

(11)   *a.* Here's the rabbi [[[whose brother's] Bar Mitzvah] we attended].
        b. Here's the rabbi [[[[whose brother's] son's] Bar Mitzvah] we attended].
        c. Here's the rabbi [[[[[whose brother's] son's] friend's] Bar Mitzvah] we attended].
        d. Here's the minister [[in [the middle [of [whose sermon]]]] the dog barked].

The NONLOCAL Feature Principle thus provides the basis for a unified treatment of filler-gap dependencies and the '*wh*-percolation' phenomenon customarily referred to (following Ross (1967)) as 'pied piping.'

Although the inheritance of SLASH and REL specifications is effected by a single mechanism in this theory, the fact remains that the latter is more constrained than the former. In particular, the phenomenon of 'parasitic' relatives in English (the analogs of parasitic gaps) is much less robust, as noted by Kayne (1983: 238) and Sells (1985):

(12)   *a.* ?John Smith, whose wife's feelings about whom have changed but little over the years, . . . (Kayne 1983: 239)
        b. the same Monseigneur, the preparation of whose chocolate for whose lips had once occupied three strong men, . . . (Jespersen 1965: 3:203; cited by Sells 1985)

If nothing further is added to our account of English relative clauses, such sentences will be permitted.[1] However, if we choose to describe a variety of English that systematically avoids such multiple relative words, then some further constraint must be assumed. One formulation of such a constraint might be the following Relative Uniqueness Principle:

(13)   RELATIVE UNIQUENESS PRINCIPLE:

        A member of the INHERITED | REL set on a headed constituent may be inherited from (i.e. may belong to the INHERITED | REL set of) at most one daughter.

1. And Kayne's observation that (i) is ungrammatical can be explained in terms of a Principle C violation in the binding theory of Chapter 6:

(i)   *John Smith, whose feelings about whom have changed but little over the years. . . .

This principle is sufficient to rule out all examples like those in (12) for varieties of modern English that exclude them.

Our analysis of *wh*-relative clauses is now lacking only an account of the tops of unbounded REL dependency structures. We assume that relative clauses, as nominal modifiers, will occur in structures like the following:

(14)

Like the modifiers discussed in Chapters 1 and 2, relative clauses bear a nonempty value for the attribute MOD. And this specification must serve to guarantee that all of the following are true of structures like (14): (1) the index of the daughter N' is identified with the REL value of the relative clause, (2) the INHER|REL value on the mother N' is empty (i.e. the REL dependency is terminated), and (3) the restriction set of the mother's content includes the content of the relative clause.

Perhaps the simplest way of achieving all these goals is to posit a phonetically null 'complementizer' that will serve as the head of the relative clause. We shall assign these elements to a part of speech we will call *relativizer* (*rltvzr*), which the reader should be careful to distinguish from the sort *comp*, which is used to classify certain markers. Relativizers, and other null clause projectors (if such exist), have nonempty SUBCAT lists and are specified for the attribute MOD (rather than SPEC), as shown in the lexical entry in (15):

(15)   SYNSEM value for null relativizer (preliminary version):

$$
\begin{bmatrix}
\text{LOCAL} \begin{bmatrix} \text{CAT} \begin{bmatrix} \text{HEAD}_{rltvzr} \left[\text{MOD N}' : \begin{bmatrix} \text{INDEX} & \boxed{1} \\ \text{RESTR} & \boxed{3} \end{bmatrix} \right] \\ \text{SUBCAT} \; \langle S[\textit{fin}, \text{INHER} \mid \text{REL} \; \{\boxed{1}\}] : \boxed{2} \rangle \end{bmatrix} \\ \text{CONTENT}_{npro} \begin{bmatrix} \text{INDEX} & \boxed{1} \\ \text{RESTR} & \{\boxed{2}\} \; \cup \; \boxed{3} \end{bmatrix} \end{bmatrix} \\ \text{NONLOCAL} \mid \text{TO-BIND} \mid \text{REL} \; \{\boxed{1}\}
\end{bmatrix}
$$

The similarity of this structure to that used for semantically restrictive attributive adjectives (Chapter 1, (58)) is noteworthy. The null relativizer (15) will give rise to N' structures with *wh*-relative clause modifiers like the one illustrated in (16). (Here and throughout we use RP (and, below, also R') for the phrases projected from relativizers.)

(16)

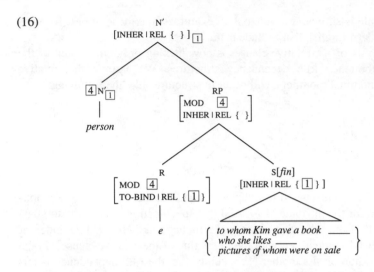

In a head-adjunct structure like this, as described in Chapter 1, section 1.9, the MOD value of the relative clause must be structure-shared with the head daughter's SYNSEM value. Because of the lexical information specified in (15), the index of the N′ head is identical to the TO-BIND | REL value of the relativizer and the INHER | REL value of the relativizer's S complement, which in turn is the index associated with the relative word within that complement. This is all in accordance with the Nonlocal Feature Principle. In addition, the CONTENT value and identities specified in (15) interact with the Semantics Principle to ensure that the CONTENT of an N′ like *person who she likes* is as shown in (17). (Here $\boxed{2}$ indicates the index associated with *she*.)

(17)

$$
\begin{bmatrix}
\text{INDEX} & \boxed{1} \\
\text{RESTR} & \left\{ \begin{bmatrix} \text{RELN } person \\ \text{INSTANCE } \boxed{1} \end{bmatrix}, \begin{bmatrix} \text{RELN } like \\ \text{LIKER } \boxed{2} \\ \text{LIKED } \boxed{1} \end{bmatrix} \right\}
\end{bmatrix}
$$

5.2.2 'CP-IP' Structures

But there is reason to question this approach to *wh*-relatives. Consider the problem illustrated by data such as (18):

(18)   *a.* *Here's the student [Kim likes whom].
       b. *Here's the student [bagels, Sandy gave to whom].
       c. *Here's the student [Dana met whose sister].

If clauses bearing nonempty values for INHER | REL are to be allowed in the grammar of English, then why are examples like these, whose structure is illustrated in (19) and (20), ill-formed?

(19)

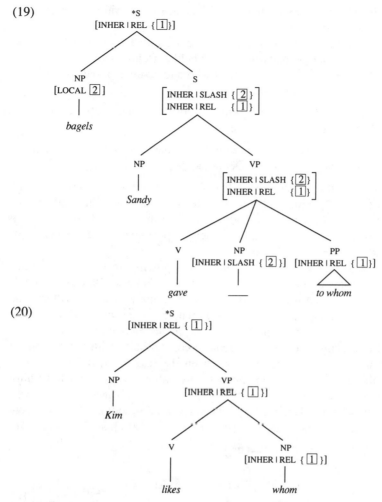

(20)

In order to prevent relative clauses like these, one would need to introduce some further constraint on the inheritance of REL values. Such a constraint is rather difficult to state in a natural way; it would have to be something like (21):

(21)   No member of the INHERITED | REL set on a headed constituent may be inherited from (i.e. belong to the INHERITED | REL set of) a daughter that is the head of S.

But (21) fails to apply to all the cases where REL inheritance (pied piping) is blocked, for example the cases in (22), all of which involve REL inheritance through an S node:

(22)   a.   *Here is the student [[to claim who was unpopular] would be ridiculous].

    b. *Here is the student [[that Lee claimed who was crazy] nobody
       could believe ___].
    c. *The elegant parties, [for us to be admitted to one of which] was
       a privilege, had usually been held at Delmonico's.
    d. *Here are the students [[for whom to be invited to the party]
       would bother Dana].

Note further that (22c) contrasts with the following acceptable example, as
noted by Nanni and Stillings (1978):[2]

(23)   The elegant parties, [to be admitted to one of which] was a privilege,
       had usually been held at Delmonico's.

What contrasts like this suggest is that finite or nonfinite clauses in English
(as opposed to VPs) require the value of INHER | REL to be the null set. But
this generalization seems impossible to express in the GPSG-style analysis
just sketched, because that analysis crucially posits Ss that have nonempty
INHER | REL values, as in (16) above.

    However, as noted by Borsley (1989), it is possible to incorporate within
HPSG certain key insights of the 'CP-IP' analysis (Chomsky 1986b) commonly
assumed within much work in GB. This style of analysis, as we will see, has
the virtue that it allows an account of *wh*-relative clauses that avoids introduc-
ing sentences bearing nonempty INHER | REL values. Here we modify Borsley's
proposal in certain minor ways to achieve compatibility with the analysis of
adjuncts developed in Chapter 1, based on the feature MOD. We begin by
revising the lexical entry for the phonetically null relativizer, which we illus-
trated in (15) above. Instead of subcategorizing for an S[INHER | REL {XP}]
complement, the new lexical entry subcategorizes for both an XP with a non-
empty INHER | REL value and an S[INHER | SLASH {XP}], as shown in (24):[3]

(24)   SYNSEM value for null relativizer (revised):

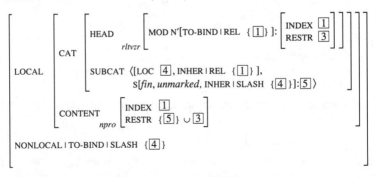

2. The Nanni-Stillings analysis, as they themselves note (1978: 217, n. 4), fails to
extend to account for the deviance of (70d).

3. As this volume went to press, it came to our attention that this lexical entry violates the Raising Principle as stated in Chapter 3, (117), for the first complement is not

On this double-complement analysis, the relativizer combines first with an S[INHER | SLASH {XP}] by Schema 2 and then with an appropriate phrase containing a relative constituent by Schema 1, to form a saturated relative clause (RP), as illustrated in (25):

(25)

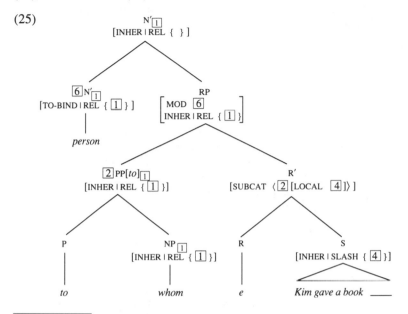

assigned a semantic role in the relativizer's CONTENT value, nor does the other complement bear a nonempty SUBCAT list whose member is identified with the first complement. We believe the solution to this problem lies in the direction of replacing the Raising Principle with a more general principle to the effect that, for each lexical entry and for each *synsem* object on the SUBCAT list of that entry that is not specified to be expletive, some provision be made for that *synsem* object to make a contribution to the CONTENT value of the lexical entry. Of course the usual provision is simply to assign the INDEX value of the *synsem* object to one of the features (semantic roles) of the psoa that forms the CONTENT value of the lexical entry in question. Failing that, another option for satisfying the principle would be to identify the *synsem* object with the SUB-CAT value of some other element of the SUBCAT list, thereby in effect passing the responsibility for making sure the principle gets satisfied to the head of the other SUBCAT element; it is this option that we have called 'raising.' The problematic entry (24) appears to present a third option for satisfying the principle: to identify (the LOCAL value of) the *synsem* object with the SLASH value of another element of the SUBCAT list. (The forms of *be* that give rise to the *it*-cleft construction may be another instance of this option.) This third option, like the second, will also result in the CONTENT value of the *synsem* object in question figuring into the content of the head that subcategorizes for that object. We leave open here the precise formulation of this more general principle, but note in passing its resemblance to the principle called 'full interpretation' in current GB theory.

The relativizer in (24) binds off the SLASH dependency of its S complement at the node labelled R′. The INHER | REL value of the PP complement, however, is inherited by the RP as a whole, and is bound off at the highest level of structure in (25), in accordance with the conditions imposed on the N′ by the RP, which, because MOD is an attribute of HEAD, are exactly those inherited from the RP's empty head. The resulting CONTENT for (25) is (26):

$$
(26) \quad \mathit{npro} \begin{bmatrix} \text{INDEX} & \boxed{1} \\ \\ \text{RESTRICTION} & \left\{ \begin{bmatrix} \text{RELN } \mathit{person} \\ \text{INST } \boxed{1} \end{bmatrix}, \begin{bmatrix} \text{RELN } \mathit{give} \\ \text{GIVER} \boxed{5} \\ \text{GIFT } \boxed{3} \\ \text{GIVEE} \boxed{1} \end{bmatrix} \right\} \end{bmatrix}
$$

Note that since the revised null relativizer requires a subject whose INHER | REL value is nonempty, it follows that examples like (19) and (20) are correctly avoided, as neither *bagels* in (19) nor *Kim* in (20) (the NPs that would have functioned as subject of the relativizer) contains a relative word. Likewise the examples in (27) are blocked because they violate the Relative Uniqueness Principle stated above:

(27)   *a.* *Here's the student [whose friends like whom].
       b. *Here's the student [whose bagels Sandy gave to whom].
       c. *Here's the student [whose sister met whose husband in Omaha].

Since the relativizer in (24) takes two complements (unlike the null relativizer in the GPSG-style analysis considered in the previous section), it may undergo the Subject Extraction Lexical Rule. The result is shown in (28):

(28)   SYNSEM value for null relativizer (SELR output):

$$
\begin{bmatrix} \text{LOCAL} \begin{bmatrix} \text{CAT} \begin{bmatrix} \text{HEAD} \begin{bmatrix} \text{MOD } \text{N}'[\text{TO-BIND I REL } \{\boxed{1}\}] : \begin{bmatrix} \text{INDEX } \boxed{1} \\ \text{RESTR } \boxed{3} \end{bmatrix} \end{bmatrix}_{\mathit{rltvzr}} \\ \text{SUBCAT } \langle \boxed{7}\text{NP}[\text{INHER I REL } \{\boxed{1}\}], \\ \qquad \text{VP}[\mathit{fin}, \text{SUBCAT } \langle \boxed{7} [\text{LOC } \boxed{4}] \rangle] : \boxed{5} \rangle \end{bmatrix} \\ \text{CONTENT} \begin{bmatrix} \text{INDEX } \boxed{1} \\ \text{RESTR } \{\boxed{5}\} \cup \boxed{3} \end{bmatrix} \end{bmatrix} \\ \text{NONLOCAL} \begin{bmatrix} \text{TO-BIND I SLASH } \{\boxed{4}\} \\ \text{INHER I SLASH } \{\boxed{4}\} \end{bmatrix} \end{bmatrix}
$$

Several properties of this lexical entry are noteworthy. First, the CONTENT of the VP is correctly incorporated into the RESTRICTION set of the *npro* that serves as the CONTENT value of the RP and the N′ that it builds. Second, the SUBCAT value of the relativizer's VP complement is identified with the relativizer's first SUBCAT member. This is a consequence of the Raising Principle (Chapter 3, section 5) and the fact that the relativizer's subject is not assigned any semantic role in (28). Third, in virtue of this identity, the SLASH value bound off by the relativizer at the R' level is the LOCAL value of the subject NP.[4] Fourth, in consequence of this last fact, it follows that in examples like (29) the INHER | REL value bound off by the N' that combines with the relative clause is the index of the subject NP, which in turn is the index that the VP assigns its subject role:

(29)

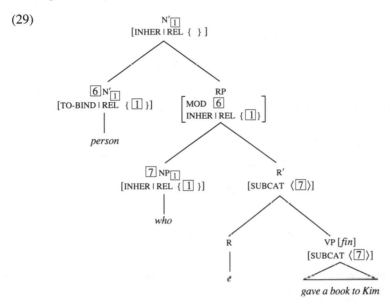

The CONTENT of this N' is the *npro* object shown in (30):

(30)

$$\begin{bmatrix} \text{INDEX} & \boxed{1} \\ & \\ \text{RESTRICTION} & \left\{ \begin{bmatrix} \text{RELN } \textit{person} \\ \text{INSTANCE } \boxed{1} \end{bmatrix}, \begin{bmatrix} \text{RELN } \textit{give} \\ \text{GIVER } \boxed{1} \\ \text{GIVEN } \boxed{4} \\ \text{GIVEE } \boxed{5} \end{bmatrix} \right\} \end{bmatrix}_{npro}$$

4. To see this, consider the following facts: (1) the SELR input specifies structure sharing between the TO-BIND | SLASH value and the first complement's LOCAL value; (2) SELR specifies structure sharing between the output's INHER | SLASH value and the LOCAL value of its VP complement's SUBCAT value; and (3) the Raising Principle requires that there be structure sharing between the LOCAL value of the VP complement's SUBCAT value and the LOCAL value of the first complement. (In identifying *synsem* objects, the Raising Principle of course identifies the LOCAL values within these *synsem* objects.) Hence it follows from the transitivity of equality that all four structures are identical (structure-shared).

This analysis of *wh*-relatives, based on the projection of a relative phrase from a null lexical head (as in GB), thus interacts with other aspects of our treatment of English in highly desirable ways. The double complement-taking null relativizer undergoes the Subject Extraction Lexical Rule and, in so doing, acquires the further SUBCAT specification necessary to complete the analysis of finite *wh*-relatives. That analysis in turn allows us to state the following language-particular constraint (recall that this constraint was inconsistent with the GPSG-style analysis sketched above):

(31)   CLAUSAL REL PROHIBITION:

    The INHER | REL value of S must be empty.

As we shall see, the presence or absence of this constraint is a parameter of variation that is independent of various others that we will consider in the sections that follow.

5.2.3 Non-*Wh*-Relative Clauses

It is usual to classify all the following as non-*wh*-relative clauses:

(32)   *a.* Here's the student [that I was telling you about ___].
        b. Here's the student [I was telling you about ___].
        c. Here's the student [that was telling you about cell structure].

Our somewhat unorthodox view of these data is that only (32a, b) are true non-*wh*-relatives. Examples like (32c) are handled perfectly in our view by assuming that Modern English has a *wh*-relative word *that*, whose CASE value is *nominative*. The lexical entry for this relative *that* is sketched in (33):

(33)   Relative *that* as it appears in the lexicon:

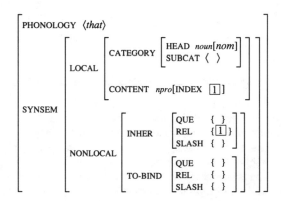

Under this proposal, which owes a certain debt to that of Gazdar (1981) (who, however, assumes that *all* occurrences of *that* in relative clauses are nominals, rather than markers), the lexical entry in (33) is compatible with the null relativizer sketched in (28) (the SELR output), and hence can appear in structures like (34):

(34)

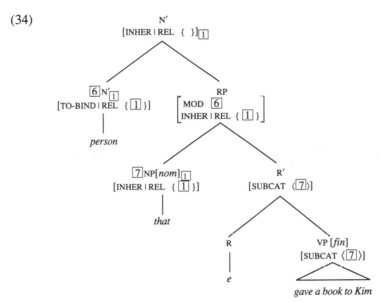

Note that since (33) contains the specification [CASE *nom*], it follows without anything further being said that relative *that* can appear neither as the object of a verb or preposition nor as a possessor, and hence can never give rise to un-wanted pied piping of the sort shown in (35):

(35)   *a.* *Here's the student [[to that] I was talking].
        b. *The elegant parties, [to attend that] was a privilege, had usually
             been held at Delmonico's.
        c. *Here's the student [[that's bagels] Sandy gave to Kim].
        d. *Hand me the reports [[the height of the lettering on the covers of
             that] the government prescribed].

As for the types of relative clauses illustrated in (32a, b), these can both be treated by positing a second null relativizer, shown in (36); this should be com-pared with the *wh*-null relativizer given in (24):[5]

5. As it stands, this lexical entry violates the Subject Condition (Chapter 4, (84)). A solution to this problem will be given in Chapter 9.

(36)   SYNSEM value for second null relativizer:

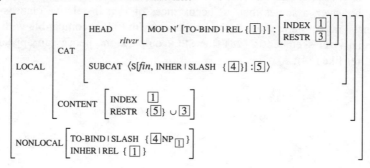

The subcategorized complement in (36) is required to be finite, but its value for the attribute MARKING is left unspecified. Hence these complement clauses may have two possible values for MARKING: *unmarked* and *that*. We thus allow for both kinds of relative clause shown in (37):

(37)

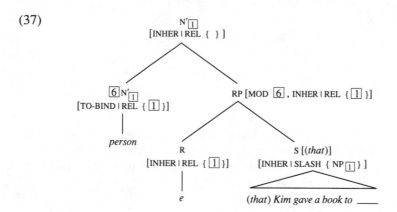

But because the Subject Extraction Lexical Rule applies only to lexical forms whose S[*fin*] complement is not the first member of the SUBCAT list, it follows that examples like (38), often ruled out only by appeal to imprecisely formulated processing strategies, are immediately predicted to be ungrammatical:[6]

(38)   *a.* *Here is the [book [pleased Sandy]].
        b. *I met a [lawyer [helped me a lot]].

6. Examples like (38b) are acceptable in some varieties of English, a fact we return to briefly in section 2.3 of Chapter 9.

5.2.4 Relative Clauses and the Complex NP Constraint

In Chapter 4 (section 4.6.2) we noted that extractions from adnominal factitive clauses are in principle grammatical (modulo considerations of definiteness and other nonstructural factors), though they were regarded by Ross (1967) (and much subsequent literature) as ungrammatical on structural grounds, that is, as violations of the CNPC:

(39) *a.* ?*Here is the book that Leslie denied [the claim [that Kris had written __]].

  b. Which Middle East country$_i$ did you hear [rumors [that we had infiltrated __$_i$]]?

The part of the CNPC involving extraction out of relative clauses, on the other hand, for example, the deviance of examples like those in (40), seems in need of grammatical explanation:

(40) *a.* *Which student$_i$ did you find [a book$_j$ [which$_j$ [Pat gave __$_j$ to __$_i$]]?

  b. *Which proposal$_i$ did you find [students$_j$ [who$_j$ [they had talked to __$_j$ about __$_i$]]?

  c. *Which student$_i$ did you find [a book$_j$ [(that) Pat gave __$_j$ to __$_i$]]?

   Notice that the basic lexical entries for the null relativizers formulated in the previous sections immediately entail the ungrammaticality of the examples in (40), for these elements subcategorize for an S complement whose INHER | SLASH value contains exactly one member (i.e. they take complements whose INHER | SLASH value is specified as {$\boxed{4}$}, rather than {$\boxed{4}$, . . . }). For instance, the first null relativizer, whose lexical entry ((24) above) contains the SUBCAT list in (41a), can never give rise to the doubly slashed S illustrated in (41b):

(41)   a.   SUBCAT ⟨ [LOC $\boxed{4}$, INHER I REL {$\boxed{1}$}] , S[*fin*, INHER I SLASH {$\boxed{4}$}] ⟩

b.

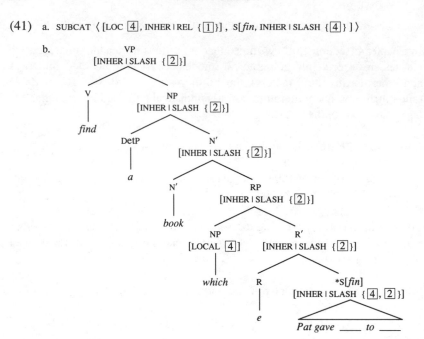

And the same is true for the basic lexical entry for the second null relativizer
((36) above). The SUBCAT list in (42a) contains a complement whose INHER |
SLASH value is singleton, and hence can never give rise to a structure like (42b).

(42)   a.   SUBCAT ⟨S[*fin*, INHER I SLASH {$\boxed{4}$}]⟩

b.

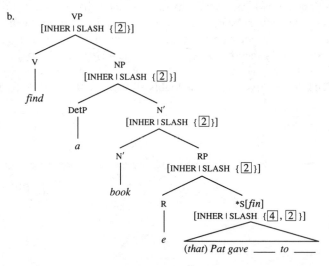

Although we have written the relevant lexical entries so as to stipulate the single-
ton INHER | SLASH value of the sentential complement, perhaps the single-

ton nature of this set should be made to follow from a more general principle, as discussed at the end of section 3 of Chapter 4.

Consider now the following examples, pointed out by Chung and McCloskey (1983: 708):

(43)   a. That's one trick that I've known a lot of people who've been taken in by ___.
         b. This is a paper that we really need to find someone who understands ___.
         c. This is the one that Bob Wall was the only person who hadn't read ___. (McCawley (1981: 108))
         d. Tony, let me ask you about a rumor that I've never been able to find anybody who would confirm ___. (Dick Cavett)

Chung and McCloskey discuss a variety of English where such examples are presumed to be grammatical, though other speakers systematically judge these as unacceptable.

The analysis of relative clauses outlined above treats these as ungrammatical, for as stated the Subject Extraction Lexical Rule (Chapter 4, section 4) requires that the VP complement of the SELR output must be [INHER | SLASH { }]. Thus, for example, structures like that in (44b) are rendered ill-formed by the SUBCAT list in the (SELR output) null relativizer shown in (44a):

(44)   a.   SUBCAT ⟨ 7 [INHER I REL { 1 }], VP[*fin*, SUBCAT ⟨7⟩, INHER I SLASH { }]⟩

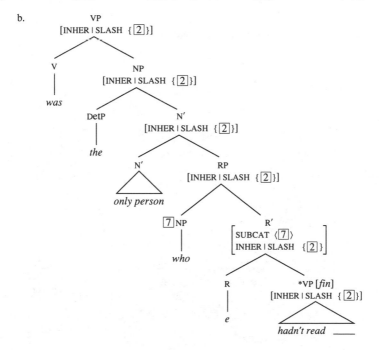

Similar remarks hold for examples like (45):

(45)   *Moby Dick,* I was the only person that hadn't read ___.

Consider, however, a minimally different grammar, one where the Subject Extraction Lexical Rule did not require that the second complement of the SELR output be specified as [INHER | SLASH { }]. Then all the examples in (43),
but none of those in (40), would be treated as grammatical. This would correspond precisely to the variety of English discussed by Chung and McCloskey.

Such an analysis of this variety of English would also explain the contrast between (46) and (47), pointed out by Elisabet Engdahl:

(46)   Which woman$_i$ do men who meet ___ $_i$ usually ask ___$_i$ out?

(47)   *Which woman$_i$ do men who meet ___$_i$ usually leave town?

In (46), the parasitic gap happens to be inside a relative clause like the one sketched in (44), but no other constraint is violated, rendering that example grammatical. (47), on the other hand, is ungrammatical not because of the relative clause, but because the SUBCAT list of the verb *leave* contains a slashed subject and no other slashed complement, in violation of the Subject Condition (Chapter 4, (84)).

Additionally, we observe that if nothing further were said, this analysis would predict the possibility of parasitic gap examples like (48a), with structures as shown in (48b):

(48)   a. ?Here are the Hollywood models$_i$ that I know artists whose pictures of ___$_i$
          flatter ___$_i$.

          b.

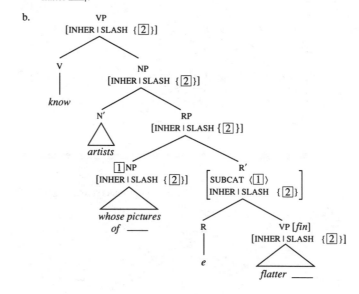

Indeed, such a revision to the SELR might also be independently motivated by apparently acceptable examples unrelated to relativization such as (49) where the VP complement of a SELR output (in this case the verb *thought*) contains an unbound trace:

(49)   ?Which papers do you remember who Mary thought [$_{VP}$ might be willing to review ___]?

There is a technical obstacle to removing the [INHER | SLASH { }] specification from the output of SELR, however. To see why, consider once more the application of SELR, so modified, to the null relativizer (24). Since this lexical entry itself specifies that its second complement (the finite S) must bear a nonempty SLASH value, it would appear (given the standard assumption about lexical rules that they change only those features of the input that are explicitly mentioned in the output part of the rule) that the null relativizer output on this application would itself be specified as always bearing a nonempty INHER | SLASH value, a clearly undesirable result.

Assuming that the facts are indeed as shown in (43)–(49), the problem can be stated as follows: we do not actually want to rule out the possibility of the SELR output null relativizer having a nonempty INHER | SLASH value in its VP complement; we simply want to prevent the VP complement from having the 'same' element in its INHER | SLASH set that the input has (namely, the one that also appears in the TO-BIND | SLASH value of both the input and the output forms). However, we have not as yet seen how to reformulate the SELR, or how to characterize the principles that govern lexical rule application, in order to achieve this effect. We leave this problem open.

5.3 Relative-Correlative Constructions

Our discussion of relative clauses has thus far been restricted to a particular kind of construction that we may refer to as the *externally headed relative clause construction*.[7] In this construction type, familiar from English and many other languages, the relative clause is properly contained within a phrase that also contains a nominal head external to the relative clause. In this section, we examine a relative clause construction that is superficially quite different, showing how the same analytic tools introduced for English can be successfully applied.

Some languages, including many of the Indian subcontinent, exhibit a kind of parataxis involving a relative and a nonrelative clause. Such *relative-correlative* constructions, which represent an ancient Indo-European construction type, are illustrated in (50)–(51):

7. We thank Smita Joshi and Mary Dalrymple for valuable discussions of the material presented in this section.

(50)   Hindi (Andrews 1975: 61, ex. 95b; Srivastav 1991a, 1991b):
          [Mere pas jo   ləṛka rəhta hai] vəh mera choṭa
          me   near which (rel) boy   lives aux [he my   little
          bhaii   hai
          brother is]
          'The boy who lives next door to me is my little brother.'
          ('Which boy lives near me, he is my little brother.')

(51)   Marathi (Andrews 1975; Dalrymple and Joshi 1986):
          [jaa mulaa-nii   jaa mulii-laa   paahile] [tyaa-nii
          which boy-ERG which girl-ACC saw   he-ERG
          ti-laa   maagNii ghaatlii]
          her-DAT   proposed
          'The boy who saw the girl$_i$ proposed to her$_i$.'
          ('Which boy$_j$ saw which girl$_i$, he$_j$ proposed to her$_i$.')

The Marathi relative-correlative construction is particularly interesting, because, as (51) illustrates, it may involve a relative clause containing multiple
relative words, each of which is associated with a correlative pronoun in the
correlative clause. Srivastav (1991a, 1991b) discusses analogous examples in
Hindi.

    These languages instantiate a rule schema that we have not yet encountered,
which we may refer to as the *Parataxis Rule*. The Indo-Aryan instantiations of
the Parataxis Rule may be viewed as setting language-particular parameters
involving the binding of two NONLOCAL features—REL and CORREL. The basic form of these structures (as defended in essential respects by Srivastav
(1991a, 1991b)) is illustrated in (52):[8]

(52)

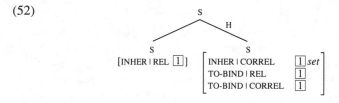

Our analysis (which follows in crucial respects that of Dalrymple and Joshi
(1986)) treats the correlative clause as the head. Thus the TO-BIND specifications on the correlative clause in (52) bind off both the REL and the CORREL
dependencies, in accordance with the NONLOCAL Inheritance Principle. Non-
empty INHER | CORREL values, as in the case of REL, arise from a closed class
of lexical items (the correlative pronouns). The value of INHER | REL on the
relative clause and that of INHER | CORREL on the correlative clause (both sets of

    8. Srivastav provides considerable evidence distinguishing left-adjoined relative
structures like those illustrated here from extraposed relative clauses in Hindi.

of indices—as in the case of English INHER | REL values) are inherited from the relative and correlative words they contain, again in virtue of the NONLOCAL Inheritance Principle. This is illustrated in (53) for the Marathi example in (51):

(53)

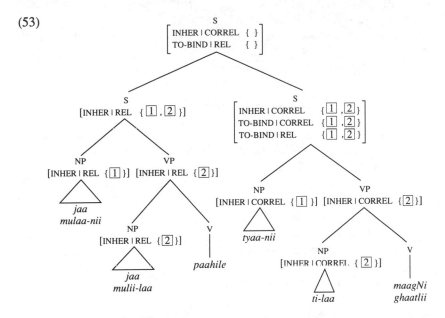

In identifying the INHER|REL value of the relative clause with the INHER| CORREL value of the correlative clause, the Parataxis Rule in Marathi identifies two sets of indices. Not only does this identify the index of each relative pronoun with that of a correlative pronoun, but it also guarantees that there will be exactly as many correlative pronouns as relative pronouns in a structure like (53).[9] We will turn to a class of apparent counterexamples to this prediction in a moment.

Marathi and Hindi thus differ from English two ways: (1) they employ a different rule schema (the Parataxis Rule) for binding off REL (and CORREL) dependencies, and (2) they do not obey the Singleton REL Constraint—that is, they allow nonsingleton INHER | REL (and INHER | CORREL) values. However, the fundamental mechanism underlying the grammar of relative clauses both in English and in the modern Indo-Aryan languages is the inheritance of REL values, in accordance with the NONLOCAL Feature Principle (Chapter 4 (16)).[10]

9. In addition, given the treatment of agreement features presented in Chapter 2, it immediately provides the basis for an account of the agreement between relative and correlative phrases discussed by Srivastav (1991a: 653ff.).

10. Chris Culy reports to us that Bambara has a relative-correlative construction, but appears not to allow nonsingleton INHER | REL values.

Predictably, there is a third difference between English and (at least) Marathi. As we saw in the previous section, English obeys the Clausal REL Prohibition. But given the paratactic relative binding structures of Marathi, which on our analysis involve Ss that have nonempty INHER | REL values, no such condition could possibly be assumed for Marathi. This in turn leads to the prediction that REL inheritance should be possible from Marathi embedded clauses. In fact, this prediction is correct, as the following example, due to Smita Joshi (personal communication, 1991), demonstrates:

(54)   [[jaa maaNsaa-laa John-nii   maarle he] Tom-laa   mahit aahe]
        which man-ACC   John-ERG hit   that Tom-DAT known is
        [tyaa maaNsaa-nii Bill-laa   paahile]
        that man-ERG   Bill-ACC saw
        'The man who Tom knows that John hit saw Bill.'
        ('Tom knows that John hit which man$_i$, that man$_i$ saw Bill.')

This is not to say, of course, that inheritance is completely unconstrained in Marathi, only that REL inheritance out of embedded clauses is possible in principle. Certain embedded environments, for example, the one illustrated in (55) and (56), in fact seem to systematically block both REL and CORREL inheritance, as noted by Dalrymple and Joshi (1986):

(55)   *[[jaa maaNsaa-laa John-nii   maarle] hyaa-war Tom-caa
        which man-ACC   John-ERG hit   this-on   Tom-GEN
        wiśwaas naahii] [tyaanii Bill-laa   paahile]
        belief   is-not he-ERG Bill-ACC saw
        'The man who Tom didn't believe that John hit saw Bill.'
        ('Tom didn't believe (it) that John hit which man$_i$, he$_i$ saw Bill.')

(56)   *[jaa maaNsaa-nii Bill-laa   paahile] [Tom-caa hyaa-war
        which man-ERG   Bill-ACC saw   Tom-GEN this-on
        wiśwaas naahii kii [John-nii tyaa-laa   maarle]]
        belief   is-not that John-ERG him-ACC hit
        'The man who saw Bill, Tom didn't believe that John hit (him).'
        ('Which man$_i$ saw Bill, Tom didn't believe (it) that John hit him$_i$.')

Clearly some extraneous factor, perhaps involving the appositive status of these embedded clauses, is responsible for the impossibility of REL inheritance in cases such as this.

A further interesting property of Marathi relative-correlative constructions is the possibility, in certain clearly definable circumstances, of extraneous relative words, that is, relative words that are not linked to any correlative pronoun. Dalrymple and Joshi cite examples like (57) as well-formed:

(57)   [[[jaa maaNsaa-caa jaa mulaa-caa] jo abhyaas]   mii
        which man-GEN   which boy-GEN   which homework I-ERG
        karuun ghetlaa] [to kathiiN hotaa]
        do   had   it   difficult was
        'The homework I had that man's son do was difficult.'
        ('I had done which man's which son's which homework$_i$, it$_i$ was
        difficult.')

Notice that the interpretation of the extraneous relative words in this example is essentially that of a demonstrative.

The only relative words that can be extraneous, according to Dalrymple and Joshi, are those that occur within possessive phrases in construction with a relative determiner. Thus the following example, where the subject NP contains a relative word not associated with any correlative pronoun, is ungrammatical:

(58)   *[jaa maaNsaa-nii [[jaa mulaa-caa] jo abhyaas]   mii
        which man-ERG   which boy-GEN   which homework I-ERG
        karuun ghetlaa] [to kathiiN hotaa]
        do   had   it   difficult was
        'Which man I had do which son's which homework, it was
        difficult.'

To account for these facts, we may assume that relative determiners optionally bind off the INHER | REL value of the possessor phrase they combine with, as illustrated in the following lexical entry (note that we are assuming that determiners like *tyaa* 'that' and *jo* 'which' optionally subcategorize for a genitive NP to form determiner phrases (DetPs) that serve as complements of nouns):

(59)   SYNSEM value for lexical representation of Marathi relative determiner *jo*:

$$
\begin{bmatrix}
\text{LOCAL | CAT} & \begin{bmatrix} \text{HEAD } det[\text{SPEC N}'_{\boxed{2}}] \\[4pt] \text{SUBCAT } \langle(\text{NP}[gen, \text{INHER | REL } \boxed{1}])\rangle \end{bmatrix} \\[20pt]
\text{NONLOCAL} & \begin{bmatrix} \text{INHER | REL} & \{\boxed{2}\} \\ \text{TO-BIND | REL} & \{\boxed{1}\} \vee \{\ \} \end{bmatrix}
\end{bmatrix}
$$

Examples like (57) thus arise when the relative determiner binds off its complement's REL dependency, as shown in (60):

(60)

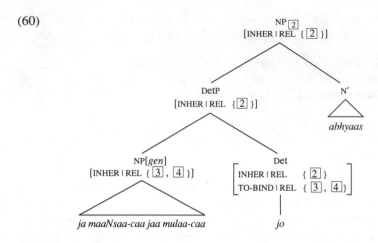

Note that the ungrammatical (58) will not be generated under this analysis. Only when a relative word occurs inside a complement to a relative determiner can its INHER | REL value be bound off lower than the top of the relative clause (which renders the relative(s) extraneous). In addition, this analysis treats the indices of extraneous relatives as free variables, hence allowing them to receive either a demonstrative interpretation (as reported for Marathi by Dalrymple and Joshi) or else an indefinite interpretation, assuming an account of indefinites like that available within discourse representation theory (Kamp 1981; Heim 1982). This appears to be the correct result for other Indo-Aryan languages, as pointed out to us by Alice Davison (personal communication, 1992).[11]

5.4 Internally Headed Relative Clauses

There is another type of relative clause construction, distinct from both the English type of relative clause and the relative-correlative constructions just discussed, that has been dubbed the *internally headed relative clause* (IHRC).[12] IHRCs, which occur in a variety of languages from unrelated language families (including Lakhota, Dogon, and Quechua), are nominalized sentences that combine with a determiner, with no overt head noun, to form an NP. A typical example, from Donno Sɔ (a variety of Dogon, a language of Mali), is given in (61):

11. We will not present a semantic analysis of correlative constructions here. For a concrete proposal, see Srivastav 1991a, 1991b.
12. We thank Chris Culy for valuable discussions of the material presented in this section. From our perspective, the terminology 'internally headed' is unfortunate, as the hallmark of IHRCs is the absence of a nominal head daughter. We will follow standard usage, however, and refer to the nominal within the IHRC that is modified by the IHRC containing it as the 'internal head'.

(61)   [ya   indɛ   mi   wɛ   gɔ] yimaa   boli.
          yesterday person 1sg see-PN-∅ DEF die-PSP go-PN-3sg
          'The person I saw yesterday is dead.'

In a recent study of IHRCs, Culy (1990) argues that the correct analysis of IHRCs involves no phonetically empty external NP heads, as has been assumed by a number of researchers (e.g. Cole 1987). Rather, according to Culy, the basic structure of IHRCs (as instantiated by (61)) is as shown in (62):

(62)

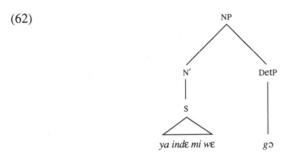

According to Culy's analysis, IHRCs exemplify an exocentric construction type, where N' expands simply to S. In addition to the absence of a head noun, another noteworthy property of IHRCs like (62) is the absence of a relative word.

Adapting Culy's HPSG analysis to the present framework, the schema for this exocentric construction would be as given in (63): [13]

(63)   EXOCENTRIC IHRC SCHEMA (after Culy 1990):

$$N_{\boxed{1}}$$
$$\begin{bmatrix} \text{INH} \mid \text{REL} \boxed{3} - \{\boxed{1}\} \\ \text{CONTENT} \mid \text{RESTR} \{\boxed{2}\} \end{bmatrix} \rightarrow S[\text{INH} \mid \text{REL} \boxed{3}]{:}\boxed{2}$$

The assumptions that underlie this analysis are the following. First, common nouns in a language like Donno Sɔ optionally introduce a nonempty INHER | REL value (and become the internal head in so doing),[14] which is inherited up to S in accordance with the NONLOCAL Feature Principle. Second, the rule in (63) removes the index of the N' ($\boxed{1}$ in (63)) from the INHER | REL value of the N' ('−' in (63) designates set difference). This binding is not the effect of the NONLOCAL Feature Principle, as the schema in (63) does not define a headed constituent. Third, (63) identifies the index that is bound off with that of the N' and makes the CONTENT of the S a restriction on that index.

13. We assume, following Culy and much recent work on the grammar of particular constructions in a variety of languages, that universal grammar makes available a small number of nonheaded schemata like (63).

14. An alternative analysis, whose consequences have not yet been adequately explored, is to treat internal heads as the result of combining a noun with a null relative determiner whose nonempty INHER | REL value introduces the relative dependency.

This adaptation of Culy's analysis is illustrated for the NP in (62) in (64):

(64)

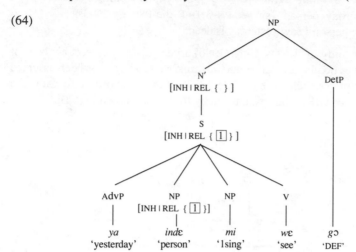

The CONTENT of the N' in (64), identical to that of the NP, is a nom-obj that contains roughly the content of *person that I saw*.[15]

Assuming Culy's analysis, it is clear that languages that have IHRCs cannot obey the Clausal REL Prohibition, for the IHRC schema itself involves an S whose INHER | REL value is nonempty. Thus we predict that, modulo other factors, inheritance of REL from subordinate clauses should in general be possible. This prediction is also correct. For example, Cole (1987) cites Imbabura Quechua examples like (65), where the internal head is in an embedded clause within the IHRC:

(65)   [Marya [Juan wawa-ta   riku-shka]   -ta
        Maria   Juan child-ACC see-NOMINAL -ACC
        ni-shka]   llugsh-irka
        say-NOMINAL leave-past
        'The child that Maria said that Juan saw left.'

Here a nonempty REL value has been inherited from an S complement within the IHRC—and this in turn requires that the embedded S bear a nonempty INHER | REL value.[16]

As the literature on IHRCs makes clear, there are a number of further constraints that have considerable cross-linguistic application. First, a conjunct

15. We will not pursue the interesting semantic properties of IHRCs here, referring the reader instead to Culy's discussion (1990: chap. 3 and appendix 2).

16. There remains the further matter of alleged subject-object asymmetries regarding relativization of embedded elements within IHRCs. For some discussion, see Culy (1990: 116ff.).

may not serve as the sole internal head of an IHRC, a fact noted for Navajo by Platero (1974) and for Quechua by Cole (1982). This fact follows directly from the coordination theory sketched in Chapter 4, section 6.1.

Second, in many languages that have IHRCs, the internal head may not be embedded in a subordinate relative clause. Thus in Navajo, examples like the following are ungrammatical:

(66) *[[hastiin łééchąą'´i bishxash-ę́ę] be'eldǫǫh
      man   dog   3:perf:3:bite-REL gun

      néidiitą́-(n)ęę]   nahał'in
      3:perf:3:pick:up-REL imp:3:bark

'The dog that the man who was bitten by picked up the gun is barking.'

Facts such as this follow directly from the supposition that Navajo, like most languages with IHRCs, are like English in obeying the Singleton REL Constraint. Thus examples like (66), if they were well-formed, would have to exploit structures like (67), where the indicated relative clause bears a doubleton specification for INHER | REL:

(67)

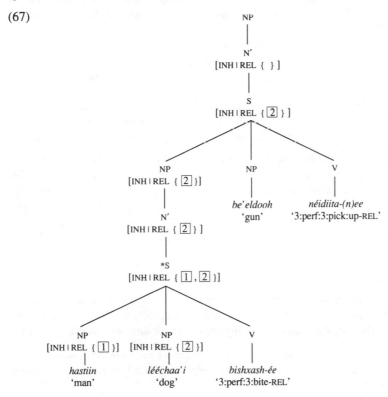

However, structures of just this sort, that is, structures like (67), are apparently allowed in Lakhota, for examples like (68) are fully grammatical (Williamson 1987: 177; Culy 1990: chap. 2):

(68)   [[wichota   wowapi wą yawa pi cha] ob   wo?ųglaka pi ki
        many-people paper   a   read Pl Ind with we-speak   Pl the

        he] *L.A. Times* e
        that *L.A. Times* be

        'The newspaper that we talk to many people who read (it) is the *L.A. Times.*'

And this is precisely the prediction that is made if Lakhota is treated (like Marathi) as allowing doubleton REL values. That is, if a language utilizes the IHRC schema and in addition is not subject to the Singleton REL Constraint, then (in the absence of further constraints) it will also allow the internal heads of IHRCs to be contained within an embedded relative clause. Thus we see that there is no universal prohibition against the internal head of an IHRC being properly contained within an internal IHRC.[17] Whether this is possible in a given language depends on whether the language allows nonsingleton values for REL, and this is a parameter of variation independent of the availability of the IHRC schema.

Finally, as shown by Cole, IHRCs may be islands with respect to extraction. The following example from Ancash Quechua (Cole 1987: 287) illustrates the impossibility of forming a question by extracting out of an IHRC:

(69)   *pi-ta-taq   [qanyan   wamra rika-nqa-n-ta]   kuya-nki
        who-ACC-WH yesterday child   see-NOMINAL-3-ACC love-2
        'Who do you love the child that saw yesterday?'

Following Culy, we might develop an account of such facts in terms of a constraint barring a constituent from having nonempty specifications for both INHER|REL and INHER|SLASH (a constraint proposed independently for English by GKPS). The more difficult question of why some languages, and not others, would have this constraint on their IHRCs remains unanswered for the moment.

5.5 Conclusion

In the preceding sections we have examined, however briefly, three kinds of relative clause constructions: (1) the familiar externally headed relative clauses found in English and many other languages, (2) the ancient relative correlative

---

17. Of course, other factors may conspire to further constrain the possible realizations of internal heads, e.g. to guarantee that only one relative head appears at each level of embedding within the relative clause.

construction still preserved in modern Indo-Aryan languages, and (3) the internally headed relative clauses found in diverse language groups throughout the world. On our theory, despite wild divergence in superficial appearance, the relative clause grammar of all three types of construction relies crucially on a single principle of universal grammar: the NONLOCAL Feature Principle.

To account for the cross-language variation we have encountered, we have posited several cross-linguistic options that languages may avail themselves of. These are summarized in (70):

(70)   Cross-language variation in relative clause constructions:

	ENGLISH	MARATHI	NAVAJO	LAKHOTA	BAMBARA
Parataxis Rule	N	Y	N	N	Y
Singleton REL Constraint	Y	N	Y	N	Y
Clausal REL Prohibition	Y	N	N	N	N
Exocentric IHRC Schema	N	N	Y	Y	N

We know that some of these patterns are systematic. In particular, we know that any language that avails itself of the Parataxis Rule or the Exocentric IHRC Schema will not be subject to the Clausal REL Prohibition and hence will allow relative dependencies to penetrate into embedded clause environments. This correlation follows from our theory, as the very nature of these two rule schemata requires the supposition of some S constituents with nonempty INHER| REL values, which in turn means that the language in question can have no systematic prohibition against such constituents. On the other hand, we know that some of the variation in (70) follows from the interaction of independent parameters. The Singleton REL Constraint, the Parataxis Rule, and the Exocentric IHRC Schema, for example, are linguistic constraints whose presence or absence in a given language is not mutually dependent, as we have seen. We leave to future research the investigation of further patterns of systematic cross-linguistic variation.

6

Binding Theory

6.1 Introduction

In this chapter we consider some questions that are standardly discussed under the rubric of binding theory. Roughly speaking, binding in this sense has to do with the classification of referentially dependent elements, such as personal pronouns and reflexive pronouns, according to syntactic constraints on the distribution of their possible antecedents. The overall plan of the chapter is as follows. In section 6.2, we review the GB binding theory presented in Chomsky 1986a. We take the liberty of assuming a general familiarity with the nature and goals of GB theory, but not with its technical details; relevant portions of the theory are reviewed as needed. In section 6.3, we examine a wide range of English data that suggest that the GB binding theory, which is based on the configurational notion of c-command, is on the wrong track. In section 6.4, we present an alternative binding theory that is based not on c-command, but rather on the relative obliqueness of grammatical relations. In section 6.5, we consider the interaction between our binding theory and the expletive pronouns *it* and *there*. In section 6.6, we explain how our binding theory accounts for the problematic data. In section 6.7, we consider some nonsyntactic factors that figure in the determination of antecedents for anaphors that are exempt (in a sense to be made precise) from our binding theory. Finally, in section 6.8, we compare our own account with some recent alternative proposals.

6.2 The Binding Theory of Chomsky 1986a

In Chomsky 1986a, noun phrases are cross-classified by the two binary features a (anaphor) and p (pronominal), as shown in (1):

(1)   GB typology of noun phrases:

Empty:

	+a	−a
+p	PRO	*pro*
−p	NP-trace	variable

Overt:

	+a	−a
+p		*he*
−p	*himself* *each other*	*john*

We will discuss the details of this typology presently. Now the key idea of Chomsky's binding theory is that +a (anaphoric) elements have to be bound within a certain local domain, but +p (pronominal) elements must *not* be bound within a certain other local domain. Here the notion *bound* is defined as in (2):

(2)   Y *binds* Z just in case:
       i. Y and Z are coindexed; and
       ii. Y c-commands Z.

And c-command is a configurational notion, defined in (3):

(3)   Y *c-commands* Z just in case:
       i. Z is contained in the least maximal projection containing Y; and
       ii. Z is not contained in Y.

Thus a binding configuration has the general form shown in (4):

(4)   Y binds z.

Now Chomsky's binding theory is especially concerned with A-*binding*, where the binder is in an A (argument) position, that is, subject, object, or object of a preposition. Z is called A-*bound* if it is bound by a Y in an argument position. Otherwise, Z is called A-*free*.

We now explain the typology of noun phrases in (1). NPs can be either *overt* (i.e. have phonetic content) or else *empty*. We consider first overt NPs. An ordinary personal pronoun like *he* is a *pure pronominal*, that is $(+p, -a)$. A reflexive pronoun like *himself* or the reciprocal *each other* is a *pure anaphor*, that is, $(+a, -p)$. A name like *John*, or a quantified NP like *every student*, is neither anaphoric nor pronominal, that is, $(-a, -p)$. And there are no overt NPs that are both pronominal and anaphoric; we shall return to this point shortly.

In the case of empty NPs, all four types are assumed to exist. The empty pure pronominal, called (little) *pro*, does not occur in English, but it is assumed to be present in languages such as Italian that permit empty subjects of finite clauses. The empty pure anaphor, called *NP-trace,* is assumed to be the empty element left behind by *NP*-movement, the species of movement that is assumed to take place when an NP that was not assigned case is forced to move to an A-position. NP movement is involved in the GB analysis of both passive and raising to subject. *Variables* are the traces left behind by elements that undergo *wh-movement*, the species of movement where the landing site is an Ā (nonargument, i.e. topic or operator) position. Variables are supposed to be neither pronominal nor anaphoric. And finally, there is an empty pronominal anaphor called (big) PRO. PRO is assumed to be the subject of infinitive clauses, such as the complements of control verbs like *try* and *persuade*.

We turn now to the GB binding theory itself, which accounts for the distribution of these elements. Two preliminary notions are required. First, an *indexing* of a phrase is an assignment of indices to all the NPs in the phrase. But there is one technical detail to note that has to do with the inflection element called Infl (I). Here it must be recalled that in GB, sentences are commonly assumed to be maximal projections of Infl, as shown in (5):

(5)   Coindexing of Infl's AGR with subject:

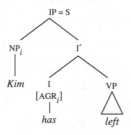

Now Infl is a bundle of features, and in cases like (5), it includes the agreement feature AGR, which is reflected morphologically by the agreement inflection on the finite auxiliary. The technical detail about indexings is that when Infl contains an AGR feature, then the AGR feature is assigned an index, just as if it were an NP; moreover, AGR is required to be coindexed with the subject of the sentence.

The second of the two preliminary notions is the configurational relationship of *government*, defined in (6):

(6)   G *governs* Z just in case one of the following three conditions obtains:

     a. G and Z c-command each other, Z is a maximal projection, and G is either a lexical category (N, A, V, or P) or a projection of one. For the purposes of this definition, AGR counts as an N.

     b. Z is the head of an element governed by G.

     c. Z is the specifier (including subject) of an element governed by G.

The key examples of government are that a lexical head governs its (nonsubject) complements, and that the AGR element within finite Infl governs the subject. But the infinitive Infl element *to* has no AGR element, so it does not govern the subject (PRO) position of the infinitive clause.

With this background, we are now in a position to state Chomsky's binding theory. This is formulated as a condition on permissible indexings, as in (7):

(7)   GB BINDING THEORY:

Let I be an indexing of the NPs (and AGRs, if any) in an expression E, and Z an NP in E. Then:

A. If Z is +a and governed by G, then Z is A-bound (under I) in the least maximal projection M containing a subject and G *for which there is an indexing J such that Z is A-bound (under J) in M.*

B. If Z is +p and governed by G, then Z is A-free (under I) in the least maximal projection M containing a subject and G.

C. 1. If Z is (−a, −p) and heads its own chain, then Z is A-free (under I) in E.

   2. If Z is (−a, −p) and does not head its own chain, then Z is A-free (under I) in the domain of the head of the chain of Z.

There are three cases to consider here; we begin with the simplest one, Condition B. This says that if Z is a governed pronominal, then it has to be A-free in its *governing category*, which for pronominals is taken to be the least maximal projection containing a subject and the pronominal's governor. This predicts, for example, that (8a) is bad, since the governing category for *him* is the sentence itself. But (8b) is grammatical, since the governing category for *their* is the NP *their friends*; here the noun *friends* is the governor:

(8)   *a.* *John$_i$ likes him$_i$.

       b. [The children]$_i$ like their$_i$ friends.

Next, we consider Condition A, which requires that a governed anaphor be A-bound in its governing category. This condition is more complicated than Condition B, because the definition of governing category for anaphors contains the additional clause indicated by italics. We will return to this point presently. Condition A predicts that (9a) is good, since the governing category of *himself* is the sentence. Example (9b), on the other hand, is bad, since here the governing category of *himself* is the embedded sentence, but *himself* is not bound within it:

(9)   *a.* John$_i$ likes himself$_i$.

       b. *John$_i$ knows Bill$_j$ likes himself$_i$.

       c. [$_S$ The children$_i$ like [$_{NP}$ [each other's]$_i$ friends]].

But now why is an additional clause needed in the definition of governing category for anaphors? This requires that in addition to containing a subject and the governor for the anaphor, the governing category M be such that there is some indexing J for M—not necessarily the same as the indexing I under consideration—such that the anaphor would be A-bound in M under J. To understand the motivation for this, consider sentence (9c). If the governing category for anaphors were defined the same way as for pronominals, then the theory would wrongly predict that *each other's* must be bound within the NP *each other's friends*. But with the extra condition, the governing category will be not this NP but rather the whole sentence, because there is no way to index the phrases in this NP that binds the anaphor. On the other hand, there *is* a way to index within the S that makes the anaphor come out bound, so the S is the governing category. As a matter of fact, according to this account not only is the binding shown in (9c) permissible, it is actually obligatory, because *the children* is the only potential binder for the anaphor. We will come back to this point in due course.

Finally, we consider Condition C, which treats elements that are neither pronominals nor anaphors, which Chomsky calls *R-expressions*. Here the *chain* associated with an element is the element together with any trace positions it occupies as it moves from its original A-position in D-structure to its final $\overline{A}$ landing site. The R-expressions that head their own chains include ordinary names like *John* or quantified NPs like *every student*; and the ones that do not head their own chains are the variables (*wh*-traces). The first clause of Condition C predicts the badness of (10a) and (10b), since in both cases *John* fails to be A-free. And the second clause predicts the contrast between the grammatical (10c) and the ungrammatical 'strong crossover' sentence (10d). In (10d), the head of the chain is *John*, and its domain is the clause indicated by square brackets; the sentence is ruled out because the variable is bound by *he* within this domain:

(10)   *a.* *He_i likes $John_i$.
        b. *He_i knows that Mary likes $John_i$.
        c. $John_i$, [I like e_i].
        d. *$John_i$, [he_i said you like e_i].

Thus far Chomsky's theory appears to be doing the job that it was designed to do. There is one additional theoretical point that we would like to raise here, which has to do with the consequences of Chomsky's theory for elements that are both pronominal and anaphoric, such as the empty element PRO. Chomsky argues as follows that PRO cannot appear in a governed position (such as the subject position of a finite clause): Suppose there were a PRO in a governed position. Then the binding theory must apply to it. Since PRO is an anaphor, it must be A-bound in its governing category. On the other hand, since PRO is a pronominal, it must be A-free in its governing category. But this is a contradiction; so the assumption that there is a PRO in a governed position must have been false. Hence PRO must always be ungoverned. This argument is referred to as the 'PRO theorem.' Similarly, it is argued that there can be no overt pronominal anaphor. This is because an independently motivated principle of GB theory, the *Case Filter*, requires that every overt NP be assigned abstract CASE, and CASE is assumed to be assigned only under government.[1]

1. For some critical discussion of the Case Filter, see Chapter 3, section 4.

6.3 Problems for Chomsky's Binding Theory

We now turn to what we see as problems for the GB binding theory. We consider first two theoretical points that strike us as ad hoc complications; and then we present several classes of empirical problems.

The first theoretical point has to do with the status of the PRO 'theorem.' As we just noted, Chomsky argues that PRO must be ungoverned, because otherwise it would have to be both A-free and A-bound in its governing category. This does not quite follow, however. The reason it does not is that according to (7), a PRO could well have two different governing categories, one as a pronominal and another, more inclusive, one as an anaphor. For example, consider (11a):

(11)   *a.* [John$_i$ said that [PRO$_i$ has eaten]].
        b. PRO$_j$ has[AGR$_j$] eaten.

It appears to follow from the definitions that the embedded S is the governing category for PRO as a pronominal and that the matrix S is the governing category for PRO as an anaphor. Then why isn't (11) grammatical? For Chomsky's argument to work, the two governing categories have to be the same.

Chomsky's solution to this problem is to say that indeed the embedded clause is the governing category for the anaphor. To make this work, he has to make the assumption, artificial by Chomsky's own admission, that the AGR element of Infl is allowed to count as a binder of the subject when the possible alternative indexings J are considered in Condition A; that is, the embedded clause is the governing category for the anaphor subject because there is a possible indexing for it that binds the anaphor, namely the one shown in (11b).

Chomsky appeals to this same argument to explain the ungrammaticality of (12a):

(12)   *a.* *Himself$_i$ has[AGR$_i$] eaten.
        b. He$_i$ has[AGR$_i$] eaten.

What seems questionable to us is the status of this notion of possible alternative indexings that bind a subject, which are not possible *real* indexings that bind the subject. For example, consider (12b). According to this notion, the indicated indexing has to be counted as a possible indexing that binds the subject. In fact, given the condition stated in (5), this indexing has to be the *actual* indexing. But considered as an actual indexing, the AGR is not allowed to count as binding the subject; for if it did, this sentence would be ruled ungrammatical by Condition B. Thus the status of the alternative indexings employed in the statement of Condition A seems most unclear. We therefore regard the PRO 'theorem' and the analogous argumentation for the nonexistence of overt pronominal anaphors as highly suspect.

Now the second theoretical point. Let us consider the grammatical sentences in (13), which Chomsky discusses at length:

(13)   *a.* [The children]$_i$ thought that [[each other's]$_i$ pictures were on sale].
      b. [The children]$_i$ thought that [pictures of [each other/themselves]$_i$ were on sale].

The difficulty presented by such examples is that, according to Condition A, the embedded clause should count as the governing category for the anaphor, since the anaphor could have been coindexed with the AGR element of *were*; but in each case the anaphor is clearly not bound in the embedded clause.

Chomsky's way out of this difficulty is to assume that when Condition A considers possible alternative indexings, it does not entertain any indexings that result in a violation of the '*i-within-i*' Condition given in (14a):

(14)   i-WITHIN-i CONDITION:
    a. $*[_{X_i} \ldots Y_i \ldots]$
    b. [[each other's]$_i$ pictures]$_i$ were [AGR$_i$] on sale.

Another way to say the same thing is that in order for an assignment of indices to the NPs (and AGRs) in a phrase to count as an indexing, it must not give rise to any instances of the configuration illustrated in (14a). That is, no indexing can result in some NP being coindexed with an NP that contains it.[2]

At first blush, this move appears to solve the problem, because as (14b) shows, coindexing the anaphor with the AGR in (13) does violate the i-within-i Condition. This is because AGR is also coindexed with the subject containing the anaphor, in accordance with the condition stated in (5). But the i-within-i Condition is clearly ad hoc. Moreover, as Chomsky has remarked elsewhere (Chomsky 1981: 229, n. 63), the version of the i-within-i Condition as stated in (14a) wrongly rules out examples like (15):

(15) $[_{NP_i} [_{NP_i}$ the man] [who$_i$ [e$_i$ saw himself$_i$]]]

Chomsky proposes to solve this problem by amending the i-within-i Condition to the form shown in (16):

(16)   i-WITHIN- CONDITION (revised):
    $*[[_{X_i} \ldots Y_i \ldots] \ldots Z_i \ldots]$ unless Y$_i$ is the head of X.

But this even more complicated restriction also follows from nothing in the theory; it is just a stipulation to force the binding in sentence (13).

    2. Chomsky (1986a: 175–176), modifying an earlier proposal due to Lebeaux (1983), sketches a possible alternative theory that (inter alia) obviates the need for an i-within-i Condition, or for the assumption that AGR can be a binder. On this alternative account, it is assumed that anaphors undergo movement to AGR at the level of LF. We will return to this proposal briefly in section 6.8.1.

We turn now to some problematic facts. To begin with, even if Chomsky's revised i-within-i Condition could be made to follow from something deeper in the theory, it is easy to find grammatical sentences that violate Condition A (incorporating the revised i-within-i Condition). Some examples are given in (17):

(17) a. [John and Mary]$_i$ knew that [the journal had rejected [each oth-er's]$_i$ papers].

b. Why are [John and Mary]$_i$ letting [the honey drip on [each oth-er's]$_i$ feet]? (Chomsky 1973: 261)

c. John suggested that [tiny gilt-framed portraits of [each other]$_i$ would amuse [the twins]$_i$].

d. John suggested that [tiny gilt-framed portraits of [each other]$_i$ would make ideal gifts for [the twins]$_i$].

e. The agreement that [Iran and Iraq]$_i$ reached guaranteed [each other's]$_i$ trading rights in the disputed waters until the year 2010.

f. John's campaign requires that pictures of himself$_i$ be placed all over town. (Lebeaux 1984: 358)

g. Mary still hadn't decided about birthday presents for the twins$_i$. Tiny gilt-framed portraits of [each other]$_i$ would be nice, but there was also that life-size stuffed giraffe.

h. Iran$_i$ agreed with Iraq$_j$ that [each other's]$_k$ shipping rights must be respected. (k = Iran and Iraq)

i. John$_i$ told Mary$_j$ that there were some pictures of themselves$_k$ in-side. (k = John and Mary)

j. John$_i$ asked Mary$_j$ to send reminders about the meeting to every-one on the distribution list except themselves$_k$. (k = John and Mary)

In (17a) and (17b), the anaphor is bound only in the matrix clause, not in the embedded clause as Chomsky's theory says it must be.

In (17c) the anaphor is coindexed with the NP *the twins* within the anaphor's governing category, but this does not satisfy Condition A of the binding theory because *the twins* does not c-command the anaphor and therefore fails to bind it. Indeed, (17c) is structurally identical to the sentence (13b) above that pro-vided the original motivation for the i-within-i Condition. This shows that in fact there is no obligatory binding in examples of this kind, so that the i-within-i Condition is not only ad hoc, but also empirically wrong. And despite sug-gestions by Belletti and Rizzi (1988) and Pesetsky (1987), counterexamples to Condition A like (17c) cannot be explained on the basis of properties of 'psych' verbs like *amuse*, as is clearly shown by examples like (17d). In (17e) and (17f), the antecedent of the anaphor fails to bind it because it is properly con-tained within an NP that c-commands it.

Discourses like the one in (17g) show that anaphors do not even have to have an antecedent within the same sentence. A somewhat different kind of counter-example to Condition A is provided by the split antecedent sentences in (17h–j) (see Lebeaux 1984: 346; also Bouchard 1984). Here the antecedent of the anaphor cannot even be found in prior linguistic context, but has to be inferred from the presence of two distinct noun phrases (e.g. *Iran* and *Iraq* in (17h)).

A rather different kind of Condition A violation is illustrated by the examples in (18). On a GB analysis, the structure of (18a) is as shown in (19):

(18) *a.* Mary talked to John$_i$ about himself$_i$.
      b. I spoke to [John and Bill]$_i$ about each other$_i$.

(19)

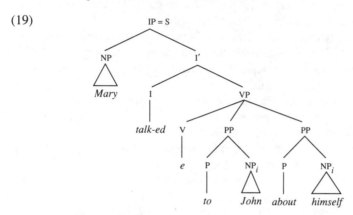

The trouble with this example is that even though the antecedent of the anaphor is within the governing category (namely the S), it does not qualify as a binder since it is the object of the preposition *to* and therefore fails to c-command the anaphor. This problem has been noted by Chomsky, who suggested the possibility of reanalyzing *spoke to* as a verb; but as Chomsky observes, such an account is implausible in the light of examples like (20):

(20)   I spoke angrily to the men$_i$ about each other$_i$. (Chomsky 1981: 226).

Analogous difficulties for Chomsky's Condition B are posed by examples like those in (21):

(21)   *a.* *Mary$_i$ talked to John$_j$ about him$_j$.
        b. *Mary$_i$ talked about him$_j$ to John$_j$.

Here the problem is that the examples are wrongly ruled to be grammatical. This is because *John* fails to c-command the personal pronoun, so that the latter is A-free within the sentence as required by Condition B.

We conclude this section by exhibiting some examples that are problematic for Chomsky's Condition C, beginning with the first clause, which requires that an R-expression other than a variable be A-free. Consider the examples in (22):

(22)   a. *Mary$_i$ talked about John$_j$ to him$_j$.
         b. *Mary$_i$ talked to him$_j$ about John$_j$.

These are wrongly predicted to be grammatical, since in both cases the pronoun fails to c-command *John*, so that the latter is A-free as required by Condition C.

We consider finally the second clause of Condition C, which requires that a variable not have a binder in an argument position that is c-commanded by the final S-structure position corresponding to the variable. Now here is the problem: if the *wh*-moved phrase—the head of the chain—happens to be a pronoun or an anaphor, then this condition can be violated. An example where the head of the chain is a pronoun is given in (23a), and an example where the head of the chain is an anaphor is given in (23b):

(23)   a. [Senator Dole]$_i$ doubted that the party delegates would endorse his wife. But HIM$_i$, he$_i$ was sure they would support t$_i$.
         b. [John and Mary]$_i$ are stingy with their children. But THEM-SELVES$_i$/[EACH OTHER]$_i$, they$_i$ pamper t$_i$.

It is interesting to observe that examples like these seem to behave as if the *wh*-moved pronoun or anaphor were actually returned (or in GB parlance, reconstructed) to the trace position that it is assumed to have originally moved from. For example, the coindexing shown in (23b) is exactly what Condition C would predict if the anaphor were returned to the trace position before the binding theory applied. Unfortunately, this approach creates as many problems as it solves. To see why, consider the grammatical sentences in (24):

(24)   a. I wonder [which of Claire's$_i$ friends]$_j$ [we should let her$_i$ invite t$_j$ to the party]?
         b. [Which of Claire's$_i$ friends]$_j$ [do you think she$_i$ would like to invite t$_j$ to the party?]

If reconstruction takes place before the binding theory applies, then the binding theory should apply to the postreconstruction structures sketched in (25):

(25)   a. I wonder [we should let her$_i$ invite [which of Claire's$_i$ friends] to the party?]
         b. Do you think she$_i$ would like to invite [which of Claire's$_i$ friends]$_j$ to the party?]

But these are Condition C violations, since now the R-expression *Claire* is A-bound by the pronoun. Hence the reconstruction analysis wrongly predicts that the sentences in (24) are ungrammatical.

Reconstruction also fails to explain the well-known interpretational freedom of anaphors contained within *wh*-moved phrases. For example, sentence (26) is ambiguous:

(26)   John$_i$ wondered [which picture of himself$_{i/j}$]$_k$ Bill$_j$ would prefer t$_k$.

But on a reconstruction analysis, the coindexation of *John* with the anaphor should produce a Condition A violation.

And finally, consider the sentences in (27):

(27)   *a.* [Which picture of herself$_i$]$_j$ does Mary$_i$ think John likes t$_j$?
         b. [Which picture of herself$_i$]$_j$ does John think Mary$_i$ likes t$_j$?
         c. [Which picture of herself$_i$]$_j$ did John say Mary$_i$ was afraid he
              had t$_j$?

On a reconstruction analysis, only (27b) should be possible; (27a) and (27c) produce Condition A violations. But in fact all three are perfectly grammatical.

6.4 A Nonconfigurational Binding Theory

In this section we propose an alternative binding theory that solves all of the problems discussed above. The key idea is to replace the configurational notion of c-command by a different relation called *obliqueness-command* or *o-command*, which is based not on tree configurations but rather on the relative obliqueness of grammatical functions.[3]

As a point of departure, recall that the CONTENT value of every NP is an object of (some subsort of) the sort *nominal-object* (*nom-obj*) and that the internal structure of a nominal-object is as sketched in (28):

(28)

$$
\textit{nom-obj}\begin{bmatrix} \text{INDEX} & \textit{index}\begin{bmatrix} \text{PER} \\ \text{NUM} \\ \text{GEND} \end{bmatrix} \\ \text{RESTRICTION } \{\ldots\} \end{bmatrix}
$$

---

3. The need for stating conditions on anaphors in terms of some form of the relational hierarchy has been recognized at least since Ross's (1974) discussion of primacy relations. Our analysis builds directly on treatments of reflexivization developed within the tradition of relational grammar, e.g. that of Johnson (1977: 167ff.), which have consistently been based on such a hierarchy.

For present purposes, there are two important properties of the analysis of nominal-objects that we developed in Chapters 1 and 2: (1) nominal-objects bear *indices*, which play much the same role as the NP indices widely employed in transformational theory; and (2) there are different sorts of nominal-objects, corresponding to different kinds of NPs with differing referential properties. We consider these points in turn.

As shown in (28), the index of a nominal-object itself has internal structure, namely, the features PERSON, NUMBER, and GENDER (informally, *agreement* features). It is token-identity (structure sharing) of indices that corresponds in our theory to the notion of coindexing for NPs. The semantic import of indices (as noted in section 4 of Chapter 2) is simply this: if an NP is referential (or quantificational), then any NP coindexed with it must have the same reference (or covary over the same domain of quantification). Since the agreement features belong to the internal structure of indices, it follows immediately that coindexed NPs (such as an anaphor and its antecedent) necessarily bear identical specifications for person, number, and gender.

Second, recall our classification of nominal-objects into sorts on the basis of the referential properties of the NPs that bear them. At the top level of the classification, we posit a distinction between nominal-objects that are pronominal (*pron*) or nonpronominal (*npro*); pronominal-objects in turn are either anaphoric (*ana*) or personal-pronominal (*ppro*) (i.e. pronouns that are not anaphors). The full classification of nominal-objects we introduced in Chapter 1 (see also section 5 of Chapter 3) is recapitulated in (29):

(29)   Sortal hierarchy of nominal-objects:

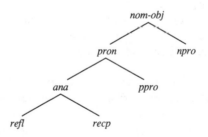

For overt nominals, the three sorts of nominal-objects *npro, ana,* and *ppro* correspond to Chomsky's three-way classification of NPs as R-expressions, anaphors, or pronominals. However, it should be recalled here that Chomsky's classification results from the reduction of a four-way classification to a three-way one, based on reasoning that we questioned at the beginning of section 6.3. We find it much more straightforward to simply posit these three kinds of NP.

By way of illustration, the nominal-objects of representative NPs are given in (30):

(30)

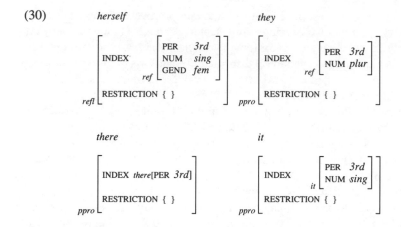

The classification of nominal-objects presented here is partly independent of the classification of indices into the three subsorts *referential, there*, and *it*. This enables us to assign the CONTENT value of expletives to the sort *ppro*[4] (as shown in (30)). This classification is independently motivated by the tag question construction, where expletives may appear as the subject of the tag, an environment where otherwise only elements assigned to the sort *ppro* may appear:

(31)   *a.*   The dogs/they will bark, won't they?
        b.   *The dogs/they will bark, won't the dogs?
        c.   There is a riot in the park, isn't there?
        d.   *There is a riot in the park, isn't one/a riot?
        e.   It bothers you that we lost, doesn't it?
        f.   *It bothers you that we lost, doesn't that/the fact?

    To place these notions within a sentential context, recall from Chapter 1 that the lexical head of a phrase (the verb in a simple sentence) identifies the referential indices of its complements with argument positions in its own CONTENT. In addition, the Semantics Principle ensures that (in the absence of adjuncts) the verb's content is identified with that of the sentence it heads. Thus, for example, the CONTENT of the sentence *Fido chased himself* is as indicated in (32):

---

4. Given that this classification of sorts of nominal-objects (which differs from the hierarchy of parameter sorts presented in Pollard and Sag 1992) groups expletives together with referential pronouns, the sort name *personal pronominal* is perhaps somewhat less than perspicuous.

(32)

$$
\begin{bmatrix}
\text{RELATION } chase \\[2pt]
\text{CHASER} \quad ref\begin{bmatrix} \text{PER} & 3rd \\ \text{NUM} & sing \end{bmatrix} \\[10pt]
\text{CHASED} \quad ref\begin{bmatrix} \text{PER} & 3rd \\ \text{NUM} & sing \\ \text{GEND} & masc \end{bmatrix}
\end{bmatrix}
$$

What is missing in (32) is precisely the information that binding theory should supply—namely, that the two indices must be identical.

On the account that we will set forth presently, it is the lists of *synsem* objects that form the SUBCAT values of lexical heads that provide the appropriate hierarchical structure for the formulation of the principles of binding theory. For example, in the sentence just discussed, the SUBCAT list of the verb *chased* will be as in (33):

(33) $\langle$ NP: *npro*, NP: *ana* $\rangle$

Hence Principle A can be stated simply as a constraint requiring coindexing between an NP:*ana* and a less oblique phrase on the same SUBCAT list (the precise formulation will be given in (40) below). This will in turn ensure that the two indices in a structure like (32) will be token-identical.

We next consider empty NPs. As we saw above, Chomsky distinguishes four kinds, shown in the left-hand box of (1): PRO, *pro*, NP-trace, and variable. We can begin by eliminating NP-trace, which figures in the analysis of passive and raising. As noted in P&S-87 (Chapter 8, sec. 3.6), in our lexical analysis of passive, there is no sense in which the passive subject is moved from an object position at any level of representation. And, as shown in Chapter 3, section 5, we assume that in raising, the subject SUBCAT element of the controlled complement is structure-shared with the (SYNSEM value of) the controlling NP. Thus there is no place for NP-trace in our theory.

The closest analogs of PRO in our theory are the subject SUBCAT elements of controlled complements of equi verbs such as *promise, persuade, try,* and *want.* Unlike Chomsky, however, we consider such elements to be not pronominal anaphors (which do not exist, on our account) but simply anaphors, more specifically reflexives (sort *refl*). The consequences of this assumption are explored in Chapter 7.

Another difference between our analysis and Chomsky's is that we allow the possibility that unexpressed subjects of some nonfinite VPs, such as those in (34), are (nonanaphoric) pronominals (we postpone detailed discussion of these and related examples until Chapter 7):

(34) *a.* The professors$_i$ knew that Kim had helped get themselves$_i$ plusher offices. (acceptable only in a context where Kim is one of the professors)

    b. Bill$_i$ knew she had said to behave himself$_j$.
    c. Fred$_i$ realized that Jane had signalled to position himself$_i$ under the table.
    d. It would help Bill's$_i$ development to behave himself$_i$ in public.
    e. Mary$_i$ knows that it would help Bill to behave herself$_i$ in public.

We also assume (as does Chomsky) that there are phonetically unrealized pronominal (*ppro*) constituents, for example, null subjects of finite clauses in languages like Italian.

Are there empty nonpronominals? It might be expected that we would adopt such an analysis of the traces employed in our analysis of unbounded dependency constructions (Chapters 4 and 5). However, it should be recalled that in filler-gap (or strong UDC) constructions, the LOCAL value of the filler is structure-shared with that of the gap. Since the NP's CONTENT value is internal to the LOCAL value, it follows that the nominal-object must also be shared between the filler and the gap. It follows in turn that a gap in a strong UDC is nonpronominal only in case the filler is. As we shall see in the following section, this has important empirical consequences.

There may also be a place for nontrace empty nonpronominal constituents in the analysis of some languages. For example, it has been claimed (Huang 1982) that empty objects in Chinese cannot be bound by arguments, but can be bound only by topics or empty operators. This claim has been disputed by Xu (1986) and by Zhang (1988), but let us suppose for the sake of argument that Huang's claim is correct. Huang accounts for this (putative) fact by assuming that Chinese empty objects are variables, or traces, in our terms. Now if these empty objects are really traces, we would expect them to obey Subjacency, or in our terms (see Chapter 4), the Subject Condition. But there is evidence that they do not; a relevant example due to Xu and Langendoen (1985) is given in (35):

(35)   [Zheben shu]$_i$ wo renwei du-guo e$_i$ de ren   bu duo.
        this book   I think   read-ASP ATTR person not many
        'I think the people that have read this book are few.'

On the other hand, if these empty elements are not traces but rather empty nonpronominals—the phonetically null equivalents of names—then they would be expected to occur in positions like the one in (35); at the same time their inability to be A-bound would be a consequence of Principle C of the binding theory (in either Chomsky's formulation or our version, to be presented immediately below).

The foregoing discussion of NP typology is summarized in the chart in (36):

(36)

Corresponding GB features	$+a, -p$	$-a, +p$	$-a, -p$	$+a, +p$
HPSG *nom-obj* sort	*ana*	*ppro*	*npro*	
Overt examples	*himself*	*him*	*John*	
Empty examples	subject of complement of *promise, try*, etc.	null subject of finite clause	Chinese zero object	

We are now in a position to present our binding theory. This is formulated in terms of the relation called *local obliqueness-command* (or *local o-command*), which is defined in (37):

(37)   Let Y and Z be *synsem* objects with distinct LOCAL values, Y referential. Then Y *locally o-commands* Z just in case Y is less oblique than Z.

Here it should be recalled that a *synsem* object Y is less oblique than a *synsem* object Z just in case it precedes Z on the SUBCAT list of some lexical head; a *synsem* object is called referential if it has an index of sort *ref*.[5]
    Local o-command is a special case of a more general relation called simply *o-command*, whose definition is given in (38):

(38)   Let Y and Z be *synsem* objects with distinct LOCAL values, Y referential. Then Y *o-commands* Z just in case Y locally o-commands X dominating Z.

Hence local o-command is just the special case of o-command where X = Z.[6] The intuitive idea of (38) is that Y o-commands everything that is, or is contained in, a more oblique complement of the same head; and Y locally o-commands the more oblique complements of the same head.

5. The purpose of the requirement that Y and Z have distinct LOCAL values is to exclude cases where Y and Z would be analyzed in GB terms as belonging to the same chain. One such case is that of nonsubject *wh*-relatives like *politician [who, Kim met ___,]* (where Y = *who,* and Z = ___,). (Another case, that of raising, will arise in section 6.8.3.) Without this requirement, such examples would wrongly be ruled out as Principle C violations.

6. Since *synsem* objects do not have daughters, domination of one *synsem* object Z by another *synsem* object X has to be understood in terms of domination of corresponding signs. More precisely, X is defined to dominate Z just in case there are signs X' and Z', with X and Z the SYNSEM values of X' and Z' respectively, such that X' dominates Z'.

Our analog of Chomsky's A-binding is the notion of *o-binding*, defined in (39):

(39)   Y *(locally)* *o-binds* Z just in case Y and Z are coindexed and Y (locally) o-commands Z. If Z is not (locally) o-bound, then it is said to be *(locally)* *o-free.*

It is important to note that o-commanders, and thus o-binders, must be referential; the significance of this fact will become clear in the following section when we consider expletive pronouns.[7]

Our binding theory is now stated in its entirety in (40); this should be compared with the GB binding theory in (7):

(40)   HPSG BINDING THEORY:

Principle A. A locally o-commanded anaphor must be locally
             o-bound.
Principle B. A personal pronoun must be locally o-free.
Principle C. A nonpronoun must be o-free.

It should be observed that our Principles A and B are stated in terms of the nonconfigurational relations local o-command and local o-binding. Only Principle C appeals to any tree-configurational notion; this is because o-freeness is defined in terms of (not necessarily local) o-command, which in turn depends on the relation of domination.[8]

Let us now consider how the theory presented in the preceding section accounts for the standard binding facts. We begin with the examples (8) above, repeated here as (41):[9]

(41)   *a.* *John$_i$ likes him$_j$.
        b. [The children]$_i$ like their$_i$ friends.

(42)   *a.* *[SUBCAT $\langle$ NP$_i$, NP:*ppro$_i$* $\rangle$]
        b. [SUBCAT $\langle$ DetP:*ppro$_i$* $\rangle$]

First, (41a) is ruled out because *him* is locally o-bound by the subject *John* in violation of our Principle B; the offending SUBCAT value for the head verb

7. Cf. Rizzi's (1990: 87) definition of binding in terms of *referential* indices.

8. The idea that only Principle C (not Principles A or B) is configurational has been proposed independently by K. P. Mohanan (personal communication, 1990), who suggests within the LFG framework that Principles A and B be stated in terms of the functional notion of *f-command*, but that Principle C be treated at the level of c-structure. In section 6.8.3 below, we consider a reformulation of binding theory that makes no appeal to tree configurations.

9. Here, again following the notational conventions introduced earlier, XP:*sort$_i$* abbreviates an XP whose CONTENT is of sort *sort* bearing the index *i*.

likes is shown in (42a). But (41b) is grammatical, because *the children* does not locally o-command the *ppro* determiner *their* (although it does o-command it); indeed, (the SYNSEM value of) *their* occurs only on the SUBCAT list of *friends*, shown in (42b). Here it should be recalled that (as discussed in section 8 of Chapter 1) possessives like *their* are treated as determiner phrases (DetP), not NPs. Nevertheless, since their CONTENT values are of sort *nom-obj*, and in particular bear referential indices (hence causing them to enter into local o-command relations), the three-way classification of referential NPs into anaphors, personal-pronominals, and nonpronominals is equally applicable to possessives.

We assume that the classification of referential NPs by nominal-object sorts is likewise applicable to PPs headed by nonpredicative ('case-marking') prepositions. More precisely, we assume that the head preposition makes no contribution to the CONTENT of the PP, so that the latter is structure-shared with the CONTENT of the prepositional object.[10] As a consequence, our Principle B also rules out coindexings like the one shown in (43):

(43)   *a.* *John$_i$ depends [on him]$_i$.
        b. *[SUBCAT $\langle$ NP$_i$, PP:*ppro$_i$* $\rangle$]

In addition, if a verb subcategorizes for both a primary object NP and a more oblique referential complement (either a secondary NP object or a nonpredicative PP) and the latter is a personal pronoun, then it must not be coindexed with either the subject or the primary object, as shown in (44) and (45):

(44)   *a.* *Mary$_i$ described Bill$_j$ to her$_i$/him$_j$.
        b. *[SUBCAT $\langle$ NP$_i$, NP$_j$, PP[*to*]:*ppro$_{i/j}$* $\rangle$]

(45)   *a.* *He$_i$ sold the slave$_j$ him$_{i/j}$.
        b. *[SUBCAT $\langle$ NP$_i$, NP$_j$, NP:*ppro$_{i/j}$* $\rangle$]

Next, we return to the examples in (9a, b), repeated here as (46):

(46)   *a.*   John$_i$ likes himself$_i$.
        b.   *John$_i$ knows Bill$_j$ likes himself$_i$.

Our Principle A predicts that the coindexing in (46a) is obligatory. This is because the anaphor is locally o-commanded by *John* and therefore has to be locally o-bound; but *John* is the sole local o-commander, and therefore the only potential local o-binder. Similarly, the coindexing in (46b) is illicit, since *him-*

---

10. The technical details underlying this assumption are discussed in section 2.2 of Chapter 9.

self is only o-bound by *John*, but not locally o-bound as Principle A requires. The corresponding SUBCAT lists for the two occurrences of *likes* are shown in (47):

(47)   *a.*   [SUBCAT ⟨ NP:*npro*$_i$, NP:*ana*$_i$ ⟩]
        b. * [SUBCAT ⟨ NP:*npro*$_j$, NP:*ana*$_i$ ⟩]

Similarly, since (as just noted) nonpredicative PPs share their CONTENT value—and therefore the sort of their CONTENT value—with the prepositional object, analogous predictions are made with respect to the examples in (48); the corresponding SUBCAT lists are shown in (49):

(48)   *a.*   John$_i$ depends [on himself]$_i$.
        b. * John$_i$ knows Bill$_j$ depends [on himself]$_i$.

(49)   *a.*   [SUBCAT ⟨ NP:*npro*$_i$, PP[*on*]:*ana*$_i$ ⟩]
        b. * [SUBCAT ⟨ NP:*npro*$_j$, PP[*on*]:*ana*$_i$ ⟩]

If a verb subcategorizes for both a primary object NP and a more oblique referential complement (either a secondary NP object or a nonpredicative PP) and the latter is an anaphor, then it must be coindexed with either the subject or the primary object, as shown in (50) and (51):

(50)   *a.*   Mary$_i$ described Bill$_j$ to herself$_i$/himself$_j$.
        b.   [SUBCAT ⟨ NP$_i$, NP$_j$, PP[*to*]:*ana*$_{i/j}$ ⟩]

(51)   *a.* * John$_k$ forgot that Mary$_i$ had described Susan$_j$ to himself$_k$.
        b. * [SUBCAT ⟨ NP$_i$, NP$_j$, PP[*to*]:*ana*$_k$ ⟩]

On our account, (52) is analogous to (50) as far as binding theory is concerned; we attribute the relative unacceptability of such examples to the oddness of their meaning. (See section 6.8.2 for further discussion of such examples.)

(52)   *a.*   ?John$_i$ sold the slave$_j$ himself$_{i/j}$.
        b.   [SUBCAT ⟨ NP$_i$, NP$_j$, NP:*ana*$_{i/j}$ ⟩]

We reconsider next example (9c), repeated here as (53):

(53)   [$_S$ The children$_i$ like [$_{NP}$ [each other's]$_i$ friends]].

According to Chomsky's Condition A, the indicated coindexing is obligatory; indeed, the extra clause in the definition of governing category for anaphors (which requires the consideration by Condition A of possible alternative indexings) is expressly designed to require coindexing of the kind exemplified here. But as examples like (17a–b), repeated here as (54a–b), and the structurally similar (54c) show, there can be no syntactic constraint making such coindexations obligatory. Thus Chomsky's extra clause in the definition of governing category for anaphors is an empirically unmotivated complication:

(54) *a.* [John and Mary]$_i$ knew that [the journal had rejected [each other's]$_i$ papers].

 b. Why are [John and Mary]$_i$ letting [the honey drip on [each other's]$_i$ feet]?

 c. [Bush and Dukakis]$_i$ charged that [General Noriega had secretly contributed to [each other's]$_i$ campaigns].

By contrast, according to our formulation of Principle A, the anaphors in examples (53) and (54) are actually *exempt* from the requirement of being locally o-bound, for the simple reason that they are not locally o-commanded. This in turn is because in each case the anaphor is the subject of the NP, and nothing can locally o-command a subject. As a consequence, the antecedents of the anaphors in these examples are not determined by binding theory, but rather by other, nonsyntactic factors.[11] (In section 6.7 we consider in some detail what factors contribute to the determination of antecedents for anaphors that are exempt in this sense from Principle A.)

We now reexamine the examples in (10), repeated here as (55):

(55) *a.* *He$_i$ likes John$_i$.

 b. *He$_i$ knows that Mary likes John$_i$.

 c. John$_i$, [I like e$_i$].

 d. *John$_i$, [he$_i$ said you like e$_i$].

We predict that (55a) and (55b) are ungrammatical because in both cases the nonpronoun *John* is o-bound, in violation of our Principle C. In each of (55c) and (55d), the trace has its LOCAL value (and hence also its CONTENT value) structure-shared with that of the filler, the nonpronoun *John*, so the trace itself must also be a nonpronoun. In (55c), the trace is o-free, so the sentence is grammatical, but the crossover sentence (55d) is ruled out because the trace is o-bound, in violation of Principle C. It should be observed in this connection that, unlike Chomsky's formulation, our version of Principle C does not neces-

11. Roughly this division of labor between principles of binding theory and interacting factors was arrived at independently by Tanya Reinhart and Eric Reuland (see Reuland and Reinhart 1991; Reinhart and Reuland, to appear), whose theory is formulated in terms of a dichotomy between logophoric and nonlogophoric anaphor binding. A related proposal, with slightly different consequences, is made by Dalrymple (1990).

sitate separate clauses for traces and nontraces. This is because the structure
sharing between the filler and the gap ensures that relevant information from
the filler is present at the trace site, which in turn is subject to Principle C. We
return to this point in section 6.6, in connection with the question of
reconstruction.

6.5 Binding Theory and Expletive Pronouns

We now turn to the binding properties of the expletive NPs *it* and *there*. As
noted by Freidin and Harbert (1983) and by Kuno (1987: 95ff.), an anaphor
does not require a local binder in the extraposition construction. Kuno cites the
following examples of anaphors with nonlocal antecedents:

(56)   *a.* They$_i$ made sure that it was clear to each other$_i$ that this needed to
        be done.
        b. They$_i$ made sure that it was clear to themselves$_i$ that this needed
        to be done.
        c. They$_i$ made sure that it wouldn't bother each other$_i$ to invite their
        respective friends to dinner.

This observation follows immediately from our theory. As we proposed in
section 6 of Chapter 3, the lexical entries for verbs and adjectives taking *it*-
subjects and extraposed clausal complements are derived via lexical rule from
verbs that take sentential subjects.[12] The SUBCAT lists of these derived lexical
entries are illustrated in (57) and the structure that arises from (57a) is illustrated in (58). ($\bar{S}$ here abbreviates S[*comp*]; see Chapter 3.)

(57)   *a.* [SUBCAT ⟨ NP$_{it}$, NP, $\bar{S}$ ⟩]
        b. [SUBCAT ⟨ NP$_{it}$ (, PP[*to*]), $\bar{S}$ ⟩]

(58)

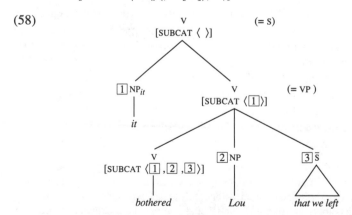

12. As is well known, some extraposition verbs (e.g. *seem*) cannot be so derived,
and hence must be listed in the lexicon with appropriate SUBCAT values.

Kuno's examples thus involve SUBCAT lists of the sort illustrated in (59):

(59) a. [SUBCAT $\langle$ NP$_{it}$, NP:ana, $\bar{S}$ $\rangle$]
         b. [SUBCAT $\langle$ NP$_{it}$, PP[to]:ana, S $\rangle$]

In (59a, b), the anaphors are not locally o-commanded, because the subject's index is nonreferential. Therefore, these anaphors are not required to be locally o-bound, that is, they are exempt from Principle A.

Similar predictions are made about sentences involving the expletive pronoun *there*, though these are somewhat more difficult to test because of the conflict between the definiteness of anaphors and the 'definiteness restriction' on the postcopular NP in *there*-constructions. Note first that anaphors embedded within the postcopular NP (e.g. those in (60)) are not at issue here:

(60) a. The men$_i$ knew that there were pictures of each other$_i$ on sale.
         b. John$_i$ knew there was a picture of himself$_i$ in the post office.
         c. John$_i$ realized that the fact that there were pictures of each other$_j$ in their$_j$ dressing rooms would annoy [the two male leads]$_j$.

Because these anaphors have no local o-commander within the picture NP, they are exempt from Principle A, as explained earlier, and are free to take nonlocal antecedents, as they do in these examples.

What is at issue is the status of examples like (61):

(61) a. ?John$_i$ knew that there was only himself$_i$ left.
         b. ?John realized that there was only each other$_i$ preventing [Kim and Sandy]$_i$ from realizing their goals.
         c. ?John$_i$ was devastated by the loss of his entire family. Now there was only himself$_i$ remaining.

These are not ruled out by Principle A, as the SUBCAT list in question, that of the verb *be* in its *there*-subject use, is the one shown in (62):

(62)   [SUBCAT $\langle$ NP$_{there}$, NP:ana, XP[+PRD] $\rangle$]

Because the index of *there* is not referential, the anaphor in (62) has no local o-commander and therefore need not (indeed cannot) be locally o-bound. As the examples in (61) show, this is the correct result (modulo definiteness effects): the antecedent of a postcopular anaphor in the *there* construction may be in a higher clause, in a non-c-commanding position, or even in prior discourse.

It is interesting to observe that sentences containing meteorological verbs with *it* subjects exhibit binding properties different from those just considered. When an anaphor is properly contained within the argument of a meteorological predicate, it appears to be exempt from Principle A:

(63)   *a.* John*ᵢ* knew that it would rain on that picture of himself*ᵢ* that was
         sitting on the patio.

         b. The men*ᵢ* knew that it would rain on each other's*ᵢ* parades.

This is just as predicted by our account.

But an anaphor argument of a meteorological verb seems not to allow a
remote antecedent, as the following examples show:

(64)   *a.* *John*ᵢ* knew that it would rain on himself*ⱼ*.

         b. *The men*ᵢ* knew that it would rain on each other*ⱼ*.

If these judgments are correct, then perhaps the solution is to treat meteorological *it* as a referential (nonexpletive) pronoun, as suggested by Bolinger
(1973). On Bolinger's analysis, this pronoun is treated as *ambient*, that is, as
involving environmental reference. Once we treat such *it* subjects in terms of
referential indices, then the anaphors in (64) are locally o-commanded and
must be locally o-bound, which they cannot be because of semantic and agreement conflicts. This proposal, however speculative, would account for the deviance of the examples in (64).

It-clefts appear to behave in a manner analogous to *there*-sentences. The
subject pronoun in examples like (65) is an expletive:

(65)   *a.* It was herself*ᵢ* that Mary*ᵢ* liked best.

         b. It was each other*ᵢ* that the twins*ᵢ* liked best.

On one possible analysis of *it*-clefts, the relationship between the postcopular
(clefted) phrase and the gap is analogous to that between a filler and a gap in a
strong UDC (see Chapter 4). On this analysis, the SUBCAT list for the examples
in (65) is as shown in (66):

(66)   [SUBCAT $\langle$ NP*ᵢₜ*, NP[LOC $\boxed{1}$]:*ana*, S̄[INH | SLASH {$\boxed{1}$}] $\rangle$]

The basic idea here is that the copula that figures in the cleft construction subcategorizes for an expletive *it* subject, some second complement (the 'focus'),
and a finite clause (the 'presupposition') containing a trace whose LOCAL value
is structure-shared with that of the second complement. Since the anaphor on
this SUBCAT list is not locally o-commanded, it might appear at first blush that
it is predicted to be exempt from Principle A.[13] However, inasmuch as the LO-
CAL value, and therefore the CONTENT, of the focus complement is, by assumption, shared with that of the trace, it follows that the trace too has an
anaphoric CONTENT value, as shown in (67):

13. We observe in passing that anaphors appear to be exempt quite generally in copular constructions. Thus our account does not yet explain why anaphors in examples like
*The one who John*ᵢ* likes best is himself*ᵢ* are exempt. This suggests that the notion of
exempt anaphor is in need of a deeper explanation, one that is able to exploit properties
of the argument structure of the copula.

(67)

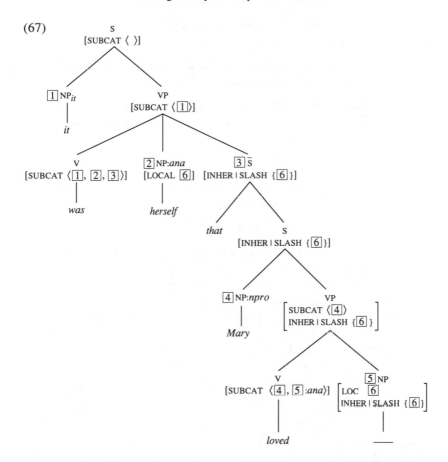

This in turn has as a consequence that the SUBCAT list of the lower verb in (67) contains an anaphor (indicated by the tag '⑤') with a local o-commander (*Mary*, indicated by the tag '④'). Principle A will therefore require that this anaphor trace be coindexed with *Mary*. Since the content of the trace *is* the content of *herself*, it follows that *Mary* and *herself* must be coindexed in (67). In essence, what we have here is the effect of a reconstruction analysis.

It is not entirely clear that this is the right prediction. The critical data are those in (68):

(68)   *a.* It was herself; that Mary; thought Bill; admired t; most.
         b. It was himself; that Mary; thought John; admired t; most.

The proposal just outlined predicts that only (68b) is grammatical, for the anaphor on the SUBCAT list of the most deeply embedded verb in (68a) would not be locally o-bound, in violation of Principle A. This prediction seems to be correct for some speakers. For other speakers, however, not only are both (68a, b) possible, but so are the examples in (69):

(69)   *a.* It was himself$_j$ that John$_i$'s fantasies most centrally concerned.
         b. John$_i$ knew that it was himself$_i$ that they were after.

These differing patterns of data find a relatively straightforward alternative analysis that is still consistent with the version of Principle A that we have proposed. On this alternative analysis, the relationship between the postcopular phrase and the gap is analogous to a weak UDC in the sense that the SUBCAT list for *be* (in its *it*-cleft function) would not identify the LOCAL values of the postcopular NP and the INHER|SLASH value, but instead would merely require them to be coindexed, as shown in (70):

(70)   [SUBCAT ⟨ NP$_{it}$, NP$_i$, S̄[INHER | SLASH {NP$_i$}] ⟩]

Since the CONTENT of the trace is now distinct from (but coindexed with) the postcopular NP (the second NP in (70)), when the latter is an anaphor, the former need not be. Consequently, Principle A will be in force neither in the higher structure (the cleft structure) nor in the lowest structure (the one containing the trace). As a result, a postcopular anaphor will be entirely exempt from Principle A, which in turn means that all the examples in (68) and (69) will be allowed, as desired. In short, we take these variations in judgment to be a consequence of minor idiolectal differences in the lexical entry for the copula involved in the cleft construction.

6.6 The Facts Explained

We now consider how the problematic facts discussed in section 6.3 are explained within our binding theory. We begin with (12a), repeated as (71):

(71)   *Himself$_i$ has eaten.

Recall that Chomsky's analysis of this example appeals to the assumption, which we argued to be dubious even on GB-internal theoretical considerations, that AGR of Infl can be a binder in a possible alternative indexing. Our explanation, following Brame (1977), is much simpler: (71) is bad because the English reflexive lacks a nominative form. As would be expected from its morphology, *himself* is accusative, and therefore is disallowed from serving as the subject of a finite verb. On the other hand, our Principle A does not prevent anaphors from serving as subjects of nonfinite clauses where, on independent grounds, we know that the subject must be in the accusative case, as shown in (72):

(72)   *a.* John wanted more than anything else for her/*she to get the job.
         b. The men preferred for him/*he to do the hard work.

The question then arises whether the anaphors in examples like (73) should be subject to Principle A: [14]

(73) *a.* John$_i$ wanted more than anything else for himself$_i$ to get the job.
      b. The men$_i$ preferred for each other$_i$ to do the hard work.

On standard GB accounts, this question is answered affirmatively. But there is good reason to question the correctness of such accounts. Whatever factors are at work to determine the coindexing indicated in such examples, such factors are also at work in examples like (74):

(74) *a.* What John$_i$ would prefer is for himself$_i$ to get the job.
      b. The thing [Kim and Sandy]$_i$ want most is for each other$_i$ to succeed.

In these examples, no appeal to Principle A (however it is formulated) would appear to be possible. Yet the indicated coindexing seems just as obligatory as it does in (73). For this reason, it would be missing a generalization to formulate Principle A so as to include in its domain examples like (73) (but not examples like (74)). However, on our account the anaphors in all these examples, being subjects, are exempt from Principle A. Hence one must appeal to other factors to explain what appears to be obligatory binding in both kinds of cases. [15]

We consider next the sentences in (13), repeated here as (75):

(75) *a.* [The children]$_i$ thought that [[each other's]$_i$ pictures were on sale].
      b. [The children]$_i$ thought that [pictures of [each other/themselves]$_i$ were on sale].

It should be recalled here that examples such as these constituted the principal motivation for Chomsky's stipulative i-within-i Condition in (16), which forces the indicated coindexings. However, as we pointed out earlier, Chomsky's proposal is directly counterexemplified by example (17c), repeated here as (76), which has exactly the same structure as (75b) but a different indexing:

(76) John suggested that [tiny gilt-framed portraits of [each other]$_i$ would amuse [the twins]$_i$].

On the other hand, our formulation of Principle A predicts that both (75) and (76) are possible. This is because none of the anaphors in these examples are

14. Notice that in such examples, the reflexive subject must bear contrastive pitch accent, which in turn is associated with interpretive focus. For example, in (73a) the interpretation is that John wants himself to get the job as opposed to anyone else getting the job. This should be compared with *John wanted more than anything else to get the job*, where the interpretation is that John wants to get the job as opposed to wanting something else.

15. For further discussion of this point, see Pollard and Sag 1992.

locally o-commanded, and therefore they are exempt from the requirement of being o-bound. Likewise, all of the anaphors in examples (17d–j), which were wrongly ruled out by Chomsky's binding theory, are exempt from our Principle A and therefore correctly predicted to be grammatical.

We now reconsider (18a), here repeated as (77), which is wrongly ruled out by Chomsky's condition A because the antecedent fails to c-command the anaphor:

(77)   Mary$_i$ talked to John$_j$ about himself$_j$.

On our analysis, however, both *to John* and *about himself* are headed by non-predicative prepositions and therefore structure-share their CONTENT values with their respective prepositional objects. Adopting the standard assumption that *to*-phrases are less oblique than *about*-phrases,[16] the SUBCAT value of *talked* in (77) is as shown in (78):

(78)   [SUBCAT⟨ NP$_i$, PP[*to*]$_j$, PP[*about*]:*ana$_j$* ⟩]

Thus the anaphor satisfies Principle A, as required. Similarly, our account makes the following additional predictions:

(79)   *a.*   Mary$_j$ talked to John$_i$ about herself$_j$.
          b.   *John$_k$ thought that Mary$_j$ had talked to Susan$_i$ about himself$_k$.
          c.   *Mary$_j$ talked about John$_i$ to himself$_i$.
          d.   *Mary$_j$ talked to himself$_i$ about Bill$_i$.

Here, (79a) is good because *Mary* locally o-binds *about herself*. But in (79b–d), the phrase coindexed with the anaphoric PP fails to o-command it. In (79b) this is because the coindexed phrase is an argument of the matrix verb; in (79c–d) it is because the PP[*about*] is more oblique than the PP[to].[17]

As we have seen, examples such as those in (21), repeated here as (80), are wrongly predicted to be good by Chomsky's Condition B. On our account, though, such examples are ruled out by Principle B because the personal-pronominal PP[*about*] is locally o-bound by the less oblique PP[*to*]:

(80)   *a.*   *Mary$_i$ talked to John$_j$ about him$_j$.
          b.   *Mary$_i$ talked about him$_j$ to John$_j$.

16. See, e.g., the relational grammar analyses of '3-to-2 advancement' (Perlmutter and Postal 1977, 1983), which presume that *to*-phrases are *terms*, and hence less oblique than *about*-phrases.

17. The theory presented here fails to explain the badness of **Mary$_j$ talked about himself$_i$ to John$_i$*, as compared with *Mary talked about the boat to John*, which seems acceptable (if not impeccable), particularly in case *to John* bears contrastive pitch accent. It seems clear that the relative order of anaphor and antecedent must somehow come into play in the analysis of this example, but our obliqueness-based account is insensitive to such effects.

Analogously, the examples in (22), repeated here as (81), which were wrongly predicted to be grammatical by Chomsky's Condition C, are correctly ruled out by our Principle C because the nonpronominal PP[*about*] is illicitly o-bound by the less oblique PP[*to*]:

(81)   *a.* *Mary$_i$ talked about John$_j$ to him$_j$.
         b. *Mary$_i$ talked to him$_j$ about John$_j$.

The key point to be noted with respect to all these examples is that it is local o-command, not c-command, that is relevant to the proper characterization of syntactic domains that bear on binding theory.

We now return to the examples in (23), repeated here as (82), that were wrongly ruled ungrammatical by the second clause of Chomsky's Condition C:

(82)   *a.* [Senator Dole]$_i$ doubted that the party delegates would endorse his wife. But HIM$_i$, he$_i$ was sure they would support t$_i$.
         b. [John and Mary]$_i$ are stingy with their children. But THEM-SELVES$_i$/[EACH OTHER]$_i$, they$_i$ pamper t$_i$.

This difficulty arose because on Chomsky's account, all traces are considered to be R-expressions and therefore subject to Condition C. But on our account, as we have seen, the content sort of a trace in a filler-gap (strong UDC) construction is determined by the content sort of the filler. It follows that (82a) is grammatical: in this case the trace is a personal pronoun, so our Principle C does not apply to it. (Instead Principle B applies, and is satisfied, inasmuch as the trace is locally o-free.) (82b) is also grammatical. That is because in this case the trace is an anaphor, and is therefore required to satisfy only our Principle A (not Principle C). And this it does, since it is locally o-bound by *they*.

As we pointed out above, it is possible in GB theory to make correct predictions about the examples in (82), provided we assume that the fillers are 're-constructed' to the trace position before the binding theory applies. The trouble with this move is that reconstruction wrongly predicts that sentences like (24a) and (27a), repeated here as (83) and (84), are ungrammatical: (83) then violates GB Condition C, while (84) violates GB Condition A. Perhaps surprisingly, however, although our theory produces the desired effect of reconstruction in (82), it successfully avoids the undesirable effects of reconstruction in (83) and (84). Let us consider the latter two examples in turn:

(83)   I wonder [which of Claire's$_i$ friends]$_j$ [we should let her$_i$ invite t$_j$ to the party]?

(84)   [Which picture of herself$_i$]$_j$ does Mary$_i$ think John likes t$_j$?

First, in (83), the filler *which of Claire's friends* has its LOCAL value structure-shared with that of the trace. But there simply is no sense in which the NP *Claire* is contained within the trace position. That is because subconstituents of a sign are part of the DAUGHTERS value of that sign, which is not contained in the LOCAL value of the sign. Hence there is also no sense in which *Claire* is o-commanded by *her*. Consequently, (83) does not lead to a violation of Principle C as we have formulated it, and is therefore predicted to be grammatical.

Similarly, in the case of (84), even though the LOCAL structure of the filler *which picture of herself* is shared with the trace, there is no sense in which the anaphor *herself* is contained within the trace position. In fact, even if it were, our Principle A would not apply to it, since it would still not be locally o-commanded. So (84) is also grammatical.

The conclusion is this. In GB, the binding theory is formulated in terms of tree-configurational notions like c-command, government, and A-binding, resulting in a large array of seemingly intractable theoretical and empirical problems. We think this shows that GB theory is on the wrong track, and that configurational notions of this kind do not really have any deep linguistic significance. On our account, on the other hand, the binding theory is formulated in terms of the relative obliqueness of grammatical functions. With the binding theory formulated in these terms, the problems that we have considered here simply disappear.

6.7 Nonsyntactic Factors in the Distribution of Exempt Anaphors

As we have noted at several points in the preceding section, our version of Principle A differs from Chomsky's, and indeed from most theories of anaphor distribution since Lees and Klima 1963, insofar as it constrains only those anaphors that have a less oblique referential coargument. For other anaphors, which we have called *exempt*, such as those in (17), we believe that the determination of the antecedent must be made by other, nonsyntactic factors.[18] In this section we discuss both processing (*intervention*) and discourse (*point of view*) constraints on exempt anaphors.

18. As Zribi-Hertz (1989) points out, examples of nonexempt anaphors that nevertheless violate our version of Principle A (and virtually all previous treatments of English reflexives) are attested in the works of various writers:

(i)   Clara$_i$ did not know whether to regret or to rejoice at their arrival; she$_i$ did not get on well with either of them . . . , and yet, on the other hand their presence did not intensify the difficulty, but somehow dissipated and confused it, so that at least its burden did not rest upon herself$_i$ alone. (Margaret Drabble)

(ii)   Not till she had, with difficulty, succeeded in explaining to him$_i$ that she had done nothing to justify such results and that his$_i$ wife was equally incredulous of her innocence and suspected himself$_i$, the pastor, to be the cause of her distress, did his$_i$ face light up with understanding. (William Gerhardie)

(iii)   Whom he$_i$ [Philip] was supposed to be fooling, he$_i$ couldn't imagine. Not the twins, surely, because Désirée, in the terrifying way of progressive Ameri-

Why have most analyses of anaphor binding in the past attempted to explain the distribution of coargument anaphors and exempt anaphors by a single principle? The reason is that in simple examples like (85), the observed coindexing seems obligatory:

(85)   *a.* John$_i$ found [a picture of himself$_i$].
        b. The women$_i$ selected [pictures of each other$_i$].
        c. The men$_i$ admired [each other's$_i$ trophies].
        d. The men$_i$ introduced the women$_j$ to [each other's$_{i/j}$ spouses].

Similarly, in examples like (86), it appears that the minimal c-commanding NP (i.e. *Tom*) is the only possible antecedent for the anaphor:

(86)   *a.* Bill remembered that Tom$_i$ saw [a picture of himself$_i$] in the post office.
        b. What Bill remembered was that Tom$_i$ saw [a picture of himself$_i$] in the post office.
        c. What bothered Bill was that Tom$_i$ had seen [a picture of himself$_i$] in the post office.
        d. Bill remembered that Tom$_i$ said that there was [a picture of himself$_i$] in the post office.
        e. What Bill remembered was that Tom$_i$ said that there was [a picture of himself$_i$] in the post office.

These facts are predicted by standard versions of binding theory, such as that of Chomsky discussed above, in which Principle A is formulated so as to ig-

---

        can parents, believed in treating children like adults and had undoubtedly explained to them the precise nature of her relationship with himself$_j$. (David Lodge)
(iv)   But Rupert$_i$ was not unduly worried about Peter's opinion of himself$_i$. (Iris Murdoch)
(v)   Miss Stepney$_i$'s [heart was] a precise register of facts as manifested in their relation to herself$_i$. (Edith Wharton)

It is interesting to note that none of her examples are from spoken language, an idiom that seems to exclude the possibility of such violations of Principle A; indeed, such examples are uniformly judged ungrammatical by American speakers (insofar as we have been able to ascertain). These facts suggest either (1) that there exist differences among varieties of English with regard to the precise formulation of Principle A, or (2) that grammatical constraints can sometimes be relaxed by writers who exercise certain license with their language. The latter possibility seems particularly plausible if there is an inherent association of reflexives with point of view. This association works in tandem with Principle A in everyday language use, but may provide an overarching strategy for reflexive interpretation in highly stylized narrative that supersedes Principle A.

nore the distinction between exempt and nonexempt anaphors. The restricted
formulation of Principle A we have offered does not guarantee the coindexings
indicated in these examples.

This, however, is a virtue of our analysis. Although there are diverse factors
that interact to cause the coindexings indicated in these examples to be favored,
these coindexings are not absolute. Hence they should not be enforced by principles of grammar, which state absolute constraints on binding. To see this,
note first that changing the intervening NP *Tom* to an inanimate NP improves
the acceptability of picture noun reflexives with nonlocal antecedents: [19]

(87)   *a.* ?Bill$_i$ remembered that *the Times* had printed [a picture of him-
              self$_i$] in the Sunday edition.
        b. ?What Bill$_i$ remembered was that *the Times* had printed [a picture
              of himself$_i$] in the Sunday edition.
        c. ?What bothered Bill$_i$ was that *the Times* had printed [a picture of
              himself$_i$] in the Sunday edition.
        d. Bill$_i$ suspected that *the silence* meant that [a picture of himself$_i$]
              would soon be on the post office wall.

Quantified intervenors also enhance acceptability, as do expletive intervenors
(also noted by Kuno (1987)):

(88)   *a.* Bill$_i$ thought that *nothing* could make [a picture of himself$_i$ in
              the *Times*] acceptable to Sandy.
        b. ?What Bill$_i$ wasn't sure of was whether *any newspaper* would put
              [a picture of himself$_i$] on the front page.
        c. Bill$_i$ suspected that *there* would soon be [a picture of himself$_i$]
              on the post office wall.
        d. Bill$_i$ knew that *it* would take a [picture of himself$_i$ with Gor-
              bachev] to get Mary's attention.

These facts are reminiscent of those cited in the literature on 'Super Equi NP
Deletion' (Grinder 1970, 1971; Kimball 1971; Clements 1975; Jacobson and
Neubauer 1976). Super-Equi is a nonlocal anaphoric relation between the
unexpressed subject of a gerund or infinitive phrase and an NP higher in the
tree structure:

(89)   *a.* Mary$_i$ knew [that [PRO$_i$ getting herself arrested] would be
              unpleasant].
        b. John$_i$ thought [that the fact [that [PRO$_i$ criticizing himself] was
              hard] surprised Mary].

Super Equi, though unbounded in principle, is subject to an *Intervention Constraint* (Grinder 1970), which rules out the possibility of a nonlocal controller

19. Closely related examples are noted by Kuno (1987: 95).

when another possible controller intervenes, as shown in (90) (examples from Jacobson and Neubauer (1976: 434ff.)):

(90)   a.   *John$_i$ thought [that Mary would be bothered by [PRO$_i$ shaving himself]].
         b.   *John$_i$ thought [that Mary was surprised by the fact [that [PRO$_i$ criticizing himself] was hard]].

The Intervention Constraint, in our view, is plausibly viewed as a processing-based factor that interacts with grammatical constraints in such a way as to render unacceptable a family of sentences that are otherwise grammatical.[20]

Now as the literature on Super Equi makes clear, there are certain intervenors that do not inhibit long-distance control, for example, expletives:

(91)   a.   John$_i$ thought [that it would be illegal [PRO$_i$ to undress himself]]. (Clements 1975)
         b.   John$_i$ thought [that it was likely [to be illegal [PRO$_i$ to undress himself]]].
         c.   Mary$_i$ knew [that there would be no particular problem in [PRO$_i$ getting herself a job]].

And it is straightforward to show that inanimate intervenors also increase acceptability:

(92)   a.   John$_i$ thought [that Proposition 91 made [PRO$_i$ undressing himself] illegal].
         b.   Mary$_i$ knew [that the prevailing political climate would ensure [that [PRO$_i$ getting herself arrested] would be unpleasant]].

The similarity between the way intervenors affect Super Equi sentences and the observed facts of exempt anaphors is striking. In fact, Jacobson and Neubauer (1976: 435) suggest in passing that (for many speakers) picture noun reflexives and Super Equi are governed by the very same Intervention Constraint. Once this insight is appreciated, we can begin to understand how many researchers have mistakenly thought that exempt anaphors obey the same constraints as nonsubject coargument anaphors. Structures containing animate intervenors define environments virtually identical to those where Principle A does hold. It is only when we consider examples lacking strong (typically animate) intervenors that we see that the constraint in question is weaker than Principle A.

Another factor that appears to affect the acceptability of exempt anaphors is the nature of the determiner. Changing the determiner of a picture noun phrase

20. See the closely related proposal by Kuno (1987: 74ff.), stated in terms of Langacker's (1969) notion of *chain of command*.

to *the* or *that*, that is, making the phrase more definite, often improves acceptability:

(93)   *a*. What Bill$_i$ finally realized is that the *Times* was going to print
            [that picture of himself$_i$ with Gorbachev] in the Sunday edition.
        b. Bill$_i$ finally realized that if the *Times* was going to print [that pic-
            ture of himself$_i$ with Gorbachev] in the Sunday edition, there
            might be some backlash.
        c. Bill$_i$ suspected that the silence meant that [the picture of himself$_i$
            with Gorbachev] had already gone to press.

These examples also demonstrate another important factor that has long been recognized to be relevant to the acceptability of picture noun reflexives: *point of view*. The differences between reportive and nonreportive style and their importance for the statement of linguistic principles have been discussed at length in the literature.[21] The conclusion reached within this tradition of research, by and large ignored in current discussions of binding theory, is that reflexive pronouns, in particular (exempt) picture noun reflexives, often are assigned an antecedent on the basis of point of view, the reflexive taking as its antecedent an NP whose referent is the individual whose viewpoint or perspective is somehow being represented in a given text. We will make no attempt here to summarize the evidence for this conclusion except to cite two further pieces of evidence supporting it.

Consider the discourse in (94):

(94)   John$_i$ was going to get even with Mary. That picture of himself$_i$ in
        the paper would really annoy her, as would the other stunts he had
        planned.

In the most natural interpretation of (94), the narrator has taken on John's perspective, or viewpoint. This perspective is moreover maintained throughout the two-sentence text. And the picture noun reflexive is naturally interpretable as referring to John.

Compare this with the discourse in (95), where Mary's viewpoint is presented:

(95)   *Mary was quite taken aback by the publicity John$_i$ was receiving.
        That picture of himself$_i$ in the paper had really annoyed her, and
        there was not much she could do about it.

---

21. A few relevant references are Kuroda 1965, 1973; Kuno 1972, 1975, 1983, 1987; Kuno and Kaburaki 1977; Cantrall 1974; Banfield 1982; Sells 1987; Zribi-Hertz 1989; and Iida 1992.

Here the picture noun reflexive with *John* as antecedent is unacceptable. In order to refer to John in such a text, a nonreflexive pronoun must be used, as in (96):

(96)   Mary was quite taken aback by the publicity John$_i$ was receiving. That picture of him$_i$ in the paper had really annoyed her, and there was not much she could do about it.

This kind of observation strongly suggests that when a reflexive is exempt from Principle A, it is constrained, in part, to take as its antecedent an NP referring to the individual whose viewpoint the text presents.

In addition, it is generally assumed in discourse studies that each sentence (or clause) presents at most one viewpoint.[22] This assumption, taken together with the claim that exempt anaphors refer to the individual whose viewpoint is expressed, leads to the conclusion that if a single clause has more than one such anaphor, they will be referentially identical. This conclusion appears to be correct for English, as the unacceptability of the following examples shows:[23]

(97)   *a.* *John told Mary that the photo of himself with her in Rome proved that the photo of herself with him in Naples was a fake.
        b. *John traded Mary pictures of herself for pictures of himself.

English psych verbs (e.g. *bother*) present another case in which failure to consider a sufficiently wide range of data has led previous analyses to overlook the possible role of viewpoint in determining the antecedent of anaphors. It is natural to assume that the bearer of the experiencer role (e.g. the primary object of *bother*) is the individual whose viewpoint is being reflected. And so we observe contrasts like (98a, b):

(98)   *a.* The picture of himself$_i$ in *Newsweek* bothered John$_i$.
        b. *The picture of himself$_i$ in *Newsweek* bothered John$_i$'s father.

Although, as we noted above in connection with (17c), attempts have been made to reanalyze such examples syntactically in order to reconcile them with Principle A, it might just as plausibly be maintained that (98b) is bad precisely because sentences containing verbs like *bother* tend to present the experiencer's (John's father's) viewpoint (not John's). This account is further supported by the grammaticality of examples such as those in (99):

22. Kuno (1987: 207ff.) discusses related facts in terms of his Ban on Conflicting Empathy Foci.

23. It may be the case that complex sentences contain embedded domains where distinct viewpoints are presented. We have not systematically explored this issue.

(99)   *a.* The picture of himself$_i$ in *Newsweek* dominated John$_i$'s thoughts.
        b. The picture of himself$_i$ in *Newsweek* made John$_i$'s day.
        c. The picture of himself$_i$ in *Newsweek* shattered the piece of mind
             that John$_i$ had spent the last six months trying to restore.

Note that (99a) and (99b) are structurally the same as (98b); the difference is
that in all the examples in (99), it is John whose viewpoint is reflected. It is
difficult to imagine any principle involving a configurationally determined notion of binding domain, however formulated, that would account for such facts.

6.8 Alternatives

6.8.1 Movement to AGR

As we noted in section 6.3, Chomsky (1986a) sketches a possible alternative
theory of anaphor binding wherein anaphors undergo movement to AGR of Infl
at the level of LF. Together with the assumption (see (5) above) that AGR is
coindexed with the subject, such a theory would appear to predict that all anaphors are bound by subjects unless something else is said. In support of the
movement-to-AGR account, Chomsky (1986a: 174–175) cites example (100),
noting that 'here the binder of *each other* must be *they*, not *us*, as the sense
makes clear':

(100)   They told us that pictures of each other would be on sale.

However, as Chomsky acknowledges in a footnote, 'the relevant facts are less
clear than the exposition assumes.' Accepting this assessment, we find the reading of (100) where *us* antecedes the reciprocal to be quite acceptable. Indeed,
in structurally identical examples such as (101), the matrix object is the preferred antecedent:

(101)   *a.* John told his two daughters that each other's pictures were
             prettier.
         b. The matchmakers told Zhang Xiansheng and Li Xiaojie that each
             other's parents were richer than they really were.

On the basis of such facts, as well as the numerous other types of English
examples we have examined wherein anaphors are bound by objects, are coindexed with a non-c-commanding NP, or else have a discourse antecedent, we
consider an account of long-distance anaphor binding based on movement to
AGR (or some analog in terms of structure sharing) to be untenable.

Accounts of this kind have also been proposed to deal with so-called long-
distance anaphors in languages such as Chinese, Japanese, and Korean (Battistella 1987; Cole et al. 1990), for which it is often claimed that only
c-commanding subject antecedents (possibly in a superordinate clause) are

possible. However, on the basis of examples like the following (where the antecedent has no plausible analysis as a subject at any stage of derivation), it is now generally agreed that at least some cases of *zibun* binding are governed by discourse, rather than structural conditions:

(102)   [zibun$_i$-no buka-no   husimatu-ga]   Taroo$_i$-no
        self$_i$-of   subordinate-of misconduct-SUBJ Taroo-of

        syusse-o   samatagete-simatta.
        promotion-OBJ   blocked-have

        'Misconduct of his$_i$ subordinate has blocked Taroo$_i$'s promotion.'

But, as Iida (1992) demonstrates, 'mixed' theories of *zibun* binding—those that assume two distinct *zibun*-binding mechanisms (one based on structure, one on discourse)—are too weak. They fail to provide an adequate account of the full range of restrictions on possible antecedents. In the analysis that Iida develops, a unified account of *zibun* binding is offered in terms of a contextual index that encodes *deictic perspective*.[24] An instance of *zibun* always takes as its antecedent an NP whose referent is the individual whose deictic perspective is presented by a sentence or an NP containing that instance. The choice of such deictic perspective will also determine the interpretation of expressions like *migigawa* 'the right side.' Hence on Iida's account, two occurrences of a reflexive in a simple clause must be coreferential. To put it another way, a Japanese sentence can contain two noncoreferential occurrences of *zibun* just in case they occur in different phrases each of which presents a distinct deictic perspective. Thus (103) can convey that Taroo could not defend Hanako from the criticism of her (Hanako's) friend, but (103) cannot convey that Taroo could not defend Hanako against the criticism of his (Taroo's) friend:

(103)   Hanako-wa [Taroo-ga   zibun-o zibun-no tomodati-no
        Hanako-TOP Taroo-SUBJ self-OBJ self-of   friend-of

        hihan-kara   mamorikir-e-nakatta] koto-o sitteita.
        criticism-from defend-could-not   CMP   knew

        'Hanako$_i$ knew that Taroo$_j$ couldn't defend her$_i$ against her$_i$/*his$_j$ friend's criticism.'

But in an example like (104), where the embedded *no*-clause may induce a shift in perspective, no such constraint is to be observed:

(104)   Hanako$_i$-wa [zibun$_i$-ga sono toki sudeni [Taroo-ga$_j$
        Hanako-TOP   self-SUBJ   that time already Taroo-SUBJ

---

24. Iida distinguishes deictic perspective from point of view, arguing that the former, not the latter, is relevant for *zibun* interpretation.

zibun$_{i/j}$-o kiratteiru-no]-o sitteita koto]-o mitometa-gara-nakat-ta.
self-OBJ hate-CMP-OBJ   knew CMP-OBJ admit-want-not-past

'Hanako$_i$ did not want to admit that she$_i$ already knew at the time that Taroo$_j$ hated her$_i$/himself$_j$.'

In the case of Chinese, a movement-to-AGR account of anaphor binding runs afoul of examples such as (105)–(107) (due to Tang (1989)), where the subject antecedent fails to c-command the anaphor:

(105) [Zhangsan$_i$ de   jiaoao]$_j$ hai le   ziji$_{i/*j}$.
       Zhangsan PART pride   hurt PER self

       'Zhangsan's pride harmed him.'

(106) [Wo$_i$ ma   ta$_j$]$_k$ dui ziji$_{i/*j/*k}$ meiyou   haochu.
       I   scold he to self   not-have advantage
       'That I scolded him did me no good.'

(107) [[[Zhangsan$_i$ de]   baba$_j$ de]   qian]$_k$ bei
       Zhangsan   PART father PART money BEI

       ziji$_{*i/j/*k}$ de   pengyou touzou le.
       self   PART friend   steal   PER
       '[[Zhangsan$_i$'s father]$_j$'s money]$_k$ was stolen by his$_{*i/j/*k}$ friend.'

Tang proposes an alternative account whereby, in case a c-commanding subject fails to be animate, antecedency can pass to the highest animate subject (or possessor) embedded within it.

However, as noted by Wang (n.d.), Tang's judgments seem to reflect only preferences, which may be overridden by pragmatic factors. Tang's example in (107), for example, may occur in discourses like the one in (108):

(108) Zhangsan$_i$ de baba de qian   bei ziji$_i$ de pengyou touzou le.
       Zhangsan$_i$'s father's money BEI self$_i$'s friend   steal PER
       Mama de shu ye   bei ziji$_i$ de pengyou touzou le.
       mother's book also BEI self's friend   steal PER
       'Zhangsan$_i$'s father's money was stolen by his$_i$ friend. (His) mother's books were also stolen by his$_i$ friend.'

And here it is clear that *ziji* can take *Zhangsan* as its antecedent. Moreover, in examples like the following (also due to Wang (n.d.)) *ziji* can be coindexed only with *Zhangsan*:

(109) [Zhangsan$_i$ de baba de   qian he mama de   shu]
       Zhangsan PART father PART money and mother PART book
       dou   bei [ziji$_i$ de   pengyou] touzou le.
       both/all BEI self PART friend   steal   PER

'Zhangsan$_i$'s father's money and (his) mother's books were both
stolen by his$_i$ friend.'

One such factor proposed by Wang is discourse topic; we would suggest that
point of view may play a role here as well.

6.8.2 A Thematic Alternative to Principle A?

It is tempting to try to derive the effect of the obliqueness hierarchy from other
primitives. As some people have suggested,[25] certain conditions on anaphor
binding might be seen in terms of a hierarchy of thematic relations, rather than
a hierarchy of grammatical relations such as we have proposed. Jackendoff
(1972), for example, seeks to explain constraints on reflexives by appeal to a
thematic hierarchy (Agent < Location, Source, Goal < Theme) together with
a condition that a reflexive cannot thematically outrank its antecedent.[26] A proposal of this sort makes many of the same predictions as our own analysis.

Thus, the deviance of the examples in (110), which we explain in terms of
the obliqueness hierarchy, might also be explained in terms of Jackendoff's
thematic hierarchy, as in fact it is in the analysis of Wilkins (1988):

(110)   *a.* *I sold himself$_i$[GOAL] the slave$_i$[THEME].
        b. *Mary talked about John$_i$[THEME] to himself$_i$[GOAL].

Because the hierarchy of grammatical relations bears a close relation to the
thematic hierarchy, it is often difficult to distinguish the predictions made by
these two approaches, though a reduction of our *local o-command* account to
one stated in terms of the thematic hierarchy would of course be welcome
progress.

The problems we see facing such a reduction of local o-command to the
thematic hierarchy are the following. First, the examples in (111) are predicted
to be ungrammatical by the thematic analysis (the reflexives in (110) are agents
and therefore outrank their antecedents on the thematic hierarchy), a prediction
argued to be correct by Jackendoff (1972):

(111)   *a.* John was shaved by himself.
        b. John was hit by himself.

Such examples, judged in isolation, are often considered to be deviant. But, as
noted already by Morgan (1969), this judgment is questionable. Examples like
(112), well-formed for virtually all speakers, are incorrectly ruled out by analyses based on the thematic hierarchy:

25. See, inter alia, Jackendoff 1972, Wilkins 1988, and Hellan 1988.

26. See also Jackendoff's (1992) alternative formulation of binding theory in terms
of hierarchical relations stated on conceptual structure, an alternative we have not yet
systematically compared with our own proposals.

(112)   *a.* The only barber who was shaved by himself was Figaro.
         b. The only pitcher who was ever hit by himself was Cy Young.

Whatever deviance inheres in examples like (111a, b) must have some other explanation.
   Second, consider (113a–c):

(113)   *a.*   I sold the slave$_i$ [THEME] to himself$_i$ [GOAL].
         b.   I sold the slave$_i$ [GOAL] himself$_i$ [THEME].
         c. *I sold himself$_i$ [GOAL] the slave$_i$ [THEME].

These contrasts would appear to pose a paradox for any account of reflexive binding stated in terms of the thematic hierarchy. If GOAL is higher than THEME on the thematic hierarchy, then why is (113a) possible? If the THEME is higher than GOAL, then why is (113b) good and (113c) impossible? The answer to these questions offered by Wilkins (1988) is that the THEME argument in (113a) and the GOAL arguments in (113b, c) are also PATIENTs. And, since PATIENT is higher on the thematic hierarchy than GOAL or THEME, these examples constitute no violation of the thematic hierarchy condition.[27]

   This multiple θ-role approach may ultimately prove to be successful, yet one cannot help but observe (as noted by Wilkins (1988: 209)) that in all relevant examples, the PATIENT turns out to be the NP adjacent to the verb, that is, the primary object, which in turn is less oblique than the anaphor it binds, just as predicted by our obliqueness-based account.

   We should add that examples like (114) may also pose difficulties for accounts stated in terms of a thematic hierarchy condition:

(114)   *a.*   John$_i$ seems to himself$_i$ to be unproductive.
         b.   John$_i$ seems to be unproductive to himself$_i$.

Although similar examples involving first-person reflexives are cited as ungrammatical by Postal (1971: 35), (114) seems to be only as peculiar as the message it conveys (compare the grammatical deviance of *Mary talked about John to himself*). Consequently, (114a, b) should in all likelihood be treated as grammatical, in particular as not being ruled out by Principle A. The problem that examples like this pose is simply that the subject bears no thematic role, and hence presumably is thematically outranked by the role-assigned reflexive that it binds, in violation of the thematic hierarchy condition.

   Other problematic cases include examples like (115):

(115)   *a.*   Max strikes himself as qualified for the job.
         b.   He looks funny to himself.
         c.   Schwarz is acceptable to himself (just as he is).

27. Wilkins, following Jackendoff (1987), suggests as a criterion for patienthood the possibility of occurring in the X position in such sentence frames as *What happened to X is . . .* or *What Y did to X is . . . .*

Again, Postal (1971: 47) treats examples like these as ungrammatical (and as providing motivation for the transformation of *Psych movement*, applying subject to his *Crossover Constraint*). And again, it seems clear that these examples are only pragmatically deviant. The difficulty in interpreting the examples in (115) is precisely the difficulty of imagining an appropriate context. In order to interpret (115a), for example, one must imagine that Max is somehow disassociated from himself, or in some other peculiar mental state where he gets only fleeting impressions of himself. If Max were in a more familiar mental state, where he has reasonable self-knowledge, we would be likely to report that *Max believes himself to be qualified for the job*. The deviance of (115a) is thus attributable to a conflict between the meaning of *strike* and customary assumptions about people's self-knowledge. Once this is appreciated, binding theory is seen to play no role in the explanation of (115a). And much the same is true of (115b, c), whose grammaticality (pace Postal) can be appreciated with little or no contextualization.

But given that these examples should not be ruled out by Principle A, the problem they pose is the same as that posed by the examples in (114). Either the subject antecedent of the reflexive bears no θ-role, or else it is a theme. In either case, the reflexive it antecedes outranks it on the thematic hierarchy, in violation of the thematic hierarchy condition.

In sum, though it is tempting to speculate that a thematically based condition on anaphors might replace the condition we have formulated in terms of the hierarchy of grammatical relations, there remain a number of outstanding problems that must first be solved before any version of the thematic hierarchy condition can be maintained.

6.8.3 A Totally Nonconfigurational Binding Theory?

In section 6.4, we presented a version of binding theory wherein Principles A and B were formulated in terms of the nonconfigurational notion of local command; only Principle C appealed to tree structure, inasmuch as the definition of (general) o-command made reference to the domination relation. In this section, we propose a possible modification to our binding theory that obviates the need for any recourse to domination. The basic idea here is to minimally extend local o-command in such a way that unexpressed reflexive subjects of VP and predicative complements become subject to Principle A. As will be shown in the next chapter, such an extension is motivated by the desire to derive via binding theory certain important generalizations about complement control, such as Manzini's Generalization (that VP complements are controlled by an argument of the governing verb) and Visser's Generalization (that subject-control verbs do not passivize). However, once local o-command is extended in this way, a natural definition of (general) o-command suggests itself that does not require reference to domination.

We begin by considering the following revision to the definition of local o-command (cf. the original definition in (37)):

(116)   DEFINITION OF LOCAL O-COMMAND (revised):

Let Y and Z be *synsem* objects with distinct LOCAL values, Y referential. Then Y *locally o-commands* Z just in case either:

  i. Y is less oblique than Z; or
  ii. Y locally o-commands some X that subcategorizes for Z.

The effect of the new (second) clause is that now a referential complement will locally o-command not only more oblique complements, but also the subject SUBCAT element of a more oblique unsaturated complement, provided such exists.[28] Let us now assume that, in the case of equi control verbs, such SUBCAT elements are reflexive, an assumption anticipated by Helke (1971) and Fodor (1975), who treat equi constructions in terms of a rule deleting *for self*, and also suggested by the GB treatment of PRO as a pronominal anaphor. Then as it stands, our Principle A will entail that such elements must be coindexed with (i.e. controlled by) an argument of the governing verb; no changes are required to the definitions of (locally) o-bound, (locally) o-free, or (general) o-command.[29]

28. Another effect of clause (ii) is to give rise to another class of cases that are excluded as instances of local o-command by the requirement that Y and Z have distinct LOCAL values, namely, cases where Y is a raising controller and Z is the unexpressed complement subject. Without this requirement, examples like (i) would wrongly be ruled out as Principle C violations:

(i)   Leslie seems to be nice.

29. We are well-aware that in many languages that have possessive reflexives, such possessives are standardly assumed to be subject to Principle A. Latin *suus, -a, -um* is one such case, as illustrated in (i) (adapted from a Martial epigram):

(i)   [Hic homo]$_i$ [suos$_i$ dentes] habet.
      this man   self's teeth   has
      'This man has his own teeth.'

There are various ways to extend our definition of local o-command so that Principle A extends to cases such as these. One proposal might be to replace clause (ii) in (116) with the following condition:

(ii)′ Y locally o-commands some X whose head's initial SUBCAT member is Z.

As stated, this modification would cover not only cases like (i), but also cases like (73) above. It would also exclude long-distance binding of anaphors analogous to the occurrences of *each other's* in (17) above. Perhaps this is the correct result for languages that have possessive reflexives. It is also possible that the correct extension of local o-command should take the notion of modifier into account, as *suus* functions essentially like an adjective in examples like these, as do, e.g., Hindi *apnaa* and possessive reflexives in numerous other languages. We will not attempt to resolve this matter here.

However, once local o-command is redefined as in (116), a natural way of redefining (general) o-command recursively suggests itself. This is given in (117) (cf. (38)):

(117)   DEFINITION OF O-COMMAND (revised):

Let Y and Z be *synsem* objects, with distinct LOCAL values, Y refer-ential. Then Y *o-commands* Z just in case either:
  i. Y is less oblique than Z; or
  ii. Y o-commands some X that subcategorizes for Z; or
  iii. Y o-commands some X that is a projection of Z (i.e. the HEAD values of X and Z are token-identical).

It is clear from the forms of these definitions that local o-command is a special case of o-command; indeed the cases of local o-command are just those cases of o-command whose verification does not involve recourse to the recursion clause (iii).

By way of illustration, consider example (118):

(118)   Kim thinks John kissed Mary.

First, note that *Kim*, as the subject of *thinks*, must (locally) o-command the sentential complement *John kissed Mary*; this is a consequence of clause (i). Next, by an application of clause (iii), we establish that *Kim* o-commands the head verb of the embedded clause *kissed*. And finally, by an application of clause (ii), we conclude that *Kim* o-commands both *John* and *Mary*, since *kissed* subcategorizes for both.

We conclude this section by calling attention to a rather subtle point involv-ing strong crossover that provides independent motivation for the totally non-configurational binding theory sketched immediately above. As we noted above, with o-command defined as in (38), our formulation of Principle C pre-dicts the ungrammaticality of (55d), repeated here as (119):

(119)   *John$_i$, he$_i$ said you like ___$_i$.

This is because the trace, which shares the content sort *npro* with the filler *John*, is illicitly o-commanded by the coindexed *he*. It is natural to assume that an entirely analogous explanation exists for the fact that *he* in (120) cannot be coindexed with *John* in (120):

(120)   *John$_i$, he$_i$ claimed left.

Recall, however, that (as explained in section 4 of Chapter 4) we follow GPSG in assuming that English has no subject traces. Instead, the structure of (120) is roughly as shown in (121), where the head verb *claimed* is produced by the Subject Extraction Lexical Rule:

(121)

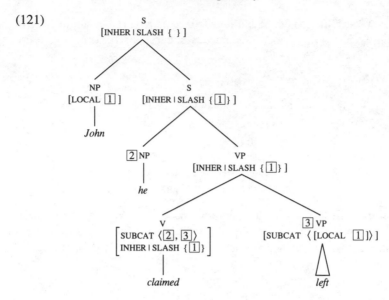

It is easy to see that as long as o-command is defined in terms of tree configurations, Principle C cannot yield an account of (120) analogous to that for
(119), since the crucial trace does not exist. But with o-command redefined as
in (117), this problem disappears. To see why, consider the SUBCAT value of
claimed, shown in more detail in (122):

(122)   [SUBCAT ⟨ [2]NP, [3]VP[SUBCAT ⟨[LOCAL [1]]⟩]⟩]

Suppose now that *he* (= [2]) and *John* are coindexed. Since the LOCAL value
of *John* coincides with the INHER | SLASH element of *claimed*, which in turn is
lexically specified to be identical with the LOCAL value on the subject SUBCAT
element of the finite VP *left* (= [3]), the SUBCAT list in (122) now constitutes a
violation of Principle C. This is because (i) [2] is less oblique than [3], which
in turn subcategorizes for the [LOCAL [1]] subject of *left*, so that [2] o-commands the subject of *left*; (ii) *John* and the [LOCAL [1]] subject of *left* are
coindexed; and (iii) the [LOCAL [1]] subject of *left* shares with *John* the content
sort *npro*. It follows that, with o-command redefined as in (117), (120) is ruled
out by Principle C, as desired.

6.9 Conclusion

The binding theory we have presented in this chapter makes no use of configurational notions like c-command, and possibly (section 6.8.3) requires no appeal to phrase structure constructs of any kind. Replacing such constructs in

our binding theory have been the notions of o-command and local o-command. These notions, together with a variety of processing and discourse factors, have been argued to provide an account of English binding superior to that developed within GB by Chomsky (1986a) (sections 6.4 and 6.6) or to binding theories based on the hierarchy of thematic relations first presented in Jackendoff (1972) (section 6.8.2).

7

Complement Control

7.1 Introduction

We now return to the topic of controlled complements.[1] In the analysis presented in Chapter 3, we assumed that the fundamental mechanism of control was coindexing between the unexpressed subject of an unsaturated complement and its controller. This rather traditional view of control has been challenged by a number of researchers working within the tradition of Montague grammar, where controlled complements are analyzed semantically as properties (rather than propositions or psoas) and control is treated simply as a lexical entailment. On the property-based account, the unexpressed subject of, for example, an infinitival complement is never directly identified (via coindexing or any other grammatical mechanism) with the controller, which merely participates in certain entailments guaranteed by meaning postulates. The property-based theory of control is defended by a number of researchers, perhaps most notably by Chierchia (1984a, 1984b) (see also Dowty 1985; Chierchia and Jacobson 1986; and Jacobson 1990), who argues that it provides an immediate account of inference patterns like those in (1):

(1)   Jean tried to play Paganini.
       René tried everything that Jean tried.
       Therefore, René tried to play Paganini.
       (*Therefore, René tried for Jean to play Paganini.)

Whereas it is true that the property-based theory of control provides an elegant account of such patterns of argument validity, it is not the only possible approach in light of the fact, discussed in detail by Chierchia (1990), that verbs taking full clausal complements also admit the possibility of such 'sloppy' inference patterns when a pronoun coindexed with the matrix subject is present within the embedded clause, as in (2):

1. This chapter is a revised version of Ivan A. Sag and Carl Pollard, 'An Integrated Theory of Complement Control,' *Language*, 67, no. 1(1991): 63–113; it appears here with appropriate permissions. We would particularly like to thank Gennaro Chierchia, Georgia Green, and Paul Kroeger for helpful discussion of the material presented in this chapter.

(2)   Pavarotti$_i$ believes he$_i$ is a genius.
          Domingo believes everything that Pavarotti believes.
          Therefore, Domingo$_j$ believes that he$_j$ is a genius.

Chierchia (1990) presents an analysis of such cases, based on Lewis's (1979) notion of belief *de se*, wherein embedded clauses may be analyzed as properties, as an alternative to their customary interpretation as propositions. But an alternative approach to this entire problem seems equally plausible—namely, to treat inferences like the one illustrated in (2) as the result of an interpretational indeterminacy that arises from whatever factors lead to strict/sloppy ambiguities in general. This approach would open the door to retaining a version of the traditional analysis of the infinitivals in (1), as long as control theory can be called on to explain the unacceptability of the unwanted inference in (1), where no reindexing has affected the complement of *try*. In light of the existence of examples like (2), it seems that some other evidence must be found in order to choose between the property-based analysis of unsaturated infinitive phrases defended by Chierchia and Dowty and the familiar proposition-based (or psoa-based) approach we adopted in Chapter 3.

We think that the facts of agreement provide just such evidence. One crucial aspect of the property-based theory of control is that there is no direct link between the semantic argument position of the controller and that of the unexpressed subject of the controlled complement; the only relation between these two argument positions is inferential. But recall that there is agreement of person, number, and gender throughout control structures, for example, as shown in (3):

(3)   *a.*   He$_i$ tried to find himself$_i$.
          b.   *He$_i$ tried to find herself$_i$/themselves$_i$/itself$_i$.
          c.   *He$_i$ tried to find myself$_i$/yourself$_i$/yourselves$_i$.

The property theory of control thus appears to require a purely semantic approach to agreement, along the lines proposed by Dowty and Jacobson (1989), where all agreement distinctions, even grammatical gender, are treated exclusively in terms of denotational restrictions.

As we have already shown in considerable detail, there are a host of unsolved problems facing any purely semantic theory of agreement like Dowty and Jacobson's (see section 7 of Chapter 2 for a summary). However, under the assumption that control involves structure sharing between two indices (one the index of the controller, the other the index within the embedded psoa that corresponds to the unexpressed subject of the VP complement), the observed agreement phenomena are completely explained by the theory of agreement outlined in Chapter 2. Because agreement features are attributes of indices, coindexed phrases must always have compatible specifications for all agreement features. This important result follows (see section 7.2) under the assumptions of our psoa-based theory of control, and not from the property-based account, which, though otherwise compatible with our overall theory of grammar, we are constrained to reject.

In Chapter 3, we also assumed that the mechanism for determining which coargument was the controller (in cases of obligatory control) was simple lexical stipulation. In the analysis presented in this chapter, however, essentially all such word-specific control stipulations are eliminated in favor of a small number of semantically based principles of controller assignment. This follows the insights of Jackendoff (1972: 214ff.), who first suggested that controller assignment is determined by semantic (or *thematic*) roles, rather than by purely syntactic factors (e.g. structural configurations or grammatical relations), as has frequently been assumed (Lakoff 1965; Rosenbaum 1967; Williams 1980; Chomsky 1980; Bresnan 1982; Larson 1988). Jackendoff observed, for instance, that controller choice in the following examples can be predicted in a uniform manner:

(4)   *a.* Joe got furious at Henry.
      b. John promised to leave.
      c. Frank got Joe furious at Henry.
      d. John promised Bill to leave.

Jackendoff's treatment involves role-based constraints to the effect that the controller of the unexpressed subject of the complement of *get* is always the individual playing the role of THEME, whereas in the case of *promise* (Jackendoff 1974: 503), it is the AGENT (or SOURCE) that must be the controller. These constraints remain constant across different subcategorizations of the 'same' verb, as illustrated.

Our analysis will build on Jackendoff's insight, extending his semantic view of control constraints to a range of data broader than that standardly considered in such discussions. Our semantic constraints eliminate the need for any stipulations associated with specific lexical items (e.g. the verb *promise* or the noun *appeal*) and provide a unified account of sets of data such as the following:

(5)   *a.* Sandy promised Tracy to leave the party early.
      b. Sandy's promise to Tracy to leave the party early caused quite an uproar.
      c. The promise by Sandy to leave the party early caused quite an uproar.
      d. The promise that Sandy made, to leave the party early, caused quite an uproar.
      e. Sandy made Tracy a promise. It was to leave the party early.

(6)   *a.* Sandy appealed to Tracy to leave the party early.
      b. Sandy's appeal to Tracy to leave the party early was untimely.

c. The appeal that Sandy made to Tracy, to leave the party early, was untimely.

d. Sandy made an appeal to Tracy. It was to leave the party early.

(7)   a. Dana wished to leave the party early.

b. The wish that Dana made, to leave the party early, was fulfilled.

c. Dana made a wish. It was to leave the party early.

Further, our semantically based principles of controller assignment, taken together with the theory of binding presented in Chapter 6, allow us to explain the apparent shifts of control in examples like (8), first noted by Hust and Brame (1976):

(8)   a. Lee promised Pat to be allowed to leave.

b. Pat was promised to be allowed to leave.

As noted by Jackendoff (1987: 370), such examples have not been adequately explained by previous theories of control, which we will survey. On our account, these examples involve no control shift at all. Rather, the semantic content of the infinitival complement, a (nonintentional) state, has been 'coerced' to an action in order to achieve semantic compatibility with promising (the semantics of *promise to* crucially involves a commitment to act, not a commitment to truth). On our analysis, (8a), for example, is treated roughly on a par with *Lee promised Pat to cause him (Pat) to be allowed to leave*. The interpolated causer in the complement's semantics is thus identified with the appropriate matrix argument by the same semantic principles that determine controller assignment quite generally.

Finally, we will offer some speculative remarks on the consequences of our account with respect to the question of controller realization, with particular attention to a proposal of Manzini's (roughly, that the unexpressed subject of a VP complement must be controlled within the minimal clause containing it), and to the phenomenon that Bresnan (1982) has dubbed *Visser's Generalization*, that is, the general incompatibility of subject control and passivizability, as illustrated in (9) and (10):

(9)   a.   Lee persuaded Pat to leave.

b.   Pat was persuaded to leave (by Lee).

(10)   a.   Lee promised Pat to leave.

b.   *Pat was promised to leave (by Lee).

7.2 The Semantic Nature of Controller Assignment

The principles of controller assignment are nonarbitrary. Radford (1981: 381) offers the following critical observation:

Firstly, arbitrary lists of properties associated with predicates have no predictive or explanatory value: ask the question 'How do you know this is a verb of subject control?' and you get the answer 'Because it's listed as a verb of subject control in the lexicon.' Secondly, treating *control . . .* as a *lexically governed* phenomenon implies that control properties are entirely arbitrary, and hence will vary in random fashion from dialect to dialect, or language to language: this would lead us to expect that the counterpart of *Fred persuaded Mary to give him title to her estate* in some other dialect or language would have subject control rather than non-subject control. . . . But as far as we know, this is not the case.

The point here is that many widely accepted analyses of control phenomena stipulate precisely what is to be explained, namely that in a clear, uniform, and consistent manner, verbs of a certain semantic type take 'subject control,' while those of a different semantic type take 'object control.' To illustrate this point, made also by Comrie (1984), consider the following classes of verbs, which exhibit uniform control constraints:

(11)   *order/permit* type (object control):

order, persuade, bid, charge, command, direct, enjoin, instruct, advise, authorize, mandate, convince, impel, induce, influence, inspire, motivate, move, pressure, prompt, sway, stir, talk (into), compel, press, propel, push, spur, encourage, exhort, goad, incite, prod, urge, bring, lead, signal, ask, empower, appeal (to), dare, defy, beg, prevent (from), forbid, allow, permit, enable, cause, force

(12)   *promise* type (subject control):

promise, swear, agree, contract, pledge, vow, try, intend, refuse, choose, decline, decide, demand, endeavor, attempt, threaten, undertake, propose, offer, aim

(13)   *want/expect* type (subject control):

want, desire, fancy, wish, ache, hanker, itch, long, need, hope, thirst, yearn, hate, aspire, expect

Verbs of the *order/permit* type all submit to a semantic analysis involving psoas where a certain participant (the referent of the object) is influenced by another participant (the referent of the subject) to perform an action (characterized in terms of the psoa denoted by the VP complement). The influencing participant may be an agent (as in *Kim persuaded Sandy to leave*) or a nonagent (as in *Ignorance of thermodynamics compelled Pat to enroll in a poetry class*). The semantics of every verb in this class thus involves a psoa whose relation is of the sort *influence*. With respect to such psoas, we may identify three semantic roles, which we will refer to as INFLUENCE (the possibly agentive influencer), INFLUENCED (the typically animate participant influenced by the

INFLUENCE), and SOA-ARG (the action that the INFLUENCED participant is influenced to perform (or, in the case of verbs like *prevent* and *forbid, not* to perform)).[2] In the case of the relations involved in the semantic analysis of verbs like *allow, permit, cause,* and *force,* the INFLUENCED participant need not be present; in such cases these verbs are raising verbs (e.g. *The police permitted there to be a demonstration in the park*).[3] In addition, in relations of this class the SOA-ARG argument need not be an action, as examples like *His pituitary condition caused him to be nine feet tall* show.

The *promise*-type verbs also exhibit semantic uniformity. The semantic analysis of these verbs involves psoas that contain a relation of a sort that we may refer to (perhaps somewhat inaccurately) as *commitment.* Commitments involve a typically animate participant that we may identify as COMMITTOR, and a SOA-ARG, in this case the action the COMMITTOR commits to performing (or to *not* performing, in the case of verbs like *refuse* or *decline*). Some *commitment*-sort relations also allow a third role, which we may refer to as COMMISSEE, the individual to whom the commitment is made.

Similarly, the *want/expect*-type verbs all involve desire, expectation, or similar mental orientation toward a given psoa. For these relations, we posit a third sort—*orientation*—whose associated roles will be characterized as EXPERIENCER (the participant who experiences the appropriate orientation) and SOA-ARG (here the psoa toward which the EXPERIENCER is oriented).

(14) summarizes this classification of *control-relations*:[4]

(14) Sortal hierarchy of control relations:

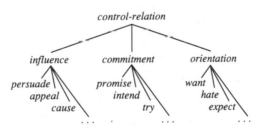

This hierarchy of relations is the basis for the determination of which relations take which roles. In addition, it plays a crucial role in the formulation of control theory, which we state as in (15):

2. For a different characterization of our notion of 'action' in terms of Castañeda's notion (see Castañeda 1975) of 'practition,' see the HPSG control theory developed by Clements and Wettengel (1989).

3. For some discussion, see Schmerling 1979.

4. At present, the motivation for this particular classification of relations is entirely intuitive. It is clearly desirable to develop further tests for classifying control relations. However, we will not embark on that important line of research here.

(15)   CONTROL THEORY (preliminary version):

If the CONTENT of an unsaturated phrase is the SOA-ARG in a psoa
whose relation is a control relation, then the subject SUBCAT element
of that phrase is coindexed with the INFLUENCED, COMMITTOR, or
EXPERIENCER participant in that psoa, according as the control relation is of sort *influence, commitment,* or *orientation,* respectively.

The role-based generalizations in (15) are adapted from Jackendoff
(1972, 1974), and the characterization of the relevant classes of relations is
adapted in part from Foley and Van Valin (1984). Our notion of *influence*-sort
relation (and, by extension, *influence*-sort psoa) is intended to be more general
than Foley and Van Valin's notion of *directive*, and our category of *commitment*
extends their category of *commissive* to include, for example, attempts as well
as promises. We distinguish *orientation*-sort relations from commitments on
the grounds that the latter do not involve agents and actions, but rather exper-
iencers and psoa arguments that may be either actions or states.[5]

One important property of the controller assignment principles in (15) is that
they apply whenever the content of an unsaturated phrase (e.g. an infinitival
VP) occurs in a particular semantic context. The condition in (15) constrains
any lexical entry whose relation is of one of the three sorts indicated above, for
example, the lexical entry for the verb *persuaded*. This is sufficient to guarantee that a sentence like (16) will have the CONTENT value sketched in (17):

(16)

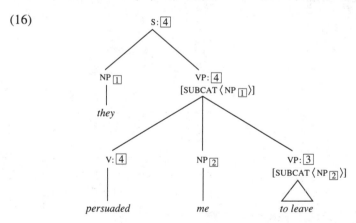

5. Here and throughout, the reader will notice that we have made cautious use of
generalized semantic (or thematic) roles. Our use of the notions of INFLUENCE, COM-
MITTOR, EXPERIENCER, and the like implies a commitment only to the idea that there
are semantic regularities that hold over the particular sorts of relations and psoas that
we consider, i.e. over psoas whose relation is of *influence, commitment,* and *orientation*
sort. For a critical discussion of thematic roles that we are in sympathy with, see Ladusaw and Dowty 1988.

(17)

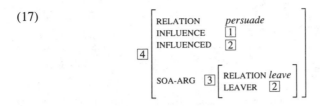

Thus (15) makes no mention of particular verbs; the controller assignment principles constrain the entire class of affected verbs in virtue of the nature of their semantic relation. As we shall see directly, the effect of these constraints is even more general.

Infinitival VPs also occur as dependents of nominal expressions, as illustrated in (18):

(18)   *a.* Sandy's promise/attempt to leave the party early caused quite an uproar.
       b. Chris's desire/wish to leave the party bothered Pat.
       c. Rene's signal/appeal to Jean to leave the room was noticed by everyone.

There is no apparent difference between the *semantic* function of these infinitival phrases within nominal constituents and their semantic function within VPs. The infinitival VPs in (18a) and (5a), for example, both designate the content of a promise made by an individual named Sandy. There is one important syntactic difference, however: within NPs these infinitival phrases are always optional.

It is evident that the unexpressed subjects of infinitival phrases within the NP are governed by the very same semantic principles that determine controller assignment for verbs.[6] In (18a) it is Sandy, the COMMITTOR of the promise, who controls the missing subject; in (18b) the controller is Chris, the EXPERIENCER of the desire or wish; and in (18c) it is Jean, the INFLUENCED participant in the *influence*-sort situation, who serves as controller. These observations show beyond any reasonable doubt that semantic control constraints function identically within nominal and verbal constituents. Within nominal constituents, however, the location of the semantically relevant NP cannot be specified in syntactic terms, as the examples in (19) show:

(19)   *a.* Sandy's promise to Tracy to leave the party early caused quite an uproar.
       b. The promise by Sandy to leave the party early caused quite an uproar.

6. The observation that verbal and nominal constructions obey similar control constraints was made by Higgins (1973) and by Jackendoff (1972, 1974). See also Williams 1985.

   c. The promise that Sandy made, to leave the party early, caused
       quite an uproar.
   d. The promise to leave the party early, which Kim knew would be
       immediately forthcoming from Sandy, was going to cause quite
       an uproar.

In all of these examples, the content of the promise, speaking informally, is that Sandy, the COMMITTOR of the promise, leave the party early. In (19a) the controller is realized as a possessor; in (19b) it is realized as the object of a *by*-phrase; in (19c–d) the COMMITTOR of the promise is not realized as any dependent of the noun *promise*. Rather, in (19c–d) it is only through integration of the content of the relative clause that the identity of the implicit COMMITTOR argument is determined.

   Of course the semantically determined controller need not be expressed within the NP at all:[7]

(20)   The whole room was focussed on Sandy. A promise now to endow
        the center would ensure the success of the funding drive.

In this context, Sandy is the most likely choice for controller of the unexpressed subject of the infinitival phrase in the second sentence. Yet, even if prior context clearly establishes someone other than Sandy (say someone whose promise would have an immediate and observable impact on Sandy), it remains true that that individual will be taken as the COMMITTOR of the promising as well as the controller of the unexpressed subject of the infinitival phrase. The two argument positions are inextricably linked. In fact, this link between unexpressed subject and the COMMITTOR of a promise can be observed even in the absence of a discourse referent, as in the examples in (21), discussed by Chomsky (1981), Heim (1982), Huang (1983), and Lebeaux (1984):

(21)   *a.* A promise to endow the center would indicate a desire to help the
            campaign.
        b. A promise to endow the center would mean a commitment to
            success.

It is never possible to construct a context where the COMMITTOR of the promise is disassociated from the controlled subject of the infinitival phrase. Thus examples like (22) are systematically ill-formed:

(22)   *a.* *Mary knew that a promise by John to get herself arrested would
            be extremely unfortunate.
        b. *John was quite upset. A promise by Mary to get himself arrested
            would be extremely unfortunate.

   7. Such examples are also noted by Williams (1985).

It is straightforward to demonstrate analogous application of control constraints within nominal constituents whose semantics involves relations of *orientation* or *influence* sort:

(23)   a. The wish/desire on Dana's part to leave the party early had no sensible basis.

        b. The wish that Dana made, to leave the party early, was fulfilled.

        c. Dana's wish/desire/preference to leave the party early had gone unnoticed.

        d. A wish to leave the party early would make perfect sense.

(24)   a. Sandy's appeal/instruction/signal to Tracy to leave the party early was untimely.

        b. The appeal that Sandy made to Tracy, to leave the party early, was untimely.

        c. The appeal/signal/instruction to leave the party early went unnoticed.

In (23a–c), the content of the wish/desire being described is that Dana leave a certain party early; the content of the wish in (23d) is that whoever is the experiencer of the wish leave the party early. Similarly in (24a, b) the content of the appeal/signal/instruction being described is that Tracy leave the party early. In (24c), the implicit INFLUENCED argument (which could have been realized as the object of a *to*-phrase, as in (25)) is unambiguously the controller of the unexpressed subject of the infinitival phrase:

(25)   The appeal/signal/instruction to the kids to leave the party early went unnoticed.

Note in fact that once the INFLUENCED argument is expressed, no other choice of controller is possible in examples like (26):

(26)   Mary realized that the appeal/signal/instruction to the kids to get her/*herself to leave the party early went unnoticed.

In sum, the semantically based principles of controller assignment posited for the various verb classes also function within nominal constituents.

Higgins (1973: 80, 89) observed that control constraints also hold across the copula in examples like (27) and across clause boundaries in examples like (28):

(27)   His promise was to reform himself.

(28)   a. I don't quite remember what John's plan was, but I think it was to leave himself at least two hours to get there.

        b. If there's one vice she will admit to, it is that of dosing herself too liberally with laudanum.

    c. If I remember his aims correctly, they were to proclaim himself
      emperor and to march on Moscow.

And the 'connectivity' of control constraints discussed by Higgins is even
more extensive than these examples would suggest. The phenomenon extends
across sentence boundaries in discourse, as the data in (29)–(30) show:[8]

(29)   *a*. Sandy made Tracy a promise. It was to leave the party early.
      b. Tracy made an appeal to Sandy. It was to leave the party early.
      c. Sandy wanted/desired/wished for something. It was to leave the
         party early.

(30)   A: Sandy promised Tracy something.
      B: What was it?
      A: I think it was to leave the party early.

    Here we observe exactly the same interpretational restrictions that are char-
acteristic of complement control. The unexpressed subject of the VP *to leave
the party early* is interpreted as referring to Sandy. Following Dowty (1989),
we may refer to this discourse control phenomenon as 'remote control.'
    Our analysis of remote control proceeds roughly as follows. *It*, like other
third-person pronouns, may refer to some object made salient in the context of
utterance. In the case of (30), the salient object is the promised action (about
which little has yet been specified) of a certain promising event introduced into
the discourse by the previous utterance. The copula conveys simple identity
between this promised action and the semantic object designated by *to leave
the party early*. Combining all relevant information in this discourse yields a
promising psoa wherein the promised action is the semantic content of the infinitival VP. Control theory is now applicable: since promises are COMMIT-
MENTs, the COMMITTOR of the promise must control the unexpressed subject.
Hence the interpretational properties of remote control examples like (30) are
correctly predicted.[9]

    8. Examples like (109a) were first pointed out to us by Janet Fodor (personal com-
munication, 1984).
    9. There remains of course (as noted by Dowty (1989: 102–103)) the independent
question of when a given utterance evokes a salient object that may be referenced by
subsequent anaphoric elements. Thus Dowty points out contrasts such as the following:

(i)   John made an agreement with Mary yesterday.
         It was to perjure themselves.
(ii)   John agreed with Mary yesterday.
        *It was to perjure themselves.

Evidently, use of the verb *agreed* is insufficient to render salient the psoa that was
agreed to. This could well be because this sort of use of *agreed* conventionally impli-
cates that what was agreed to is understood from context; if this is right then the badness

Further evidence for the semantic nature of controller assignment comes from the peculiar *How's about* construction.[10] Unlike *How about*, which can be used to make suggestions of all kinds, *How's about* can be used only to make a request:

(31)   A :   How can Johnnie get the teacher to like him?
        B :   How about behaving himself, for once.
        B':   *How's about behaving himself, for once.

(32)   *a.* How's about a beer.
        b. How's about handing me the pliers.

When *How's about* takes a gerund complement, the unexpressed subject of that gerund must be controlled by the addressee, as in (33):

(33)   *a.* How's about taking *myself/yourself/*ourselves off the list right now!
        b. How's about booking yourself/*you/*myself/me on the 12:30 flight.

Since *How's about* sentences can be used only to perform a request, and request is a relation of the *influence* sort, the unexpressed subject of the gerund complement must be controlled by the INFLUENCED participant in the *influence*-sort psoa, namely the addressee. This is exactly as predicted by the semantic control constraint formulated above.

In sum, the regularities that underlie controller assignment apply not only to the complements of verbs, but also to nominal control constructions, remote control, and interpretationally restricted constructions. Controller assignment principles are tied to the psoas described by linguistic expressions rather than to linguistic expressions themselves. This has the important consequence that the lexical entries for verbs and nouns whose complements have controlled

---

of (ii) would be analogous to the badness of (iii), where similarly the identity of the job applied for must already be established:

(iii)   John finally decided to apply yesterday.
           *It was the computational ichthyology position.

In any case it is not true that remote control arises only with nominalizations of control verbs, as Dowty hints, but rather that discourse saliency is intimately tied to the difference between nominal and verbal expression. That remote control cannot be explained solely in terms of nominalizations of control verbs is demonstrated by examples like (iii), where it is the NP argument of the verb *promise* that gives rise to remote control:

(iii)   Kim promised Sandy something.
           It was to support the resolution.

10. The relevance of this construction was pointed out to us by Bill Eilfort and Jerry Sadock (personal communication, 1988).

subjects should not stipulate controller assignment. Once role-assignment is correctly guaranteed for a lexical entry, controller assignment will follow from the semantic properties of the lexical entry. Thus subject control for a verb like *promise* is derived from the interaction of two things: (1) whatever principles ensure that the subject of (the active forms of) *promise* is assigned the COM-MITTOR role, and (2) the principles of controller assignment sketched in (15) above. Only by formulating the principles of controller assignment in essentially semantic terms, as we have done, can we provide a sufficiently explanatory, unified account of control relations.

Although controller assignment is semantically determined, as we have seen, it would appear to be an inescapable fact that the controlled element (the element identified with the controller) must be identified in syntactic terms. Consider the following examples:

(34)   *a.* Lee persuaded Tracy to examine Kim.
       b. Lee persuaded Tracy to be examined by Kim.

(35)   *a.* Sandy wants to go to Rome.
       b. Sandy wants to receive an invitation.

As these examples show, the controlled element can play almost any kind of role in the complement's psoa. For this reason, we have accepted the traditional wisdom that the controlled element is to be identified as the unexpressed subject (the single SUBCAT member) of the controlled complement.

Finally, note that the semantically based principles of controller assignment given in (15) interact with Principle A of the binding theory outlined in Chapter 6 to guarantee agreement of person, number, and gender in arbitrarily complex embedded complements. To see this, consider first the indicated coindexing that must be true of the lexical entries in (36) and (37) in virtue of the principles of controller assignment:

(36)   *try*

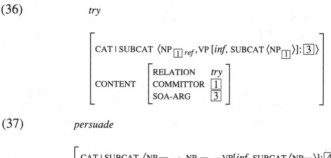

(37)   *persuade*

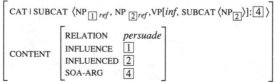

Suppose now that the VP complement of *try* or *persuade* contains an anaphor object. Principle A of our binding theory then guarantees coindexing between that anaphor and the complement's unexpressed subject. Since that unexpressed subject is coindexed with the appropriate matrix argument (by control theory), it then follows from the theory of agreement outlined in Chapter 2 that there is multiple coindexing and hence agreement as indicated in (38) and (39):

(38)

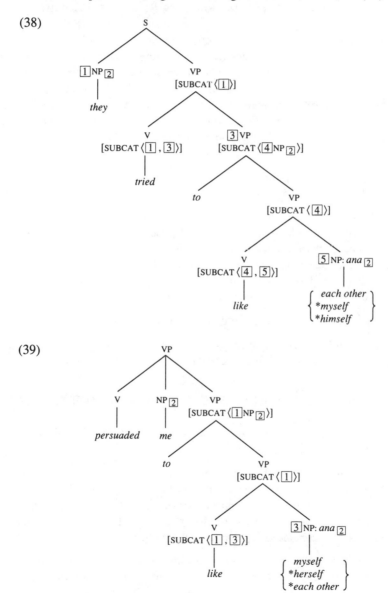

(39)

Thus binding theory and control theory interact to derive the agreement properties of English controlled complements. Note that since the infinitival element *to* is a subject raising auxiliary verb, it serves to transmit the agreement dependency between the embedded VP and the matrix environment. All raising expressions, because they structure-share their complement's unexpressed subject with another subcategorized element, will function in this way, giving rise to long-distance agreement of arbitrary complexity. Recall that raising itself is determined by a general principle of lexical argument structure (the Raising Principle—Chapter 3, section 5). Hence our account of long-distance agreement is a consequence of the interaction of the Raising Principle, control theory, the Subcategorization Principle, and Principle A of the binding theory. Unlike Gazdar et al.'s (1985) account of these facts, which is based on a stipulation called the Control Agreement Principle, our account extends to the full range of agreement phenomena in control constructions via a rather rich deductive interaction of independently motivated aspects of HPSG theory.

7.3 The Realization of Controllers: Manzini's and Visser's Generalizations

The control theory formulated in the previous section correctly identifies in semantic terms the controller of the unexpressed subject of a VP (or other predicative) complement, but it imposes no constraint on how the controller is realized, or whether it must be realized at all. However, there is evidence that some further principle is at work. For example, there are no verbs in English that exhibit the behavior of *foobar* in the following example:

(40)   Mary suspected that John would foobar Bill to behave herself.

And only a handful of verbs, such as *signal, say*, or *shout* (see below), allow what appears to be control from higher clauses or from the prior discourse context:

(41)   *a.* Mary realized that John had signalled to position herself near the door.
         b. Mary was on the alert. John had signalled to position herself behind the door.

In the vast majority of cases, when a verb allows a VP (or predicative) complement, the controller of the unexpressed subject of that complement is realized as one of the verb's complements (subject, primary object, or nonpredicative PP complement). In this section we would like to consider the tenability of the following hypothesis concerning controller realization:

(42)   In all cases of verbs whose semantics involves relations of *commitment, influence*, or *orientation* sort, the controller, if expressed, must

be less oblique (in roughly the traditional sense of the term) than the controlled complement.

We will explore the possibility of deriving this hypothesis, to the extent that it is true, from the theory of binding.

The matter of controller realization is less clear with gerund complements. As the following examples illustrate, the controller of the unexpressed subject of a gerund complement need not be an overtly expressed less oblique dependent of the verb, as in (43a, b):

(43)   *a.* Kim discussed perjuring themselves with Sandy.
        b. Mary thought John might be willing to discuss getting herself a new car.

Cross-discourse control of unexpressed gerund subjects is also possible, though examples like the following vary somewhat in acceptability across speakers:

(44)   Mary was in quite a quandary—should she get herself arrested, or not? John would find *getting herself arrested* quite objectionable, but Bill would think it was the only thing to do.

In fact verbal gerunds need not be controlled at all:

(45)   Kim and Sandy consider stuffing oneself with nachos to be offensive.

Though we assume gerunds in examples like these are to be analyzed semantically in much the same way as infinitivals, the principles of controller assignment we have articulated do not affect relations like *consider, discuss,* or *find*, and hence there is no obligatory control in these examples.[11] In the discussion that follows, however, we will confine our attention to other types of VP and predicative complements.

11. Gerund complements of verbs whose relations are of *commitment* sort sometimes appear to be subject to our principles of controller assignment, e.g., in cases like (i) and (ii):

(i)   Kim tried tying his shoes.
(ii)   I will now undertake juggling three balls with my hands tied.

However, counterexamples such as the following can be constructed:

(iii)   Mary has been working regularly with that disabled boy to help him improve his motor skills. For the past few weeks she's had him playing catch with a beachball and putting his own pants on, and next week she's planning to try tying his shoes.

7.3.1 Manzini's Generalization

Various researchers have tried to understand the constraints on controller realization. Manzini (1983: 423) offers the generalization in (46):

(46)   MANZINI'S GENERALIZATION:

Nonsubject VP complements with unexpressed subjects must have a controller within the minimal clause that contains that complement.

This conclusion is based on examples like those in (47), where in each case there is such a controller, and those in (48) where either there is no appropriate controller anywhere within the sentence, or else the appropriate controller is not in the minimal clause containing the complement:

(47)   *a.*   John asked Bill to shave himself.
        b.   John asked Bill to be allowed to shave himself.
        c.   John promised Bill to shave himself.
        d.   John promised Bill to be allowed to shave himself.

(48)   *a.* *John asked Bill to shave oneself.
        b. *John promised Bill to shave oneself.
        c. *Mary said that John asked Bill to behave herself.
        d. *Mary said that John promised Bill to behave herself.

In a similar vein, Bach (1979) has suggested that when the direct object of a verb is a controller, the verb can never undergo detransitivization, as shown by the contrast between (49) and (50):

(49)   *a.*   Kim promised Sandy to leave.
        b.   Kim promised to leave.

(50)   *a.*   Kim persuaded Sandy to leave.
        b. *Kim persuaded to leave.

Bach's Generalization can thus be seen as a subcase of Manzini's, as long as some other constraint prevents the subjects in (50) from being controllers.

We will now consider three potential problems facing Manzini's Generalization. First, there is the verb *help*, which, as noted by Mohanan (1983) and Chierchia (1984b) (see also Comrie 1984), appears to be a counterexample to Manzini's Generalization (and also to Bach's, if we assume that the *help* in question is derived from object-controlled *help* via detransitivization):

(51)   Rene helped (to) trim the sail.

Second, there are examples like (52b), which, as noted by Bresnan (1982: 373), appear to contradict Bach's Generalization:

(52)   *a.* Pat signalled Lou to leave.
        b. Pat signalled to leave.

Here it is the unexpressed primary (direct) object (or perhaps an unexpressed *to*-phrase) that controls the unexpressed subject of the VP complement. The complement thus has no controller within the minimal clause that contains it, contra Manzini. And, if (52b) involves an unexpressed object, detransitivization has applied to eliminate a controller, contra Bach.

A third class of cases to be considered concerns extraposed VPs (based on examples by Manzini (1983: 426)):

(53)   *a.* It would help Bill to behave himself in public.
        b. It would help Bill's development to behave himself in public.
        c. Mary knows that it would help Bill to behave herself in public.
        d. It reflects well on the whole corps to conduct oneself honorably in public.

In these examples as well, the controller need not be expressed as a dependent of the verb. In fact, the controller of the unexpressed subject of an extraposed VP may also be an individual evoked by the prior discourse context, as in (54):

(54)   Mary was in a quandary. It would suffice to find herself a new secretary, but the real solution was an entirely new office staff.

In order to save Manzini's Generalization in the face of examples like (51), one might suggest (as Manzini does) that *help* allows a phonetically null pronominal object to function as controller. On such an account, (51) is analogous in structure to (55):

(55)   Rene helped them (to) trim the sail.

However, this explanation is empirically untenable, as the examples in (56) show:

(56)   *a.*   John$_i$ helped the barbers (to) shave him$_i$.
        b.   *John$_i$ helped to shave him$_i$.
        c.   John$_i$ helped to shave them$_k$.

If Manzini's account were right, then we should expect (56b) to be grammatical by analogy with the well-formed (56a) and (56c); but this expectation is not borne out.

A more plausible explanation for these facts, we think, is that the *help* of (55) and (56a) is the (transitive and object-controlled) *help* of assistance, a typical *influence*-sort verb, while the *help* of participation instantiated in (51) and (56c) is simply intransitive and therefore not object-controlled. In fact, perhaps surprisingly, neither is the *help* of participation subject-controlled. For if it were, then we should expect (57a) to be grammatical and (57b) to have a reading where it is John that gets tenure:

(57)   *a.*   ? The barbers were grateful that John$_i$ had helped to shave himself$_i$.
        b.   *John helped to get tenure.

But (57a) is unexpectedly bad (for many, though not all, native speakers of English), and the intended interpretation of (57b) is in fact unavailable; rather, if (57b) has any interpretation at all, it is only the pragmatically bizarre one wherein John is a member of a collective entity that jointly gets tenure (cf. *John helped to get the grant*). We conclude therefore that participatory *help* does not involve an *influence*-sort relation, and is not subject to the control theory proposed in the previous section. Moreover, it constitutes a genuine counterexample to Manzini's Generalization.

The control properties of verbs like *signal* are also interesting. When an object or *to*-phrase is present, as in (58), that phrase may function as controller:

(58)   *a.* The captain signalled (to) Kim$_i$ to position herself$_i$ behind the door.

         b. Kim shouted to the captain$_i$ to free himself$_i$ from the ropes.

Here, *signal* and *shout* might appear at first blush to be functioning as verbs of *influence* sort, with controller assignment in accordance with the principles outlined earlier. This possibility is also preserved in examples like (59), where the verbs all seem to have an *influence*-sort interpretation:

(59)   *a.* Detective Jones$_i$ knew the captain had signalled to position himself$_i$ under the table.

         b. Bill$_i$ knew she had said to behave himself$_i$.

Thus in order to preserve Manzini's Generalization, we would have to assume that these examples contain a phonetically unrealized object that functions essentially as a pronominal.

However, this is not the only possibility for verbs like *signal*, as the following examples show:

(60)   *a.* The car signalled to turn left.

         b. Col. Jones signalled to land.

These examples are ambiguous. They allow the unexpressed object interpretation just discussed (the car in (60a) could be a stopped police car signalling an oncoming motorist to make a detour; Col. Jones could be signalling a pilot to land). But the more natural interpretations involve the car in (60a) signalling that it will make a left turn and Col. Jones signalling (perhaps to the control tower) that he will land; these readings would appear to be instances of simple subject control. Indeed, the same ambiguity persists even in the presence of an overt object, as (61) and (62) show:

(61)   *a.* The parked police car signalled (to) the oncoming motorist to turn left.

         b. The speeding car signalled (to) the startled pedestrian to turn left.

(62)   *a.* Col. Jones signalled (to) the pilot to land.
       b. Col. Jones signalled (to) the control tower to land.

And readings (with or without an overt object) are even available where control is 'split' between the signaller (subject) and the (perhaps unrealized) signallee:

(63)   Col. Jones signalled to Capt. Rogers to synchronize watches.

Can the cases involving *signal* where no overt object controller is present be accounted for in terms of a null pronominal object, along the lines proposed by Manzini for *help*? Although the facts are not inconsistent with such an account, it lacks independent motivation, and, moreover, it provides no explanation for the fact that *signal* appears to permit either subject or object control, as the examples in (64) illustrate:

(64)   *a.* Col. Jones$_i$ signalled (the control tower) to position himself$_i$ for a landing.
       b. Col. Jones$_i$ knew that the control tower had signalled (him$_i$) to position himself for a landing.

We will offer our own account of these facts presently; for the time being we simply anticipate that account by asserting that *signal* is not subject to the semantically based control constraints and also (in case no object is present) constitutes another genuine counterexample to Manzini's Generalization.

The third class of potential problems for Manzini's Generalization involves control into extraposed VPs. Thus, corresponding to the examples in (53) (repeated in (65)) are those in (66):

(65)   *a.* It would help Bill to behave himself in public.
       b. It would help Bill's development to behave himself in public.
       c. Mary knows that it would help Bill to behave herself in public.
       d. It reflects well on the whole corps to conduct oneself honorably in public.

(66)   *a.* To behave himself in public would help Bill.
       b. To behave himself in public would help Bill's development.
       c. Mary knows that to behave herself in public would help Bill.
       d. To conduct oneself honorably in public reflects well on the whole corps.

Similar examples can be constructed involving predicates like *bother, upset, foolish*, etc., as well as with the copula.

As (65) and (66) suggest, none of these expressions is subject to semantically based controller assignment. This is further supported by the examples in (67):

(67)   *a.* John knew that to behave himself in public would upset/irritate/
       annoy/bother Mary.

       b. John knew that it would upset/irritate/annoy/bother Mary to be-
       have himself in public.

       c. John was happy and excited. To have involved herself in the
       group was the most positive move his daughter could have made.

The unexpressed subject of extraposed VP complements (as well as of subject
VPs), as Manzini (1983: 424) puts it, '(co) refers freely,' even across discourse,
as Bresnan (1982: 328ff.) takes pains to establish:

(68)   *a.* Mary was happy and excited. *To have involved herself in the*
       group was a risky action. But it was proving that she could
       change her life.

       b. Tom felt sheepish. *To have pinched those elephants* was foolish.

(69)   *a.* Mary was happy and excited. It was a risky action *to have in-*
       volved herself in the group. But it was proving that she could
       change her life.

       b. Tom felt sheepish. It was foolish *to have pinched those elephants.*

It seems clear that no appeal to null pronominals can provide an appropriate
controller within the minimal clause containing these controlled complements.
Thus extraposed VP complements (and subject VPs) are subject neither to semantic controller assignment principles, nor to Manzini's Generalization.

It is our position that Manzini's Generalization obtains uniformly in those
cases where the semantic controller assignment constraints are in force. On our
view, this fact should be a consequence of binding theory, in particular, of
Principle A, which requires anaphors (reflexives and reciprocals) to be coindexed with an appropriate antecedent in a certain local domain. In the previous
chapter (section 6.8.3), we have already introduced a modification of the definition of local o-command ensuring that the unexpressed subject (single member of the SUBCAT value) of VP and other unsaturated complements is locally
o-commanded by elements less oblique than that VP. In order to complete the
analysis of control, we augment the control theory given in (15) as follows:

(70)   CONTROL THEORY (revised version):

       If the CONTENT of an unsaturated phrase is the SOA-ARG in a psoa
       whose relation is a control relation, then the subject SUBCAT element
       of that phrase is
       (i) reflexive; and
       (ii) coindexed with the INFLUENCED, COMMITTOR, or EXPERIEN-
       CER value in that psoa, according as the control relation is of
       sort *influence, commitment,* or *orientation,* respectively.

According to this revised formulation, any verb whose content is subject to the controller assignment principles given earlier will select a VP complement whose unexpressed subject must be reflexive. The various SUBCAT lists that illustrate this point are given in (71):

(71)   *promise*: SUBCAT $\langle$NP$_i$ (, NP), VP[SUBCAT $\langle$NP:*refl$_i$*$\rangle$]

       persuade: SUBCAT $\langle$NP, NP$_i$, VP[SUBCAT $\langle$NP:*refl$_i$*$\rangle$]$\rangle$

       appeal: SUBCAT $\langle$NP, PP[*to*]$_i$, VP[SUBCAT $\langle$NP:*refl$_i$*$\rangle$]$\rangle$

       try: SUBCAT $\langle$NP$_i$, VP[SUBCAT $\langle$NP:*refl$_i$*$\rangle$]$\rangle$

       want: SUBCAT $\langle$NP$_i$, VP[SUBCAT $\langle$NP:*refl$_i$*$\rangle$]$\rangle$

Note that the SUBCAT lists shown in (71) exhibit coindexings that are completely determined by control theory, but that also obey binding theory, as Principle A of the binding theory outlined in the previous chapter requires that the unexpressed reflexive subject of each subcategorized VP be coindexed with some element less oblique than that VP. The definition of local o-command in fact rules out the possibility of any SUBCAT list where a noninitial controlled complement lacks a local o-binder. Since the SUBCAT list of a verb determines which NPs will be realized in a given clause, it follows that a controlled subject will have a controller within the minimal clause containing it. To the extent that Manzini's Generalization makes correct predictions, it is thus a consequence of the interaction of control theory and Principle A of the binding theory.

But what about the several exceptions to Manzini's Generalization discussed above? We analyze these as cases where the unexpressed complement subject is specified not as reflexive, but rather as pronominal (*ppro*). We consider these in turn.

First, the *help* of participation. In this case we assume not only that the complement subject is pronominal, but moreover that this pronominal is constrained by the participatory semantics of *help* to refer to some group to which the helper belongs. It is easy to see that this assumption is consistent with all the facts about *help* above ((56b)–(57)); in addition it accounts for the otherwise puzzling fact that (72) is grammatical only on a reading where Kim is one of the professors:

(72)   The professors$_i$ knew that Kim had helped get themselves$_i$ plusher offices.

We return next to the facts about *signal* discussed in (58)–(64) above. A natural account of these facts, we believe, is that *signal* subcategorizes optionally for an object, and obligatorily for an infinitive VP complement whose unexpressed subject's CONTENT value is specified as *pron* (= *ppro* or *ana*). In the event that the unexpressed complement subject is instantiated as an anaphor (and both reflexive and reciprocal interpretations seem to be possible), then it is controlled by either the subject or the object (if any) of *signal* (cf. (61)–(62)

and (64)). But when it is instantiated as a pronominal (e.g. *the control tower signalled to land*), then Principle B of the binding theory will require that the unexpressed complement subject *not* be coindexed with any argument of *signal*.[12] The essential prediction of this analysis (that the complement subject of *signal* can be either a reflexive or a nonreflexive pronoun) is that the interpretation of the unexpressed subject is free. An alternative analysis, due to Georgia Green, would simply let *signal* be ambiguous between an *influence*-sort relation (as in (58a)) and a *commitment*-sort relation (as in (60a)).

Finally, we consider unexpressed subjects of extraposed (unsaturated) VP complements, as in (69). In such examples (just as with the VP subjects in (68)), there is no less oblique referential complement to o-command the unexpressed subject, and therefore the effect of Manzini's Generalization is not observed.[13]

7.3.2 Visser's Generalization

We now turn to the issue of Visser's Generalization, which states that 'subject-controlled' verbs cannot undergo passivization:

(73) *a.* Kim was persuaded to leave (by Dana).
  b. *Kim was promised to leave (by Dana).

Recall from Chapter 3 (section 3) that we treat passivization in terms of a passive lexical rule (PLR) that cyclically permutes SUBCAT lists, as illustrated in (74):

(74) *read, devour, . . .* :
  SUBCAT $\langle \text{NP}_{\boxed{1}}, \text{NP}_{\boxed{2}} \rangle \Rightarrow$
  SUBCAT $\langle \text{NP}_{\boxed{2}}, \text{PP}[by]_{\boxed{1}} \rangle$

  give, donate, . . . :
  SUBCAT $\langle \text{NP}_{\boxed{1}}, \text{NP}_{\boxed{2}}, \text{PP}[to]_{\boxed{3}} \rangle \Rightarrow$
  SUBCAT $\langle \text{NP}_{\boxed{2}}, \text{PP}[to]_{\boxed{3}}, \text{PP}[by]_{\boxed{1}} \rangle$

12. Recall that our formulation of Principle B requires that a pronominal not be locally o-bound.

13. On the other hand, extraposed VP complements may or may not be controlled by an object, as in (i) and (ii):

(i) It bothers me to play the guitar (when I don't have thick enough calluses on my fingers).

(i) It bothers my neighbors to play the guitar (when we have the windows open and the amp turned way up).

We assume such contrasts depend on whether the CONTENT of the understood subject is realized as a reflexive or not (nothing requires it to be).

Passivization thus creates SUBCAT lists where the *by*-phrase is the most oblique dependent element. Like similar lexical rules, passivization preserves semantic role assignment to indices.

Let us consider the passivization of control verbs in more detail. PLR applies to an object control verb like *persuade* to give a lexical entry whose SUBCAT specification is as shown in (75):

(75)   SUBCAT ⟨NP, VP[SUBCAT ⟨NP:*refl*⟩], PP[*by*]⟩

Principle A requires that the unexpressed subject of the VP complement be coindexed with the subject NP, the only available local o-commander. This coindexing also satisfies control theory: because PLR preserves semantic role assignment, the subject NP is assigned the INFLUENCED role in the passive verb's content. Binding theory and control theory thus impose the same constraint, jointly guaranteeing that the result of applying PLR to a verb like *persuade* will be a SUBCAT list like (76):

(76)   SUBCAT ⟨NP$_i$, VP[SUBCAT ⟨NP:*refl$_i$*⟩], PP[*by*]⟩

Consider now the application of PLR to *promise*. The result will be essentially the same as (75). And Principle A will again require the coindexing in (76). However, here control theory and binding theory part company. Because PLR preserves semantic role assignment, the *by*-phrase is assigned the role of COMMITTOR. Thus control theory requires that the unexpressed subject of the VP complement be coindexed with the *by*-phrase. The result will be a SUBCAT list like (77):

(77)   SUBCAT ⟨NP$_i$, VP[SUBCAT ⟨NP:*refl$_i$*⟩], PP[*by*]$_i$⟩

Now in each case, this SUBCAT list will give rise to sentences that are ruled out by independently motivated factors, namely sentences like those in (78a) and (78b):

(78)   *a.*   *Kim$_i$ was promised to leave by Sandy$_i$/Kim$_i$.
        b.   *John$_i$ was promised to leave by him$_i$.
        c.   ?*John$_i$ was promised to leave by himself$_i$.

Example (78a) is ruled out by Principle C of our binding theory, which entails that nonpronominals (including proper names and quantified NPs) can never be coindexed with a local o-commander.[14] Example (78b) is similarly ruled out by Principle B of the binding theory, which disallows the coindexing of a pronominal (an element whose CONTENT value is of sort *ppro*) with any of its local o-commanders.

14. In fact, Principle C guarantees that a nonpronominal is never coindexed with any o-commander, as discussed in Chapter 6.

This leaves the matter of (78c). Whatever the status of this example may be (and the judgments of many speakers, the authors included, are uncertain at best), there is nothing in our theory as it stands that actually rules it out. Now it has often been assumed in the literature that reflexives (for whatever reason) cannot appear in passive *by*-phrases, so it may be that (78c) is less acceptable (if indeed it is) because of other (perhaps pragmatic) constraints that are independent of control and binding.[15] If this is indeed the case, then the SUBCAT list in (77), the only PLR output that satisfies both binding theory and control theory, is one that never can appear in a well-formed linguistic structure.

There is one further problem that remains to be discussed. Visser's Generalization of course also applies to 'short' passives (those that lack a *by*-phrase) like (79):

(79)   *Dana was promised to leave.

This fact must be a consequence of a fully developed theory of complement control, as it perhaps already is under our account, given the following observations.

According to control theory, the unexpressed anaphor subject of the VP complement has to be identified with the COMMITTOR of the promising (which is not linguistically expressed); but according to Principle A, it must be bound by its (unique) referential o-commander *Dana* (the COMMISSEE of the promise). The ill-formedness of (79) thus arises from the impossibility of satisfying these conflicting demands. The trouble with this account is that it is not quite true that the demands of control theory and binding theory cannot be jointly satisfied: they could be, if Dana happened to have been the promiser. In other words, our theory as stated predicts not that (79) is ungrammatical, but rather that the only possible interpretation available for (79) is one paraphrasable as *Dana promised himself to leave.*

Yet we know independently that short passives strongly disfavor reflexive interpretations. Thus there is no way to understand (80) as a paraphrase of (81):

(80)   The only barber who was ever shaved was Figaro.

(81)   The only barber who was ever shaved by himself was Figaro.

---

15. However, in section 8.2 of Chapter 6 (see also Pollard and Sag 1992), we cited counterexamples to this constraint (of a sort noted by Morgan (1969)):

(i)   The only barber who was shaved by himself was Figaro.

One might expect that examples like (ii), analogous to (i), would be more acceptable than (78c):

(ii)   The only president who was promised by himself not to raise taxes is George Bush.

It is not clear to us if this expectation is fulfilled.

In light of this nonequivalence, it is clear that some account *must* be provided for this fact about unexpressed *by*-phrases, considerations of complement control aside. It is equally clear that virtually any such account will suffice to explain the deviance of (79).[16]

A further point warrants mention before we conclude this discussion. First, it is generally thought, on the basis of examples like (82), that subject raising verbs are also governed by Visser's Generalization:

(82)   *a.*   Sandy struck Kim as unreliable.
        b.   *Kim was struck as unreliable by Sandy.

Strike can be seen to be a subject raising verb, which assigns no semantic role to its subject, by the grammaticality of examples like (83):

(83)   *a.*   It struck me as very unlikely that Dana would get the job.
        b.   There struck Sandy as being too many Republicans on the committee.

But, as has commonly been observed, subject role assignment is an essential prerequisite for passivization:[17]

(84)   *a.*   *Our party was rained on by it.
        b.   *A furor was arisen by there.

Thus the fact that subject raising verbs fail to passivize is part of a more general constraint on passivization, one that is irrelevant to our account of Visser's Generalization.

Second, *by*-phrase controllers, though impossible in the VP, are permitted within nominal constituents, as noted by Bresnan (1982) and others (see section 7.2):

(85)   *a.*   We appreciated [the promise by Hearst to endow the center].
        b.   [A promise by Jamie not to chew gum] would have been appreciated by all.

These are correctly predicted to be grammatical under our theory, despite uncertainty as to the precise nature of nominal SUBCAT lists. Clearly, the SUBCAT list of nominals like those in (85) contains a DetP, a VP, and a PP[*by*]. A DetP

16. One speculative proposal along these lines might be that in short passives, the *by*-phrase is actually realized as a null pronominal. If this is right, it would then follow from the binding theory, as desired, that no self-promising interpretation of (80) is available. Unfortunately this proposal, essentially identical to Manzini's approach to the unrealized complements of *signal*-class verbs, lacks independent motivation.

17. In a number of recent proposals, passivization is in fact characterized as a 'demotion' (Bresnan and Kanerva 1989; Kiparsky 1987) of the 'highest' θ-role. Our passive lexical rule is easily reformulated so as to apply to only those lexical forms whose subject is assigned a semantic role.

like those in (85), viz. *the* and *a*, is not a potential binder, and hence not a local o-commander of the unexpressed subject of the VP. If the *by*-phrase locally o-commands the VP, then both binding theory and control theory are satisfied by coindexing the unexpressed subject and the *by*-phrase. If the VP is less oblique than the *by*-phrase, then the unexpressed anaphor subject of the VP is locally o-commanded by nothing and hence exempt from Principle A. In this case, that anaphor must still be coindexed with the *by*-phrase in order to satisfy control theory.

7.4 Complement Coercion

A long-standing problem in the analysis of control phenomena has been what appears to be a shift in controller assignment with certain sorts of embedded complements. The best-known examples of this phenomenon are *to be allowed to* complements of the sort illustrated in (86):

(86) *a.* Kim promised Sandy to be allowed to attend the party.
      b. Dana asked Pat to be allowed to attend the party.

In (86a) it is Sandy, the COMMISSEE of the promise, who is the controller of the unexpressed subject of the VP complement; in (86b) the controller is Dana, the INFLUENCE of the asking. These shifts in controller choice appear to violate the semantically based principles of controller assignment discussed in the previous sections.

It is sometimes thought [18] that such controller shifts occur only when the VP complement is passivized. However, passivization is neither a necessary nor a sufficient condition for controller shift, as the following examples show:

(87) *a.* Kim promised Sandy to be hassled by the police.
      b. Dana asked Pat to be hassled by the police.

(88) *a.* Grandma promised the children to be able to stay up for the late show.
      b. Montana was promised (by the doctor) to be healthy by game time on Sunday.
      c. Dana asked Pat to be able to attend the party.

In (87), the preferred controller of the unexpressed subject of the (infinitival) passive complement is the individual picked out by our semantic constraint on *commitment*-sort and *influence*-sort relations (even though the readings in question are pragmatically odd): the COMMITTOR in (87a), the INFLUENCED in (87b). But in (88), we see the same shifts in controller assignment that we saw with the *be allowed to* examples. Thus the COMMISSEE is the controller in (88a, b) (*the children* in (88a); *Montana* in (88b)), even though promise is a

18. See, e.g., the remarks made in passing by Jackendoff (1987).

relation of *commitment* sort. And *Dana* is the controller in (88c), though *ask* involves an *influence*-sort relation.

For many speakers, controller shift from subject to object is more acceptable when the matrix verb is passivized, as in (89):

(89)   Sandy was promised to be allowed to attend the party.

But even examples like (86) and (88a, c) are interpretable for such speakers, and judgments improve with proper contextualization (as noted by Farkas (1988)). Hence, we will take it as our goal to provide an account of controller shift that applies equally well to active and passive matrix structures.

Controller shift is thus closely tied to the interpretation of the controlled complement, rather than to any syntactic property it may possess.[19] Roughly speaking, controller shift takes place when the complement's content does not (quite) satisfy the semantic demands of the relation it is an argument of. In (89), for example, the relation *promise* selects an action-type psoa as its SOA-ARG, and the content of VPs like *to be allowed to X*, to be able to *X*, and so forth is a state, rather than an action. Controller shift involves a kind of 'accommodation' of interpretation, or *coercion*.[20]

19. This point is emphasized by both Růžička (1983) and Farkas (1988).

20. There is much research one can point to as identifying the need for some notion of coercion in the semantic analysis of natural languages. As Michael Herweg reminds us (personal communication, 1991), aspectual interpretations are particularly susceptible to coercion, as in phrases like *as soon as he was on the patio* or *they were in Santa Cruz within an hour*, where a state is coerced to an ingressive event-type interpretation. For further examples of this kind of phenomenon, see Moens and Steedman 1987. Partee's work on polymorphic types (e.g. Partee 1987) may also be viewed as an attempt to construct a theory of certain types of coercion, though these are somewhat different from the cases that are relevant in the present context. Also relevant here is a body of work that seeks to view reference transfer and related phenomena (e.g. *Boston called, Kim began a novel*) in terms of coercion processes. See Hobbs et al. 1988 and Pustejovsky 1991, in press, for some recent discussion. In addition, the interpretation of 'concealed' questions (Baker 1968; Grimshaw 1977, 1979) involves coercion of NP interpretations to interrogative interpretations, as in *I asked his phone number*. Equally systematic is the coercion found in the interpretation of the objects of locative prepositions (Herskovitz 1986), e.g. *The nail is in the bowl*. The situation described by this sentence might be a nail resting in the interior of a bowl, or a nail hammered into the side of a bowl. In the first case, the space that *the bowl* designates corresponds to the concavity bounded by the interior of the bowl; in the second situation, it is the region occupied by the bowl. Here again, we can view the problem in terms of adjusting the interpretation of *bowl* (positing mappings from physical objects to three-dimensional spaces that are contextually associated with them) or in terms of manipulating the interpretation of the preposition (e.g. letting the interpretation of *in* 'float' among a family of contextually determined containment relations). Other prepositions have similar effects (see Brugman 1981; Lindner 1981; and Lakoff 1987). These studies, in fact, sug-

On our view, the shift of controller in these examples is only an apparent violation of the semantically based principles of controller assignment we have put forth. The interpretation of *to be allowed to leave* is coerced into roughly the interpretation 'to cause X to be allowed to leave,' and it is the 'interpolated' causer that is identified with the appropriate participant of the embedding psoa in accordance with our semantically based principles. Under this proposal, which bears a certain similarity to the analysis of *try* put forth by Perlmutter (1968), if Jones promises Smith to be allowed to go, the action that Jones promises to perform is an action that causes Smith to be allowed to go, and it is Jones himself who must perform this action.[21] As Farkas (1988) points out,[22] a similar kind of coercion affects the interpretation of imperatives. If the VP of an imperative sentence is not sufficiently agentive, we make every effort to make it so. Thus in examples like (90), the interpretation is crudely characterizable as 'make yourself Φ,' where Φ is the state expressed by the imperative VP:

(90)   *a.*   Be optimistic!
        b.   Be careful!
        c.   ??Be allowed to go!
        d.   ?*Be tall.

As such examples suggest, VPs are graded as to how easily they allow such causative coercion.

Like the imperative construction, *commitment*-sort relations select for complements that denote actions intentionally performed by an agent—to promise to Φ is to commit to doing Φ. Many VP complements denote actions, but others (e.g. *to be tall, to resemble Kim, to be allowed to go*) do not. When such semantically mismatched VPs appear as the complements of verbs whose relation is of *commitment* or *influence* sort, they are also made to fit semantically through causative coercion, as illustrated in (91):

---

gest that interpretation is far more fluid than our discussion would imply. If this body of research is on the right track, then argument coercion of the sort employed here is just the limiting case of a highly fluid interpretation process that involves metaphors and 'radial' categories connecting core concepts in diverse and potentially complex ways. Such a conclusion would not alter in fundamental ways the nature of our proposal for complement coercion. For our present purposes, it is sufficient to establish the existence of semantic coercion, which will play a central role in our analysis of control shifts.

21. The notion of action that we appeal to is admittedly a slippery one, and may ultimately be explicated in terms of the notion 'degree of agency,' 'self-controllability,' or 'responsibility.' See Fillmore 1967, Fodor 1974, Steele et al. 1981, Comrie 1984, and Farkas 1988 for some relevant discussion.

22. See also Perlmutter 1968, 1971; Kuno 1970; and Lasnik and Fiengo 1974.

(91)   *a.*   They promised us *to be on time.*
        b.   We promised *to have the right change.*
        c.   ??He promised *to be allowed to attend the party.*

The complements in (91), taken in isolation, describe nonintentional states—states where no intentional action is implied. But in contexts like (91), these complements must be interpreted as actions. A promise by X to Φ, where Φ would otherwise describe a (nonintentional) state, is a promise by X to act in such a way as to cause Φ to hold of X.

Interpolated causation is familiar in many languages as a common way of establishing cohesion of a discourse, as in *The evidence was revealed (and) Jones resigned* (S_1 caused S_2) and *Jones resigned; The evidence was revealed* (S_2 caused S_1). Of course some things are difficult to cause, given the way the world is. Hence the causative coercion analysis provides a natural account of the difficulty people have in interpreting examples like the following:

(92)   *a.* Sandy promised Kim to be tall.
        b. Pat promised them to resemble Kim.

The difficulty one experiences in interpreting examples like these is precisely the difficulty of imagining circumstances wherein one can cause someone's height to change or someone's appearance to be altered in controllable ways. Speakers differ a great deal in how easily they can imagine such circumstances or with regard to which particular circumstances they instantiate in order to relate the state and the causal action.[23] Example (92a) might be interpreted as a promise to stand erect so as to appear tall or to eat certain foods believed to stimulate growth. The promise in (92b) might be taken to involve undergoing plastic surgery or applying makeup to alter one's appearance. These are some of the more plausible scenarios that would all count as ways of causing the state in question to come about. The assumption of causative coercion is a useful step, though admittedly just a first step, in making sense of interpretational observations such as these.

Causative coercion is also required in the case of verbs whose relation is of *influence* sort, but not for *orientation*-sort relations:

(93)   *a.* We persuaded Sandy to be on time.
        b. We persuaded Sandy to be tall.

(94)   *a.* Sandy wanted to be tall.
        b. Sandy's desire to be tall.

In (93), we see the same causative coercion as with *promise. Persuade to* involves persuading to act, and if the complement describes a state, a causation

---

23. See the discussion in Fodor (1974: 103).

of that state is interpolated, with more or less difficulty and a certain amount of variation across speakers. (93b), for example, can be interpreted only in terms of Sandy being persuaded to act in such a way as to cause it to come about that (s)he be, or appear, tall. Wanting (and similarly for other volitionals, e.g. hating), however, does not require its embedded property to be an action, and no adjustment of interpretation is observed in examples like (94).

Causative coercion is particularly robust in the case of *to be allowed to* complements of *promise*, as in (95):

(95)   *a.*   Jim promised Mary to be allowed to attend the reception.
        b.   ?Jim promised Mary to be allowed to defend himself.

In (95a), the complement undergoes causative coercion; its interpretation is roughly paraphrasable as 'to cause X to be allowed to attend the reception.' This is, in effect, the only way of reconciling the interpretation of the nonagentive VP complement with the demands of promising. And the index of the interpolated causal agent must be Jim, the COMMITTOR of the promise, by what appears to be our familiar semantic control constraint. The preferred 'causee' (i.e. the individual who is caused to be allowed to attend the reception) is Mary. However, it is also possible to interpret example (95a) in terms of a situation where Jim promises Mary that he (Jim) will cause it to come about that he (Jim) be allowed to attend the reception. Such circumstances, where X promises to cause Y to allow X to do something, are hard to imagine, precisely because they simultaneously involve X having power over Y (in order for X to cause Y to do anything) and Y having power over X (in order for Y to allow X to do anything). The complexity of such circumstances makes (95b), where this is the only option available, more difficult to assign any interpretation to at all. Nonetheless, it seems prudent to conclude that the index of the unexpressed subject of *be allowed to* Φ may in principle be associated with either the COMMITTOR or the COMMISSEE of the promise.

The claim that the *be allowed to* complements of *promise* are causative in nature perhaps requires some justification. It has been claimed (by Bresnan (1982), for example) that when *promise* takes such complements, it takes its *promise_{that}* sense, that is, the sense of *promise* that occurs with *that* clauses, whose semantics is propositional in nature. The *promise_{that}* sense does not convey a commitment to act, but rather merely a prediction about future events, as in *I promise you that it will rain.*

If this observation were true, it would of course itself require explanation, for the *promise_{to}* $\mapsto$ *promise_{that}* coercion (unlike the causative coercion we have illustrated in other contexts) lacks independent justification. But, in fact, there is evidence against the *promise_{that}* analysis of the *be allowed to* type of complement. The two senses of *promise* are difficult to tease apart, largely because when one promises that Φ, one in general *suggests* that one will in fact do something to cause Φ to come about, as in (96):

(96) I promise that you will get the job.

But this example only suggests that the speaker will act so as to enable the addressee to get the job in question. This cannot be part of the linguistic meaning of *promise*, for the *promise$_{that}$* relation can perfectly well be predicated of an inanimate argument that is incapable of performing actions, as in (97):

(97) The fortune cookie promised Montana that he would play in the Super Bowl.

If the *be allowed to* type of complement required the *promise$_{that}$* sense of *promise*, then we would expect that an example like (98) would make sense, the same sense that (97) makes:

(98) #The fortune cookie promised Montana to be allowed to play in the Super Bowl.

Example (98), however, is nonsensical. If an interpretation is forced, it could only be one where the fortune cookie somehow caused itself or Montana to be allowed to play in the Super Bowl. Observations such as these argue that the causative coercion analysis we have proposed is superior to an analysis that involves an ad hoc *promise$_{to}$* $\mapsto$ *promise$_{that}$* coercion.

Finally, we observe that similar coercion affects the *be allowed to* complements of verbs whose relation is of *influence* sort:

(99) Susie persuaded the teacher to be allowed to leave early.

(100) a. Jim asked Mary to be allowed to get himself a new dog.
b. ?Jim asked Mary to be allowed to get herself a new dog.

Example (100a) is interpreted roughly as *Jim asked Mary to cause him (Jim) to be allowed to get himself a new dog*. And the complement in (100b) (which is considerably harder to interpret) is coerced to roughly *Jim asked Mary to cause herself (Mary) to be allowed to get herself a new dog*. In both cases, it is the interpolated causer that is identified with the INFLUENCED argument of *ask* (Mary), in keeping with our semantic constraint. In the more natural (100a), the INFLUENCE of the asking psoa (Jim) is identified with the unexpressed subject of *be allowed*. In the less natural (100b), the unexpressed subject is identified with the goal of the asking psoa (Mary). The preferred interpretation for sentences whose semantics is of *commitment* or *influence* sort appears to involve identifying the index of the unexpressed subject of the *be allowed to* . . . complement with the participant of the matrix psoa that is not the controller of the interpolated causer. That is, interpretations of the sort 'X caused X to Φ' are systematically less natural.

In the next section, we put forth a speculative account of how these observations about coercion may be reconciled with our control theory.

7.5 Control Theory and Coerced Complements

The dilemma uncovered in the previous section is that certain unsaturated phrases, most notably *to be allowed to . . .* complements, allow coerced interpretations when they occur as complements of control expressions. When this phenomenon occurs, the unexpressed subject of the complement (e.g. the IN-FLUENCED argument of *to be allowed to . . .*) is no longer the controlled element. These cases thus appear to violate the semantically based controller assignment principles that are central to our control theory.

The approach to this problem that we adopt here involves a lexical rule that effects coercion. Unlike the account sketched in Sag and Pollard 1991,[24] this lexical rule affects the interpretation of the control verb, rather than that of its complement, as shown in (101):

(101)   Coercion Lexical Rule:

$$
\left[
\begin{array}{l}
\text{CATEGORY I SUBCAT } \langle \ldots , \text{ VP [SUBCAT } \langle \text{NP}_{\boxed{1}} \rangle]:\boxed{2} , \ldots \rangle \\[2ex]
\text{CONTENT} \left[
\begin{array}{l}
\text{RELN } \textit{commitment} \vee \textit{influence} \\
\text{SOA-ARG } \boxed{2}
\end{array}
\right]
\end{array}
\right] \Rightarrow
$$

$$
\left[
\begin{array}{l}
\text{CATEGORY I SUBCAT } \langle \ldots , \text{ VP [SUBCAT } \langle \text{NP} \rangle]: \boxed{3} , \ldots \rangle \\[2ex]
\text{CONTENT I SOA-ARG} \left[
\begin{array}{ll}
\text{RELN} & \textit{i-cause} \\
\text{INFLUENCE} & \boxed{1} \\
\text{SOA-ARG} & \boxed{3}
\end{array}
\right]
\end{array}
\right]
$$

We assume here that the interpolated cause relation (notated *i-cause*) is of sort *influence*. That is, perhaps unlike the relation used to analyze the English verb *cause*, this relation is always specified for the attribute INFLUENCED. The lexical rule in (101) (like all lexical rules in HPSG) preserves all properties of the input not mentioned in the rule. It will thus apply to the lexical form for *promise* sketched in (102) to give the lexical form shown in (103):

24. The present account has the virtue of eliminating the EXTERNAL ARGUMENT attribute employed in Sag and Pollard 1991, and hence purges from our analysis of content feature specifications that are not relevant to semantic interpretation. This welcome advance is matched by another: coercion is now correctly restricted to apply only in the context of relations of *influence* or *commitment* sort.

(102)   *promise*

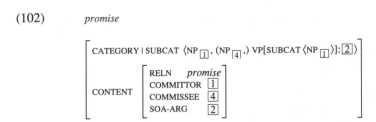

(103)   *promise* (coerced)

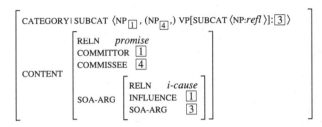

Notice that the lexical rule input in (102) must satisfy the semantically based controller assignment principles. Hence the index of the VP complement's unexpressed subject must be [1]—the index of the committor, which is also the index of the subject in (102). The lexical rule in (101) specifically mentions this index, and hence the resulting lexical form in (103) requires that the IN-FLUENCE argument within *promise*'s soa-argument is coindexed with the verb's subject, as indicated. When this same lexical rule applies to a verb like *persuade*, the embedded INFLUENCE argument is associated instead with the object NP, as that lexical rule input is subject to a different controller assignment principle. Thus the lexical rule in (101) interacts correctly with our control theory to guarantee that the interpolated causer is the same argument that would otherwise function as controller.

In addition, because *i-cause* itself is an *influence*-sort relation, the unexpressed subject of the VP on the SUBCAT list in (103) must be reflexive. This is guaranteed by the control theory introduced in section 7.3.1. Hence the unexpressed subject of the VP complement of a coerced control verb like (103) will always be subject to Principle A of the binding theory.

There are two consequences of this analysis worth pointing out. First, because the outputs of the Coercion Lexical Rule all have SUBCAT lists containing VPs whose unexpressed reflexive subjects are subject to Principle A, it follows that these subjects will always be coindexed with one of the control verb's less oblique SUBCAT members. In the case of the lexical entry in (103), our account predicts that the unexpressed subject may be coindexed with either the subject or the object of *promise*. This is indeed a correct prediction, as the following data show:

(104)   *a.*   Jim promised Mary$_i$ to be allowed to get herself$_i$ a new dog.
      b.   Jim$_i$ promised Mary to be allowed to get himself$_i$ a new dog.
      c.   *Sam$_i$ thought I$_j$ promised Mary$_k$ to be allowed to get himself$_i$ a
          new dog.

Though (104b) may be more difficult for some speakers to contextualize than
(104a) (because (104b) involves imagining a rather complex situation where
Jim causes himself to be allowed to get a new dog), it is clearly grammatical.
(104c), on the other hand, is clearly ungrammatical, as predicted by our analysis. The reflexive *himself* must be coindexed with the unexpressed subject of
get (by Principle A), which in turn is the subject of *to be allowed to get himself
a new dog*, which must (again by Principle A) be coindexed with either *I* or
Mary, which it is not in (104c).

The second consequence of our coercion-based analysis concerns its interaction with passive. Suppose the coerced lexical form in (103) undergoes the
Passive Lexical Rule. The result will be the lexical form sketched in (105):

(105)   *promised* (coerced and passivized)

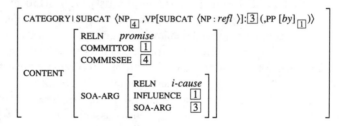

This lexical form is unproblematic. It gives rise to none of the problems
discussed in section 7.3.2 having to do with Visser's Generalization. In particular, since the content of the VP on this SUBCAT list is not assigned the SOA-ARG
role in the (highest level of the) verb's content, the semantically based controller assignment principles are no more applicable to the role attributes in
the verb's content in (105) than they were to the form that gave rise to (105)
(i.e. (103)). The *by*-phrase index is of course assigned the COMMITTOR role,
and Principle A requires the VP's unexpressed subject to be coindexed with the
only element that o-commands it, namely the (passive) subject. The index of
this NP is the COMMISSEE in (105). Control theory thus produces no potential
conflict with binding theory when coercion is involved, correctly allowing for
examples like (106).

(106)   Kim$_5$ was promised to be allowed to go by Pat$_6$.

The CONTENT value for this example is sketched in (107):

(107)

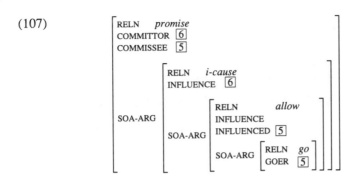

In like fashion, we obtain an immediate account of such contrasts as (108a, b):

(108) *a.* Leslie persuaded/asked the teacher to be allowed to leave early.

  b. *The teacher was persuaded/asked (by Leslie) to be allowed to leave early.

7.6 Conclusion

In this chapter we have presented an integrated theory of complement control. Central to this theory has been the interaction of semantically based principles of controller assignment with other aspects of HPSG theory. As we showed in section 7.2, our account of long-distance agreement, which eliminates all appeal to agreement-particular stipulations like GPSG's Control Agreement Principle, is a consequence of the interaction of these principles with the Raising Principle (Chapter 3), the Subcategorization Principle (Chapter 1), and Principle A of the binding theory (Chapter 6). In addition, the assumption that the unexpressed subjects of many controlled complements are reflexive anaphors further allows us to derive the correct predictions of Manzini's Generalization and many of the predictions of Visser's Generalization from the interaction of our control theory with Principle A of the binding theory. Finally, we extend our analysis to the treatment of the long-standing problem of *be allowed to . . .* complements and their apparent exceptional status with respect to Visser's Generalization. We offer a solution to this problem based on the notion of coercion of interpretation. As noted, this solution is distinct from and arguably superior to the one entertained in Sag and Pollard 1991, which should be consulted for a detailed survey of previous control theories.

8

Aspects of Interpretation

8.1 Introduction

In Chapter 1, we presented a preliminary sketch of a semantic analysis of determiners and NPs that made use of Robin Cooper's (1975, 1983) notion of quantifier storage. In section 8.2, we refine and formalize this account. Section 8.3 treats the related issue of scope of modification. In section 8.4, we consider the role of context in interpretation. And in section 8.5, we attempt to tie up a few loose ends and delineate some topics for further study.

Throughout this volume, we have treated the value of a sentence's CONTENT as an object of the sort *parameterized-state-of-affairs* (*psoa*). These psoas (or, as they are often referred to—after Devlin (1991)—*infons*) determine in part the type of situation described by an utterance of the relevant type of sentence. In situation semantics, meaning in general is analyzed as a relation between situation types: linguistic meaning relates utterance situation types to described situation types (with truth being an ancillary matter having to do with how a particular described situation relates to the real world). Utterance situation types, on our theory, will be determined by the value of a sentence's CONTEXT value—by the particulars of who is speaking, who is being addressed, which background assumptions (appropriacy conditions) are required, and so forth (see section 8.4). In this way, the various semantic attributes of HPSG signs are intended to fit into a rigorously specified, highly context-dependent definition of meaning, content, and truth.

It will doubtless be a disappointment to some readers—and a relief to others—that we will not attempt here to formulate in precise terms the principles that relate our linguistic descriptions to any one version of situation semantic analysis, referring the interested reader instead to Barwise 1989, Robin Cooper et al. 1990, and, especially, Richard Cooper 1990. Our goal here will be rather to offer examples of how certain familiar analytic insights of a semantic nature can be integrated with the syntactic treatments of the earlier chapters.

8.2 Quantificational Content and Nuclear Content

In section 7 of Chapter 1, we presented the following principle governing the semantic content of phrasal signs:

(1)   SEMANTICS PRINCIPLE (second version):

In a headed phrase, the CONTENT value is token-identical to that of
the adjunct daughter if the DTRS value is of sort *head-adj-struc*, and
with that of the head daughter otherwise.

This principle suffices to determine the CONTENT value for a large class of
structures. In addition, quantificational content was determined in part by the
Quantifier Inheritance Principle (QIP), which we formulated informally as
follows:

(2)   QUANTIFIER INHERITANCE PRINCIPLE (QIP, informal version)

The QUANTIFIER-STORE (QSTORE) value of a phrasal node is the
union of the QSTORE values of the daughters less those quantifiers
that are retrieved at that node.

These principles are intended to interact in the fashion sketched in (3):

(3)

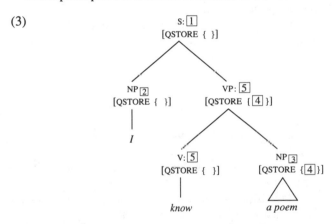

All quantifiers 'start out in storage' (see Chapter 1, section 7), are inherited by
successively larger phrases (in accordance with the QIP), and are 'retrieved' at
an appropriate higher level of structure, whose CONTENT value will be a quantified psoa. If quantified psoas are analyzed in the style of P&S-87, then the
CONTENT value of the sentence *I know a poem* will be roughly as shown in (4):

(4)

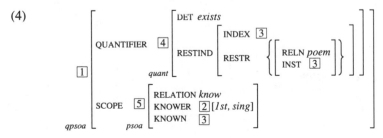

But this assumption contradicts the formulation of the Semantics Principle given in (1), as the CONTENT value of the S in (3) is no longer identical to that of its head daughter—the VP *know a poem*. Clearly, some revision must be made to the principles that relate QSTORE and CONTENT values.

One possibility, which we will not explore here, involves introducing non-branching structures solely for the purpose of retrieving quantifiers from quantifier storage:

(5)
$$\text{S:[QUANT } \boxed{4}, \text{ SCOPE } \boxed{3}]$$
$$\text{QSTORE } \Sigma - \boxed{4}$$
|
$$\text{S:}\boxed{3}$$
$$\text{QSTORE } \Sigma$$

Various analyses incorporating quantifier storage have employed a retrieval rule of this sort.[1] Our approach, by contrast, employs no otherwise unmotivated syntactic structures like (5).

We begin by restructuring the feature-structure representation of (possibly quantified) psoas. In particular, we propose to replace the old sorts *psoa* and *qpsoa* with a new sort *psoa* of *possibly quantified psoa*, with internal structure as shown in (6):

(6)
$$psoa \begin{bmatrix} \text{QUANTIFIERS} & \text{(list of quantifiers)} \\ \text{NUCLEUS} & \text{(}qfpsoa\text{)} \end{bmatrix}$$

The key difference is that in the new representation, quantificational information—QUANTIFIERS (QUANTS)—is segregated from the nonquantificational core, called the NUCLEUS. Here the QUANTS value is a list of quantifiers (in order of scope); and the NUCLEUS value is of a new sort called *quantifier-free psoa* (*qfpsoa*). Thus the CONTENT of *I know a poem* is analyzed as shown in (7), where the tag $\boxed{4}$ indicates the quantifier shown in (8):

(7)
$$psoa \begin{bmatrix} \text{QUANTS } \langle \boxed{4} \rangle \\ \\ \text{NUCLEUS} \quad qfpsoa \begin{bmatrix} \text{RELATION } know \\ \text{KNOWER } \boxed{2} \; [1st, sing] \\ \text{KNOWN } \boxed{3} \end{bmatrix} \end{bmatrix}$$

(8)
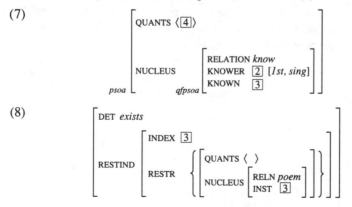

1. All following, in essence, Robin Cooper (1975, 1983).

Note that the RESTRICTION value of a quantifier's restricted index is a set of possibly quantified psoas, each of which may itself be quantified, thus allowing for the analysis of NPs like *a poem that is liked by every person* or *every teacher who many students like*. For ease of notation, (8) will be abbreviated as in (9):

(9) $(\exists x_3 | \{ poem(x_3) \})$

And the nested quantification of (10) will be abbreviated as in (11):

$$(10)\quad \begin{bmatrix} \text{DET } few \\[2pt] \text{RESTIND} \begin{bmatrix} \text{INDEX } \boxed{3} \\[2pt] \text{RESTR} \left\{ \begin{bmatrix} \text{QUANTS } \langle\ \rangle \\[2pt] \text{NUCLEUS} \begin{bmatrix} \text{RELN } poem \\ \text{INST } \boxed{3} \end{bmatrix} \end{bmatrix}, \begin{bmatrix} \text{QUANTS } \langle(\ \forall x_2\ |\{ student\,(x_2\,) \}) \rangle \\[2pt] \text{NUCLEUS} \begin{bmatrix} \text{RELN } like \\ \text{LIKER } \boxed{2} \\ \text{LIKED } \boxed{3} \end{bmatrix} \end{bmatrix} \right\} \end{bmatrix} \end{bmatrix}$$

$(11)\,(few\ x_3 | \{ poem(x_3),\ (\forall x_2 | \{ student(x_2) \}) like(x_2,\ x_3) \})$

Fundamental to our analysis are principles that constrain the relation between QSTORE and QUANTS in such a way as to guarantee that quantifiers are assigned a scope (i.e. appear within the QUANTS value) precisely where they are 'removed from storage.' This is illustrated in (12) (the RETRIEVED attribute will be explained presently):

(12)

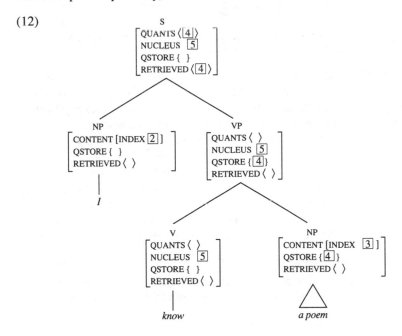

Here $\boxed{4}$ is the quantifier shown in (8) and (9), and $\boxed{5}$ is the quantifier-free psoa given in (13):

(13)
$$\begin{bmatrix} \text{RELATION } know \\ \text{KNOWER} \quad \boxed{2} \\ \text{KNOWN} \quad \boxed{3} \end{bmatrix}$$

Once quantifiers are separated from other aspects of content, the remaining information—the NUCLEUS values ($\boxed{5}$)—of the headed phrases in (12) are simply identified with the NUCLEUS values of their respective head daughters.

In (12), the only nonhead daughters are complements. However, as we noted in Chapter 1, in a head-adjunct-structure it is the adjunct daughter, rather than the head daughter, that determines the (nonquantificational part of the) CONTENT of the mother. Hence the general principle governing the CONTENT value of headed structures, given in (15a), makes reference to the notion of *semantic head* defined in (14):

(14)   The *semantic head* of a headed phrase is
         (1) the adjunct daughter in a head-adjunct structure,
         (2) the head daughter otherwise.

(15)   *a.* CONTENT PRINCIPLE:

         In a headed phrase,
         (Case 1) if the semantic head's CONTENT value is of sort *psoa*,
         then its NUCLEUS is token-identical to the NUCLEUS of the
         mother;
         (Case 2) otherwise, the CONTENT of the semantic head is
         token-identical to the CONTENT of the mother.

Note that (15a) divides into two cases according as the CONTENT of the semantic head is a psoa (e.g. a constituent headed by a verb or by a predicative adjective, preposition, or noun) or not (e.g. a constituent headed by a nonpredicative noun or preposition). The key point is that in the former case only the NUCLEUS (but not necessarily the QUANTS) is identified between the mother and the semantic head; this will allow for the possibility of quantifier retrieval.

More precisely, we now introduce a new attribute of signs called RE-TRIEVED-QUANTIFIERS (RETRIEVED), whose value will be a list of quantifiers. We now posit two more universal constraints whose effect is to require that all retrieved quantifiers be properly scoped. The first of these is our old Quantifier Inheritance Principle (QIP), now formalized as in (15b):

(15)   *b.* QUANTIFIER INHERITANCE PRINCIPLE (QIP, formal version):

         In a headed phrase, the RETRIEVED value is a list whose set of
         elements forms a subset of the union of the QSTOREs of the

daughters, and is nonempty only if the CONTENT of the semantic
head is of sort *psoa*; and the QSTORE value is the relative complement of the RETRIEVED value.

The other principle is the Scope Principle stated in (15c):

(15)   *c.* SCOPE PRINCIPLE:

In a headed phrase whose semantic head is of sort *psoa*, the
QUANTS value is the concatenation of the RETRIEVED value with
the QUANTS value of the semantic head.

The combined effect of the three principles (15a–c) can be obtained by a
single, revised Semantics Principle that supersedes the simplified formulation
given in Chapter 1. The reformulated Semantics Principle is stated in (16):

(16)   SEMANTICS PRINCIPLE (final version):

In a headed phrase:
a. the RETRIEVED value is a list whose set of elements forms a subset of the union of the QSTOREs of the daughters; and the QSTORE
value is the relative complement of that set; and
b. (Case 1) if the semantic head's CONTENT value is of sort *psoa*,
then the NUCLEUS value is identical with that of the semantic
head, and the QUANTS value is the concatenation of the RE-
TRIEVED value and the semantic head's QUANTS value;
(Case 2) otherwise the RETRIEVED value is empty and the
CONTENT value is token-identical to that of the semantic
head.

The reformulated Semantics Principle provides a correct account of the relation that holds among the QSTORE and CONTENT values in (12). In addition,
it allows a sentence like (17) to have either of the distinct CONTENT values in
(18) and (19):

(17)   Every student knows some poem.

(18) $(\forall x_1 |\{ student(x_1) \})(\exists x_2 |\{ poem(x_2) \}) know(x_1, x_2)$

(19) $(\exists x_2 |\{ poem(x_2) \})(\forall x_1 |\{ student(x_1) \}) know(x_1, x_2)$

This effect of the Semantics Principle is illustrated in (20), where the tags
$\boxed{4}$ and $\boxed{6}$ refer to the quantifiers in (21). For ease of notation, empty QSTORE
or RETRIEVED values are not shown:

(20) a.

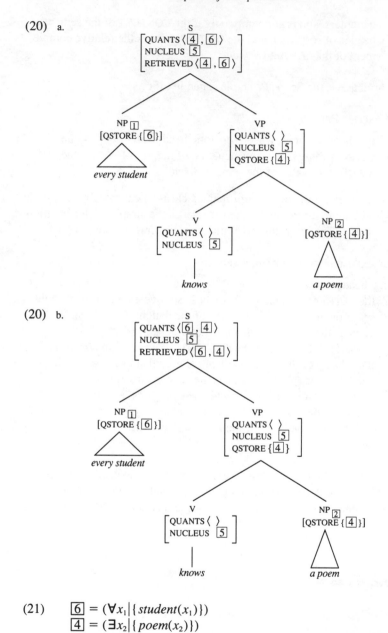

(20) b.

(21) $\boxed{6}$ = ($\forall x_1 | \{student(x_1)\}$)
          $\boxed{4}$ = ($\exists x_2 | \{poem(x_2)\}$)

Of course nothing requires that all quantifiers be retrieved at the same node, or that the QSTORE be emptied at all nodes of a certain category. Subject to various constraints that we will not attempt to make precise here, either of the quantifiers in (20) could remain in storage to be retrieved at a higher level of structure. One such possibility allowed by our analysis is sketched in (22), where the resulting CONTENT value is as shown in (23):

(22)

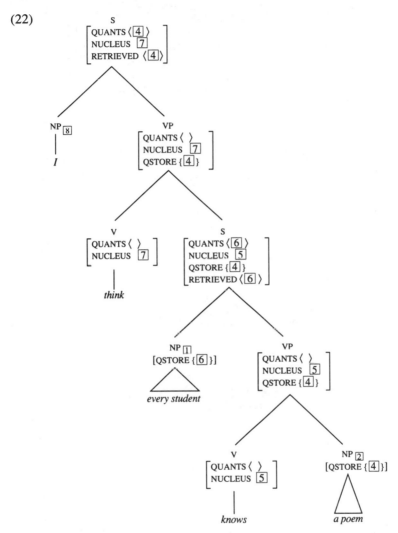

(23) $(\exists x_2|\{poem(x_2)\})think(x_8, (\forall x_1|\{student(x_1)\})know(x_1,x_2))$

The quantifier retrieval analysis just sketched also allows a quantifier within a VP complement to take narrow scope, as illustrated in (24)–(25), where the tag $\boxed{3}$ refers to the quantifier $(\forall x_2|\{teacher(x_2)\})$:

(24)   *Kim tries to please every teacher.*

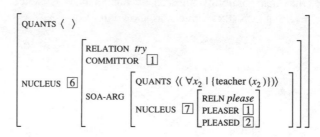

(25)

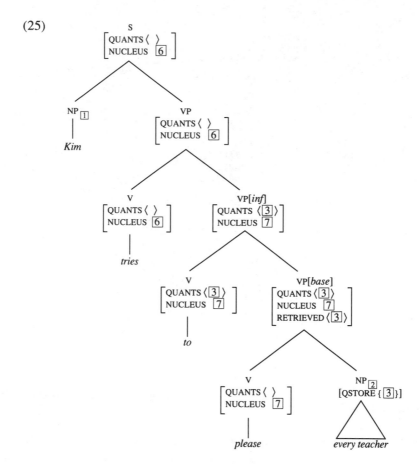

Note that the auxiliary element *to* has nonempty QUANTS and NUCLEUS values because its lexical entry remains as follows (see section 5 of Chapter 3), despite the introduction of QUANTS and NUCLEUS:

(26)   *to*

$$
\left[
\begin{array}{l}
\text{CAT}
\left[
\begin{array}{l}
\text{HEAD}
\left[
\begin{array}{l}
\text{VFORM } \textit{inf} \\
\text{AUX} +
\end{array}
\right] \\[6pt]
\text{SUBCAT } \langle \boxed{2}\text{NP, VP}[\textit{base}, \text{SUBCAT } \langle \boxed{2} \rangle]{:}\boxed{1} \rangle
\end{array}
\right] \\[12pt]
\text{CONTENT } \boxed{1}
\end{array}
\right]
$$

In identifying the CONTENT value of *to* with that of its VP complement, we thereby identify respective QUANTS and NUCLEUS values. In this way, the Semantics Principle guarantees that the QUANTS value of the phrase *to please every teacher* is the result of appending the empty list (of retrieved quantifiers) to the nonempty QUANTS of the semantic head *to*, as shown in (25).

Consider now the problem posed by the following examples:

(27)   *a.* One of her$_i$ students approached [each teacher]$_i$.
          b. The picture of himself$_i$ in his office delighted [each dictator]$_i$.
          c. [Each man]$_i$ talked to a friend of his$_i$.

It is clear that the indicated coindexings restrict the scope assignments that can be assigned to these examples. In each case, when the pronoun whose index is contained within an existential quantifier is anaphoric to (coindexed with) a universal quantifier, the universal quantifier must have wide scope.

What such examples show is that we must impose a further condition on quantifier retrieval to prevent a quantifier from having a scope that is not wide enough to bind all 'occurrences' of the index that 'belong' to it.[2] This condition is stated informally in (28) as a global well-formedness condition on CONTENT values:

(28)   QUANTIFIER BINDING CONDITION:

          Given a quantifier contained within a CONTENT value, every occurrence within that CONTENT value of the quantifier's index must be captured by that quantifier.

Here it should be noted that the only place a quantifier can occur within a CONTENT value is on a QUANTS list (at some level of embedding). We understand a quantifier on a QUANTS list of a psoa to *capture* an occurrence of the index that belongs to it provided the occurrence is either (1) in the RESTRICTION of the quantifier, (2) in another quantifier to the right of the quantifier in

2. Of course, in actuality a CONTENT value is a graph, so a given index can really occur only once within it. Here when we speak of 'occurrences,' we really mean paths within that graph that have the index in question as their value. The index that 'belongs to' a quantifier is the one that is its RESTIND|INDEX value.

question on the same QUANTS list, or (3) in the NUCLEUS of the psoa in question. Here it seems evident that we are attempting to capture an essentially semantic generalization in terms of a condition on 'the syntax of logical form.' We hope that eventually a system of model-theoretic interpretation for CONTENT values will eliminate the need for such a constraint, in the sense that any CONTENT containing a quantifier that fails to meet this condition would simply be uninterpretable. Such a project must await the development of a suitable model-theoretic interpretation for the language of situation theory.[3]

The analysis of quantification we have sketched in this section is Russellian in character insofar as it treats indefinite NPs in terms of existential quantifiers, rather than *reference markers* of the sort proposed within discourse representation theory (Kamp 1981) or file change semantics (Heim 1982). Instead, in order to account for the coindexed interpretation of such classic examples as (29), our treatment would have to rely either on an 'E-type' analysis of pronoun interpretations (Evans 1977, 1980; Heim 1990) or else on a 'dynamic' approach to the interpretation of the appropriate existential quantifiers (see, e.g., Groenendijk and Stokhof 1990, 1991):

(29)   Every man who owns [a donkey]$_i$ beats it$_i$.

Finally, it should be clearly understood that the proposal made in this section is quite programmatic and is intended only as a point of departure, not as a complete treatment of quantifier scope in English. The numerous factors that appear to affect the determination of quantifier scope include lexical differences (e.g. in many contexts, *each* has a stronger tendency to take wide scope than *every* does), length of NP (long indefinite NPs may tend to take wide scope), linear order (at the same level of embedding, earlier quantifiers tend to take scope over those that follow), depth of embedding (less embedded quantifiers tend to take scope over more deeply embedded ones), and scope islands

3. One potential defect of the analysis we have sketched arises from the interaction with raising verbs:

(i)   A unicorn appears to be approaching.
(i)   Sandy believes each painting to be fraudulent.

Assuming the analysis of raising presented in Chapter 3, the Semantics Principle allows no interpretation of these examples where the quantifier is within the scope of the raising verb. Yet the standard treatment of such examples is to predict the failure of existential generalization and substitutivity by allowing precisely such a scope assignment. This observation suggests that a reformulation of the Semantics Principle may be required wherein more quantifier scoping options are available than are permitted by the mechanism of retrieval at phrase-structural nodes that dominate the NP giving rise to the quantifier in question. We offer no such reformulation here, but note that the scope-based account of such examples is challenged by Zalta (1988: 216–219), whose alternative account is in principle compatible with our treatment of raising.

(complex NPs may constitute environments that delimit scope possibilities). The Quantifier Binding Condition is intended to provide only one constraint on quantifier interpretation that interacts with such additional factors.

8.3 Modifiers Revisited

In Chapters 1 and 2, we presented an analysis of adjectival modifiers that included lexical entries like the following (suitably modified to reflect the new QUANTS/NUCLEUS encoding of psoas):

(30)   LOCAL value of the lexical entry for the (attributive) adjective *red*

$$
\begin{bmatrix}
\text{CATEGORY} & \begin{bmatrix} \text{HEAD} & adj & \begin{bmatrix} \text{MOD N}' : \begin{bmatrix} \text{INDEX } \boxed{1} \\ \text{RESTR } \boxed{3} \end{bmatrix} \end{bmatrix} \\ \text{SUBCAT } \langle \ \rangle \end{bmatrix} \\
\text{CONTENT} & \begin{bmatrix} \text{INDEX } \boxed{1} \\ \text{RESTR} & \left\{ \begin{bmatrix} \text{QUANTS } \langle \ \rangle \\ \text{NUCLEUS} \begin{bmatrix} \text{RELN } red \\ \text{INST } \boxed{1} \end{bmatrix} \end{bmatrix} \right\} \cup \boxed{3} \end{bmatrix}
\end{bmatrix}
$$

Adjectives like (30) combine with nominal N′ constituents to form N′s whose index's restriction set includes one psoa stemming from the adjective and one stemming from the N′'s head noun, as illustrated in (31):

(31) $x_1 | \{ book(x_1), red(x_1) \}$

In our earlier discussion we treated only adjectives like *red*, whose interpretation is correctly modelled by the analysis in (31), which imposes multiple restrictions on the anchor of a parameter. Such an analysis seems appropriate, even in the face of the well-known fact that color terms might make reference to a hidden parameter whose value fixes a scale relative to which redness is determined. Thus, we may assume that the relation *red* has an additional role— let us call it STANDARD—whose value is some contextually determined property that provides the standard with respect to which redness will be determined.

By appealing to a 'hidden' parameter providing a contextually determined standard, we may also extend the multiple restrictions analysis to adjectives like *good*. On the basis of contrasts like (32), it is often thought that an adjective like *good* must be treated in terms of a function taking as argument the property associated with the noun it modifies:

(32)   *a.* Churchill was a good orator.
     b. This is a good cookie.
     c. A good speedboat is rare.

That is, it is often thought that the content of *good X* depends crucially on the meaning of X.

But the content of *good X* does not always depend on the meaning of X. Consider the following example (similar to those pointed out by McConnell-Ginet (1979)):

(33)   The Linguistics Department has an important volleyball game coming up against the Philosophy Department. I see the Phils have recruited Julius to play with them, which means we are in real trouble unless we can find a good linguist to add to our team in time for the game.

Here it seems clear that the standard of goodness is not at all determined by the modified noun (*linguist*). Rather, the relevant property (*volleyball player*) is supplied by the prior context. This is exactly as predicted by the multiple restrictions approach, once *good*, like most other adjectives, is analyzed in terms of a contextually determined standard. This standard (the anchor of the parameter that serves as the value of the STANDARD attribute) is commonly determined by the property (relation) of the modified noun, but not in cases like (33), where the standard is contextually supplied.

This general treatment of adjective modifiers also allows an account of adjectives like *alleged* and *fake*. These seem to be inconsistent with the multiple restriction analysis for the simple reason that *alleged* Xs need not be Xs. However, the lexical entry of an adjective need not specify a restriction set that the modified nominal's restriction set is part of. Rather, the lexical entry for an adjective like *alleged* may embed the nominal's restriction set as an argument of the *alleged* relation, as shown in (34):

(34)   LOCAL value of the lexical entry for the (attributive) adjective *alleged*

$$
\begin{bmatrix}
\text{CATEGORY} & \begin{bmatrix} \text{HEAD} & \begin{bmatrix} & \text{MOD N}': \begin{bmatrix} \text{INDEX} & \boxed{1} \\ \text{RESTR} & \boxed{3}\,set \end{bmatrix} \end{bmatrix}_{adj} \\ \text{SUBCAT} \langle\ \rangle \end{bmatrix} \\[4ex]
\text{CONTENT} & \begin{bmatrix} \text{INDEX} & 1 \\ \text{RESTR} & \left\{ \begin{bmatrix} \text{QUANTS} \langle\ \rangle \\ \text{NUCLEUS} \begin{bmatrix} \text{RELN } alleged \\ \text{SOA-ARG} & \boxed{3} \end{bmatrix} \end{bmatrix} \right\} \end{bmatrix}
\end{bmatrix}
$$

In this way, the content of an N' like *alleged criminal* is the nom-obj shown in (35):[4]

---

4. A technical complication evident here is that the value of the SOA-ARG role is a (singleton) set of psoas, not simply a psoa as we assumed in Chapter 7. This complication is a consequence of our having treated restrictions on indices as *sets* of psoas rather

(35) $x_1|alleged(\{criminal(x_1)\})$

The individual referred to by a use of this type of nominal is thus subject only to the condition that some contextually determined individual have *alleged* that that individual be a criminal, not that (s)he actually *be* a criminal. This is the desired result.

The theory of quantifier retrieval presented in the previous section interacts correctly with the analysis of modifiers just sketched. Consider the structure in (36), where the head of the relative clause is the null relativizer output from the SELR (see Chapter 5, section 2.2, (28)):

(36)

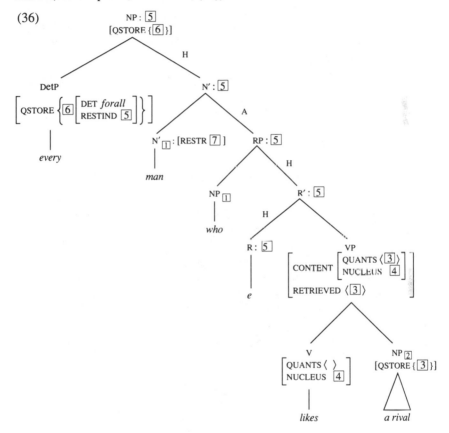

than simply as psoas. One obvious solution to this problem is to treat restrictions on indices as (possibly conjunctive) psoas rather than as sets. In this case our unions in modifier contents must be replaced with conjunctions. A second possibility would be to employ a set algebra (along the lines of Quine 1980), wherein the singleton of an element is not distinguished from the element itself (see Schwarzschild 1991 for some discussion in the context of the semantics of group expressions). We will not attempt to resolve this issue here.

Here the existential quantifier $\boxed{3}$, shown in (37), is retrieved at the VP level within the relative clause. The resulting CONTENT $\boxed{5}$ for the null relativizer, shown in (38), is shared with the R′, the RP, the higher N′, and the root NP, all courtesy of the Semantics Principle (the relevant semantic heads are indicated as either H (head-daughter) or A (adjunct-daughter) in (36):

(37) $(\exists x_2 | \{ rival(x_2) \})$

(38) $x_1 | \{ man(x_1), (\exists x_2 | \{ rival(x_2) \}) like(x_1, x_2) \}$

And the quantifier cannot be retrieved at any higher level of structure in (36), because at each higher level of structure, the CONTENT value is an npro, rather than a psoa. Thus NPs like *a rival* in (36) give rise to two kinds of interpretation. Example (36) illustrates early retrieval, where the quantifier is part of the restriction set of the npro. And if retrieval is postponed, as is natural in the case of examples like (39), the quantifier takes scope in the higher clause containing the relativized NP:

(39)   Most companies fired every man who likes a (certain) rival. The rival was. . . .

8.4 Contextual Information

8.4.1 Background Conditions

Throughout the previous chapters, we have made use of the attribute CONTEXT. The values of this attribute—objects of sort *context*—take the two attributes C-INDICES and BACKGROUND. As noted in section 3 of Chapter 1, the values of C-INDICES are specified for a number of attributes that give linguistically relevant information about the circumstances of utterance, for example, SPEAKER, ADDRESSEE, and UTTERANCE-LOCATION (U-LOC). The attribute BACKGROUND, as discussed in Chapter 2, takes as value a set of psoas corresponding to what are best thought of as the appropriateness conditions associated with an utterance of a given type of phrase. Objects of the sort *context* are thus structured as shown in (40):

(40)
$$
\begin{bmatrix}
\text{C-INDICES} & \begin{bmatrix} \text{SPEAKER} & \boxed{1}\,ref \\ \text{ADDRESSEE} & \boxed{2}\,ref \\ \text{U-LOC} & \boxed{3}\,ref \end{bmatrix} \\
\text{BACKGROUND} \ \{ \boxed{4}\,psoa, \ldots \}
\end{bmatrix}
$$
context

For example, in Chapter 2, we used background conditions to provide an account of various phenomena, specifically polite pronouns in German and French and honorific agreement in languages like Korean. This kind of analysis of course presupposes some method for accumulating the various background conditions that pieces of a sentence might engender, that is, of guaranteeing that a given sentence acquires all the background conditions of its component parts. The simplest way of guaranteeing this, given the assumptions we have made about the nature of *context*-sort objects, would be to establish the following principle:

(41)   PRINCIPLE OF CONTEXTUAL CONSISTENCY:

The CONTEXT | BACKGROUND value of a given phrase is the union of the CONTEXT | BACKGROUND values of the daughters.

The principle in (41) requires that all of the contextual assumptions associated with any part of an utterance will be inherited as part of the set of background conditions associated with the utterance as a whole, as illustrated in (42):

(42)

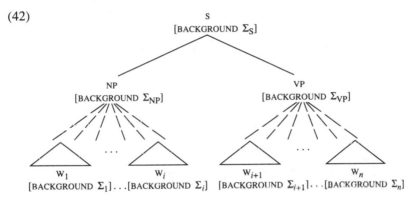

Where $\Sigma_S = (\Sigma_{NP} \cup \Sigma_{VP}) = (\Sigma_1 \cup \ldots \cup \Sigma_i \cup \ldots \cup \Sigma_n)$

(41) is a very strong theory of presupposition inheritance. Unfortunately, it is known to be incorrect. Minimally, it fails to allow for certain expressions that systematically block the inheritance of the presuppositions associated with specific parts of an utterance. Most notable among these are the 'plugs' of Karttunen (1973a) (e.g. the connective *if* (. . . *then*)) and verbs of saying or propositional attitude (e.g. *say* or *believe*). Thus in the following sets of examples, the (a) and (b) sentences differ in that only the former have as a presupposition the proposition expressed by the (c) sentence:

(43)   *a.* Pat regrets that Terry is dead.
        b. If Terry is dead, then Pat regrets that Terry is dead.
        c. Terry is dead.

(44)   *a.* Pat regrets that Terry is dead.
        b. Kim fears that Pat regrets that Terry is dead.
        c. Terry is dead.

It was once widely believed that phenomena such as these were best analyzed in terms of some theory of the 'projection problem' for presuppositions,
that is, the problem of stating the conditions under which the presuppositions
of components of utterances are either inherited or discarded by successively
larger components of utterances. Karttunen's (1973a) approach was to classify
connectives and other clause-embedding expressions as 'plugs,' 'holes,' and
'filters,' according to how they affected presuppositional inheritance. In a similar vein, Karttunen and Peters (1979), who treated the majority of presuppositional phenomena as conventional implicatures, assigned to all such
expressions an appropriate 'heritage property' that plays a role in a general
theory determining the conventional implicatures of sentences in a compositional fashion.

Clearly, any theory of this kind could easily be expressed within the general
framework for contextual information that we have set forth here. The cancellation of presuppositions bears a strong resemblance to the removal of quantifiers from QSTORE values, as discussed in section 8.2. Indeed it is also similar
to the removal of NONLOCAL feature values that takes place in our analysis of
the binding of SLASH (Chapter 4) and REL (Chapter 5) dependencies. Formally,
much the same technique could be applied in an effort to weaken the Principle
of Contextual Consistency to allow specific elements (the plugs) to remove
members from the inherited set of appropriacy conditions.

We will not formulate such a theory here, however, as the view of presupposition and presupposition inheritance just described has been widely recognized as inadequate and has largely given way to a quite different conception.
As Karttunen (1973b, 1974) was already aware (see also Stalnaker 1973), plug-
ging is not an absolute matter. For verbs of propositional attitude—in (45a),
for example—the presupposition of the most deeply embedded clause ((45b))
is not simply plugged:

(45)   *a.* Kim fears that Pat will stop protecting Sandy.
         b. Pat is protecting Sandy.
         c. Kim believes that Pat is protecting Sandy.

That is, (45a) is not without presupposition; rather, it presupposes (45c), where
the presupposition of the most deeply embedded clause of (45a) must be in the
set of the fearer's (Kim's) beliefs.

Subsequent literature on presupposition (e.g. Gazdar 1979a, 1979b; Soames
1982; Heim 1983) responded in part to the need to provide a systematic account of facts such as these. It was also motivated by the desire to eliminate the
arbitrariness of theories like Karttunen's original proposal or the theory of
Karttunen and Peters (1979), where the presuppositional inheritance properties
of various expressions are stipulated in a way that appears unrelated to their
meaning. In Heim's theory, for example, the familiar conception of semantics
based on the static (albeit context-dependent) notion of content was abandoned

in favor of a conception of linguistic meaning based on the notion of context change potential (CCP). A compositional assignment of CCPs, as Heim shows, can serve to predict both the truth conditional aspect of an utterance's meaning and its presuppositional inheritance. Her account of the CCP of *if*, for example, is as shown in (46):

(46)   c + if A,B = c − (c + A − (c + A + B)).

This is to be interpreted as defining the result of executing the CCP of *if* A,B on a context c (where c is a set of possible worlds and − is set difference). The definition in (46) says that c admits *if* A,B only if c admits A and c + A admits B. The inheritance property of *if* (that the presuppositions of B entailed by A are filtered), as well as its truth conditional import, falls out of (46).

We believe that an approach along these lines holds considerable promise not only for the theory of presuppositions, but for semantic theory in general. And the precise determination of which background conditions of the parts of an utterance are inherited by the utterance as a whole may well require such a wholesale shift in the nature of the semantic objects we have assumed. However, exploring such modifications is well beyond the scope of the present study. We have entered into this discussion, admittedly somewhat of a digression, in an effort to make clear some of the problems that must be addressed in developing an adequate theory of contexts, which seem to play an increasingly important role in linguistic description.

8.4.2 Contextual Indices

A deictic expression might be defined as one that identifies some part of its content with some part of its context. For example, the first person pronoun *I*, as discussed in Chapter 2, identifies indices as shown in (47):

(47)
$$
\begin{bmatrix}
\text{CONTENT} \ \ ppro \ [\text{INDEX} \ \boxed{1}[1st, sing]] \\
\\
local \ \ [\text{CONTEXT I C-INDICES I SPEAKER} \ \boxed{1}]
\end{bmatrix}
$$

But, in general, any occurrence of the word *I* (or *me, my*, or *myself*) within a given utterance makes reference to the same individual—the speaker of that utterance. That is, in examples like (48a, b), the first-person pronouns all corefer because there is only one speaker per utterance, not one for each phrase within the utterance:

(48)   a. I_i thought they would never do that to me_i.
         b. My_i friends say that there is no way anyone can do anything to make Kim stop believing that Sandy resents me_i.

Is this fact due to some linguistic constraint that must be assumed in addition to the basic meaning of the first-person singular pronoun? Probably not: in those cases where more than one individual collaborates in the utterance of a single sentence, the reference of a particular occurrence of *I* must be the utterer of that particular occurrence. In examples like the following, for example, the deictic orientation is that of the second collaborator—the one who actually utters the deictic expression:[5]

(49)   A: Well, do you think they're gonna . . .
        B: . . .   fire me [= B]?

(50)   A: Well, do you think they're gonna . . .
        B: . . .   fire you [= A]?

Thus it would seem that the coreference indicated in (48a, b) follows directly from the lexical entry for the first-person pronoun (cf. (47)) and the fact that those examples are normally considered as single speaker utterances, rather than as collaborations like (49) and (50).

Much the same is true of other deictic expressions. In fact, the word-by-word variation in reference of non-first-person deictic expressions requires less in the way of exotic contextualization. Examples like (51), for example, where each occurrence of *you* has a different reference, involves nothing more than a little ostension on the speaker's part:

(51)   For this detail, I will need the assistance of you_1, you_2, you_3, and you_4.

And without the possibility of fine-grained, word-by-word, context individuation, the following examples would all be highly redundant or nonsensical:

(52)   *a.* I want telephone jacks installed here, here, here, and here.
        b. I'll schedule appointments for her, him, him, her, and her.
        c. That is larger than that or that.

Analogous examples involving temporal deixis may be more difficult to contextualize, but a likely explanation is that we do not customarily communicate ostensively about minute time intervals. Nonetheless, an example like (53) seems to exhibit just the same contextual granularity as those in (52):[6]

(53)   It seems to be louder *now* . . . than it is *now*. (listening to a malfunctioning auto alarm emitting a complex sound pattern)

Clearly, each word of an utterance—in principle at least—introduces its own contextual parameters that may be relevant for the interpretation of deictic expressions. This means that the standard methods for bringing contextual in-

---

5. Collaborative utterances of this sort are not at all unusual. For some discussion, see Wilkes-Gibbs 1986, Lerner 1987, and Clark and Schaefer 1989.

6. Further examples of this sort are discussed by Fodor and Sag (1982). See also Green (1989: chap. 2).

formation into the model-theoretic semantic analysis of natural language, for example, the *indices* of Montague (1974), the *'expanded'* indices of Lewis (1972), or the *contexts* of Kaplan (1979), do not do justice to the subtle nature of deictic context dependence. Any account of meaning that simply relativizes a recursive truth definition to a single set of contextual elements (speaker, addressee, etc.) associated with (an utterance of) an entire sentence embodies a gross simplification of the linguistic data.

The analog in our system of this simplified approach to deixis would be to identify the C-INDICES value of all daughters in a given phrase with that of the phrase itself, that is, with the mother in (54):

(54)

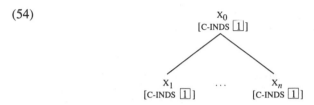

In an effort to adopt a more realistic notion of context, one that can begin to address the kinds of complexities of deictic usage just observed, we will not identify the C-INDS values of daughters and mothers. Rather, we will assume that each part of an utterance (at least each lexeme) has its own C-INDICES value, and that the commonalities that exist among such values are simply due to the nature of utterances. Thus, because speakers generally utter sentences unassisted (let us assume) to a particular addressee in a time frame that seldom requires reference to finely grained subintervals of an utterance, it follows that all relevant information contained within C-INDICES values are typically identified within an utterance. We may, in fact, generally identify whole values of C-INDS, as in (54), but it should always be born in mind that this is not due to any principle or constraint that is part of the linguistic system that we have herein set out to describe, nor of any other. As we have seen, any such constraints are in principle defeasible, and hold only in virtue of typical properties of discourse situations—tendencies totally external to language.

8.5 Some Analytic Alternatives

In this section, we will discuss briefly various possible modifications of the basic semantic analysis presented throughout this volume.

8.5.1 Relations and Qfpsoas

The first of these (first presented in Pollard (1989)) has to do with the way individual relations select their roles. Throughout this volume (as well as in other writings), we have assumed that objects of sort *quantifier-free parame-*

trized state of affairs (qfpsoa, called simply psoas in Chapters 1–7) are specified for the attribute RELATION, and that the objects that serve as the values of
this attribute are of various (atomic) sorts corresponding to individual relations
(e.g. *persuade, investigate, book).* The qfpsoas we have assumed in our examples all exhibit relation-specific role selections. That is, the semantic roles appropriate for a given qfpsoa depend crucially on which relation appears as the
value of the RELATION attribute. Thus we have assumed that our theory of
qfpsoas and relations will ensure that qfpsoas like those in (55) are well-
formed, while the ones in (56) are not.

(55)   a.
$$
qfpsoa \begin{bmatrix} \text{RELATION} & love \\ \text{LOVER} & ref[\ ] \\ \text{LOVED} & ref[\ ] \end{bmatrix}
$$
b.
$$
qfpsoa \begin{bmatrix} \text{RELATION} & persuade \\ \text{INFLUENCE} & ref[\ ] \\ \text{INFLUENCED} & ref[\ ] \\ \text{SOA-ARG} & [\ ] \end{bmatrix}
$$

(56)   a.
$$
qfpsoa \begin{bmatrix} \text{RELATION} & persuade \\ \text{LOVER} & ref[\ ] \\ \text{LOVED} & ref[\ ] \end{bmatrix}
$$
b.
$$
qfpsoa \begin{bmatrix} \text{RELATION} & person \\ \text{INFLUENCE} & ref[\ ] \\ \text{INFLUENCED} & ref[\ ] \\ \text{SOA-ARG} & [\ ] \end{bmatrix}
$$

But these assumptions present a technical difficulty. Totally well-typed feature
structures of the kind employed in our framework (see section 2 of Chapter 1) must satisfy the condition that they bear all and only those features that
are appropriate to their sort. But then there is no natural way to reflect the fact
that what roles appear in a qfpsoa depend on that qfpsoa's relation.

A solution to this technical problem would be to eliminate the attribute RE-
LATION. The atomic sorts *persuade, love, person,* etc. would become subsorts
of the sort *qfpsoa.* Instances of each of these subsorts could then bear only the
appropriate attributes. Technically, the appropriate sorts for each relation (subsort of *qfpsoa)* would be declared in a hierarchy of sorts like the one in (57).
As a result, we would permit only qfpsoas like those in (58) where all and only
the appropriate attributes appear.

(57)

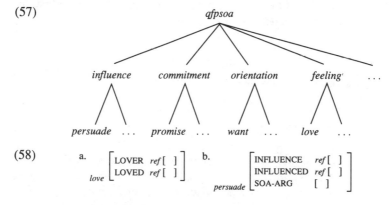

(58)   a.
$$
love \begin{bmatrix} \text{LOVER} & ref[\ ] \\ \text{LOVED} & ref[\ ] \end{bmatrix}
$$
b.
$$
persuade \begin{bmatrix} \text{INFLUENCE} & ref[\ ] \\ \text{INFLUENCED} & ref[\ ] \\ \text{SOA-ARG} & [\ ] \end{bmatrix}
$$

8.5.2 Propositions and Types

Our treatment of CONTENT values in terms of psoas (infons), which we have adopted primarily for expository reasons, is by no means the only analysis possible within HPSG. As Richard Cooper (1990, chap. 7) has shown, it is straightforward to modify the lexical entries of verbs in such a way that general principles of HPSG theory, in particular the Semantics Principle in (16) above, cause sentences to have propositions (in the situation-theoretic sense) as their CONTENT value, rather than psoas. In (59), we adapt the lexical entry he gives (p. 145) for a simple transitive verb:[7]

(59)
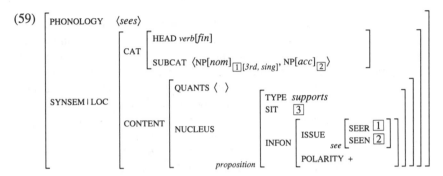

Note that the indicated structure sharing identifies the indices of subcategorized phrases with the appropriate role arguments, as before, but the NUCLEUS value of the resulting content for the sentence projected by this verb will be the proposition that the described situation ([3]) *supports* the positive state of affairs involving the appropriately anchored role arguments (the seer and the seen).[8]

Similarly, Cooper treats background assumptions as a set of parametric propositions, rather than a set of psoas. This amounts to little more than replacing specifications like (60) with those like (61):

7. Just as relations can be treated as subsorts of *qfpsoa,* so can types (in the sense of situation theory) be treated as subsorts of proposition. Thus the CONTENT in (59) could be rendered as shown in (i):

$$
\begin{bmatrix}
\text{SIT} \; \boxed{3} & \\
\text{INFON} & \begin{bmatrix} \text{ISSUE} \quad _{see} \begin{bmatrix} \text{SEER} \; \boxed{1} \\ \text{SEEN} \; \boxed{2} \end{bmatrix} \\ \text{POLARITY} \; + \end{bmatrix} \\
_{supports} &
\end{bmatrix}
$$

8. Unlike our implicit treatment of polarity in the previous chapters, Cooper systematically separates POLARITY from semantic roles.

(60)

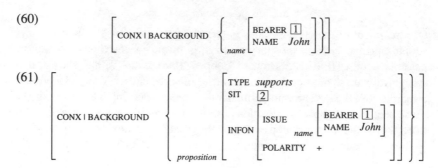

$$\left[\text{CONX | BACKGROUND}\ \left\{ {}_{\textit{name}}\begin{bmatrix} \text{BEARER}\ \boxed{1} \\ \text{NAME}\ \ \textit{John} \end{bmatrix} \right\} \right]$$

(61)

$$\left[\text{CONX | BACKGROUND}\ \left\{ {}_{\textit{proposition}}\begin{bmatrix} \text{TYPE}\ \ \textit{supports} \\ \text{SIT}\ \ \boxed{2} \\ \text{INFON}\ \begin{bmatrix} \text{ISSUE}\ \ {}_{\textit{name}}\begin{bmatrix} \text{BEARER}\ \boxed{1} \\ \text{NAME}\ \ \textit{John} \end{bmatrix} \\ \text{POLARITY}\ \ + \end{bmatrix} \end{bmatrix} \right\} \right]$$

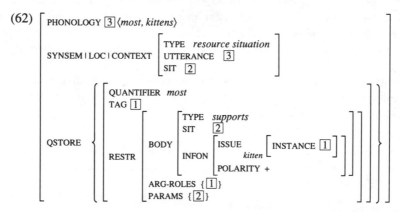

A further restriction is required to guarantee that index $\boxed{2}$ in (61) is anchored to the relevant resource situation. Aside from minor additions of this sort, it would appear that nothing in the previous chapters need be changed in order to incorporate these basic changes in semantic analysis.

A third proposal of Cooper's, however, may give rise to certain difficulties. His semantic analysis treats the restrictions of quantifiers as complex types formed by abstraction over certain role arguments. To deal with complex types, three attributes are introduced: BODY, ARG-ROLES, and PARAMS. In a quantifier like the one described in (62), it is the ARG-ROLE value that tells us that the parameter $\boxed{1}$ is abstracted over, and the PARAMS value that tells us that the parameter $\boxed{2}$ 'is a parameter of' (the situation semantics analog of 'occurs freely in') the quantifier's restriction:

(62)

$$\begin{bmatrix} \text{PHONOLOGY}\ \boxed{3}\ \langle \textit{most, kittens} \rangle \\ \text{SYNSEM | LOC | CONTEXT}\ \begin{bmatrix} \text{TYPE}\ \ \textit{resource situation} \\ \text{UTTERANCE}\ \ \boxed{3} \\ \text{SIT}\ \ \boxed{2} \end{bmatrix} \\ \text{QSTORE}\ \left\{ \begin{bmatrix} \text{QUANTIFIER}\ \ \textit{most} \\ \text{TAG}\ \boxed{1} \\ \text{RESTR}\ \begin{bmatrix} \text{BODY}\ \begin{bmatrix} \text{TYPE}\ \ \textit{supports} \\ \text{SIT}\ \ \boxed{2} \\ \text{INFON}\ \begin{bmatrix} \text{ISSUE}\ \ {}_{\textit{kitten}}\begin{bmatrix} \text{INSTANCE}\ \boxed{1} \end{bmatrix} \\ \text{POLARITY}\ + \end{bmatrix} \end{bmatrix} \\ \text{ARG-ROLES}\ \{\boxed{1}\} \\ \text{PARAMS}\ \{\boxed{2}\} \end{bmatrix} \end{bmatrix} \right\} \end{bmatrix}$$

Here the situation parameter $\boxed{2}$ is a parameter of ('free in') the proposition that is the value of BODY, of the type that restricts the quantifier, and ultimately of the entire utterance. That parameter is contextually constrained, however, to be a resource situation appealed to by the utterance of *most kittens*. The ARG-ROLES value tells us which parameters of the BODY are absorbed by the type abstraction; thus in the present case the restriction of the stored quantifier is the type of being a $\boxed{1}$ such that the resource situation $\boxed{2}$ supports $\boxed{1}$ being a kitten. The semantics of *most kittens* will thus be specified in terms of this property.

In our treatment of quantification, we have assiduously avoided the use of complex types of this sort (or the closely related complex relations formed by abstraction over infons instead of propositions), though they are often employed by recent work in situation semantics (see, e.g., Gawron and Peters 1990). The reasons that have led us away from such constructs have to do with agreement phenomena. As we saw in Chapter 2, agreement phenomena cannot be purely semantic in nature; that is, they cannot be adequately treated solely in terms of conditions on the denotations of linguistic expressions. An important subset of agreement relations requires nonsemantic agreement information associated with the *indices* that appear as the INDEX values of linguistic expressions. Consider, for example, the sentences in (63):

(63)   *a*. Most people that take/*takes this class introduce themselves.
        b. A person that takes/*take this class introduces himself/herself/
             *themselves.
        c. Every woman who enrolls herself distinguishes herself/*himself/
             *themselves.

On our analysis, the reflexive pronouns in the matrix clause of examples like these must be coindexed with the subject (by binding theory—see Chapter 6), and because of the constraints on relative clauses (Chapter 5), these subjects must be coindexed with the subject inside the relative clause. There is agreement in all these examples because the covarying forms all must make use of the same index. Hence because indices are systematically related to referents, the theory establishes a principled relation between agreement and coreference. This is precisely the relation exhibited by the relevant agreement phenomena.

But this link between reference and agreement is absent from the account offered by Cooper. In fact, it would be semantically unobjectionable (if not customary) to employ distinct indices in the case of distinct instances of abstraction. If his analysis is to describe the basic facts of agreement in English, he must either (1) treat all agreement patterns in terms of denotational (in)compatability (cf. the Dowty-Jacobson position we argued against in Chapter 2), or else (2) state some semantically unnecessary and otherwise unmotivated condition requiring identity of two indices. Cooper appears to have some condition of the latter sort in mind, judging from his use of the attribute TAG, but the precise nature of his proposal is unclear to us.

In this section, we have examined several revisions of semantic analysis introduced by Richard Cooper (1990). Two of these, having to do with replacing psoas (i.e. infons) with parametrized propositions, seem quite compatible with the analyses we have proposed in previous chapters. Cooper's third proposal, to treat quantifier restrictions in terms of types rather than psoas (or parametrized propositions), presents certain difficulties in light of the conclusions we reached in Chapter 2 about the nature of agreement phenomena in English and other languages.

8.5.3 Roles and Subcategorization

Another change in semantic analysis that might be entertained concerns the content of subcategorized dependents. Our approach to dependent NPs and dependent PPs headed by nonpredicative prepositions has been to treat them as contributing an index (of the object NP or the prepositional object) that is assigned a semantic role in the CONTENT value of the verb. This analysis leaves no room for assigning interpretations to nonpredicative prepositions. There is a clear intuition that *to*-marked, *for*-marked, and *of*-marked phrases, for example, are role-restricted (none can take an object that will be assigned what is intuitively an agentive role, e.g.). At present, this fact follows from nothing in our theory.

Suppose, however, that thematic roles of the familiar sort could be used to classify the fine-grained semantic roles we have employed throughout this volume. That is, suppose we had a way of classifying the GIVEE, DONATEE, HANDEE roles (and their like) as different realizations of a more general (or superordinate) role called GOAL. Such a classification might involve a limited second-order extension of the general theory of feature structures we have been assuming. Given such an extension, we could perhaps use sort compatibility to provide the beginning of an account of the role restrictions that nonpredicative prepositions seem to obey.

Suppose the lexical form for a nonpredicative preposition is as shown in (64):

$$(64) \qquad to \quad \begin{bmatrix} \text{CAT} \begin{bmatrix} \text{HEAD} & prep \\ \\ \text{SUBCAT} \langle \text{NP}[acc]_{\boxed{1}} \rangle \end{bmatrix} \\ \\ \text{CONTENT} \mid \text{NUCLEUS} \underset{transfer}{\begin{bmatrix} \text{GOAL} & \boxed{1} \end{bmatrix}} \end{bmatrix}$$

This preposition, whose CONTENT | NUCLEUS value is a qfpsoa of the supersort *transfer* (making the revisions suggested in section 8.5.1, but not those suggested in section 8.5.2), assigns its object's index to the GOAL role in the indicated transfer situation.

In consequence of this analysis, a PP headed by the preposition in (64) will have as its content nucleus a transfer-sort qfpsoa, and hence when it combines with a verb, that verb must identify its own content with that of the preposition. Such a revision is sketched in (65) for the transfer-sort verb *give*:

(65)

$$\text{give}\begin{bmatrix} \text{CAT} \begin{bmatrix} \text{HEAD} \quad verb[\textit{fin}] \\ \text{SUBCAT} \langle \text{NP}_{\boxed{2}}, \text{NP}[acc]_{\boxed{3}}, \text{PP}[to]: \boxed{4} \rangle \end{bmatrix} \\ \text{CONTENT} \mid \text{NUCLEUS} \boxed{4} \underset{give}{\begin{bmatrix} \text{GIVER} \quad \boxed{2} \\ \text{GIFT} \quad \boxed{3} \end{bmatrix}} \end{bmatrix}$$

Although (65) assigns no semantic role directly to the argument of the preposition, this role assignment comes about indirectly. In consequence of the structure sharings specified in (64) and (65), the content nucleus for a phrase of the relevant sort (e.g. *give a book to Pat*) will be as shown in (66):

(66)

$$\underset{give}{\begin{bmatrix} \text{GIVER} \quad \boxed{2} \\ \text{GIFT} \quad \boxed{3} \\ \text{GIVEE} \quad \boxed{1} \end{bmatrix}}$$

In order for this treatment to succeed, the specification $\boxed{4}$[GOAL $\boxed{1}$], taken together with the specification $\boxed{4}$ *give* and the information that the attribute GIVEE is a subfeature of the attribute GOAL, must be sufficient to determine the information in (66). This treatment also raises a number of questions about how o-command, as well as the other constructs of binding theory, are to be redefined. We will not resolve these matters here.

8.6 Conclusion

Though the analyses presented in this chapter are in the main rather sketchy, they nonetheless illustrate a method that we believe can be extended to the full range of semantic problems in natural language. Following the leading ideas of situation semantics, we have assumed that linguistic meaning is in essence a set of constraints that define a relation between contexts of utterance (CON-TEXT values) and interpretation (CONTENT values). This *relational theory of meaning*, as it is often called, is one that, to our knowledge, has not previously been coupled with detailed syntactic analysis. In this chapter, we have tried to take a few preliminary steps in remedying that defect, by sketching how the relational theory of meaning can be coupled with the detailed syntactic analyses we have provided in the previous chapters. But a very great deal remains to be done.

9

Reflections and Revisions

9.1 Introduction

In P&S-87, and in the foregoing chapters of this volume, we have taken the position that there is nothing special about subjects, other than the fact that (by definition) they are the least oblique complements of the heads that select them. Technically, of course, on our account this amounts to identifying the subject of a given head as the first (i.e. leftmost) member of that head's SUBCAT list. However, most other current syntactic frameworks treat subjects as fundamentally different from complements. Thus, for example, in GPSG, complement selection takes place by keying lexical heads to a certain set of lexical ID rules by means of specific integer values for a certain syntactic feature (called SUB-CAT, but rather different in character from the SUBCAT feature that we have been employing); but subject selection (and concomitantly, subject-verb agreement) is mediated by two distinct features (SUBJ and AGR). In some versions of GB, as discussed in section 1.5, subjects are distinguished from objects in the respect that the former are specifiers in terms of the tree-configurational position that they occupy relative to the X′ schemata; but the latter are complements according to the same criterion. And in LFG, not only are subjects distinguished from objects; rather, each of the full inventory of LFG grammatical functions (classically, SUBJ, OBJ, OBJ2, etc.) is distinguished from the others via a different feature (or, within recent versions of lexical mapping theory (Bresnan and Kanerva 1989; Bresnan and Zaenen 1990) via a bundle of features) at the level of f(unctional)-structure.

Indeed, even in the theory that we have presented thus far, there are a number of notions and constraints that require specific reference to the first member of the SUBCAT list. Among these are the Raising Principle (Chapter 3, (117)), which identifies an unexpressed subject with a semantically unassigned complement; the notion of strict subcategorization employed in the English-specific version of the Trace Principle (Chapter 4, (33)) in order to block extraction of subjects; the Subject Extraction Lexical Rule (SELR), which permits certain apparent exceptions to the Trace Principle; the Subject Condition (Chapter 4, (84)), which permits appropriately licensed extractions from subjects; and the revised definition of local o-command (Chapter 6, (116)), whose purpose is to ensure that local o-command holds between a referential NP (or nonpredicative PP) argument and the unexpressed subject of a more oblique complement.

In a series of important and provocative papers, Robert Borsley (1987, 1989, 1990, to appear) has argued for a version of HPSG, alternative to the one that we have thus far presented here, that builds in a fundamental distinction between subjects and complements into the theory in the most direct way possible: by positing distinct corresponding features SUBJ and COMPS.[1] Although Borsley has persisted in making us aware of various advantages of this theoretical move beginning as early as 1986, we have been equally persistent in choosing to work out the empirical consequences of the simpler hypothesis that all complements are selected via a single list-valued feature, and that is the course we have followed thus far.

Nevertheless, in the course of the six years that have elapsed since the publication of P&S-87, we have gradually become persuaded that the overwhelming weight of evidence favors Borsley's view of this matter. The careful reader has surely noticed that, throughout the preceding chapters of this volume, we have pointed out (either parenthetically or in footnotes) various difficulties with the theory presented there whose resolution is deferred to Chapter 9. These promissory notes must now be paid, and it is in the currency of Borsley's SUBJ versus COMPS distinction that we will now redeem them.

The remainder of this chapter is organized as follows. In section 9.2, we summarize and extend Borsley's own arguments for distinguishing subjects from complements, and sketch a revised form of HPSG that incorporates this change. In section 9.3, we briefly consider some further advantages of Borsley's proposal that arise in the analysis of Welsh. (A terminological note: for expository convenience, we will follow Borsley's terminology in referring to the version of the theory that we have presented so far (the one in which SUBJ and COMPS are *not* distinguished) as 'standard' HPSG, although one of the chief purposes of this chapter is to argue *against* that version, not for it.) In section 9.4, we will present arguments in favor of making a further featural distinction between subjects (SUBJ) and specifiers (SPR), as proposed by Borsley (to appear), and show that specifiers share certain properties with heads on the one hand and with markers on the other. In section 9.5, we lead from the assumption that SUBJ and COMPS are distinct into an analysis of unbounded dependency constructions that obviates the need for traces. And finally, in section 9.6, we speculate as to whether there is a sense in which subjects and the fillers in UDCs should be regarded as subcases of a single phenomenon.

1. Borsley himself actually employs the names SUBJ and SUBCAT for the features corresponding to subjects and (nonsubject) complements, respectively. We prefer the names SUBJ and COMPS, so that the latter will be clearly distinguished from our own SUBCAT feature.

Throughout this chapter, a cautionary note is in order: we are attempting here to give a tentative sketch of how the theory presented so far might be modified in certain ways, while preserving as much as possible of what is right about the standard theory. But as yet, many of the technical details of the revised theory have not been worked out, and it remains to be seen to what extent the proposals set forth here can be made consistent with the assumptions and analyses presented in preceding chapters.

9.2 On Borsley's Arguments from English

9.2.1 The Notion of Possible Nonhead Category

Borsley (1987) observes that standard HPSG 'does not permit as simple a characterization of the notion possible nonhead category as some other frameworks', for example, in GPSG, nonheads are either (minor) lexical categories like Det or else maximal projection (i.e. ⟨bar, 2⟩) categories. Similarly, the usual X' schemata employed in GB together with the assumption that movement applies only to lexical heads or maximal projections has similar consequences; and if it is further assumed that lexical heads move only from one head position to another, then in fact all nonheads would be maximal projections. However, in standard HPSG, nonheads may be either lexical (e.g. markers), saturated (e.g. S, NP), or almost-saturated (e.g. VP, predicative AP). Borsley's proposal to distinguish SUBJ from COMPS eliminates this complication, as now nonheads (other than markers) can be characterized simply as [COMPS ⟨ ⟩] phrases. Indeed, it seems that a further simplification is available: inasmuch as all phrases will now be [COMPS ⟨ ⟩], we might incorporate this specification into the definition of the sort *phrase*. In this case we can simply say that nonheads (other than markers) are phrasal.[2]

---

2. Citing examples such as those in (i)–(iii), Borsley attempts to mount an independent argument that standard HPSG 'does not treat VP and S as a natural class' and therefore 'cannot provide a satisfactory account of the various contexts in which both subjectless infinitives and clauses can appear':

(i)   *a.* John expects to be here.
        b. John expects that Mary will be here.

(ii)   *a.* John wondered whether to leave.
        b. John wondered whether he should leave.

(iii)   *a.* John arranged to see Mary.
        b. John arranged for Bill to see Mary.

To the extent that it is correct, this critique appears to us to be a special case of the argument just given. Thus, e.g., in the case of (iii), we can simply say that *arrange* requires an infinitive phrase as complement. The fact that this complement must be [COMPS ⟨ ⟩] is just a consequence of the fact that it (like all complements) is a phrase;

9.2.2 Nonpredicative Prepositions

As Borsley (1987) points out, there is no reasonable basis for assuming that nonpredicative prepositions subcategorize for two complements. But if there is only one complement, then the prepositional object would really be a subject; consequently one might expect that whatever principle orders subjects before verb phrases (P&S-87, Chapter 7) would also order prepositional objects before the prepositions. This is a flaw in standard HPSG: if nonpredicative *on* is lexically specified as [SUBCAT ⟨NP[*acc*]⟩], then the grammar proposed in Chapter 1 runs the danger of predicting, for example, that (1a) is good and (1b) bad:

(1) *a.* *Kim depends [Sandy on].
     b. Kim depends [on Sandy].

But if the lexical entry for nonpredicative *on* is instead as shown in (2),[3] then this problem is readily disposed of provided we reformulate Schemata 1 and 2 (Chapter 1, (22)) along the lines indicated in (3):[4]

(2)
$$
\begin{bmatrix}
\text{CAT} & \begin{bmatrix} \text{HEAD } prep[on,\ -\text{PRD}] \\ \text{SUBJ } \langle\ \rangle \\ \text{COMPS } \langle \text{NP } [acc]: \boxed{1} \rangle \end{bmatrix} \\
\text{CONTENT } \boxed{1}
\end{bmatrix}
$$

(3)   Schema 1 (revised version): a phrase with DTRS value of sort *head-subj-struc* in which the HEAD-DTR value is a phrasal sign.

---

and nothing constrains the SUBJ value. In the case of (ii), the argument seems to us to lack force, in the absence of a precise account of what is a possible interrogative phrasal projection of V; e.g., on what basis are the nonsentences in (iv) to be ruled out?

(iv) *a.* *John wondered whether for Bill to leave.
      b. *John wondered whether Bill leave.
      c. *John wondered whether Bill leaving.

Similarly, in the case of (i) it is not enough to say simply that *expect* takes a verbal complement; more needs to be said to rule out the nonsentences in (v):

(v)   *a.* *John expects for Bill to be here. (ungrammatical in the authors'
           idiolects)
      b. *John expects that Bill be here.
      c. *John expects that Bill being here.

3. Lexical entries like this one, together with the Semantics Principle (Chapter 8, (16)), also provide for the sharing of CONTENT values between nonpredicative PPs and their prepositional objects (Chapter 6, section 4).

4. A revision of Schema 3 will also be needed. We return to this question in section 9.6.

Schema 2 (revised version): a phrase with DTRS value of sort *head-comp-struc* in which the HEAD-DTR value is a lexical sign.

For these schemata to work, some of the technical assumptions of Chapter 1 need to be modified slightly.[5] For example, we must assume a new feature of headed structures called SUBJECT-DAUGHTER (SUBJ-DTR) as well as a new subsort of *headed-structure* called *head-subject-structure* whose SUBJ-DTR value is specified as a singleton list (and whose COMP-DTRS value is specified as the empty list). In addition, the Subcategorization Principle (Chapter 1, (15)) must be replaced with a principle along the lines of (4):

(4)   VALENCE PRINCIPLE:

In a headed phrase, for each valence feature F, the F value of the head daughter is the concatenation of the phrase's F value with the list of SYNSEM values of the F-DTRS value.

For the time being, F ranges over the 'valence features' SUBJ and COMPS; in section 3, following another suggestion of Borsley's (Borsley, to appear), we will also consider the addition of a third valence feature SPR (SPECIFIER).[6]

9.2.3 Blocking Subject Traces

Another of Borsley's (1987) criticisms of standard HPSG, which has to do with the ad hoc fashion in which subject traces are disallowed, is based on an early version of standard HPSG (Pollard 1985), but the stipulative nature of this aspect of the theory is nevertheless preserved in our English-specific version of the Trace Principle (Chapter 4, (33)), which requires that traces be *strictly* subcategorized (i.e. a noninitial member of a SUBCAT list). On the revised account, we require only that traces be complements (in the stricter sense of being on a COMPS list).

This revision, together with the revised treatment of nonpredicative prepositions in the preceding subsection, solves the problem raised in Chapter 4 (nn. 12 and 25) with respect to preposition stranding in examples like (5):

5. We return briefly in section 9.4.5 to the matter of how obliqueness relations relevant to binding theory are to be reconstructed within the revised theory we are exploring here.

6. For the sake of uniformity, we assume here that all the valence features take list values. In the case of SUBJ and SPR, we assume further that the length of the list can be at most one. But there may be some room for argument here. For example, Grover and Moens (1990) assume that the SUBJ feature (or, as they call it, the EXTERNAL feature) can have length up to two, an assumption that they exploit in their analysis of missing object constructions.

(5)   What$_i$ [were you thinking of ___$_i$]?

In standard HPSG, the trace is, technically speaking, not in a strictly subcate-gorized position and therefore should be disallowed; but on the revised ac-count, it (or rather, its SYNSEM value) is on the COMPS list of *of*, as required.

One other topic that warrants mention in connection with the blocking of subject traces is that of apparent exceptions, such as those in (6a–c), to the generalization that 'extraction' of or from subjects is disallowed in English:

(6)   *a.*   Who do you think left?
        b.   How many guests did you tell Sandy were coming to the reception?
        c.   Which rebel leader did rivals of ___ assassinate ___?
        d.   *Which rebel leader did rivals of ___ assassinate the British consul?

As explained in Chapter 4, examples like those in (6) are handled in standard HPSG by the Subject Extraction Lexical Rule (SELR, Chapter 4, (35)), re-peated here as (7):

(7)   SUBJECT EXTRACTION LEXICAL RULE (SELR):

$$X$$
$$[\text{SUBCAT} \langle Y, \ldots, S[unmarked], \ldots \rangle]$$

$$\Downarrow$$

$$X$$
$$\begin{bmatrix} \text{INHER I SLASH} & \{\boxed{1}\} \\ \text{SUBCAT} \langle Y, \ldots, \begin{bmatrix} & VP & \\ \text{SUBCAT} \langle [\text{LOC } \boxed{1}] \rangle \\ \text{INHER I SLASH} & \{ \ \ \} \end{bmatrix}, \ldots \rangle \end{bmatrix}$$

Here the variable Y (ranging over *synsem* objects) is necessary in order to guarantee that the unmarked S in the lexical rule input is a noninitial member of the SUBCAT list (i.e. a nonsubject). This apparently ad hoc restriction was crucially appealed to in Chapter 5 in order to block the application of SELR to the non-*wh* null relativizer, thereby ruling out non-*wh* subject relatives such as (8) and (9):

(8)   *I met a lawyer [helped me a lot].

(9)   *The neighbor [borrowed my drill] never brought it back.

In the revised theory, however, following Borsley (to appear), we can refor-mulate the SELR as in (10), where the feature COMPS guarantees that the af-fected S is a *non-subject* complement:

(10)   S<small>UBJECT</small> E<small>XTRACTION</small> L<small>EXICAL</small> R<small>ULE</small> (SELR, revised version):

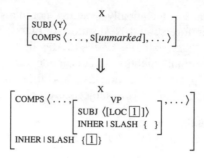

This formulation does embody the correct generalization.[7]

The familiar parasitic gap contrast in (6c–d) is accounted for in standard HPSG by the Subject Condition, which was formulated (Chapter 4, (84)) as in (11):

(11)   S<small>UBJECT</small> C<small>ONDITION</small> (standard version):

The initial element of a lexical head's S<small>UBCAT</small> list may be slashed only if that list contains another slashed element.

But once S<small>UBJ</small> and C<small>OMPS</small> are distinguished, this constraint can be given the more concise formulation in (12):

(12)   S<small>UBJECT</small> C<small>ONDITION</small> (revised version):

A lexical head's subject can be slashed only if one of its complements is.

This also correctly allows for preposition stranding.

To conclude this subsection, we point out that the reformulation of the Subject Condition given in (12) leads to a solution of another problem noted in Chapter 5 (n. 5), which arose in connection with the analysis of relative clauses like the one in (13):

(13)   Here's the student [(that) I was telling you about].

Here it should be recalled that such examples were analyzed in terms of a null relativizer (Chapter 5, (36)) that subcategorizes only for a slashed S[*fin*]. The problem was that, by definition, this S[*fin*] is the subject of the null relativizer and therefore constitutes an unintended violation of the Subject Condition

---

7. Note that the specification [S<small>UBJ</small> ⟨Y⟩] on the input of (10) is necessary in order to prevent the second null relativizer (section 2.3 of Chapter 5) from undergoing SELR and hence giving rise to examples like (8). Varieties of English where examples like (8) are well-formed can be adequately described by simply dropping the [S<small>UBJ</small> ⟨Y⟩] condition on the SELR input.

(Chapter 4, (84)). The solution, of course, is for the null relativizer to select the slashed S[*fin*] via the COMPS feature. The fact that there is no less oblique complement then simply has no bearing; what matters is that the S[*fin*] is a complement, not a subject.[8]

9.3 The SUBJ/COMPS Distinction in the Analysis of Welsh

How should a nontransformational theory account for the facts of a language like Welsh, where finite clauses (whether root or embedded) are typically VSO, as shown in (14)?[9]

(14)   *a.* Gwelodd Emrys y   ddraig.
           saw   Emrys the dragon
           'Emrys saw the dragon.'

        b. Rhoddodd Gwyn y   llyfr i Megan.
           gave   Gwyn the book to Megan
           'Gwyn gave the book to Megan.'

        c. Ceisiodd Emrys [ysgrifennu llythyr].
           tried   Emrys write   letter
           'Emrys tried to write a letter.'

        d. Perswadiodd Gwyn Megan i [fynd adref].
           persuaded   Gwyn Megan to go home
           'Gwyn persuaded Megan to go home.'

        e. Disgwyliodd Emrys i [Gwyn weld Megan].
           expected   Emrys to Gwyn see Megan
           'Emrys expected Gwyn to see Megan.'

        f. Dywedodd Gwyn [fod Emrys yn ddiog].
           said   Gwyn be Emrys in lazy
           'Gwyn said Emrys was lazy.'

        g. Dywedodd Gwyn y   [gwelodd ef y bechgyn].
           said   Gwyn MRKR saw he the boys
           'Gwyn said that he saw the boys.'

In Chapter 1, we proposed to handle such facts by the same device that we employed in the analysis of English inverted sentences: Schema 3, repeated below as (15):

(15)   SCHEMA 3:

    A [SUBCAT ⟨ ⟩] phrase with DTRS value of sort *head-comp-struc* in which the head daughter is a lexical sign.

8. This null relativizer will also be specified as [SUBJ ⟨ ⟩]. This will ensure that it does not undergo the SELR (as revised in (10) above).

9. Welsh data cited in this subsection are all taken from Borsley (1989, 1990). We thank Steve Harlow and Bob Borsley for their help with the Welsh data.

Assuming that we now follow Borsley's suggestion to replace the SUBCAT feature with distinct SUBJ and COMPS features, the most obvious adaptation of this schema would be the one given in (15′):

(15′)   SCHEMA 3 (revised version):

A [SUBJ ⟨ ⟩] phrase with DTRS value of sort *head-subj-comp-struc* in which the head daughter is a lexical sign.

Here we have introduced a new subsort of *headed-structure, head-subject-complement-structure*, whose SUBJ-DTR is a singleton list and whose COMP-DTRS is a (possibly empty) list; the specification [COMPS ⟨ ⟩] is not needed since we are now assuming this is included in the definition of a phrase. It follows from the Valence Principle that any phrase instantiating the revised Schema 3 will have a single subject daughter and as many complement daughters as the (lexical) head selects.

Although (15′) appears to be the schema of choice for handling English inverted clauses, Borsley (1989) argues that Welsh VSO clauses are best analyzed not by Schema 3 but rather by (the revised version of) Schema 2. On his account, what are usually considered subjects of the main clauses in (14) are actually least oblique complements. More precisely, the finite verbs heading the main clauses in (14) differ from the corresponding nonfinite verbs, from which they are derived by lexical rule, in the respect that their SUBJ values are empty and their COMPS lists contain an additional element corresponding to the subject of the nonfinite form. The lexical rule in question can be stated as in (16) (for expository convenience, only affected features are shown in lexical rules): [10]

(16)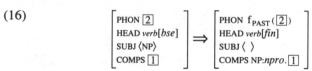

Here the operation f_{PAST} produces the (nonagreeing) past form from the base form.[11] One point to be noted here is that the finite output form of this lexical rule is specified to take a nonpronominal 'subject'; for pronominal subjects, a different set of finite forms, presumably derived by other lexical rules, will be needed. We will return to this point presently.

For example, the derivation of the finite verb *gwelodd* 'saw' in (14a) from the base verb *gweld* is shown in (17):

10. The '.' notation in (16) denotes the 'cons' operation of adding an element to the beginning of a list, e.g. W . ⟨X, Y, Z⟩ = ⟨W, X, Y, Z⟩.

11. For simplicity we ignore the possibility of irregular past tense formation. To take this into consideration, the operation f_{PAST} must actually be allowed to take a second argument, namely, the irregular nonagreeing past form (if any). See P&S-87, pp. 210–213; and Flickinger 1987.

(17)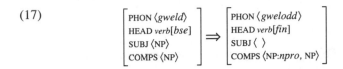

The resulting structure for (14a), shown in (18), is then an instance of Schema 2: [12]

(18)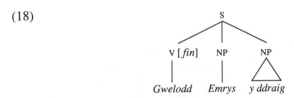

Why should we assume that the lexical rules that derive finite verbs rearrange the argument structure of the base form in this way? Why not just analyze VSO clauses as instances of Schema 3 instead, as we have done for inverted clauses in English? In order to understand the motivation for this analysis, we need to consider a wider range of facts.

First, as noted above, the finite forms discussed above do not occur with pronominal subjects (or, on Borsley's analysis, least oblique complements). Instead, we have the overtly inflected forms in (19):

(19)   *a.* gwelais i   *d.* gwelasom ni
           saw-1S I   saw-1P   we
           'I saw'   'we saw'

        b. gwelaist ti   *e.* gwelasoch chwi
           saw-2S   you   saw-2P   you
           'you(sing) saw'   'you(plur) saw'

        c. gwelodd ef/hi   *f.* gwelasant hwy
           saw-3S   he/she   saw-3P   they
           'he/she saw'   'they saw'

Second, many Welsh prepositions, such as *wrth* (by, near) take only non-pronominal prepositional objects, as illustrated in (20):

(20)   *a.* Mae 'r ty   wrth yr afon.
              is   the house near the river
              'The house is near the river.'

12. In accordance with the adoption of the SUBJ vs. COMPS distinction, we must now systematically reinterpret abbreviations such as 'VP,' 'S,' etc. introduced in Chapter 1, (7). Thus 'VP' now denotes a phrase specified [HEAD *verb*, SUBJ ⟨*synsem*⟩], 'S' denotes a phrase specified [HEAD *verb*, SUBJ ⟨ ⟩], etc.

b. *Mae 'r ty   wrth ef.
    is   the house near he

With pronominal objects (and only with pronominal objects), the inflected forms shown in (21) are used:

(21)   *a.* wrthyf i   *e.* wrthym ni
            near-1S I   near-1P we
            'near me'   'near us'
    b. wrthyt ti   *f.* wrthych chwi
            near-2S you   near-2P you
            'near you(sing)'   'near you(plur)'
    c. wrtho   ef   *g.* wrthynt hwy
            near-3SM he   near-3S they
            'near him'   'near them'
    d. wrthi   hi
            near-3SF she
            'near her'

The parallelism between the inflected forms in (19) and (21), not just in grammatical function but also in the phonetic form of the suffixes for the plural forms, suggests the generalization in (22):

(22)   Certain categories of Welsh predicates agree with a least oblique pronominal complement.

Of course, this generalization has a natural formulation only if 'subjects' of finite verbs are taken to be complements.

    Support for this hypothesis comes from the phenomenon of clitic doubling, which occurs in three different kinds of environments. First, nonfinite verbs, such as *gweld* 'see' in (14e) cannot, on their own, occur with pronominal objects, as shown in (23): [13]

(23)   *Disgwyliodd Emrys i   Gwyn weld hi.
       expected   Emrys that Gwyn see she
      'Emrys expected Gwyn to see her.'

Rather, the verb must be immediately preceded by a clitic that agrees with the pronominal object, as shown in (24):

    13. Because of this, the lexical category for *gweld*, given as the lexical rule input in (17), must be amended to the form:

$$\begin{bmatrix} \text{HEAD } verb[bse] \\ \text{SUBJ } \langle NP \rangle \\ \text{COMPS } \langle NP{:}npro \rangle \end{bmatrix}$$

(24)   *a.* Ceisiodd Emrys fy ngweld i.
         tried   Emrys 1S see   I
         'Emrys tried to see me.'
      b. Ceisiodd Emrys dy weld di.
         tried   Emrys 2S see   you(sing)
         'Emrys tried to see you.'
      c. Ceisiodd Emrys ei   weld ef.
         tried   Emrys 3SM see   he
         'Emrys tried to see him.'
      d. Ceisiodd Emrys ei   gweld hi.
         tried   Emrys 3SF see   she
         'Emrys tried to see her.'
      e. Ceisiodd Emrys ein gweld ni.
         tried   Emrys 1P see   us
         'Emrys tried to see us.'
      f. Ceisiodd Emrys eich gweld chwi.
         tried   Emrys 2P see   you
         'Emrys tried to see you.'
      g. Ceisiodd Emrys eu gweld hwy.
         tried   Emrys 3P see   they
         'Emrys tried to see them.'

Second, possessor 'subjects' of possessed nouns immediately follow the noun, as shown in (25):

(25)   darlun Gwyn o Megan
        picture Gwyn of Megan
        'Gwyn's picture of Megan'

But if the possessor is a pronoun, the head noun must be preceded by a clitic agreeing with the possessor, as in (26):

(26)   *a.* fy narlun i o Megan
         1S picture I of Megan
         'my picture of Megan'
      b. dy ddarlun di   o Megan
         2S picture you(sing) of Megan
         'your picture of Megan'
      c. ei   ddarlun ef o Megan
         3SM picture he of Megan
         'his picture of Megan'
      d. ei darlun hi o Megan
         3SF picture she of Megan
         'her picture of Megan'

    e. ein darlun ni o Megan
        1P picture we of Megan
        'our picture of Megan'
    f. eich darlun chwi   o Megan
        2P   picture you(plur) of Megan
        'your picture of Megan'
    g. eu darlun hwy o Megan
        3P picture they of Megan
        'their picture of Megan'

And third, unique among nonfinite verbs, *bod* 'be' can form verb-subject clauses, such as the embedded clause in (14f) above. But if the subject of *bod* is a pronoun, then *bod* must be preceded by a clitic agreeing with that subject, as shown in (27):

(27)   *a.* Dywedodd Gwyn [fy mod i yn ddiog].
        said   Gwyn 1S be   I in lazy
        'Gwyn said I was lazy.'
    b. Dywedodd Gwyn [dy fod di   yn ddiog].
        said   Gwyn 2S be   you(sing) in lazy
        'Gwyn said you were lazy.'
    c. Dywedodd Gwyn [ei   fod ef yn ddiog].
        said   Gwyn 3SM be   he in lazy
        'Gwyn said he was lazy.'
    d. Dywedodd Gwyn [ei bod hi   yn ddiog].
        said   Gwyn 3SF be   she in lazy
        'Gwyn said she was lazy.'
    e. Dywedodd Gwyn [ein bod ni yn ddiog].
        said   Gwyn 1P be   we in lazy
        'Gwyn said we were lazy.'
    f. Dywedodd Gwyn [eich bod chwi   yn ddiog].
        said   Gwyn 2P   be   you(plur) in lazy
        'Gwyn said you were lazy.'
    g. Dywedodd Gwyn [eu bod hwy yn ddiog].
        said   Gwyn 3P   be   they in lazy
        'Gwyn said they were lazy.'

To account for this array of facts, Borsley assumes that in all three cases where an element normally analyzed as the subject follows the head (subject of finite verb, possessor-subject of noun, and subject of nonfinite clause-initial *bod*), that element is to be analyzed not as a subject but rather as a least oblique complement. The facts in (24), (25), and (27) can then be seen as instances of the generalization stated in (22) above—that certain categories of Welsh predicates agree with a least oblique pronominal complement. The only difference between these facts and the agreement facts cited in (19) and (21) above is that in the latter case, we have inflecting categories (finite verb and preposition), so the agreement is shown by suffixation, but in the former case, we have noninflecting categories (nonfinite verbs and nouns), so the agreement is shown by cliticization.

To be specific, in both the inflection and the cliticization cases, we can account for the agreement by lexical rules.[14] For example, the clitic + verb sequence *eich gweld* in (24f) would be an instance of the output produced by the lexical rule (28):

(28) SECOND-PLURAL CLITIC RULE:

$$
\begin{bmatrix} \text{PHON } \boxed{1} \\ \text{HEAD } \textit{verb[bse]} \\ \text{COMPS } \langle \text{NP: } \textit{npro}, \ldots \rangle \end{bmatrix} \Rightarrow \begin{bmatrix} \text{PHON } f_{eich}\,(\boxed{1}) \\ \\ \text{COMPS } \langle \text{NP: } \textit{ppro[2nd, plu]}, \ldots \rangle \end{bmatrix}
$$

Here the morphological operation f_{eich} prepends the clitic *eich* to its argument. Of course this rule is just one member of a schema of seven (one for each of the pronominal clitics).[15] Similarly, the inflected form *gwelasoch* in (19e) would be an instance of the output produced by the lexical rule (29):

(29) SECOND-PLURAL PAST INFLECTIONAL RULE:

$$
\begin{bmatrix} \text{PHON } \boxed{2} \\ \text{HEAD } \textit{verb[bse]} \\ \text{SUBJ } \langle \text{NP} \rangle \\ \text{COMPS } \boxed{1} \end{bmatrix} \Rightarrow \begin{bmatrix} \text{PHON } f_{2P\text{-}PAST}\,(\boxed{2}) \\ \text{HEAD } \textit{verb[fin]} \\ \text{SUBJ } \langle \; \rangle \\ \text{COMPS NP: } \textit{ppro[2nd, plu]}.\ \boxed{1} \end{bmatrix}
$$

By the way, it should not be assumed that the subjectless analysis of finite clauses is appropriate only for VSO languages like Welsh. Rather, such an analysis is worth considering for any clausal structures that are arguably 'flat' (in the sense of not having a VP as an immediate constituent), be they head-initial such as Welsh finite clauses or German polar questions; head-final as in

14. The lexical rules proposed here differ in technical details from the account of Borsley (1989).

15. Andreas Kathol (personal communication, 1992) points out that the set of cliticization rules can be collapsed into a single schematic lexical rule as follows:

SECOND-PLURAL CLITIC RULE:

$$
\begin{bmatrix} \text{PHON } \boxed{1} \\ \text{HEAD } \textit{verb[bse]} \\ \text{COMPS } \langle \text{NP: } \textit{npro}_{\boxed{2}}, \ldots \rangle \end{bmatrix} \Rightarrow \begin{bmatrix} \text{PHON } f_{\text{clitic}}\,(\boxed{1}, \boxed{2}) \\ \\ \text{COMPS } \langle \text{NP: } \textit{ppro }_{\boxed{2}}, \ldots \rangle \end{bmatrix}
$$

where f_{clitic} is a function that yields as value the result of prepending a clitic bearing the agreement features $\boxed{2}$ to the base form $\boxed{1}$.

Japanese and Korean (cf. Chung, to appear); [16] or verb-second as in German declarative main clauses, which are now standardly treated via 'extraction' from a head-initial clause (cf. den Besten 1983; Uszkoreit 1984; Pollard 1989). The assumption that only nonfinite predicates (i.e. nonfinite verbs and nonverbal predicatives) have a nonempty SUBJ attribute, as reflected in the lexical rule (16) above, can also be profitably carried over into such languages. (See, e.g., the analyses of German passives in Kathol 1991 and Pollard, to appear.)

In the other direction, it must not be assumed that the subjectless analysis of finite clauses is necessarily optimal for all VSO languages. For example, Borsley (n.d., b) argues, principally on the basis of clitic behavior, that Syrian Arabic is best analyzed in terms of the head-subject-complement schema. [17] In section 9.6, we will consider the question of whether the subjectless analysis is appropriate for inverted clauses in English.

9.4 The Status of Specifiers

What is the status of elements traditionally identified as specifiers, such as the italicized expressions in (30)–(34)?

(30)   *a.* Kim saw [*some/the/many/six* unicorns].
       b. [*Every/a/no* student] signed the petition.

(31)   *a.* John is [*very/too/six feet* tall].
       b. Kim is [*much/two inches* taller (than Sandy)].

(32)   *a.* Mary's office is [*just/right* around the corner].
       b. Chris lives [*30 miles* nearer to Chicago] than Dana does.

(33)   *a.* Kim ran [*so/too* fast].
       b. Kim drives [*much/20 miles per hour* faster (than Sandy)].

(34)   *a.* [*A dozen/many* fewer] people came to the reception than had been
          expected.
       b. Bozo is [*much* more] intelligent than Bonzo.

As indicated, the elements specified by specifiers can be nouns, adjectives, prepositions, adverbs, or even other specifiers (about whose categorial status we reserve judgment for the time being). Other than the specifiers of nouns (exemplified in (30)), which are standardly identified as determiners, specifiers are little discussed in recent syntactic literature, but it is generally assumed that,

16. The similarity of this proposal to the GB analyses of Japanese proposed by Kitagawa (1986), Fukui (1986), and Kuroda (1988) should be noted.

17. This analysis presumably would also be appropriate for the grammar of Chamorro, which is VSO but shows subject-nonsubject asymmetries (as shown by Chung (1990)).

cross-categorially, one and the same grammatical relation holds between the specifier and the element that it specifies. On the most widely accepted view (exemplified, say, by Chomsky (1981, 1986b)), the specified element is the head, and the specifier bears the same grammatical relation (namely the SPE-CIFIER relation) with respect to that element that subjects bear with respect to the finite VP (or, in GB terms, the I'). That relation, of course, is considered to be defined configurationally by the X'-schemata in (35):

(35)   a. $X'' \rightarrow$ Y'' , X'
                      SPECIFIER
         b. $X' \rightarrow$ $Y''*$, X^0
                      COMPLEMENTS

The obvious analog of this position within the theory advocated so far in this chapter is to treat specifiers in terms of the SUBJ feature. Thus, for example, a singular count noun would bear the specification [SUBJ ⟨DetP⟩]. An alternative view, advocated by Brame (1982), Hoeksema (1984), Abney (1987), and numerous others, holds that the relation between specifier and specified is one of head to complement. In this section, we will argue in favor of a third position due to Borsley (to appear), namely, that specifiers, although nonheads, should be regarded in terms of a grammatical relation distinct from subject, and therefore treated by a distinct feature, here called SPR.[18]

9.4.1 Why Specifiers Are Not Subjects

Pretheoretically, specifiers appear to differ from subjects in the important respect that they lack the potential to be semantic arguments; instead, their semantic contribution is more abstract, typically quantificational or degree-denoting in nature. (Exceptional in this respect are possessives—if indeed they are specifiers rather than subjects (see section 9.4.5).) Another difference, evidently related, is that the specifier positions do not seem to be available for obligatory control as subjects are; nor do we find raising of specifiers to an argument position of a higher predicate.[19]

But even if we do not regard semantic considerations as criterial for the determination of grammatical relations, a purely syntactic difficulty arises from attempting to identify subjects and (traditional) specifiers as instances of the same grammatical relation, as pointed out by Borsley (to appear). Consider the examples in (36)–(38):

(36)   a. [John] is *an* idiot.

18. Borsley's original name for this feature is SPEC, but that term has already been preempted for the feature by which markers and determiners select their heads.

19. A possible exception might be cases of 'possessor ascension,' but again there is some question whether possessors are actually specifiers.

    b. We consider [John] *an* idiot.

    c. [His father] *a* lifelong Elk, John was assured admission to the brotherhood.

(37)   *a.* [John] is *six feet* tall.

    b. We consider [Sandy] *too* radical.

    c. With [Butch] *so* competent, why do we need another computational ichthyologist?

(38)   *a.* [Kim's place] is *two blocks* nearer campus than Sandy's.

    b. We found [Chris's place] to be *as* near campus as Dana's.

    c. With [the cops] *right* around the corner, we better not try anything funny.

In each case, we have a predicative noun, adjective, or preposition, whose specifier is indicated in italics. The difficulty is that each of these predicatives also has a subject (indicated in square brackets), be it raised to subject (as in the (a) examples), raised to object (as in the (b) examples), or realized within the (small) clausal projection of the predicative itself (as in the (c) examples).[20]

    What such examples suggest is that, cross-categorially, both specifiers and subjects can appear with the same head. Inasmuch as we already have pretheoretical motivations for distinguishing subjects from specifiers, it would appear that the most obvious solution to this problem is simply to posit distinct

---

20. As yet, we lack a worked out account of predicative NPs. The problem is not that of accounting for the subject position; adapting a suggestion of Borsley's (to appear), this can be accomplished by a lexical rule of roughly the form (i):

(i)   Predicative NP Lexical Rule:

    $N[-PRD, SUBJ \langle\ \rangle]:[RESTRICTION\ \boxed{2}]_{\boxed{1}} \Rightarrow$
    $N[+PRD, SUBJ\ \langle XP_{\boxed{1}} \rangle]:\boxed{2}$

    However, this lexical rule fails (on semantic grounds) to account for predicative proper nouns, as in *Cicero is Tully*. Another difficulty arises in accounting for which determiners can accompany predicative NPs (see (ii)), and for how these determiners make their semantic contribution:

(ii)   *a.* John is [a/the/*every/*each Republican].
    b. Kim, Sandy, and Dana are [the/three/*few/*most/*all Republicans].

A third difficulty is that predicative NPs also allow additional degree specifiers, as shown in (iii)–(iv):

(iii)   *a.*   John is *such* a fool.
    b. * *Such* a fool walked in.

(iv)   *a.*   Mary is *too much* (of) a Republican for my taste.
    b. * *Too much* (of) a Republican walked in.

We leave these problems open.

grammatical relations (and therefore, distinct valence features) SPR and SUBJ. (It remains to consider the alternative that specifiers are heads. We return to this matter in section 9.4.3.)

Under this assumption, which we now adopt without further argument, the Valence Principle ((4) above) will guarantee that specifications for required subjects, complements, and specifiers that appear on the head word of a constituent are uniformly removed on the phrasal projections of that head as they become satisfied, as illustrated in (39):

(39) a.

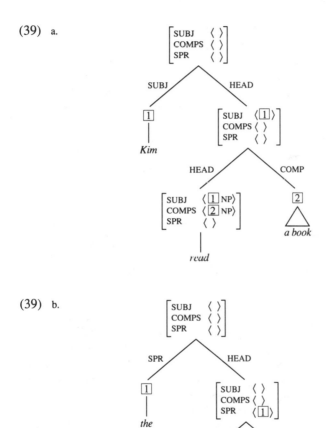

(39) b.

(In order to license phrases like (39b), we will require a head-specifier schema this will be introduced presently.) The three valence features and the Valence Principle supersede the SUBCAT feature and the Subcategorization Principle in standard HPSG.[21]

9.4.2 A Lexically Based X′-Theory

Using the valence features COMPS, SPR, and SUBJ, we can reconstruct a version of X′-theory as follows. We begin by assuming that the lexicon provides us with words (X⁰), whose requirements for selected dependents are given by their valence features, and that all other constituents are phrases (XP) built up from phrase-structural schemata (to be given). Within phrases, we make a distinction between those that are specifier-saturated ([SPR ⟨ ⟩]), called X″, and those that still seek a specifier phrase ([SPR ⟨X″⟩]), called X′. In other words, X⁰ abbreviates *word*, XP abbreviates *phrase*, X″ abbreviates *phrase*[SPR ⟨ ⟩], and X′ abbreviates *phrase*[SPR ⟨Y″⟩]. We now introduce our first three schemata, shown in (40) (the remaining schemata will be given in subsequent sections):

(40)   Three schemata for local selection of nonhead by head:

Head-Subject Schema   X″[SUBJ ⟨ ⟩] → $\boxed{1}$Y″ , X″[SUBJ ⟨$\boxed{1}$⟩]
                                                          SUBJ   HEAD

Head-Specifier Schema X″ → $\boxed{1}$Y″[SPEC $\boxed{2}$] , $\boxed{2}$X′[SPR ⟨$\boxed{1}$⟩]
                                         SPR   HEAD

Head-Complement   XP → $\boxed{1}$,   X⁰[COMPS $\boxed{1}$]
Schema   COMPS   HEAD

A number of remarks are in order here. First, as a consequence of the Valence Principle, these schemata are all 'local' in the sense that the valence specifications that they satisfy cannot propagate beyond the largest constituent headed by the word that introduced them (the word's 'maximal projection', on one use of that term). This distinguishes the valence features from nonlocal features used by heads to select nonheads, such as the SLASH feature, which we will consider in a new light in the following section.

Second, the Head-Complement Schema is the analog of the schema (35b) of standard X′-theory. The tag $\boxed{1}$ here ranges over lists of X″, selected as complements by various words. There is no requirement that the X⁰ additionally select a subject or specifier; thus *pictures of Mary* and Welsh *gwelodd emrys y ddraig*

---

21. Alternatively, we can view COMPS as the analog of the GPSG SUBCAT feature and SUBJ as doing the work done jointly in GPSG by the SUBJ and AGR features.

(saw Emrys the dragon: 'Emrys saw the dragon') are perfectly good X″ even though *pictures* (in this case) does not require a specifier and *gwelodd* (saw) does not require a subject (on the analysis presented in section 9.3). The mother is called XP because this subsumes both of the possibilities X′ and X″, corresponding to the cases where the X⁰ does or does not require a specifier, respectively.

Third, between them, the Head-Subject Schema and the Head-Specifier Schema cover roughly the same ground as Schema 1 of standard HPSG (Chapter 1, (22)) or the X′ schema (35a) in pre-*Barriers* GB. (In *Barriers* and most subsequent GB work, the coverage of this X′-schema is wider, also taking in the territory of the Filler-Head Schema to be discussed in Section 9.6.) With respect to the Head-Subject Schema, it should be observed that gaining its subject does not affect a phrase's bar level (as defined here). For example, both S and VP are X″, differing only as to whether they are [SUBJ ⟨ ⟩] or [SUBJ ⟨Y″⟩]. This is much the same as the [+SUBJ] vs. [−SUBJ] distinction in GPSG. By the way, the [SUBJ ⟨ ⟩] specification on the left-hand side of the Head-Subject Schema is redundant (since it is a consequence of the Valence Principle), but it is added for perspicuity.

Fourth, unlike the situation with respect to subjects, the acquisition of a specifier by a phrase has the effect of promoting it from X′ to X″. This, of course, is quite different from GB theory, where subjects are considered to be a kind of specifier. (But see Richard Cooper's (1990) different approach to reconstructing X′-theory out of valence features, one that follows GB in treating subjects as a kind of specifier.)

Fifth, another important difference between the Head-Specifier Schema and the Head-Subject Schema is that, in the former, not only does the head select the nonhead via a valence feature (SPR and SUBJ, respectively), but also the specifier can exert a reciprocal selection for the head, via the SPEC feature. (This is a property we take specifiers to share with markers, a point to which we will return in due course.) This selection was motivated by semantic considerations in Chapter 1; syntactic motivation will be provided in section 9.4.4. It is this mutual selection, we suggest, that has accounted for the general lack of consensus as to whether the determiner or the N′ is the head of a noun phrase.

9.4.3 Why Specifiers Are Not Heads

We have claimed (and will later argue) that specifiers share with markers the property of selecting their head sisters. In this subsection, we argue that specifiers share with markers the further property of being nonheads. Nevertheless, specifiers and markers must be clearly distinguished. One important respect in which specifiers differ from markers is that, contrary to conventional wisdom, specifiers need not be words. There can be specifier phrases of great complexity, complete with their own lexical heads, complements, and specifiers; some examples will be given shortly. A second difference is that markers tend to be semantically vacuous, or else their semantic contributions are of a logical nature, for example, the boolean connectives (if indeed they are markers) and the complementizer *whether* (if indeed it is a complementizer). However, although some determiners have essentially logical semantic content (e.g. *every, some, no*), many specifiers have semantic contents (typically of degree-specifying nature) with semantic constituents that refer to any imaginable subject matter (again, examples will be forthcoming presently). Third, specifiers do not mark their sisters; thus, there are no words that require as complement a noun phrase with a certain determiner. And fourth, specifiers participate in the syntactic phenomenon of comparative subdeletion, to be discussed below.

To illustrate the foregoing points, it is useful to move beyond the oft-discussed one-word determiners like *every, some*, and *no*, to complex specifier phrases of the kind that abound in degree constructions, in difference comparative (*more/er . . . than*) constructions, and in factor comparative (*as . . . as*) constructions. The first thing to note is that degree count determiners like *many* and *few* (and their mass counterparts such as *much* and *little*) form one of two major classes of specifiers. The second major class is constituted by such expressions as *how, very, as* (. . . *as* . . .), *too* (. . . (*for* NP) *to* . . .), and *so* (. . . *that* . . .), hereafter called degree expressions (Deg).

These classes can be characterized distributionally in the following way. First, determiners serve as specifiers for nouns and comparative forms of gradable words, which may be adjectives (*taller*), prepositions (*nearer*), adverbs (*later*), count determiners (*more, fewer*), mass determiners (*more, less*), or degree words (*more, less*):

(41)   *a.* many/few/a few/more/fewer students
        b. much/little/a little/more/less wine
        c. much/little/a little taller (than Kim)
        d. much/little/a little nearer Chicago (than Cleveland)
        e. much/little/a little later (than 5:00 P.M.)
        f. [many fewer] students (than professors)
        g. [much more] beer (than wine)
        h. [much more] intelligent (than Sandy)

Second, it should be noted that *more* can be either a degree word or a determiner (as if it were the comparative form of *many* or *much*, blocking the nonexistent **manier* and **mucher* (cf. Bresnan 1973)); *less* is similar, except that in some varieties it cannot be a count determiner (being superseded in that role by *fewer*):

(42)   *a.* more students
         b. more wine
         c. more intelligent.

(43)   *a.* fewer students
         b. less students (nonstandard varieties only)
         c. less wine
         d. less intelligent

A third important fact, clearly semantic in nature, is that count nouns and comparative count determiners take count determiner specifiers, while mass nouns and comparatives other than count determiners take mass determiner specifiers:

(44)   *a.* many/*much/*very students
         b. many/*much/*very fewer students
         c. [*many/much/*very less] wine
         d. *many/much/*very taller
         e. *many/much/*very nearer Chicago
         f. *many/much/*very later
         g. [*many/much/*very more] intelligent (than Sandy)

Fourth, positive (i.e. noncomparative) forms of gradable words take degree, not determiner, specifiers:

(45)   *a.* very/*much/*many tall
         b. very/*much/*many near
         c. very/*much/*many late
         d. very/*much intelligent
         e. [very/*much/*many few] students
         f. [very/*much/*many little] wine
         g. [very/*much/*many very] intelligent

Fifth, scalar numbers have the same potential to serve as specifiers that (count) determiners have, while nonscalar measure phrases (e.g. two feet, 400 horsepower) have the potential to serve as specifiers in the same environments that either (mass) determiners or degree expressions do (except that with mass nouns, a partitive construction is required):[22]

(46)   *a.* three gallons of wine
         b. [[three gallons] less] wine (than beer)
         c. three feet tall/taller

22. As defined by Rich Thomason (personal communication), a milliHelen is the degree of beauty required to launch one ship.

      d. three hours late/later
      e. three miles beyond Chicago
      f. three miles nearer Chicago
      g. three feet wide/wider
      h. three milliHelens more beautiful

(47)   *a.* three students
       b. [three fewer] students (than professors)

For expository convenience, we will refer to the categories of scalar numbers and nonscalar measures as *Scal* and *Meas*, respectively.

Now one very interesting consequence of these facts is that degree specification can be recursive. That is, degree specifiers can bear other degree specifiers, which in turn can bear still further degree specifiers. Thus we have examples such as the following:

(48)   *a.* [[Many [more [than 50]]] men] appeared on the horizon.
      b. [[[[How much] more] comfortable] [than the first chair]] was the other chair?
      c. This table is [[[[three times] as] long] [as that one is Δ wide]].
      d. This factory is [[[[[very many] times] as] productive] [as that one]].
      e. Kim is [[[50 IQ points] more] less] intelligent [than Sandy] [than Chris is [Δ less] intelligent than Dana].
      f. Kim is [[[[three times] as] much] more] intelligent [than Sandy] [as Chris is [Δ more] intelligent than Dana].

Here the 'Δ' notation indicates sites of comparative subdeletion, which will be discussed presently. As discussed by Bresnan (1973), Pollard (1990), and Chae (to appear), the right-peripheral *than* and *as* phrases containing the subdeletion sites are licensed (one each) by a comparative word.[23]

Recursive specification examples such as (48e–f) are discussed at length by Bresnan (1973). We follow Bresnan in treating such examples as fully grammatical; however, the analyses we advocate are essentially similar to the left-branching analyses attributed by Bresnan (1973: 289ff.) to unpublished work of J. Bowers and of E. Selkirk (and argued against by Bresnan). The degraded acceptability of such examples reported by some speakers is probably due to

23. The mechanism by which this licensing takes place is a fascinating topic in its own right (see the references just cited), but one that must be set aside here. Briefly, *than-* and *as*-phrases can be analyzed in some cases as extraposed complements and in others as unbounded dependents licensed by a new nonlocal rightward-looking selectional feature (say, EXTRA); for present purposes, we will assume the latter without argument, although the difference is not really germane in the present setting.

the mathematical complexity of their semantic content, which requires that the results of two comparisons be in turn compared. For such speakers, acceptability may be restored by appropriate contextualization, as in (49):

(49)   John: What a mismatched couple! I really don't see what a
              reasonably intelligent person like Chris sees in an intellectual
              zero like Dana.
       Mary: Well, if you think *they're* mismatched, what about Kim and
              Sandy?
       John: What do you mean? Do you think there's more of an
              intellectual gap between Kim and Sandy than there is between
              Chris and Dana?
       Mary [pulling IQ test results out of file]: Sure! In fact, according
              to these tests, Kim, Sandy, Chris, and Dana have IQs of 150,
              90, 115, and 95, respectively. So Kim is actually three times
              as much more intelligent than Sandy as Chris is (more
              intelligent) than Dana.

We now need to consider the internal structure of the specifier phrases themselves. We begin with a relatively simple example, given in (50). (Here, adapting a distinction proposed by Hankamer (1973), we analyze the *as* and *than* that introduce the phrases licensed by comparative words sometimes as markers, and sometimes as prepositions.)

(50)

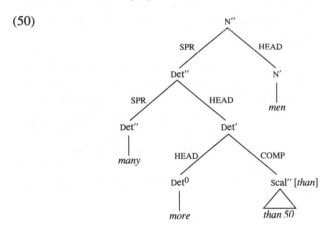

This is merely intended to illustrate that determiner phrases can be cleanly analyzed in terms of the same valence-based revision of X'-theory that we have employed above for the so-called 'major' phrasal categories.

To take a more interesting example, under the same analysis, the predicative A" in (48d) has the structure shown in (51):

(51)

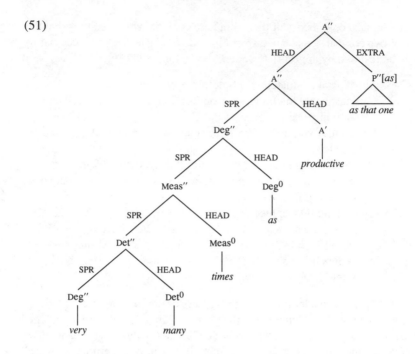

Here the extraposed *as* phrase is licensed by the degree word *as*. We assume that the Deg^0 *as* optionally selects a factor-denoting Meas″ specifier, the $Meas^0$ *times* obligatorily selects a Scal″ or Det″ specifier, and that the Det^0 *many* optionally selects a Deg″ specifier.[24]

The massive cross-categorial parallelism exhibited in degree specification suggests very strongly a parallel internal syntactic structure for the various types of specified phrases, for example, Det + N′, Det″ + (comparative) X′ (X = A, P, Adv, Det, or Deg), and Deg″ + (positive) X′. More specifically, if one of them is nonhead + head (or head + nonhead), then it seems natural to assume that they all are. Further support for this assumption is provided by the phenomenon of comparative subdeletion, illustrated in (48) above. Although the subdeletion sites in these examples are positions corresponding to specifiers of Deg words (*less* and *more*), subdeletion is actually a cross-categorial phenomenon, as illustrated in (52):

24. A detailed syntactic and semantic analysis of degree specification and a very wide range of difference and factor comparative constructions, based on the foregoing assumptions, have been implemented in an experimental computational linguistic system by the Natural Language group at Hewlett-Packard Laboratories (Dan Flickinger, Mark Gawron, John Nerbonne, Marilyn Walker, Carl Pollard, and others). See also Pollard (1990).

(52) *a.* Hewlett-Packard employs more consultants than [Xerox employs [Δ engineers]]. (Δ = specifier of N)

  b. Kim is as wide as [Sandy is [Δ tall]]. (Δ = specifier of A)

  c. Kim lives as near Chicago as Sandy lives [Δ near] Detroit]. (Δ = specifier of P)

  d. Kim drinks as quickly (in ounces per seconds) as [Sandy drinks [Δ rudely] (in belches per second)]. (Δ = specifier of Adv)

  e. Kim is as much more intelligent than Sandy as [Chris is [Δ more] intelligent than Dana]. (Δ = specifier of Deg)

  f. Hewlett-Packard hired as many more consultants than Xerox as [DEC fired [Δ more] engineers than Sun]. (Δ = specifier of Det)

The apparent generalization here is that subdeletion affects specifier positions.[25]

Now the fact that a very detailed syntactic and semantic analysis can be provided for the foregoing facts based on the assumption that the specifiers are nonheads does not constitute a proof that no analysis can be provided based on the contrary assumption (that the specifiers are heads). But the obstacles to such an analysis would appear to be very great indeed. By way of illustration, let us return to the example in (48d). Disregarding the extraposed phrases (which are optional, in any case), just how are we to analyze the lowermost A″, under the assumption that determiners and degree phrases are heads?

It will not do to simply retain the tree geometry of (51) while relabelling all specifiers and heads as heads and complements, respectively, as shown in (53):

(53)

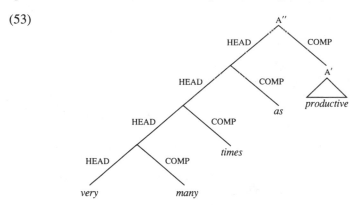

That would lead to the conclusion that *very* is an adjective that selects four complements (which are shown here as selected one at a time, but positing a

25. In the detailed analysis of comparatives just mentioned, this is accounted for in terms of a distinct nonlocal selectional feature that carries information about the missing specifier up to the point where the marker *than* or *as* adjoins to the extraposed clause; it is at this point that the unbounded dependency becomes (both syntactically and semantically) bound.

flat structure instead will not help). Similar reanalysis of the examples in (48e) and (48f) will lead to the conclusion that scalar expressions (e.g. *three*) are adjectives selecting five complements. In fact, by parallelism and recursion, for every category X in the set {N, A, P, Adv, Det, Deg} and every natural number n, we can now construct a similar example to show that all scalar, measure, determiner, and degree words are of category X and select n complements. This strikes us as an unacceptable consequence.

By considerations of parallelism, the only other clear alternative is to propose for (48d) a uniformly right-branching structure, as shown in (54):

(54)

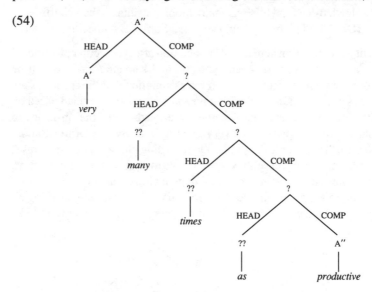

Suppose this is the right structure. Then *productive* is an A″, and the whole phrase is an A″; but what is more important, it is clear that the whole phrase is an A″ precisely *because productive* is an A″ (to see this, simply replace *as productive* with *as much wine, as many barrels,* or *as often* in this structure). Moreover, it is clear on distributional grounds that all the internal nodes on the right branch (labelled '?') must be A″, and by hypothesis about where the heads lie, it also follows that the terminals of all the left branches (labelled '??') must be A⁰. This leads to the conclusion that degrees (*very, as*), determiners (*many*), measures (*times*), and so forth are all adjectives when they appear in a structure like this one; but we can also construct parallel examples to show that all these words, as well as scalars like *three*, are nouns, prepositions, or adverbs. These considerations show that, under the assumption that specifiers are heads, specifiers really have no inherent category at all, but instead are like wild cards that get their gross category assignments from the phrases they specify. But then there is clearly no basis for calling the specifiers heads. By reductio ad absurdum, we conclude that all the classes of specifiers discussed here are non-heads with their own inherent category assignments, except that, as noted above, *more* still has to be taken as ambiguous between a degree and a determiner ('manier/mucher').

9.4.4 The German NP Revisited

Must determiners be able to select their N′ sisters? English gives little guidance on this question. Since English nouns do not inflect for gender, case, or declension class, the only relevant feature that might be selected is number. Certain determiners (*the, some, no*) can occur with nouns of either number, while certain others (the demonstratives *this/these* and *that/those*) covary in form with the number of the head noun. But the majority occur either only with singulars (*a, one, each, every*) or else only with plurals (*all, two, few, many*). Although we might take this last fact as an indication that the determiners select the nouns, it is also clear that the selection involved is largely semantic in nature; there is nothing to suggest an actual syntactic dependency.[26]

However, evidence of syntactic selection of the N′ by the determiner is forthcoming from German. By way of background, we review briefly some basic facts of German inflectional morphology (see Chapter 2 for further details). Determiners inflect for case, number, and gender; nouns inflect for case and number, and (except for a small subclass of *variable* nouns, neglected in Chapter 2, but to be discussed presently) have an inherent gender; and (attributive) adjectives inflect for case, number, gender, and a fourth dimension here called (governed) declension type (DECL), which can be either *weak* or *strong*.

Determiners and all common nouns other than the exceptional ones just mentioned also inherently belong to declensional paradigms. Inherent declension type of nouns has no bearing on the present discussion; but we will be directly concerned with the declension class of determiners, which (in the terminology of Zwicky (1986)) may be either I (undeclinables like *zwei* 'two'), II (such as *der* 'the'), or III (such as *kein* 'no'). As Zwicky points out, there is no semantic basis for the classification of determiners into declension classes.

In a noun phrase, determiner, adjectives, and noun must agree in case, number, and gender. More important for present purposes, the presence or absence of the determiner, and (in case it is present) its inherent declension class, deter-

---

26. In Chapter 2, this was captured by assuming, e.g., that determiners like *every* select via the SPEC feature a noun whose index is token-identical with, and therefore has the same NUMBER specification as, the index of the determiner itself. More generally, we assumed in Chapter 1, on the basis of theory-internal semantic considerations, that determiners must have access to their N′ sister, but we did not provide any argument that the dependency in question had any syntactic correlate.

mines the declension class of the adjective (or adjectives) as follows: (1) if there is no determiner (which, as in English, is permissible for mass and plural nouns), or a class I determiner, or else a zero-inflected (singular nonfeminine nominative or singular neuter accusative) class III determiner, then the adjective is in a [DECL *strong*] form; and (2) if the determiner is of class II or else a nonzero-inflected form of class III, then the adjective is in a [DECL *weak*] form.

This pattern of adjective declension government by the determiner seems problematic, since under standard X′-theoretic assumptions about noun phrase structure (which are in main outline endorsed in this chapter) the adjective is a niece of the determiner and therefore neither 'has its hands' directly on the other. Now in Chapter 2 we accounted for these facts in the following way: although we did not employ a DECL feature, we assumed that the adjective forms here identified as [DECL *strong*] used the MOD feature to select as modified heads only those N′s that in turn selected (via the SUBCAT feature) either no determiner at all or else a [DTYPE *weak*] determiner; and the forms identified here as [DECL *weak*] modified only N′s that subcategorized for a [DTYPE *strong*] determiner.

Suppose, however, as suggested by Maier and Steffens (1989) and Kathol (n.d.), that the declension type of the adjective were actually a property not just of the adjective itself but rather of the N′ that it forms together with the noun. Technically that would amount to saying DECL is a head feature of nouns and adjectives.[27] If that were the case, then we could simply say that some determiners (class I and zero-inflected class III) were specified as [SPEC N′[DECL *strong*]], and others (class II and nonzero-inflected class III) as [SPEC N′[DECL *weak*]].[28]

But is there any evidence that the declension class of the adjective is a property of the N′? Interestingly, there is. As pointed out to us by Andreas Kathol (personal communication, 1991), there is a small number of German stems, such as *Beamt-* 'government official appointed for life' and *Verwandt-* 'relative,' that inflect for gender and declension class, much as if they were adjectives. However, as their capitalization in standard German orthography suggests, these elements are best analyzed as nouns, not adjectives;[29] for unlike German adjectives, they are able to govern a complement to the right (e.g.

27. Of course, now we must ensure that attributive adjectives agree with the nouns they modify not only for gender, number, and case, but also for DECL; this would be handled via the MOD feature on the adjective just as for the three other features.

28. The SPEC feature might also be used to effect the case/number/gender agreement between the determiner and the noun; but this could just as well be done in the other direction via the SPR feature on the noun. We are not aware of any arguments one way or the other.

29. Indeed, the participial adjective stem related to the (archaic) verb *beamten* is *beamtet-*, not *beamt-*; and in the case of *verwandt*, the verbal 'source' does not exist.

Verwandte von mir 'relatives of mine').[30] Crucially, determiners govern declension class on such variable nouns just as they do on adjectives, and this holds true whether or not the noun is modified by an adjective (and in the latter case, the adjective agrees with the noun not only in case, number, and gender, but also in declension class). This fact, which is not explained by the analysis of Chapter 2 (reviewed above), shows that the declension class governed by the determiner is a property of the whole N'. It just happens that the declension class of the N' (which must be distinguished from the syntactically irrelevant inherent declension class or paradigm of typical nouns that do not inflect for declension) is usually reflected morphologically only on the adjective.

Of course this account requires accepting that the vast majority of nouns (the nonvariable ones) bear a feature DECL whose value is not specified as either *weak* or *strong*, but is instead supplied by the syntactic context without any morphological reflex on the noun itself; that is (except for *Beamt*-class nouns), governed declension of nouns is a 'construction feature,' not a morphosyntactic one. This strikes us as a harmless consequence; in any case, this proposal must be evaluated in comparison with the available alternatives.

One technical problem remains. How do we prevent mass or plural NPs that are weak (by virtue either of being headed by a weak variable noun or of being modified by a weak adjective) from forming determinerless N" on their own? In the first case, we can simply say that the weak forms of variable nouns obligatorily select a determiner via the SPR feature. In the second case, the adjective itself can select, via the MOD feature, an N' head that in turn obligatorily selects a determiner via the SPR feature. In either case, the weak N' will demand a determiner specifier, as required.

To conclude, we have proposed a new analysis of German determiner-adjective declension government based on the assumption that determiners share with markers the ability to select syntactic features of their head sisters (via the SPEC feature). A question that immediately suggests itself is the following. Instead of assimilating this kind of selection to the SPEC feature mechanism, why not assume (as many have) that NP = DP, that is, that determiners head NPs and simply subcategorize for their sisters? Of course, it is precisely this position that we have argued against in the preceding section. We suspect that the analogous arguments can be constructed for German, but whether this is indeed the case remains to be seen.[31]

---

30. This was pointed out to us by Klaus Netter (personal communication, 1991). Compare *ein mit mir verwandter*, where *verwandter* is an adjective; this can be understood only as a case of null N' anaphora.

31. In this context, it is worth mentioning that Netter (in press) sets forth an HPSG-based account of German NP structure that does adopt the hypothesis that NP = DP; unfortunately, we have not yet had an opportunity to study the final version of this analysis at length.

9.4.5 Are Possessives Subjects or Specifiers?

In the foregoing discussion of specifiers, we have deliberately neglected possessives like *my* and *the mayor of Boston's*. There is a reason for this: there is
some question as to whether possessors are best treated as specifiers or as subjects. This problem is perhaps best appreciated at an intuitive level by considering the status of the occurrences of *Pat('s)* in (55):

(55)   *a.*   *Pat's* tasteless portrait of Bush as a mendicant created quite a
              stir. (NOUN)
       b.   *Pat's* tasteless portrayal of Bush as a mendicant created quite a
              stir. (DEVERBATIVE NOUN)
       c.   ?*Pat's* tasteless portraying of Bush as a mendicant created quite a
              stir. (NOMINAL GERUND)
       d.   *Pat's* tastelessly portraying Bush as a mendicant created quite a
              stir. (VERBAL GERUND)
       e.   *Pat* tastelessly portraying Bush as a mendicant would create
              quite a stir. (VERBAL GERUND)
       f.   *Pat* tastelessly portrayed Bush as a mendicant. (FINITE VERB)

Now in theories such as GB (at least those varieties where determiners are
not analyzed as heads) there is no problem: they are all specifiers, since the
specifier/subject distinction has no theoretical status. But once these notions
have been distinguished, as we have advocated above, where is the line to be
drawn? For anyone who accepts the validity of the distinction, it is perhaps
natural to assume that in (a)–(c) *Pat's* is a specifier, and in (e)–(f) *Pat* is a
subject; but how is the case (d) to be adjudicated? If we make the determination
on the basis of the gross categorial identity of the head (i.e. nominal gerunds
count as nouns, verbal gerunds as verbs), then *Pat's* in (d) counts as a subject.
But if the presence of *-'s* is taken as criterial, then it counts as a specifier, so
that verbal gerunds would take either subjects or specifiers.[32]

Without taking a position on this particular issue (whose empirical consequences, if any, are not clear to us), we believe that—at least in the cases of
English and German—there are good reasons to treat possessives of nominals
as specifiers. In German, for example, possessives inflect just as nonpossessive
determiners do, and observe the same general patterns of distribution, agreement, and government. And in both languages, complications are introduced
by assigning possessives and nonpossessive determiners to different grammatical relations. For example, the traditional notion of N′ could be expressed only
as the disjunction of NP[SUBJ $\langle$ [ ] $\rangle$, SPR $\langle$ $\rangle$] and NP[SUBJ $\langle$ $\rangle$, SPR $\langle$ [ ] $\rangle$].

However, it could well be that the issue is resolved the other way in other

---

32. This choice, however analyzed, seems often to correlate with a semantic definite/
indefinite or realis/irrealis distinction. We have no explanation for this fact.

languages. For example, in Welsh, as Borsley points out, nonpossessive determiners precede the noun; but possessives follow the noun and (when pronominal) trigger clitic doubling (see (25) and (26) above), suggesting that they are 'subjects' (i.e. least oblique complements). And as discussed at length by Abney (1987: 37–53), in many languages possessor-possessed constructions pattern like subject-verb constructions with respect to agreement, case marking, or both. Thus in Yup'ik, possessed nouns agree in number with possessors via the same agreement morphemes by which verbs agree with subjects (while their inherent number is reflected by the same agreement morphemes employed by transitive verbs for object agreement); and the possessor, like the subject of a transitive verb, is in ergative case. Similarly, in Hungarian, the possessed noun agrees with the possessor in a way that parallels subject-verb agreement morphologically, and the possessor is case-marked like a subject (in the instance of Hungarian, nominative). For such languages, the analysis of possessors as subjects appears to be well-motivated.

There is one last point that needs to be addressed here before we close our discussion of valence dependencies. Thus far it would appear that the use of distinct features SUBJ, SPR, and COMPS obviates the need for a feature, such as our old SUBCAT feature, that represents all the selectional requirements of a lexical head within a single list. This is not quite the case, however; for the entire binding theory set forth in Chapter 6 is formulated in terms of the less-oblique-than relation, which in turn is defined in terms of just such a SUBCAT feature. In order for the binding theory to carry over into the revised framework sketched in this chapter, then, we must ensure that the less-oblique-than relation is still well-defined and still covers the same cases that it did before. That is, complements further left on the COMPS list must be less oblique than those further right; a subject must be less oblique than any complement; and a specifier (e.g. possessive determiner) must be less oblique than any complement.

The most straightforward way we know to get this effect is simply to retain a SUBCAT feature, whose value is canonically defined for words as the list concatenation of the values for SUBJ, SPR, and COMPS, in that order. Although it is obvious that SUBJ and SPR must be ordered before COMPS on the SUBCAT list, it is less obvious, but nevertheless true, that SUBJ and SPR must also be ordered with respect to each other. This is because when both are nonempty on the same lexical head, as with a predicative NP that has a possessive determiner, facts such as those in (56)–(58) show clearly that subjects are less oblique than specifiers:

(56)   a.   With [Kim and Sandy]$_i$ each other's$_i$ closest confidants, it will be good for them to have a chance to do some travelling together.

  b.   *With Kim$_i$ his$_i$ greatest admirer, it's obvious that he isn't going to win any popularity contests.

(57)   *a.*   [Kim and Sandy]$_i$ are each other's$_i$ greatest admirers.
       b.   *[Kim and Sandy]$_i$ are their$_i$ greatest admirers. (cf. [Kim and
              Sandy]$_i$ met their$_i$ greatest admirers.)

(58)   *a.*   We$_j$ consider [Yeltsin and Gorbachev]$_i$ to be [each other's]$_{i/*j}$
              greatest potential allies.
       b.   We$_j$ consider Gorbachev$_i$ to be our$_j$/*his$_i$ greatest admirer. (We
              consider Gorbachev$_i$ to have met his$_i$ greatest admirer.)

Since the satisfaction of valence requirements is now mediated by the features SUBJ, SPR, and COMPS, there is no longer any need for the SUBCAT feature
to play any role in this task. Thus we might assume that SUBCAT is a head
feature: that is, the valence requirements of lexical heads would be reflected
also on all their phrasal projections. This would be a highly undesirable result,
however, for endowing phrases with such information would make it available
for subcategorization, allowing the possibility of verbs that subcategorized for
clauses headed by ditransitive verbs or verbs subcategorizing for NPs that contained no specifiers (e.g. those headed by mass nouns or bare plurals). As we
argued in Chapter 1, such nonlocal subcategorizations are in principle impossible and should be ruled out by a correct theory of the organization of linguistic information, as it is in standard HPSG. For this reason, it would seem
preferable to accept an alternative proposal, suggested to us by Klaus Netter
(personal communication, 1991), according to which the SUBCAT feature is
appropriate only for words (not for phrases).

9.5 Extraction Revisited

9.5.1 Complement Extraction and Subject Extraction

As we have seen in the preceding sections, the three valence features SUBJ,
SPR, and COMPS are all local in the sense that they do not propagate beyond the
maximal projections of the words on which they originate. In this section, we
reconsider the SLASH feature (introduced in Chapter 4 for the analysis of unbounded dependency constructions) in relation to these valence features. The
formal connection is simply that, like the valence features, SLASH (here, we
refer specifically to the path SYNSEM|NONLOCAL|INHER|SLASH) is employed
by heads to select a nonhead sister. The key difference, of course, is that SLASH
is a nonlocal feature, not a valence feature, and can therefore propagate beyond
the smallest maximal projection in which it originates.

Unbounded dependencies are usually assumed, within both GB and PSG
accounts (including our account in Chapter 4), to originate from a phonetically
null constituent (a variable or (*wh*-)trace). These null constituents are further-
more standardly assumed to play a direct role in on-line human sentence
processing. Roughly, the assumption is that traces have a detectable psycholin-

guistic reality. The comprehension of a filler-gap sentence is complete, for example, only when a trace is processed and identified with the filler (hence giving rise to various reactivation effects).

However, in an interesting study, Pickering and Barry (1991) have demonstrated a potential problem for this widely held view of the role of traces in human sentence processing. Consider first the example in (59):

(59)   Which box did you put the cake in ___?

Here it is evident that comprehension is not complete until the preposition is encountered. The filler *which box* is intuitively held in some kind of storage cell by the sentence processor, and complete comprehension requires removing that element from that cell when an appropriate location, presumably the location of a trace, is encountered. Thus a sentence like (60) is extremely awkward, because the filler must be held in store until a trace is encountered, and there is a long and complicated NP that intervenes between the filler and its trace:

(60)   Which box did you put the very large and beautifully decorated wedding cake bought from the expensive bakery in ___?

Now consider Pickering and Barry's (1991: 233) example in (61):

(61)   In which box did you put the very large and beautifully decorated wedding cake bought from the expensive bakery?

The surprising thing about this example is that it is easy to process, even though the PP trace would not be encountered until the very end of the sentence. If comprehension really involves holding the filler in storage until an appropriate trace position is encountered, then why is (61) so much easier to process than (60)?[33]

The answer to this question suggested by Pickering and Barry is that there are no traces in filler-gap constructions.[34] On their view, comprehension is completed not when a trace position is found, but rather when an appropriate

---

33. Pickering and Barry are careful to exclude any possible alternative explanation of these contrasts based on the hypothesis that they involve the complex NP shift phenomenon (discussed in Chapter 3), which would position the trace in immediate postverbal position. *Give*, e.g., does not allow complex NP shift, as (i) shows:

(i)   *I gave [   ] the book the woman in the heavy winter coat.

Yet relevant examples with *give* exhibit the same ease of processing as (61):

(ii)   Which book did you give the woman in the heavy winter coat?

34. Or in any other, though that is not of immediate relevance to the issue at hand.

lexical element, for example, the verbal head whose complement is associated with the filler, is processed.

In this section, we will offer a revised theory of filler-gap constructions that begins to make sense of the Pickering-Barry results. We will outline a PSG based traceless account of UDCs of a kind that has been suggested a number of times since the mid-1980s.[35] The basic idea is that SLASH originates not on traces, but rather from the head that licenses the 'missing' element.

Technically, the most straightforward way to implement this idea is by lexical rules. Thus, in order to handle complement gaps, we assume there is a lexical rule, along the lines shown in (62), that takes as input a lexical entry with a certain COMPS list and returns as output a lexical entry that is just the same except that one element has been removed from the COMPS list and placed within the INHER | SLASH value:[36, 37]

(62)   COMPLEMENT EXTRACTION LEXICAL RULE:

$$
\begin{bmatrix}
\text{SUBCAT} \; \langle \ldots, \boxed{3}, \ldots \rangle \\
\text{COMPS} \; \langle \ldots, \boxed{3}[\text{LOC } \boxed{1}], \ldots \rangle \\
\text{INHER | SLASH } \boxed{2}
\end{bmatrix}
\Rightarrow
$$

$$
\begin{bmatrix}
\text{SUBCAT} \; \langle \ldots, \boxed{4}[\text{LOC } \boxed{1}, \text{INHER | SLASH } \{\boxed{1}\}], \ldots \rangle \\
\text{COMPS} \; \langle \ldots \ldots \rangle \\
\text{INHER | SLASH } \{\boxed{1}\} \cup \boxed{2}
\end{bmatrix}
$$

35. For example, in Gazdar et al. 1984; Borsley n.d., a; and Richard Cooper 1990. Distinct traceless analyses of UDCs have also been proposed within LFG and categorial grammar. See, for example, Kaplan and Zaenen 1989 and Steedman (1987, 1991).

36. The intended interpretation of the lexical rule is that all occurrences of $\boxed{3}$ in the input (except for the one on the COMPS list, which is eliminated in the output) are to be replaced in the output by a specification $\boxed{4}$, which is exactly like $\boxed{3}$ except that it bears the additional specification [INHER|SLASH {$\boxed{1}$}]. This will ensure, for example, that in the case of a raising-to-object verb, the complement subject synsem object remains token-identical with the SUBCAT element corresponding to the "extracted" subject (e.g., in who I expected ___ to come.). We are grateful to Tilman Höhle for clarifying discussion of this point.

37. Of course the operation of this lexical rule has to be constrained in certain ways. For example, we cannot topicalize a VP[*inf*] complement of a verb:

(i)   * To be a genius, we believed Kim.

(ii)   * To attend the lecture, Kim tried/condescended/managed.

We set this problem aside here; in any case, an analogous problem must also be solved within any trace-theoretic account of UDCs.

The rule in (62) eliminates the need for traces, and also for the Trace Principle (Chapter 4, (94b)).[38] By way of illustration, extraction of the secondary object of a double-object verb would instantiate this lexical rule as shown in (63):

(63)

$$
\begin{bmatrix}
\text{V} \\
\text{SUBCAT} \langle \boxed{1}, \boxed{2}, \boxed{3} \rangle \\
\text{SUBJ} \quad \langle \boxed{1}\,\text{N}'' \rangle \\
\text{COMPS} \quad \langle \boxed{2}\,\text{N}'', \boxed{3}\,\text{N}''[\text{LOC}\,\boxed{4}\,] \rangle \\
\text{INHER} \mid \text{SLASH} \ \{ \ \}
\end{bmatrix}
$$

$$\Downarrow$$

$$
\begin{bmatrix}
\text{V} \\
\text{SUBCAT} \langle \boxed{1}, \boxed{2}, [\text{LOC}\,\boxed{4}, \text{INHER} \mid \text{SLASH}\,\{\boxed{4}\}] \rangle \\
\text{SUBJ} \quad \langle \boxed{1} \rangle \\
\text{COMPS} \quad \langle \boxed{2}\,\text{N}'' \rangle \\
\text{INHER} \mid \text{SLASH} \ \{\boxed{4}\}
\end{bmatrix}
$$

The INHER | SLASH value on this new lexical head would be passed up in the usual way by the Nonlocal Feature Principle (Chapter 4, (94a)) and, in the case of strong (i.e 'filler-gap') UDCs, discharged in the usual way by the Head-Filler Schema (repeated in (65b) below). A simple topicalization example employing this analysis is sketched in (64):

38. It also illustrates the issue discussed in the previous section of how the COMPS and SUBJ lists relate to the SUBCAT list, assuming that the latter is retained for purposes of binding theory. It would appear that the lexical rule in (62) will give rise to verbs whose SUBJ and COMPS lists form a proper sublist of the SUBCAT value, i.e. verbs that violate the canonical relation among such elements. On the other hand, the outputs of a lexical rule like passive would seem to obey the canonical relation among SUBJ, COMPS, and SUBCAT lists. As yet, we have no general theory of such differences. It is well-known, however, that some languages allow the equivalent of passive *by*-phrases (so called logical subjects) to antecede less oblique reflexive coarguments. Such phenomena could well be analyzed in terms of a lexical rule that rearranges SUBJ and COMPS lists, leaving the SUBCAT list intact. A similar approach might be explored with regard to unaccusative phenomena.

(64)

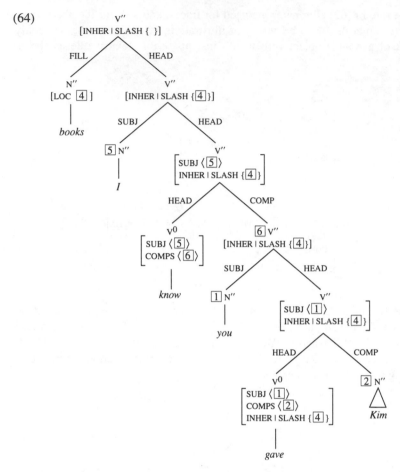

For expository clarity both the SUBCAT feature and selection features with empty values are omitted. All phrasal nodes in this structure are licensed by either the Head-Subject Schema, the Head-Complement Schema, or the Head-Filler Schema.[39]

39. As pointed out to us by Tilman Höhle, the assumption that complement traces do not exist necessitates a further revision to the Subject Condition (9.2.3, (12)). He suggests a reformulation along the following lines:

> SUBJECT CONDITION (second revision):
> A slashed subject can be realized as a constituent only if it locally o-commands a slashed element.

This entails that for any word token with a slashed SUBJECT value element, there must be another (more oblique) member of that word's SUBCAT list that is also slashed in order for that SUBJECT element to be the SYNSEM value of an actual sign.

There is a certain similarity between the Head-Filler Schema and the Head-Subject Schema, repeated in (65) to facilitate comparison:

(65)   *a*. Head-Subject Schema   X″ → $\boxed{1}$Y″, X″[SUBJ ⟨$\boxed{1}$⟩]
                                            SUBJ   HEAD

        b. Head-Filler Schema   X″ → Y″[LOC $\boxed{1}$],
                                           FILLER

                                          V″[SLASH {. . ., $\boxed{1}$, . . .}]
                                          HEAD

They are so similar, in fact, that one might be tempted to suggest that they are actually the same schema, if only SLASH and SUBJ were the same feature.[40] Such a suggestion (which we will not adopt) is reminiscent of categorial grammar, which might be characterized as a theory of grammar with only one valence feature (categorial SLASH). It is also reminiscent of Chomsky's *Barriers* system, where both subjects and fillers are treated as specifiers, and both subject-head and filler-head structures (in our terms) are taken to be licensed by the standard X′ schema (35a). Of course, the *Barriers* treatment of fillers as specifiers is dependent on the identification of (possibly empty) complementizers as the heads of complementized clauses, a position we argued against in Chapter 1.

In spite of the apparent obstacles to collapsing the Head-Subject and Head-Filler Schemata, perhaps they should be regarded as a natural class. (Technically, this suggestion could be implemented by positing a new subsort of *headed-structure*, *head-topic-struc*, with *head-subj-struc* and *head-filler-struc* as immediate subsorts.) The two schemata certainly have much in common (other than similar syntactic form). In English, for example, they share the following traits: (1) the nonhead daughter is realized to the left; (2) the nonhead

---

This analysis eliminates the problem, pointed out in Chapter 4, n. 34, that the Subject Condition wrongly blocks the extraction of objects of raising-to-object verbs. For example, in the sentence *I wonder who he expected to win*, the form of *expected* is an output of the Complement Extraction Lexical Rule specified as V[SUBJ ⟨NP⟩, COMPS ⟨VP[SUBJ ⟨[LOC $\boxed{1}$]⟩], INHER | SLASH {$\boxed{1}$}⟩}], so that the slashed complement subject is no lot realized as a daughter of the matrix VP.

40. This is actually proposed, albeit very speculatively, by Richard Cooper (1990). Among the numerous obstacles in reconciling this proposal with other assumptions that we have made here, the following four are rather immediately apparent: (1) head-filler structures appear to be limited to V″ heads; (2) SLASH value elements and SUBJ value elements are of different sorts (*local* vs. *synsem*); (3) for English and many other languages, the subject must be realized locally (i.e. not as a filler) if its clause is marked with a complementizer; (4) the value of SLASH is a set, while the value of SUBJ is a (singleton) list. In spite of these difficulties, it might be worthwhile to explore ways of dispensing with these assumptions in order to collapse the two schemata.

daughter can be a *wh*-phrase, and accordingly both schemata can be instantiated as constituent questions; (3) the same categories are disallowed as non-head daughters in these two construction types (but not in head-complement constructions), namely, bare-infinitive VPs, finite VPs, and complementizerless sentences, as illustrated in (66)–(68):[41]

(66)   *a.*   To make mistakes is human.
       b.   *Make mistakes is human.
       c.   *Made mistakes was expected.
       d.   For Kim to make mistakes is common.
       e.   *Kim to make mistakes is common.
       f.   That Kim would make mistakes was obvious.
       g.   *Kim would make mistakes was obvious.

(67)   *a.*   To make mistakes, nobody would aspire.
       b.   *Make mistakes, nobody would aspire to.
       c.   *Made mistakes, I wonder who they thought.
       d.   For Kim to make mistakes, nobody would like.
       e.   *Kim to make mistakes, nobody would like.
       f.   That Kim would make mistakes, nobody had anticipated.
       g.   *Kim would make mistakes, nobody had anticipated.

(68)   *a.*   Nobody would aspire to make mistakes.
       b.   We saw Kim make mistakes.
       c.   Who do they think made mistakes?
       d.   Nobody would like for Kim to make mistakes.
       e.   Nobody wants Kim to make mistakes.
       f.   Nobody had anticipated that Kim would make mistakes.
       g.   Nobody had anticipated Kim would make mistakes.

It should be observed that the lexical rule given in (62) above gives rise only to complement gaps. For subject gaps, another lexical rule, introduced in (10) above and repeated in a slightly revised form as (69), is needed:[42]

41. Dale Russell (personal communication, 1992) points out that in some cases, for which we have no explanation, complementizerless sentential subjects appear, e.g. (i):

(i)   It's nothing serious. I'm just tired is all.

42. Note that the assumption in (10) that the affected complement (X″) of the output word as an empty SLASH value has been dropped. This is to allow for the possibility of examples such as (i):

(i)   These rare old books, I wonder who John thinks ___ stole ___ .

(69)   SUBJECT EXTRACTION LEXICAL RULE:

$$\begin{bmatrix} \text{SUBJ } \langle \text{Y}'' \rangle \\ \text{COMPS } \langle \dots, \text{X}'' \, [\textit{unmarked}] \,, \dots \rangle \\ \qquad\qquad [\text{SUBJ } \langle \, \rangle] \end{bmatrix}$$

$$\Downarrow$$

$$\begin{bmatrix} \text{COMPS } \langle \dots, \qquad \text{X}'' \qquad\quad ,\dots \rangle \\ \qquad\qquad [\text{SUBJ } \langle [\text{LOC } \boxed{2}] \rangle] \\ \text{INHER I SLASH } \{\boxed{2}\} \end{bmatrix}$$

The basic idea of this rule is that if we have a word that takes a clausal complement (which need not be headed by a verb, but might instead be a 'small clause' headed by a predicative noun, adjective, or preposition) then there is a valence alternant of that word that takes a VP (or predicative NP, AP, or PP) complement; but now the 'missing' complement subject must be sought further afield via the SLASH feature. Generalizing the rule to small clause complements is intended to account for examples like (70c–d), as well as the more familiar (70a–b):

(70)   *a.* Which candidate did Sandy tell you impresses him the most?
       b. I forgot which guests you said are here.
       c. These patients, I want well by next week.
       d. I wonder who Kim wants in the club?

For example, the *wh*-complement clause in (70b) will have the structure shown in (71):

(71)

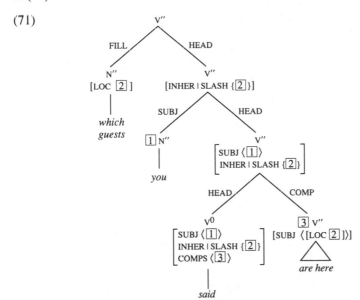

The rule in (69) is more complex than the Complement Extraction Lexical Rule: the latter 'gaps out' complements of the word to which it applies, but the former affects not the subject of the word to which it applies (here indicated by $\boxed{1}$) but rather the subject of that word's clausal complement (whose LOCAL value is indicated by $\boxed{2}$). Such indirection is required in order to prevent giving rise to 'complementizer-trace filter' violations like those in (72):

(72)   *a.* *Which candidate did Sandy say that impressed him the most?
          b. *Who would you prefer for to get the job?

9.5.2 Adjunct Extraction

There is general agreement that adjuncts select (both syntactically and semantically) the heads that they modify. By way of review, in Chapter 1, we posited the head feature MOD for this purpose. Thus, for example, attributive adjectives bear the specification [MOD N']. To license adjunct-head structures, we then posited the schema given in Chapter 1, (60), repeated here in a slightly different format as (73):

(73)   Head-Adjunct Schema: XP $\rightarrow$ Y''[MOD $\boxed{3}$], $\boxed{3}$XP

Given that adjuncts can be (or, as we assume here, must be) phrasal, it is easy to see that MOD must be a head feature. This is because the MOD specification on an adjunct like *very expensive* must be propagated onto the phrase from its lexical head. An analogous argument can be used to show that the SPEC feature by which determiners select the heads they specify must also be a head feature.[43] (Thus, features employed by nonhead phrases to select heads must be head features.) Both cases are illustrated in (74):

---

43. This question does not arise with markers, since they lack phrasal projections.

(74)

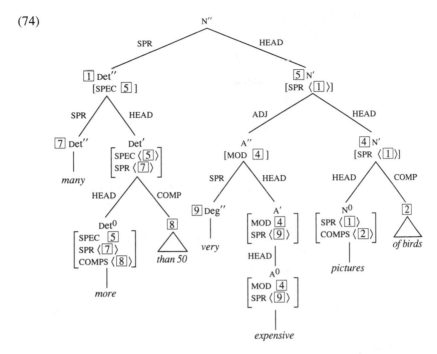

The key points to be noted here are the following. First, dependents selected by heads (here complements and specifiers) are selected by features (here SPR and COMPS) that obey the Valence Principle. Second, dependents selected by nonheads (here specified heads of specifiers and modified heads of adjuncts) are selected by features (here SPEC and MOD) that obey the Head Feature Principle. (In particular determiners and nouns select each other, but the syntactic evidence for this supplied by German declension government is missing in English.)

We turn now, as promised at the end of Chapter 4, section 4, to the extraction of adjuncts. We begin by briefly reviewing relevant points from Chapter 4. Usually, fronted adjuncts (especially if they are *wh*-phrases) are matrix modifiers (semantically speaking), so there is nothing to explain: we can simply analyze examples like those in (75) as head-adjunct structures:

(75)   *a.* On Saturday, will Dana go to Spain?
        b. When will Dana go to Spain?

On the basis of contrasts like those in (76), it is often held that adjuncts do not participate in unbounded dependencies; that is, fronted adjuncts are *always* matrix modifiers:

(76)   *a.* *How long ago will you deny that John left?

   b. Why do you doubt that John burned down the building?
      —Because I have always known him to be a decent fellow.
      #—To collect the insurance.
   c. When do you deny that your husband is planning to leave you?
      —Whenever I can manage to delude myself.
      #—When he gets enough money to manage on his own.

Of course, this view has to somehow be squared with the existence of apparent counterexamples like (77):

(77)   *a.* How long ago do you believe that John left?
       b. Why do you suppose that John burned down the building?
          —Because he smelled sooty and didn't have a good alibi.
          —To collect the insurance.
       c. When do you think your husband is planning to leave you?
          —Whenever I get depressed.
          —When he gets enough money to manage on his own for a
          while.

Such facts have been attributed to special properties of so-called bridge verbs like *believe, suppose,* and *think,* such as the ability to function in parenthetical tags illustrated in (78):

(78)   *a.* How long ago did John leave, do you believe?
       b. Why did John burn down the building, do you suppose?
       c. When is your husband planning to leave you, do you think?
       d. *How long ago did John leave, do you deny?
       e. *Why did John burn down the building, do you doubt?
       f. *When is your husband planning to leave you, did you whisper?

However, it is possible to construct acceptable examples with fronted adjuncts that modify sentential complements of nonbridge verbs, as shown in (79):

(79)   *a.* While their parents are in town next week, I doubt that the twins
          will attend any lectures.
       b. During my term as president of this university, I categorically
          deny that there were any improper appropriations of federal
          funds.
       c. With no tools but a crowbar and a ballpeen hammer, I'm not very
          confident that Butch is going to be able to fix that disk drive.

On balance, then, it must be concluded that fronted adjuncts need not be matrix modifiers, though the possibilities for embedded modification are subject to severe semantic and pragmatic constraints, which we do not attempt to characterize here.[44] To account for such possibilities, we posit the lexical rule shown in (80):[45]

(80)   ADJUNCT EXTRACTION LEXICAL RULE:

$$\begin{bmatrix} \text{COMPS} & \langle \ldots, & \boxed{2}\,\text{V}'' & , \ldots \rangle \\ & & [\text{SUBJ} \langle \ \rangle] \\ \text{INHER} \mid \text{SLASH} & \{ \ \} \end{bmatrix}$$

$$\Downarrow$$

$$\begin{bmatrix} \text{COMPS} & \langle \ldots, \boxed{2}, \ldots \rangle \\ \text{INHER} \mid \text{SLASH} & \{\text{Y}''[\text{MOD}\,\boxed{2}]:\boxed{3}\} \\ \text{CONTENT} \mid \text{SOA-ARG} & \boxed{3} \end{bmatrix}$$

This rule gives rise to traceless structures like the one in (81), in which an adverbial filler modifies an embedded clause:

(81)

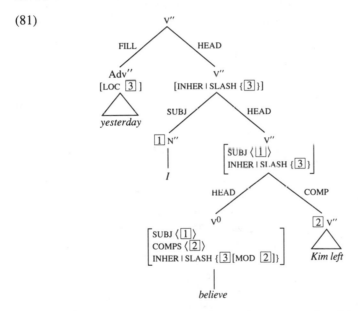

Here the verb *believe* has the valence alternant produced by the Adjunct Extraction Lexical Rule. But the restriction of this rule to S ($= \text{V}''[\text{SUBJ} \langle \ \rangle]$) complements (a restriction that should ultimately follow from more general

44. But see n. 21 of Chapter 4.

45. Note that the content of the output form has to be identified with that of the 'missing' adjunct. This ensures that the extracted adjunct will have semantic scope over the phrase that it modifies.

principles) rules out the possibility of extracting modifiers of (say) NP or V″[SUBJ ⟨[ ]⟩], as in (82):

(82) *a.* *Red, I saw the ball.
   b. *Who shot the sheriff, I met the man.
   c. *Last Monday, I will never forget Kim leaving.
   d. *Quickly, I asked Sandy to run down to the corner store. (*quickly* modifies *run*)

9.6 Inversion Revisited

In Chapter 1, we analyzed English subject-auxiliary inversion in terms of a schema (there called Schema 3) that licensed a word together with all its complements (including the least oblique one, or subject). In order to carry this analysis over into the revised framework of this chapter, we need to reformulate this schema along the lines suggested by Borsley (1987), shown in (83):

(83) HEAD-SUBJECT-COMPLEMENT SCHEMA

$$X'' \rightarrow \quad X^0 \quad , \quad Y'' \quad , \quad Z''*$$
$$ \text{HEAD} \quad \text{SUBJ} \quad \text{COMPS}$$

This schema[46] is an odd man out in the context of our revised framework, since all our other schemata (Head-Subject, Head-Complement, Head-Specifier, Head-Filler, Head-Adjunct, and Head-Marker) license only one kind of nonhead daughter. General considerations of parallelism, then, suggest that we should attempt to eliminate this schema.

The obvious thing to try here is to follow the lead of Borsley's analysis of Welsh finite clauses. That is, we would posit a lexical rule along the lines shown in (84) (cf. (15′) above):

(84) SUBJECT-AUXILIARY INVERSION LEXICAL RULE:

$$\begin{bmatrix} \text{HEAD } verb[\text{+AUX}, -\text{INV}, fin] \\ \text{SUBJ } \langle N''[nom]\rangle \\ \text{COMPS } \boxed{1} \end{bmatrix} \Longrightarrow \begin{bmatrix} \text{HEAD } verb[\text{+AUX}, +\text{INV}, fin] \\ \text{SUBJ } \langle \ \rangle \\ \text{COMPS } N''[nom] . \boxed{1} \end{bmatrix}$$

46. By the Valence Principle, this is equivalent to (i):

(i) $X''[\text{SUBJ } \langle \ \rangle] \rightarrow X^0[\text{SUBJ } \langle\boxed{1}\rangle, \text{COMPS } \boxed{2}], \boxed{1}Y'' \ , \ \boxed{2}Z''$
   $\phantom{X''[\text{SUBJ } \langle \ \rangle] \rightarrow}$ HEAD SUBJ COMPS

In English, this schema must be limited to the cases where X^0 is a [+INV] finite auxiliary.

By way of illustration, the noninverted auxiliary *can* of *Kim can go* would give rise, via this lexical rule, to the inverted *can* of *can Kim go*, as shown in (85):

(85)

$$\begin{bmatrix} \text{HEAD } verb[\text{+AUX}, -\text{INV}, fin] \\ \text{SUBJ } \langle \boxed{1}\text{N}''[nom] \rangle \\ \text{COMPS } \langle \text{V}''[bse, \text{SUBJ } \langle \boxed{1} \rangle] \rangle \end{bmatrix}$$

⇓

$$\begin{bmatrix} \text{HEAD } verb[\text{+AUX}, +\text{INV}, fin] \\ \text{SUBJ } \langle \ \rangle \\ \text{COMPS } \langle \boxed{1}\text{N}''[nom], \text{V}''[bse, \text{SUBJ } \langle \boxed{1} \rangle] \rangle \end{bmatrix}$$

Indeed, just such a lexical rule was proposed by Bach (1983) in a categorial grammar setting, and more recently by Richard Cooper (1990) in an HPSG framework.

Appealing as it may appear, this lexical approach to English inversion is problematic in the following respect: it predicts a spurious structural ambiguity for such sentences as *John must leave*. One analysis, of course, is the usual head-subject analysis (86a). But under standard assumptions about the extract-ability of complements (including the ones adopted here), we also have the head-filler analysis shown in (86b):[47]

(86)

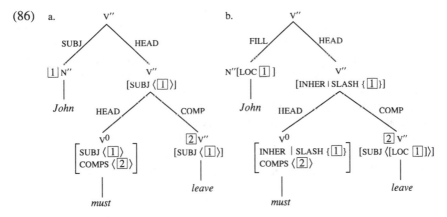

Here the auxiliary in (86b) arises from applying the Complement Extraction Lexical Rule (62) to the output of the Subject-Auxiliary Inversion Lexical Rule.

What are our options for eliminating this ambiguity? Perhaps the most obvious is to collapse the Head-Subject and Head-Filler Schemata, so that (86a)

47. As pointed out by Soames (1989), the standard GPSG analysis of inversion suffers from an analogous spurious ambiguity. See also Chapter 4, section 4.5.

and (86b) become one and the same analysis. Unfortunately, as we saw in the preceding section, there are a number of technical problems in getting this to work, whose solutions are not at all obvious.

A second possibility, inspired by McCawley's (1971) analysis of English as 'underlyingly VSO,' is to eliminate analysis (86a) by assuming that all finite auxiliaries are subjectless, just as all Welsh finite verbs are on the analysis of section 9.3. That is, an auxiliary like *has* would be derived from base forms not by a lexical rule like that in (87a) (as assumed in P&S-87), but rather by one like that in (87b): [48]

(87)   a. $\begin{bmatrix} \text{PHON } \boxed{2} \\ \text{HEAD } verb[bse] \end{bmatrix} \Rightarrow \begin{bmatrix} \text{PHON } f_{3rdsng}(\boxed{2}) \\ \text{HEAD } verb[fin] \end{bmatrix}$

        b. $\begin{bmatrix} \text{PHON } \boxed{2} \\ \text{HEAD } verb[bse, +AUX] \\ \text{SUBJ } \langle N'' \rangle \\ \text{COMPS } \boxed{1} \end{bmatrix} \Rightarrow \begin{bmatrix} \text{PHON } f_{3rdsng}(\boxed{2}) \\ \text{HEAD } verb[fin, +AUX, +INV] \\ \text{SUBJ } \langle \ \rangle \\ \text{COMPS } N'' \cdot \boxed{1} \end{bmatrix}$

On this account, the auxiliary in *Kim has left* would arise from the output of (87b) via the Complement Extraction Lexical Rule.

However, this account is also problematic in at least two respects. First, note that the output of (87b) includes the head feature [+INV]. This is required since the outputs of this rule will head clauses like *has Kim left*, which must be somehow identifiable as inverted (so that they can be selected against by verbs that take uninverted clausal complements). But now *Kim has left* will also bear the head feature [+INV], clearly a wrong result.

And second, if inverted subjects are treated as complements, then there is no obstacle to extracting constituents from within them; but then it is wrongly predicted that examples such as (6d), repeated here as (88), are grammatical:

(88)   *Which rebel leader did rivals of assassinate the British consul?

In the face of such difficulties, we conclude that, in spite of the asymmetry that it introduces into the set of schemata, there is no obvious way to eliminate the need for the Head-Subject-Complement Schema in English.

---

48. Thus, the finite inflectional rules of P&S-87 would apply only to [-AUX] base verbs.

9.7 Classifying Headed Structures

In the revised theory sketched in this chapter, we posit six kinds of nonhead daughters. These are listed with examples in (89):

(89)   Types of nonhead daughters:

Daughter Type	Abbreviation	Examples
COMPLEMENT-DAUGHTER	COMP-DTR	saw *John* must *leave* (Welsh VSO clause 'subjects')
SUBJECT-DAUGHTER	SUBJ-DTR	*John* saw Mary
ADJUNCT-DAUGHTER	ADJ-DTR	*probably* left *red* ball
SPECIFIER-DAUGHTER	SPR-DTR	*two* books *two feet* tall *six feet* under the ground
MARKER-DAUGHTER	MARK-DTR	*that* John left *for* Mary to come (Dan is wider) *than* Derek is tall Naomi-*ga* (Japanese 'case' markers)
FILLER-DAUGHTER	FILL-DTR	*Who* did John see *Bagels* I like

Headed constructions are then classified according to the kind of nonhead daughter(s) they have, as shown in (90):

(90)   Sorts of headed constructions:

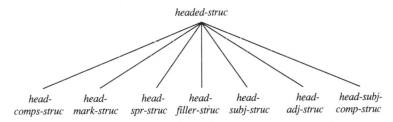

headed-struc

head-comps-struc *head-mark-struc* *head-spr-struc* *head-filler-struc* *head-subj-struc* *head-adj-struc* *head-subj-comp-struc*

Of the seven sorts, only *head-subj-comp-struc* (employed in the analysis of English subject-auxiliary inversion) has more than one kind of nonhead daughter.[49] We consider it a desirable goal to remove this asymmetry, but we have not yet seen how to overcome the numerous technical obstacles to doing so.

For five of these basic construction types, we assume that the head daughter selects the nonhead(s), in the sense that the latter is (are) partially specified by

49. But see Kasper (to appear) for a proposal that the positioning of adverbs in the German Mittelfeld be treated by a schema that introduces both complements and adjuncts as sisters of the lexical head.

a feature that appears on the former. Which feature is used to make the selection depends on the construction type. Of the four selectional features employed by heads, the first three (COMPS, SUBJ, and SPR) form a natural class, called VALENCE features. The notion of relative obliqueness, which underlies our binding theory, is defined in terms of the SUBCAT feature of lexical heads, whose value is the concatenation of the SUBJ, SPR, and COMPS values. Valence features express the 'local combinatory potential' of words and of the phrases that they head, by virtue of satisfying the Valence Principle, repeated in (91):

(91)   VALENCE PRINCIPLE:

In a headed phrase, for each valence feature F, the F value of the head daughter is the concatenation of the phrase's F value with the list of SYNSEM values of the F-DTRS value.

But the features used by nonheads to select the head sisters that they specify or modify must be head features, not valence features. These are the features MOD, through which adjuncts select the heads they modify, and SPEC, through which specifiers and markers select the heads on which they depend. Of the seven basic headed construction types, only in specifier-head constructions do the head and nonhead reciprocally select; and in English, the selection from specifiers to heads might as well be assumed to involve only semantic content.

To summarize, we have posited seven basic types of headed constructions. Their basic properties are shown on the table in (92):

(92)   Summary of basic construction types:

Type of Nonhead DTR	Bar Level of Nonhead DTR(S)	Bar Level of Head DTR	Semantic Head	Syntactic Selector	Selecting Feature(s)
COMPLEMENT	Y''	X^0	Head	Head	COMPS (V)
SUBJECT and COMPLEMENT	Y''	X^0	Head	Head	SUBJ (V) COMPS (V)
SUBJECT	Y''	X''	Head	Head	SUBJ (V)
SPECIFIER	Y''	X'	Head	Head Nonhead	SPR (V) SPEC (H)
FILLER	Y''	X''	Head	Head	SLASH (N)
MARKER	Y^0	X''	Head	Nonhead	SPEC (H)
ADJUNCT	Y''	XP	Nonhead	Nonhead	MOD (H)

Here the parenthesized designation following the selecting feature indicates which feature propagation principle the feature is subject to, as follows: V = Valence; N = Nonlocal, H = Head. The following generalizations can be noted (exclusive disjunctions): nonheads are either X″ or markers; semantic functors are either heads or adjuncts.

9.8 Conclusion

In this somewhat speculative chapter, we have explored a number of revisions of HPSG theory that allow important syntactic generalizations to be expressed and that lead to improved accounts of a rather wide range of syntactic phenomena that we have considered. Most notable among these changes is the separation of SUBCAT selection into SUBJ, COMPS, and SPR selection, an innovation pioneered by Robert Borsley. In the process of developing these ideas, we have also been led to examine closely the hypothesis that specifiers are heads of their phrases, concluding that, although this commonplace assumption leads to unacceptable consequences, in some languages (such as German), specifiers can share with markers the ability to select syntactic features of their phrasal (head) sisters. Relatedly, we have concluded that possessor NPs in English and German should be treated as specifiers, though they may well be subjects in other languages. The assumptions that we have explored here, however speculatively, lead to a lexically based version of X′-theory that we believe merits careful consideration relative to other currently available alternatives. Additionally, they have led us, at least tentatively, to a trace-free account of unbounded dependency constructions, which we also believe is well worth considering as an alternative to current trace-based accounts. Finally, we have proposed a universal typology of headed constructions into seven schemata, all but one of which license the combination of a head with one kind of nonhead sister (subject, complement, specifier, filler, marker, or adjunct).

Appendix

We present here the final version of the English grammar employed in the first eight chapters of this book. A fuller version of this grammar would also include a hierarchy of lexical sorts (subsorts of *word*) and a set of lexical rules, roughly as described in P&S-87, Chapter 8. Also not treated here are linear precedence (LP) principles; for discussion, see P&S-87, Chapter 7.[1]

The grammar consists of a *sort hierarchy* and a set of *principles*. The sort hierarchy is presented as a taxonomic tree, with the root labelled *object* (the sort of all linguistic entities with which the grammar deals). For each local tree in the hierarchy, the sorts $\sigma_1, \ldots, \sigma_n$, which label the daughters, partition the sort σ, which labels the mother; that is, they are necessarily disjoint subsorts of σ that exhaust σ. For two sorts σ and τ, τ is a *subsort* of σ if and only if it is dominated by σ; sorts that label terminal nodes are called *maximal* (in the sense of maximally informative or maximally specific). A *feature declaration* of the form

$$\sigma: \begin{bmatrix} F_1 & \tau_1 \\ \ldots \\ F_n & \tau_n \end{bmatrix}$$

where $\sigma, \tau_1, \ldots, \tau_n$ are sorts and $F_1, \ldots, F_n$ are feature labels, signifies that for each $i = 1, \ldots, n$, (1) the feature F_i is appropriate for all objects of sort σ, and (2) for any such object, the value of the F_i feature must be an object of sort τ_i.

If sorts σ_1 and σ_2 bear declarations $[F\ \tau_1]$ and $[F\ \tau_2]$ for the same feature F and σ_2 is a subsort of σ_1, then τ_2 must be a subsort of τ_1. A sort inherits the feature declarations of its supersorts; hence any feature that is defined for a given sort is defined for all of that sort's subsorts. By convention, the features that are declared for a maximal sort (including those inherited from its supersorts) are the only features defined for that sort. A

---

1. Three lexical rules are introduced in this volume: the Extraposition Lexical Rule (Chapter 3, section 6); the Subject Extraction Lexical Rule (Chapter 4, (35)); and the Coercion Lexical Rule (Chapter 7, (101)). Although the operation of lexical rules is well-understood from the procedural point of view (see P&S-87, Chapter 8), we lack as yet any satisfactory declarative formalization (but see Shieber et al. 1983). The fundamental difficulty here is that lexical rules must be seen as implicative relationships between lexical entries; but lexical entries themselves are constraints on feature structures (not feature structures themselves), so evidently a higher-order formalism must be developed within which such relationships can be expressed. A promising avenue of investigation, we think, would be to treat a set of lexical rules as essentially a closure operator that embeds a basic lexicon (conceived of as an exclusive disjunction of descriptions) into a full lexicon (a larger disjunction).

special case is that of *atomic* sorts or simply *atoms*, maximal sorts for which no features are defined.

Feature structures, which serve as our mathematical models of token linguistic objects, and which are the entities constrained by the grammar, are required to be *sort-resolved* and *totally well-typed*. That is, every node q in the feature structure must be labelled by a maximal sort σ (depending on q); for each node q and for each feature F that is defined for the sort σ labelling q, q must have exactly one outgoing arc labelled by F; and the sort that labels the node at which that arc terminates must be a maximal subsort of the sort τ that was defined to be appropriate for feature F relative to sort σ.

Among the principles, some are distinguished as *parochial* (English-specific); all others can be assumed to be universal. Among the universal principles, the Immediate Dominance (ID) Principle is given in disjunctive form, and each of its disjuncts is called an ID schema. For ease of reference, the ID schemata are listed separately after the principles. In certain cases, a given principle or schema will have both a universal version and a more specific parochial version.

A.1 The Sort Hierarchy

PARTITIONS:

Partition of *object: list(σ)*, *set(σ)*, *boolean (bool)*, *sign, phoneme-string (phonstring)*, *constituent-structure (con-struc)*, *mod-synsem, local (loc)*, *nonlocal (nonloc)*, *nonlocal1 (nonloc1)*, *category (cat)*, *head, marking, verbform (vform)*, *case, preposition-form (pform)*, *content (cont)*, *context (conx)*, *contextual-indices (c-inds)*, *quantifier-free-parametrized-state-of-affairs (qfpsoa)*, *semantic-determiner (semdet)*, *index (ind)*, *person (per)*, *number (num)*, *gender (gend)*

Partition of *list(σ): nonempty-list(σ) (nelist(σ))*, *empty-list (elist or ⟨ ⟩)*

Partition of *set(σ): nonempty-set(σ) (neset(σ))*, *empty-set (eset or { })*[2]

Partition of *boolean: plus (+)*, *minus (−)*

Partition of *sign: word, phrase*

Partition of *mod-synsem: syntax-semantics (synsem)*, *none*

Partition of *head: substantive (subst)*, *functional (func)*

Partition of *substantive: noun, verb, adjective (adj)*, *preposition (prep)*, *relativizer (reltvzr)*

Partition of *functional: marker (mark)*, *determiner (det)*

Partition of *marking: unmarked, marked*

Partition of *marked: complementizer (comp)*, *conjunction (conj)*, . . .[3]

Partition of *complementizer: that, for*

Partition of *case: nominative (nom)*, *accusative (acc)*

Partition of *vform: finite (fin)*, *infinitive (inf)*, *gerund (ger)*, *base (bse)*, *present-participle (prp)*, *past-participle (psp)*, *passive-participle (pas)*

Partition of *pform: to, of*, . . .[4]

2. We employ limited parametric polymorphism for lists and sets as follows: where σ is a metavariable over (nonparametric) sorts, we partition *list(σ)* into *elist* and *nelist(σ)* and declare *nelist(σ)*[FIRST σ, REST *list(σ)*]; likewise we partition *set(σ)* into *eset* and *neset(σ)*.

3. We leave open the question of what other markers English has besides complementizers and conjunctions.

4. We lack as yet an exhaustive list of all forms of English nonpredicative prepositions.

Partition of *phonstring*: kIm, sændi, krIs, . . . [5]

Partition of *con-struc: headed-structure (head-struc), coordinate-structure (coord-struc)* [6]

Partition of *head-struc: head-complement-structure (head comp-struc), head-marker-structure (head-mark-struc), head-adjunct-structure (head-adj-struc), head-filler-structure (head-filler-struc)*

Partition of *content: parametrized-state-of-affairs (psoa), nominal-object (nom-obj), quantifier (quant)*

Partition of *semdet: forall, exists, the, . . .* [7]

Partition of *index: referential (ref), there, it*

Partition of *person: 1st, 2nd, 3rd*

Partition of *number: singular (sing), plural (plur)*

Partition of *gender: masculine (masc), feminine (fem), neuter (neut)*

Partition of *qfpsoa: control-qfpsoa, . . .* [8]

Partition of *control-qfpsoa: influence, commitment, orientation*

Partition of *influence: persuade, appeal, cause, . . .*

Partition of *commitment: promise, intend, try, . . .*

Partition of *orientation: want, hate, expect, . . .*

Partition of *nom-obj: nonpronoun (npro), pronoun (pron)*

Partition of *pron: personal-pronoun (ppro), anaphor (ana)* [9]

Partition of *ana: refl, recp*

FEATURE DECLARATIONS:

$$nonempty\text{-}list(\sigma): \begin{bmatrix} \text{FIRST } \sigma \\ \text{REST } list(\sigma) \end{bmatrix}$$

5. In principle, the infinite set of well-formed English phoneme strings should be generated by a distinct phonological subgrammar, but for simplicity we assume there is a finite set of well-formed phonetic strings that can be exhaustively listed; thus subsorts of *phonstring* are taken to be atomic.

6. We leave open the question of what subsorts of *con-struc* exist other than *head-struc*. We tentatively assume that coordinate structures constitute one such sort, but we do not yet have a formal theory of these. To put it another way, except for the roughly formulated section 6.1 of Chapter 4, our fragment of English is limited to headed structures.

7. In our fragment, we can get by with a small finite number of atomic subsorts of *semdet*. A more complete grammar would require a separate subgrammar for an infinite set of semantic determiners (including, e.g., cardinality determiners for each natural number).

8. We adopt here the proposal that semantic relations be treated as subsorts of *qfpsoa*, thereby eliminating the RELATION feature. We make no effort to exhaustively classify subsorts of *qfpsoa*. Such knowledge should probably not be regarded as strictly linguistic, but rather part of a distinct module of encyclopedic knowledge with which linguistic knowledge interfaces. Likewise we do not declare here what features ('semantic roles') are appropriate for various subsorts of *qfpsoa*; but we do assume that for each subsort of *qfpsoa*, the only sorts of values that are available for these features are either *ref* or *psoa*.

9. The sort name *personal-pronoun* is misleading, since it includes expletives as well as items traditionally considered to be (nonreflexive) personal pronouns. A more precise, but unwieldy, alternative name would be *nonanaphoric-pronoun*.

$$sign: \begin{bmatrix} \text{PHONOLOGY } list(phonstring) \\ \text{SYNSEM } synsem \\ \text{QSTORE } set(quantifier) \\ \text{RETRIEVED } list(quantifier) \end{bmatrix}$$

$$synsem: \begin{bmatrix} \text{LOCAL } local \\ \text{NONLOCAL } nonlocal \end{bmatrix}$$

$$nonlocal: \begin{bmatrix} \text{TO-BIND } nonlocal1 \\ \text{INHERITED } nonlocal1 \end{bmatrix}$$

$$nonlocal1: \begin{bmatrix} \text{SLASH } set(local) \\ \text{REL } set(ref) \\ \text{QUE } set(npro) \end{bmatrix}$$

$$local: \begin{bmatrix} \text{CATEGORY } category \\ \text{CONTENT } content \\ \text{CONTEXT } context \end{bmatrix}$$

$$context: \begin{bmatrix} \text{BACKGROUND } set(psoa) \\ \text{CONTEXTUAL-INDICES } c\text{-}inds \end{bmatrix}$$

$$c\text{-}inds: \begin{bmatrix} \text{SPEAKER } ref \\ \text{ADDRESSEE } ref \\ \text{UTTERANCE-LOCATION } ref \\ \cdots \end{bmatrix}^{10}$$

$$substantive: \begin{bmatrix} \text{PRD } boolean \\ \text{MOD } mod\text{-}synsem \end{bmatrix}^{11}$$

$$functional: [\text{SPEC } synsem]$$

$$category: \begin{bmatrix} \text{HEAD } head \\ \text{SUBCAT } list(synsem) \\ \text{MARKING } marking \end{bmatrix}$$

$$noun: [\text{CASE } case]$$

$$verb: \begin{bmatrix} \text{VFORM } vform \\ \text{AUX } boolean \\ \text{INV } boolean \end{bmatrix}$$

$$preposition: [\text{PFORM } pform]$$

$$phrase: [\text{DAUGHTERS } con\text{-}struc]$$

$$head\text{-}struc: \begin{bmatrix} \text{HEAD-DTR } sign \\ \text{COMP-DTRS } list(phrase) \end{bmatrix}$$

$$head\text{-}mark\text{-}struc: \begin{bmatrix} \text{HEAD-DTR } phrase \\ \text{MARKER-DTR } word \\ \text{COMP-DTRS } elist \end{bmatrix}$$

10. We have not attempted to make an exhaustive list of contextual indices.

11. Substantives that are not adjuncts are assumed to be [MOD *none*]. It follows that substantive words whose phrasal projections may or may not be adjuncts must have both [MOD *none*] and [MOD XP] entries (for suitable XP).

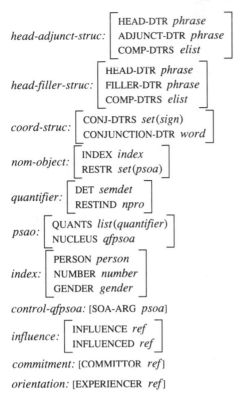

head-adjunct-struc:
$$\begin{bmatrix} \text{HEAD-DTR } \textit{phrase} \\ \text{ADJUNCT-DTR } \textit{phrase} \\ \text{COMP-DTRS } \textit{elist} \end{bmatrix}$$

head-filler-struc:
$$\begin{bmatrix} \text{HEAD-DTR } \textit{phrase} \\ \text{FILLER-DTR } \textit{phrase} \\ \text{COMP-DTRS } \textit{elist} \end{bmatrix}$$

coord-struc:
$$\begin{bmatrix} \text{CONJ-DTRS } \textit{set}(\textit{sign}) \\ \text{CONJUNCTION-DTR } \textit{word} \end{bmatrix}$$

nom-object:
$$\begin{bmatrix} \text{INDEX } \textit{index} \\ \text{RESTR } \textit{set}(\textit{psoa}) \end{bmatrix}$$

quantifier:
$$\begin{bmatrix} \text{DET } \textit{semdet} \\ \text{RESTIND } \textit{npro} \end{bmatrix}$$

psao:
$$\begin{bmatrix} \text{QUANTS } \textit{list}(\textit{quantifier}) \\ \text{NUCLEUS } \textit{qfpsoa} \end{bmatrix}$$

index:
$$\begin{bmatrix} \text{PERSON } \textit{person} \\ \text{NUMBER } \textit{number} \\ \text{GENDER } \textit{gender} \end{bmatrix}$$

control-qfpsoa: [SOA-ARG *psoa*]

influence:
$$\begin{bmatrix} \text{INFLUENCE } \textit{ref} \\ \text{INFLUENCED } \textit{ref} \end{bmatrix}$$

commitment: [COMMITTOR *ref*]

orientation: [EXPERIENCER *ref*]

A.2 The Principles

In the following statements of the principles, a *headed phrase* is a *phrase* whose DAUGHTERS value is of sort *headed-structure*.

THE HEAD FEATURE PRINCIPLE (p. 34):

In a headed phrase, the values of SYNSEM | LOCAL | CATEGORY | HEAD and
DAUGHTERS | HEAD-DAUGHTER | SYNSEM | LOCAL | CATEGORY | HEAD
are token-identical.

THE SUBCATEGORIZATION PRINCIPLE (p. 34):

In a headed phrase, the list value of
DAUGHTERS | HEAD-DAUGHTER | SYNSEM | LOCAL | CATEGORY | SUBCAT
is the concatenation of the list value of SYNSEM | LOCAL | CATEGORY | SUBCAT with the list consisting of the SYNSEM values (in order) of the elements of the list value of DAUGHTERS | COMPLEMENT-DAUGHTERS.

THE ID PRINCIPLE (p. 38):

Every headed phrase must satisfy exactly one of the ID schemata.

THE MARKING PRINCIPLE (p. 45n):

In a headed phrase, the MARKING value is token-identical with that of the MARKER-DAUGHTER if any, and with that of the HEAD-DAUGHTER otherwise.

THE SPEC PRINCIPLE (p. 51):

In a headed phrase whose nonhead daughter (either the MARKER-DAUGHTER or COMPLEMENT-DAUGHTERS | FIRST) has a SYNSEM | LOCAL | CATEGORY | HEAD value of sort *functional*, the SPEC value of that value must be token-identical with the phrase's DAUGHTERS | HEAD-DAUGHTER | SYNSEM value.

THE NONLOCAL FEATURE PRINCIPLE (p. 164):

In a headed phrase, for each nonlocal feature F = SLASH, QUE, or REL, the value of SYNSEM | NONLOCAL | INHERITED | F is the set difference of the union of the values on all the daughters and the value of SYNSEM | NONLOCAL | TO-BIND | F on the HEAD-DAUGHTER.

THE TRACE PRINCIPLE (p. 172):

The SYNSEM value of any trace must be a (noninitial) member of the SUBCAT list of a substantive word.[12]

THE SUBJECT CONDITION (parochial) (p. 195):

If the initial element of the SUBCAT value of a word is slashed, then so is some other element of that list.[13]

THE WEAK COORDINATION PRINCIPLE (p. 203):

In a coordinate structure, the CATEGORY and NONLOCAL values of each conjunct daughter are subsumed by those of the mother.[14]

THE SINGLETON REL CONSTRAINT (parochial) (p. 211):

For any sign, the SYNSEM | NONLOCAL | INHERITED | REL value is a set of cardinality at most one.

THE RELATIVE UNIQUENESS PRINCIPLE (parochial, limited to certain dialects) (p. 212):

For any phrase, a member of the set value of SYNSEM | NONLOCAL | INHERITED | REL may belong to the value of that same path on at most one daughter.

12. By definition, a sign is a *trace* just in case it satisfies the description (15) of Chapter 4. A *substantive* word is one whose SYNSEM|LOCAL|CATEGORY|HEAD value is a subsort of *substantive*. The parenthesized 'initial' appears in the parochial version of the principle but not in the universal version.

13. A *synsem* object is said to be *slashed* if its NONLOCAL|INHERITED|SLASH value is a non-empty set.

14. This principle as yet lacks a precise formal interpretation, because of the foundational problems mentioned in Chapter 4, n. 38.

THE CLAUSAL REL PROHIBITION (parochial) (p. 220):

For any *synsem* object, if the LOCAL | CATEGORY | HEAD value is *verb* and the LOCAL | CATEGORY | SUBCAT value is ⟨ ⟩, then the NONLOCAL | INHERITED | REL value must be { }.

THE BINDING THEORY (p. 254):

Principle A. A locally o-commanded anaphor must be locally o-bound.
Principle B. A personal pronoun must be locally o-free.
Principle C. A nonpronoun must be o-free.

DEFINITIONS FOR THE BINDING THEORY:

A *synsem* object is an *anaphor* (respectively, a *personal pronoun, nonpronoun*), provided its LOCAL | CONTENT value is of sort *ana* (respectively, *ppro, npro*); a *synsem* object is *referential* provided its LOCAL | CONTENT | INDEX value is of sort *ref*.

One *synsem* object is *more oblique* than another provided it appears to the right of the other on the SUBCAT list of some word.

One referential *synsem* object *locally o-commands* another provided they have distinct LOCAL values and either (1) the second is more oblique than the first, or (2) the second is a member of the SUBCAT list of a *synsem* object that is more oblique than the first.

One referential *synsem* object *o-commands* another provided they have distinct LOCAL values and either (1) the second is more oblique than the first, (2) the second is a member of the SUBCAT list of a *synsem* object that is o-commanded by the first, or (3) the second has the same LOCAL | CATEGORY | HEAD value as a *synsem* object that is o-commanded by the first.[15]

One referential *synsem* object (*locally*) *o-binds* another provided it (locally) o-commands and is coindexed with the other. A referential *synsem* object is (*locally*) *o-free* provided it is not (locally) o-bound. Two *synsem* objects are *coindexed* provided their LOCAL | CONTENT | INDEX values are token-identical.

THE CONTROL THEORY (p. 302):

If the SOA-ARG value of a *control-qfpsoa* is token-identical with the CONTENT value of a *local* object whose CATEGORY | SUBCAT value is a list of length one, then the member of that list is (1) reflexive, and (2) coindexed with the INFLUENCED (respectively, COMMITTOR, EXPERIENCER) value of the *control-qfpsoa* if the latter is of sort *influence* (respectively, *commitment, orientation*).

THE SEMANTICS PRINCIPLE (p. 323):

(a) In a headed phrase, the RETRIEVED value is a list whose set of elements is disjoint from the QSTORE value set, and the union of those two sets is the union of the QSTORE values of the daughters.

---

15. We adopt here the revised definitions of o-command and local o-command in Chapter 6, section 8.3.

(b) If the semantic head's SYNSEM | LOCAL | CONTENT value is of sort *psoa*, then the SYNSEM | LOCAL | CONTENT | NUCLEUS value is token-identical with that of the semantic head, and the SYNSEM | LOCAL | CONTENT | QUANTS value is the concatenation of the RETRIEVED value and the semantic head's SYNSEM | LOCAL | CONTENT | QUANTS value; otherwise the RETRIEVED value is the empty list, and the SYNSEM | LOCAL | CONTENT value is token-identical with that of the semantic head.[16]

QUANTIFIER BINDING CONDITION (p. 327):

Let X be a *quantifier*, with RESTINDEX | INDEX value Y, on the QUANTS list of a *psoa* Z, and P a path in Z whose value is Y. Let the address of X in Z be QUANTS | Q | FIRST. Then P must have a prefix of one of the following three forms:

    (1) QUANTS | Q | FIRST | RESTINDEX | RESTRICTION;
    (2) QUANTS | Q | REST; or
    (3) NUCLEUS.

PRINCIPLE OF CONTEXTUAL CONSISTENCY (p. 333):

The CONTEXT | BACKGROUND value of a given phrase is the union of the CONTEXT | BACKGROUND values of the daughters.

A.3 The ID Schemata

SCHEMA 1 (HEAD-SUBJECT SCHEMA) (p. 38):

The SYNSEM | LOCAL | CATEGORY | SUBCAT value is ⟨ ⟩, and the DAUGHTERS value is an object of sort *head-comp-struc* whose HEAD-DAUGHTER value is a phrase whose SYNSEM | NONLOCAL | TO-BIND | SLASH value is { }, and whose COMPLEMENT-DAUGHTERS value is a list of length one.

SCHEMA 2 (HEAD-COMPLEMENT SCHEMA) (p. 38):

The SYNSEM | LOCAL | CATEGORY | SUBCAT value is a list of length one, and the DAUGHTERS value is an object of sort *head-comp-struc* whose HEAD-DAUGHTER value is a word.

SCHEMA 3 (HEAD-SUBJECT-COMPLEMENT SCHEMA) (p. 40):

The SYNSEM | LOCAL | CATEGORY | SUBCAT value is ⟨ ⟩, and the DAUGHTERS value is an object of sort *head-comp-struc* whose HEAD-DAUGHTER value is a word.[17]

SCHEMA 4 (HEAD-MARKER SCHEMA) (p. 46):

The DAUGHTERS value is an object of sort *head-marker-struc* whose HEAD-DAUGHTER | SYNSEM | NONLOCAL | TO-BIND | SLASH value is { }, and whose MARKER-DAUGHTER | SYNSEM | LOCAL | CATEGORY | HEAD value is of sort *marker*.

---

16. In a headed phrase, the *semantic head* is the ADJUNCT-DAUGHTER if any and the HEAD-DAUGHTER otherwise.

17. In the parochial versions of Schemata 1 and 2, the SYNSEM | LOCAL | CATEGORY | HEAD | INV value, if any, must be *minus*; in the parochial versions of Schema 3, it must be *plus*.

SCHEMA 5 (HEAD-ADJUNCT SCHEMA) (p. 56):

The DAUGHTERS value is an object of sort *head-adjunct-struc* whose HEAD-DAUGH-TER | SYNSEM value is token-identical to its ADJUNCT-DAUGHTER | SYNSEM | LOCAL | CATEGORY | HEAD | MOD value and whose HEAD-DAUGHTERS | SYNSEM | NONLOCAL | TO-BIND | SLASH value is { }.

SCHEMA 6 (HEAD-FILLER SCHEMA) (p. 164):

The DAUGHTERS value is an object of sort *head-filler-struc* whose HEAD-DAUGHTER | SYNSEM | LOCAL | CATEGORY value satisfies the description [HEAD *verb*[VFORM *finite*, SUBCAT ⟨ ⟩], whose HEAD-DAUGHTER | SYNSEM | NONLOCAL | INHERITED | SLASH value contains an element token-identical to the FILLER-DAUGHTER | SYNSEM | LOCAL value, and whose HEAD-DAUGHTER | SYNSEM | NONLOCAL | TO-BIND | SLASH value contains only that element.

A.4 The Raising Principle (p. 140)

Let E be a lexical entry in which the (description of the) SUBCAT list L contains (a description corresponding to) a member X (of L) that is not explicitly described in E as an expletive. Then in (the description of) the CONTENT value, X is (described as) assigned no semantic role if and only if L (is described as if it) contains a nonsubject whose own SUBCAT value is ⟨X⟩.[18]

---

18. It should be noted that the Raising Principle has a different logical status than the other principles and is therefore listed separately. This is because the other principles are constraints on feature structures, but the Raising Principle is a constraint on the form of lexical entries, which themselves are constraints on feature structures of sort *word*. Thus, given a specific syntax for the encoding of lexical entries, the Raising Principle constitutes a syntactic well-formedness constraint on the lexical entries themselves, *not* on the feature structures representing lexical tokens that satisfy (or instantiate) those entries.

References

Abney, Steven P. 1987. *The English Noun Phrase in Its Sentential Aspect*. Doctoral dissertation, MIT.

Adams, Douglas, Mary Ann Campbell, Victor Cohen, Julie Lovins, Edward Maxwell, Carolyn Nygren, and John Reighard, eds. 1971. *Papers from the Seventh Regional Meeting of the Chicago Linguistic Society*. Chicago: Chicago Linguistic Society.

Aissen, Judith. 1975. Presentational *There*-Insertion: A Cyclic Root Transformation. In *Papers from the Eleventh Regional Meeting of the Chicago Linguistic Society*, ed. Robin Grossman, L. James San, and Timothy Vance. Chicago: Chicago Linguistic Society.

Ait-Kaci, Hassan, and R. Nasr. 1986. LOGIN: A Logical Programming Language with Built-In Inheritance. *Journal of Logic Programming* 3:187–215.

Akmajian, Adrian. 1984. Sentence Types and the Form-Function Fit. *Natural Language and Linguistic Theory* 2:1–23.

Anderson, Stephen, and Paul Kiparsky, eds. 1973. *A Festschrift for Morris Halle*. New York: Holt, Rinehart & Winston.

Andrews, Avery. 1975. *Studies in the Syntax of Relative and Comparative Clauses*. Doctoral dissertation, MIT. (Published in 1985 by Garland.)

Andrews, Avery. 1982. The Representation of Case in Modern Icelandic. In Bresnan 1982b.

Bach, Emmon. 1977. Review of *On Raising*, by Paul Postal. *Language* 53:621–654.

Bach, Emmon. 1979. Control in Montague Grammar. *Linguistic Inquiry* 10:515–531.

Bach, Emmon. 1983. Generalized Categorial Grammars and the English Auxiliary. In *Linguistic Categories*, vol.2, *Auxiliaries and Related Puzzles*, ed. F. Heny and B. Richards. Dordrecht: Reidel.

Baker, C. Leroy. 1968. *Indirect Questions in English*. Doctoral dissertation, University of Illinois at Urbana-Champaign.

Banfield, Ann. 1982. *Unspeakable Sentences*. London: Routledge & Kegan Paul.

Barlow, Michael. 1988. *A Situated Theory of Agreement*. Doctoral dissertation, Stanford University.

Bartsch, Renate. 1973. The Semantics and Syntax of Number and Numerals. In *Syntax and Semantics*, vol. 2, ed. John Kimball. New York: Seminar Press.

Barwise, Jon. 1989. *The Situation in Logic*. CSLI Lecture Notes no. 17. Stanford: Center for the Study of Language and Information (distributed by the University of Chicago Press).

Barwise, Jon, and Robin Cooper. 1981. Generalized Quantifiers and Natural Languages. *Linguistics and Philosophy* 4:159–219.

Battistella, Edward 1987. Chinese Reflexivization. Paper presented at the second Harbin Conference on Generative Grammar, Heilongjiang University, Harbin, People's Republic of China. (MS available from the University of Alabama at Birmingham.)

Belletti, Adriana, and Luigi Rizzi. 1988. Psych-Verbs and θ-Theory. *Natural Language and Linguistic Theory* 6:291–352.

den Besten, Hans. 1983. On the Interaction of Root Transformations and Lexical Deletive Rules. In *On the Formal Syntax of the Westgermania: Papers from the 3rd Groningen Grammar Talks, Groningen, January 1981*, ed. Werner Abraham. Amsterdam and Philadelphia: Benjamins.

Bolinger, Dwight P. 1973. Ambient *It* Is Meaningful Too. *Journal of Linguistics* 9: 261–270.

Bolinger, Dwight P. 1975. On the Passive in English. In *The First LACUS Forum*, ed. Adam Makkai and Valerie Makkai. Columbia, S.C.: Hornbeam Press.

Borer, Hagit. 1986. I-Subjects. *Linguistic Inquiry* 17:375–416.

Borsley, Robert. 1987. Subjects and Complements in HPSG. Technical report no. CSLI-107-87. Stanford: Center for the Study of Language and Information.

Borsley, Robert. 1989. Phrase-Structure Grammar and the *Barriers* Conception of Clause Structure. *Linguistics* 27:843–863.

Borsley, Robert. 1990. Welsh Passives. In *Celtic Linguistics: Readings in the Brythonic Languages, a Festschrift for T. Arwyn Watkins*, ed. Martin J. Ball, James Fife, Erich Poppe, and Jenny Rowland. Philadelphia and Amsterdam: Benjamins. (Published as vol. 68 of *Current Issues in Linguistic Theory*.)

Borsley, Robert. To appear. Subjects, Complements, and Specifiers in HPSG. In *Readings in Head-Driven Phrase Structure Grammar*, ed. Carl Pollard and Ivan A. Sag.

Borsley, Robert. n.d., a. An HPSG Approach to Welsh Unbounded Dependencies. Unpublished manuscript, University of Wales.

Borsley, Robert. n.d., b. NPs and Clauses in Welsh and Syrian Arabic. Unpublished manuscript, University of Wales.

Bouchard, Denis. 1984. *On the Content of Empty Categories*. Dordrecht: Foris.

Brame, Michael. 1976. *Conjectures and Refutations in Syntax and Semantics*. New York and Amsterdam: Elsevier North Holland.

Brame, Michael. 1977. Alternatives to the Tensed-S and Specified Subject Conditions. *Linguistics and Philosophy* 1:381–411.

Brame, Michael. 1982. The Head-Selector Theory of Lexical Specifications and the Nonexistence of Coarse Categories. *Linguistic Analysis* 8(4):321–325.

Bresnan, Joan. 1968. Adsententials. Unpublished manuscript. MIT.

Bresnan, Joan. 1972. *Theory of Complementation in English Syntax*. Doctoral dissertation, MIT. (Published in 1979 by Garland.)

Bresnan, Joan. 1973. Syntax of the Comparative Clause Construction in English. *Linguistic Inquiry* 4(3):275–343.

Bresnan, Joan. 1976. Nonarguments for Raising. *Linguistic Inquiry* 7:485–501.

Bresnan, Joan. 1978. A Realistic Transformational Grammar. In *Linguistic Theory and Psychological Reality*, ed. Morris Halle, Joan Bresnan, and George Miller. Cambridge, Mass.: MIT Press.

Bresnan, Joan. 1982. Control and Complementation. *Linguistic Inquiry* 13:343–434. (Reprinted in Bresnan, ed., 1982.)

Bresnan, Joan, ed. 1982. *The Mental Representation of Grammatical Relations*. Cambridge, Mass.: MIT Press.

Bresnan, Joan. n.d. Levels of Representation in Locative Inversion: A Comparison of English and Chichewa. Unpublished manuscript, Stanford University.

Bresnan, Joan, and Jane Grimshaw. 1978. The Syntax of Free Relatives in English. *Linguistic Inquiry* 9:331–392.

Bresnan, Joan, and Jonni Kanerva. 1989. Locative Inversion in Chichewa: A Case Study of Factorization in Grammar. *Linguistic Inquiry* 20:1–50.

Bresnan, Joan, and Ronald M. Kaplan. 1982. Introduction. In Bresnan, ed., 1982.

Bresnan, Joan, and Sam Mchombo. 1987. Topic, Pronoun and Agreement in Chicheŵa. *Language* 63:741–782.

Bresnan, Joan, and Annie Zaenen. 1990. Deep Unaccusativity in LFG. In *Grammatical Relations: A Cross-Theoretical Perspective*, ed. Katarzyna Dziwirek, Patrick Farrell, and Errapel Mejías-Bikandi. Stanford: Stanford Linguistics Association.

Brugman, Claudia. 1981. *Story of 'Over'*. M.A. thesis, University of California, Berkeley. (Published by Garland in 1989)

Calcagno, Michael, Andreas Kathol, and Carl Pollard, compilers. 1993. Bibliography of Published Works in or on HPSG. In *OSU Working Papers in Linguistics #42: Papers in Syntax*, ed. Andreas Kathol and Carl Pollard. Columbus: Department of Linguistics, Ohio State University.

Cantrall, William. 1974. *Viewpoint, Reflexives, and the Nature of Noun Phrases*. The Hague: Mouton.

Carpenter, Bob. 1990. Typed Feature Structures: Inheritance, (In)Equations, and Extensionality. In *Proceedings of the First International Workshop on Inheritance in Natural Language Processing*. Tilburg: University of Tilburg.

Carpenter, Bob. 1992. *The Logic of Typed Feature Structures*. Cambridge Tracts in Theoretical Computer Science no. 32. New York: Cambridge University Press.

Carpenter, Bob, and Carl Pollard. 1991. Inclusion, Disjointness, and Choice: The Logic of Linguistic Classification. In *Proceedings of the 29th Annual Meeting of the Association for Computational Linguistics*. Morristown, N.J.: Association for Computational Linguistics.

Carpenter, Bob, Carl Pollard, and Alex Franz. 1991. The Specification and Implementation of Constraint-Based Unification Grammars. In *Proceedings of the Second International Workshop on Parsing Technology*. Carnegie Mellon University School of Computer Science.

Castañeda, Hector-N. 1975. *Thinking and Doing*. Dordrecht: Reidel.

Cattell, Ray. 1978. On the Source of Interrogative Adverbs. *Language* 54:61–77.

Chae, Hee-Rahk. To appear. English Comparatives and an Indexed Phrase Structure Grammar. In *Proceedings of the 18th Regional Meetings of the Berkeley Linguistics Society*. Berkeley: University of California, Berkeley.

Chafe, Wallace. 1970. *A Semantically Based Sketch of Onondaga*. Part 2. *Language*, suppl.

Chierchia, Gennaro. 1984a. Anaphoric Properties of Infinitives and Gerunds. In *Proceedings of the Third West Coast Conference on Formal Linguistics*, ed. Mark Cobler, Susannah MacKaye, and Michael Wescoat. Stanford: Stanford Linguistics Association.

Chierchia, Gennaro. 1984b. *Topics in the Syntax and Semantics of Infinitives and Gerunds*. Doctoral dissertation, University of Massachusetts at Amherst.

Chierchia, Gennaro. 1988. Aspects of a Categorial Theory of Binding. In *Categorial Grammars and Natural Language Structures*, ed. Richard Oehrle, Emmon Bach, and Deirdre Wheeler. Dordrecht: Reidel.

Chierchia, Gennaro. 1990. Anaphora and Attitudes *De Se*. In *Language and Contextual Expressions*, ed. Renate Bartsch, Johan van Benthem, and P. Van Ende Boas, Dordrecht: Foris.

Chierchia, Gennaro, and Pauline Jacobson. 1986. Local and Long Distance Control. In *Papers from the Sixteenth Annual Meeting of the North Eastern Linguistic Society*, ed. S. Berman, J. Choe, and J. McConough. Amherst: GLSA, University of Massachusetts.

Chierchia, Gennaro, Barbara Partee, and Raymond Turner, eds. 1989. *Properties, Types and Meaning II*. Dordrecht: Kluwer.

Chomsky, Noam. 1955. The Logical Structure of Linguistic Theory. Unpublished manuscript, MIT. (Published in 1975 by Plenum.)

Chomsky, Noam. 1957. *Syntactic Structures*. The Hague: Mouton.

Chomsky, Noam. 1965. *Aspects of the Theory of Syntax*. Cambridge, Mass.: MIT Press.

Chomsky, Noam. 1973. Conditions on Transformations. In Anderson and Kiparsky 1973.

Chomsky, Noam. 1977. On *Wh*-Movement. In Culicover et al. 1977.

Chomsky, Noam. 1980. On Binding. *Linguistic Inquiry* 11:1–46.

Chomsky, Noam. 1981. *Lectures on Government and Binding*. Dordrecht: Foris.

Chomsky, Noam. 1982. *Some Concepts and Consequences of the Theory of Government and Binding*. Cambridge, Mass.: MIT Press.

Chomsky, Noam. 1986a. *Knowledge of Language*. New York: Praeger.

Chomsky, Noam. 1986b. *Barriers*. Cambridge, Mass.: MIT Press.

Chomsky, Noam. 1991. Some Notes on Economy of Derivation and Representation. In *Principles and Parameters in Comparative Grammar*, ed. Robert Friedin. Cambridge, Mass.: MIT Press.

Chomsky, Noam. 1992. A Minimalist Program for Linguistic Theory. Unpublished manuscript, MIT.

Chomsky, Noam, and Howard Lasnik. To appear. Principles and Parameters Theory. In *Syntax: An International Handbook of Contemporary Research*, ed. J. Jacobs, Arnim von Stechow, W. Sternefeld, and Theo Vennemann. Berlin: Walter de Gruyter.

Chung, Chan. To appear. Korean Auxilliary Verb Constructions without VP nodes. In *Harvard Studies in Korean Linguistics*, vol. 5, *Proceedings of the 1993 Workshop on Korean Linguistics*, ed. Susumo Kuno et al. Cambridge, Mass.: Harvard University, Department of Linguistics.

Chung, Sandra. 1990. VP's and Verb Movement in Chamorro. *Natural Language and Linguistic Theory* 8:559–619.

Chung, Sandra, and James McCloskey. 1983. On the Interpretation of Certain Island Facts in GPSG. *Linguistic Inquiry* 14:704–713.

Cinque, Guglielmo. 1990. *Types of Ā Dependencies*. Cambridge, Mass.: MIT Press.

Clark, Herbert, and Edward Schaefer. 1989. Contributing to Discourse. *Cognitive Science* 13:259–294.

Clements, George N. 1975. Super-Equi-NP-Deletion and the Intervention Constraint. In *Papers from the Fifth Annual Meeting of the North Eastern Linguistic Society*, ed. Ellen Kaisse and Jorge Hankamer. Cambridge, Mass.: Harvard University.

Clements, Clancey, and Gerrard Wettengel. 1989. Verb-Dependent Control Phenomena with Infinitive Clauses. Unpublished manuscript, Indiana University.

Cole, Peter. 1982. *Imbabura Quechua. Lingua* Descriptive Studies, vol. 5. Amsterdam: North Holland.

Cole, Peter. 1987. The Structure of Internally Headed Relative Clauses. *Natural Language and Linguistic Theory* 5:277–302.

Cole, Peter, Gabriella Herman, and L.-M. Sung. 1990. Principles and Parameters of Long-Distance Reflexives. *Linguistic Inquiry* 21:1–22.

Comrie, Bernard. 1984. Subject and Object Control: Syntax, Semantics and Pragmatics. In *Proceedings of the Tenth Annual Meeting of the Berkeley Linguistics Society*. Berkeley, Calif.: Berkeley Linguistics Society.

Cooper, Richard. 1990. *Classification-Based Phrase Structure Grammar: An Extended Revised Version of HPSG*. Doctoral dissertation, University of Edinburgh.

Cooper, Robin. 1975. *Montague's Semantic Theory and Transformational Syntax*. Doctoral dissertation, University of Massachusetts at Amherst.

Cooper, Robin. 1983. *Quantification and Syntactic Theory*. Dordrecht: Reidel.

Cooper, Robin, Kuniaki Mukai, and John Perry, eds. 1990. *Situation Theory and Its Applications*. CSLI Lecture Notes no. 22. Stanford: Center for the Study of Language and Information (distributed by the University of Chicago Press).

Corbett, Greville. 1988. Agreement: A Partial Specification Based on Slavonic Data. In *Agreement in Natural Language: Approaches, Theories, Descriptions*, ed. Michael Barlow and Charles Ferguson. Stanford: Center for the Study of Language and Information.

Couper-Kuhlen, Elizabeth 1979. *The Prepositional Passive in English*. Tübingen: Max Niemeyer Verlag.

Crow, Judith. 1990. Locations Now and Then. In Cooper et al. 1990.

Culicover, Peter, Adrian Akmajian, and Thomas Wasow, eds. 1977. *Formal Syntax*. New York: Academic Press.

Culy, Chris. 1990. *The Syntax and Semantics of Internally Headed Relative Clauses*. Doctoral dissertation, Stanford University.

Dalrymple, Mary. 1990. *Syntactic Constraints on Anaphoric Binding*. Doctoral dissertation, Stanford University.

Dalrymple, Mary, and Smita Joshi. 1986. Relative Clauses and Relative Clause Linking in Marathi. Unpublished manuscript, Stanford University.

Davis, Steven, ed. 1991. *Pragmatics—a Reader*. New York and Oxford: Oxford University Press.

Davison, Alice. 1980. Peculiar Passives. *Language* 56: 42–66.

Devlin, Keith. 1991. *Logic and Information*. Vol. 1 *Situation Theory*. Cambridge: Cambridge University Press.

Downing, Pamela. 1977. On the Creation and Use of English Compound Nouns. *Language* 53:810–842.

Dowty, David. 1982a. Grammatical Relations and Montague Grammar. In Jacobson and Pullum 1982.

Dowty, David. 1982b. More on the Categorial Analysis of Grammatical Relations. In *Subjects and Other Subjects*, ed. Annie Zaenen. Bloomington: Indiana University Linguistics Club.

Dowty, David. 1985. On Recent Analyses of the Semantics of Control. *Linguistics and Philosophy* 8:291–331.

Dowty, David. 1989. On the Semantic Content of the Notion 'Thematic Role.' In Chierchia et al. 1989.

Dowty, David, and Belinda Brodie. 1984. The Semantics of 'Floated' Quantifiers in a Nontransformational Grammar. *Proceedings of the Third West Coast Conference on Formal Linguistics*, ed. Mark Cobler, Susannah MacKaye, and Michael Wescoat. Stanford: Stanford Linguistics Association.

Dowty, David, and Pauline Jacobson. 1989. Agreement as a Semantic Phenomenon. *Proceedings of the Fifth Eastern States Conference on Linguistics (ESCOL '88)*, ed. Joyce Powers and Kenneth de Jong. Columbus: Ohio State University.

Eilfort, William, Paul Kroeber, and Karen Peterson, eds. 1985. *Papers from the 21st Regional Meeting of the Chicago Linguistic Society*. Chicago: Chicago Linguistic Society.

Emonds, Joseph. 1976. *A Transformational Approach to English Syntax: Root, Structure-Preserving, and Local Transformations*. New York: Academic Press.

Engdahl, Elisabet. 1983. Subject Gaps: An Asymmetry between Questions and Relatives in Norwegian. In *Papers from the Fourteenth Annual Meeting of the North Eastern Linguistic Society*, ed. Charles Jones and Peter Sells. Amherst, Mass.: GLSA, University of Massachusetts at Amherst.

Evans, Gareth. 1977. Pronouns, Quantifiers and Relative Clauses. *Canadian Journal of Philosophy* 7:467–536.

Evans, Gareth. 1980. Pronouns. *Linguistic Inquiry* 7: 337–362.

Farkas, Donka. 1988. On Obligatory Control. *Linguistics and Philosophy* 11:27–58.

Farkas, Donka, Daniel Flickinger, Gerald Gazdar, William Ladusaw, Almerindo Ojeda,

Jessie Pinkham, Geoffrey K. Pullum, and Peter Sells. 1983. Some Revisions to the Theory of Features and Feature Instantiation. Unpublished manuscript, UCLA.

Fenstad, Jens-Erik, Per-Kristian Halvorsen, Tore Langholm, and Johan van Benthem. 1987. *Situations, Language, and Logic*. Dordrecht: Reidel.

Fillmore, Charles. 1967. The Case for Case. In *Universals in Linguistic Theory*, ed. Emmon Bach and Robert Harms. New York: Holt, Rinehart & Winston.

Fillmore, Charles, and Paul Kay. To appear. Construction Grammar. Unpublished manuscript, University of California, Berkeley.

Flickinger, Daniel. 1987. *Lexical Rules in the Hierarchical Lexicon*. Doctoral dissertation, Stanford University.

Flickinger, Daniel P., and John Nerbonne. 1992. Inheritance and Complementation: A Case Study of *Easy* Adjectives and Related Nouns. *Computational Linguistics* 18: 269–309.

Flickinger, Daniel, Carl Pollard, and Thomas Wasow. 1985. Structure Sharing in Lexical Representation. In *Proceedings of the 23rd Annual Meeting of the Association for Computational Linguistics*. Morristown, N.J.: Association for Computational Linguistics.

Fodor, Janet D. 1974. Like Subject Verbs and Causal Clauses in English. *Journal of Linguistics* 10:95–110.

Fodor, Janet D. 1978. Parsing Strategies and Constraints on Transformations. *Linguistic Inquiry* 9:427–473.

Fodor, Janet D. 1992. Islands, Learnability and the Lexicon. In *Island Constraints: Theory, Acquisition and Processing*, ed. Helen Goodluck and Michael Rochemont. Dordrecht: Kluwer.

Fodor, Janet, and Ivan A. Sag. 1982. Referential and Quantificational Indefinites. *Linguistics and Philosophy* 5:355–398.

Fodor, Jerry A. 1975. *The Language of Thought*. New York: Crowell.

Foley, William, and Robert Van Valin. 1984. *Functional Syntax and Universal Grammar*. Cambridge: Cambridge University Press.

Fraser, Norman, and Richard A. Hudson. 1992. Inheritance in Word Grammar. In *Inheritance in Natural Language Processing*, ed. W. Daelemans and Gerald Gazdar. (Published as a special issue of *Computational Linguistics*.)

Freidin, Robert, and Wayne Harbert. 1983. On the Fine Structure of the Binding Theory. In *Proceedings of the Thirteenth Annual Meeting of the North Eastern Linguistic Society*, ed. Peter Sells and Charles Jones. Amherst, Mass.: GLSA, University of Massachusetts at Amherst.

Fukui, Naoki. 1986. *A Theory of Category Projection and Its Applications*. Doctoral dissertation, MIT.

Gawron, Jean Mark, and Stanley Peters. 1990. *Anaphora and Quantification in Situation Semantics*. CSLI Lecture Notes no. 19. Stanford: Center for the Study of Language and Information (distributed by the University of Chicago Press).

Gazdar, Gerald. 1979a. *Pragmatics: Implicature, Presupposition, and Logical Form*. New York: Academic Press.

Gazdar, Gerald. 1979b. A Solution to the Projection Problem. In Oh and Dineen 1979.

Gazdar, Gerald. 1981. Unbounded Dependencies and Coordinate Structure. *Linguistic Inquiry* 12:155–184.

Gazdar, Gerald. 1982. Phrase Structure Grammar. In Jacobson and Pullum 1982.

Gazdar, Gerald, Ewan Klein, Geoffrey K. Pullum, and Ivan A. Sag. 1984. Foot Features and Parasitic Gaps. In *Sentential Complementation*, ed. W. Geest and Y. Putseys. Dordrecht: Foris.

Gazdar, Gerald, Ewan Klein, Geoffrey K. Pullum, and Ivan A. Sag. 1985. *Generalized*

Phrase Structure Grammar. Oxford: Basil Blackwell; Cambridge, Mass.: Harvard University Press.

Gazdar, Gerald, and Geoffrey K. Pullum. 1982. *Generalized Phrase Structure Grammar: A Theoretical Synopsis.* Bloomington: Indiana University Linguistics Club.

Gazdar, Gerald, Geoffrey K. Pullum, Robert Carpenter, Ewan Klein, Thomas E. Hukari, and Robert D. Levine. 1988. Category Structures. *Computational Linguistics* 14: 1–19.

Gazdar, Gerald, Geoffrey K. Pullum, and Ivan A. Sag. 1982. Auxiliaries and Related Phenomena in a Restricted Theory of Grammar. *Language* 58:591–638.

Gazdar, Gerald, Geoffrey K. Pullum, Ivan A. Sag, and Thomas Wasow. 1982. Coordination and Transformational Grammar. *Linguistic Inquiry* 13:663–676.

Ginzburg, Jonathan. 1992. *Questions, Queries, and Facts: A Semantics and Pragmatics for Interrogatives.* Doctoral dissertation, Stanford University.

Goldsmith, John. 1985. A Principled Exception to the Coordinate Structure Constraint. In Eilfort et al. 1985.

Goodall, Grant. 1987. *Parallel Structures in Syntax.* Cambridge: Cambridge University Press.

Green, Georgia M. 1989. *Pragmatics and Natural Language Understanding.* Hillsdale, N.J.: L. Erlbaum Associates.

Grimshaw, Jane. 1977. *English Wh-Constructions and the Theory of Grammar.* Doctoral dissertation, University of Massachusetts at Amherst.

Grimshaw, Jane. 1979. Complement Selection and the Lexicon. *Linguistic Inquiry* 10: 279–326.

Grinder, John. 1970. Super-Equi-NP-Deletion. In *Papers from the Sixth Regional Meeting of the Chicago Linguistic Society*, ed. Mary Ann Campbell, James Lindholm, Alice Davison, William Fisher, Louanna Furbee, Julie Lovins, Edward Maxwell, John Reighard, and Stephen Straight. Chicago: Chicago Linguistic Society.

Grinder, John. 1971. A Reply to Super Equi-NP Deletion as Dative Deletion. In Adams et al. 1971.

Groenendijk, Jeroen, Theo Janssen, and Martin Stokhof, eds. 1981. *Formal Methods in the Study of Language.* Amsterdam: Mathematical Centre Tracts.

Groenendijk, Jeroen, and Martin Stokhof. 1990. Dynamic Montague Grammar. In *Papers from the Second Symposium on Logic and Language*, ed. László Kálmán and László Pólos. Budapest: Akadémiai Kiadó.

Groenendijk, Jeroen, and Martin Stokhof. 1991. Dynamic Predicate Logic. *Linguistics and Philosophy* 14:39–100.

Grosu, Alexander. 1972. *The Strategic Content of Island Constraints.* Ohio State Working Papers in Linguistics no. 13. Columbus: Ohio State University.

Grosu, Alexander. 1973. On the Nonunitary Nature of the Coordinate Structure Constraint. *Linguistic Inquiry* 4:88–92.

Grosu, Alexander. 1974. On the Nature of the Left Branch Condition. *Linguistic Inquiry* 5:308–319.

Grover, Claire, and Marc Moens. 1990. Missing Objects and Control. Unpublished manuscript, University of Edinburgh Computer Laboratory and University of Edinburgh Center for Cognitive Science, 30 November.

Gunji, Takao. 1987. *Japanese Phrase Structure Grammar.* Dordrecht: Reidel.

Haegeman, Liliane. 1991. *Introduction to Government and Binding Theory.* Oxford and Cambridge, Mass.: Basil Blackwell.

Hale, Kenneth. 1973. Person Marking in Warlpiri. In Anderson and Kiparsky 1973.

Halvorsen, Per-Kristian. 1983. Semantics for Lexical-Functional Grammar. *Linguistic Inquiry* 14:567–616.

Han, Eunjoo. 1990. Honorification in Korean. Unpublished manuscript, Stanford University.

Hankamer, Jorge. 1973. Why There Are Two *Than*'s in English. In *Papers from the Ninth Regional Meeting of the Chicago Linguistic Society*, ed. Claudia Corum, Timothy Smith-Stark, and Ann Weiser. Chicago: Chicago Linguistic Society.

Hankamer, Jorge, and Ivan A. Sag. 1976. Deep and Surface Anaphora. *Linguistic Inquiry* 7:391–426.

Hegarty, Michael. 1990. On Adjunct Extraction from Complements. Unpublished manuscript, MIT.

Heim, Irene. 1982. *The Semantics of Definite and Indefinite Noun Phrases*. Doctoral dissertation, University of Massachusetts at Amherst.

Heim, Irene. 1983. On the Projection Problem for Presuppositions. In Barlow et al. 1983. (Reprinted in Davis 1991.)

Heim, Irene. 1990. E-Type Pronouns and Donkey Anaphora. *Linguistics and Philosophy* 13:137–178.

Helke, Michael. 1971. *The Grammar of English Reflexives*. Doctoral dissertation, MIT.

Hellan, Lars. 1986. The Headedness of NPs in Norwegian. In *Features and Projections*, ed. Pieter Muysken and Henk van Riemsdijk. Dordrecht: Foris.

Hellan, Lars. 1988. *Anaphora in Norwegian and the Theory of Grammar*. Dordrecht: Foris.

Herskovitz, Annette. 1986. *Language and Spatial Cognition*. Cambridge: Cambridge University Press.

Higgins, Francis Roger. 1973. *The Pseudo-Cleft Construction in English*. Doctoral dissertation, MIT.

Hirst, Graeme. 1987. *Semantic Interpretation and the Resolution of Ambiguity*. Cambridge: Cambridge University Press.

Hobbs, Jerry, Mark Stickel, Paul Martin, and Douglas Edwards. 1988. Interpretation as Abduction. In *Proceedings of the 26th Annual Meeting of the Association for Computational Linguistics*. Morristown, N.J.: Association for Computational Linguistics.

Hoeksema, Jack. 1983. Plurality and Conjunction. In *Studies in Model-Theoretic Semantics*, ed. Alice ter Meulen. Dordrecht: Foris.

Hoeksema, Jack. 1984. *Categorial Morphology*. Doctoral dissertation, Rijksuniversiteit te Groningen.

Höhfeld, Markus, and Gert Smolka. 1988. Definite Relations over Constraint Languages. LILOG Report no. 53. Stuttgart: IBM Deutschland.

Huang, James. 1982. *Logical Relations in Chinese and the Theory of Grammar*. Doctoral dissertation, MIT.

Huang, James. 1983. A Note on the Binding Theory. *Linguistic Inquiry* 14:554–561.

Hudson, Richard. 1984. *Word Grammar*. Oxford: Basil Blackwell.

Hudson, Richard. 1990. *English Word Grammar*. Oxford: Basil Blackwell.

Hudson, Richard. 1992. The Case against Case. Unpublished manuscript, University College London. (Presented at the spring meeting of the Linguistic Association of Great Britain, Brighton.)

Hukari, Thomas, and Robert Levine. 1987a. Parasitic Gaps, Slash Termination, and the C-Command Condition. *Natural Language and Linguistic Theory* 5:197–222.

Hukari, Thomas, and Robert Levine. 1987b. Rethinking Connectivity in Unbounded Dependency Constructions. In *Proceedings of the Sixth West Coast Conference on Formal Linguistics*, ed. Megan Crowhurst. Stanford: Stanford Linguistics Association.

Hukari, Thomas, and Robert Levine. 1991. On the Disunity of Unbounded Dependency Constructions. *Natural Language and Linguistic Theory* 9:97–144.

Hust, Joel, and Michael Brame. 1976. Jackendoff on Interpretive Semantics. *Linguistic Analysis* 2:243–277.

Iida, Masayo. 1992. *Context and Binding in Japanese*. Doctoral dissertation, Stanford University.

Jackendoff, Ray. 1972. *Semantic Interpretation in Generative Grammar*. Cambridge, Mass.: MIT Press.

Jackendoff, Ray. 1974. A Deep Structure Projection Rule. *Linguistic Inquiry* 5:481–506.

Jackendoff, Ray. 1985. Multiple Subcategorization and the θ-Criterion: The Case of *Climb*. *Natural Language and Linguistic Theory* 3:271–295.

Jackendoff, Ray. 1987. The Status of Thematic Relations in Linguistic Theory. *Linguistic Inquiry* 18:369–411.

Jackendoff, Ray. 1992. Mme. Tussaud Meets the Binding Theory. *Natural Language and Linguistic Theory* 10:1–32.

Jacobson, Pauline. 1983. Phrase Structure and Grammatical Relations. Unpublished manuscript, Brown University. (Portions presented as a colloquium talk at the 1983 Meeting of the Linguistic Society of America, Minneapolis.)

Jacobson, Pauline. 1984. Connectivity in Phrase Structure Grammar. *Natural Language and Linguistic Theory* 1:535–581.

Jacobson, Pauline. 1987. Review of *Generalized Phrase Structure Grammar*, by Gerald Gazdar et al. *Linguistics and Philosophy* 10: 389–426.

Jacobson, Pauline. 1990. Raising as Function Composition. *Linguistics and Philosophy* 13:423–475.

Jacobson, Pauline. 1992. The Lexical Entailment Theory of Control and the *Tough*-Construction. In Sag and Szabolcsi 1992.

Jacobson, Pauline, and Paul Neubauer. 1976. Strict Cyclicity: Evidence from the Intervention Constraint. *Linguistic Inquiry* 7:429–462.

Jacobson, Pauline, and Geoffrey K. Pullum, eds. 1982. *The Nature of Syntactic Representation*. Dordrecht: Reidel.

Jespersen, Otto. 1937. *Analytic Syntax*. Copenhagen: Levin & Munksgaard.

Jespersen, Otto. 1965. *A Modern English Grammar*. London: Allen & Unwin.

Johnson, David. 1974. On the Role of Grammatical Relations in Linguistic Theory. In La Galy et al. 1974.

Johnson, David. 1977. On Relational Constraints on Grammars. In *Syntax and Semantics*, vol. 8, *Grammatical Relations*, ed. Peter Cole and Jerrold M. Sadock. New York: Academic Press.

Johnson, David, and Paul Postal. 1980. *Arc Pair Grammar*. Princeton: Princeton University Press.

Johnson, Mark. 1984. Grammatical Gender and Pronoun Reference. Unpublished manuscript, Center for the Study of Language and Information, Stanford.

Johnson, Mark. 1988. *Attribute-Value Logic and the Theory of Grammar*. CSLI Lecture Notes no. 14. Stanford: Center for the Study of Language and Information (distributed by the University of Chicago Press.)

Johnson, Mark. 1991. Features and Formulae. *Computational Linguistics* 17:131–151.

Joseph, Brian. 1979. Raising to Oblique in Modern Greek. In *Proceedings of the Fifth Annual Meeting of the Berkeley Linguistics Society*. Berkeley: Berkeley Linguistics Society.

Kamp, Johan A. W. 1981. A Theory of Truth and Semantic Representation. In Groenendijk et al. 1981. (Reprinted in *Truth, Interpretation and Information*, ed. Jeroen Gr enendijk, Theo Janssen, and Martin Stokhof. Dordrecht: Foris, 1984.)

Kang, Hyeonseok. 1991. Subject Honorification in Korean in Terms of Point of Unpublished manuscript, Ohio State University.

Kaplan, David. 1979. On the Logic of Demonstratives. *Contemporary Perspectives in the Philosophy of Language*, ed. Peter French, Theodore Uehling, and Howard Wettstein. Minneapolis: University of Minnesota Press.

Kaplan, Ronald, and Annie Zaenen. 1989. Long-Distance Dependencies, Constituent Structure, and Functional Uncertainty. In *Alternative Conceptions of Phrase Structure,* ed. Mark Baltin and Anthony Kroch, 17–42. Chicago: University of Chicago Press.

Karttunen, Lauri. 1973a. Presuppositions of Compound Sentences. *Linguistic Inquiry* 4:169–193.

Karttunen, Lauri. 1973b. Remarks on Presuppositions. In *Proceedings of the Texas Conference on Performatives, Presuppositions, and Conversational Implicatures,* ed. J. Murphy, Andrew Rogers, and Robert Wall. Washington D.C.: Center for Applied Linguistics.

Karttunen, Lauri. 1974. Presupposition and Linguistic Context. *Theoretical Linguistics* 1:181–194. (Reprinted in Davis 1991.)

Kartunnen, Lauri, and Stanley Peters. 1979. Conventional Implicature. In Oh and Dinneen 1979.

Kasper, Robert. To appear. Adjuncts in the Mittelfeld. In Nerbonne et al. to appear.

Kasper, Robert, and William Rounds. 1986. A Logical Semantics for Feature Structures. In *Proceedings of the 24th Annual Meeting of the Association for Computational Linguistics.* Morristown, N.J.: Association for Computational Linguistics.

Kathol, Andreas. 1991. Verbal and Adjectival Passives in German. In *Proceedings of the Third Student Conference in Linguistics.* MIT Working Papers in Ling uistics no. 14. Cambridge: Department of Linguistics, Massachusetts Institute of Technology.Kathol, Andreas. n.d. Agreement in HPSG Revisited. Unpublished manuscript, Ohio State University.

Katz, Jerrold, and Paul Postal. 1991. Realism and Conceptualism in Linguistics. *Linguistics and Philosophy* 14:515–554.

Kayne, Richard. 1983. Connectedness. *Linguistic Inquiry* 14(2): 223–250. (Also in Kayne 1984a.)

Kayne, Richard. 1984a. *Connectedness and Binary Branching.* Dordrecht: Foris.

Kayne, Richard. 1984b. Two Notes on the NIC. In Kayne 1984a.

Keenan, Edward L. 1987. A Semantic Definition of 'Indefinite NP.' In Reuland and ter Meulen 1987.

Kimball, John. 1971. Super-Equi-NP-Deletion as Dative Deletion. In Adams et al.1971.

King, Paul. 1989. *A Logical Formalism for Head-Driven Phrase Structure Grammar.* Doctoral dissertation, University of Manchester.

Kiparsky, Paul. 1987. *Morphology and Grammatical Relations.* Unpublished manuscript, Department of Linguistics, Stanford University.

Kitagawa, Yoshihisa. 1985. Small but Clausal. In Eilfort et al. 1985.

Kitagawa, Yoshihisa. 1986. *Subjects in English and Japanese.* Doctoral dissertation, University of Massachusetts at Amherst.

Klein, Ewan H., and Ivan A. Sag. 1985. Type-Driven Translation. *Linguistics and Philosophy* 8:163–201.

Koster, Jan. 1987. *Domains and Dynasties.* Dordrecht: Foris.

Koster, Jan, and Robert May. 1982. On the Constituency of Infinitives. *Language* 58: 116–143.

Kroch, Anthony. 1989. Amount Quantification, Referentiality, and Long *Wh*-Movement. Unpublished manuscript, University of Pennsylvania.

Kuno, Susumu. 1970. Some Properties of Non-Referential Noun Phrases. In *Studies in General and Oriental Linguistics,* ed. Roman Jakobson and Shigeo Kawamoto. Tokyo: TEC Co.

Kuno, Susumu. 1972. Pronominalization, Reflexivization, and Direct Discourse. *Linguistic Inquiry* 3:161–195.

Kuno, Susumu. 1973. Constraints on Internal Clauses and Sentential Subjects. *Linguistic Inquiry* 4:363–385.

Kuno, Susumu. 1975. Three Perspectives in the Functional Approach to Syntax. In *Papers from the Parasession on Functionalism*, ed. Robin Grosman, L. James San, and Tomothy Vance. Chicago: Chicago Linguistic Society.

Kuno, Susumu. 1983. Reflexivization in English. *Communication and Cognition* 16 (1/2): 65–80.

Kuno, Susumu. 1987. *Functional Syntax*. Chicago: University of Chicago Press.

Kuno, Susumu, and E. Kaburaki. 1977. Empathy and Syntax. *Linguistic Inquiry* 8: 627–672.

Kuroda, Sige-Yuki. 1965. *Generative Grammatical Studies in the Japanese Language*. Doctoral dissertation, MIT.

Kuroda, Sige-Yuki. 1968. English Relativization and Certain Related Problems. *Language* 44:244–266.

Kuroda, Sige-Yuki. 1973. Where Epistemology, Grammar, and Style Meet: A Case Study from Japanese. In Anderson and Kiparsky 1973.

Kuroda, Sige-Yuki. 1988. Whether We Agree or Not: A Comparative Syntax of English and Japanese. In *Papers from the 2nd International Workshop on Japanese Syntax*, ed. William Poser. Stanford, Calif.: Center for the Study of Language and Information.

Ladusaw, William. 1988. A Proposed Distinction between Level and Stratum. In *Linguistics in the Morning Calm 2*, ed. the Linguistic Society of Korea. Seoul: Hanshin Publishing Co.

Ladusaw, William. n.d. Variation in Negative Concord Systems. Unpublished manuscript, University of California, Santa Cruz.

Ladusaw, William, and David Dowty. 1988. Towards a Non-Semantic Account of Thematic Roles. In *Syntax and Semantics* vol. 21, *On the Nature of Thematic Roles*, ed. Wendy Wilkins. New York: Academic Press.

La Galy, Michael W., Robert A. Fox, and Anthony Bruck, eds. 1974. *Papers from the Tenth Regional Meeting of the Chicago Linguistic Society*. Chicago: Chicago Linguistic Society.

Lakoff, George. 1965. *On the Nature of Syntactic Irregularity*. Doctoral dissertation, Indiana University. (Published in 1970 as *Irregularity in Syntax*. New York: Holt, Rinehart & Winston.)

Lakoff, George. 1986. Frame Semantic Control of the Coordinate Structure Constraint. In *Papers from the 22nd Regional Meeting of the Chicago Linguistic Society*. Chicago: Chicago Linguistic Society.

Lakoff, George. 1987. *Women, Fire, and Dangerous Things*. Chicago: University of Chicago Press.

Langacker, Ronald. 1969. On Pronominalization and the Chain of Command. In Reibel and Schane 1969.

Langendoen, D. Terence, and Paul Postal. 1984. *The Vastness of Natural Language*. Oxford: Basil Blackwell.

Lapointe, Steven. 1980. *A Theory of Grammatical Agreement*. Doctoral dissertation, University of Massachusetts at Amherst.

Lapointe, Steven. 1983. A Comparison of Two Recent Theories of Agreement. In *Papers from the Parasession on the Interplay of Phonology, Morphology, and Syntax*, ed. John Richardson, Mitchell Marks, and Amy Chukerman. Chicago: Chicago Linguistic Society.

Larson, Richard. 1988. *Promise* and the Theory of Control. Lexicon Project Working Papers no. 23. Cambridge, Mass.: Center for Cognitive Science, MIT.

Lasersohn, Peter. 1988. *A Semantics for Groups and Events*. Doctoral dissertation, Ohio State University.

Lasnik, Howard, and Mamoru Saito. 1991. On the Subject of Infinitives. In *Papers from the 27th Regional Meeting of the Chicago Linguistic Society,* e.d. Lise Dobun, Lynn Nichols and Rosa Rodríguez. Chicago: CLS.

Lasnik, Howard, and Robert Fiengo. 1974. Complement Object Deletion. *Linguistic Inquiry* 5:535–571.

Lebeaux, David. 1983. A Distributional Difference between Reciprocals and Reflexives. *Linguistic Inquiry* 14: 723–730.

Lebeaux, David. 1984. Locality and Anaphoric Binding. *Linguistic Review* 4:343–63.

Lees, Robert, and Edward Klima. 1963. Rules for English Pronominalization. *Language* 39:17–28. (Reprinted in Reibel and Schane 1969.)

Lerner, G. H. 1987. *Collaborative Turn Sequences: Sentence Construction and Social Action*. Doctoral dissertation, University of California, Irvine.

Lewis, David. 1972. General Semantics. In *Semantics for Natural Language*, ed. Donald Davidson and Gilbert Harman. Dordrecht: Reidel. (Reprinted in Barbara Partee, ed. *Montague Grammar*. New York: Academic Press, 1976.)

Lewis, David. 1979. Attitudes *De Dicto* and *De Se*. *Philosophical Review* 88:513–43.

Liberman, Mark. 1973. *Some Observations on Semantic Scope*. Master's thesis, MIT.

Lindner, Susan. 1981. *A Lexico-Semantic Analysis of Verb-Particle Constructions with Up and Out*. Doctoral dissertation, University of California, San Diego.

Link, Godehard. 1983. The Logical Analysis of Plurals and Mass Terms: A Lattice-Theoretic Approach. In *Meaning, Use, and Interpretation of Language*, ed. Rainer Bäuerle, Christopher Schwarze, and Arnim von Stechow. Berlin: Walter de Gruyter.

Link, Godehard. 1987. Generalized Quantifiers and Plurals. In *Generalized Quantifiers*, ed. Peter Gärdenfors. Dordrecht: Reidel. (Also appeared as CSLI Report no. CSLI-86-87. Stanford: Center for the Study of Language and Information.)

McCawley, James. 1971. English as a VSO Language. *Language* 46:286–299.

McCawley, James. 1981. The Syntax and Semantics of English Relative Clauses. *Lingua* 53:99–149.

McCawley, James. n.d. [Unpublished list of examples.] University of Chicago.

McCloskey, James. 1984. Raising, Subcategorization, and Selection in Modern Irish. *Natural Language and Linguistic Theory* 1:441–485.

McConnell-Ginet, Sally 1979. On the Deep (and Surface) Adjective 'Good.' In *Grammatical Studies: Semantics and Syntax*, ed. Linda R. Waugh and Francis van Coetsem. Leiden: E. J. Brill.

Maier, Petra, and Petra Steffens. 1989. Zur Syntax pränominaler Elemente in einer kategorialen Unifikationsgrammatik des Deutschen. IWBS Report no. 70. Stuttgart: IBM Germany Scientific Center.

Maling, Joan. 1980. Inversion in Embedded Clauses in Modern Icelandic. *Íslenskt mál of almenn málfræði* 2: 175–193. (Reprinted in Maling and Zaenen 1990.)

Maling, Joan. 1983. Transitive Adjective: A Case of Categorial Reanalysis. In *Linguistic Categories: Auxiliaries and Related Puzzles*, ed. Frank Heny and Barry Richards. Dordrecht: Reidel.

Maling, Joan, and Annie Zaenen. 1982. A Phrase Structure Account of Scandinavian Extraction Phenomena. In Jacobson and Pullum 1982.

Maling, Joan, and Annie Zaenen, eds. 1990. *Syntax and Semantics*. Vol. 24, *Modern Icelandic Syntax*. San Diego: Academic Press.

Manzini, M. Rita. 1983. On Control and Control Theory. *Linguistic Inquiry* 14:421–446.

May, Robert. 1984. *Logical Form: Its Structure and Derivation*. Cambridge, Mass.: MIT Press.

Milsark, Gary. 1977. Toward an Explanation of Certain Peculiarities of the Existential Construction in English. *Linguistic Analysis* 3:1–29.

Moens, Mark, and Mark Steedman. 1987. Temporal Ontology and Temporal Reference. *Computational Linguistics* 14:14–28.

Mohanan, K. P. 1983. Functional and Anaphoric Control. *Linguistic Inquiry* 14:641–674.

Montague, Richard. 1974. *Formal Philosophy*. New Haven: Yale University Press.

Morgan, Jerry. 1969. On Arguing about Semantics. *Papers in Linguistics* 1:49–70.

Morgan, Jerry. 1972. Verb Agreement as a Rule of English. In *Papers from the Eighth Regional Meeting of the Chicago Linguistic Society*, ed. Paul Peranteau, Judith Levi, and Gloria Phares. Chicago: Chicago Linguistic Society.

Morgan, Jerry. 1985. Some Problems of Determination in English Number Agreement. In *Proceedings of the First Eastern States Conference on Linguistics*, ed. Gloria Alvarez, Belinda Brodie, and Terry McCoy. Columbus: Ohio State University.

Moshier, Drew. 1988. *Extensions to Unification Grammars for the Description of Programming Languages*. Doctoral dissertation, University of Michigan, Ann Arbor.

Nanni, Deborah, and Justine Stillings. 1978. Three Remarks on Pied Piping. *Linguistic Inquiry* 9:310–318.

Nerbonne, John, Klaus Netter, and Carl Pollard, eds. To appear. *HPSG for German*. Stanford: Center for the Study of Language and Information. (Distributed by University of Chicago Press.)

Netter, Klaus. To appear. Morphosyntax of German Noun Phrases. In Nerbonne et al., to appear.

Nunberg, Geoffrey. 1977. *The Pragmatics of Reference*. Doctoral dissertation, New York: CUNY Graduate Center.

Nunberg, Geoffrey. To appear. Transfers of Meaning. *Journal of Semantics*.

Nunberg, Geoffrey, Ivan A. Sag, and Thomas Wasow. In preparation. Idioms. Stanford University.

Oh, Chung-Kyu, and Daniel Dineen, eds. 1979. *Syntax and Semantics*. Vol. 11, *Presupposition*. New York: Academic Press.

Paolillo, John. 1992. *Functional Articulation in Diglossia: A Case Study of Grammatical and Social Correspondences in Sinhala*. Doctoral dissertation, Stanford University.

Park, Byung-Soo. 1992. The Semantic and Pragmatic Nature of Honorific Agreement in Korean: An Information-Based Approach. Unpublished manuscript, Kyung-Hee University, Seoul, and Stanford University.

Partee, Barbara. 1987. Noun Phrase Interpretation and Polymorphic Types. In *Groningen-Amsterdam Studies in Semantics*, vol. 8, *Studies in Discourse Representation Theory and the Theory of Generalized Quantifiers*, ed. Jeroen Groenendijk, Dick de Jongh, and Martin Stokhof. Dordrecht: Foris.

Peeters, Bert. 1989. *Commencement, Continuation, Cessation: A Conceptual Analysis of a Set of English and French Verbs from an Axiological Point of View*. Doctoral dissertation, Australian National University.

Pereira, Fernando, and Stuart Shieber. 1987. *PROLOG and Natural Language Analysis*. CSLI Lecture Notes no. 10. Stanford: Center for the Study of Language and Information (distributed by the University of Chicago Press.)

Perlmutter, David. 1971 *Deep and Surface Structure Constraints in Syntax*. New York: Holt, Rinehart & Winston.

Perlmutter, David. 1968. *Deep and Surface Structure Constraints in Syntax*. Doctoral dissertation, MIT. (Published in revised form as Perlmutter 1971.)

Perlmutter, David, ed. 1983. *Studies in Relational Grammar 1*. Chicago: University of Chicago Press.

Perlmutter, David, and Paul Postal. 1977. Toward a Universal Characterization of Passivization. In *Proceedings of the 3rd Annual Meeting of the Berkeley Linguistics Society*. Berkeley: University of California, Berkeley. (Also in Perlmutter ed. 1983.)

Perlmutter, David, and Paul Postal. 1983. Some Proposed Laws of Basic Clause Structure. In Perlmutter 1983.

Pesetsky, David. 1987. Binding Problems with Experiencer Verbs. *Linguistic Inquiry* 18: 126–40.

Pickering, Martin, and Guy Barry. 1991. Sentence Processing without Empty Categories. *Language and Cognitive Processes* 6(3): 229–259.

Platero, Paul. 1974. The Navaho Relative Clause. *International Journal of American Linguistics* 40:202–246.

Pollard, Carl. 1984. *Generalized Context-Free Grammars, Head Grammars and Natural Language*. Doctoral dissertation, Stanford University.

Pollard, Carl. 1985. Phrase Structure Grammar without Metarules. In *Proceedings of the Fourth West Coast Conference on Formal Linguistics*, ed. Jeffrey Goldberg, Susannah MacKaye, and Michael Wescoat. Stanford: Stanford Linguistics Association.

Pollard, Carl. 1989. The Syntax-Semantics Interface in a Unification-Based Phrase Structure Grammar. KIT-Report no. 74. Technische Universität Berlin.

Pollard, Carl. n.d. Sorts in Unification-Based Grammar and What They Mean. Unpublished manuscript, Carnegie-Mellon University.

Pollard, Carl. To appear. Toward a Unified Account of German Passive. In Nerbonne et al. to appear.

Pollard, Carl. 1990. Notes on the Syntax and Semantics of Comparatives. Unpublished manuscript, Hewlett-Packard Laboratories, Palo Alto.

Pollard, Carl, and Bob Carpenter. 1990. Extensionality in Feature Structures and Feature logic. Paper presented at the Workshop on Unification and Generation, Bad Teinach, Germany, November.

Pollard, Carl, and Drew Moshier. 1990. Unifying Partial Descriptions of Sets. In *Vancouver Studies in Cognitive Science*, vol. 1, *Information, Language and Cognition*. Vancouver: University of British Columbia Press.

Pollard, Carl, and Ivan A. Sag. 1987. *Information-Based Syntax and Semantics, Volume 1: Fundamentals*. CSLI Lecture Notes no. 13. Stanford: Center for the Study of Language and Information (distributed by the University of Chicago Press.)

Pollard, Carl, and Ivan A. Sag. 1992. Anaphors in English and the Scope of Binding Theory. *Linguistic Inquiry* 23:261–303.

Pollock, Jean-Yves. 1989. Verb Movement, Universal Grammar, and the Structure of IP. *Linguistic Inquiry* 20:365–424.

Postal, Paul. 1971. *Crossover Phenomena*. New York: Holt, Rinehart & Winston.

Postal, Paul. 1974. *On Raising*. Cambridge, Mass.: MIT Press.

Postal, Paul. 1977. About a 'Nonargument' for Raising. *Linguistic Inquiry* 8:141–154.

Postal, Paul. 1986. Studies of Passive Clauses. Albany: State University of New York Press.

Postal, Paul, and Geoffrey K. Pullum. 1988. Expletive Noun Phrases in Subcategorized Positions. *Linguistic Inquiry* 19:635–670.

Pullum, Geoffrey K. 1982. Syncategorematicity and English Infinitival *To*. *Glossa* 16: 181–215.

Pustejovsky, James. 1991. The Generative Lexicon. *Computational Linguistics* 17: 409–441.

Pustejovsky, James. In press. Type Coercion and Lexical Selection. In *Semantics and the Lexicon*, ed. James Pustejovsky. Dordrecht: Kluwer.

Quine, Willard van Orman. 1980. *Set Theory and Its Logic*. Rev. ed. Cambridge, Mass.: Harvard University Press.

Radford, Andrew. 1981. *Transformational Grammar*. Cambridge: Cambridge University Press.

Reibel, David, and Sanford Schane, eds. 1969. *Modern Studies in English*. Englewood Cliffs, N.J.: Prentice-Hall.

Reinhart, Tanya, and Eric Reuland. 1991. Anaphors and Logophors: An Argument Structure Perspective. In *Long Distance Anaphora*, ed. Jan Koster and Eric Reuland. Cambridge: Cambridge University Press.

Reinhart, Tanya, and Eric Reuland. To appear. Reflexivity. *Linguistic Inquiry*.

Reuland, Eric. 1983. Governing - *ing*. *Linguistic Inquiry* 14:101–136.

Reuland, Eric, and Tanya Reinhart. 1991. Binding Conditions and Chains. In *Proceedings of the Tenth West Coast Conference on Formal Linguistics*. Stanford: Stanford Linguistics Association.

Reuland, Eric, and Alice ter Meulen, eds. 1987. *The Representation of (In)Definiteness*. Cambridge, Mass.: MIT Press.

Richardson, John. 1988. *Free Choice Interrogatives*. Doctoral dissertation (draft), University of Chicago.

Riddle, Elizabeth, and Gloria Sheintuch. 1983. A Functional Analysis of Pseudo-Passives. *Linguistics and Philosophy* 6:527–563.

Rizzi, Luigi. 1982. Negation, *Wh*-Movement and the Null Subject Parameter. In *Issues in Italian Syntax*. Dordrecht: Foris.

Rizzi, Luigi. 1990. *Relativized Minimality*. Cambridge, Mass.: MIT Press.

Roberts, Craige. 1987. *Modal Subordination, Anaphora, and Distributivity*. Doctoral dissertation, University of Massachusetts at Amherst.

Rosenbaum, Peter S. 1967. *The Grammar of English Predicate Complement Constructions*. Cambridge, Mass.: MIT Press.

Ross, John R. 1967. *Constraints on Variables in Syntax*. Doctoral dissertation, MIT. (Published as *Infinite Syntax!* Norwood, N.J.: Ablex, 1986.)

Ross, John R. 1974. There, There, (There, (There, (There, . . .))). In La Galy et al. 1974.

Rothstein, Susan. 1981. Preposition Stranding and the Status of PP as a Bounding Node in English. Unpublished manuscript, MIT.

Růžička, R. 1983. Remarks on Control. *Linguistic Inquiry* 14:309–324.

Sag, Ivan A. 1987. Grammatical Hierarchy and Linear Precedence. *Syntax and Semantics*, vol. 20, *Discontinuous Constituency*, ed. Geoffrey Huck and Almerindo Ojeda. New York: Academic Press.

Sag, Ivan A., Ronald Kaplan, Lauri Karttunen, Martin Kay, Carl Pollard, Stuart Shieber, and Annie Zaenen. 1985. Unification and Grammatical Theory. In *Proceedings of the Fifth West Coast Conference on Formal Linguistics*, ed. Mary Dalrymple, Jeffrey Goldberg, Kristin Hanson, Michael Inman, Chris Piñon, and Stephen Wechsler. Stanford: Stanford Linguistics Association.

Sag, Ivan A., Lauri Karttunen, and Jeffrey Goldberg. 1992. A Lexical Analysis of Icelandic Case. In Sag and Szabolcsi 1992.

Sag, Ivan A., and Ewan Klein. 1982. The Syntax and Semantics of English Expletive Pronoun Constructions. In *Stanford Working Papers in Grammatical Theory*, vol. 2, *Developments in Generalized Phrase Structure Grammar*, ed. Michael Barlow, Daniel Flickinger, and Ivan A. Sag. Bloomington: Indiana University Linguistics Club.

Sag, Ivan A., and Carl Pollard. 1989. Subcategorization and Head-Driven Phrase Structure. In *Alternate Conceptions of Phrase Structure*, ed. Mark R. Baltin and Anthony S. Kroch. Chicago: University of Chicago Press.

Sag, Ivan A., and Carl Pollard. 1991. An Integrated Theory of Complement Control. *Language* 67:63–113.

Sag, Ivan A., and Anna Szabolcsi, eds. 1992. *Lexical Matters*. CSLI Lecture Notes no. 24. Stanford: Center for the Study of Language and Information (distributed by the University of Chicago Press.)

Saussure, Ferdinand de. (1916) 1959. *Course in General Linguistics*. New York: McGraw-Hill.

Scha, Remko. 1981. Distributive, Collective, and Cumulative Quantification. In Groenendijk et al. 1981.

Schmerling, Susan. 1979. Synonymy Judgments as Syntactic Evidence. In *Syntax and Semantics*, vol. 9, *Pragmatics*, ed. Peter Cole. New York: Academic Press.

Schwarzschild, Roger. 1991. *On the Meaning of Definite Plural Noun Phrases*. Doctoral dissertation, University of Massachusetts at Amherst.

Sells, Peter. 1984. *Syntax and Semantics of Resumptive Pronouns* . Doctoral dissertation, University of Massachusetts at Amherst.

Sells, Peter. 1985. Pied Piping and the Feature *WH*. Unpublished manuscript, Stanford University.

Sells, Peter. 1987. Aspects of Logophoricity. *Linguistic Inquiry* 18:445–479.

Shieber, Stuart. 1986. *An Introduction to Unification-Based Approaches to Grammar*. CSLI Lecture Notes no. 4. Stanford: Center for the Study of Language and Information (distributed by the University of Chicago Press.)

Shieber, Stuart, Hans Uszkoreit, Jane Robinson, and Mabry Tyson. 1983. The Formalism and Implementation of PATR-II. In *Research on Interactive Acquisition and Use of Knowledge*. Menlo Park, Calif.: Artificial Intelligence Center, SRI International.

Soames, Scott. 1982. How Presuppositions Are Inherited: A Solution to the Projection Problem. *Linguistic Inquiry* 13: 483–545. (Reprinted in Davis 1991.)

Soames, Scott. 1989. Subject-Auxiliary Inversion and Gaps in Generalized Phrase Structure Grammar. *Linguistics and Philosophy* 12(3): 373–382.

Soames, Scott, and David Perlmutter. 1979. *Syntactic Argumentation and the Structure of English*. Berkeley and Los Angeles: University of California Press.

Sproat, Richard. 1985. Welsh Syntax and VSO Structure. *Natural Language and Linguistic Theory* 3:173–216.

Srivastav, Veneeta. 1991a. The Syntax and Semantics of Correlatives. *Natural Language and Linguistic Theory* 9:637–686.

Srivastav, Veneeta. 1991b. Wh- *Dependencies in Hindi and the Theory of Grammar*. Doctoral dissertation, Cornell University.

Stalnaker, Robert. 1973. Presuppositions. *Journal of Philosophical Logic* 2:447–457.

Steedman, Mark. 1987. Combinatory Grammars and Parasitic Gaps. *Natural Language and Linguistic Theory* 5:403–439.

Steedman, Mark. 1990. Structure and Intonation. *Language* 67:262–296.

Steele, Susan, et al. 1981. *An Encyclopedia of* AUX. *Linguistic Inquiry* Monograph no. 5. Cambridge, Mass.: MIT Press.

Stowell, Timothy. 1981. Origins of Phrase Structure. Doctoral dissertation, MIT.

Stowell, Timothy. 1983. Subjects across Categories. *Linguistic Review* 2:285–312.

Szabolcsi, Anna, and Frans Zwarts. 1991. Unbounded Dependencies and Algebraic Semantics. Lecture notes, Third European Summer School in Language, Logic, and Information, Saarbrücken.

Tang, C. C. Jane. 1989. Chinese Reflexives. *Natural Language and Linguistic Theory* 7:93–121.

Thomason, Richmond. 1974. Some Complement Constructions in Montague Grammar. In La Galy et al. 1974.

Thráinsson, Höskuldur. 1979. *On Complementation in Icelandic*. New York: Garland.

Tomabechi, Hideto. 1989. A Uniform Treatment of Japanese Postpositions Using the Head-Marker Structure in HPSG. Unpublished manuscript, Carnegie Mellon University.

Uszkoreit, Hans. 1982. German Word Order in GPSG. In *Proceedings of the First West Coast Conference on Formal Linguistics*, ed. Daniel Flickinger, Marlys Macken, and Nancy Wiegand. Stanford: Stanford Linguistics Association.

Uszkoreit, Hans. 1984. *Word Order and Constituent Structure in German*. Doctoral dissertation, University of Texas at Austin. (Published in revised form as CSLI Lecture Notes no. 8. Stanford: Center for the Study of Language and Information [distributed by the University of Chicago Press], 1987.)

Wang, Jinhao. n.d. *Ziji*: A Chinese Long-Distance Anaphor. Unpublished manuscript, Program in Computational Linguistics, Carnegie Mellon University.

Warner, Anthony R. 1992. English Auxiliaries: A Lexical Account in HPSG. Research Paper YLLS/RP 1992-1. Department of Language and Linguistic Science, University of York.

Warner, Anthony R. To appear. *English Auxiliaries: Structure and History*. Cambridge: Cambridge University Press.

Wechsler, Stephen. 1991. *Argument Structure and Linking*. Doctoral dissertation, Stanford University.

Wierzbicka, Anna. 1988. *The Semantics of Grammar*. Amsterdam: John Benjamins.

Wilkes-Gibbs, Deanna. 1986. *Collaborative Processes of Language Use in Conversation*. Doctoral dissertation, Stanford University.

Wilkins, Wendy. 1988. Thematic Structure and Reflexivization. *Syntax and Semantics*, vol. 21, *Thematic Relations*, ed. Wendy Wilkins. New York, Academic Press.

Williams, Edwin S. 1980. Predication. *Linguistic Inquiry* 11:203–238.

Williams, Edwin S. 1983. Against Small Clauses. *Linguistic Inquiry* 14:287–308.

Williams, Edwin S. 1985. PRO and Subject of NP. *Natural Language and Linguistic Theory* 3:297–316.

Williams, Edwin S. 1989. The Anaphoric Nature of θ-Roles. *Linguistic Inquiry* 20: 425–56.

Williamson, Janis. 1987. An Indefiniteness Restriction for Relative Clauses in Lakhota. In Reuland and ter Meulen 1987.

Wunderlich, Dieter. 1988. Einige Bemerkungen über Kongruenz. Unpublished manuscript, Heinrich Heine–Universität.

Xu, Liejiong. 1986. Free Empty Category. *Linguistic Inquiry* 17:75–93.

Xu, Liejiong and D. Terrence Langendoen. 1985. Topic Structure in Chinese. *Language* 61: 1–27.

Zaenen, Annie, Joan Maling, and Höskuldur Thráinsson. 1985. Case and Grammatical Functions: The Icelandic Passive. *Natural Language and Linguistic Theory* 3:441–483. (Reprinted in Maling and Zaenen 1990.)

Zalta, Edward. 1988. *Intensional Logic and the Metaphysics of Intentionality*. Cambridge, Mass.: Bradford/MIT.

Zhang, Shi. 1988. Argument Drop and *pro*. In *Proceedings of the Seventh West Coast Conference on Formal Linguistics*, ed. Hagit Borer. Stanford: Stanford Linguistics Association.

Zhang, Shi. 1990. The Structure of *Mad* Magazine Sentences and Unmarked Accusative Case. In *Proceedings of the Western Conference on Linguistics*, vol. 3, ed. Grant Goodall et al. Fresno: California State University at Fresno.

Zhang, Shi. 1992. CP-Adjoined Structure and Unmarked Accusative Case: Pros and Cons. In *Proceedings of the Tenth West Coast Conference on Formal Linguistics*, ed. Dawn Bates. Stanford: Stanford Linguistics Association.

Ziv, Yael, and Gloria Sheintuch. 1981. Passives of Obliques over Direct Objects. *Lingua* 54: 1–17.

Zribi-Hertz, Anne. 1989. Anaphor Binding and Narrative Point of View: English Reflexive Pronouns in Sentence and Discourse. *Language* 65:695–727.

Zwicky, Arnold. 1986. German Adjective Agreement in GPSG. *Linguistics* 24:957–990.

Index of Names

Index of Languages

Index of Subjects